THE OXFORD HANDBOOK OF
APPLIED LINGUISTICS

THE OXFORD HANDBOOK OF
APPLIED LINGUISTICS

EDITED BY

Robert B. Kaplan

EDITORIAL ADVISORY BOARD

William Grabe

Merrill Swain

G. Richard Tucker

OXFORD
UNIVERSITY PRESS

2002

OXFORD
UNIVERSITY PRESS

Oxford   New York
Athens   Auckland   Bangkok   Bogotá   Buenos Aires   Cape Town
Chennai   Dar es Salaam   Delhi   Florence   Hong Kong   Istanbul   Karachi
Kolkata   Kuala Lumpur   Madrid   Melbourne   Mexico City   Mumbai   Nairobi
Paris   São Paulo   Shanghai   Singapore   Taipei   Tokyo   Toronto   Warsaw

and associated companies in
Berlin   Ibadan

Copyright © 2002 by Oxford University Press

Published by Oxford University Press, Inc.
198 Madison Avenue, New York, New York 10016

Oxford is a registered trademark of Oxford University Press

Library of Congress Cataloging-in-Publication Data
The Oxford handbook of applied linguistics / edited by Robert B. Kaplan;
editorial advisory board, William Grabe, Merrill Swain, G. Richard Tucker.
p. cm.
Includes bibliographical references and index.
ISBN 0-19-513267-X
1. Applied linguistics.   I. Kaplan, Robert B.
P129 .O95 2002
418—dc21   2001036839

1 3 5 7 9 8 6 4 2

Printed in the United States of America
on acid-free paper

PREFACE

....

THE work of organizing this volume began in the fall of 1998. Peter Ohlin, of Oxford University Press (OUP), contacted me to indicate his interest in organizing *The Handbook of Applied Linguistics*. The suggestion was of interest to me—after all, I had been the editor of the *Annual Review of Applied Linguistics* from 1980 to 1991 and had continued on the editorial board through 2000 (Kaplan and Grabe 2000); in addition, in 1980 I had edited *On the Scope of Applied Linguistics* (Kaplan 1980), and, in 1991, together with William Grabe I had co-edited the *Introduction to Applied Linguistics* (Grabe and Kaplan 1992); finally, together with Henry Widdowson, I had served as co-editor for applied linguistics for the *International Encyclopedia of Linguistics* (IEL), edited by William Bright (Kaplan and Widdowson 1992), and at present I'm engaged again in the same context for the second edition of the IEL (Kaplan and Grabe in preparation), this time under the general editorship of William Frawley and with William Grabe serving as co-editor for applied linguistics in lieu of Henry Widdowson. In other words, I've been interested in the scope of applied linguistics for more than twenty years.

In October 1998, a preliminary proposal for the *Handbook* was developed, and, following appropriate review, in November a contract with OUP was signed. William Grabe, Merrill Swain, and G. Richard Tucker were invited to constitute an editorial advisory board for the project. In December 1998 and January 1999, the Editorial Advisory Committee and I developed a revised outline for the volume and identified 43 contributors to write for the *Handbook* (out of a tentative list of more than 100 applied linguists who constituted a preliminary pool of potential contributors). Three contributors dropped out along the way. The first letters of invitation were mailed out in February 1999. Through March, April, and May 1999, negotiations were carried out; in June, the list of contributors was finalized. Contributors were asked to write scholarly articles on the topics for which they were responsible, placing their topics within the field of applied linguistics and, in so far as possible, suggesting the ways in which the several subdisciplines might develop in the future. Contributions began to arrive during late December 1999, though the deadline for contributions had been set for March 2000; contributions trickled in through March, April, and May 2000, and the last contribution was received in November 2000.

A book of this type will be judged not only on what it includes, but also on what it excludes. There are at least three holes in the design of this volume: work with the deaf, with teacher education, and with corpus development—papers which unfortunately were never delivered. The editorial group spent quite a bit of time debating whether critical (applied) linguistics/critical pedagogy/critical discourse analysis should be included; on the grounds that critical applied linguistics rejects all theories of language, expresses "skepticism towards all metanarratives" (Lyotard 1984), and rejects traditional applied linguistics as an enterprise because it has allegedly never been neutral and has, rather, been hegemonic (Rampton 1997b), the editorial group decided not to include the cluster of "critical" activities. Despite some omissions, the coverage is wide and comprehensive.

In a way, the editorial group assembled for this volume is less than ideal. Tucker had been president of the Center for Applied Linguistics (CAL) from 1978 and 1992; Swain, working at the Ontario Institute for Studies in Education (OISE), in Toronto, together with Michael Canale, had authored the seminal "Theoretical bases of communicative approaches," which had appeared in volume 1, number 1 of the journal *Applied Linguistics*; Grabe was the second editor of the *Annual Review of Applied Linguistics*, serving from 1991 to 2000. Both Swain and Grabe had at various times been elected to the presidency of the American Association for Applied Linguistics (AAAL), as had I, and Tucker, in his CAL role, had served for a number of years as an ex officio member of its governing board. As a matter of fact, I happen to be the eldest of the editorial group by at least a dozen years; indeed, I am since 1995 formally retired from the University of Southern California (USC), holding the title professor emeritus.

Thus, the editorial group represents an enormous amount of experience; its four members have lived through much of the past three or four decades of the development of applied linguistics not only in the United States but throughout the world (through their participation in the International Association of Applied Linguistics [AILA] and their wide individual and collective familiarity with applied linguists around the world), and they unquestionably know the history of applied linguistics and how and why applied linguistics has arrived at its present stage of development. In sum, the editorial board reflects a good overview of the field, and the contributors, representing the best scholarship, are drawn from diverse backgrounds—in every sense of the term. The members of the editorial group may, however, be less well qualified to discuss the future of applied linguistics. That is a task for younger scholars. As a result, every effort has been made to allow a mix of younger and more established scholars to have their say through the 39 contributions to this volume. (Five of the chapters have two collaborating authors.) The distribution of scholars reflects diversity; 43 percent of contributors are women, and 45 percent are drawn from countries other than the United States (Australia, Belgium, Canada, Hungary, the Netherlands, and the United Kingdom), although all contributions are written in English and edited to U.S. conventions.

Applied linguistics is a difficult notion to define; indeed, it should not be assumed that this volume will provide a definitive definition of the field. Rather, this volume offers a snapshot of some of the subfields of applied linguistics at the beginning of the third millennium—and, thus, a kind of overview of the field. The term *applied linguistics* came into existence in the 1940s through the efforts of language teachers who wished to ally themselves with "scientific" linguists and to disassociate themselves from teachers of literature. By the mid-1950s, the term was given credence by the opening of the School of Applied Linguistics at the University of Edinburgh (1956) and by the creation of the Center for Applied Linguistics (CAL, 1959) in the United States. Soon thereafter, during the 1960s, the term was institutionalized in the International Association of Applied Linguistics (Association Internationale de Linguistique Appliquée, [AILA] 1964) and in the evolution of a series of national associations of applied linguistics (e.g., the British Association of Applied Linguistics, 1967). Further, the field was given scope and substance by the publication of *Introducing Applied Linguistics* (Corder 1973) and by the publication of *The Edinburgh Course in Applied Linguistics* (Allen and Corder 1973/1975). The range and quality of research was soon being identified through the founding of a number of journals, including *Language Learning* (1948), *TESOL Quarterly* (1967), *Applied Linguistics* (1980), and the *Annual Review of Applied Linguistics* (1980).

Because the field came into being during the ascendancy of the structuralist linguistics movement, of Skinnerian psychology, and of the audiolingual method—a combination that gave rise to the notion that linguistic and psychological theory could easily be translated into practice—early applied linguistics was dominantly associated with language teaching. Indeed, while that relationship continues in the present (see, e.g., Davies 1999; Spolsky 1999), the field has diversified, with some segments splitting off to become essentially independent: Language testing has its own organization and its own journal; second language acquisition has its own journal, though not yet an independent organization; and language policy and planning commands several journals (e.g., *Current Issues in Language Planning, New Language Planning Newsletter*) and a web site (http://cilp.arts.usyd.edu.au/), but as yet no independent organization.

The current diversity of the field can be seen in the range of topics included in this volume, in the list of the scientific commissions of AILA, and in summary pieces written at various times over the past decade or so by Angelis (1987), by Grabe and Kaplan (1991: 3–6), by Kaplan (1999), by Kaplan and Grabe (2000), and by others (cf. Davies 1999). It is clear that applied linguistics lacks a central organizing theory. In some ways, the field seems to be fragmenting into segments. At the twelfth World Congress of AILA, held in Tokyo in August 1999, there were a number of fairly heated public discussions on the nature and scope of applied linguistics; there was little consensus among the participants in these discussion, but in part at least the lack of agreement may have been the result of the fact that five quite different questions were being addressed simultaneously:

1. What is the place of applied linguistics in the architecture of the "university"?
2. Where does applied linguistics fit in the sociology of knowledge?
3. What are the kinds of questions that applied linguistics ought to be addressing? That is, what are the dominant paradigms guiding research in the field?
4. What part(s) of linguistics can be applied to the real-world, language-based problems that applied linguistics presumes to mediate?
5. What kind(s) of problems can be solved through the mediation of applied linguistics?
6. What does an aspiring applied linguist need to know? That is, what should the content of graduate curricula in applied linguistics contain?

These questions are impacted by the assumption that applied linguistics ought to be unitary; that is:

- The training of incipient applied linguists ought to be based on the notion of a curriculum in which "one size fits all."
- The work of applied linguists ought to be driven by a single unified theoretical paradigm.
- The place of applied linguistics in the academy ought to be conceived in terms of a model of the traditional academic department.

This assumption is quite ironic, since applied linguists have repeatedly argued that their field is not merely "linguistics applied" but rather is, by definition, multidisciplinary and interdisciplinary. English departments, for example, exist whose charge includes at least:

American literature (divided into chronological components)
Comparative literature
Creative writing
English literature (divided into chronological components—sometimes with Anglo-Saxon language and literature and Middle English language and literature as separate components, sometimes with special components in Irish language and literature, sometimes with special components in EL2 literatures)
History of English language
Journalism
Rhetoric and composition
Teaching English as a first language
Teaching English as a second language
World literature

Such hydra-like monstrosities do exist (not always happily). If applied linguistics is to be conceived as having a traditional academic departmental structure, one could conceive of something as diverse and ecumenical as that suggested earlier. While such a structure is not to be highly recommended, it does illustrate the point that diversity is possible in an administrative sense.

Because the real-world language-based problems that applied linguists try to mediate are enormously diverse, having in common only the probability that they are language based, it is unlikely that any single paradigm can speak to the diverse activity of the field. Depending on the setting of a given problem, the applied linguist practitioner may be expected to know something about at least the following:

Anthropology	Planning
Economics	Policy development
Education theory	Political science
Gerontology	Psychology and neurology
History	Public administration
International relations	Sociology
Language learning and teaching	Teacher training
Lexicography	Text production

Indeed, Christian (1999: 7) points out that the current staff of the Center for Applied Linguistics includes individuals holding graduate degrees in particular languages, psychlogy, bilingual education, health administration, cognitive and social psychology, educational multicultural education, and educational measurement, in addition to linguistics, applied linguistics, and sociolinguistics. In sum, the applied linguist has to have a broad exposure to all the social sciences. Of course, since the common element is language, the applied linguist ought to be well grounded in linguistics, psycho- and neurolinguistics, and sociolinguistics, including literacy, individual bilingualism, and societal multilingualism. And all applied linguists must be highly computer literate and able to deal with statistical data.

With respect to the training of incipient applied linguists, a curriculum grounded in linguistics and its various hyphenated subcomponents should be considered basic. Beyond that, perhaps a wide variety of academic minors ought to be available, or, alternatively, joint degrees in applied linguistics and any of the fields mentioned ought to be possible, assuming that bureaucratic obstacles can be overcome. "While these demands on new students may seem daunting, they are probably no more demanding than new and increasing expectations in other disciplines. It is an exciting time to be an applied linguist, and also an exciting time to become one" (Kaplan and Grabe 2000: 16).

The contributions to this volume, I hope, explicate and demonstrate the breadth of applied linguistics and the depth of knowledge required of one who aspires to practice this discipline in the real world. While the field is diverse and multidisciplinary, it need not be thought of as Balkanized. While there is no unifying paradigm yet, it is likely that one may evolve in the future. What is unlikely, however, is that applied linguistics and autonomous linguistics will merge into a single enterprise. That is so because the two activities take quite distinct views of language; for the autonomous linguist, language is self-contained and independent of human use, while for the applied linguist language must be considered primarily in the context of its uses and users (Grabe, in Grabe and Kaplan 1992; 35–60; Kaplan 1993; 375–378).

Each of the contributions to this volume may be taken as a complete, free-standing discussion, yet every effort has been made to integrate the contributions into a coherent whole. Each is printed with its own endnotes (if any are used), but the reference lists are compiled into one single alphabetical list at the end of the volume. This compilation of references is provided in part to eliminate duplication but in part also to give a sense of the scope of the field, of the key players, and of the disciplinary history; it constitutes an abbreviated citation index as well as an extensive reference list to much current literature. There is also an index at the end of the volume, and a brief biographical listing of the contributors follow the contents. The biographic entries were written by the contributors. Each entry provides an e-mail address at which the author can be contacted. Aside from these features, the approach is intentionally conservative, offering no special features and deliberately avoiding cross reference among the contributions. In sum, this volume is not just a compilation of thirty-nine unrelated articles; it is, as noted previously, a comprehensive overview of the field of applied linguistics at the beginning of the third millennium. Readers are invited to contact the editor or the members of the editorial based with questions or comments.

CONTENTS

....

PART IV. THE STUDY OF
SECOND LANGUAGE LEARNING

PART V. THE STUDY OF
SECOND LANGUAGE TEACHING

CONTRIBUTORS

COLIN BAKER is professor of education in Bangor, North Wales (UK), and holds a Personal Chair at the University of Wales. He is the author of books on bilingualism and bilingual education, notably *Foundations of Bilingual Education and Bilingualism* (1996, 2nd ed.) and the *Encyclopedia of Bilingualism and Bilingual Education* (1998, with Sylvia Prys Jones). He is editor of the *International Journal of Bilingualism and Bilingual Education* and is co-editor, with Nancy Hornberger, of a book series on bilingualism and bilingual education. He can be reached at eds009@bangor.ac.uk.

RICHARD B. BALDAUF, JR., is associate professor and director of the University of Sydney Language Centre and president of the Applied Linguistics Association of Australia. He has published numerous articles in refereed journals and books. He is co-editor of *Language Planning in Australasia and the South Pacific* (1990), principal researcher and editor of the *Viability of Low Candidature LOTE Courses in Universities* (1995), and co-author, with Robert Kaplan, of *Language Planning from Practice to Theory* (1997). He can be reached at richard.baldauf@language.usyd.edu.au.

KATHLEEN BARDOVI-HARLIG is professor of linguistics and TESOL and of applied linguistics at Indiana University, where she teaches and conducts research in second language acquisition. Her work on interlanguage pragmatics and on the acquisition of pragmatics has appeared in *Studies in Second Language Acquisition, Language Learning, TESOL Quarterly, Discourse Processes, ROLSI,* and several volumes of the monograph series *Pragmatics and Language Learning*. She can be reached at bardovi@indiana.edu

GEOFF BRINDLEY is a senior lecturer in the department of linguistics and research coordinator at the National Centre for English Language Teaching and Research (NCELTR) at Macquarie University, Sydney, Australia. He has worked as an EFL and ESL teacher, teacher trainer, researcher, test developer, and program administrator in Europe, North America, Asia, and Australia. He is the author and editor of a variety of publications on TESOL curriculum design, second language acquisition, and language proficiency assessment. His research interests include the role of assessment in the improvement of learning, the testing of listening comprehension assessment, and the interfaces between language research and policy. He can be reached at gbrindle@laurel.ocs.mq.edu.au.

JILL BURSTEIN received a Ph.D. in linguistics from the City University of New York, Graduate Center, in 1992. Dr. Burstein is currently a researcher at Educational Testing Service. Her research applies natural language processing methods to the development of text assessment applications. Dr. Burstein is co-inventor of *e-rater*, an automated essay scoring system, currently used to score essays on the Graduate Management Admissions Test, and of *Criterion*, a web-based writing instruction system. She can be reached at jburstein@ets.org

MARTIN BYGATE lectures in TESOL at the School of Education, University of Leeds. His main areas of interest are instructed second language acquisition, oral second language proficiency, and the role of tasks in language learning. He has directed research projects, co-edited two volumes, and published a book and various research articles on the teaching and learning of oral skills. Prior to his appointment at Leeds, he taught in France, Morocco, and Brazil and at the Universities of Reading and London. He is currently co-editor of *Applied Linguistics* journal. He can be reached at m.bygate@education.leeds.ac.uk.

MICHELINE CHALHOUB-DEVILLE is an associate professor of foreign language and ESL education at the University of Iowa. Dr. Chalhoub-Deville, who received her Ph.D. from Ohio State University, is recognized internationally for her work in the field of second language assessment. She has published in various journals, including *Language Testing, Language Learning, Annual Review of Applied Linguistics*, and *Foreign Language Annals*. She has also edited a book on computer adaptive testing, entitled *Issues in Computer-Adaptive Testing of Reading Proficiency* (1999). Dr. Chalhoub-Deville has received the International Language Testing Association Award for Best Article on Language Testing. She has been serving on the TOEFL Committee of Examiners and Policy Council. She can be reached at m-chalhoub-deville@uiowa.edu.

CAROL A. CHAPELLE is professor of TESL/applied linguistics at Iowa State University. Recent papers on CALL appear in *Language Learning and Technology*, and her recent book is titled *Computer Applications in Second Language Acquisition: Foundations for Teaching, Testing and Research*. She is currently editor of *TESOL Quarterly*. She can be reached at carolc@iastate.edu.

MARTIN CHODOROW received a Ph.D. in cognitive psychology from the Massachusetts Institute of Technology in 1976. After completing a postdoctoral research assignment at IBM's Thomas Watson Research Center, he joined the faculty of the psychology department at Hunter College of the City University of New York. Dr. Chodorow has worked on a number of natural language processing projects at IBM, at Princeton University's Cognitive Science Laboratory, and, most recently, at Educational Testing Service. He can be reached at martin. chodorow@hunter.cuny.edu.

KEES DE BOT graduated from the University of Nijmegen in general linguistics and applied linguistics. His recent research interests include foreign language attrition, the maintenance and shift of minority languages, and the psycholinguistics of bilingual language processing. He is chair of applied linguistics and head of the department, as well as director of the School of Language, Communication, and Information Sciences, at the University of Nijmegen. He was reviews editor for *Applied Linguistics* until 1998, and he is currently co-editor of the series *Studies in Bilingualism* with John Benjamins. He has published several books and journal articles on various topics in applied linguistics, and he is coordinator of an AILA scientific commission and a member of the AILA Executive Board. His address for correspondence is: Department of Applied Linguistics, University of Nijmegen, Erasmusplein 1, 6525 HT Nijmegen, the Netherlands. He can be reached at c.debot@let.kun.nl.

TON DIJKSTRA is a senior staff member at the Nijmegen Institute for Cognition and Information (The Netherlands). His principal research interests are monolingual and bilingual visual and auditory word recognition, but he makes occasional side trips to other domains, such as language production and morphological processing. As a strong believer in the heuristic value of modeling, he has been engaged in the development of a computer model for bilingual word recognition and has edited a book on computational psycholinguistics (with K. de Smedt). He wrote two books in Dutch on psycholinguistics (with G. Kempen as a co-author), one of which was translated into German. He can be reached at dijkstra@nici.kun.nl.

PATRICIA A. DUFF is associate professor of language and literacy education at the University of British Columbia. Her main areas of interest are second language acquisition, language socialization, qualitative research methods, and classroom discourse in a variety of educational contexts, including second/foreign language courses and mainstream and L2-immersion content-based courses. Her work has appeared in *Studies in Second Language Acquisition, Journal of Multilingual and Multicultural Development, Modern Language Journal, TESOL Quarterly, Canadian Modern Language Review,* in numerous edited volumes, and in a forthcoming book on case study research in second language acquisition. She is editor of the Research Issues section of the *TESOL Quarterly.* She can be reached at pduff@interchange.ubc.ca.

WILLIAM G. EGGINGTON is professor of English language and linguistics and associate chair of the English department at Brigham Young University. Originally from Australia, he received his M.A. and his Ph.D. in linguistics from the University of Southern California. He specializes in studying macrorelationships between language and society, specifically language policy and planning. He has published nationally and internationally in language planning, with his most recent publication being a co-edited book, *The Sociopolitics of English Language Teaching* (2000). He is actively involved in professional organizations, including TESOL International, having served as Chair of the Sociopolitical Concerns Committee and Chair of the Applied Linguistics Interest Section. He can be reached at william_eggington@byu.edu.

CHRISTIAN FALTIS is professor of education in the program in multicultural education at Arizona State University, Tempe, Arizona. He received his Ph.D. from Stanford University. From 1998 to 2001, he served as editor of *Educational Researcher*, Research News and Comments Section. He has authored and edited eleven books and written more than sixty articles and chapters on the topics of bilingual education, second language acquisition, and English as a second language. His most recent works are *Joinfostering: Teaching and Learning in a Multilingual Classrooms* (2001) and, with P. Wolfe, *So Much to Say: Adolescents, Bilingualism and ESL in the Secondary School* (1999). He can be reached at cfaltis @asu.edu.

OFELIA GARCIA is presently the dean of the School of Education at the Brooklyn campus of Long Island University. She has published extensively in the areas of bilingualism, bilingual education, sociology of language, and U.S. Spanish. She is the editor of the new journal *Educators for Urban Minorities*, published by LIU Press. She can be reached at ogarcia@hornet.liunet.edu.

ROBERT C. GARDNER is a professor emeritus in psychology at the University of Western Ontario. He has written two books, co-authored a third one, and co-edited another. In addition, he has published approximately 150 journal articles and book chapters. The majority of his publications are concerned with the role of attitudes and motivation in second language learning, but in addition he has made contributions to the literature on ethnic relations, ethnic stereotypes, and ethnic attitudes, psycholinguistics, and statistics. In 1999, he was honored by the Canadian Psychological Association with the Award for Distinguished Contributions to Education and Training. He can be reached at gardner@julian.uwo.ca.

SUSAN GASS is University Distinguished Professor in the department of English at Michigan State University. She is the director of the English Language Center and codirector of the Center for Language Education and Research. She has published widely in the field of SLA, focusing on a number of different areas, including language transfer, language universals, and input and interaction. She is author *of Input, Interaction, and the Second Language Learner* (1997) and co-author, with Larry Selinker, of *Second Language Acquisition: An Introductory Course* (1994). She can be reached at gass@pilot.msu.edu.

WILLIAM GRABE is professor of English at Northern Arizona University. He is interested in all aspects of reading and writing abilities: L1 and L2, child and adult, and theory and practice. He is also interested in issues pertaining to literacy, language policy, and applied linguistics more generally. He has co-authored *Theory and Practice of Writing* (1996, with Robert B. Kaplan). He is currently working on a book, *Applied Linguistics in Action: Researching Reading* (with Fredricka Stoller). He has just concluded his ten-year tenure as editor of the *Annual Review of Applied Linguistics*. He can be reached at William.Grabe@NAU.EDU.

MICHAEL HARRINGTON is a senior lecturer in second language acquisition at the University of Queensland, Brisbane, Australia. He has an M.A. in English as a second language (ESL) from the University of Hawaii and a Ph.D. in experimental psychology from the University of California, Santa Cruz. His research and teaching interests are in second language acquisition, research methods, second language vocabulary development, Japanese as a second language, and computer-mediated language processing and use. He has published articles and chapters in the areas of second language cognitive models, working memory, sentence processing, and computer-mediated second language acquisition. He can be reached at mwharr@cltr.uq.edu.au.

NANCY H. HORNBERGER is professor of education and director of educational linguistics at the University of Pennsylvania Graduate School of Education, where she also convenes the annual Ethnography in Education Research Forum. She specializes in sociolinguistics and linguistic anthropology, language planning and educational policy, bilingualism and biliteracy, and educational policy and practice for the indigenous and immigrant language minorities in the United States and internationally. Recent publications include *Sociolinguistics and Language Teaching* (1996, co-edited with S. McKay) and *Research Methods in Language and Education* (1997, co-edited with D. Corson). Professor Hornberger co-edits a book series on bilingualism and bilingual education. She can be reached at nancyh@gse.upenn.edu.

ALAN JUFFS is currently associate professor and chair of the department of linguistics at the University of Pittsburgh. His research interests include the semantics-syntax interface and second language sentence processing. He has published in a variety of journals. He is also the director of the English Language Institute at the University of Pittsburgh and co-editor of the Pitt Series in ESL textbooks, published by the University of Michigan Press. He maintains a keen interest in classroom research and materials development. He can be reached at juffs+@pitt.edu.

ROBERT B. KAPLAN is emeritus professor of applied linguistics in the department of linguistics at the University of Southern California. He was the founding editor of the *Annual Review of Applied Linguistics* and has served as an editor of the applied linguistics entries for both the first and second editions of the *International Encyclopedia of Linguistics*. In addition, he is founding co-editor (with Richard B. Baldauf, Jr.) of *Current Issues in Language Planning*. He is the author or editor of 35 books and more than 140 articles in scholarly journals and as chapters in books. He has served as president of NAFSA (1983–1984), TESOL (1989–1990), and AAAL (1993–1994). He can be reached at rkaplan@olypen.com.

JUDITH F. KROLL is professor of psychology at Pennsylvania State University (USA). Her research is focused on the cognitive processes that support the acquisition of a second language by adult learners and the fluent use of two languages among proficient bilinguals. She is the editor (with A. de Groot) of *Tutorials in Bilingualism: Psycholinguistic Perspectives* (1997) and a co-editor (with F. Grosjean, J. Meisel, and P. Muysken) of the journal *Bilingualism: Language and Cognition*. She can be reached at j.kroll@nici.kun.nl.

JAMES P. LANTOLF is professor of applied linguistics and Spanish and director of the Center for Language Acquisition at the Pennsylvania State University. He was on the faculty of Cornell University from 1991 to 1999, and from 1980 to 1991 he was on the faculty of the University of Delaware. He has held visiting appointments at the University of Auckland, Notthingham University, the University of Melbourne, the University of Rome (*La Sapienza*), and Kassel University. He is past co-editor of *Applied Linguistics* and continues to serve on its editorial panel, as well on the editorial boards of *the Modern Language Journal* and *Spanish Applied Linguistics*. His research focus is on sociocultural and activity theory and second language acquisition. He can be reached at JPL7@psu.edu.

ILONA LEKI is professor of English and director of ESL at the University of Tennessee. Her books include *Understanding ESL Writers: A Guide for Teachers*, *Academic English*, and *Reading in the Composition Classroom* (with Joan Carson). She co-edits (with Tony Silva) the *Journal of Second Language Writing*. Her research interests center around the development of academic literacy, and she is winner of the 1996 TESOL/Newbury House Distinguished Research Award. She can be reached at leki@utkux.utk.edu.

TONY LYNCH is senior lecturer at the Institute for Applied Language Studies, University of Edinburgh, Scotland, where he is involved primarily in directing and teaching EAP courses and in teacher education. He has written two books on listening—a lecture comprehension course (*Study Listening*, 1983) and a teaching methodology book, co-authored with Anne Anderson (*Listening*, 1988)—and his most recent book is *Communication in the Language Classroom* (1996). He is currently investigating the benefits of different forms of language 'recycling' in task-based classroom learning. He can be contacted at A.J.Lynch@ed.ac.uk

MARY MCGROARTY, professor in the applied linguistics program of the English department at Northern Arizona University, Flagstaff, teaches courses in sociolinguistics and language pedagogy and assessment. She has also been on the faculty at the University of California, Los Angeles. Her research addresses language policy, pedagogy, and assessment and has appeared in *Applied Linguistics, Bilingual Review, Language Learning, TESOL Quarterly,* and several anthologies. President of the American Association for Applied Linguistics in 1997–1998, she has served on the editorial boards of *Applied Linguistics* and *TESOL Quarterly* and is current editor of the *Annual Review of Applied Linguistics.* She can be reached at Mary.McGroarty@nau.edu.

PÉTER MEDGYES is the director of the Centre for English Teacher Training at Eötvös Loránd University, Budapest. Previously, he was a schoolteacher, teacher trainer, vice rector of his university, and deputy state secretary at the Hungarian Ministry of Culture and Education. Professor Medgyes has written numerous books and articles, including *The Non-Native Teacher* (1994, winner of the Duke of Edinburgh Book Competition), *Changing Perspectives in Teacher Education* (1996, co-edited with Angi Malderez), and *The Language Teacher* (1997). His main professional interests lie in curriculum studies, language policy, and teacher education. He can be reached at medgyes@ludens.elte.hu.

PETER MÜHLHÄUSLER was born in Freiburg/Black Forest (Germany), where he completed his Abitur at the Humanistische Bertholdsgymnasium in 1966. He received his university education at Stellenbosch (Hons–B.A. 1969), Reading (M.Phil. 1972), and the Australian National University (Ph.D. 1976). He was a lecturer at the Technical University of Berlin from 1976 to 1979 and the University Lecturer in General Linguistics at the University of Oxford from 1979 to 1992. He is now the Foundation Professor of Linguistics at the University of Adelaide, remaining a supernumerary fellow of Linacre College, Oxford. He has lectured on most areas of linguistics and published on pidgins and creoles, language contact, language planning, missionary linguistics, and ecolinguistics, among other subjects. His current research projects are a social and linguistic history of the languages of Norfolk Island and a volume on missionary writing systems. He can be reached at pmuhlhau@arts.adelaide.edu.au.

PETER HANS NELDE is currently professor and chair of German and general linguistics at the Katholieke Universiteit Brussel (Belgium) and visiting professor in Nijmegen (the Netherlands) and Leipzig (Germany). In 1977, he founded the Research Centre on Multilingualism and has been its director ever since. His main research areas are multilingualism, contact linguistics, language policy, and language planning. Peter Nelde is a member of different linguistic societies (e.g., the Linguistic Society of America) and a member of the editorial board of several linguistic periodicals (e.g., *Multilingua*). He is also one of the editors of *Sociolin-*

guistica: *International Yearbook of Sociolinguistics* (Niemeyer, Tübingen) and the editor in chief of *Contact Linguistics: An International Handbook of Contemporary Research* (vol. 1, 1996, and vol. 2, 1997). He can be reached at peter.nelde @kubrussel.ac.be.

MARIANNE NIKOLOV teaches pre-service, in-service, and doctoral courses on applied linguistics at the University of Pécs. She is the author of various teaching materials of English as a foreign language and articles on child second language acquisition, classroom-based research, and the Hungarian Examination Reform. Doctor Nikolov edited the journal *NovELTy* for three years and also edited books on a variety of topics of language education.

BONNY NORTON is associate professor in the department of language and literacy education at the University of British Columbia, Vancouver, Canada. She has published widely in the area of identity, language learning, and critical research. She was guest editor of the special issue of *TESOL Quarterly* on language and identity, published in 1997, and recently authored *Identity and Language Learning: Gender, Ethnicity and Educational Change* (2000). She would like to acknowledge the help of Lynne McGivern, her research assistant on this project, as well as funding from UBC/HSS research grant # S99–0111. She can be reached at bonny. norton@ubc.ca.

TERENCE ODLIN is associate professor of English and adjunct associate professor of linguistics at Ohio State University. He has also taught in Washington, D.C., Texas, Algeria, Iran, France, Ireland, and Finland, where he was a Fulbright Scholar in 1997. Along with the psycholinguistic issues involved in language transfer and contrastive analysis, his research interests are focused on sociohistorical factors in language contact situations in the Celtic lands and elsewhere. He is the author of *Language Transfer* (1989), the editor of *Perspectives on Pedagogical Grammar,* and a co-editor of *Language Contact, Variation, and Change.* He can be reached at odlin.1@osu.edu.

REBECCA L. OXFORD, Ph.D., holds two degrees in foreign languages and two degrees in educational psychology. She is currently director of second language education (TESOL and Foreign Languages) at the University of Maryland, College Park, a similar post to the one she held at Teachers College at Columbia University, New York City. At the University of Alabama she served in several roles at different times: associate dean, foreign language education coordinator, TESOL coordinator, and teacher education area head. Her books include *Language Learning Strategies: What Every Teacher Should Know* (1990); *Language Learning Strategies around the World: Crosscultural Perspectives* (1996); *Language Learning Motivation: Pathways to the New Century* (1996); *Patterns of Cultural Identity; Simulation, Gaming, and Language Learning* (with David Crookall, 1990); and *The Tapestry of*

Language Learning (with Robin Scarcella, 1992). She has written many articles and chapters on learning strategies, styles, motivation, anxiety, and related themes. She can be reached at ro38@umail.umd.edu

DEBORAH POOLE is an associate professor of applied linguistics at San Diego State University, where she has taught since 1989. Her interests include classroom discourse, language socialization, and second language pedagogy. Her present research is focused on the ways spoken and written language interact in classroom literacy events and the implications for both discourse analysis and literacy instruction. Her publications include articles in *Language and Education, Cognition and Instruction, Language Learning,* and *Quantitative Studies in Education.* She has co-authored several ESL textbooks and co-edited a special issue of the *CATESOL Journal* dealing with intersegmental articulation. She can be reached at dpoole @mail.sdsu.edu.

DENNIS R. PRESTON is professor of linguistics at Michigan State University. His major research interests are sociolinguistics, dialectology, ethnography and discourse analysis, folk linguistics, and second language acquisition. His most recent monograph publications are *Folk Linguistics* (with Nancy Niedzielski, 1999) and *A Handbook of Perceptual Dialectology* (1999). He is vice president and president-elect of the American Dialect Society, hosted the 2000 NWAV, and will direct the 2003 LSA Summer Institute at Michigan State. In two recent National Science Foundation awards, he has focused on discourse representations of folk linguistics and has developed a number of quantitative and qualitative approaches to discourse study, with a special view of substantiating content as well as structure in discourse. He has had considerable experience in leading both faculty and student research teams in the collection and analysis of spoken language data, not only in the projects listed but also in foreign and second language settings as well (e.g., in Brazil and Poland). He can be reached at preston@pilot.msu.edu.

RODA P. ROBERTS, a certified translator, is a full professor at the School of Translation and Interpretation of the University of Ottawa, where she was director from 1979 to 1989. She has taught languages, translation, and interpretation at a number of universities in Canada, the United States, and India. In addition, she has trained translation and interpretation trainers in Canada, the United States, and Mexico and has served as curriculum consultant to various educational institutions. She has written numerous articles on translation theory, translator/interpreter training, terminology, and lexicography. She is presently director of the Bilingual Canadian Dictionary Project, an interuniversity lexicographic project that has centers at the University of Ottawa, the University of Montreal, and Laval University. She can be reached at roberts@uottawa.ca.

NANCY L. SCHWEDA NICHOLSON is professor of linguistics and cognitive science at the University of Delaware. She is widely published in the areas of simultaneous and consecutive interpretation theory, training, and evaluation, as well as language planning for court interpretation services in the United States and abroad. Professor Schweda Nicholson was a Fulbright Scholar in Denmark in 1995 and a Fellow of the Salzburg Seminar in 1999. She is a member of the Editorial Board of *Language Problems and Language Planning* and has served as a consultant and trainer for the Executive Office for Immigration Review and the Federal Bureau of Investigation. She can be reached at nsn@UDel.Edu.

JEFF SIEGEL, currently associate professor of linguistics at the University of New England in Australia, has an M.A. in English as a second language from the University of Hawai'i and a Ph.D. in linguistics from the Australian National University. He has done extensive research on pidgins, creoles, and other language contact varieties and their use in education and is author of *Langauge Contact in a Plantation Environment* (1987) and *Vernacular Education in the South Pacific* (1996). Since 1990, he has been editor of the *Pidgin and Creoles in Education (PACE) Newsletter*. He can be reached at jsiegel@metz.une.edu.au.

PETER SKEHAN is professor of applied linguistics at King's College, London, and holds a University of London Ph.D. He has taught EFL in France, ESL in the United Kingdom, and EAP in British universities. His current interests are in language testing, individual differences, and task-based instruction. His book, *A Cognitive Approach to Language Learning*, published by Oxford University Press, appeared in 1998. He can be reached at Peter.Skehan@tvu.ac.uk.

JAMES W. TOLLEFSON is professor of English, adjunct professor of linguistics, and professor at the Jackson School of International Studies at the University of Washington. He is the author or editor of six books, including *Language Policies in Education: Critical Issues: Power and Inequality in Language Education* (1995); *Planning Language, Planning Inequality* (1991); and *Alien Winds: The Reeducation of America's Indochinese Refugees* (1989). His articles appear in *TESOL Quarterly, Language Problems and Language Planning, Studies in Second Language Acquisition,* and many other journals. He can be reached at tollefso@u.washington.edu.

KELLEEN TOOHEY is associate professor in the faculty of education at Simon Fraser University in Burnaby, British Columbia, Canada. Interested in language education generally, she has worked with English, heritage, and First Nations language teachers in a variety of settings. A recent publication, *Learning English at School: Identity, Social Relations and Classroom Practice* (2000), investigates the learning of English by young children in mainstream English-medium classrooms. Her current research involves teachers and researchers in collaborative projects designed to support children of minority language backgrounds in their struggle to appropriate English in their public school classrooms. She can be reached at kelleen_toohey@sfu.ca.

MARJORIE BINGHAM WESCHE is a professor at the University of Ottawa (Second Language Institute, cross-appointed to Graduate Studies in Education) and former director of the Institute, where she joined the faculty in 1978. Her research and teaching interests involve second language acquisition, instruction, and assessment, focusing on content-based language instruction (school immersion and postsecondary initiatives), performance and aptitude testing, linguistic input and interaction in language acquisition, and vocabulary acquisition. She has published widely on these topics, co-authored *Content-Based Second Language Instruction*, and co-edited *Second Language Performance Testing* (1985) and *Incidental L2 Vocabulary Acquisition: Theory, Current Research and Instructional Implications* (1999). She can be reached at mwesche@aix1.uottawa.ca.

PART I

INTRODUCTION

CHAPTER 1

APPLIED LINGUISTICS: AN EMERGING DISCIPLINE FOR THE TWENTY-FIRST CENTURY

WILLIAM GRABE

A realistic history of the field of applied linguistics would place its origins at around the year 1948 with the publication of the first issue of the journal *Language Learning: A Journal of Applied Linguistics*. While there are certainly other possible starting points, particularly from a British perspective, this time still accords roughly with any discussion of the beginning of applied linguistics.

Over the years, the term *applied linguistics* has been defined and interpreted in a number of different ways, and I continue that exploration in this overview. In the 1950s, the term was commonly meant to reflect the insights of structural and functional linguists that could be applied directly to second language teaching, and also, in some cases, to first language (L1) literacy and language arts issues as well. In the 1960s, the term continued to be associated with the application of linguistics-to-language teaching and related practical language issues (Corder 1973; Halliday, McIntosh and Strevens 1964; Rivers 1968). At the same time, applied linguists became involved in matters of language assessment, language policies, and a new field of second language acquisition (SLA), focusing on learning, rather than on teaching. So, by the late 1960s, one saw both a reinforcement of the centrality of second language teaching as applied linguistics, and also an expansion into other realms of language use. In this respect, applied linguistics began to emerge as a genuine problem-solving enterprise.

In the 1970s, the broadening of the field of applied linguistics continued, accompanied by a more overt specification of its role as a discipline that addresses real-world language-based problems. While the focus on language teaching remains central to the discipline, it takes into its domain the growing subfields of language assessment, SLA, literacy, multilingualism, language-minority rights, language planning and policy, and teacher training (Kaplan 1980; Kaplan et al. 1981; Widdowson, 1979/1984). The notion that applied linguistics is driven first by real-world problems rather than theoretical explorations, has had four major consequences:

- The recognition of locally situated contexts for inquiry and exploration, and thus the importance of needs analyses and variable solutions in differing local contexts.
- The need to see language as functional and discourse based, thus the re-emergence of systemic and descriptive linguistics as resources for problem-solving, particularly in North American contexts.
- The recognition that no one discipline can provide all the tools and resources needed to address real-world problems.
- The need to recognize and apply a wide array of research tools and methodologies to address locally situated language problems.

These trends took hold and evolved in the 1980s as major points of departure from an earlier, no longer appropriate, "linguistics applied" perspective. The central issue remained the need to address language issues and problems as they occur in the real world. Of course, since language is central to all communication, and since many language issues in the real world are particularly complex and long-standing, the emerging field has not simply been reactive, but rather, has been, and still is, fluid and dynamic in its evolution. Thus, definitions of applied linguistics in the 1980s emphasized both the range of issues addressed and the types of disciplinary resources used in order to work on language problems (Grabe and Kaplan 1992; Kaplan 1980). In the 1980s, applied linguistics truly extended in a systematic way beyond language teaching and language learning issues to encompass language assessment, language policy and planning, language use in professional settings, translation, lexicography, multilingualism, language and technology, and corpus linguistics (which has continuously held a far greater attraction for applied linguistics than for theoretical linguists). These extensions are well documented in the first ten years of the journal *Applied Linguistics* and in the *Annual Review of Applied Linguistics (ARAL)*.

By the close of the 1980s, a common trend was to view applied linguistics as incorporating many subfields (as indicated earlier) and as drawing on many supporting disciplines in addition to linguistics (e.g., psychology, education, anthropology, sociology, political science, policy studies and public administration, and English studies, including composition, rhetoric, and literary studies). Combined with these two foundations (subfields and supporting disciplines) was the view of applied linguistics as problem driven and real-world based rather than theory driven and disconnected from real language use (Kaplan and Widdowson 1992; Strevens 1992). Applied linguistics evolved further in the 1990s, breaking away from the common framing mechanisms of the 1980s. These changes are taken up in later sections. A parallel co-evolution of linguistics itself also needs to be commented upon to understand why and how linguistics remains a core notion for applied linguistics.

Where Is Linguistics?
The 1970s, 1980s, and 1990s

Beginning in the 1960s, generative linguistics in the United States came to dominate formal linguistic theorizing for the next forty years. So pervasive was its influence that few other competing theories of language knowledge or language analysis were able to resist its dominance. Many applied linguists, particularly in the United States, were led to believe that generative linguistics was the only real foundation for understanding language form, expression, and acquisition. Chomskian linguistics—first transformational, then Government and Binding, then Minimalism—was seen as the leading direction for understanding the fundamental nature of language knowledge (or, perhaps, syntactic knowledge). Despite schisms and alternatives within this framework, the basic tenets have remained thoroughly generative (rule-based systems that, in principle, derive all of the grammatical sentences of a language). While there are obvious problems with generative linguistics—(1) the suspect status of data and evidence, (2) the assumption of competence apart from performance, (3) the notion of the idealized speaker, (4) the default genetic (non)explanation for language acquisition, and (5) the minimal interface with real-world uses (and abuses) of language—generative linguistics remains a powerful influence over linguists and nonlinguists alike. It has also had an undeniable impact on applied linguists of all persuasions, as Widdowson (2000a) points out, some aspects of which are clearly positive. However, as most trained applied linguists are well aware, a number of competing orientations and approaches have survived the onslaught and now are gaining ground among applied linguists, for the very practical reasons that they are more useful for solving language-based problems.

Among these competing frameworks for linguistic analysis, growing recognition is being given to systemic linguistics, descriptive and corpus linguistics, and functional linguistics. All three have demonstrated that they can be effective approaches for the analysis of language data collected in a range of language-use contexts. They provide socially relevant and accessible reference points for interpretation of language data that can be connected to language-based issues in other disciplines. They also relocate the basic unit of analysis from the clause unit to the discourse or textual unit, reflecting again a closer link to language use in the real world.

Anthropological linguistics and sociolinguistics have similarly adopted more functional and descriptive approaches to language and analyze discourse-level data that reflect the settings in which the data were collected. To a lesser extent, pragmatics and psycholinguistics have moved toward more descriptive data and away from theory-internal research assumptions, this being particularly true for the subfield of cross-cultural pragmatics (which may be more appropriately interpreted as a subfield within applied linguistics, rather than as formal linguistics). This shift in linguistic research subfields indicates a growing recognition that relevant language data and use occurs in real-world contexts and must be analyzed in ways that recognize these situations.

For applied linguistics research, the shift to discourse analysis, descriptive data analysis, and interpretation of language data in their social/cultural settings all indicate a shift in valuing observable language data over theoretical assumptions about what should count as data (Beaugrande 1997; Van Lier 1997). One of the most useful perspectives to have arisen out of this evolution of a more relevant linguistics has been the development of register analysis and genre analysis as they apply to a wide range of language use situations (Johns 2001). Both of these approaches, along with more refined techniques for discourse analysis, are now hallmarks of much applied linguistics research. In fact, many applied linguists have come to see the real-world, problem-based, socially responsive research carried out in applied linguistics as the genuine role for linguistics, with formal linguistics taking a supporting role. As Van Lier (1997) notes:

> I think that it is the applied linguist, who works with language in the real world, who is most likely to have a realistic picture of what language is, and not the theoretical linguist who sifts through several layers of idealization. Furthermore, it may well be the applied linguist who will most advance humankind's understanding of language, provided that he or she is aware that no one has a monopoly on the definitions and conduct of science, theory, language research, and truth. (1997: 103)

Some second language educators have gone even further in suggesting that language teachers actually do not need any real training in linguistics and language awareness (see Crandall 2000).

TRENDS AND PERSPECTIVES IN THE 1990S

In this section, I only note various developments that emerged in the 1990s and that will continue to define applied linguistics through this decade. The present volume provides the details to much of the brief sign-posting that this section provides. For much the same reason, I refrain from a long catalog of appropriate references on the assumption that these ideas will be well-referenced elsewhere.

Under the umbrella of applied linguistics, research in language teaching, language learning, and teacher education is now placing considerable emphasis on notions of language awareness, attention and learning, "focus on forms" for language learning, learning from dialogic interactions, patterns of teacher-student interaction, task-based learning, content-based learning, and teacher as researcher through action research. Research in language learning has shifted in recent years toward a focus on information processing, the emergence of language ability from extended meaningful exposures and relevant practice, and awareness of how language is used and the functions that it serves (see Doughty and Williams 1998b; N. Ellis 1999; Gass 1997; MacWhinney 1999; McCarthy and Carter, 1994; Robinson 2001; Schmidt 1995; Van Lier 1995, 1996; Van Lier and Corson, 1997). Instructional research and curricular issues have centered on task-based learning, content-based learning, dialogic inquiry, and a return to learning centered on specific language skills (Grabe et al. 1998; Skehan 1998b; Snow and Brinton 1997; Swain 2000; Wells 1999).

Language teacher development has also moved in new directions. Widdowson (1998a) has argued forcefully that certain communicative orientations, with a pervasive emphasis on natural language input and authenticity, may be misinterpreting the real purpose of the language classroom context and ignoring effective frameworks for language teaching. He has also persuasively argued that applied linguists must support teachers through their mediation with all aspects of Hymes's notion of communicative competence, balancing language understanding so that it combines grammaticality, appropriateness, feasibility, and examples from the attested (Widdowson, 2000a). A further emphasis for language teacher education has been the move to engaging teachers in the practice of action research. The trend to train teachers as reflective practitioners, inquiring into the effectiveness of teaching and learning in local classroom settings, will increase in the new decade.

A second major emphasis that has taken hold in discussions among applied linguists themselves is the role for critical studies; this term covers critical awareness, critical discourse analysis, critical pedagogy, student rights, critical assessment practices, and ethics in language assessment (and language teaching) (Davies

1999b; Fairclough 1995; McNamara 1998; Pennycook 1997b; Rampton 1997b; Van Lier 1995, 1997). At the same time, there are a number of criticisms of this general approach and its impact on more mainstream applied linguistics that highlight weaknesses in much of the critical studies theorizing (Widdowson 1998b, 1998c). At present, critical studies is also an emphasis that has not demonstrated strong applications in support of those who are experiencing "language problems" of various types. The coming decade will continue this debate.

A third emphasis is on language uses in academic, disciplinary, and professional settings. This research examines the ways in which language is used by participants and in texts in various academic, professional, and occupational settings. It also emphasizes how language can act as a gatekeeping mechanism or create unfair obstacles to those who are not aware of appropriate discourse rules and expectations. In academic settings, the key issue is understanding how genres and register expectations form the basis for successfully negotiating academic work (Hyland 1999; Johns 1997, 2001; Swales 2000). Analyses of language uses in various professional settings are described in Atkinson (1999a), Gibbons (1999), Hyden and Mishler (1999), and Swales (2000). More specific to English for Special Purposes (ESP), Swales (2000) and Dudley-Evans and St John (1998) provide strong overviews.

A fourth emphasis centers on descriptive (usually discourse) analyses of language in real settings and the possible applications of analyses in corpus linguistics, register variation, and genre variation. A breakthrough application of corpus linguistics is the recent *Longman Grammar of Spoken and Written English* (Biber et al. 1999): It is based entirely on attested occurrences of language use in a very large English corpus. The key, though, is not the corpus data themselves but the innovative analyses and displays that define the uniqueness of the grammar. Other important applications of corpus linguistics include the teacher-friendly introduction to discourse analysis by McCarthy and Carter (1994) and their more recent description and resource materials for the study of spoken English (Carter and McCarthy 1997; McCarthy 1998).

A fifth emphasis in applied linguistics research addresses multilingualism and bilingual interactions in school, community, and work and professional settings, or in policy issues at regional and national levels. Since the majority of people in the world are bilingual to some extent, and this bilingualism is associated with the need to negotiate life situations with other cultures and language groups, this area of research is fundamental to applied linguistics concerns. Multilingualism covers issues in bilingual education, migrations of groups of people to new language settings, equity and fairness in social services, and language policies related to multiple language use (or the restriction thereof). Key issues are addressed in Baker and Jones (1998), Grabe et al. (1997), and Rampton (1995b).

A sixth emphasis focuses on the changing discussion in language testing and assessment. In the past ten years, the field of language assessment has taken on a number of important issues and topics that have ramifications for applied linguistics more generally. Validity is now powerfully reinterpreted and, in its new interpretation, has strong implications for all areas of applied linguistics research and data collection (Bachman and Palmer 1996; Chapelle 1999a). Similarly, emphases on technology applications, ethics in assessment, innovative research methodologies, the roles of standardized testing and alternative assessment, standards for professionalism, and critical language testing are all reshaping language assessment and, by extension, applied linguistics (Clapham 2000; Clapham and Corson 1997; McNamara 1998).

A seventh and final emphasis addresses the role of applied linguistics as a mediating discipline and applied linguists as mediators. Over the past decade, discussions about the role of applied linguists, as a bridge between research and practice, have been raised by Widdowson and a number of other scholars (Beaugrande 1997; Widdowson 2000b). At issue is not only the work of applied linguists but also the status of applied linguistics as an academic enterprise (Rampton 1997b; Tucker 2000; Van Lier 1997; Widdowson 1998c; Wilkins 1999). In some of these debates, there are still discussions of the applied linguist as an "MA generalist" or "language teacher." It should be clear from this review that applied linguists in the modern world require training and expertise far beyond such outmoded designations. (And, for this reason, master's degree programs, in and of themselves, are not the appropriate locus of training for applied linguists [Grabe and Kaplan 1992].)

THE PROBLEM-BASED NATURE OF APPLIED LINGUISTICS: THE PROBLEMS, NOT THE DISCIPLINES

In the many discussions of trends, and disciplines, and subfields, and theorizing, the idea is sometimes lost that the focus of applied linguistics is on trying to resolve language-based problems that people encounter in the real world, whether they be learners, teachers, supervisors, academics, lawyers, service providers, those who need social services, test takers, policy developers, dictionary makers, translators, or a whole range of business clients. A list of major language-based problems that applied linguistics typically addresses across a wide range of settings follows. The list is necessarily partial, but it should indicate *what* it is that applied linguists try to do, if not *how* they go about their work. Applied linguists address subsets of the following problems:

- Language learning problems (emergence, awareness, rules, use, context, automaticity, attitudes, expertise)
- Language teaching problems (resources, training, practice, interaction, understanding, use, contexts, inequalities, motivations, outcomes)
- Literacy problems (linguistic and learning issues)
- Language contact problems (language and culture)
- Language inequality problems (ethnicity, class, region, gender, and age)
- Language policy and planning problems (status planning and corpus planning; ecology of language)
- Language assessment problems (validity, reliability, usability, responsibility)
- Language use problems (dialects, registers, discourse communities, gatekeeping situations, limited access to services)
- Language and technology problems (learning, assessment, access, and use)
- Translation and interpretation problems (on-line, off-line, technology assisted)
- Language pathology problems (aphasias, dyslexias, physical disabilities)

These categories could be expanded further, and ideas in each category could be elaborated into full articles in and of themselves. The key point, however, is to recognize that it is the language-based problems in the world that drive applied linguistics. These problems also lead applied linguists to use knowledge from other fields, apart from linguistics, and thereby impose the interdisciplinarity that is a defining aspect of the discipline.

DEFINING APPLIED LINGUISTICS

In this chapter, I have defined applied linguistics as a practice-driven discipline that addresses language-based problems in real-world contexts. However, this general definition does not come to terms with many of the claims that applied linguistics is not a discipline. Critics note that applied linguistics is too broad and too fragmented, that it demands expert knowledge in too many fields, and that it does not have a set of unifying research paradigms. However, it is possible to interpret applied linguistics as a discipline much in the way that many other disciplines are defined. It has a core and a periphery, and the periphery blurs into other disciplines that may or may not want to be allied. This picture may not be very different from those of several other relatively new disciplines in academic institutions. The following points reflect commonalities that most applied linguists would agree on:

1. Applied linguistics has many of the markings of an academic discipline: professional journals, professional associations, international recognition for the field, funding resources for research projects, a large number of individuals who see themselves as applied linguists, trained professionals who are hired in academic institutions as applied linguists, students who want to become applied linguists, and a recognized means for training these students to become applied linguists.

2. Applied linguistics recognizes that linguistics must be included as a core knowledge base in the work of applied linguistics, although the purpose of most applied linguists' work is not simply to "apply" linguistics to achieve a solution.

3. Applied linguistics is grounded in real-world, language-driven problems and issues (primarily by linkages to practical issues involving language use, language evaluation, language contact and multilingualism, language policies, and language learning and teaching). There is also, however, the recognition that these practically driven problems have extraordinary range, and this range tends to dilute any sense of common purpose or common professional identification among practitioners.

4. Applied linguistics typically incorporates other disciplinary knowledge beyond linguistics in its efforts to address language-based problems. Applied linguists commonly draw upon and are often well trained in psychology, education, anthropology, political science, sociology, measurement, computer programming, literature, and/or economics.

5. Applied linguistics is, of necessity, an interdisciplinary field, since few practical language issues can be addressed through the knowledge resources of any single discipline, including linguistics.

6. Applied linguistics commonly includes a core set of issues and practices that is readily identified as work carried out by many applied linguists (e.g., language teaching, language teacher preparation, and language curriculum development).

7. Applied linguistics generally incorporates or includes several further identifiable sub-fields of study: second language acquisition, forensic linguistics, language testing, corpus linguistics, lexicography and dictionary making, language translation, and second language writing research. Some members of these fields do not see themselves as applied linguistics, though their work clearly addresses practical language issues.

8. Applied linguistics often defines itself broadly in order to include additional fields of language-related studies (e.g., language pathology, natural language processing, first language literacy research, and first language

composition studies). The large majority of members of these fields do not see themselves as applied linguistics, but the broad definition gives license for applied linguists to work with and borrow from these disciplines for their own goals.

These eight points indicate the emerging disciplinary nature of applied linguistics. There are certainly difficulties for the field and problems with defining the core versus the periphery. There are also problems in deciding how one becomes an applied linguist and what training (and what duration of training) might be most appropriate. But these problems are no more intractable than those faced by many disciplines, even relatively established ones (e.g., education, psychology).

CONCLUSION

The coming decade of research and inquiry in applied linguistics will continue the lines of investigation noted in the second and third sections of this chapter. Applied linguists will need to know more about corpus linguistics, computer applications for research purposes, and new ways to examine language data. Testing and assessment issues will not be limited to testing applications but will have a much greater influence on other areas of applied linguistics research (Clapham 2000): Issues such as validity, fairness in testing, and ethics (Chapelle 1999a, McNamara 1998) will extend to other areas of applied linguistics (e.g., Bachman and Cohen 1998). These issues will also lead to continued discussions on the most appropriate research methods in different settings (Hornberger and Corson 1997). Applied linguistics will also direct more attention to issues of motivation, attitude, and affect as they potentially influence many language-based problems. Similarly, learning theories will become a more central concern in language learning and teaching. There has been relatively little attention explicitly given to learning theories as they are debated in educational and cognitive psychology.

All of these issues also ensure that applied linguistics will remain interdisciplinary. The resolution of language-based problems in the real world is complex and difficult. It is only appropriate that applied linguists seek partnerships and collaborative research if these problems are to be addressed in effective ways.

CHAPTER 2

RESEARCH APPROACHES IN APPLIED LINGUISTICS

PATRICIA A. DUFF

In a field as vast as applied linguistics (AL), representing the range of topics featured in this volume, an overview of research approaches must be highly selective, a mere sampling and culling of major trends and developments in research perspectives and methods in a number of areas. In this chapter, I discuss recent quantitative and qualitative approaches to AL research and consider some future directions for the field.

Interestingly, no existing textbook provides a comprehensive treatment of contemporary quantitative and qualitative research approaches in AL, although many previous publications have dealt with aspects of AL research methodology, such as quantitative research design and statistics (e.g., Brown 1988; Hatch and Lazaraton 1991); research methods in language and education (Hornberger and Corson 1997); and approaches to research in second language (L2) studies specifically (e.g., Johnson 1992; Kasper and Grotjahn 1991; Nunan 1992; Seliger and Shohamy 1989). Furthermore, no methods textbook in AL is devoted to qualitative research methods, although some volumes (e.g., Bailey and Nunan 1996; Chaudron 1988; Johnson 1992; Larsen-Freeman and Long 1991; Nunan 1992; Seliger and Shohamy 1989; Van Lier 1988) and articles (e.g., Cumming 1994; Davis 1995; Edge and Richards 1998; Lazaraton 1995, 2000) discuss qualitative methods such as case study and ethnography and look at related methodological issues. Many other publications have highlighted specific analytical approaches or methods for conducting research, typically within a particular realm of AL, such as L2 classroom research; these include ethnomethodology and conversation analysis (Markee

2000); case study research (Duff forthcoming); corpus linguistics (Biber, Conrad, and Reppen 1998); ethnography (Van Lier 1988; Watson-Gegeo 1988); L1, L2, and interlanguage analysis (Gass and Selinker 1994; Kasper and Grotjahn 1991; Larsen-Freeman and Long 1991; Pica 1997a), stimulated recall (Gass and Mackey 2000); discourse analysis (Schiffrin 1994); critical discourse analysis (Fairclough 1989; Pennycook 1999b); survey methods (Baker 1997); verbal reports (Cohen 1991; Kasper 1998); and elicited imitation and grammaticality judgment tasks in SLA and the use of VARBRUL in sociolinguistics (Tarone, Gass, and Cohen 1994). Some of these methods can be used in either quantitative or qualitative research, depending on the nature of the research question.

RESEARCH APPROACHES: CONTRASTING, COMBINING, AND EXPANDING PARADIGMS

Most research methodology textbooks in education and the social sciences (e.g., Creswell 1994; Gall, Borg, and Gall 1996; Neuman 1994; Palys 1997), and therefore in some of the AL overview texts referred to earlier, distinguish between quantitative (nomothetic) and qualitative (hermeneutic) research as two distinct approaches to scientific enquiry. They also emphasize that the approach or method is crucially linked to the kind of research question or problem under investigation, the purpose of the study (e.g., exploratory, interpretive, descriptive, explanatory, confirmatory, predictive), and the type of data and population one is working with. Quantitative research is often associated with experiments and qualitative research with ethnography or case study. This is, of course, an oversimplification, yet one that persists. Each paradigm actually represents a collection of approaches to research that share some common principles but reflect major differences as well. Increasingly, quantitative and qualitative approaches are seen as complementary rather than fundamentally incompatible, and more mixed-paradigm research is recommended (Miles and Huberman 1994), although not as much combination of the two occurs in AL as one might hope (Lazaraton 1995). Thus, discussing approaches in terms of the quantitative-qualitative dichotomy, as current research methods textbooks do, can be both useful and problematic.

Any research paradigm or approach reflects a number of components, including:

- A philosophical basis or belief system regarding epistemology, or the nature of truth and of knowing (e.g., that research is ideally objective, unbiased, and value free vs. more subjective);

- An ideology concerning ontology, or the nature of reality (e.g., that an objective reality exists, or that reality is constructed socially and that multiple perspectives on reality exist);
- A corresponding methodology (e.g., one that is experimental/manipulative and hypothesis testing, or not) with various designs, methods, techniques, and devices for eliciting and analyzing phenomena (Cohen and Manion 1994; Denzin and Lincoln 1994).

Therefore, there are many levels at which research can be analyzed and categorized. Comparison and categorization in AL tends to be based primarily on methods or techniques, with less reflection on epistemological and ontological issues.[1] Quantitative approaches tend to be associated with a positivist or postpositivist orientation, a realist ontology, an objectivist epistemology, and an experimental, manipulative methodology. Qualitative approaches, on the other hand, are more often associated with an interpretive, humanistic orientation, an ontology of multiple realities, a nonobjectivist epistemology, and a naturalistic, nonmanipulative methodology (Guba and Lincoln 1994). However, what is ostensibly quantitative research may involve qualitative analysis (e.g., discourse analysis) and vice versa. Case study, for example, normally considered qualitative research, may actually reflect a more positivist approach than an interpretive one (Yin 1994), or it may be part of a quantitative one-shot (experimental) case study or a single- or multiple-case time series design (e.g., Mellow, Reeder, and Forster 1996). Similarly, statistical techniques can be used in both quantitative and qualitative research, but inferential statistics are mostly associated with quantitative research (Gall, Borg, and Gall 1996).

Quantitative research includes a variety of approaches, designs, and tools, such as correlations, surveys, and multifactorial studies, in addition to experimental or quasi-experimental studies. Despite its underrepresentation in AL, qualitative research encompasses a broad, expanding assortment of approaches, including narrative research, life history, autobiographical or biographical accounts, content analysis, historical and archival studies, conversation analysis, microethnography, and discourse analysis, drawing on such traditions as ethnomethodology, symbolic interactionism, structuralism, poststructuralism, phenomenology, hermeneutics, feminism(s), social/educational anthropology, and cultural studies, as well as case study and ethnography (Bogdan and Biklen 1992; Denzin and Lincoln 1994; LeCompte, Millroy, and Preissle 1992).

Quantitative research has traditionally enjoyed a more elevated status within education and the social sciences because it is considered by some researchers to be more robust, rigorous, scientific, theoretical, and generalizable, and, therefore, it is argued, it has more to contribute to knowledge and theory than qualitative research. Of course, none of these claimed attributes should be taken for granted in quantitative research—they must, rather, be demonstrated by the researcher.

Neither should it be assumed that qualitative research is atheoretical, unscientific, lacking in rigor or generalizability (transferability), or intellectually insignificant; again, the onus is on the researcher to demonstrate the credibility and importance of the methods and findings.

Qualitative research of different types has gained a major foothold in AL in the past ten years, however. Yet quantitative approaches are still considered "mainstream" by some AL scholars, while other more interpretive or critical approaches are cast as "alternative(s)" (Pennycook 1994a). This perceived imbalance is, moreover, supported by a recent survey of research articles in AL (Lazaraton 2000) revealing a disproportionate number of quantitative studies in AL journals compared with qualitative ones.

Some research methodologists outside AL posit the existence of not just two research paradigms and perspectives, but three or more. These include:

- Positivist, interpretive, and critical (Jackson 1995)
- Positivist, postpositivist, critical (and related ideological positions), and constructivist (Guba and Lincoln 1994)
- Positivist/postpositivist, constructivist, feminist, ethnic, Marxist, and cultural studies (Denzin and Lincoln 1994)

In AL, Seliger and Shohamy (1989) contrast qualitative research (participant observation, ethnography), descriptive research (case or group studies, tests, surveys, questionnaires, self-reports, interviews, observation, correlation and multivariate analysis), and experimental research (different designs). Larsen-Freeman and Long (1991) compare cross-linguistic (more quantitative) and longitudinal (more qualitative) approaches, and they depict research methodologies along a continuum (from qualitative to quantitative) with the following methods: introspection, participant observation, nonparticipant observation, focused description, preexperimental, quasi-experimental, and experimental. Cumming's (1994) survey of TESOL research approaches includes the categories descriptive (analysis of learner language, verbal reports, text analysis), interpretive (classroom interaction analysis, ethnography), and ideological (critical pedagogy, participatory action research).

Critical (or "ideological") research is sometimes accorded a category of its own, as in the previous example, apart from quantitative and qualitative paradigms. Perhaps this is so because certain approaches to research constitute explicitly ideological lenses or frames (e.g., critical or feminist) through which any data or situation can be analyzed; other studies also reflect an ideology, but one that is simply not explicated. Thus, critical perspectives can be applied to ethnography, and feminist perspectives can be applied to surveys or case studies. On the other hand, it might be claimed that these overtly ideological perspectives constitute different approaches, purposes, underlying assumptions, methods, subject matter, and reporting styles and that they are therefore not simply new lenses, frames, or values to be applied to otherwise orthodox academic pursuits with reified categories and objectification. Finally, additional categories sometimes discussed separately in research methods textbooks (especially in L2 education) include action research, collaborative research, and teacher research; program evaluation; language policy research; and historical, archival, and (other) library research (Johnson 1992; Nunan 1992).

Developments in Quantitative Research

The 1980s and 1990s were a very productive time in the development, explanation, and application of quantitative research design and statistics and other analytical techniques in AL research using a variety of types of research: experimental, quasi-experimental, correlational, survey, and other carefully controlled, sometimes multivariate designs. As a result, greater attention has been paid to the reliability and validity of research constructs, instruments, scales, rating protocols, and analytical procedures; sampling procedures; measurement; variables; and parametric and nonparametric statistics (Brown 1988; Hatch and Lazaraton 1991; Lazaraton 2000). I consider some additional developments in this section.

Ellis (1999) discusses three quantitative approaches to cognitive and psycholinguistic research: Observational research (e.g., using language corpora), experimentation (e.g., in studies on form-focused instruction and SLA; Doughty and Williams 1998b), and simulations (e.g., connectionist models of SLA; Gasser 1990; Kempe and MacWhinney 1998). Although there is a greater understanding among applied linguists of the criteria of good quantitative research now, it is also evident that true experimental research is often difficult to conduct for logistical and ethical reasons, particularly in research with children or adults in educational contexts. In many institutions, for example, pretesting, random assignment to treatment types (e.g., instructional interventions or experimental stimuli), and control or normative/baseline groups may be difficult to arrange. Norgate (1997) provides an interesting example of this dilemma in research on the L1 development of blind children. Rather, quasi-experimental research examining cause-effect relationships among independent and dependent variables and research looking for other kinds of relationships among variables predominate. Experimental SLA laboratory studies are an exception; that research often involves artificial or semiartificial L2 structures, control groups, random assignment, and pre- and posttesting (e.g., Hulstijn and DeKeyser 1997). The downside of this carefully controlled research is that it lacks ecological validity because the language(s), contexts, and activities do not represent those ordinarily encountered by language learners and users.

In another area of AL, language testing, Kunnan (1999) describes new quantitative methods, such as structured equation modeling, that permit sophisticated analyses of relationships among groups of learner (test taker) variables such as L2 proficiency, language aptitude and intelligence (e.g., Sasaki 1993). In L1/L2 survey research, Baker (1997) describes large-scale and small-scale initiatives in Europe, South America, and elsewhere, dealing with such issues as language vitality among minority language groups and social-psychological variables (e.g., attitudes and motivation) connected with successful L2 learning. He also illustrates how more readily available census data with specific items about language has facilitated certain kinds of analysis for language policy and planning purposes (see Clément, Dörnyei, and Noels 1994; Johnson 1992; and Schumann 1997 for other examples of survey research).

DEVELOPMENTS IN
QUALITATIVE RESEARCH

Despite the widespread use of some forms of qualitative research in AL historically, as in case studies (Hatch 1978) which have had considerable impact within SLA, discussions of qualitative approaches to research were almost nonexistent in general AL research methods textbooks before 1989 and still appear to be uncommon in many AL graduate programs. The current expansion of qualitative approaches in AL reflects trends across the health sciences, social sciences, humanities, and education in recent years (Denzin and Lincoln 1994; LeCompte, Millroy, and Preissle 1992; Miles and Huberman 1994) and a growing interest in ecological validity and in the social, cultural, situational, embodied, and performative nature of language, knowledge, and learning.

Ethnographies of language learning and teaching, literacy practices, and workplace encounters and methodological discussions about cultural aspects of knowledge and behavior have become more prominent and commonplace since Watson-Gegeo's (1988) influential article first appeared (e.g., Duff 1995; Harklau 1994; Ramanathan and Atkinson 1999; Roberts, Davies, and Jupp 1992). In addition, a burgeoning interest in poststructural, postcolonial, and critical L2 research (e.g., Pennycook 1994b, 1998, 1999) is evident in many areas of AL. Critical and poststructural perspectives have been applied to ethnographies (e.g., Canagarajah 1993b; Goldstein 1997), to studies of language and social identity (e.g., Norton 1997b; Peirce 1995), and to research on language and gender (e.g., Cameron 1992; Ehrlich 1997; Freeman 1997; Mills 1995), some of which is explicitly feminist, emancipatory, reflexive, and postmodern.

Thus, whereas qualitative AL research in the past may have leaned toward (post)positivism and structuralism, relying on researchers' structured elicitations, analyses, and interpretations of a relatively narrow band of observed linguistic (or other) behavior sometimes designed to test specific hypotheses, current strands of research lean toward more unapologetically subjective, dialectical accounts, incorporating different, sometimes contradictory perspectives of the same phenomenon and grappling more intentionally with issues of position, voice, and representation (Edge and Richards 1998). The personal accounts and narratives of the experiences of language teachers, learners, and others, often across a broader span of time, space, experience, and languages, have now become a major focus in some qualitative research. Evidence of this are first-person narratives, diary studies, autobiographies, and life histories of developing, teaching, or losing aspects of one's language, identity, and affective orientation (e.g., Bailey and Nunan 1996; Kouritzen 1999; Schumann 1997); studies now examine individuals using language in and across social contexts that were investigated to a lesser degree in the past (e.g., in professional or academic settings [Spack 1997], in the home/family, community, workplace, and other social institutions).

While interesting and compelling in many cases, the newer approaches are not necessarily supplanting existing ones but rather complementing them and providing alternatives to traditional approaches, topics, genres, analyses, and conclusions, and notions of authenticity and legitimacy (Edge and Richards 1998). In addition to these emerging narrative approaches to exploring linguistic experience, other important but less emic accounts of language and behavior have attracted renewed attention from scholars across disciplines, particularly in studies of the discursive structure and social-interactional accomplishment of narrative texts (e.g., Bamberg 1998).

There is a growing emphasis on social, cultural, political, and historical aspects of language and language research, in addition to narrative aspects (Hinkel 1999; McKay and Hornberger 1996; Tollefson 1995). Categorical labels and unacknowledged bias have therefore been the subject of analysis and critique (in connection with, e.g., race, class, culture, language, gender, heterosexism, native versus nonnative speakers, inner and outer circle in World Englishes). Drawing on different (psychological) traditions but also concerned with social aspects of language and literacy are neo-Vygotskyan, sociocultural, and constructivist accounts, which have been adopted by growing numbers of applied linguists over the past decade (Lantolf 1994, 2000), particularly in research in classrooms, therapeutic or counseling encounters, and community settings. Like other primarily qualitative approaches, sociocultural research often involves conversation analysis, discourse analysis, narrative analysis, and microethnography and examines language and content in an integrated manner.

Reflecting another change in AL research approaches and objects of study, text and discourse analyses now investigate not only the structure of, say, scientific research articles but also the linguistic messages, symbols, and genres associated with ostensibly nonscientific discourse(s) and interactions, such as in popular culture, mass media, and everyday social encounters (e.g., dinnertime discussions). Some of this research is framed in terms of critical or poststructural theory, and the constructs of literacy and discourse, like that of identity, have been theorized and analyzed as plural, not singular entities, and as social, multifaceted and fluid (Gee 1996). Finally, the concern for understanding contextual features of linguistic phenomena that is the hallmark of much qualitative (or at least nonquantitative) AL research has also been applied to analyses of the historical, political, social, cultural, rhetorical, and intellectual contexts and consequences of AL theories, research, and practice/praxis (Crookes 1997; Rampton 1995a; Thomas 1998; and the paradigm debates in AL in note 1).

THE IMPACT OF TECHNOLOGICAL ADVANCES ON RESEARCH APPROACHES IN AL

Technological and computational advances have also played an important role in the ongoing transformation of AL research and thus merit some discussion. For example, the recent availability of high-quality, affordable tape recorders, digital video cameras, personal and handheld computers, scanners, and means of incorporating data of different types from multiple sources in computer files and in publications (e.g., with accompanying compact disks) has major practical and theoretical implications, particularly in applied psycholinguistics, corpus linguistics, discourse analysis, and testing (Ellis 1999; Grabe et al. 1996). These innovations have also enhanced research with minority populations in AL, such as the blind and deaf (Hornberger and Corson 1997). In addition, the use of data management and analysis software designed specifically for qualitative research is also increasing (e.g., Weitzman and Miles 1995). Similarly, the development and accessibility of L1 and L2 acquisition databases such as CHILDES (MacWhinney 1995a), corpora from oral and written texts (Biber, Conrad, and Reppen 1998;

Thomas and Short 1996), new databases resulting from the use of computers in language testing, and online language interactions in CALL or other electronic networks have also engendered new possibilities for AL research in such diverse fields as language acquisition, text analysis, syntax and semantics, assessment, sociolinguistics, and language policy. Future AL research will no doubt continue to be greatly influenced by ongoing technical developments in natural language processing, machine and other translation systems, artificial intelligence, brain imaging techniques, CALL, aural/visual recognition and transcription devices, and AL-tailored statistical packages and procedures. Also, as more research focuses on languages other than English—including signed and other languages with different orthographies—and seeks to accommodate a greater range of information about messages (e.g., phonetic, temporal, visual, contextual, material), new electronic tools and theoretical insights will result.

Conclusion

In this short chapter, I have provided an overview of both dominant and emerging approaches to AL research, particularly those typically described as quantitative or qualitative, and how these have been discussed and utilized in the field. Here I provide some concluding remarks about current and future trends and directions in AL research.

The research topics and approaches discussed, much like the field of AL, involve various philosophical and theoretical commitments, as well as methodological preferences and practices. Generally speaking, AL research has begun to show greater pluralism and rigor, an increased sensitivity to the contexts of research, the characteristics of research participants, the need to draw meaningful theoretical insights from findings and to consider carefully constraints on generalizability (or transferability) of results. There is now a growing recognition of and respect for fundamental issues of ethics, fairness, and validity in AL research and practice (e.g., Cameron et al. 1992; Davis 1995; Davies 1997b) and an awareness that some issues, populations, languages, and geographical areas receive considerable research attention (and funding), while others have remained invisible or on the margins. This point not only suggests imbalances in the global research enterprise but also has implications regarding the limitations of the theoretical conclusions drawn from work confined to particular areas, languages, and participants.

The development of criteria for exemplary quantitative research and reporting has resulted in many carefully conceived quantitative research studies and programs of research. Now parallel work needs to be done with other (e.g., qualitative) approaches to research, some of which are only just appearing in AL (Edge and Richards 1998). In addition, a greater collective awareness and understanding (and, ideally, genuine appreciation) of different research methods and areas of study would be helpful to the field at large. Along the same lines, collaboration among researchers looking at similar phenomena in different (socio)linguistic, cultural, and geographical contexts (e.g., Blum-Kulka, House, and Kasper 1989) would certainly benefit theory development and practical applications. Combining the expertise of applied linguists espousing different research paradigms in complementary types of analysis of the same phenomenon would also yield richer analyses of complex issues (Koshmann 1999). Furthermore, multiperspective research with researchers from different traditions and primary areas (e.g., anthropology, psychology, education, and linguistics) examining the same data from their own disciplinary frames of reference would be both interesting and timely. Although much AL research is chiefly concerned with abilities, behaviors, or sociolinguistic conditions and phenomena at one point in time (typically the present and/or immediate past or future), more research sustained over larger periods of time, space, and activities is also needed; for example, research that examines the long-term effects of certain interventions or establishes developmental patterns across oral and written structures and genres (Heath 2000). Replication studies, meta-analyses, crosslinguistic, cross-generational, and cross-medium (e.g., oral/written) studies have been used in limited ways in AL, with particular combinations of languages, media, and age groups. In addition, more multimethod AL research would provide a greater triangulation of findings. Research has started to take into greater account not only individual (e.g., cognitive, linguistic, affective) and group aspects of language behavior and knowledge but also sociocultural, historical, political, and ideological aspects. More emphasis is therefore being placed on the multiple, sometimes shifting identities, perspectives, and competencies of research participants and researchers and on the multiple contexts in which language is learned, produced, interpreted, translated, forgotten, and even eliminated.

Finally, all basic or pure research is meant to contribute to the knowledge base and theoretical growth of a field; thus, with more conceptually sound research, new discoveries, insights, and applications are certainly in store for the field of AL. In applied research that aims to yield a greater understanding of phenomena in the mind/world and also help improve some aspect of the human condition, increased social and political intervention and advocacy may also be warranted. These, then, are just some of the issues and challenges that applied linguists must address in the future from different perspectives and using a variety of approaches. Indeed, as perspectives, methods, genres, and media for conducting, reporting and disseminating research are transformed, new areas for AL research and new challenges, too, will surface for the evaluation of innovative, nontraditional forms of research.

NOTE

1. Discussions and debates concerning philosophical and theoretical foundations of AL research (particularly SLA)—a phenomenon dubbed the "paradigm wars" (e.g., Edge and Richards 1998)—have tended to take place apart from discussions of particular methods (e.g., Beretta 1993; Beretta, Crookes, Gregg, and Long 1994; Block 1996; Gregg, Long, Jordan, and Beretta 1997; Van Lier 1994).

PART II

THE FOUR SKILLS:
SPEAKING, LISTENING,
READING, AND
WRITING

CHAPTER 3

....

SPEAKING

....

MARTIN BYGATE

THE study of speaking—like the study of other uses of language—is properly an interdisciplinary enterprise. It involves understanding the psycholinguistic and interpersonal factors of speech production, the forms, meanings, and processes involved, and how these can be developed. This chapter views speaking as a multilevel, hierarchical skill, in which high-level plans, in the form of speaker intentions, are realized through the processes of formulation and articulation under a range of conditions. For the purposes of this chapter, spoken language is taken to be *colloquial* in the two senses of representing dialogue and of representing the features typically associated with the everyday use of language.

This chapter first outlines the need for an integrated account of oral language processing. It then presents such an account, considers the range of formal features which characterize spoken language, and reviews oral language pedagogy in the light of this account. The conclusion outlines issues for further exploration.

ASPECTS OF SPOKEN LANGUAGE

....

We start from the distinction between language as system and language in contexts of use. A speaker's language proficiency can be seen as a pool of systemic resources and the ability to use them in real contexts. Systemic knowledge can be described in relatively decontextualized terms, as in a grammar or dictionary. To communicate, speakers have to exploit those resources for real purposes and under real constraints. An applied linguistic model of speaking needs to explain how and why speakers adapt systemic knowledge of language to real world use, involving judgments of appropriacy at all levels, whether discourse, lexicogrammatical, or articulatory.

Consider the following example, from a recording of a family evening meal:

Example

Mother: Oh:: you know what? you wanna tell Daddy what happened
to you today?=   (Ochs and Taylor 1992: 324)

We can assume that behind the mother's utterance lie a number of intentions:

• To attract attention
• To announce a potentially interesting topic
• To indicate familiarity with it
• To invite her child to recount it
• To invite others present to listen.

In other words, the content of the communication reflects judgments of appropriacy based on speaker intention.

In addition, formulation of the message is also subject to judgments of appropriacy based on the speaker's intentions. For example, the speaker chose to formulate her intentions through uninverted questions (requiring the realization of appropriate intonations). Other choices include the use of the first question to announce a new topic; use of the word 'Daddy' rather than, say, 'your father'; and 'you wanna' as an invitation implying strong encouragement. Issues of appropriacy, then, are not limited to the level of discourse structure or message content but permeate the processes of message formulation and phonological articulation.

This example suggests the desirability of an account that presents the speaker's judgments of feasibility, appropriacy, and frequency as affecting the whole speech process. Although underlying this process there must be a robust systemic knowledge of the language, this chapter focuses on how our systemic resources are used across the full hierarchy of language levels.

AN INTEGRATED MODEL OF ORAL LANGUAGE PRODUCTION

An account of oral language production needs to represent the main types of decision that speakers typically make. Building on the work of Levelt (1989), Levelt et al. (1999; see also Poulisse [1997] and Scovel [1998] for an accessible introduction), these can be accommodated to a considerable extent in terms of four different *levels* of decision making: discourse modeling, message conceptualization, message formulation, and message articulation. We consider each of these in turn.

Discourse Modeling

In speaking, we have to construct a discourse plan that represents a number of general intentions: our overall topic and intended outcome, the way we would like the interaction to proceed, our relationships with our interlocutor(s), our personality, and our relationship with the world. One aspect of this concerns the kinds of relationships, identity, and formality we wish to establish and maintain. This dimension has been researched in relation to cross-cultural talk and its capacity to lead to misleading perceptions of the speakers in various contexts (e.g., in relation to communication at the workplace, in the law courts, in the context of academic tutorials, in doctor-patient interviews). Studies have shown how language is used to negotiate particular interactional roles and relationships in the family, and studies in cross-cultural pragmatics have explored the ways in which speakers negotiate the dimension of face (see Scollon and Scollon 1983; Spolsky 1998).

A second dimension concerns the expected patterns of oral discourse (Hoey 1991). Studies have demonstrated the structuring of classroom talk (e.g., Coulthard 1991; Sinclair and Coulthard 1975) and of service encounters and have shown the differences in the organization of talk across cultures and from a cross-cultural perspective (e.g., Gumperz 1983). This suggests differences in cultural expectations toward particular types of interpersonal interactions or discourse types (such as narrative structure), which can give rise to significant misinterpretations.

A third dimension, content knowledge, is clearly also relevant to managing communication on different topics (e.g., Selinker and Douglas 1985). Speakers' knowledge of their topic has been shown to have an impact on their ability to speak. To participate in any form of interaction, then, speakers need knowledge of types of identity and relationship, knowledge of discourse patterns and patterns of interaction, and topic structures.

Further, in practice, these aspects of discourse have to be negotiated by speakers through joint interaction, rather than being decided on the basis of unilateral decisions by individual speakers or by the application of fixed patterns. Speakers might therefore commonly develop strategic routines for purposes such as the offering of invitations, or the giving of directions, including preparatory as well as summarizing moves (Widdowson 1983). Speakers improvise around familiar structures in order to achieve satisfactory outcomes. In addition, in interacting with others, we commonly identify discourse features preferred by our interlocutors. We can borrow or adopt these ourselves, if we feel that by so doing interaction will be facilitated. This is referred to as the process of "converging" or "diverging" from the dialect feature of one's interlocutor (Preston 1989; Spolsky 1998).

So, the discourse level provides speakers with frames of reference for planning their utterances, anticipating interlocutors' knowledge and expectations, evaluating utterances produced, and deciding whether any repair work might be needed. It provides, then, a key reference point for the production process.

Message Conceptualization

The production of specific utterances begins by conceptualization of the particular pragmatic purpose, content, speaker orientation, and appropriate speech acts in terms of contextual appropriacy and relevance (Yule 1996). This is undertaken against a mapping of the preceding discourse and with anticipation of the interlocutors' knowledge and expectations and of the likely ensuing talk. The output from this phase is the mental activation of a set of lexical concepts (Levelt et al. 1999: 9).

This level is important for two main reasons. First, whether we are concerned with first or second language production, it is important be able to work with the notion that thought underlies talk. Work with first language users in secondary school, or more generally with second language users, might, for instance, aim to raise awareness among students of the strategic implications of the choice of different kinds of content that they could select in particular contexts (such as contexts of group work, formal presentation, or different kinds of interview situations). See Bardovi-Harlig and Hartford (1990) for a discussion of these issues in the context of student/tutor advising sessions and L. Cameron et al. (1996) on the language of study among British ESL students in secondary classrooms.

Second, it provides a basis for understanding how speakers solve communication problems through the use of communication strategies. Communication strategies are part of the formulation phase and involve improvising the communication of meanings where conventional language is lacking. This can occur only if speakers already have a meaning to convey. This is the framework proposed by Faerch and Kasper (1983a) for the study of communication strategies. (See also Bialystok 1990; Færch and Kasper 1983b; Kasper and Kellerman 1997.) Dörnyei and Kormos (1998) use this as a basis for bringing together all problem-solving processes, whether these are pre-articulatory or postarticulatory and whether they resolve problems in the speaker's own output or in that of their interlocutor. Conceptualization then provides a basis for formulation, pre- and postarticulatory monitoring, and, if necessary, reformulation or reconceptualization.

Formulation

Formulation is the phase where speakers select language to convey the conceptual content of their intended message. This involves accessing speakers' systemic language store and making a number of distinct but interrelated decisions. Levelt et al. (1999) consider that this involves the following processes:

The selection of lemmas—identifying a relevant lexical family
The formation of a rough syntactic frame on the basis of initial awareness
    of the word classes needed
The selection of relevant lexemes, including multiword items
The selection of grammatical lexemes
The accessing of relevant grammatical morphemes, such as inflections
The preparation of a phonological plan for the utterance.

The process has a strong pragmatically developed dimension. Several aspects of native-speaker production appear to be based on speakers' prototypical memories of the characteristics of different lexical items (such as the likelihood of their occurring as singular or plural nouns, and their typical meanings). Further, many decisions depend on the use of rapidly fading traces—on the part of speaker and listener—in short-term memory (e.g., in the production of anaphoric and cataphoric markers, relative clauses, or verb-adverbial particle combinations). In addition, accessing involves drawing on a range of different types of collocational information (Lennon 1996, 1998; Pawley and Syder 1983; Wray 2000; see later discussion). We should note that it is not known how far the precise characteristics of native speaker processing can, or need be, replicated by nonnative learners, but clearly the process is complex and demanding.

The complexity and time pressures may help explain why unscripted spoken language is typically found to be less dense than written language (Biber et al. 1994; Brown and Yule 1983b; Chafe 1985). It also provides an explanation for why patterns of pausing typically change as speakers become more proficient: On the one hand, too much intra-clause pausing will interfere with various aspects of processing, providing an in-built motivation to increase fluency; on the other hand, more intra-clause pausing can be predicted where speakers need more accessing time, whereas, as accessing becomes quicker and other processing loads get lighter, pausing will retreat to clauses boundaries, resulting in longer runs. This occurs whether the talk is produced by native speakers (Beattie 1980) or by less proficient nonnative speakers (Lennon 1990; Towell, Hawkins, and Bazergui 1996).

It is evident from this account that relevant practice should engage speakers as active decision makers in the task of formulation. Rote repetition clearly cannot provide sufficient appropriate practice (although thought-provoking types of "drill" are useful if they involve learners in active decisions of linguistic appropriacy).

Articulation

Articulation involves the execution of the pre-articulatory plans prepared in the formulation phase. Just two points need noting here about this phase of operation. First, articulation is generally a relatively automated phase. By this is meant that plans can be executed with minimal conscious attention. An indication of this is the fact that speakers often fail to correct their speech errors, and when they do, it is with a delay, suggesting that errors are picked up after, rather than during, articulation.

The fact of automation is important, particularly within a limited capacity model of attention, according to which channeling attention to articulation would divert it from the phases of conceptualization and formulation where it is particularly needed (Levelt 1989). However, although articulation in proficient speakers is usually automated, articulation is nonetheless open to some degree of active monitoring. This can be seen in speakers' articulation when addressing children or when speaking against background noise or to those thought to have comprehension difficulties. A limited capacity model suggests that attention to pronunciation will be difficult when learners are simultaneously encountering other problems in oral communication and that articulatory skills need integrating into the full hierarchy of oral production, rather than relying on pronunciation practice in isolation.

Monitoring

From the foregoing account it is clear that all aspects of speech production are subject to active monitoring (see particularly Dörnyei and Kormos 1998). In this view, maintaining formal accuracy is only one facet of the more general process of ensuring that conceptualization, formulation, and articulation of the message conforms to the speaker's underlying intentions. That is, accuracy (Hymes's category of "possibility") joins feasibility, appropriacy, and frequency in being subject to on-line monitoring.

Processing Demands and Quality of Performance

Drawing on current views of cognition and memory, Skehan (1998a) proposes an account of language processing that describes quality of performance in terms of fluency, accuracy, and complexity. Skehan suggests that in producing language, speakers have two kinds of memory to draw on (Peters 1983). One is an extensive memory store of lexical items, including formulaic 'chunks' (Bolinger 1975; Nattinger and DeCarrico 1992; Pawley and Syder 1983; Wray 2000). The second is a lexicogrammatical repertoire for generating novel utterances. According to this view, speakers can access their item store for rapid production, avoiding the trouble of having to assemble novel lexicogrammatical combinations. The item store then enables speakers to maintain fluency of output.

However, this resource is not without limitations. These are, first, that formulaic phrases may not be appropriate to any particular communicative intentions and, second, that they may contain inaccuracies, constituting a source of communication problems or impeding the learner's development. In contrast, although generating new utterances is more time consuming, it is more likely to enable learners to monitor the accuracy of their output and to develop new ways of expressing themselves. Working within a limited capacity model, Skehan suggests that effort in each of the dimensions of fluency, accuracy, and complexity can affect our capacity to process the others, suggesting the possibility of a tradeoff in performance between them.

There is growing evidence to support this account of language processing. However, Robinson (2000) argues for a multiple capacity model, suggesting that by manipulating task factors, speakers can be induced to increase fluency and complexity without loss of accuracy. Clearly, this issue remains to be resolved. However, three points need making. First, the existence of a tradeoff effect should not distract from the fact that fluency, accuracy, and complexity have to be managed simultaneously in any circumstances, and it is far from clear how they can be effectively integrated in language learning. Second, it is worth noting that language use is typically a constant blend of the formulaic and the generative, speakers being unable to rely exclusively on either one or the other in the vast majority of situations. And, third, the construct of "complexity" requires investigation, given that it sometimes involves complex language but sometimes involves the complex matching of simple language to new concepts. Nonetheless, the framework discussed here is one with clear interest for teachers and testers, and with considerable potential for development.

FORMS OF ORAL LANGUAGE

Finally the lexicogrammatical features of speech need consideration. Most speech conditions affect the patterning of grammar and vocabulary in four major ways.

First, as Brown and Yule (1983b) point out, the lack of planning time for the speaker, combined with the fact that, in most speech, the listener has to cope with a fleeting and often imperfect signal, leads speech to be less lexically dense, notably with less noun premodification (Chafe 1985). These conditions also account for the fact that speakers often repeat and rephrase aspects of their message and help to explain part of the function of pausing (Pawley and Syder 1983). A second important condition is the fact that speech is usually situated in the same time and space for both speaker and listener. This means that speakers can typically refer directly to the environment ("this here") and can orient to the same temporal context ("now") without having to make these points of reference explicit (Chafe 1985). A further effect of this condition is that speakers assume the shared knowledge and cooperation of the listener, which enables various forms of ellipsis (Chafe 1985; Eggins and Slade 1997). The third important condition of speech is that the interlocutors are both normally involved and have speaking rights during the event. This has the effect that the speaker can typically refer directly to the listener (using second-person pronouns), and that the speaker can expect the listener to take turns at talk. Finally, the fact that the speaker knows the listener and the context of the interaction enables a wide range of informality in speech style (Preston 1989).

These four conditions can clearly affect writing, as well as speech. However, the range of speech functions is wider than that in writing, and the informal end of the range is more common in speech. (See the findings of corpus linguistics; e.g., Biber 1988.) However, while education needs to consider the informal aspects of speech, other features are also important for learners, such as more formal speech styles and contexts and the ability to handle cross-cultural or cross-dialectal differences. Hence, these should not be neglected. Features of spoken language are explored in Carter and McCarthy (1997) and in Eggins and Slade (1997) and are reviewed in Riggenbach (1999).

PEDAGOGY

Against this background, it is instructive to consider developments in the teaching of spoken language. It can be argued that, in most approaches to language pedagogy, the teaching of speaking began to emerge as a concern in its own right only in the 1940s. For one thing, many approaches to language teaching had largely ignored speech, as in the grammar-translation method, and most were based on the use of texts (apart from the use of phrase books and written dialogues—

according to Howatt [1984: 8] a tradition going back to the Middle Ages). It is true that the European reform movement had as two of its three main principles the primacy of speech and the centrality of an oral methodology in the classroom (Howatt 1984: 171). However, even within this context, speech was used first (particularly because of its "here-and-now" dimension) as an effective conduit for presenting and demonstrating grammatical structures without using the first language, as in the direct method, and in Palmer's use of question-answer sequences in his "oral method" (e.g., Palmer 1930) and, second, as a way of facilitating memorization. Spoken discourse, then, was mainly represented through question-answer interactions or the use of written dialogues.

These assumptions continued through the audiolingual approach of the 1940s. Building on the insights of the reform movement, this approach began from the insistence that new language should be taught initially through listening and speaking. The reasons for this, however, had little to do with the aim of fostering spoken interaction. Rather, it was based on the assumptions that accurate speaking depended on habit formation, which was taken to imply a need for substantial practice at responding to oral stimuli, that the orthography of a language was likely to interfere with the development of accurate pronunciation, and that oral drills were an effective way of promoting memorization (Fries 1945). This approach could be described, then, as one that used oral activities as a way of teaching pronunciation skills and grammatical accuracy and of promoting memorization. The language content of materials was substantially (e.g., Broughton 1968–1970) or even exclusively (e.g., Lado and Fries 1957; or *English 900* [English Language Services 1964]), defined in terms of the formal grammatical structures of the language, although often the structures were to some extent related to typical conversation patterns (e.g., Alexander 1967).

Clearly, this neglected significant aspects of speaking as a skill. During the 1960s, there was a growing awareness that drills were inadequate for real-world needs and that it would be necessary to try to prepare learners to handle a range of commonly occurring real-life situations in terms of dialogues (e.g., Ockenden 1972; O'Neill 1970; 1981). In the 1970s, critics began to suggest that audiolingual drills were also limited in that they failed to teach the typical forms and functions of oral language, and that a "functional" approach might be more effective (e.g., Munby 1978; Wilkins 1976). This led to the introduction of drills and exercises that taught learners to express a range of speech functions (such as invitations, requests, apologies, offers, refusals) and to vary the degrees of formality (particularly in terms of politeness; e.g., Abbs and Freebairn 1977; O'Neill 1981), though some began to include role play activities (e.g., Morrow and Johnson 1979). The nature of spoken language was, then, one of the central concerns of this period, but the issue was addressed mainly in terms of identifying typical speech acts. The kinds of *activity* provided for learners to practice on still mainly took the form of drills.

To summarize developments so far, speaking was attended to in terms of system rather than contextual appropriacy. Audiolingual approaches aimed to develop speaking only in terms of pronunciation and fluent, accurate manipulation of grammar. Situational approaches introduced dialogue patterns into the range of features to be taught, and functional approaches added speech acts into the syllabus. However, these approaches, on the whole, omitted to develop the interactive grammar and discourse patterns of typical speech; that is, they neglected typical "modes" of speech. Further, the types of exercise used to practice them omitted to situate practice within the contexts of genuine communication. In terms of the integrated model outlined in this chapter, audiolingual, situational, and functional approaches concentrated on providing practice at the levels of formulation and articulation; the level of conceptualization was broadly ignored, so practice was largely isolated from the conceptual planning and decision making typical of the communicative use of language. To resolve this problem required the development of different kinds of activities and not merely a broadening of the scope of drills. Awareness of this need led to the development of a communicative approach to language teaching.

The communicative approach stressed the importance of enabling learners to develop fluency and not just accuracy (e.g., Brumfit 1984) and advocated exercises containing problems to resolve and requiring learners to communicate with each other in order to resolve them (Allwright 1984). Littlewood (1981) outlined the possibility of a range of different types of oral exercise: precommunicative, communicative, and sociointeractional. Brown and Yule (1983b) sketched the elements of an oral syllabus, including the desirability of teaching short turns, long turns, interactional language, and transactional language. A key area of concern for them was that of "reference"—the ability to identify effectively referents (such as participants in a narrative), time, and place. (See also Yule 1997.)

These general developments resulted in the publication of supplementary materials (e.g., Dörnyei and Thurrell 1992; Geddes and Sturtridge 1979, 1981; Hadfield 1987; Klippel 1984; Matthews and Read 1981; Porter-Ladousse 1987; Ur 1981) that were largely based on the use of various kinds of jigsaw or opinion-gap tasks in the context of pair and group work. (See Pica, Kanagy, and Falodun 1993 for an attempt to map an extensive inventory of task types.) Course books similarly incorporated many of these insights (e.g., Abbs and Sexton 1978; Geddes 1986; Richards, Hull, and Proctor 1991), the output of one task often serving as input to the next (e.g., Nunan 1995b; Swan and Walter 1992; Willis and Willis 1988).

The communicative movement was also sensitive to the fact that speaking in a second language can be stressful, particularly if it is not supported by adequate exposure to the vernacular forms of the language. This insight gave rise to a movement that favored delaying oral production at the beginning of language programs, instead introducing students to the oral language through a more or less extensive period of listening activities (e.g., Asher 1977). Concern for the per-

sonal affective aspects of language learning gave rise to the development of materials with subject matter likely to engage learners' personal interest and curiosity
(e.g., Geddes 1986; Legutke and Thomas 1991; Maley, Duff, and Grellet 1980; Riggenbach and Samuda 2000).

CONCLUSION

Most of the conditions of speech have been broadly attended to in these pedagogical developments, although perhaps issues of identity, register, topic familiarity, and discourse type have been less well addressed than the contextualized practice of formulation skills. In addition, broader scale methodological controversies
also remain.

A central concern lies in the ways in which the different parts of the skill
hierarchy can best be practiced. While it is agreed that the main teaching and
learning objective is for learners to be able to exploit all levels of the hierarchy in
order to be able communicate, five alternative approaches have been proposed.
One is that oral skills should first be learned in a controlled form, essentially at
the level of lexicogrammatical system, before extending into the broader areas of
spoken discourse. This is suggested by Widdowson (1998a), drawing on Rivers
and Temperley's (1978) distinction between "skill-getting" and "skill-using" phases
of learning. This view seems to see it as preferable to practice speaking initially
in a decontextualized manner, bringing communication tasks into operation only
once the "skill" has been learnt.

A second view is that, provided that the conceptual load is constrained so as
to enable learners to focus on particular aspects of the lexicogrammar and to
avoid overloading them with complex communication problems, it would be perfectly possible to follow the use of a communication task with a decontextualized
grammar practice activity. This has been described as a "whole-skill: part-skill"
approach (Littlewood 1981), the decontextualized activities being used to provide
"part-skill" practice, while the communication tasks provide "whole-skill" practice.

A third approach argues that it is possible to use tasks to provide a context
in which the focus can alternate between different aspects of language performance, such as fluency, accuracy, and complexity. Skehan (1998a), Bygate (1996,
1999), and Lynch and Maclean (2001) suggest that adjusting task variables (such
as the provision of planning time, structuring, relevant background knowledge,
and task repetition) can be deployed to vary the focus on language in similar
ways; some suggest ways teachers can switch students' attention from discourse

pattern and function to formal features within (Samuda 2001) or around (Willis 1996) a given task. Similarly Johnson (1996) argues that it is possible for a speaker either to proceduralize declarative knowledge or to start with proceduralized knowledge and work at analyzing it.

The fourth approach, stressing the importance of integrating attention to form and attention to meaning, argues that attention to language form should be handled only within the context of a focus on meaningful communication (e.g., papers in Doughty and Williams 1998b). Finally outlining a fifth approach, Brumfit's (1984) account argues for seeing the contrast from a number of perspectives. For one thing, the same task may be accuracy focused for some students, and fluency focused for others, depending on their language and content knowledge; further, the overall language program might best be characterized by a proportionate shift from a concern with accuracy in the early stages toward a predominant focus on fluency as students become more advanced.

It is worth noting that these controversies are far from adequately researched and recalling the well-documented failure to find clearcut results in favor of one pedagogical approach or another (Ellis 1994: 571). Further, they do not address the broader issues of the potential interactive content of the oral language syllabus. While, as we have seen earlier, this issue has not been totally ignored, much remains to be done in this area if the potential content of the oral syllabus is to be as thoroughly mapped as those in the areas of reading and writing. It is the range of areas that deserve attention, rather than the particular route to be adopted in addressing them, that this chapter has aimed to highlight.

CHAPTER 4

LISTENING: QUESTIONS OF LEVEL

TONY LYNCH

A common thread in the past decade's work on listening comprehension is the notion of "level," in various senses. Listening involves the integration of whatever cues the listener is able to exploit—incoming auditory and visual information, as well as information drawn from internal memory and previous experience. The scale of the task, especially in real time and under social pressure in the case of face-to-face listening, means that comprehension can be achieved only by massively parallel, interactive processing. Research into listening has recently concentrated on the question of what distinguishes skilled from unskilled listening behavior: Is it primarily a difference in individuals' ability to deal with the lower-level components of incoming speech, or their ability to apply higher-level meaning-based skills such as prediction and inference (Tsui and Fullilove 1998). At the same time, there is a related debate going on in the pedagogic context over whether it is more effective to raise learners' level of listening through a focus on skill or on strategy (e.g., Mendelsohn 1998; Field 2000).

Despite the well-attested complexity of comprehension processes, we are generally unaware of serious problems in everyday listening—at least in our first language (L1) and under reasonable acoustic conditions. However, listening in another language (L2) is a qualitatively different experience, requiring more conscious attention to information at different levels, especially when the linguistic cues are made inaccessible by limited grammatical and lexical knowledge. At the same time, listening to the L2 is recognized as playing a key role in language learning (e.g., Ellis et al. 1994; Faerch and Kasper 1986). In this article I concentrate mainly on the case of L2 listening, though much of the discussion also applies to L1 listening (cf. Anderson and Lynch 1988; Brown 1995; Brown and Yule 1983b).

RESEARCH INTO LISTENING

Modeling the Process

The dominant paradigm in listening comprehension is that of information processing, derived from Anderson's three-stage comprehension model: *Perception—Parsing—Utilization* (Anderson 1985). Although this implies that understanding is achieved through a linear series of steps, it is clear that the only way that listeners can cope with the task is by some form of parallel distributed processing (PDP). PDP models of language processes, based on neural networks, (e.g., Sharkey 1996) are biologically plausible because they resemble the way brain cells work—in particular, their capacity for the simultaneous integration of information from multiple sources. However, such models have been criticized for creating a narrow view of humans as limited-capacity processors and not much else. Barsalou (1999) has adopted an evolutionary perspective to argue that the purpose of comprehension is not primarily to "archive" information, as computer-analogous models assume, but to prepare the individual for real-world action.

Levels of Processing

The levels at which spoken information is available for interpretation include (at least) phonetic, phonological, prosodic, lexical, syntactic, semantic, and pragmatic. For reasons of space, I briefly comment on the lowest and highest of those levels. At the phonetic, even sublexical, level of conversation, speakers need to attend to a number of signals of their interlocutor's attitude to the current topic; e.g., *Hm, Hmhm,* and *Uhuh.* Gardner (1998) analyzed the functional complexity of such signals in English, which can present problems of interpretation for nonnative speakers. At the higher level, research into sociopragmatics has revealed the extent to which listeners' experience of their own culture can hinder understanding in another (e.g., Bremer et al. 1996; Kasper 1997; Rampton 1997a; Williams, Inscoe, and Tasker 1997). Bremer et al. (1996) investigated immigrant workers' transactional L2 experiences in gatekeeping situations such as job interviews. Among

their conclusions was that implicit high-level factors strongly influence understandings and misunderstandings, reflecting "linguistic difficulties and imbalances,
social and cultural differences and power relations which structure individual encounters in hierarchical ways" (Bremer et al. 1996: 10).

Accessing the Process

Not the least of the problems facing the listening researcher is the fact that listening is unobservable. Several strategies have been adopted to access mental activity
during listening tasks, such as introspection with an interviewer (Ross 1997) and
other types of self-report, including journal writing (Goh 1997; Rost 1994). A
particularly enlightening study is that of Ross (1997), which explored the hypothesis that listeners at different levels of L2 proficiency use different processing
strategies. Ross asked Japanese learners of English to match an array of icons (e.g.,
a train) with a recorded message in English (e.g., about a rail journey) and then
to introspect in Japanese about how they decided which icon to choose. Their
self-reported strategies suggested eight "processing stages," ranging from the more
primitive and unsuccessful to more complex and successful:

1. *Noise*—no response
2. *Distraction*—process overload
3. *Syllable restructuring*—mishearing
4. *Syllable identification*
5. *Key word association*
6. *Linking* with more than one key words
7. Recognition of *phrases*
8. Recognition of *whole utterances.*

Ross found that Stage 5, key word association, was the commonest level of
processing for the weaker listeners, who produced an initial mental model and
kept to it without searching for confirming cues; the more proficient listeners also
frequently operated at Stage 5 but had sufficient capacity to hold the key word in
short-term memory while they searched for support in the message.

Factors That Influence Processing

Rubin (1994) pinpointed five characteristics that affect the ease or difficulty of
listening: text, speaker, task, listener, and process. These apply in both L1 and L2;
work done by Brown and associates on the intrinsic cognitive difficulty of a listening text has been based on interactive tasks carried out by fully competent

native speakers (Brown 1986, 1995, Brown and Yule 1983b), providing baseline data against which to evaluate the performances of L1 speakers undergoing communication skills training, as well as those of L2 learners (Lynch 1991). Among the other sources of difficulty are the listener-based factors—not just their ability to listen (phonological decoding ability) but also their relevant topical knowledge, which has been shown to exert a powerful influence on success in listening (e.g., Long, D., 1990; Jensen and Hansen 1995). As far as L2 level is concerned, there are divergent views as to what happens when a listener of limited L2 proficiency tries to process L2 text, as we see in the section on the Testing of Listening.

Coping with the Process: Skills and Strategies

Level also comes to the fore in the analysis of the attributes that allow successful listening, whether in L1 or L2. The components of listening ability can be arranged hierarchically from lower order subskills (for example, decoding and literal recognition of an utterance), through to higher order subskills, such as inferencing, interpretation, and critical evaluation. The most accessible description of this hierarchy is that of Rost (1990: 152–153), where listening skills are grouped into three clusters of subskills, related to perception, interpretation, and enacting.

Some recent research has focused on learners' use of listening strategies, categorized into three main groups drawn from the wider framework of language learning strategy research: *metacognitive*—those to do with planning, regulating, and managing; *cognitive*—those that facilitate comprehension, such as conscious use of context or background knowledge; and *social and affective*—for example, requests for clarification and positive self-talk. The consensus from studies such as Thompson and Rubin (1996) and Goh (1997) is that more conscious and effective use of strategies increase the chances of success in L2 listening. A series of related studies of listening strategy training (Vandergrift 1997a, 1997b, 1999) supports the claim that metacognitive strategy use increases with learner proficiency level.

THE TESTING OF LISTENING

It is not easy to design listening comprehension tests that reflect the purposes of real-life listening, partly because most routine listening tasks require either no response or a minimal response from the listener, such as the acknowledgment tokens investigated by Gardner (1998). Most of us are unlikely to find ourselves needing to match incoming speech against alternative written options (as in multiple-choice item tests) or to absorb and reproduce detailed information without being able to make notes, yet both activities are standard practice in tests of listening. Apart from the fact that tests involve comparatively unnatural tasks, the test designer also faces the problem of the inevitable indirectness of the act of assessment:

> To a complex enough model of speaker/writer, text and understander, we add several more critical parts: A tester who becomes speaker/writer and creator of a second text that sets tasks for the understander, a third text produced by that understander, a reader/interpreter of that new text (the tester or marker), and a fourth text, a mark or score or grade that awaits the interpretation of an additional participant, the test user. (Spolsky 1994: 147)

Given what we know about the bundle of processes and sources involved in comprehension, it is difficult to design a pure test of listening, free of interference from other cognitive skills or knowledge (Thompson 1995). In attempting to prevent "contamination" from individual attributes such as memory and background knowledge (Call 1985; Long 1990), the test designer may well remove factors that, although they represent confounding variables for assessment, would be helpful resources for the listener under normal circumstances.

Life is made still more difficult for the test designer by the contemporary view of the listener as active creator of meaning, rather than passive recipient; if higher level and lower level processing are engaged simultaneously and interactively in ordinary listening, then it is hardly possible to distinguish between different levels of processing or to attribute test responses to any one skill. This also casts serious doubt on descriptions of listening ability expressed in terms of upward progression on proficiency rating scales (Brindley 1998a).

Influences on Listening Test Performance

Among the key variables that affect listening test scores are those related to the *input* (e.g., speech rate, length of the text, lexical and syntactic characteristics, accent, register, propositional density, amount of redundancy), to the *task* (e.g., amount of context provided, clarity of instructions, output required), and to the *listener* (e.g., memory, topic-relevant knowledge, motivation). Until recently, relatively few studies had explored these variables in any depth (Buck 1990; Shohamy and Inbar 1991); for a comprehensive review, see Brindley (1998a). But three studies of listening test performance (Buck and Tatsuoka 1998; Tsui and Fullilove 1998; and Wu 1998) have addressed the issue of level of item difficulty in relation to candidates' success.

Wu (1998) stressed that most studies of the effect of test method on candidates' performance had been psychometric—manipulating methods and measuring effects on scores. In contrast, he adopted a mentalistic approach, which he aligns with Buck's (1990) verbal introspection study. Wu applied a similar retrospective commentary method to performance on a multiple choice listening test by ten relatively advanced Chinese learners of English, to explore their use of linguistic and nonlinguistic processing. Wu's analysis of his subjects' test performance and retrospective commentaries showed that:

1. Partial success in linguistic processing often forced the listeners to activate general knowledge, as compensation for linguistic failings.
2. Partial success in linguistic processing could also lead them to override what they had correctly abstracted from that processing, in favor of schema-based interpretation.

He concluded that for L2 listeners, linguistic processing is basic, in two senses:

1. Failure or partial success in it may result in learners allowing activated schematic knowledge to dominate their decision making inappropriately.
2. Competence in linguistic processing constrains but does not rule out nonlinguistic activation.

In a study on a very different scale, sampling roughly 150,000 item performances, Tsui and Fullilove (1998) investigated whether the difference between successful and unsuccessful L2 listening performance could be ascribed to failure in either top-down or bottom-up processing. They considered two possible reasons, derived from reading comprehension research, for poor comprehension ability. First, it might be rooted at the "bottom" level: Poor readers are unable to recognize words rapidly and construct an accurate representation, and therefore they have to rely more on contextual information and guessing to understand the text. Alternatively, poor readers might fail because they are overreliant on *either* the top-down or the bottom-up route.

Tsui and Fullilove compared listening test items where the correct answer matched the likely schema with items where the answers conflicted with the schema. They found that the candidates who got the correct answer for nonmatching schema items tended to be more skilled listeners; presumably, the less skilled could rely on guessing for the matching items, but not for nonmatching ones. Bottom-up processing seemed to be more important than top-down processing in discriminating the listening performance on test items; one pedagogic implication is that, as less skilled L2 listeners are weak at the bottom level, they need to be helped to rely less on contextual and topical guessing and to rely more on rapid and accurate linguistic decoding, a point we return to in the section on the teaching of listening.

Buck and Tatsuoka (1998) applied the "rule-space" statistical technique to language testing for the first time; previously it had been used to assess mastery of skill components in other academic subjects. The technique breaks test items down into cognitive attributes that represent the underlying knowledge and skills that the items assess, and then analyzes each candidate's pattern of responses to calculate an individual's chances of having mastered each attribute. Buck and Tatsuoka established fifteen attributes, which accounted for virtually all the variance in the performance of the test population. These attributes involved the ability:

- To recognize the task by deciding what constitutes task-relevant information
- To scan fast spoken text automatically and in real time
- To process a substantial information load
- To process medium information load
- To process dense information
- To use previous items to locate information
- To identify relevant information without explicit markers
- To understand and utilize heavy stress
- To process very fast text automatically
- To make text-based inferences
- To incorporate background knowledge into text processing
- To process L2 concepts with no literal equivalent in L1
- To recognize and use redundancy
- To process information scattered throughout a text
- To construct response quickly and efficiently. (Buck and Tatsuoka 1998: 141–142)

They concluded that "second-language listening ability is not a point on one linear continuum, but a point in a multi-dimensional space, and the number of dimensions is large" (1998: 146).

THE TEACHING OF LISTENING: SKILLS AND/OR STRATEGIES

As in other areas of language teaching, the teaching of listening has been prone to pendulum movements of theory, "evidence," and fashion. In the case of listening, the swing has been from a focus on linguistic processing to a preoccupation with schematic processing, or as Field (1998) puts it, from "skills" to "strategies." For example, the first edition of *Listening to Spoken English* (Brown 1977) devoted 150 pages to the linguistic features of natural speech and ten pages to the teaching of comprehension. This contrasts sharply with a recent teacher education text (Mendelsohn 1994) that acknowledges Brown's influence but adopts a strategy-based approach to listening: It presents a rationale for a listening course in which only one unit is devoted to "linguistic proficiency" (the ability to cope with word boundaries, weak forms, elision, assimilation, and so on) and all the others concentrate on fostering strategy use and "metastrategic awareness."

Field (1998, 2000) has argued that the (mainly) strategic approach has been taken too far and that a better balance should be struck between skills and strategies. He points out that the evidence for the effectiveness of strategic training in listening is very mixed—a point admitted even by its proponents (cf. Rubin 1994). In essence, Field's argument is this:

1. The *skills* of listening are competencies that native speakers have acquired and L2 learners still need to acquire.
2. *Strategies* are compensatory and, as learners' ability improves, can and should be discarded, except in emergencies.
3. Teachers should aim to help students enhance their bottom-level linguistic processing skills, as well as encouraging strategic listening—temporarily—but ought not to regard strategies as a *substitute* for skills.

As we have seen, Field's position finds support in the research findings of Wu (1998) and Tsui and Fullilove (1998): that what differentiates skilled and unskilled listeners is the ability to cope with linguistic processing, rather than the ability to use higher-level strategies.

Problem Orientation

Another strand in current discussions of teaching listening is what we might think of as a "problem-oriented" approach, in contrast with a "solution-oriented" approach of strategy-based teaching. This focus on problems is not a new concern and can be traced back, for example, to Brown (1986):

> Comprehension teaching ... is very much a hit-or-miss affair.... Until the teacher is provided with some sort of method of investigating the student's problems the teacher is really not in the position of being able to help the student 'do better....' We need to move to a position where the teacher is able to recognize particular patterns of behavior in listening manifested by an unsuccessful listener and to provide exercises for the student which will promote superior patterns of behavior. (Brown 1986: 286)

Although those words were written in the mid-1980s, it is only quite recently that a number of teachers and teacher educators have taken up the call for a classroom approach that features the diagnosis and remedy of specific and even individual problems (e.g., Field 1998; Lynch 1997; Tauroza 1997; White 1998). They share a concern to establish a principled way of tackling processing problems at local and text level. Tauroza (1997), for example, questions the value of a pre-emptive approach to teaching listening, in which the teacher tries to identify potential problems in listening materials before using them in class. This is not a practical solution for many teachers, he argues, since it adds considerably to lesson preparation time. Instead, he has developed the three-phase remedial technique (for occasional use) of "troubleshooting":

1. Identifying the students' listening problems
2. Finding out how many students share the problems
3. Focusing students' attention on the problem points.

The technique gives a key role to the *repetition* of spoken/recorded material, with the aim of helping learners work out what is being said as a prerequisite to understanding what is being meant. Repetition is something that many language teachers avoid, by intuition or training, but there is increasing evidence from a wide variety of research that repetition and recycling can assist "noticing," for example, in the form of replay (Field 2000), transcribing (Clennell 1999), and dictogloss (Swain and Lapkin 2001).

CONCLUSION

As we have seen, recent work on listening comprehension makes clearer than ever the complexity of its component processes, even in L1 listening. To make sense of speech, the listener has to apprehend, notice, and act on information from a variety of sources and normally has to do so in real time. In the case of reciprocal interaction, listeners carry the additional burden of having to formulate an appropriate response. This brief survey has highlighted the notion of *level*, in different senses. First, listening involves physiological and cognitive processes at different levels (perception, recognition, interpretation). Second, all but the most basic spoken messages carry multiple levels of meaning. Third, in the L2 setting, although language teaching institutions tend to group learners into different proficiency levels, the relationship between overall L2 proficiency and the ability to understand the spoken language is far from straightforward. Last, there are questions as to how top (expectation-based) and bottom (text-based) levels interact in the listener's efforts to understand and, therefore, doubts about the optimal balance between skill practice and strategy practice in the listening classroom.

Looking ahead, we can see likely avenues for future work in listening research, testing, and teaching. First, there will probably be a expansion in research adopting a more or less mechanistic view of (human) listening, in the form of studies of comprehension in naturalistic or real-life settings, as opposed to laboratory-type experiments. It will emphasize the social, cultural, and affective factors in listening performance as a counterbalance to computing-influenced concepts (such as *input*, *processing*, and *output*). Second, in the area of testing and assessment, we may well see further research into the skill componential analysis of test items and hence into the extent to which the end-user of a test score can be confident that it provides an accurate evaluation of the candidate's ability to cope with real-life listening tasks. Third, I think that teachers will become more aware of the pedagogic potential of misunderstandings and noncomprehension as starting points for the improvement of perception and recognition skills—what I referred to as a problem-oriented approach to teaching listening. This might involve bursts of intensive work at the "bottom" level (e.g., short sequences of detailed practice in microlevel dictation), complemented by perhaps more selective training in coping strategies than is currently discussed in the pedagogic literature, particularly in North America (Field 2000).

There is, of course, no doubt that all three areas will be affected by advances in technology, which have not been touched on here; however, for recent discussion of the role of technological applications in research, assessment, and teaching, see Lynch (1998), Brindley (1998a), and Mendelsohn (1998), respectively. There will be a growing influence of the computer and multimedia listening applications already available, not to mention those still to be invented. For example, there is enormous potential in the capacity for interactive PC-linked video to deliver higher quality sound and picture, and to do so with a variety of replay modes—with subtitles or translation, with graphic representations of speech, and so on. As Brindley (1998a) points out, although 'manual' video has been widely used for the teaching of listening for many years, the use of PC-mediated video for the testing of listening is still relatively unexplored. Watch the screens.

Vandergrift's recent comment that "Listening is hard work, and deserves more analysis and support" (Vandergrift 1999: 168) neatly encapsulates the themes I have touched on in this chapter: the "effort after meaning" made by listeners, the importance of the empirical investigation and assessment of listening by researchers, and the need to develop more effective materials and techniques for language teachers.

CHAPTER 5

READING IN A SECOND LANGUAGE

WILLIAM GRABE

THE ability to read in a second language (L2) is one of the most important skills required of people in multilingual and international settings. It is also a skill that is one of the most difficult to develop to a high level of proficiency. Any current understanding of reading requires attention to a number of basic issues: (1) different purposes for reading, (2) definitional criteria for fluent reading, (3) processes that underlie reading as an individual skill, (4) social context influences on L2 reading, (5) unique features of L2 reading (as opposed to L1 reading) and difficulties central for L2 reading instruction, and (6) L2 research implications for improving instruction and student learning. These topics form the framework for the discussion to follow.

DIFFERENT PURPOSES FOR READING

People read for a variety of purposes, and many of these purposes require distinct combinations of skills in order to achieve the reader's purpose. Because of this variation, it is not easy to define L2 reading as a single notion or a unitary ability. It is true that differing purposes draw on many of the same cognitive processes, but they do so to differing extents, and sometimes in different ways. Having said this, I nonetheless state that the most fundamental ability for L2 reading is basic comprehension of main ideas from a text. Few purposes for reading disregard this ability, and most purposes build upon this foundation (cf. Alderson 2000; Urquhart and Weir 1999 for other discussions of reading purposes).

Purposes for reading can include the following: reading to find information (scanning, searching), reading to learn, reading to critique and evaluate, and reading for basic comprehension. (There are other purposes.) In the case of *reading to find information*, the crucial skill is to scan for a specific word, phrase, form, or number. Meaning in the text is not critical, though a reader may slow down to skim (a different purpose) to see if he or she is perhaps in the right neighborhood. This skill is typically carried out at a very fast rate of words per minute (WPM) processing of the text. *Reading to learn*, in contrast, requires reading for the main ideas, but, in addition, it requires awareness of many of the details of the text and a strong organizing frame in which to relate the various meanings of the text. Such textual coherence increases the text's memorability and aids recall when the relevant information is needed. The cognitive processing is carried out at a relatively slow rate of WPM processing (perhaps around 175–200 WPM for fluent L1 readers, much slower for most L2 readers). *Reading to critique and evaluate* requires, in addition, reflections and elaborate connections to prior knowledge and an integration with prior knowledge, including the reader's attitudes, emotions, motivations for reading, and level of topic-specific background knowledge. Reading rate is likely to be even slower for this purpose.

The most common, and most basic, reading purpose is *reading for general understanding*. It is saved for last in this discussion because it is the primary goal for most L2 reading instruction, even though it may not be the easiest type of reading to teach. Reading for general understanding is typically carried out at about 250–300 WPM by fluent readers (but this rate holds for relatively few L2 readers). This purpose satisfies most reading expectations for understanding main ideas and a subset of supporting ideas and information. While it is often noted as "basic," and "general," it is by no means easy to carry out fluently. Reading for general understanding, under normal processing rates, requires a very large recognition vocabulary, automaticity of word recognition for most of the words in the text, a reasonably rapid overall reading speed for text-information integration, and the ability to build overall text comprehension under some time pressure. This set of processing abilities is the common goal of most L2 reading instruction, though most reading teachers and curriculum developers have only a limited concept of the processing demands of reading for general comprehension under relatively rapid time demands. Instead, most instructors and text materials end up teaching slow translation of texts, a possible purpose for reading, though perhaps a skill entirely outside standard purposes for reading. This mismatch is explored in more detail in the two following sections.

A DEFINITION OF READING

Reading can easily be defined simply as the ability to derive understanding from written text. However, this simple definition belies the complexity inherent in the ability to read (now assuming reading for general understanding as the primary purpose). L2 reading can best be understood as a combination of skills and abilities that individuals bring to bear as they begin to read. The following five abilities should be seen as definitional, though others can be added under a finer specification of reading: a rapid and automatic process, an interacting process, a flexible and strategic process, a purposeful process, and a linguistic process (cf. Grabe 1999).

First, fluent reading is by definition *a rapid process*: The various bits of information being activated at any moment in working memory (Carpenter et al. 1994) need to be active simultaneously if the information (from both the text and reader background knowledge) is to be integrated for understanding. Slow reading rates make the assembling of text comprehension a very inefficient and laborious process. Assisting in a rapid and efficient process is the ability to recognize words automatically; reading, in any normal sense, is not possible without this ability. Second, *reading is an interactive process* in two ways. Reading requires many skills and abilities to be carried out simultaneously, some of which are automatic and some of which are attentional—where we focus our attention. At the same time, the higher level comprehension process, such as deciding the main ideas of the text, require an interaction of textual information and background knowledge. This latter interaction is also needed to decide whether immediate goals are being met and whether strategies for reading are being used effectively to achieve the reading purpose.

Third, *reading is strategic and flexible* in that readers assess whether or not they are achieving their purposes for reading. If not, readers must then flexibly adapt various processing and monitoring activities. This ability to adapt strategically is the hallmark of a good reader. Fourth, *reading is purposeful* in the ways noted at the outset of this discussion; it is also purposeful in a more immediate way. As readers, we monitor not only our efficiency of processing but also whether the immediate activity fits with our larger expectations, whether the task is sufficiently interesting to continue, and whether our purposes might be better served by changing the current activity or task. It is also worth noting that the most central purpose for reading is comprehending the text. Fifth and finally, *reading is a linguistic process* (as opposed to a reasoning process). Fundamentally, we derive understanding and new meaning as we interact with the text information by means of linguistic processing. It is sometimes said that if meaning is to be developed from text, reading must be primarily a reasoning activity. However, this view is the result of researchers who are fluent readers and who cannot recognize the obvious struggles that a beginning reader or an L2 reader has with texts. One has only to try to read a text in Chinese when one knows no Chinese characters to realize that reading is first and foremost a linguistic processing activity.

How Reading Works:
Individual Processes in Reading

Fluent reading requires efficient cognitive processing. Two basic types of processing are required: *lower level processing* and *higher level processing* (without assuming that either type is more difficult than the other type; they are just different). Within lower level processing, readers must be rapid and automatic word recognizers, they must be able to pull out and use basic structural information, and they must begin to assemble clause-level meaning units (Adams 1990). Within higher level processing, readers must be able to assemble clause-level information into a text model of their understanding—strengthening repeated and salient ideas and pruning ideas that do not get reactivated. They also need to build an interpretation of the text that conforms with their goals, attitudes, and background knowledge (a situation model of interpretation). They also have to make appropriate inferences and to determine whether they are staying on task and achieving their reading purpose (Grabe 1999; Kintsch 1998).

Lower level processes most importantly involve *activating word meanings* for use in working memory. In this respect, reading centrally involves word recognition, even though all researchers recognize that *word recognition* itself is not the "reading comprehension" process. However, many researchers argue that reading comprehension cannot be carried out without strong word recognition and lexical access skills (potentially two separable abilities for L2 readers) (Stanovich and Stanovich 1995). The average fluent L1 reader can recognize four to five words per second and actually take time to look at these words each and every second of reading. This fact may well be the central miracle of a human's fluent reading abilities. Moreover, the words and meanings are accessed automatically in the vast majority of cases, since readers do not take the time to think consciously about what each new word means (Samuels and Flor 1997). Research has shown that fluent readers cannot suppress the activation of known word meanings when they are visually exposed to a word for a little as a twentieth of a second. (Automaticity entails an inability to suppress information.)

The *syntax and semantics of clauses* in a text also play a role in lower level processing. As a clause is read, information about word order (and which word or phrase is the subject), main versus adjunct phrase, and relations among phrases in the unit are all extracted in fluent reading. Usually this process is attempted quickly in line with certain default expectations, so syntactic information is pulled automatically from a clause, assuming there is no complication that confuses the reader's processing. At the same time, basic information about the word meanings, in combination with the syntactic information, leads to the assembly of initial meaning units (*propositional units*). Unless there is some complication of unexpected outcomes of these processes, they take place relatively automatically; that is, we don't have to think about them (and actually can't think about them very easily).

The higher level processing that a reader carries out includes the combining of clause-level meaning information into a basic text representation (*a text model of reading*). This text model represents that basic "summary" of the text as the reader understands it to be intended by the author. At the same time, a more elaborate copy is created that combines the text model with stronger reader views about the purposes of the author in writing the text, the attitude of the reader to the material in the text, past experiences with reading similar texts, reader motivations for reading, and reader evaluation of the text itself (likes, agreements, interests, surprises, supports for opinions, disagreements with the text). This second model is often described as *a situation model of text interpretation* (Grabe 1999; Kintsch 1998). Thus, a good reader creates two levels of comprehension for a text. Both levels of text understanding require processing interactions with reader knowledge; both levels require extensive *inferencing* and reasoning about the text (and *reasoning* becomes important at this point). Finally, a fluent reader is able to monitor his or her reading (*an executive control process*) to decide whether it is achieving the intended purpose and, if needed, to take some actions to make adjustments for better understanding.

SOCIAL FACTORS THAT INFLUENCE READING

One outcome of this explanation of fluent reading processing is the impression that learning to read is an individual process. It is true that at any given moment that a reader engages with a text, reading is primarily a cognitive activity, but the longer developmental process cannot be understood without recognizing social influences on reading development. Social contexts that influence reading include those of the home, the school and other institutions, peers, and student-teacher interactions. Much research has shown that home factors in early reading development have a significant and lasting impact, though in many complex ways, depending on the settings and interactants (Snow et al. 1991; Snow et al. 1998). Peer interactions over time and student-teacher interactions also have a major role to play in a developing reader's motivations, attitudes, task successes, and reading experiences. The educational institutional setting more generally also plays a powerful role. Students develop differing proficiencies in reading depending on school administrations, library resources, classroom resources, amount of curricular time set aside specifically for reading development, teacher training, teacher practices and preferences, and teacher interest in books and student learning. The picture is very complex and difficult to sort through, but that does not give anyone the right to ignore such major influences on a person's learning to read.

In L2 reading contexts, the picture becomes even more complex, because readers deal with two languages, with two general educational experiences (including patterns of success and failure on a wide range of learning tasks), with varying motivations and attitudes toward tasks in both L1 and L2 contexts, with different impositions by an L2 culture, and with differing levels of expected success in L2 instruction. Moreover, in many L2 academic settings, the assumption is made that L2 reading abilities (often poorly defined) can be acquired in a much briefer time span than typically occurs in L1 contexts, creating unrealistic expectations and often destroying motivation for reading in the L2. Complicating the fact that there are unending variations in L2 social contexts for reading, there are also relatively few empirical studies on social context influences. Nonetheless, most L2 reading researchers recognize the powerful impact of social contexts on L2 reading development.

SPECIFIC L2 READING ISSUES

To this point, the discussion of reading has been general, combining L1 and L2 reading issues. However, the purposes, processes, and practices of L2 reading invoke a number of specific issues that deserve attention. Among these issues are the more limited language knowledge of the L2 reader (compared with the L1 reader), the relative importance of L2 language proficiency versus L1 reading abilities as the strongest factor in L2 reading development, the issues surrounding transfer of skills more generally, the role of strategy uses unique to L2 learners (bilingual dictionaries, cognates, mental translation, glosses), the recognition that texts and educational institutions themselves may work differently for learners, and the more limited total exposure of learners to the L2 and L2 reading experiences.

In comparison with L1 readers, L2 readers begin to learn to read without the initial language base that can be assumed for L1 readers. Most L1 readers begin their instruction with at least 6,000 words already known in their language and with a firm tacit knowledge of most basic grammatical structures of the language. The L2 reader, in contrast, may have relatively little spoken language knowledge of the L2 at the time reading instruction begins. As a learner gains L2 reading abilities, a major debate has arisen as to the primary way that L2 reading development is supported—L2 language knowledge (knowledge of L2 vocabulary, L2 structure, L2 task successes, exposure to L2 reading) or prior L1 reading skills (reading strategies, metalinguistic knowledge, task successes, word learning skills). This debate is otherwise known as the Language Threshold Hypothesis. Over the past ten years, the evidence has grown steadily that L2 language knowledge plays a much greater role until some general (and very variable) threshold of language knowledge is passed, confirming a general version of the Language Threshold Hypothesis. For most L2 students, the key is to develop a large recognition vocabulary, a reasonable command of language structure and discourse marking devices, and many positive experiences with manageable L2 reading tasks. At some point at which most words are recognized rapidly and automatically, and most structural parsing automatically provides the needed processing information, the reader will be more successful in using the full range of reading skills and strategies that support successful fluent L1 reading.

More generally, the issue of L1 transfer has also been explored extensively, and a useful set of findings can be offered at this point. It appears that L2 readers do transfer L1 syntactic knowledge of various types to their L2 reading, even at relatively advanced stages. Sometimes the transferred knowledge is supportive and sometimes it causes interference (Durgunoglu and Verhoven 1998; MacWhinney 1997; Nagy et al. 1997). On this issue, L2 reading strongly overlaps with SLA research on transfer. More specifically for reading, research on orthographic transfer seems to show an impact at early stages of L2 reading, though less of an impact at advanced levels. Much of this research can be linked to the Orthographic Depth Hypothesis, which states that readers of differing orthographies will develop somewhat different word recognition processing skills depending on the L1 orthography. There is growing evidence that this hypothesis does reflect the learning behavior of certain groups of beginning L2 readers (e.g., Japanese readers of English, English readers of Japanese, Spanish readers of English, English readers of Hebrew) (see Koda 1996, 1997; Nagy et al. 1997; Shimron and Savon 1994).

Another area that focuses specifically on L2 reading issues involves the use of certain reading strategies and the role of bilingual resources for reading. In strategy research, for example, it is found that mental translation (a uniquely L2 strategy) is not necessarily a "poor habit" but can be a useful early L2 reading strategy for students who are dealing with difficult texts. Strategies for the use of cognates has also proven to be important for L2 readers, but often only after learners receive explicit instruction in recognizing and using potential cognates. Bilingual dictionaries and the use of word glosses for comprehension purposes are two further resources for L2 reading not common to L1 reading instruction. The use of bilingual dictionaries has been an ongoing issue for many teachers. Research over the past decade suggests that dictionaries can be useful supports for L2 reading; however, students should be trained how to use dictionaries effectively. Recent research on the use of glosses with L2 reading texts have demonstrated that glosses can provide some benefit and do not seem to interfere with reading comprehension tasks.

Another issue that concerns L2 readers uniquely concerns the patterns of text organization that may be uncommonly read by learners in their L1 contexts. Students moving to L2 reading may encounter text organization that is unfamiliar to them or that they have not had extensive exposure to and practice with. In some cases, the cultural and literacy practices of a culture privilege certain types of text patterns and organization structures, particularly with informational expository prose texts. The point is not that such texts cannot be understood by L2 readers but that learners will need more explicit instruction in how texts are structured and how information is organized. In some cases, the issue is not a matter of having no exposure to rhetorical preferences in the L2, but a need for more practice with such texts. This problem is part of a more general problem of L2 exposure.

L2 readers are almost always at some disadvantage (in comparison with L1 readers) because they seldom have exposure to similar amounts of text for L2 reading purposes. Given that reading efficiency is dependent on rapid and automatic word recognition and a large recognition vocabulary, extensive exposure to L2 texts through reading is the only learning option available to L2 students. Yet most L2 students do not receive nearly the amount of exposure to L2 texts that would be necessary for the development of fluent L2 reading skills. A large factor in this L2 issue is that most teachers, curricula, and instructional materials do not recognize the severely limiting impact of relatively low amounts of exposure to L2 reading texts. The solution, theoretically, is obvious and simple; in practice, however, the solution (reading extensively) is quite difficult to implement for a variety of reasons.

Overall, the research on L2 reading shows that the factors that influence reading development are quite complex. One example involves transfer: Research shows that the transfer of L1 reading skills and strategies is itself complex. One cannot assume that the transfer of all reading skills and strategies from the L1 is easy, automatic, or uniformly positive. Only two useful generalizations can be made at present. The first is that many instances of transfer lead to interference for L2 reading comprehension. The second is that researchers do not know the full range of situations in which positive transfer does or does not occur, or when transfer occurs. A second example involves extensive exposure to L2 reading material. A reading specialist would be hard pressed to miss the linkage in research between amount of exposure texts and reading development. However, the goal of increasing the amount of learners' exposure to L2 reading material is commonly resisted in instructional practice and curriculum planning, or it is given a low priority. A third example involves vocabulary development. Vocabulary knowledge is at the heart of fluent reading abilities—a large recognition vocabulary is essential. Yet vocabulary growth and vocabulary instruction are not emphasized in most L2 instruction, even in L2 reading curricula. Admittedly, vocabulary instruction is not an easy instructional focus, but ignoring the need will not solve the learner's difficulties in this area.

READING INSTRUCTION

On the basis of research in both L1 and L2 reading contexts, a number of general implications for L2 reading instruction can be established. These implications, many of which have been supported in the discussion in this chapter, provide guidance for the development of reading curricula and instructional practices (even if each teaching context is unique and requires its own combination of instructional emphases). The following ten implications offer a useful starting point for instructional practice:

1. The need for a large recognition vocabulary
2. The need to provide explicit language instruction to help students move through the L2 language threshold
3. The need for knowledge of discourse organizing principles
4. The usefulness of graphic representations for comprehension instruction
5. The importance of metacognitive awareness and strategy learning—the need for students to become strategic readers
6. The need for practice in reading fluency to develop automaticity
7. The importance of extensive reading and broad exposure to L2 texts
8. The benefits of integrating reading and writing instruction in academic settings

9. The need to develop effective content-based instruction for reading development
10. The need to motivate students to read

Describing in detail how such implications can be transformed into applications would require another full chapter. However, some comments on these implications are in order. Points one and two follow directly from research on the reading processes of the individual; a large recognition vocabulary and reasonable structural knowledge are central resources for reading improvement. Points three and four follow from the need to work with academic texts or text types that learners may not have received sufficient exposure to, particularly in reading-to-learn situations (see also point eight) (Pearson and Fielding 1991; Pressley 1998). Point five highlights the need to develop the strategic reader (rather than reading strategies), a key aspect of skilled reading comprehension, especially in academic settings (Kucan and Beck 1997; Pressley 1998; Pressley and Woloshyn 1995). Points six and seven highlight the importance of reading efficiency, appropriate reading rates, automaticity, and broad exposure to L2 texts (Krashen 1993; Stahl et al. 1997; Samuels and Flor 1997). Point eight stresses the link between reading and writing, the academic and occupational demands that assume this linkage, and the need to develop skills for linking reading and writing (Grabe 2001). Points seven, nine, and ten also combine under the need to motivate student to read in the L2. Extensive reading provides learners with opportunities to become engaged with interesting ideas and topics as does the framework provided by effective content-based curricula. Both reinforce motivation for L2 reading, a crucial component of any successful L2 reading instruction (Csikszentmihalyi 1990). More generally, content-based instruction, if done well, provides an effective curricular framework for carrying out all of the ten implications for L2 reading instruction noted earlier.

FURTHER ISSUES FOR CONSIDERATION

There are a number of further issues that should be addressed in a longer review of L2 reading. These include reading assessment, reading and writing interactions, materials development, teacher training, curriculum space issues, the role of authentic materials, motivational factors, and the need for instructional resources. Recent volumes by Alderson (2000), Chalhoub-DeVille (1999), and Urquhart and Weir (1999) offer important insights into assessment research and practice. Grabe (2001) addresses reading writing relations in considerable detail. Day and Bamford

(1998) and Widdowson (1998a, 2000a) make powerful arguments for rethinking simplistic notions about authenticity for reading instruction and reading materials. Issues concerning motivation in L2 reading contexts are relatively untouched but need serious exploration. There is also relatively little in the reading literature with respect to teacher training, curricular space, and instructional resources in various L2 reading contexts (cf. Grabe 1996).

CONCLUSION

One outcome of a careful review of L2 reading is that it is almost impossible to get a firm grasp on all the issues and complexities that influence learner success or failure, particularly in the endlessly varying L2 settings. But complexity, in and of itself, should not be a cause for despair. The situation of L2 reading instruction may actually be generally positive. Despite all the complexities and difficulties that can go into reading success or failure, it is extraordinary that so many L1 and L2 learners become good readers. We should celebrate this miracle at the same time that we look for ways to improve this pattern of success for more learners.

CHAPTER 6

SECOND LANGUAGE WRITING

ILONA LEKI

IN his discussion of theoretical issues in L2 writing, Cumming comments that "Writing is text, is composing, and is social construction" (1998: 61). His analysis is appropriate not only synchronically, as he uses it in his discussion of current theoretical issues, but also diachronically. Modern L2 writing instruction and research have gradually broadened their perspective by shifting focus from texts, to processes (i.e., composing), to disciplinary and sociopolitical contexts (i.e., social construction).

The fortunes of L2 writing have certainly expanded in modern times. Once writing was viewed as no more than a handmaid (Rivers 1968) to all other language skills, a means of reinforcing the acquisition of grammatical and vocabulary knowledge. Now construed primarily as composing, writing is considered by some as a privileged or particularly potent means for effecting democratic change toward a more just and equitable sociopolitical order (Clark and Ivanic 1997) through the potential participation of traditionally dominated voices in public written debate. Less grandly, L2 writing is also constructed as a primary means for participation in international disciplinary conversations through writing for international disciplinary journals. On the other hand, and more ominously, because of writing's usefulness as a gatekeeping mechanism, writing is at the center of the contested terrain of access to knowledge, power, and resources (see Leki submitted; see also Crowley 1998 and Russell 1991 for discussion of this issue for English L1 writing).

While for many users—perhaps most, outside academic circles—L2 writing may be limited to functions such as writing short notes or even simply filling out forms, the vast majority of published research on L2 writing has dealt with extended writing in academic (particularly tertiary) and professional settings. The goal of research into extended L2 writing has often centered on how best to teach L2 writing. This research question, however, is premature since, before teaching L2 writing, it would seem necessary to understand and characterize good writing, even to specify what it means to be a good writer. Yet, while examples of admired texts and writers abound, it has eventually become clear that the answer to these questions is slippery, perhaps unspecifiable, because decontextualized good writing cannot exist. In fact, given current understandings of meaning as constructed (rather than as residing in text), the goodness of writing (or of a writer) comes into being only in the reading of a text. In a postmodern intellectual climate, the insight that judgments about the quality of writing depend on the context in which the writing is done and read seems unobjectionable, even trivial. However, these questions—What is good writing? What is good writing good *for*? What does it mean to be a good writer? How can we teach good writing? Even *can* good writing be taught, particularly by an L2 writing teacher?—have rather profound implications and continue to be at the center of intellectual and disciplinary debates about L2 writing research and instruction.

Although the themes that thread through historical and current L2 writing research and instruction overlap and cross-fertilize, making division into separate strands difficult, I have attempted to group these themes into four orientations representing primary concerns of L2 writing practitioners and researchers in modern times (i.e., in the past fifty years):

1. Text- and classroom-based orientations
2. Process-based orientations
3. Budding sense of disciplinarity
4. Growing orientation to sociopolitical issues.

TEXT- AND CLASSROOM-BASED ORIENTATIONS

The core of text-based issues in L2 writing has been made up of concerns about error in writing, contrastive rhetoric, response to writing, and assessment. Although each of these threads has persisted over time, the degree of attention each commands has shifted considerably and in parallel with pedagogical focuses in L2 writing.

Arguably, the overriding issue of concern in early modern L2 writing instruction, interest in errors in writing and in how to correct them or reduce their number, has fluctuated considerably. These fluctuations have followed trends in part from language teaching (from an emphasis on error in, for example, A-LM, to a de-emphasis in communicative approaches) and in part from L1 English writing instruction (also moving from emphasis to de-emphasis). The professional conversation about L2 writing errors moved from how best to deal with them in L2 student writing to whether to bother dealing with them at all and then back, at least to some degree, to how to deal with them again. The more recent perspective, however, gives errors far less importance and exhibits far less faith that error correction can really have much of an effect on reducing numbers of errors. Although students express a desire for error correction, among researchers the debate about the effectiveness of attention to errors has continued (Ferris 1999; Truscott 1996).

As L2 writing instruction was pondering its initial move away from a focus on sentence-level error, a new interest had begun to captivate L2 writing teachers and researchers, contrastive rhetoric, or the idea that different cultures produce culturally influenced and rhetorically distinguishable types of text (Kaplan 1966). Since providing students with model texts to imitate was a familiar feature of L2 writing classrooms of the 1960s and 1970s, contrastive rhetoric's focus on organizational patterns smoothed its ready incorporation into those classrooms. As with error correction, however, after a period of fairly intense interest, arguments began to emerge in the professional literature that challenged the validity of early contrastive rhetoric research and ultimately granted it a much diminished pertinence to L2 writing instruction. However, the kernel insight of contrastive rhetoric, that cultures affect texts, has recently dovetailed with and been partially subsumed by current interest in the idea that knowledge (and judgments about the quality and appropriateness of texts) is socially constructed, a notion introduced into L2 writing primarily though genre studies. More sophisticated approaches to textual variation now get beyond the essentializing cultural explanations that characterized early contrastive rhetoric and explain cross-cultural variation in text as arising from a response to organizational setting and history (see, e.g., Thatcher 2000).

How readers respond to a writer's text probably has more influence on a writer's motivation and progress than any other single feature of writing instruction. With the arrival of process approaches to teaching writing and their emphasis on multiple drafting, it eventually became clear that merely giving L2 writers model texts to imitate and marking their errors did not produce better writers. Thus, the attention of researchers and teachers turned to investigations of other kinds of responses to L2 writing, by teachers (Conrad and Goldstein 1999) and by peers (Nelson and Carson 1998), in writing (Ferris 1997) and in oral conferences (Goldstein and Conrad 1990), that would lead to appropriate revision beyond sentence-level corrections. Results of these investigations reveal the complexity of the impact of response to L2 writing. L2 writers advanced in their disciplines may resist teacher suggestions beyond the level of grammar/mechanical errors (Radecki and Swales 1988); writers may also resist suggestions for revision targeting macro text features that would require revisions deemed too extensive (Leki 1990). Writing teachers are warned not to substitute their own "ideal" text for the emerging texts their L2 students are creating but also are urged to realize that intervention in writing is not the same as appropriating text (Reid 1994). Peer response is sometimes too gentle (Nelson and Carson 1998), sometimes too forceful (Nelson and Murphy 1992), sometimes ignored in preference to teacher response (Zhang 1995). Oral conferencing appears to work best when the students actively invest themselves in the conference rather than simply accept teacher commentary (Goldstein and Conrad 1990). Some evidence suggests that self-directed revision, without response from any reader at all, also results in improvement in subsequent drafts (Polio, Fleck, and Leder 1998). Finally, even response that corresponds to a student's expressed desire for response type may lead to unanticipated and adverse affective reactions in the writer (Hyland 1998). Although L2 writing professionals now have some idea about effective response strategies, given the central importance of responding to writing and the complexity of its effects, it is clear that, just as there is no prototypical good text, there is no simple relationship between response and writing improvement. Furthermore, L2 writing professionals are beginning to recognize that writing response is crucially embedded in complex and inescapable disciplinary, social, and political contexts that may be out of the control of both the writer and the teacher.

In most academic contexts (and less directly in professional settings), writing is evaluated. Like all forms of assessment, L2 writing assessment serves a sorting and gatekeeping function. However repugnant such a function may be, if assessment is unavoidable (an arguable supposition), it is the responsibility of L2 practitioners, as Hamp-Lyons asserts (2001), to do it well. One of several tortured issues in writing assessment is what is a fair text, a fair sample of writing, to assess. Single-shot exams written within a restricted period of time on an arbitrarily chosen topic that the writer sees for the first time at the exam session, such as in the Test of Written English? Tests based on a reading passage from the test taker's disciplinary area (Hamp-Lyons 1991a)? Revised texts? Portfolios of a variety of writing produced over time?

Each of these types of evaluative measures has been used at one time or another to decide the educational fate of L2 writers. In addition to the problem of which texts to evaluate comes the question of who should evaluate them. Research studies have shown the results of allowing inappropriate raters to evaluate texts—for example, language teachers who evaluate texts in disciplinary areas where they have no expertise, as has happened with the ELTS exam (Hamp-Lyons 1991b), or L1 writing teachers (and teachers from other disciplinary areas) who evaluate L2 writing with no understanding of L2 writing issues, as may happen in exit or proficiency exams (Sweedler-Brown 1993). When the same writing proficiency exam is used with L1 and L2 writers, problems arise with selecting culturally appropriate writing topics, and these problems tend to disadvantage the L2 writers (Johns 1991b). Finally, when L1 and L2 writers are tested together, the question arises of whether different standards should be used to evaluate the writing. Balancing between a perceived need, or institutionally enforced requirement, to test writing and a desire to be fair to L2 writers, L2 writing professionals do not appear to have consistent, satisfactory answers to these vexed questions of what is an appropriate text to rate, who should read it, what writing topic is fair, and what accommodations should be made in rating L2 writers' texts.

PROCESS-BASED ORIENTATIONS

Questions about texts, tests, and teaching methodologies continue. However, these issues were displaced from center stage by explorations oriented toward individual writers, first synchronically toward their cognitive processes while writing and then diachronically toward their development as writers and as initiates into academic and professional disciplines. Emulating Emig's seminal (1971) study of English L1 high school students' cognitive processes while writing, L2 writing researchers developed a significant body of research reviewed in, for example, Krapels (1990), focusing on such topics as writing processes of strong L2 writers (Zamel 1983), those of less proficient L2 writers (Raimes 1985), planning in L1 versus L2 (Friedlander 1990), use of L1 in L2 writing (Roca, Murphy, and Manchon 1999), and threshold levels of L2 proficiency (Cumming 1989). Pursuit of the question of how mental processes are engaged in L2 writing has somewhat tapered off; nevertheless, the most significant results of these studies include the findings:

- That proficient L2 writers focus on content, and not only on form, as they write
- That L2 writers need to reach a threshold level of proficiency in L2 before they can engage the efficient writing processes they use in L1
- That writers' processes vary fairly widely across individuals though they may remain more or less consistent from L1 to L2 (Arndt 1987)

• That shifting to L1 can be a very useful strategy for generating ideas and stimulating more complex thinking in L2.

Such writing process studies looked at L2 writers at a single moment in time. As a clearer picture of L2 writers' mental processes began to develop, disciplinary interest shifted toward the question of how individuals' writing processes and skills developed over time, as opposed to how they might be instantiated in a single moment of writing. Consistent with a growing trend in L2 writing research away from decontextualized examinations of texts or of the writing processes of disembodied writers, the focus on L2 writers' development has revealed how personal, social, and educational contexts are necessarily entwined. In broadening their scope to include more than just learners' L2 writing, studies of L2 writers' development have given the field a look at how specific individuals, with names, histories, personalities, and voices, negotiate their way, over time, through educational institutions in the L2 toward academic literacy. (See Harklau 2000 for high school students in the United States and Leki 1999 and Spack 1997 for college students in the United States.) Other studies have looked at how individuals come to be initiated into disciplinary domains. Here, personal intellectual, academic, and literacy growth is shown to be actively and firmly shaped by the chosen academic disciplines. These studies focus on graduate students and professionals working in L2 English, tracing such formative experiences as writing for graduate seminars (Prior 1998; Riazi 1997), experiencing conflicting assumptions about the chosen discipline (Casanave 1998), writing dissertations in L2 (Belcher 1997), writing in L2 on the job (Parks 2000), and publishing in L2 (Flowerdew 1999).

BUDDING SENSE OF DISCIPLINARITY

If disciplinarity is marked by, among other things, a theoretical foundation and a disciplinary history, L2 writing may be at the brink of disciplinarity, and perhaps at the same time, at a moment of crisis. Although both Cumming and Riazi (2000) and Silva (1993) argue that L2 writing as yet does not have agreed-upon models or theories, borrowings (from L1 English) and fragments of models are surfacing, as are disciplinary histories (Matsuda 1998, 1999). Yet, at the same time, as several researchers have pointed out, the number of L2 teacher-education programs that offer courses in teaching L2 writing and the number of L2 writing researchers in Ph.D. programs who can develop a new generation of L2 writing researchers remain relatively small, prompting some to express concern about the future of the field (Santos et al. 2000). Atkinson (in Santos et al. 2000) calls for an intellectual infusion into L2 writing that might move the field away from perennial rehashing of process approach issues. Two likely infusion donors might be socio-cognitive/sociocultural studies (discussed later) and second language acquisition (SLA).

Perhaps oddly, there has thus far been little interdisciplinary cross-fertilization between SLA and L2 writing, little examination, for example, of language acquisition through L2 writing (see, however, Weissberg 2000, who argues that new L2 forms first emerge in writing, not in speech).[1] The implications for writing of current models of second language acquisition, such as parallel distributed processing (PDP), also remain unexplored. No doubt part of this astonishing lack of interdisciplinary interface is the result of L2 writing's historical, and sometimes misguided, dependence on L1 writing research; another part is perhaps SLA's historical focus primarily on speech, rather than on writing. Be that as it may, two features of PDP, or connectionist, explanations for brain processes should interest L2 writing researchers and practitioners: first, how neurons work to mediate the relationship between outside world stimulus to a person and the actions that person then takes, and, second, how such materialistic views of mind, memory, and learning have been interpreted as supporting social constructionist views of knowledge.

In talking about language learning in *Language Teaching*, Lado (1964) asserted, following behaviorists, that contact with new language forms leaves traces in the mind/memory and that repeated stimulation or contact with that same form intensifies the traces and results in deeper, more permanent learning. But current PDP discussions of learning describe a far more complex system in which not only are multiple links made to multiple neural sites at once but also these links carry varying weights, causing differential stimulation. A better grasp among L2 writing researchers of the complexity of PDP descriptions might help us to clarify, for example, the apparent disconnect students appear to experience between the writing done for L2 writing classes and that done in other disciplinary areas, for which, presumably, the L2 writing classes purportedly prepare them (Leki and Carson 1997). In other words, it might help us to understand why what is learned in L2 writing classes seems somehow not to transfer to other writing contexts.[2]

The second perspective that comes from interpretations of connectionism links up directly with preoccupations of L2 writing researchers and practitioners, but it too has not yet been influential, so far finding its way into L2 writing through, for example, the work of Atkinson (1999b) and perhaps best expressed in Gee (1996). Gee argues that the theoretical interest of connectionism to social constructionists is that it demonstrates how it might be possible that thought, memory, learning, and other functions of the mind are located not in the physical brain but in the social world. All that the brain holds is multiple series of neural networks linked thousands of times over to the other series of neural networks in the brain. If memories, then, cannot be properly thought of as somehow physically stored in the brain, where are those memories and that learning? Gee explains that an individual's experiences and the meanings associated with them create the links among networks of neurons and the varying strength at which any input neurons will fire. Since these experiences with the outside, particularly the social, world set these weights and stimulate excitation levels, meaning can reside only in those sociocultural groups or communities into which a person has been initiated.

Again, while these views have not yet played much of a role in L2 writing research and practice, they dovetail well with the influences already felt in L2 writing of both postmodern and sociopolitical/critical pedagogical perspectives, as discussed later. The convergence of these three perspectives (connectionist, postmodern, and sociopolitical) also seems to me to offer an opening into the most exciting, least pedestrian future directions for L2 research and practice. (See later discussion.) What needs to be worked out, for example, is how the insights from these domains can be applied to practical, everyday, working world contacts between L2 writing students and the social world that surrounds their L2 writing and their other activities.

GROWING ORIENTATION TO
SOCIOPOLITICAL ISSUES

The separation of this last group of themes related to sociopolitical orientation into a category distinct from the ones discussed earlier is problematic. It should not be construed as suggesting that these political dimensions exist apart from the issues discussed earlier or that any of those issues can be viewed apolitically. That is, sociopolitical concerns are not on a par with such aspects of L2 writing as assessment, revision, or error correction. Rather, political dimensions subsume and permeate all the focuses, concerns, and themes discussed earlier, whether or not we choose to recognize this, as so aptly argued by Benesch (1993).

Reflecting a growing awareness of the interested or nonneutral nature of education, increasing numbers of L2 writing researchers have begun to address sociopolitical questions, in some cases primarily in relation to cross-cultural issues and stereotyping (for example, Kubota 1999). Others, however, have dealt more directly with L2 writing. Angelil-Carter (1997) deals with identity issues and how one South African L2 writer consciously decides where and how to ally himself politically through his writing choices. Canagarajah (1993a) introduces the pointed question of the role of local knowledge in L2 English writing as a means of resisting the spread of the hegemonic and normative influences of Western academic writing. Pennycook (1997a) exposes historical, cultural, and economic roots of Western notions of plagiarism in an effort to reveal its situatedness and to resist the hysteria that sometimes surrounds plagiarism. Clark and Ivanic (1997), though not specifically addressing writing issues in L2, analyze the politics of writing from a variety of dimensions, arguing for increased access to public voice for subalterns (which includes L2 writers) as a democratizing effort. Benesch (1993) has argued for a critical pedagogy that would encourage and instruct L2 students in the use of writing to counter economic and political forces that have a negative impact on their lives. Australian genre researchers (for example, Cope and Kalantzis 1993) have all argued for the empowerment of the disempowered, particularly children from nonprivileged classes, through teaching them the power genres. References in L2 writing research to theorists and researchers of critical language awareness and the new literacies movements, such as Street, Rampton, Gee, Fairclough, though not yet frequent, are increasing. Many of these writers have reflected postmodern perspectives, which have helped to deepen our understanding of certain writing issues. Postmodernism challenges the belief in individual agency, in the unitary self, and in freely chosen, self-motivated actions, feelings, and opinions. The speaker/writer is viewed instead as a juncture of shifting experiences, beliefs, and ideological discourses. Such a perspective works against the ever-present temptation to exoticize L2 learners and to essentialize their home cultures.

Thus, the historical trajectory of L2 writing has moved from narrow focuses and tight control over L2 writing toward a growing interest in the context in which that writing takes place, both the individual context and the broad sociopolitical and historical context. We have partial answers to such central questions as what good writing is and what good writing is good for, how L2 writing is done, and how we should teach L2 writing. But explorations continue from perspectives that shift over time, as they should. Perhaps disciplines evolve in ways similar to the ways natural language acquisition takes place, with each important new perspective unsettling and causing a salutary restructuring of previous and presumed-settled understandings.

NOTES

1. One notable exception to this generalization is the impact of Krashen's SLA work, which certainly did its part to move L2 writing teachers away from a narrow focus on language errors toward a more comprehensive understanding of L2 writing. Krashen's (1984, 1993) interest in literacy and the power of reading has also influenced L2 writing.

2. Connectionist computer simulations attempting to model what happens in the mind suggest something like the following (Churchland 1995). Each neuron in a set of (simulated) input neurons receives an outside stimulus. Each one of these input neurons is linked to another set of hidden simulated neurons with different strengths or weights. These weights or strengths in real humans might be based on any number of things, for example, past experience or importance of that particular outside world stimulus to the system/person. Each neuron in this input layer not only is linked with differing strengths to the second hidden layer but also can fire its signal at varying degrees of excitement or intensity to that hidden layer. In the simulations, neurons in the hidden layer then fire, with the same possibilities for variation in link weight and firing strength, to an output layer that governs, for example, muscle movement or speech.

Even in this most radically simplified version of what may go on in the mind, such a conceptualization already helps us see why simple repetition, as in giving corrective feedback on errors in writing, for example, cannot guarantee learning or any more or less permanent change in how the writer handles that feature of language.

PART III

DISCOURSE ANALYSIS

CHAPTER 7

DISCOURSE ANALYSIS AND APPLIED LINGUISTICS

DEBORAH POOLE

STREVENS's early characterization of applied linguistics (AL) as a dynamic discipline that "redefines itself afresh for each task" (1980: 19) aptly captures its disciplinary link with discourse analysis (DA). For more than twenty years, their relationship has been a fluid and multifaceted one, driven by a variety of theoretical perspectives across an increasingly diverse range of contexts. As such, locating a unified body of work to represent the AL/DA interface proves elusive, although connections between them are substantive and well-established.

From its initial—and still largely central—focus on second language learning, applied linguistics (AL) is now more widely seen as relevant to any real-world, language-related problem that an interdisciplinary, as opposed to purely linguistic, approach can address. This view has been widely articulated (e.g., Brumfit 1997; Gunnarsson 1997; Widdowson 1980) for some time and, with an explosion of work in the 1990s (Kramsch 2000b), been realized with more frequency throughout the discipline. The expanded focus has resulted in closer ties with DA, as its potential to specify how language is integral to the constitution and maintenance of complex social phenomena has become clearer. With DA increasingly a methodology of choice for investigating broader AL concerns such as the language of politics, professions, or family, their relationship is poised to deepen over the next decade. This promise is a qualified one, however, in that the theoretical perspectives underlying the newer applications have yet to fully cohere with the ways DA has been employed in the more traditional AL areas of second language teaching and learning.

The potential for discord marks several recent discussions that take issue with the sort of DA traditionally assumed AL (e.g., Fairclough 1997; Pennycook 1994a; Wodak 1995).[1] Pennycook, for example, draws from statements by Hatch (1992), Cook (1989), Brown and Yule (1983a), and others to demonstrate that the analysis of language use beyond the level of the sentence constitutes a widely agreed-upon definition. He suggests that this perspective contributes to the "political quietism" (1994a: 120) of AL as a discipline and in its place proposes a more far-reaching DA that relates features of language use to multiple contextual dimensions such as ideological orientation, relations of power, or institutional constraints. In the intervening years, a modified version of this perspective has motivated much of the growing discourse analytic work within AL, work which holds promise for linking the traditional and more recent contexts where DA and AL converge. With views similar to Pennycook's echoed elsewhere, however, the potential for both growth and division within AL seems clear.

The following discussion seeks to specify areas of commonality and difference across these varied contexts and subsequently to suggest how the interdisciplinary promise of the DA/AL interface might be fulfilled without creating unbridgeable gaps in the field. To begin, I focus much of the discussion on the ways DA has been employed in the traditional second language focused areas of AL. This body of work, though narrower than the whole, remains their most fully developed area of interface (cf. Kaplan and Widdowson 1992) and is itself characterized by considerable variation in terms of what counts as DA and the purposes for which it is used. The complexities marking this variation provide a background for more recent AL developments; they also suggest several potentially fruitful lines of inquiry that have been marginalized or ignored.

Language Learning and Discourse Analysis

Discourse analysis and L2 concerns have converged most prominently in the domains of communicative language teaching, English for specific purposes, contrastive rhetoric, classroom-based research, and interlanguage pragmatics. Across these areas, applied linguists have drawn from multiple perspectives associated with the analysis of natural language use: speech act theory, functional linguistics, conversation analysis,[2] the ethnography of speaking, and text linguistics. (See, e.g., Coulthard 1977; Hatch 1992; Hatch and Long 1980; Widdowson 1978.) Hence, even though the traditional definition of DA identified earlier usually pertains, the types of analysis have varied widely and included such disparate foci as form-function relations of grammatical features, the lexical and grammatical characteristics of texts, written text structure, the sequential organization of talk in speech activities, and the frequency, scope, and distribution of specific interactional sequences or speech acts. The complexity of these applications is deepened by the ongoing question of whether data should be analyzed quantitatively, with a focus on counting discrete language features, or qualitatively, with a focus on fine-grained, contextualized descriptions of language in use.

Across these domains and types of L2 discourse inquiry, the unifying feature has been the goal of drawing pedagogical implications from a research base in actual language use. On the whole, however, sustaining an ongoing connection between DA and L2 classroom practice has proved difficult, despite the best and most explicit of intentions.

DA in Communicative Language Teaching and English for Specific Purposes

The tendency for discourse analytic theory and research to distance itself from classroom practice can be observed in the literatures of both communicative language teaching (CLT) and English for specific purposes (ESP). These related movements, with their focus on learner goals, or the language that learners *aim for*, were among the most significant initial influences of discourse analysis on second language teaching. Early CLT, especially in the oral/aural domain, strove for a pedagogical "authenticity" oriented to classroom language use that paralleled speech events and activities beyond the classroom setting. Hence, in developing prescriptions for syllabi and pedagogy, language teaching theory turned to perspectives focused on language use in settings beyond the classroom, especially to the work of Austin (1962), Searle (1969), Halliday (1978), and Hymes (1971b). As has been widely documented, speech act theory in particular motivated the development of functional-notional syllabi, which in turn were appropriated by a more broadly focused approach drawing from Hymes's notion of communicative competence and from the Hallidayan perspective of language as a system of meaning potential through which individuals and communities can fulfill their communicative purposes.

The tenets and methodologies of the communicative approach arguably constitute the dominant paradigm in current English language teaching. However, although its pedagogical theory derived largely from theories and analyses of discourse, CLT was not tied to an explicit research agenda. The consequence has been that, over time, the original link between DA and the communicative teaching of spoken language has receded in importance (Riggenbach [1999] provides an exception), and comparative analyses of recommended classroom practices and the authentic communication on which they are purportedly based have been rare.

Within the ESP movement, the connection between DA and classroom practice has fared somewhat differently, largely because ESP itself was predicated on a discourse analytic research agenda (Widdowson 1978). The original linking of student goals to settings in science and technology prompted discourse inquiry into the texts and contexts associated with those settings. The subsequent turn to quantitative accounts of grammatical and lexical features sought to characterize the sorts of texts students would need to read and write within their chosen disciplines. However, the quantitative and highly specialized nature of the early findings tended to ignore the organizational features of texts (Johns 1991a), making widespread application to classroom practice difficult to sustain. A later tendency, as Johns and Dudley-Evans note, has been the "danger of over-dependence on the materials writers' intuitions about what is involved in such activities, rather than upon research and analysis of representative discourse" (1991: 307). Ironically, recent research in ESP has moved toward more descriptive discourse analyses, which, while increasing in frequency and sophistication, are simultaneously becoming more distant from their original link to the goals of second language learning (B. Samraj, personal communication).

The exception to this is seen in the genre analysis domain of ESP (Johns 1997, Swales 1990), which may represent the best-realized link between discourse analysis and contemporary L2 pedagogy. Genre analysis has provided, for example, analyses of academic texts and their subparts that have been widely used for purposes of graduate writing instruction. Perhaps more importantly, it has offered writing instructors the analytical tools to analyze new genres as well as to teach a pedagogically appropriate form of discourse awareness to their students.

Contrastive Rhetoric

A complementary thread in the discourse analysis of written texts is that of contrastive rhetoric (Connor 1996; Kaplan 1966), where the connection between DA and AL predates the others discussed throughout this chapter. Contrastive rhetoric represents the first serious contemporary study of second language writing, as well as the only early paradigm where prominence was given to cross-cultural research. In contrast to the initial goal orientation of ESP, contrastive rhetoric has been concerned largely with the process of learning to write in a second language, particularly with how that process is affected by differences in text characteristics across languages and cultures. Its effect on pedagogy has primarily been to create teacher awareness of specific or potential differences in the nature of written text, rather than to recommend specific teaching practices (Connor 1996; 1991).

Over time, areas of overlap between contrastive rhetoric and ESP have begun to emerge, with both now focusing on genre-comparisons across languages (Connor 1996), and ESP giving increased attention to learners' developmental processes (e.g., Swales 1990). In addition, the importance that ESP assigns to discourse communities in the social construction of texts (Johns 1997) resonates with the contrastive rhetoric concern for how texts are culturally constructed and embedded. Recent discussions such as those by Connor (1996) and Leki (1991) focus on these areas of similarity and offer promise of increased coherence between the two approaches.

The Separation of Speech and Writing

The discussion of these interrelated approaches points to the fact that, for purposes of L2 pedagogy, a good deal more discourse analysis has focused on written language than on spoken language. The tendency to separate the two in research, however, supports their separation in practice and serves to undermine one of the original premises of CLT, that everyday language use involves the complex interplay of both speech and writing (Savignon 1991). This perspective is well represented in the pedagogical literature which argues for an integrated skills approach to language teaching (e.g., Scarcella and Oxford 1992; Stoller 1999), in large-scale multidimensional discourse analyses that fail to find distinct linguistic differences between spoken and written genres (Besnier 1988; Biber 1986), and in ethnographic research that documents the interconnectedness of spoken and written language (Heath 1982; Scribner and Cole 1981) and rejects a strict distinction between them as "a construct of researchers, not an accurate portrayal of reality across cultures" (Heath 1982: 73). However, such a view has yet to be more than minimally reflected in research, materials, or program planning within AL.

Discourse Analysis and Classroom Interaction

The comparatively greater focus on DA and the teaching of writing can also be viewed in light of the classroom as social context. Written genres, including those typical of nonschool settings, can be taught through the practice of routine classroom interaction so that the norms of classroom speaking are largely unaffected. In spoken language instruction, however, inherent differences characterize the authentic language representing the goals of instruction and the authentic interactional environment of the classroom (cf. Ellis 1990; Sinclair 1987; Widdowson 1978).

The analysis of classroom discourse has the potential to address this contradiction by revealing how communicative tasks affect interaction and, in turn, how that interaction compares with traditional language learning activities and more authentic contexts beyond the classroom. However, the fundamental characteristics of classroom discourse and its realizations in foreign/second language settings have, for the most part, remained marginal to mainstream L2 pedagogical concerns.

A sizable body of work (e.g., Cazden 1987; Mehan 1979; Sinclair and Coulthard 1975) exists in this area, some directly focused on the L2 context (Coulthard 1977; Sinclair 1987; Van Lier 1988). This work has identified what Cazden has termed the "default" script of classroom interaction, in that it is "what happens unless deliberate action is taken to achieve some alternative" (1987: 53). In the default script, the teacher constructs the overwhelming proportion of initiating and responding turns, as well as framing utterances that function to bring the activity into being, move it forward, and draw it to a close. The teacher also has the right to determine when and how to relinquish the floor to a student, as well as select which student can respond. In such a sequence, the student's verbal role can be a limited one (i.e., a response to the teacher's initiation) so that the full repertoire of communicative acts needed for L2 competence becomes, for all practical purposes, impossible to practice and thus unlikely to be achieved.

For CLT, the relevance of the default pattern further lies in its differences from interaction beyond the classroom—exactly the sort CLT tries to teach in the name of authenticity. In face-to-face conversation, initiations and responses are shared between and among interlocutors, a speaker can select him- or herself as next speaker, and a single turn often includes both a response and subsequent initiation (Sacks, Schegloff, and Jefferson 1974). Hence, in classrooms, the dispreference for student self-selection as next speaker, the low proportion of student initiation turns, and the unlikelihood of a student responding and initiating in the same utterance mark the interaction as fundamentally distinct from most nonclassroom talk.

Hints of this mismatch emerged in at least one early study (Long and Sato 1983), which found that interaction in communicative classrooms bore little resemblance to conversations but were characterized by more typical teacher-talk features, such as display questions. As a result, Long and Sato suggested that "contrary to the recommendations of many writers on SL teaching methodology, communicative use of the target language makes up only a minor part of typical classroom activities. 'Is the clock on the wall?' and 'Are you a student?' are still the staple diet, at least for beginners" (1983: 280). Seen in light of the differences between the default pattern of classroom interaction and the characteristic features of face-to-face interaction, however, their findings are not surprising, since the teachers in their study acted appropriately according to the norms of classroom speech activities (cf. Poole 1992).

The attempt in CLT to facilitate language learning useful for nonclassroom contexts has been represented through the use of role plays, jigsaw activities, and various types of pair and small-group work, since these allow students to assume interactional roles outside those afforded by the default script. The problem however, reminiscent of the caution offered by Johns and Dudley-Evans (1991), is that much of CLT practice draws from intuitive responses to activities and intuitive notions of interaction beyond the classroom but is not tied to a research base. Exceptions are found in the work of Nunan (1991), Duff (1993), and Kinginger and Savignon (1991) who have investigated the interactional effects of L2 pedagogical tasks. However, this body of work is not yet sufficiently cohesive to provide clear implications for practice. The substantial work that *does* exist in the area of L2 classroom-based research has been less concerned with pedagogy per se than with what classroom practices will motivate second language acquisition (SLA). The result is that its findings are addressed in the SLA, rather than a pedagogical, literature and have yet to make a significant impact on L2 classroom practice, despite the impressive efforts of some (e.g., Chaudron 1988; Ellis 1990; Van Lier 1988) to link the two.

Discourse Analysis in Classroom-Based Research

Most L2 classroom-based research has been grounded in the assumption that learners' interactional modifications, including phenomena such as clarification requests, confirmation checks, and repair sequences, promote acquisition of the target language. It has focused on various task-types and speaker-configurations, largely in the search for what conditions result in the most interactional modifications. The argument rests on the notion, sometimes termed the 'interaction hypothesis,' that more modifications elicit more comprehensible input, which in turn promotes better or faster acquisition. As Ellis has noted, however, "the lack of research lending direct support to the interaction hypothesis has not inhibited researchers from basing classroom research on it. The general assumption is that the greater the amount of interactional modification there is, the more rapid and successful acquisition will be" (1990: 111).

Perhaps because of its relatively narrow focus, the substantial body of L2 classroom-based research has had surprisingly little effect on classroom practice. For example, one of the most widely cited findings (Doughty and Pica 1986) is that "two-way" tasks (such as information-gap or jigsaw activities) promote more interactional modifications than "one-way" tasks (such as decision making and problem solving) and are therefore preferable.[3] However, pedagogical prescriptions in AL (e.g., Nunan 1991; Ur 1996) seldom recommend one task type over the other, stressing instead the importance of task variety. In addition, even a cursory survey of current textbooks reveals little preference for two-way tasks.

The goal in L2 classroom-based research of locating interactional modifications has necessitated a form of discourse analysis based on quantification of predetermined categories. As a whole, it is also grounded in the ubiquitous input-output metaphor of SLA research. In both senses, it differs from the tradition of classroom discourse described earlier (Cazden 1987; Mehan 1979), as well as from recent qualitative analyses that view interaction as the joint, embedded activity of all coparticipants and employ analytical categories only as they emerge from a body of data.

New Directions in Classroom-Based Research

Over the past decade, there have been indications of a shift in the focus of classroom-based L2 research as the number, scope and depth of interactional analyses have increased. This newer work investigates L2 classrooms without the motive of locating interactional modifications or even of relating its findings to SLA theory and research. Hence, it represents a departure from what has traditionally motivated the study of talk in second language classrooms and offers a new orientation to the link between analysis of spoken discourse and L2 pedagogy.

From a conversation-analytic point of view, for example, Koshik (1999) has considered how display questions can assist student performance in teacher-student writing conferences, thus calling into question the longheld disdain with which they have been viewed. Another study (Sorjonen 1999) investigates the interaction surrounding a "discourse chain," a common CLT activity in which students use textual cues to construct a semispontaneous dialog. Through close analysis of student talk, Sorjonen documents the problematic, normally dispreferred, dimensions of the interactional sequence demanded by the discourse chain. In an interactional study of pair work interaction across several task types, Kelley (2000) reveals that learners have the flexibility to turn interaction in "one-way" tasks (as defined by Doughty and Pica) into "two-way" exchanges, suggesting that the "one-way/two-way" distinction can be difficult to discern in the face of more qualitative analysis (cf. January 1996). These and other recent studies not only have important implications for pedagogy, but also point to the need for a more widely focused DA in classroom-based L2 research.

Cross-Cultural Perspectives

Perhaps the most important extension of classroom-based research would include its application to a wider range of cultural contexts. However, throughout the history of the AL/DA interface, the notion that classroom practices might differ cross-culturally has received scant attention.

More than a decade ago, Chick argued for the importance of understanding classroom interactional differences across cultures but lamented that the research perspectives and methodologies employed in AL "tend to be narrow" (1988: 3). His analysis focused on student choral responses in a KwaZulu classroom and grew from his participation in a CLT program dedicated to the improvement of English language teaching in South Africa. From his perspective, this program tended to view existing teaching practices as incompatible with (and inferior to) those advocated in CLT. Chick considered the chorusing practices from the perspective of politeness theory (Brown and Levinson 1988) and pointed to their role in satisfying wider sociocultural norms for preserving face. He called for applied linguists to view such phenomena with deeper understanding of their underlying dimensions, rather than from a "deficit" perspective toward practices seemingly at odds with communicative ideology (cf. Chick 1996; Poole 1992).

The sort of cross-cultural perspective recommended by Chick has seldom been realized in AL research, and, to date, only a few studies (e.g., Chen 1999; Cook 1999; Duff 1995; Duff and Uchida 1997) have considered classroom interaction in non-English speaking environments. Duff, for example, considers a dual-language program in Hungary, documenting the changing interactional characteristics of a recitation event and linking them to the rapid sociopolitical changes characteristic of the school's wider context. In an analysis of Japanese teacher-student interaction, Cook considers an interactional sequence in which one student is called upon to comment on a previous student's utterance. She interprets this sequence as a linguistic means through which students are socialized to the importance of listening in order to interpret nuances of another speaker's intended meaning (cf. Anderson 1995). Chen's study of Chinese TEFL classrooms recalls Chick's in considering the predominance of student choral responses and the corresponding low frequency of individual student responses. These and similar studies follow from work in constitutive ethnography (Mehan 1979) and language socialization (Ochs 1988; Schieffelin and Ochs 1986). As such, they are undertaken in part to dispel cultural stereotypes through in-depth contextualized analyses that can support grounded, but not deterministic, understanding of cross-cultural differences.[4]

Despite the relevance of these sorts of classroom-based studies for the process of language learning in formal contexts, the question of whether they will find a more central place as a domain of L2 inquiry remains an open one. With the exception of work in contrastive rhetoric, AL has traditionally resisted focusing on cross-cultural differences. This has begun to change with a growing interest in language socialization, which explores the role of language in the socialization of novices to group membership (Ochs 1988; Schieffelin and Ochs 1986). At present, however, language socialization is largely viewed as part of the expanded focus of AL, rather than as a relevant area for L2 learning.[5]

New Connections between DA and AL

As indicated earlier, the focus of AL has now broadened to include issues related to "communication in institutions, media discourse, political discourse, discourse, and gender (and) racist discourse" (Wodak 1995: 1), as well as to topics more readily linked to traditional AL concerns, such as bilingualism, language minority issues, and NS classroom interaction. (See Gunnarsson [1997] for an excellent overview.)

Multiple perspectives and methodologies underlie this work, but it is unified in its assumption that language use is inextricably linked with features of context. In essence, this view considers language and context to be mutually constitutive phenomena (Goodwin and Duranti 1992), although perspectives on relevant contextual features vary widely. At one end of the spectrum, a range of approaches assumes that broader (i.e., institutional, historical, ideological, or cultural) dimensions of context are reflected and sustained through features of language use. At the other, conversation analysis considers the most relevant contextual features to include gesture, gaze, bodily orientation, and the turn-by-turn unfolding of a sequence of talk. Both perspectives, however, differ from the traditional role of DA within AL. Conversation analysis, although often referred to and nominally appropriated for language teaching purposes (e.g., Richards 1990), has seldom been employed as a research methodology within AL. Only recently, in fact, has its appropriateness for L2 research purposes been seriously considered (e.g., Firth 1996). Conversely, the more expansive approaches consider multiple layers of context in much broader ways than the traditional AL definition of DA has allowed. Moreover, they take the notions of discourse community and social embeddedness of language as relevant to both spoken *and* written language, as well as to the ways they interact.

The sort of transcendent perspective now called for is represented, potentially at least, in the work of a new generation of applied linguists who have investigated L2 settings in ways that show the relation of language use to a variety of contextual phenomena, from microlevel features such as the interplay of text, gaze, and gesture in an ESL pair work activity (e.g., Olsher 2000) to the more global level of political change in a recitation event (Duff 1995). Related approaches in language minority school settings have identified other compelling connections. Rymes (1998), for example, interprets students' oral narratives about past drop-out experiences as reflecting the conflicting institutional goals of the charter school which they attend. Patthey-Chavez (1993), in a study combining analysis of written discourse with ethnographic observation in a Los Angeles high school, identifies routine contexts where Anglo and Latino cultural identities collide and where the boundary between them is negotiated. Poole (1994a, 1994b) identifies how interaction in a routine testing event functions to recreate and maintain both the social differentiation of students and the view of knowledge most valued in school. In a college ESL setting, Patthey-Chavez and Ferris (1997) analyze the effect of students' divergent backgrounds on the outcomes of teacher-student writing conferences (cf. Patthey-Chavez and Clare 1996).

Through the type of analysis that characterizes it, this work—which considers a range of both spoken and written discourse types—offers the possibility of a more broadly focused DA across several L2 domains of inquiry. And, although close to the traditional concerns of AL, it transcends its historic boundaries in terms of its methodology and the sorts of questions that drive it, offering links to the newer concerns and approaches of AL, including the sort of political DA advocated by Pennycook at the beginning of this chapter.

FUTURE DIRECTIONS

As the disciplinary boundaries of AL expand, they also become increasingly blurred, a tendency amplified through its closer association with DA. Large bodies of research, in areas such as the ethnography of education or doctor-patient communication, employ some form of DA on which to base implications for real-world situations. This work has a tradition outside of AL, however, and has not typically acknowledged AL as a home discipline. Hence, the potential exists for nonreciprocal relationships with a number of fields whose purposes of inquiry match those of AL.

The excitement generated as interdisciplinary connections are expanded is also tempered by the fact that they threaten to form separate subdisciplines within AL with few ties to its historic second language base.[6] These separate interests recently prompted Ochs (1997) to observe the "parallel neighborhoods" in AL and to call for intentional efforts at communicating across the growing intradisciplinary boundaries. One could say that these separations call for an "applied linguistic" solution, as it is currently defined.

In fact, the potential for connections across the various communities of AL appears to be readily available. The current conceptions of discourse and applications of discourse analysis across AL resonate with similar themes that suggest intra-disciplinary links not currently acknowledged or sought (cf. Kaplan 1990). The discourses *about* discourse repeatedly echo notions such as the sociocultural embeddedness of language use, the mutually constitutive relationship of language and context, the importance of discourse community, and the role of joint activity and negotiation in the creation of meaning. These notions, though articulated in slightly different ways and to different degrees across the domains of interest, provide obvious and increasingly substantial points of departure for more coherence among the areas where DA and AL converge.

NOTES

1. It should be noted that these authors do not propose the same sort of DA. Fairclough, e.g., argues for a 'critical discourse analysis' that has the goal of revealing social inequality. Pennycook, drawing from Foucault (e.g., 1972), rejects this view as too deterministic, arguing for a form of DA that assumes the potential of human agency while identifying connections between language features and various contextual phenomena.

2. Applied linguists have traditionally included conversation analysis as one type of discourse analysis. This view is not widely shared among conversation analysts, however. See Levinson (1983) for discussion.

3. Two-way tasks, it is argued, necessitate an exchange of information that is optional, though encouraged, in one-way tasks. Doughty and Pica (1986; cf. Pica 1987) have argued that it is the *requirement* to exchange information that promotes more interactional modifications in two-way tasks.

4. This work assumes the possibility of change and human agency, as well as the influence of novices on the socialization process. Duff's (1995) study is an especially strong example of this.

5. Recent work in interlanguage pragmatics (Kasper and Blum-Kulka 1993) has also begun to highlight the role of cross-cultural research for SLA. Like contrastive rhetoric, interlanguage pragmatics takes the perspective that discourse norms in the first language—in this case, interactional, rather than written—can influence a learner's acquisition of related norms in the second.

6. Work in second language acquisition is a case in point, which, it has been argued (Firth 1996), is in danger of losing contact with research on language and social interaction.

PART IV

THE STUDY OF SECOND LANGUAGE LEARNING

CHAPTER 8

FORMAL LINGUISTIC PERSPECTIVES ON SECOND LANGUAGE ACQUISITION

ALAN JUFFS

BEFORE considering the contributions of formal linguistics to the study of second language acquisition (SLA), a definition of formal linguistics is necessary. Linguists disagree on the scope of formal linguistics (even within a theory of syntax [Van Valin and La Polla 1997: 12–15]), so any definition will be controversial. For clarity, this chapter understands formal linguistics to be a theory of the capacity underlying the grammars of natural languages that meets the requirements of "explanatory adequacy" (Chomsky 1981, 1986; Hall C., 1995; Van Valin and La Polla 1997). A formal grammar is an explicit description of a speaker's knowledge of his or her language(s); this means that all the properties are specified fully and precisely as a system of operations on linguistic categories (Hall, C., 1995: 171). The grammar will achieve explanatory adequacy if linguistic expressions can be derived from the grammar *and* if the theory accounts for how the grammar might have arisen in the mind of the speaker (Van Valin and La Polla 1997: 8). Formal linguistics, then, seeks the answers to two main questions: "What does it mean to say we 'know' a language?" and "How does that knowledge arise in the mind of the speaker; that is, how is it acquired?"

Many researchers have written on the relationship between formal linguistics and second language acquisition; this review owes much to previous work, which readers should also consult (Cook 1988, 1993; Epstein, Flynn, and Martohardjono 1996; Flynn 1988, 1996; Gregg 1989, 1996; Lightbown and White 1987; Rutherford 1983; White 1989, 1996b). Lightbown and White (1987: 483) wrote that (formal) linguistic theories have an "essential but not exclusive" role to play in studies of language acquisition. This position is adopted in this overview; formal theories have a major role to play in one subdomain of a general theory of SLA: the development and ultimate attainment of linguistic competence. Linguistic competence is the tacit knowledge of the abstract properties of the language(s) we speak. Formal linguistics does not address issues of language *use* directly; that is, it claims to be a comprehensive theory not of communicative competence (Canale and Swain 1980; Hymes 1972) but of one subcomponent of communicative competence. It is worth emphasizing, as others have, that formal approaches neither deny the importance of pragmatics and sociological constraints in language use and learning nor do they underestimate their importance in a unified theory of SLA; they simply do not claim to address them (Flynn 1996: 122; Gregg 1996; Schwartz 1999).[1]

This chapter concentrates on the clause and sentence for morphosyntax and the segment and the syllable where phonology is concerned. One short essay obviously cannot do justice to work of an entire field over the past decade. For detailed discussion of points raised in this brief chapter, readers should refer to other research, notably the following works: Archibald 2000, Beck 1998b, Clahsen 1996, Flynn, Martohardjono, and O'Neill 1998, Juffs, Talpas, Mizera, and Burtt 2000, Klein and Martohardjono 1999, Ritchie and Bhatia 1996.

Formal linguistics has contributed to SLA in the following ways:

- It has provided a detailed account of the principles that underlie human languages, some of which will be described later. By doing so, it makes possible falsifiable claims about the nature of second language (L2) competence that lead directly to empirical studies. In particular, controlled experiments are not possible without a specific theory of the structure to be acquired. It also provides a framework for investigating how that knowledge is related to native language competence.
- Through this theoretical framework, researchers have been able ask questions and discover facts about second language grammars that had not previously been described, much less explained.
- Research that is grounded in formal linguistics has created an evolving methodology for evaluating L2 grammar. In some cases, questions in formal linguistics have led to the development of materials used in empirical studies in classroom studies of second language acquisition (Trahey and White 1993; White 1991a, 1991b).

Morphosyntax

Most formal linguistic research in second language acquisition has been conducted within the Principles and Parameters paradigm (Chomsky 1981, 1986) and its successor theory, Minimalism (Chomsky 1995; Marantz 1995).[2] I focus on two main areas. The first strand concentrates on the development of functional categories and the relationship between the acquisition of these categories, and the acquisition of morphology, and word order; the second focuses on second language learners' knowledge of constraints on moved constituents or constraints on coreference of noun phrases.

Functional Categories and the Development of Morphosyntax

In Principles and Parameters (P&P) syntax, syntactic categories are divided into two basic kinds: open-class, lexical categories (noun, verb, adjective, adverb) and closed-class, functional categories (FCs). Functional categories are proposed as the hosts for free and bound morphemes such as determiners (the, a), complementizers (whether, that), negation, tense, aspect, agreement, and so on. Early formulations of P&P syntax contained two functional categories: the complementizer phrase (CP), which introduced the clause, and the inflectional phrase (IP), which was the host of tense, number, and agreement. Pollock (1989) and Chomsky (1991) proposed that IP be split into separate categories of tense, and agreement. Hence, the formal description of a clause for English will appear as in Figure 8.1 (Marantz 1995: 364), where AgrS = Subject agreement, and AgrO = Object agreement. Functional categories, and the "split" INFL categories in Figure 8.1, are important because, by the mid-1990s, linguistic theory had identified them as part of Universal Grammar where constrained variation among languages is accounted for.[3] For most researchers, these functional categories are assumed to exist in all languages, even when those languages do not have overt morphological reflexes of them.[4] The claim is that they form the common core of the syntactic computational component of the language module. In order to understand the role of functional categories in word order variation, consider first the sentences from French and German in (1) and (2). The descriptive generalization to be made is that the verb 'eat' is not next to the object NP, 'beef,' in sentences with questions, negation, and with an adverb.

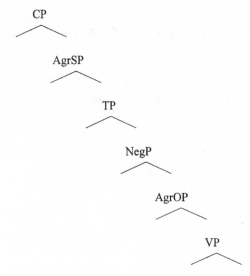

Fig. 8.1. Split Inflectional Phrase (IP or INFL)

(1) a. *Mange- t-il   le   boeuf?*
         eats   he   the   beef
         'Does he eat beef?'
     b. *Il   (ne) mange pas le   boeuf.*
         he   (ne) eats   not the   beef
         'He doesn't eat beef.'
     c. *Il   mange souvent le   boeuf.*
         he   eats   often   the   beef
         'He often eats beef.'
     d. *Il   a   mangé le   boeuf*
         he   has eaten the   beef
         'He has eaten the beef.'

(2) a. *Iβt   er   Rindfleisch?*
         eats he   beef
         'Does he eat beef?'
     b. *Er   iβt   nicht Rindfleisch.*
         he   eats not   beef
         'He doesn't eat beef.'
     c. *Er   iβt   oft   Rindfleisch.*
         he   eats often beef
         'He often eats beef.'
     d. *Er   hat   das   Rindfleisch gegessen.*
         he   has   the   beef   eaten
         'He has eaten the beef.'

Hence, both French and German permit the verb to be separated from the object in main and subordinate clauses. However, German differs from French in that in German the verb phrase is head-final. This is clear from (2d), where 'eaten' appears after the object NP 'the beef.' Normally the finite verb in German moves to the head of the TP and then to the head position of CP in main clauses. This movement makes German main clauses superficially similar to their French counterparts. I will say more about this directly.

In contrast, languages like English require the verb to be next to the object. The English glosses and translations of the examples in (1) and (2) show that English employs 'do' support for questions and negation. The examples in (3) through (6) show that Chinese behaves much like English with respect to the placement of the main verb and the object; however, negation precedes the verb without 'do' support in Chinese. Instead of 'do' support for 'yes/no' questions, Chinese uses the sentence-final question particle *ma*.

(3) a. *Bao Yu xihuan Dai Yu ma?*
    Bao Yu like   Dai Yu Question Part
    'Does Bao Yu like Dai Yu?'

 b. **Xihuan Bao Yu Dai Yu.*
    like   Bao Yu Dai Yu
    Intended: 'Does Bao Yu like Dai Yu?'

(4) *Zhang San bu xihuan niurou.*
    Zang San not like   cow-meant
    'Zhang San does not like beef.'

(5) a. *Li Si changchang chi jüzi.*
    Li Si often   eat oranges
    'Li Si often eats oranges.'

 b. **Li Si chi changchang jüzi.*
    Li Si eat often   oranges
    Intended: 'Li Si often eats oranges.'

(6) *Huangdi zuotian qu le Nanyue.*
    emperor yesterday go ASP South Mountain.
    'The Emperor yesterday went to the South Mountain.'

The theory of functional categories explains these differences in word order as follows: Functional categories may be "strong" or "weak" in different languages (Chomsky 1995: 348–354). In French and German the functional category TENSE is [+STRONG]; in English and Chinese it is [-STRONG]. The specific tense value, for example, [±PAST], on the verb must agree with the [±PAST] tense value of the functional category TP; otherwise, the representation will be ungrammatical. This agreement occurs through a process of "checking" in which the verb "moves" up to the Functional Category. Features in [+STRONG] functional categories must be checked *before* the representation is encoded in the phonology. The result is that the finite main verb appears in a position that is not adjacent to its NP arguments in questions and in negative sentences. Weak features are checked *after* phonological processing, so the verb usually cannot appear in a position that is nonadjacent to its arguments. Hence, the difference between French and German and between English and Chinese can be represented schematically in (7) and (8). In French, V raises to C for yes/no questions. In German, the finite verb always moves to C, even in declarative, finite main clauses because tense must be checked in 'C.' This property of German explains the requirement that the verb is always the second constituent in a finite main clause.

(7) Strong: $[CP \ [C \ [TP \ [T \cdot \ [_T V_i] \quad [ADV/NEG] \quad [VP \ [V' \ [t_i] \ NP]]]]]$

Verb raises from VP to TP for checking

(8) Weak: $[CP \ [TP \ [T \cdot [_T \ \varnothing] \quad [ADV/NEG] \quad [VP \ [V' \ [V] \ NP]]]]$

This theory has several strengths for SLA researchers. It *describes* structure with details that can handle a range of unrelated languages. The theory provides precisely defined categories and a single operation carried out on those categories to explain cross-linguistic variation in word order. It reduces several superficially unrelated structures (word order in question formation, negation, and declarative clauses) to one simple property of the grammar, [±STRONG] functional category. The grammar is *learnable* based on pre-existing knowledge of the categories provided by UG and the binary values of the categories. In addition, the data available to the learner—for example, exposure to simple, every day sentences such as those in (1) through (6) in the appropriate language—will *trigger* the correct strength value.

Not surprisingly, these proposals have formed the basis of intense debate in SLA about the status of such categories in second language development and the relationship of such knowledge to the acquisition of inflectional morphology and the position of the verb in the clause. The theory permits questions such as:

- Do second language learners show evidence of acquiring the correct strength value(s) of the language they are learning *across a range of structures?*
- Do strength values of FCs transfer from the L1 to the L2 (White 1991a, 1991b; Schwartz and Sprouse 1996)?
- Does the acquisition of tense and agreement morphology coincide with the correct placement of verbs (Lardiere 2000, Sprouse 1998)?

- Is there an advantage for native speakers of a language with a strong or a weak functional category system?

Such questions are more precise than a range of similar, but purely descriptive questions:

- Are second language learners able to acquire tense and agreement?
- Can second language learners acquire new word orders?

A significant finding of research on the knowledge of functional categories in SLA since the work of White (1991a, 1991b, 1992) is that second language grammars seem to exhibit an optionality that first language grammars do not always show, at least in the end state (Sorace 2000). For instance, it appears that learners of English as a second language permit the verb to appear both adjacent and nonadjacent to the direct object. This behavior violates the expected pattern if learners know that weak features must be checked after phonological processing. Violations are even claimed to occur with learners whose L1 (e.g., Chinese) is also a weak feature language (Eubank et al. 1997).

The acquisition of German has been the focus of intense scrutiny because of its variable word order, richer (than English) inflectional morphology, and the availability of a large corpus of data from a variety of learners (Eubank 1993; Schwartz and Sprouse 1994). As pointed out already, in German the verb raises to the head of the CP (complementizer) in German main clauses, but not in subordinate clauses. The finite verb must be the second constituent, but infinitives remain in the verb phrase, which is head-final. At the beginning stages, second language learners of German often fail to "raise" finite verbs; moreover, these verbs appear to lack inflectional morphology. To account for these facts, Vainikka and Young-Scholten (1994, 1996, 1998) have proposed that the *gradual* emergence of functional categories is the best account for the developmental facts both for morpheme order development and knowledge of L2 word order. They claim that L2 learners begin by building a grammar of the L2 that has only the lexical VP, as in Figure 8.1. The initial acquisition of agreement would trigger the development of a functional projection and permits optional raising of the verb; this initial FP is not specified in terms of type but provides a position to which a verb may move and is the source of initial agreement marking. The acquisition of full inflectional paradigms would result in fully specified functional projections and obligatory raising if that is required by the language. Zobl (1998) adopts a similar proposal in his account of the acquisition order of morphemes in English by two Russian speakers.

In contrast, Schwartz and Sprouse (1994, 1996) argue that all functional projections that are present in the L1 are transferred and available in the L2; in other words, the final state of the L1 serves as the basis for the beginning of the L2 grammar. Development is based on a restructuring of the values of the functional categories or the addition of new ones from UG to cope with the new demands of the L2 input data.

Eubank (1993/1994), Eubank et al. (1997), and Beck (1998a) adopt a third position: Knowledge of the functional categories exists, but the values [±STRONG] are somehow impaired. Eubank's claim seeks to account for the variability in the interlanguage data—that is, sometimes morphemes are supplied correctly, sometimes the verb is in the correct position with regard to its complements; at other times learners make errors. Eubank does not attribute these errors to performance but instead claims that variability is inherent in the grammar and therefore must be accounted for in terms of the system of categories and features.

Most recently, Prévost and White (2000) have challenged proposals such as those by Eubank and Beck with data from learners of German and French as a second language. They explore the knowledge learners have of the overt morphology associated with tense and agreement. Since by definition the morphophonological forms of tense and agreement vary from language to language (e.g., -ed in English,-te in German), they must be learned. Hence, if learners do not produce them correctly, it does not necessarily mean that the knowledge of the abstract categories *themselves* is deficient. Prévost and White argue that, if the strength values are missing or impaired in some way, the position of finite and nonfinite verbs should be random and not predictable on the basis of the type of inflection they carry. However, they claim that their data show that "finite verb forms are associated with finite features and appear in raised positions. Nonfinite forms appear correctly in non-finite contexts and also as a default in finite positions" (Prévost and White 2000: 119).

Although these researchers do not yet agree on the exact status of the development of functional categories, the framework nevertheless provides a way for these researchers to debate what learners know and when they know it. It is worth re-emphasizing that this theory permits researchers to ask questions about second language development *in general,* and not just questions concerning the acquisition of a specific language or a specific structure. To the extent that learners demonstrate knowledge of functional categories, similar processes can be inferred to occur in both first and second language acquisition. Global questions are made possible because Functional Category theory is a theory about all human languages, not just English for example. As such, the use of the theory has been a significant step toward a general theory of SLA for this domain.

Binding Theory

The study of the syntax of human languages has focused to a large degree on clause structure and the constraints that govern the interpretation and the ordering of constituents within and across clause boundaries. It has been argued that some of the constraints must be part of a specific linguistic endowment—namely, Universal Grammar (UG) (Chomsky 1981, 1986, 1995; papers in Hornstein and Lightfoot 1981). This claim is based on the fact that adult speakers know more about the clause structure and meanings of their native language than they could possibly have induced from the input they receive. This argument is now well known as the "poverty of the stimulus" or the "logical problem of language acquisition."[5]

Hence, the second question that formal theories of morphosyntax have sought to answer is whether learners of a second language have knowledge of constraints on representation that native speakers of that language have (White 1989). Examples of this come from properties of co-reference of reflexives, pronouns, and full noun phrases. It is well known that English reflexive pronouns must usually have a co-referent in the same clause (9a), and may co-refer with an object (9b). (Subscripts are used to indicate the intended co-reference. This co-reference is referred to as "binding." Hence, *Peter* in (9a) binds the reflexive, but *John* cannot.)

(9)   a.   John$_i$ noticed that Peter$_j$ gave himself $^*_{i/j}$ a raise.
      b.   John$_i$ noticed that Peter$_j$ gave Fred$_k$ a book about himself $_{*i/j/k}$.

However, in Japanese the reflexive pronoun *zibun* 'self' may co-refer with a subject NP inside or outside the clause in which the reflexive occurs, such as (10a). However, it may never co-refer with an object, even one that is inside the same clause (10b) (Thomas 1993: 125).

(10) a.   Taroo   wa$_i$ [IP Mika ga$_j$ zibun o$_{i/j}$ aishite-iru]   to   omotte iru.
           Taro   TOP   Mika NOM   self-ACC   love-PROG   QT   think-PROG
           'Taro thinks that Mika loves self.'
      b.   Taroo   wa$_i$ Masanobu ni$_j$ zibun no$_{i/*j}$ syashin o   misete-shimata.
           Taro-   TOP   Masanobu-DAT   self GEN   photo ACC   showed
           'Taro showed Masanobu self's picture.'

Theoretical developments of the early 1990s proposed that the difference between English and Japanese is that in Japanese the morpheme *zibun* 'self' is a simple morpheme (technically a X° 'head'). It must raise to INFL (the head position of IP) to check person and number features at an abstract semantic level called Logical Form (LF) in Principles and Parameters (e.g., Cole and Sung 1994; Cole, Hermon, and Sung 1990). This movement puts the morpheme in a structural position that precludes any co-reference with the object. This is so because an antecedent of a reflexive must be higher in the syntactic structure (in a technical sense it must "c-command" it, see Thomas 1993: 23). The object is too low in the syntactic tree to c-command the reflexive if the reflexive has moved to INFL and is therefore higher in the tree.

Moving to INFL also permits more long-distance movement to another, higher, clause (precise details need not concern us here) and therefore allows the "long-distance" co-reference that Japanese exhibits in sentences such as (10a). In contrast, reflexives in English are complex NPs, or compounds. They consist of a pronoun 'X' (e.g., him, her, our) and 'self' and cannot therefore move to the head position of INFL because they are morphologically complex. Japanese also has morphologically complex anaphors, but they are not usually used; English has no equivalent of the monomorphemic 'self' *zibun* in Japanese or Chinese 'self' *ziji*, which behaves in the same way.

This difference has produced some interesting and testable hypotheses about second language development (e.g., Thomas 1991, 1993, 1995; White et al. 1997; Yip and Tang 1998). Japanese learners of English may initially misanalyze English reflexives as being simple morphemes. (This may result from an incorrect comparison with the usual Japanese *zibun* or from a failure to parse correctly the internal morphology of the English reflexive.) If this is true, they should allow long-distance co-reference, for example between *John* and *himself* in (9a); if they do, then they should *not* allow co-reference with an object, for example, *Fred* and *himself* in (9b). In contrast, if they do allow co-reference with an object, they should not allow long-distance binding. English learners of Japanese need to learn the long-distance properties of *zibun* and know that this prevents co-reference with an object (Thomas 1995). However, results of experimental studies cast some doubt as to whether all learners can successfully acquire the monomorphemic/ subject orientation of anaphors like *zibun* and whether learners of English can successfully learn the possibility that reflexives can be bound by an object (Yip and Tang 1998). It is possible that methodology in detecting preferences needs to be refined in studies of binding (White et al. 1997). Moreover, performance effects on tasks that seek to tap linguistic competence must be carefully evaluated before definitive claims can be made. (See, e.g., papers in White 1998.)

These formal descriptions of the learning problems that face second language learners have resulted in many experimental studies. They have led researchers to the following tentative conclusions about second language grammars in this domain. First, second language learners do not allow random co-reference between NPs and reflexives, nor do they have a global strategy such as binding to the "nearest NP" (Thomas 1993). Second, many learners appear to acquire the syntactic constraints in an L2, even when that L2 allows a different set of possibilities from their L1. Such results suggest that second language grammars are constrained by principles that govern first language grammars—principles that could derive only from the subtle knowledge provided by UG (Thomas 1995).

Of course, not all researchers agree with the claim that second language learners still have access to Universal Grammar (e.g., Bley-Vroman 1989; Schachter 1989, 1996). Moreover, one potential drawback to all of these findings is that linguistic theory is constantly evolving. White (2000b: 4) does not believe that such changes are always detrimental; however, Schwartz and Sprouse (2000) point out that analyses of interlanguage data that rely only on theory internal analysis cannot show conclusively that learners' grammars are, or are not, constrained by principles that constrain first language acquisition. Instead, they advocate concentrating on the logical problem of acquisition in SLA; that is, showing the learners' knowledge of the L1 either does, or does not, go beyond the input data they receive.

Semantics and the Lexicon

It is uncontroversial that the link between sounds and concepts is completely arbitrary and that new words have to be learned from the linguistic environment. However, recently some researchers have argued that not *all* aspects of lexical knowledge are entirely arbitrary (Gleitman 1990; Pinker 1989). Hale and Keyser (1993), Pinker (1989), and Jackendoff (1990) have proposed that the number of noun phrases and prepositional phrases that are permitted in a clause, as well as their position within the clause, is in part predictable from the underlying semantic representation of the main verb. For example, the verb 'put' means "to cause something to be in a place"; as a result, every sentence with the verb 'put' must contain a noun denoting the thing that is moved as well as the place the thing moves to. These semantic requirements of 'put' are the reason that a sentence such as "*John put on the shelf" is ungrammatical. Formal linguists have developed representations for decomposing the meaning of words as these meanings relate to syntax. To illustrate, consider the well-known alternation with English locative verbs. Locative verbs describe the movement of an object to a destination or location. The issue with locative verbs is that some allow one syntactic pattern, where only Theme (the moving object) can be the direct object in the syntax (11), whereas others allow only the Goal (the destination of movement) to be the direct object (12).

(11) a. John poured the soup into the bowl.
          [X CAUSE [Y GO [PATH]]]
      b. *John poured the bowl with soup.

(12) a.   John covered the bed with the blanket.
           [X CAUSE [Y GO [STATE]]]
      b.   *John covered the blanket onto the bed.

(13) a.   John sprayed insecticide onto the tree.
           [X CAUSE [Y GO [PATH]]]
      b.   John sprayed the tree with insecticide.

(14) a.   John loaded the hay onto the truck.
      b.   John loaded the truck with hay.
           [X CAUSE [Y GO [STATE]]]

Underneath each sentence, a proposed semantic decomposition is provided. Verbs that have the decomposition structure [GO[PATH]] in (11) allow only Theme direct objects; those with meaning components in (12) [GO[STATE]] allow only Goal direct objects. Verbs of both classes may allow alternations that are expressed as a rule changing semantic structure from the type in (11) and the type in (12) or vice versa. This is possible only if verbs belong to *narrow* classes within the main semantic classes of (11) and (12), where the movement of a specific type of theme is specified. For example, *spray* belongs to a class that specifies ballistic motion in a specified trajectory; *load* belongs to a class that involves a mass that is put onto/into an object intended for that use. Pinker maintains that verb learning involves acquiring these narrow range classes and that, once these classes are established, errors will cease.

Recently, knowledge of semantic constraints of this type has been investigated by researchers in SLA (Juffs 1996; Montrul 1998, 1999). Juffs (2000) provides an overview of this research and the results that have been achieved so far. Research suggests many learners begin by assuming any verb, even some intransitives, can appear in a sentence with the form NP V NP. However, such errors gradually disappear, and some learners seem to acquire new semantic structures and the constraints these structures impose on syntax by the time they are advanced learners. Such analysis has important implications for language teaching, since materials writers must ensure that the range of possible sentence types allowed for each type of verb is represented in the input provided to the learners. The important point in the context of this chapter is that these developments show the clear role theory plays in SLA research—until a theory of a certain type of linguistic knowledge develops, researchers have no way of asking interesting or important questions in the relevant domain. Formal theories are not just useful; they are a *requirement* for investigation of the nature of SLA.

PHONOLOGY

The study of L3 phonology has a long history, but there is not as much research from a UG/Principles and Parameters perspective as there is in syntax. Evidence of this imbalance can be seen from collected works such as Ritchie and Bhatia (1996), which devotes much more space to syntax than to phonology. However, with new developments in theories of the internal structure of the segment and new theories of prosody, together with developments in acoustic recording and analysis, the field of second language phonology is rapidly developing (Archibald 1998). This section highlights two areas where recent advances have been made.

Segments

Most people with a rudimentary knowledge of linguistics know that some languages employ certain segments as part of the system of contrasts (i.e., the segments are phonemes), whereas these same sounds in other languages are merely phonetic variants of an underlying phoneme (allophones). This formal distinction has been important in explaining L2 phonological development, and versions of it remain of interest in SLA to this day (e.g., Eckman and Iverson 2000). Standard generative theory, such as the Sound Pattern of English (SPE) (Chomsky and Halle 1968), proposed that segments consisted of bundles of unordered features, for example, [±voice], [±coronal]. This view of the segment was challenged because features in one segment influence other segments that are not immediately adjacent. For example, [+nasal], and [+round] can spread in predictable, but constrained, ways across multiple segments, yet SPE theory provided no principled way of accounting for these phenomena (Goldsmith 1976).

Current accounts propose that the segment has internal organization, or 'geometry' (e.g., Clements 1985; Piggott 1992). For example, one proposal is that features are organized into groups, as indicated in Figure 8.2. Like the schematic of functional categories in Figure 8.1, such geometry is assumed to be a part of Universal Grammar (UG) that limits the range of possible phonologies in human languages. Feature geometry is meant as a constraint on the hypothesis space and a guide to interpreting the data from the language that the learner hears. However, not all languages will make use of all nodes in their representation of segments. For instance, Brown (1998, 2000) suggests that Japanese does not make use of the coronal node anywhere in its feature geometry.

This theory of the internal structure of the segment has been particularly useful in giving preciseness to problematic concepts such as Flege's (1990) "old" versus "new" sounds (cf. Leather and James 1996: 276, fn. 1). Brown (2000) also

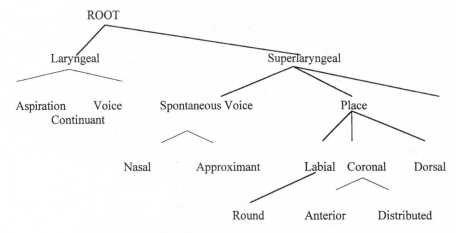

Fig. 8.2. A model of Feature Geometry (Brown 2000: 12)

uses feature geometry to discuss how the theory defines new sounds. She describes three experiments in which she claims to show that it is not at the *segmental* level, but rather at the *node* level, in features where some more satisfying explanations can be reached concerning L1 phonological effects. For example, Brown shows that the well-known difficulty that Japanese speakers have with the [l] vs. [r] contrast in English results from the absence of the coronal node in the phonological representation of their L1. Although Chinese speakers do not have segments that are exactly similar to English [l] and [r], they are nevertheless more successful than Japanese speakers because the coronal *node* is present in the phonology of Chinese.

Suprasegmentals

Suprasegmental phenomena have also seen some considerable advances recently. In addition to Archibald's (1993) work on metrical parameters, there have been other developments in approaches to suprasegmental phonology (see papers in Hannahs and Young-Scholten 1997). In their wide-ranging and thorough review, Young-Scholten and Archibald (2000) investigate knowledge of syllable structure in second language acquisition. While their review is not amenable to a simple summary, they do demonstrate that a theory of the syllable that includes internal structure (illustrated in Figure 8.3) allows for interesting crosslinguistic comparisons and predictions. The independence of syllable onsets from syllable rhymes has been especially relevant to SLA research.

     Young-Scholten and Archibald explain that segments are associated with positions in syllable structure by two principles:

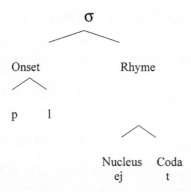

Fig. 8.3. Syllabification of the word 'plate' [plejt]

1. Segments must attach to onset first.
2. Other segments must attach to the onset until the vocalic peak is reached. This attachment must be in compliance with a segment sonority hierarchy (highest: stops-fricatives-nasals-liquids-glides VOWEL-glides liquids-nasals-fricatives-stops).

Languages vary with respect to principle 2 in the number of consonants they allow in the onset. For example, Mandarin Chinese does not allow complex onsets (other than some restricted to glides), nor does it allow consonants in coda position other than alveolar and velar nasals.

Interestingly, Young-Scholten and Archibald link syllable structure with a theory of feature geometry of the type discussed in the section on segments. It is impossible to do justice to the sophistication of their analysis here, but the broad outlines are as follows. They suggest that the acquisition of a contrast between liquids ([l] and [r]) at the level of feature geometry, and the presence of such a contrast cross-linguistically, is related to both the acquisition of complex onset clusters and the presence of such onset clusters in a particular language. In other words, the nodes used in the feature geometry of a language for phonemic contrasts have implications for syllable structure.

Korean, like Japanese, does not make the [l]/[r] distinction and also does not allow complex onsets such as that for [pl] in Figure 8.3. Finnish, however, does make the [l]/[r] contrast but does not allow complex onsets. Korean learners make syllabification errors in speaking L2 English with complex onsets containing liquids; they insert a schwa [ə] between the [f] and the [l], creating two syllables (e.g., floor [flOr], is pronounced [fəlor], and plate [plejt] is pronounced [pəlejt]). However, the Finnish learner that Young-Scholten and Archibald report on does not do this, even though complex onsets are disallowed in Finnish. Hence, according to this analysis, the errors of Korean learners are attributable more to the structure of the segment inventory than to the phonotactics of syllable onsets.

The analysis that Young-Scholten and Archibald make here is not possible with simple accounts of cross-linguistic *phonetic* contrasts; rather, they claim that an explanation is possible only with phonological representation.

METHODOLOGICAL CONTRIBUTIONS

In addition to production data, the standard tool for investigating competence has been the grammaticality judgment task. However, it is well known that there are several problems with using such tasks out of context (e.g., Birdsong 1989). In response to these difficulties, researchers have developed the use of pictures to give context to the sentences that they are investigating. In this way, they can be more certain that the intuitions that learners have are the relevant ones. Research-ers have also developed narrative contexts that force certain interpretations on the sentences that learners are supposed to judge (White et al. 1997). Bley-Vroman and Loschky (1993) suggest that this type of task may be used in developing pedagogical materials because they force learners to pay attention to both form and meaning.

CONCLUSION

Formal linguistic theory has a crucial role to play in the explanation of second language linguistic competence. Without it, researchers cannot hope to ask so-phisticated questions about what it means to know a second language. Formal theory captures generalizations about the structural properties of languages and makes it possible to ask whether these generalizations hold in the development of second language grammars as well (Schwartz 1999). As linguistic theory develops, it is becoming possible to map more and more aspects of a learner's interlanguage grammar(s). While the results of this research often do not have direct pedagogical applications, the results can inform an understanding of the process of second language acquisition and provide a background for teachers to understand the progress or lack of progress learners make in the classroom.

NOTES

1. It is possible that pragmatics and semantics cannot be completely excluded from a theory of grammar, even in the narrowest sense of constraints on formal operations on linguistic categories (e.g., Culicover and Jackendoff 1995; Givon 1979; Jackendoff 1992; Thomas 1995: 229; Van Valin and La Pola 1997).

2. Other candidate theories are Lexical-Functional Grammar (Bresnan forthcoming) and Head Driven Phrase Structure Grammar (Pollard and Sag 1994). See Borsley (1998) for a comparative treatment of generative theories. Other research has been conducted with a functional/typological framework (Eckman 1996).

3. See Juffs (1996b) for a qualification of this proposal.

4. However, it is not the case that all languages have all FCs. For example, White (1996: 341) assumes that French has functional projections which host clitic pronouns, but that English does not.

5. See Karmiloff-Smith (1994) and O'Grady (1996) for alternative views of the issue of innateness.

CHAPTER 9

SOCIOCULTURAL THEORY AND SECOND LANGUAGE ACQUISITION

JAMES P. LANTOLF

IN this chapter, I consider the growing body of research on SLA informed by sociocultural theory (henceforth, SCT). SCT has evolved two separate, but inter-related, branches of research, both with roots in the writings of L. S. Vygotsky (1978, 1987). The branch most robustly represented in SLA accepts as its basic principle that the human mind is always and everywhere *mediated* primarily by linguistically based communication. The other branch, *activity theory*, has until recently been less vigorously represented in SLA research. Activity theory also holds that mental functioning is mediated; however, it offers a coherent frame-work for theorizing mediation as embedded in, and emerging from, the experiences of others in the present (social), the experiences of others from the past (culture), and the immediate experiences of the individual with these others and with the artifacts they constructed. I believe that future SCT research on SLA needs to pay more attention to activity theory than is now the case. In what follows, I first discuss SLA as a mediated process and then consider activity theoretic research; finally, I address briefly concerns relating to SCT raised in recent books on SLA research (Ellis 1997) and theory (Mitchell and Myles 1998).

MEDIATION AND SLA

As a mediated process SLA has been viewed from three general perspectives—social mediation by experts and peers, self-mediation, and artifact mediation. Although each category can be understood, to some extent, independently of the others, all three entail symbolic (usually linguistic) mediation to a significant degree. Nevertheless, I believe it is appropriate to consider each perspective separately because, despite their common reliance on symbolic mediation, each foregrounds a specific aspect of mediated learning. In any given concrete situation, however, all three types of mediation may, and usually do, come into play.

Social Mediation

Experts and Novices

Aljaafreh and Lantolf (1994) look at mediated learning in the zone of proximal development (ZPD), which is the site where future development is negotiated by the expert and the novice and where assistance is offered, appropriated, refused, and withheld (Vygotsky 1978). Second language development moves through a sequence of stages in which mediation needs to be quite explicit to a point at which only implicit assistance, including the mere presence of an expert, is sufficient for a learner to perform appropriately in the language (Aljaafreh and Lantolf 1994). Hall's (1995) study of a secondary school Spanish FL classroom shows that a teacher's insistence on imposing his own pedagogical agenda and his subsequent unwillingness to communicate authentically (see van Lier 1996) with students can lead to considerable learner confusion and frustration and result in a missed opportunity to interact with learners in their ZPD.

Mitchell and Myles (1998: 161) suggest that, even though the learners in Aljaafreh and Lantolf's (1994) study improved their performance over time, a general causal relationship between scaffolded help in the ZPD and learning has yet to be established. However, Nassaji and Swain (2000) provide some evidence to allay Mitchell and Myles's concern. They show experimentally that negotiated mediation sensitive to a learner's ZPD is indeed more effective than randomly offered implicit or explicit assistance that fails to take account of the ZPD.

Comparative research has shed light on how teachers engage learners in their ZPD through *instructional conversations* that scaffold novices into an L2. Donato and Adair-Hauck (1992) compared the *monologic instructional talk* of one language teacher with the *dialogic* moves of another. The former failed to encourage verbal interaction between teacher and students and, more important, did not challenge the students to push their development forward. The dialogic teacher, on the other hand, exhibited frequent use of *proleptic* interaction, which, similar to elliptical speech, assumes a shared body of knowledge between interlocutors but which has the specific pedagogical aim of drawing novices into activities they are unable to perform alone (see Rommetveit 1985).

Antón compares the performance of a teacher who relied on a monologic strategy to control classroom practice and to "present himself as the absolute possessor of knowledge that he delivers to the learners" (1999: 308) with that of a teacher who, through dialogue, effectively involved students as active participants in their own learning. She achieved this not only through verbal moves but also, and importantly, through pauses and gestures, which frequently compelled the students to rely on themselves, rather than on the teacher, when performing (Antón 1999: 315)

According to Kramsch, SLA entails the acquisition of much more than new linguistic signs. Learners simultaneously become aware of, and gain control over, the "semiotic choices offered by the foreign language"; thus, it is inappropriate to separate linguistic structure from language practice (2000b: 153). Kramsch analyzes how, through dialoguing about her students' written summaries of a story, an ESL teacher not only succeeded in making students aware of the intended and potential meanings of what they had written but also scaffolded them into realizing that they could construct, exchange, and interpret signs created by someone else and could, therefore, experience themselves as authors, interpreters, narrators, and critics in their second language.

Peer Mediation

Dialogue among learners can be as effective as instructional conversations between teachers and learners. Working collaboratively, people are able to co-construct distributed expertise as a feature of the group, and individual members are then able to exploit this expertise as an occasion for learning to happen (Swain and Lapkin 1998). Learners are capable of scaffolding each other through the use of strategies that parallel those relied upon by experts.

Since Donato's (1994) important study on the collaborative construction of expert knowledge in FL group work, a number of researchers have looked more closely at the details of peer mediation. In a longitudinal project on college-level students of Japanese as a foreign language, Ohta (2001) reports that students not only bid for, and offer, mediation through direct means but, similar to teachers and other experts also make strategic use of prolepsis to scaffold each other into grammatically and pragmatically appropriate utterances. An especially effective strategy is the willingness of one peer to "wait" for the other to struggle to produce utterances without overt assistance; thus, learners appear to be aware of when, and when not, to offer assistance, and as such they seem to be sensitive to each other's ZPD (Ohta, 2001). However, Platt and Troudi (1997) report that, for some activities, elementary school children have problems scaffolding their peers, because, even though they may themselves possess the expertise to carry out a task, they are not sensitive to their classmates' ZPD (see also McLane 1987).

Swain and Lakpin (1998) studied the cognitive processes at work in "language related episodes" during collaborative dialogue of French immersion students. Upon encountering language problems, the students frequently generated talk that produced and assessed possible solutions to the problems. These were then appropriated by individual students, as determined by a set of pre- and posttests. Moreover, collaborative dialogue offers teachers, and researchers, some access to learners' cognitive processes, including those linked to language learning. In addition, Swain (2000) discusses important research that documents the effectiveness of learner verbalization of problem-solving strategies during collaborative dialogue.

Self- and other repetition also serves peer mediation as it stabilizes mutually constructed scaffolds and thus helps learners to focus their attention, to think, to evaluate, and ultimately to construct new linguistic forms (DiCamilla and Antón 1997: 617). More controversial is DiCamilla and Antón's claim that repetition functions to establish *intersubjectivity*. While this is not the venue in which to discuss the complexities affiliated with this topic, intersubjectivity is about much more than sharing information and deciding on appropriate problem-solving strategies, which is at the heart of DiCamilla and Antón's claim. As Wertsch puts it, true intersubjectivity consists of "two voices coming into contact and interanimating one another" (1991: 73), and it is about exposing and critiquing one's own and the other's viewpoint. It is difficult to see how simple repetition accomplishes this. Nevertheless, the topic is important and needs to be explored more fully.

Learners also seem to be effective at mutually mediating their writing activity. Villamil and de Guerrero (1996: 61) identify a number of mediational strategies that Spanish L1 ESL learners deployed when assisting each other in revising a composition. Not too surprisingly, the learners relied on concrete artifacts (e.g., dictionaries, textbooks) and sought help from their teacher. While learners frequently offered implicit and explicit assistance, their assistance, as attested in the work of Aljaafreh and Lantolf and of Ohta, was as *contingent;* that is, it was withheld at critical junctures (de Guerrero and Villamil 2000). The modifications (74 percent) attended to during peer revision were incorporated into the final versions of the compositions. Moreover, the writers introduced additional revisions when working alone on the final version. This could well indicate development as the writers moved from other- to self-mediation in the final phase of the writing activity (Villamil and de Guerrero 1996).

Mediation through the L1

Use of the L1 in peer mediation has for some time been a controversial matter. For some it inhibits, but for others it promotes learning. According to Brooks and Donato (1994), learner talk during tasks does much more than encode and decode messages. It helps learners determine what the task is about and it helps them navigate (e.g., carry out lexical searches) by themselves and with each other through the task. Among beginners, this metatalk most often, but not exclusively, occurs in the L1 (Brooks and Donato 1994: 271). Not surprisingly, as learners improve their proficiency, their metatalk also shifts to the L2 (Antón and Di-Camilla 1998, Brooks, Donato and McGlone 1997). However, Swain and Lapkin's (1998, 2000) research with French immersion students presents some evidence that, even when learners clearly have the ability to use the L2 metafunctionally, they do not always do so, relying instead on their L1. Why? Perhaps they do so because, very early in our formation as human beings, we develop nonreflective control over our mental activity through our L1, and thus it becomes intimately connected with our identity as thinking agents, something that is not easily surrendered (see Pavlenko and Lantolf 2000). Antón and DiCamilla point out that to stifle the L1 as a metacognitive tool is potentially harmful to the learning process "because it discourages the employment of a critical psychological tool that is essential for collaboration" (1998: 64). This goes against the grain of much pedagogical practice, which proscribes use of the L1 under any circumstance.

Self-Mediation

Self-directed, or private, speech generally consists of elliptical utterances such as the following: "What?" "Next, an orange one," "Wait," "No," "I can't," "Done," (see Diaz and Berk 1992; Frawley 1997). It is in the process of privatizing speech that we gain control over our ability to remember, think, attend, plan, evaluate, inhibit, and learn (Vygotsky 1987). Private speech, in its planning, attending, and thinking functions, has been well attested among L2 speakers (see Appel and Lantolf 1994; de Guerrero 1999; Frawley and Lantolf 1985; Lantolf and Frawley 1984; McCafferty 1994). However, its function in internalizing or "taking in" an L2, especially among adults, is another matter. Although L1 researchers have carried out extensive studies on the effects of *language play*—privately experimenting with morphological, phonological, syntactic, or lexical features of a language—on learning, (see Kuczaj 1983; Weir 1962), L2 research in this area is still in its incipient stages.

Saville-Troike's (1988) research with L1 Chinese, Japanese, and Korean ESL children in a North American classroom shows that, at a point when the children shied away from social speech in their L2, they privately continued to experiment with the language in ways reminiscent of the play reported for L1 children. One child, for instance, walked around the classroom quietly reciting the following: "Walking, walking, walk. Walking, walking, walk" (Saville-Troike, 1988: 584). When the children later engaged in L2 social speech, many of the forms they had played with in their private speech appeared.

Broner and Tarone (2000) document similar activity among L1 English immersion learners of Spanish. The private language play of these children most often consisted of whispered repetition of lexical items introduced during content lessons. Frequently, however, the play became social and took on a ludic character as the children verbally "sparred" with each other in their L2. Peck (1980) also attests social contact play among ESL children, and Sullivan (2000) documents ludic play among students and their teacher in a Vietnamese EFL classroom.

While adults also generate private L2 language play, it has been difficult to gain direct access to this form of private speech, and much of the research has relied on questionnaires and interviews (see de Guerrero 1999; Gillette 1994; Lantolf 1997). While the data are suggestive, they don't provide the needed detail on the specific nature of language play. Despite its shortcomings, however, the survey research has brought to light two significant insights. Learners at higher proficiency levels are less likely to play with the language than learners at lower levels (de Guerrero 1999; Lantolf 1997). This is understandable, given Vygotsky's theoretical arguments about the role of play in development. Briefly, Vygotsky proposed that play opens a *zone of proximal development* in which children engage in activities beyond their daily behavior and as such "contains all of the developmental tendencies in a condensed form and as such is itself a major source of development" (1978: 103). There also appears to be a relationship between frequency of language play and learner goals and motives such that learners with an interest in learning an L2, whether it be for intrinsic or extrinsic reasons, report that they more often experiment privately with the language than do learners whose goal is to comply with a language requirement (see Gillette 1994; Lantolf 1997).

Recently, Ohta (2001) has succeeded in recording samples of adult L2 private speech in a language classroom. She found that students responded privately to corrective feedback and to questions, even when the teacher did not address them directly. Although Lantolf (1997) builds a theoretical argument that this type of private speech is a necessary condition for L2 learning, research now needs to test empirically the validity of this claim, and therefore extensive research along the lines pursued by Ohta is crucial.

McCafferty and Ahmed's (2000) work on gesture has opened a new line of research on L2 private speech. According to McNeill (1992), gesture is a form of private speech that complements and completes meaning conveyed in verbal speech. McCafferty and Ahmed point out that "speech and gesture are 'dialectically' engaged—gesture providing imagery and speech the verbal or linguistic structure to thought" (2000: 204). Unlike speech, which is hierarchical, gestures are synthetic in nature; as such, they more readily capture an entire idea. Gestures are powerful mediational artifacts in both the interpersonal and intrapersonal domains. People gesture not only when in face-to-face interaction, but even when the interlocutor is not visible, as in telephone conversations. We also gesture when we talk to ourselves. McCafferty and Ahmed (2000) report that naturalistic Japanese L1 learners of English, including those with a fairly low level of verbal proficiency, displayed American gesture patterns, while Japanese EFL students, regardless of proficiency level, continued to produce Japanese gestures in their L2.

ACTIVITY THEORY AND NONLINGUISTIC ARTIFACTS

While language is perhaps the most powerful and pervasive cultural artifact, human mental activity is also mediated by other artifacts. Language is clearly implicated in other forms of mediation, but these artifacts (e.g., computers, videos, tasks) also entail significant nonlinguistic features that justify treating them separately. Much, though not all, of the research on non-linguistic artifacts has been informed by activity theory; therefore, a brief outline of this theory will be useful.

Activity Theory

Understanding the human mind requires study of its formation and its activity, rather than its structure (Vygotsky 1978, 1987). Human activity, whether physical, social, or mental, always has a motive and is directed toward some goal. That is, we do things that have significance and make sense to us as agents active in constructing our worlds including our own learning (Taylor 1985). Motives are realized in specific goal-directed actions that are in turn carried out under particular material conditions. Thus, activities are made up of observable (material conditions) and unobservable (motives and goals) components, and, because of this, any activity cannot be fully understood without access to its motive and goal. This requires exploration of the activity's genesis or history. It is, therefore, important to distinguish "between phenotypic (descriptive) and genotypic (explanatory) viewpoints in psychology" (Vygotsky 1978: 62). This means that two students manifesting identical behaviors (e.g., negotiating meaning in an information gap task) are not necessarily engaged in the same activity, because their motives may differ. One may be striving to learn the L2, and the other may only be trying to comply with a language requirement or to satisfy the demands of the instructor; consequently, the learning outcomes are expected to differ.

Tasks

Foley (1990, 1991) sees a theoretical parallel between task-based L2 learning and L1 acquisition. Both anticipate not only the development of grammar, phonology, vocabulary, and pragmatics but also the attainment of self-regulation, or the realization of one's agency as a linguistically constituted being. Task-based learning is primarily an "enabling process" that affords learners the opportunity to realize their agency as linguistically constituted beings and, as such, to participate fully in communities of practice instead of remaining on the periphery (Foley 1991: 73; see also Lave and Wenger 1991). Coughlan and Duff (1994) discuss how different learners at the same time and in the same setting or the same learner at different times deploy their L2 agency in construing the same task, a picture narration, as different activities (i.e., they establish different motives and goals for the task). Coughlan and Duff argue that the different performances occurred because tasks are only "blueprints" for activity and not predictors of how that activity will unfold.

Roebuck (1998) investigated how FL learners positioned themselves as agents in carrying out written recall tasks and showed that learners' orientations (what they think a task is about and what counts as successful completion) were often at variance with the teacher's or researcher's and that these changed as the activity of actually implementing the task unfolded. Moreover, learners frequently reinterpreted on-line their language abilities relative to the activity. For instance, some learners oriented themselves to the goal of writing a recall of the relevant newspaper article, while others used the writing activity to comprehend what the article was about. For some learners, the goal was to fill the page with writing, because for them the text to be recalled was too difficult. Nevertheless, they refused to abandon the activity and persisted in writing, despite their inability to make sense of what they had ostensibly read. Roebuck (1998: 125) suggests this behavior may well have been engendered in the course of the learners' history as participants in classroom communities of practice in which students are expected to comply with the wishes of those with pedagogical authority. From Foley's perspective this represents a subversion of what task-based learning is about, because learners become docile bodies instead of agents. Task "performance depends crucially on the interaction of individual and task" and not on inherent properties of the task itself

(Appel and Lantolf 1994: 480). Ellis (1999) disagrees and argues that the activity theoretic perspective on task-based learning is problematic, since it fails to sustain the grading of tasks independently of learners' ZPD. He believes that certain tasks "have a *propensity* to lead to particular types of language behavior" [emphasis in original] and that therefore there are good grounds for assuming that language variables inhere in task structure. He further contends that specific outcomes are predictable if learners are given sufficient time and the opportunity to repeat tasks. This view, of course, privileges language acquisition over learner agency. While the relative merits of each stance cannot be addressed here, suffice it to say that a potential problem may arise whenever learners fail to exhibit the behaviors predicated by tasks—will the fault reside with the learners or with the task?

Technology

Thorne (1999) discusses computer-mediated communication (CMC) in his analysis of an L2 chat environment, which he claims fosters among the students an enhanced sense of freedom and diminished culpability for their utterances. For one thing, the division of labor (Engeström 1999) found in normal classrooms where the teacher as expert and omnipresent authority and the students as novices and submissive beings was undercut, despite the students' awareness that their instructor was on-line. This reconfiguration allowed the students to say things they probably would not have said in face-to-face classroom interaction. Differences appeared in behaviors such as turn taking, topic initiation and topic shift, and taking and keeping the floor. At one point, students even produced obscene language—a clear violation of the rules of engagement in traditional classrooms— but apparently not proscribed in the chat world. At this point, the teacher stepped out of the role of electronic eavesdropper and back into the role of teacher and confronted the students face-to-face for producing what in this genre would have been illegal language. This clearly changed the nature of the activity, because the rules that mediate chat discussions are different from the rules that mediate discussion in normal educational settings.

Thorne argues that the shift to electronically mediated interaction allowed the students to exercise their agency as creative linguistic beings in ways that face-to-face interaction did not. The activity of communicating took on a much more dynamic quality than occurred in the normal classroom environment. It seems clear that the communicative practices of the individuals are bound up with the materiality of their conveyance and representation (Thorne 1999).

One especially interesting question that suggests itself is whether the communicative practices encouraged by CMC are internalized and are in turn redeployed in face-to-face interactions or in other communicative genres. Salomon

(1991) hypothesizes that, aside from enhanced efficiency and accuracy, technology can actually impact on the way we as humans think and learn. One potential outcome of the person/technology "partnership," according to Salomon, is that we internalize and mentally reconstruct the mediating means arising from the technology, which then becomes "available for cognitive use" (Salomon 1991: 193). If this is indeed the case, then the findings of studies such as Thorne's need to be examined even more closely. It could be that people not only learn a new discourse genre from interacting with technology but also might well internalize this genre and then incorporate it into other genres.

CONCLUSION

Although SCT has generated much interesting research and has perhaps compelled us to think differently about what the process of acquiring and using an L2 is about, a great deal of work remains to be done within this framework. While I believe there is certainly room for much more research in all of the areas examined in the preceding discussion, in my opinion, four areas are particularly important: (1) the function of language play in SLA; (2) the appropriation and use of gestures in an L2; (3) the effectiveness of peer mediation on learning; (4) activity theory, especially with CMC and task-based learning.

As mentioned at the outset, I would like to comment on what two leading figures in SLA research have recently written with regard to SCT. Ellis (1997: 244) argues that, while SCT has something to offer L2 pedagogy, it cannot altogether replace the input metaphor as a source of applications for the language classroom. For Ellis, because SCT sees learning as a social process, the input metaphor, with its view of the learner as an "autonomous processor," is still needed to explain such phenomena as overgeneralization errors. To say that learning is a social process does not deny that it is at the same time psychological. That individuals would generalize when learning new forms is understandable from a SCT perspective, given that this is a strategy frequently encouraged in expert/novice interactions (see Wells 1999: Ch. 6). The point is that SCT does not assume that overgeneralized forms themselves must be appropriated only through social interaction, although this could happen (see Ohta, 2001). It does, however, postulate that the psychological processes that give rise to such forms are appropriated in social interaction. Ellis (1997: 244) also recognizes the importance of social identity in an L2 but questions its relevance for classroom foreign language learners. Kramsch (2000b) and Thorne (1999) both present evidence that classrooms are sites where learners can and do develop identities and agency as linguistic beings through their L2.

Finally, Mitchell and Myles (1998) argue that SCT researchers have failed to pay sufficient attention to "the nature of language as a formal system" and have instead "typically dealt in fragments of language, often isolated elements of morphology, the conventional focus of form-focused instruction." I believe that, to some extent at least, this is a valid criticism and that future work on learning in the ZPD could explore the appropriation of grammatical properties such as word order in German and pro-drop in Spanish. Because of its focus on meaning and the form/function interface, the theory of language that perhaps most appropriately meshes with SCT is the systemic grammar developed by M. A. K. Halliday and his colleagues. SCT researchers working on SLA would do well to follow the lead of scholars such as Wells (1999), who, in his studies on learning in non-L2 classrooms, has already begun to integrate the work of Halliday and Vygotsky in compelling ways.

CHAPTER 10

IDENTITY AND LANGUAGE LEARNING

BONNY NORTON
KELLEEN TOOHEY

WHEN a language learner asks, "Who am I? How do I relate to the social world? Under what conditions can I speak?" she is seeking to understand the complex relationship among identity, language, and learning. When a language learner interacts with a member of the target language group, he is not only searching for words, phrases, and idiomatic expressions; he is asking to what extent he will be able to impose reception on his interlocutor. When a language learner writes a poem, a letter, or an academic essay, she considers not only the demands of the task but how much of her history will be considered relevant to this literacy act. Language learning engages the identities of learners because language itself is not only a linguistic system of signs and symbols; it is also a complex social practice in which the value and meaning ascribed to an utterance are determined in part by the value and meaning ascribed to the person who speaks. Likewise, how a language learner interprets or constructs a written text requires an ongoing negotiation among historical understandings, contemporary realities, and future desires. Thus, language learners are not only learning a linguistic system; they are learning a diverse set of sociocultural practices, often best understood in the context of wider relations of power.

In this chapter, we defend this bold set of claims with reference to a growing body of research that seeks to develop a textured understanding of the relationship between the language learner and the sociocultural world. Such research is interested in the multiple identities of learners as, for example, gendered/raced/classed persons with diverse histories and identifications.[1] In search of insight, researchers have, in recent years, shifted their attention from the field of social psychology (see McNamara 1997) to those of anthropology, cultural studies, feminist theory, and sociology.[2] Further, in shifting from psychological to sociocultural conceptions of identity, researchers have sought to distance themselves from what Kubota calls "fixed, apolitical and essentialized cultural representations" (1999: 9). In this spirit, contemporary applied linguistic researchers have been drawn to literature that conceives of identity not as static and one-dimensional but as multiple, changing, and a site of struggle (Bordo 1990; Butler 1990; Henriques, Hollway, Urwin, Venn, and Walkerdine 1984; Weedon 1997). In recent language learning research, conceptions of identity are congruent with prevailing theories of language and learning. Thus, in order to understand current conceptions of identity and language learning, it is necessary to understand current theories of language and learning, and how these are related to theories about learners and their identities. A discussion of these follows.

THEORIES OF LANGUAGE

Poststructuralist theories of language are becoming increasingly attractive to researchers of identity and language learning. These theories build on, but are distinct from, structuralist theories of language, associated predominantly with the work of Saussure. Saussure's (1966) distinction between speech (*parole*) and language (*langue*) was an attempt to provide a way of recognizing that, despite geographical, interpersonal, and social variations, languages have shared patterns and structure. For structuralists, the building blocks of language structure are signs that comprise the signifier (or sound-image) and the signified (the concept or meaning). Saussure asserted that neither the signifier nor the signified pre-exists the other and that the link between them is arbitrary. He saw the linguistic system itself as guaranteeing the meaning of signs and each linguistic community as having its own set of signifying practices that give value to the signs in a language.

One of the criticisms poststructuralists have leveled at this notion of language is that structuralism cannot account for struggles over the meanings that can be attributed to signs in a given language. The signs /feminist/, /research/, /SLA/, for example, can have different meanings for different people within the same linguistic community. Witness, for example, debates over the meaning of "SLA theory" in the field of applied linguistics (Beretta, Crookes, Gregg, and Long 1994;

Gebhard 1999; Lantolf 1996; Van Lier 1994). Thus, while structuralists conceive of signs as having idealized meanings and of linguistic communities as being relatively homogeneous and consensual, poststructuralists take the position that the signifying practices of societies are sites of struggle and that linguistic communities are heterogeneous arenas characterized by conflicting claims to truth and power. Three poststructuralist theorists whose work has been influential in recent research on identity and language learning are Mikhail Bakhtin, Pierre Bourdieu, and Gunther Kress.

Unlike the structuralists, Bakhtin (1981, 1984) takes the position that language needs to be investigated not as a set of idealized forms independent of their speakers or their speaking but rather as situated utterances in which speakers, in dialogue with others, struggle to create meanings. For him the notion of the individual speaker is a fiction, as he sees all speakers constructing their utterances jointly, on the basis of their interaction with listeners, in both historical and contemporary, actual and assumed communities. Thus, language for him is "not a neutral medium ... [but rather] populated—overpopulated—with the intentions of others" (1981: 294). Any one utterance is for him a link in the chain of speech communication, as the context of any one utterance is past, present, and future utterances on the same topic. Bakhtin's ideas about how speakers come to participate in discourse with others help us understand why he rejects the notion that utterances are individually created, either out of their own individualized psychological reality or through application of the rules of a syntactic system. For him, language development is a matter of appropriating the words of others. Bakhtin stresses that this appropriation of the words of others is a complex and conflictual process: Because the historical, present, and future positioning of speakers and those of their interlocutors are expressed in the 'very words' of utterances, words are not neutral but express particular cognitive predispositions and value systems.

Rather than SLA as a gradual individual process of internalizing a neutral set of rules, structures, and vocabulary of a standard language, Bakhtin's work offers us ways to think about the learning of language within particular discourses and with particular interlocutors. Speakers need to struggle to appropriate the voices of others and to "bend" those voices to their own purposes. What others say, the customary discourse of any particular community, may privilege or debase certain speakers. Finding answering words for the words of others, joining the chain of speech communication, is as much a social as a linguistic struggle.

Pierre Bourdieu (1977, 1984), a contemporary French sociologist, focuses on the often unequal relationships between interlocutors and the importance of power in structuring speech. In arguing that "speech always owes a major part of its value to the value of the person who utters it" (1977: 652), Bourdieu suggests that the value ascribed to speech cannot be understood apart from the person who speaks and that the person who speaks cannot be understood apart from larger networks of social relationships. He argues that, when a person speaks, the speaker wishes not only to be understood, but to be "believed, obeyed, respected, distinguished" (1977: 648). However, speakers' abilities to "command a listener" (1977: 648) are unequally distributed because of the symbolic power relations between interlocutors. To redress the inequities between what Bourdieu calls legitimate and illegitimate speakers, Bourdieu argues that an expanded definition of competence should include the "right to speech" or "the power to impose reception" (1977: 648). Like Bakhtin, then, Bourdieu reminds the SLA theorist that language cannot be idealized and that we cannot take for granted that good faith will prevail between participants in oral or literate activities.

Gunther Kress's (1989, 1993) notion of "discourse" and "genre" is complementary to that of Bourdieu in that he sees social relationships as central to his theory of language: "Language always happens as text; and as text, it inevitably occurs in a particular generic form. That generic form arises out of the action of social subjects in particular social situations" (Kress 1993: 27). In Kress's terms, a genre is constituted within and by a particular social occasion that has a conventionalized structure and that functions within the context of larger institutional and social processes. In this formulation, the social occasions that constitute a genre may be formulaic and ritualized, such as a wedding or a committee meeting, or less ritualized, such as a casual conversation. The important point is that the conventionalized forms of these occasions, along with the organization, purpose and intention of the participants within the occasion, give rise to the meanings associated with a specific genre. Drawing on Foucault, and echoing Bourdieu, Kress (1989) argues that the power relations between participants in an interaction have a particular effect on the social meanings of the texts constructed within a given genre, whether oral or written. Like Bourdieu, Kress stresses the importance of recognizing that theories of language cannot be developed apart from an understanding of social relationships and that social relationships are rarely constituted on equal terms.

Kress's (2000) more recent work on new theories of representation offers particularly exciting possibilities for future research on identity and language learning. (See Stein 2000.) Working within the context of the Multiliteracies Project (New London Group 1996), Kress argues that, given the rapid pace of change in social, cultural, economic, and technological domains, there has been a concomitant change in the semiotic landscape that necessitates new theories of meaning. He argues, in particular, that an exclusive and extensive focus on the written word does not do justice to the multimodality that is becoming increasingly common in the electronic age. For this reason, he suggests, we need to pay greater attention to the extent to which humans, out of individual and social interest, transform the resources available to them, becoming, in this process, not critics of a stable semiotic system but designers of an ever-changing future: "An adequate theory of semiosis will be founded on a recognition of the 'interested action' of socially located, culturally and historically formed individuals, as the remakers, the transformers, and the re-shapers of the representational resources available to them" (Kress 2000: 155).

THEORIES OF LEARNING

Davis, in discussing the use of psychological research paradigms in language learning research, notes that many "theorists and researchers tend to view SLA as a mental process, that is, to believe that language acquisition resides mostly, if not solely, in the mind" (1995: 427–428). More recent work has attempted to investigate language learning as a socioculturally situated social practice. This research conceptualizes second language learning as relational activity that occurs between specific speakers situated in specific sociocultural contexts. Drawing, in different measures, on Vygotskian notions of the sociality of learning (Vygotsky 1978), these studies contest views of language learning as individual minds acquiring linguistic, or even sociolinguistic, competence. (See, for example, Kramsch 2000b; Pavlenko and Lantolf 2000.)

A shift from seeing learners as individual language producers to seeing them as members of social and historical collectivities moves observers toward examining the conditions for learning, for appropriation of practices, in any particular community. The anthropologists Jean Lave and Etienne Wenger argue that "learning [on the part of all] is an integral and inseparable part of social practice" (1991: 31) as newcomers participate in attenuated ways with old-timers in the performance of community practices. Their notion, legitimate peripheral participation, represents their view that communities are composed of participants who differentially engage with the practices of their communities and that this engagement or participation in practice is 'learning.' Stressing the importance of local analysis of communities, Lave and Wenger (1991) point out that conditions vary with regard to ease of access to expertise, to opportunities for practice, to consequences for error in practice, and so on.

From this perspective, then, educational research might focus not so much on assessing individual 'uptake' of particular knowledge or skills but rather on the social structures in particular communities and on the variety of positionings available for learners to occupy in those communities. Bakhtin asserts that language learning is a matter of appropriating the language practices of others and

Lave and Wenger (1991) argue that it is through coparticipation in community practices that learners learn. Put together, this view of language learning stresses the importance of newcomers or learners having access to the words of others in community practices. As the sociocultural theorist Ray McDermott puts it: "Language and culture are no longer scripts to be acquired, as much as they are conversations in which people can participate. The question of who is learning what and how much is essentially a question of what conversations they are part of, and this question is a subset of the more powerful question of what conversations are around to be had in a given culture" (1993: 295). From this point of view, second language researchers are interested in questions that might include the following:

- How do community practices facilitate or block access to experienced speakers?
- How do community practices structure "possibilities for selfhood"? (Ivanič 1998)
- What kinds of utterances are available for newcomers to appropriate?

Toohey (2000) investigates just these questions with respect to young English language learners. As Faltis (1997) and McGroarty (1998) argue, this sociocultural perspective offers interesting theoretical perspectives for future research in language and education.[3]

The more recent work of Wenger (1998) on learning, meaning and identity has been influential in the development of the concept of "imagined communities" with respect to the nonparticipation of learners in language classrooms (Norton, 2001).[4] In many language classrooms, all of the members of the classroom community apart from the teacher are newcomers to a set of language practices and to a community that includes those language practices in its activities. The question that arises then is, What community practices do these learners seek to learn? What, indeed, constitutes "the community" for them? Norton draws on her research with two adult immigrant language learners to argue that, while they were initially actively engaged in classroom practices, the realm of their community extended beyond the four walls of the classroom. This imagined community was not accessible to the teacher, who, unwittingly, alienated the two language learners, who then withdrew from the language classroom. Norton's research suggests that learners have different investments in particular members of the target language community and that the people in whom learners have the greatest investment may be the very people who represent or provide access to the imagined community of a given learner. Of central interest is the extent to which such investments are productive for learner engagement in both the classroom and the wider target language community.

THEORIES OF THE LEARNER

Much research on language learning has traditionally had the objective of uncovering the personalities, learning styles, motivations, and other unique characteristics of individual learners. This work sees the identity of second language learners in terms of relatively fixed and long-term traits or characteristics. Norton (2000) argues that SLA theory needs to develop a more textured understanding of the relationship between the language learners and the social world. Along with scholars such as McKay and Wong (1996) and Siegal (1996), Norton has found feminist poststructuralism, particularly the work of Christine Weedon, helpful in formulating new conceptions of the learner in the field of second language learning. Weedon appropriates the poststructuralist theory of "subjectivity," defining it as "the conscious and unconscious thoughts and emotions of the individual, her sense of herself and her ways of understanding her relation to the world" (1997: 32). Furthermore, like other poststructuralist theorists whose ideas inform her work, Weedon foregrounds the central role of language in her analysis of the relationship between the individual and the social: "Language is the place where actual and possible forms of social organization and their likely social and political consequences are defined and contested. Yet it is also the place where our sense of ourselves, our subjectivity, is constructed" (1997: 21).

Weedon (1997: 32) notes that the terms "subject" and "subjectivity" signify a different conception of the individual than that associated with humanist conceptions of the individual dominant in Western philosophy. While humanist conceptions of the individual—and many definitions of the individual in SLA research—presuppose that every person has an essential, unique, fixed and coherent "core" (introvert/extrovert; motivated/unmotivated), poststructuralism depicts the individual—the subject—as diverse, contradictory, dynamic and changing over historical time and social space. Further, in taking the position that subjectivity is multiple and a site of struggle, feminist poststructuralism highlights the changing quality of a person's identity. As Weedon (1997: 33) notes, "the political significance of decentring the subject and abandoning the belief in essential subjectivity is that it opens up subjectivity to change." This is a crucial point for second language educators in that it opens up possibilities for educational intervention.

Recent work by Gentil (2000) considers how hermeneutic perspectives on identity articulated by Taylor (1989, 1991) and Ricoeur (1992) might articulate with feminist poststructural notions of the self and, in so doing, might provide productive possibilities in investigations of second language learning. Gentil notes that moral philosopher Charles Taylor sees language as "made and remade in conversation" (1989: 525) and, further, that Taylor sees selves or identities as dialogically created in those conversations. From this perspective, one comes to understand oneself dialogically, that is, through specific conversations (Ricoeur would stress, through narratives of the self), and the specific character of those conversations or narratives over time would define for agents a moral "horizon" of commitments, values, and identifications against which they might define themselves. Gentil argues that this examination of the historical construction of a self offers potential for understanding individual agency and at the same time recognizing the complex and pervading constraints offered by social worlds.

In the field of language learning, there has been increasing interest in linking poststructuralist conceptions of identity and human agency with the notion of 'investment' (Angelil-Carter 1997; McKay and Wong 1996; Norton Peirce 1995). Departing from current conceptions of 'motivation' in the field of language learning, the concept of investment signals the socially and historically constructed relationship of learners to the target language and their sometimes ambivalent desire to learn and practice it. Investment is best understood with reference to the economic metaphors that Bourdieu uses in his work—in particular the notion of "cultural capital." Bourdieu and Passeron (1977) use the term "cultural capital" to reference the knowledge, credentials, and modes of thought that characterize different classes and groups in relation to specific sets of social forms. They argue that cultural capital is situated, in that it has differential exchange value in different social fields. If learners "invest" in a second language, they do so with the understanding that they will acquire a wider range of symbolic and material resources, which will in turn increase the value of their cultural capital. As the value of their cultural capital increases, so learners' sense of themselves and their desires for the future are reassessed. Hence the integral relationship between investment and identity.

Toward the Future

In the field of applied linguistics, interest in language and identity is growing, reflected, in part, by the number of journals with special issues on the topic. In 1996, Martin-Jones and Heller (1996) edited two special issues of *Linguistics and Education* on discourse, identities, and power, and Sarangi and Baynham (1996) edited a special double issue of *Language and Education* on the construction of educational identities. These were followed by a special issue of *TESOL Quarterly* on language and identity, edited by Norton (1997a), a special issue on gender issues in language teaching for the Japan Association of Language Teachers (JALT) journal, *The Language Teacher* (Smith and Yamashiro, 1998), and a theme issue of *Anthropology and Education Quarterly* on authenticity and identity, edited by Henze and Davis (1999). Such interest has encouraged Ricento and Wiley to found and edit the new *Journal of Language, Identity and Education*, which, at time of writing, has yet to go to press. We anticipate that this momentum will continue well into the new millennium.

The goal we see for future research on identity and language learning is to develop understandings of learners as both socially constructed and constrained but also as embodied, semiotic and emotional persons who identify themselves, resist identifications, and act on their social worlds. Learners' investments in learning languages, the ways in which their identities affect their participation in second language activities, and their access to participation in the activities of their communities, must all be matters of consideration in future research.

NOTES

1. There has been a great deal of recent research on identity and language learning from a variety of perspectives and using diverse methodologies. Apart from researchers mentioned elsewhere in this chapter are: Auerbach 1989; Benesch 1998; Blackledge 2000; Canagarajah 1997; Corson 1998; Cummins 1996; Davison 2001; Duff and Uchida 1997; Ehrlich 1997; Goldstein 1997; Harklau 1999; Heller 1999; Hunter 1997; Janks 1997; Kanno 1996; Leung, Harris, and Rampton 1997; Lin 1999; Liu 1999; Maguire 1998; Miller 1998; Morgan 1998; Mohan, Leung, and Davison 2001; Nelson 1999; Pennycook 1998; Piller 1999; Rampton 1995b; Schecter and Bayley 1997; Schenke 1996; Sharkey and Layzer 2000; Skilton-Sylvester 1997; Starfield in press; Thesen 1997; Vandrick 1998; Willett; Solsken, and Wilson-Kennan 1998.

2. Applied linguists have found useful the work of the following: Bhabha 1994; Clifford 1988; Eisenhart 1995; Foucault 1980; Gee 1990; Hall 1996; Luke 1988; Ochs 1992; Rosaldo 1993; Simon 1992.

3. See for example, Dagenais and Day 1999; Day 1999; Gutierrez, Baquedano-Lopes, and Tejeda 1999; Hall 1998; Haneda 1997; Manyak 2000; Toohey 1996, 1998.

4. Similarly, Holland et al. (1998) write about action within "figured worlds"—to explain "people's abilities to form and be formed in collectively realized 'as if' realms" (p. 49). Ibrahim (1999), picking up on Anderson (1983), uses the term "social imaginary" to reference continental African youths' appropriation in Canada of Black American stylized English, music, bodily habitus, and other communicative performatives.

CHAPTER 11

COGNITIVE PERSPECTIVES ON SECOND LANGUAGE ACQUISITION

MICHAEL HARRINGTON

A cognitive theory of second language acquisition (SLA) seeks to explicate the psychological mechanisms that underlie comprehension and production and the means by which that competence develops in the mind of the learner. The focus in this chapter is on recent research on second language sentence processing and the contribution this research can make to this endeavor. Sentence processing research seeks to identify how and when the various sources of information, syntax, semantics, context, and so on contribute to real-time processing outcomes in comprehension (Tanenhaus and Trueswell 1995) and production (Bock and Levelt 1994). Although second language sentence processing is still in its beginning, this research enterprise builds on a voluminous psycholinguistic literature on (first language) sentence processing. For reviews see Mitchell (1994), Tanenhaus and Trueswell (1995), and Harrington (forthcoming). Studies on real-time processes in second language comprehension have only recently started to appear (Juffs 1998b; Juffs and Harrington 1995, 1996). Although the investigation of on-line processing has only begun, there are a number of studies that have examined processing issues using off-line measures[1] (Gass 1987; Harrington 1987; Kempe and MacWhinney 1998; Kilborn 1989; MacWhinney 1987; Myles 1995; Rounds and Kanagy 1998; Sasaki 1994; Ying 1996).

The purpose of this chapter is to examine the emerging research literature in second language sentence processing. Two approaches to understanding real-time sentence comprehension are contrasted. The *syntax-based* approach, represented in the principle-based parsing research used in Juffs and Harrington (1995, 1996) and Juffs (1998a, 1998b), characterizes the comprehension process as the application of autonomous syntactic principles. These principles serve as the exclusive basis for initial parsing decisions, which are subsequently fed to interpretative processes that evaluate and, if necessary, revise the initial parse (Pritchett 1992). Semantics, frequency, and contextual information are assumed to play no role in initial parsing decisions.

In contrast, *constraint-based* models of sentence processing assume that comprehension is the result of the interaction of multiple sources of knowledge, linguistic, pragmatic, contextual, and real-world. This information is represented in the mind in a distributed manner and serves as probabilistic constraints on interpretation. The constraint-based approach is most readily identified with connectionist modeling (Elman 1993), which is represented in the SLA literature in studies by Broeder and Plunkett (1994), Ellis and Schmidt (1998), Gasser (1990), and Sokolik (1990), and Sokolik and Smith (1992).

Each approach is examined by first setting out the theoretical foundations and then describing how the approach investigates on-line sentence processing effects. The key questions that frame current research are identified and representative studies discussed. The strengths and limitations of the respective approaches are identified, and the chapter concludes with a discussion of the implications this line of research has for the development of a cognitive theory of SLA.

SLA as a Cognitive Science

This chapter approaches SLA as a cognitive science. Cognitive science seeks to understand the internal mental representations responsible for the higher-order mental functions (e.g., vision, language, categorization). Cognitive theory in SLA has been closely identified with the information-processing paradigm (McLaughlin and Heredia 1996). Information processing was the dominant metaphor for cognition in the 1960s and 1970s and remains so for many researchers today (Palmer and Kimchi 1986). Although the term is widely used, it is worthwhile to specify what the paradigm entails. An *information process* is the means by which a system makes systematic responses to particular environmental conditions. The responses are typically goal oriented and serve an adaptive purpose for the system or the organism, which varies its "behavior" in response to differing environmental conditions (Stillings et al. 1995). An understanding of an information process thus includes an account of the information that the system needs to achieve its goals, as well as the means by which it uses that information. These means are usually described as subskills that contribute to the higher level information process, and the approach assumes that these component skills can be studied productively in isolation from the larger system. Because information processes take place in time, reaction time becomes a key variable in understanding the subskills involved. Finally, the information-processing approach assumes that the mind is a general purpose symbol processing system that is subject to capacity constraints. The information-processing paradigm has been and continues to be a highly productive source of SLA research (Bialystok 1994; DeKeyser 1995; Hatch 1983; Hulstijn 1990; Hulstijn and Hulstijn 1984; McLaughlin 1990; O'Malley and Chamot 1990; Robinson 1996; Schmidt 1992; Skehan 1991, 1998b; Van Patten and Cadierno 1993). For a more complete description of the information-processing paradigm in SLA, see McLaughlin and Heredia (1996).

Sentence processing research draws heavily on the information processing tradition for theory and research methodology. However, it also differs in three significant ways. First, the information-processing paradigm *takes as a given* the notion that the mind is a general purpose symbol processor, an assumption that is a major issue of contention in sentence processing research (Fodor and Pylyshyn 1988). The syntax-based and constraint-based accounts described in this chapter represent, respectively, *classical* and *connectionist* views of cognition and language (MacDonald and MacDonald 1995). The classical view sees the mind as a nonprobabilistic computational machine that carries out discrete operations on symbols (Fodor and Pylyshyn 1988). The connectionist perspective, in contrast, eschews a symbolic level of representation, characterizing language knowledge instead in distributed, probabilistic terms. Over the past decade, the debate over whether human cognition requires symbolic computation has been a—if not *the*—major issue in the cognitive science of language.

Second, as an account of SLA, information-processing approaches have traditionally left unspecified the nature of the linguistic knowledge that the learner acquires and uses (Newmeyer 1987). The nature of linguistic knowledge representations and how this knowledge is exploited in real-time comprehension is of central concern in sentence processing research and has profound implications for models of how this knowledge is developed. The third way in which sentence processing research differs from traditional information-processing research concerns the temporal dimension. Integral to any sentence processing model is an account of how comprehension processes are carried out in real time. The availability and exploitation of the various sources of information contributing to comprehension (e.g., linguistic, semantic, conceptual) under the pressure of on-line performance is a central issue among competing sentence processing approaches. In contrast, the focus in SLA information-processing research has been on identifying the conditions that affect learning outcomes, as in the implicit versus explicit processing of input (Robinson 1997), or mechanisms, as in the need to attend to input (Schmidt 1990).

Although differences exist between sentence processing research and that in the information-processing tradition, the two approaches are complementary. Both will play an important role in the development of a cognitive theory of SLA. The remaining part of the chapter describe the contribution that L2 sentence processing research can make to our understanding of SLA in cognitive terms.

A Syntax-Based Approach to Sentence Processing

The syntax-based approach ascribes a central role to syntactic processes in sentence comprehension. In this section the theoretical foundation of the approach is described, and studies applying the framework to L2 processing are presented.

Language Processing as Symbol Computation

In the syntax-based processing approach, cognition and language are characterized as a symbol manipulation process (Newell, Rosenbloom, and Laird 1989). The symbolic approach assumes that knowledge is represented in the mind directly in symbols and that computations, specified in rules, are carried out on these representations. In natural language computation these symbols include phonemes, morphemes, grammar rules, and so on, and the processor works directly on these elements to yield an interpretation. The level of syntactic representation is assumed to be independent of the semantics of the specific items involved, in the same way that the computation of an algebraic equation (e.g., $a + b = c$) is the same, regardless of the specific values of a and b.

The symbolic view has been the dominant approach to cognition, and this is reflected in the sentence processing literature. Sentence processing has traditionally been characterized as a process of symbolic computation, cast in the form of structure building (Mitchell 1994). The role of syntactic structure is thus of primary concern, and from the outset the interest has been in how the sentence processor (or *parser*) builds a syntactic structure that ultimately leads to an interpretation of the sentence (Frazier 1987). Fundamental insights into how this structure building proceeds have come from examining the processing of ambiguous language structures (e.g., *visiting relatives*), where structural alternatives are thrown into sharp relief. Ambiguity resolution processes provide a window on processes that are difficult to observe otherwise.

Syntax-Based Processing

Syntax-based approaches to processing ascribe a central role to syntactic knowledge in the sentence interpretation process. Syntactic knowledge consists of an autonomous competence grammar, and a principled distinction is made between the mechanisms responsible for lexical processing (e.g., word recognition and lexical access) and syntactic processing. Often referred to as two-stage models (Frazier and Fodor 1978), the syntactic parse is carried out rapidly using the minimal syntactic category information needed to complete the initial parse. The initial parse is then output to an interpretative mechanism that matches it against semantic, contextual, and real-world information, ultimately yielding an interpretation.

Syntax-based approaches can be classified into two categories: principle-based (Crocker 1994; Frazier 1989; Pritchett 1992) and referential (Altmann and Steedman 1988; Crain and Steedman 1985). The two differ principally as to when referential context information figures in processing outcomes. In the next section, the application to second language processing of one kind of principle-based parser, the generalized theta attachment model (Pritchett 1992), is discussed.

A Syntax-Based Second Language Processing

Juffs and Harrington (1995; 1996) used a principle-based model to investigate on-line reading processes by advanced ESL learners. The generalized theta attachment (GTA) model (Pritchett 1992) was used to assess the relative contribution of processing difficulty and (UG-based) grammatical knowledge to learner performance in on-line reading and grammaticality judgment tasks. Syntactic processing in the GTA model is driven by the assignment of thematic roles (e.g., agent, theme, goal) to elements in the input string.[2] Lexical items can appear in more than one argument structure, and it is the possibility of multiple argument structure interpretations that can lead to processing ambiguities.

The GTA parser seeks to build as complete a structure as possible by assigning all thematic roles as soon as possible.[3] As each word comes through the parser, syntactic principles (e.g., theta attachment, case, binding) are assigned so as to realize the most complete structure possible for the local string. (See Juffs and

Harrington 1995 and Juffs in this volume for details.) It is assumed that every NP must eventually be associated with a specific thematic role and that the parser selects the reading that imposes the lowest cost on the system. Processing difficulties thus arise as the result of unfulfilled thematic role assignments.

Juffs and Harrington (1995) were interested in the asymmetry evident in L2 learner performance on grammatical judgements for *wh*-structures, exemplified in (1) and (2).

(1) *Who did Ann believe ___ likes her friend?* (Subject extraction from finite clause)

(2) *Who did Ann believe her friend likes ___?* (Object extraction from finite clause)

The sentences differ structurally in that (1) involves the extraction of the pronoun *who* from the subject site (indicated by the gap), while (2) involves extraction from the object site. Earlier research showed that ESL learners experience more difficulty judging the acceptability of subject extraction sentences like (1) than their object extraction counterparts in (2) (Schachter and Yip 1990). Structures that involve constraints on *wh*-movement are of interest because they provide a testing ground for the putative effects of UG in adult SLA, given that these constraints are not assumed to operate in all languages (Epstein, Flynn, and Martohardjono 1996). Poor performance on the subject extraction sentences by adult L2 learners from languages in which *wh*-movement constraints are not assumed to operate (e.g., Chinese) have thus been used as evidence for lack of access to these principles by L2 learners (Schachter and Yip 1990). However, while L2 learners did have difficulty in the subject structures (1), they were sensitive to *wh*-constraints in judgments on other types of *wh*-structures, including the object extraction types in (2). This raised the possibility that the difficulties encountered by learners on these particular structures might be due to processing deficits rather than competence deficits. It was this possibility that Juffs and Harrington (1995) explored.

Reading times and grammaticality judgments of advanced Chinese ESL learners on sentences like (1) and (2) were collected in an on-line reading task. The key area of comparison in the study was processing times for the region immediately following the main verb *believe*. In the subject extraction sentences, this region follows the extraction site (the "postgap" region). Reading times were sharply higher in the postgap region for the subject extraction from clauses in (1), the slowdown in processing mirroring the observed decline in accuracy for these forms. Given that the Chinese learners in the study showed sensitivity to *wh*-movement constraints in general, the relative difficulty encountered on the subject extraction sentences was attributed to greater processing demands that resulted from the reanalysis involved in the correct assignment of thematic roles in these structures.[4] In sentence (1), the GTA model predicts that the parser will initially interpret the main verb *believe* as an NP complement and will posit a complete grammatical sentence with an object gap, as in *Who does Ann believe_?* The appearance of the verb *like* then forces the object gap to be reanalyzed as an embedded subject trace, *Who does Ann believe_likes?*[5] The authors thus concluded that the demands of the on-line reanalysis, and not the availability of the *wh*-movement constraints, may be responsible for the observed differences in performance on the respective structures evident in the earlier research (Schachter and Yip 1990).

The GTA model was also used by Juffs to study other types of on-line processing ambiguities that have received considerable attention in the L1 sentence processing literature, including so-called garden path structures, as *Before Mary ate the pizza arrived from the restaurant.* (Juffs 1998b), and ambiguities that arise from main verb/reduced relative clause readings of the verb, as in *The leader defeated in the election*... versus *The leader defeated the amendment*... (Juffs 1998a). In both studies, the focus was on the role that L1 argument structure and UG constraints might play on L2 processing outcomes. Results from both sets of findings indicated that processing outcomes were affected by a range of factors that may involve, but are not limited to, UG-based crosslinguistic variation.

Syntax-Based Approaches in SLA

The principle-based parser used in the studies just discussed is representative of the syntax-based approach to on-line sentence processing. The studies also represent the first attempt to apply the framework to understanding second language processing issues. In this section the implications of these findings for a theory of second language processing and, in turn, to a cognitive theory of SLA are be considered.

The use of a competence-based grammar in the Juffs and Harrington (1995) study allows the interface of syntactic knowledge representations and processing mechanisms to be systematically examined. The grammar provides a formal, testable set of predictions that permits the researcher to isolate and identify the relative contribution of the grammar and the processor to real-time language comprehension. In adult L2 comprehension, the understanding of this interaction is made more complex by the wide range of individual differences in knowledge and processing across learners and by the potential effect of the first language on both these dimensions (Juffs 1998a).

However, the prominence accorded syntactic processes in the GTA model may also be problematic. In the studies cited, the processing variation evident in the word-by-word reading times, both within and across individuals, was interpreted in terms of structural complexity demands as predicted by a GB-based parsing model. However, many researchers find the assumptions made by these models to be overly restrictive or even misplaced (Tanenhaus and Trueswell 1995). Research has shown that a range of nonsyntactic information can neutralize or even overturn predicted structural processing effects (Altman and Steedman 1988). It has been demonstrated that the manipulation of prior discourse can bias responses toward or away from the main verb/reduced relative clause readings in a garden path sentence like *The waiter served calzone complained*. For example, the reduced relative clause reading can be elicited by prefacing the test sentence with *Two waiters were served different types of Italian food. The waiter served calzone . . .* (Trueswell and Tanenhaus 1994). Semantic effects can also affect initial parsing decisions. The fact that *waiter* in *The waiter served . . .* is animate makes an ambiguous reading more likely than would the presence of an inanimate noun compare *The spaghetti served . . .* (Ferriera and Clifton 1986; Trueswell, Tanenhaus, and Garnsey 1994).

The frequency with which particular verbs appear in particular argument structures can also bias sentence interpretations. The main verb interpretation of *served* in the example sentence is possible with both a transitive and intransitive argument structure, while the reduced relative clause reading requires a transitive argument structure. Verbs that appear more frequently in transitive argument structures are less likely to be given an intransitive reduced relative interpretation, despite the fact that both structural interpretations are available (Trueswell 1996). These findings indicate that sources of information excluded in the GTA account, like prior context and frequency biases, play an immediate and important role in on-line sentence interpretation.[6]

Finally, the syntax-based approach provides little insight into how knowledge of the L2 develops. Syntax-based approaches all assume some form of competence grammar, with as yet little understanding of the mechanisms by which it develops (Gregg 1996).

In the Juffs and Harrington study, for example, the subjects were advanced L2 learners, and all were considered to possess a final-state L2 grammar. The effects observed thus reflected the outcome of the learners' experience, and provide little insight into how that knowledge developed, or the course of development that took place.

In summary, syntax-based approaches like the GTA provide an explicit, testable set of processing claims. However, they also exclude factors that have been shown to play a central role in sentence processing. As a result, the contribution that this approach can make to a cognitive theory of SLA, where learning is the primary concern, remains uncertain.

A Constraint-Based Approach to Sentence Processing

Constraint-based models of sentence processing offer a sharp contrast to the syntax-based approach described in the preceding section. These models characterize sentence interpretation as a highly interactive process, in which syntactic, lexical, and semantic-conceptual information interact closely to constrain on-line comprehension (Tanenhaus and Trueswell 1995). In this section the theoretical foundation of the approach are described, and constraint-based models of L1 and L2 processing are examined.

Language as a Distributed Probabilistic System

There are several important features of the constraint-based approach that serve to distinguish it from the syntax-based approach. First, constraint-based models assume that language is represented as distributed, graded features, in contrast to the traditional symbolic view. Linguistic knowledge is represented in the mind as a complex pattern of associative links between units. These units, or *microfeatures* (Clark 1993), are smaller than the traditional units of linguistic analysis (e.g., phoneme, word, phrase, rule). The distributed knowledge representations produce rule-like behavior but do not assume the existence of explicit rules, which is the basic stuff of symbolic models of language and cognition. The effect of this experience is incremental, or *graded*, with patterns of activation corresponding to words, grammatical structures, and so on, undergoing constant modification as a result of experience. Repeated exposure strengthens the activation level of a representation, while decreasing exposure serves to weaken and, in certain cases, extinguish it. The graded nature of the representations contrasts with traditional symbolic approaches, in which these representations are assumed to be learned in an all-or-none manner (Hintzman 1993).[7]

The distributed, graded nature of knowledge representations also means that language knowledge is readily describable in *probabilistic* terms, another distinguishing feature of the approach (Seidenberg and McDonald 1999). Knowledge of a given form can range on a continuum from near certitude, where the structure is always used correctly, through an intermediate state, where appropriate usage varies, to a random state, where the incidence of correct use of the structure does not rise above chance. Probabilistic models have an advantage over rule-based models in capturing the variable nature of behavior, which is important in contexts where variation itself is of theoretical interest, as is the case in SLA. The probabilistic, statistical nature of language processing is in sharp contrast with classical symbolic models where rule knowledge is represented and processed in a discrete fashion (Fodor and McLaughlin 1990).

The final, and potentially most significant, characteristic of the constraint-based perspective is the direct relationship it assumes between processing and learning. Novel input is processed on the basis of previously stored experience, with the act of processing itself changing the strength of existing knowledge representations. As a result, the mechanisms involved in processing input are also responsible for learning new knowledge (Sharkey 1996). Furthermore, the cognitive mechanisms responsible for the development of activation strengths are not specific to language learning but are shared by other higher order cognitive processes. As a theory of language learning, it characterizes language development as the result of the interaction between the learning environment and domain-general learning capacities of the individual, or what is termed an *emergent* property of the system (Ellis 1998).[8]

Sentence Processing as Constraint Satisfaction

Sentence interpretation in the constraint-based approach is described as an interactive process of *constraint-satisfaction* (McClelland, Rumelhart, and Hinot 1986).[9] A good example is the lexicalist constraint-based model developed by MacDonald and her coworkers (MacDonald, Perlmutter, and Seidenberg 1994). In the model, units corresponding to the various information types are activated in parallel, with the strength of activation of a particular unit or set of units reflecting the type, number, and strength of the links it shares with other units in the system. Alternative structures are activated to differing degrees, and the interpretation depends on which alternative the system ultimately settles on. For example, the resolution of the temporarily ambiguous *served* in the example sentence *The waiter served calzone (complained)* involves structural decisions concerning argument structure, tense, and voice of the verb, which can be highly sensitive to frequency and context effects (Trueswell 1996).[10]

Constraint-Based Models of Sentence Processing: Connectionist Sentence Processing

In contrast to the vast sentence processing literature in the symbolic tradition, connectionist accounts of sentence processing are fewer in number (Christiansen and Chater 1999). Connectionist approaches have been highly successful in char-

acterizing learning in local domains of processing phonological, lexical, and morphosyntactic level. Models have been trained to accurately assign verb tense (Plunkett and Marchman 1993) and to resolve lexical ambiguity (Kawamoto 1993) with
a fairly simple mechanism that works on input, without recourse to prior assumptions as to the nature of the representations, such as the existence of a
competence grammar. The ability of the model to learn these domains challenges
the symbolic approach and provides a model that combines processing and learning in a single account.

Connectionist accounts of specific morphosyntactic domains in L2 development have also appeared, including the mapping of lexical items onto thematic
roles (Gasser 1990), gender (Sokolik 1990; Sokolik and Smith 1992), verb morphology (Broeder and Plunkett 1994), and number (Ellis and Schmidt 1998). A
representative application of connectionist theory and method to a domain of L2
learning is Ellis and Schmidt (1998). The focus of the study was on the frequency
by regularity interaction that has been observed in the processing of past tense
verbs in English (Prasada and Pinker 1993). English native speakers appear to
produce the past tense of regular verbs (*play-played*) and irregular verbs (*run-ran*)
differently. The time it takes to produce the past tense of an irregular verb is
closely related to its frequency: High frequency past forms are produced quickly,
and low frequency forms are much slower. Regular verbs, in contrast, do not
appear to be sensitive to stem frequency, as high-frequency and low-frequency
stems take approximately the same time to produce.[11]

This pattern of results led Pinker and others to posit two separate mechanisms
as being responsible for the production of the English past tense (Pinker and
Prince 1994). Irregular verbs, which are sensitive to frequency effects, were posited
to be stored as individual items in associative memory, with production a matter
of retrieval from memory. Regular pasts, in contrast, are generated by a rule
binding the past tense morpheme to the stem at the time of production. Beck
(1997) presented similar results for advanced L2 learners for production on the
regular verb forms but did not find a frequency effect for irregular verbs.

Ellis and Schmidt (1998) examined how these forms were learned both by
human participants and in a connectionist simulation. In the study, a group of
subjects was taught the plural morphology of an artificial language, which preserved the frequency and regularity features of the past tense verb data in Prasada
and Pinker (1993). The findings of the subsequent simulation studies also revealed
a frequency by regularity interaction similar to the earlier study.[12] This led Ellis
and Schmidt to conclude that a symbolic, rule-based approach was not needed
to account for the results (Pinker and Prince 1994).[13]

The Ellis and Schmidt study demonstrates how connectionist modeling can
yield insight into the learning of morphosyntax. However, the capacity of connectionist models to capture the kind of empirical data relevant to key issues in
sentence processing is still questionable (Carroll 1995). The challenge for these

models is to capture the complex structural relations that are integral to language but that are not readily apparent from simple co-occurrence statistics. These relations include long-distance dependencies among elements manifest in, for example, number agreement, embedding, and the filler-gap structures examined in Juffs and Harrington (1995). It has long been argued that these phenomena demand an autonomous level of syntactic representation that is represented naturally in symbolic approaches (Pinker and Prince 1988).

Early connectionist accounts of sentence-level syntax "hard-wired" the relevant linguistic structure in a distributed connectionist architecture (Small, Cottrell, and Shastri 1982). Thus, the models were not an alternative to symbolic accounts but provided a formal structure in which to implement them. Although these implementations provided insight into the interface between symbolic and connectionist accounts, a more radical goal for many connectionist researchers has been to provide an alternative to symbolic accounts of language. The attempt has been to develop models that would be able to learn linguistic structure from sequences of words, that is, without assuming an apriori competence grammar (Christiansen and Chater 1999). Two approaches have been taken.

Statistical connectionist models (Charniak 1993) extract syntactic structure by training a model on a corpus that contains sentences that are tagged for part of speech and then using it to assign the appropriate grammatical structure to novel sentences (Stolcke 1991). Although the model assumes only general learning algorithms, much of the task of extracting linguistic structure is completed in tagging the corpus on which the model is trained.

A more radical class of connectionist models attempts to learn syntactic structure from sequences of words that are not premodified. Elman (1993) used a simple recurrent network (SRN) model to predict the next word for sentences generated by a small context-free grammar that included key syntactic structures (e.g., subject-verb agreement, argument structure variation, and subject and object relative clauses). The model was able to acquire some of the regularities in the grammar, notably the ability to identify agreement relations across intervening words (Elman 1993). Elman's findings were extended by others, including Christiansen and Chater (1994), who included more complex grammatical structures, and Ellis (1997), who examined long-distance dependencies in an SLA context (Ellis and Schmidt 1997).

These findings marked an important advance for connectionist models of sentence processing but had a significant drawback. The models used a limited vocabulary and small ("toy") grammar, and great difficulty was encountered in trying to scale them up to account for the kinds of empirical data on ambiguity effects (Christiansen and Chater 1999). More recent attempts to fit on-line reading data on garden path (Tabor, Juliano, and Tanenhaus 1997) and center-embedded structures (Christiansen and Chater 1999) have had some success, but the research is still in its infancy. To date, no work has been done on second language sentence processing.

Constraint-Based Models and SLA Theory

The constraint-based approach has appeal for SLA research. The approach characterizes processing as the interaction of multiple sources of knowledge that develop in a graded, probabilistic fashion. As such, it can readily capture the variation across learners, languages, and setting that is an integral part of adult SLA. The connectionist models considered here posit a single, unified account for learning and processing and thus provides an explicit characterization of the developmental process. This is a pressing need for current cognitive SLA theory, which still knows little about the transition mechanisms responsible for the development of L2 knowledge (Gregg 1996).

However, connectionist processing accounts of key structural effects in real-time sentence processing have yet to appear. It is still uncertain whether these models can overcome the current limitations and establish themselves as legitimate alternatives to the symbolic syntax-based models of sentence processing. One alternative, not discussed here, is mixed models that combine the advantages of distributed representation with symbolic structural knowledge (Marcus 1998; Steedman 1999).

IMPLICATIONS OF SENTENCE PROCESSING RESEARCH FOR SLA THEORY

In the final section of the chapter implications of sentence processing research for a cognitive theory of SLA are briefly discussed. Areas in which research on real-time language processing will make an increasingly important impact in SLA theory are in our understanding of the effects of the L1 on L2 use, on the mechanisms responsible for L2 development, and on SLA research methodology.

Cross-Linguistic Processing

Sentence processing research affords an important window both into the workings of the human speech processing mechanism and into the organization of the mind and behavior (Carpenter, Miyake, and Just 1995). A better understanding of the explicit mechanisms responsible for the use of a second language in real time will bring more precision to the notion of processing, a term that is used in the current SLA literature with varying degrees of rigor (Sharwood Smith 1993).

The research discussed here also marks a move toward investigating possible L1-based processing effects on-line, which have not been studied in the past (e.g., Harrington 1987; Kilborn 1989; MacWhinney 1987; Sasaki 1994; Ying 1996). Recent works by Juffs (1998a, 1998b) raise important, and extremely complex, issues concerning the interaction of the L1 and the L2 in processing.

The Relationship between Processing and Learning

A fundamental difference between the two approaches discussed in this chapter concerns the relationship between processing and learning. The syntax-based approach does not directly address the issue, while the constraint-based models provide a parsimonious, if yet to be established, account of how knowledge of a second language develops. A better understanding of how and when the various sources of information are exploited in real-time will inform a model of SLA, regardless of which approach is taken.

Sentence Processing Research Methodology

The fact that SLA researchers have only started to examine sentence processing by second language learners is attributable to several factors. One limitation has been the lack of technical resources and methodological expertise required to carry out the research. Like all cognition, the processes involved in on-line sentence processing are only indirectly observable and unfold on a millisecond time scale. The technical, methodological, and, to some extent, conceptual tools needed to carry out this research have in the past not been readily available. However, that is changing with the appearance of usable and affordable data collection and analysis software tools.

Conceptually, the treatment of second language learning as a probabilistic process has major implications for research methodology and design, particularly in terms of the statistical tests used to establish reliable relationships between data. Null hypothesis testing, which has long been the statistical method of choice in experimental social science, assumes a discrete criterion value at which the null hypothesis is either rejected or retained and statistically "significant" difference inferred. Probabilistic processes, in contrast, are best described with correlational statistics, where the relative strengths (correlations) of multiple cue associations are of central theoretical interest (Howson and Urbach 1989). Sentence processing wherein multiple cues naturally occur and interact is a prime example of multiple cue interaction. Correlational statistics have traditionally been considered problematic for establishing causal relations between variables, with a resulting (pronounced) bias toward null hypothesis testing. However, the need in sentence processing models to capture the interaction of multiple variables means that probabilistic statistical techniques, notably Bayesian modeling, will increasingly vie with the traditional two-valued statistical tests like the t-test or ANOVA.

CONCLUSION

The purpose of this chapter has been to examine the emerging research on second language sentence processing. Although still in its infancy, the field should make an increasingly important contribution to our understanding of the cognitive basis of second language learning and use. In addition, findings from research on second language processing will also provide further insight into the working of the human speech processing mechanism, in particular, and language and cognition, in general.

NOTES

1. Off-line measures include grammaticality judgments, categorization tasks, and true-false measures. They are off-line in the sense that the response, in the form of a judgment, categorization, and so on, is the result of the process. It provides only indirect evidence as to how the process was carried out in real time

2. The thematic role of a phrase is the general semantic role that the phrase (called an *argument*) plays in relation to its predicate, with the various thematic roles possible for the phrase described by the argument structure of the predicate. Thematic roles (also called theta roles) include such entities as Theme (or Patient), which signals the entity that is undergoing the effect of some action, as *Tom* does in *Tom fell over*; Agent (or Causer), in which *Tom* is the instigator of an action, as in *Tom killed Bob*; and Goal, which is the entity toward which something moves, as in *home* in *Tom went*.

3. Generalized theta attachment (GTA): Every principle of the syntax attempts to be maximally satisfied at every point during processing (Pritchett 1992: 138).

4. The Chinese ESL participants in the study performed at levels comparable to native speaker controls on grammatical extractions of objects (2) but were less accurate than the native speakers on grammatical extractions of subjects in (1) (Juffs and Harrington 1995: 501).

5. The GTA assumes that the interpretation of *Who did Ann believe* ___ *likes her friend?* requires a matrix object trace to be reanalyzed as an embedded subject trace. This process is assumed to consist of three steps: a change in theta role assigner from *believe* to *like*; a change in theta role from internal to external; and a change in Case assignment from accusative to nominative. In contrast, object *wh*-extractions involve only the reassignment of theta/Case assigner from matrix verb to embedded verb and are assumed to be easier to parse (Juffs and Harrington 1995: 492–493).

6. Particulars of the GTA account itself have also been challenged. The model adopts a fairly radical approach to how and when head information is used relative to other kinds of information, especially the stipulation that a node that identifies possible thematic roles cannot be projected before the head of the phrase is encountered. It appears that this yields different processing effects in head-initial (e.g., English) and in head-final (Japanese) languages (Kamide and Mitchell 1999; Sturt and Crocker 1996). This, of course, is not a criticism of syntax-based accounts as a class.

7. It should be noted that recent symbolic models have also incorporated graded representations (Carpenter, Miyake, and Just 1995).

8. Learning outcomes reflect the individual's experience with the environment. However, the constraint-based perspective is not a tabula rasa view of language learning, in which the learner brings an empty and unstructured set of cognitive capacities to the task. Rather, the point of departure in attempting to account for learning outcomes is that innate predispositions, such as those proposed in generative theory, make only a minimal contribution to the learning task. The emergent view sees development not in terms of either nurture or nature but as a rich and complex interaction between the two dimensions (Elman et al. 1996).

9. See Rumelhart and McClelland 1986, chapter 1, for a description of constraint satisfaction models of language and cognition. The terminology can be confusing. Pritchett's 1992 model has also been called a constraint-satisfaction model, although the constraints that are satisfied are strictly defined in terms of grammatical principles (Crocker 1994: 249). This, however, is an exception, as constraint satisfaction models are usually associated with the interactive approach discussed here (Boland 1997; Clifton, Frazier, and Rayner 1994; Tanenhaus and Trueswell 1995).

10. The ambiguity encountered in structures like *The waiter served the calzone complained* is cast as a problem of lexical ambiguity (at three levels), rather than as a structural parsing or thematic role assignment problem. Three levels of lexical ambiguity that must be resolved in order to interpret *served* in *The waiter served . . .* The argument-structure level alternates between transitive (in which both an agent and a theme thematic role can be assigned) and intransitive (in which only an agent role is possible); the tense morphology level between the past tense and past participle; and the voice level between active and passive (MacDonald, Perlmutter, and Seidenberg 1994).

The interdependencies between these levels is schematically represented in the pattern of connections. For example, the reduced relative clause reading (*The waiter who was served . . .*) requires that *waiter* be in the passive voice. This places a constraint on the other two levels, as only one possible alternative exists at each of the other two levels, namely the past-participle tense morphology and the transitive argument structure. The conjunction of the passive voice and the simple past tense is not allowed (**The waiter was flew by the pilot*), nor is the passive possible with intransitive argument structure (**The waiter was slept*).

11. Clahsen et al. observed a similar interaction for number inflection in German (Clahsen, Rothweiler, Woest, and Marcus 1993).

12. Singular word stems were the input units, and the plural prefixes were the output units. The output units were either the regular plural or irregular forms. The network was trained by presenting as input the singulars, which would then activate one of the plural output units. At the outset, this process was random, with a given input stem activating any of the plural output units. Each time a given input unit activated a particular output unit, the model would compare the activation of that mapping with the activation weight of the correct output unit, given that input unit. The backpropagation learning mechanism was used to calculate the difference between the mapping produced and the desired mapping and to then make an incremental adjustment in weights. As a result, the next time the stem input was presented, it was closer to the correct output unit in terms of activation strength. All the input-output mappings were thus trained separately over many blocks of trials. In addition, Ellis and Schmidt also had a singular stem that was used to test how well the network could generalize to novel items. They found that there was a small tendency for the untrained singular to activate the regular plural (e.g., as *wugs* is given as the plural for *wug*).

13. This oversimplifies things somewhat, as there are other systematic differences between regular and irregular verbs that also led Pinker to adopt a rule-based model for the regular verbs (Pinker 1991).

CHAPTER 12

A VARIATIONIST PERSPECTIVE ON SECOND LANGUAGE ACQUISITION: PSYCHOLINGUISTIC CONCERNS

DENNIS R. PRESTON

ALTHOUGH there have been a few book-length attempts to show how the principally monolingual program of research known as "variationist" (or "Labovian") sociolinguistics may apply to SLA (e.g., Adamson 1988; Bayley 1991; Bayley and Preston 1996; Preston 1989; Tarone 1988; Young 1989), most of these have not dealt extensively with the psycholinguistic problem of variation, or, at least, with the "interface" problem between a psycholinguistically plausible account of variation and other claims concerning SLA. I believe that SLA proponents are correct in emphasizing the importance of plausible psycholinguistic accounts from any who want to enter the field, but I also believe that the major claims of variationists are, in fact, psycholinguistically plausible, however infrequently outlined.

Variationist work has focused on the correlation of social facts and linguistic forms, the influence of linguistic forms on one another, and the place of variation within the study of language change. I am aware of the fact that many see sociolinguistic work as completely focused on the first of these interests, but that is decidedly not the case. Here, however, I want to show how a plausible psycholinguistic account can be given for each of these three levels of interest and be integrated into a design of variation in SLA.[1]

LEVEL I

Although rare in variationist work, some studies have concerned themselves only with the correlation of linguistic form and social facts; I will call such studies "Level I." Of course, one may study the forms themselves with no reference whatsoever to sociocultural facts. It is only if one wants to study the *distribution* or *selection* of forms that he or she is lost without sociocultural guidance. Somebody may be going around saying that one cannot study grammatical forms at all without reference to sociocultural facts, and this must be the case, since Long (1998) complains about people who have accused SLA researchers and others who look at grammatical facts outside their sociocultural embedding of "sociolinguistic naiveté" (87–94); unfortunately, one might conclude from Long"s article that it is sociolinguists who have made this accusation. I can assure you that it is not sociolinguists from the variationist tradition I represent.

In a Level I variationist approach, sociocultural facts and linguistic forms are put in touch with each other. If one chooses to call that connection a psycholinguistic one, that is taking a broad view of psycholinguistics, and I am not opposed to it, but I want to be clear about the separateness (or "modularity") of the devices that are at stake here. Figure 12.1 (with apologies to Levelt 1989) shows what I have in mind.

After you know what you want to say and have "contextualized" it according to previous linguistic information (including your best-shot knowledge about interlocutor information, which is one of the factors that causes the "hedge" between the "information" and "sociocultural" components in Figure 12.1), you go to your "grammar" to choose those things that reveal what you intended to say (and its information organization). In many cases, there are two (or more) forms (that are not internally incompatible, no matter what view of grammar you take) available in competence. In Level I variationist studies, the choice between one or another of these forms is based on the sociocultural selection shown in Figure 12.1.

What sort of linguistic competence does Figure 12.1 suggest? I believe it accurately displays a linguistic (and I mean a strictly grammatical) competence which licenses two constructions in English. That licensing imposes no internal contradictions on the grammar, and, if by a "variable linguistic competence" one

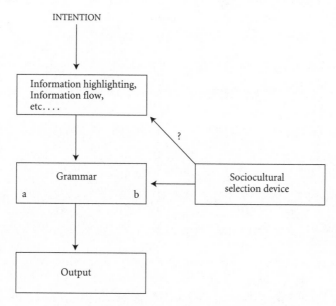

Fig. 12.1. A Level I psycholinguistic model of variation (Preston 2000)

means that two (or more) forms in the "same grammar" that can fulfill the same communicative task, then this model of Level I variation displays such a "variable linguistic competence," and I cannot think of any theoretical objections to it (except from those who might find it "uninteresting").

Figure 12.1 can be modified to take care of slightly more complex selection. Figure 12.2 shows a sociocultural selection device that has more than one grammar to select from.[2] This has to be true, or fluent speakers of two languages would not know how to use sociocultural facts in determining the appropriateness of one language or the other (and, of course, the sociocultural selection device may be divided in two to determine the sociocultural selection of forms when one is "completely within" one language or the other, as shown in Figure 12.1). Unfortunately, there has been some rather irresponsible speculation about where different grammars are necessary.

> Every human being speaks a variety of languages. We sometimes call them different styles or different dialects, but they are really different languages, and somehow we know when to use them, one in one place and another in another place. Now each of these languages involves a different switch setting. In the case of [different languages] it is a rather dramatically different switch setting, more so than in the case of the different styles of [one language]. (Chomsky 1988: 188)

Chomsky asserts that there is necessarily a different grammar every time there is a stylistic shift, but there is often no such requirement. No different switch settings (even of the less dramatic sort) are required for much variation (since

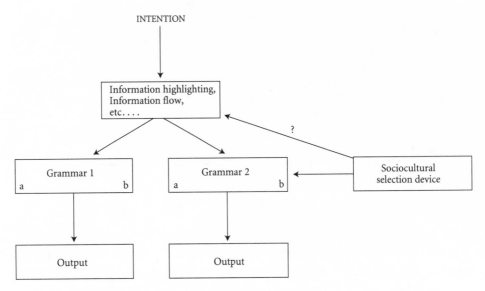

Fig. 12.2. A Level I psycholinguistic model of interlanguage variation (Preston 2000)

the choice may be between two options sanctioned by the same grammar). Of course, it is easy to imagine cases when Chomsky is exactly right. I can say "*Nobody came to my party*," but I am also a fluent speaker of the equivalent "*Didn"t nobody come to my party*." I am convinced that when I switch back and forth between those constructions that I am switching between two different grammars of English (using the same sort of sociocultural selection device represented in Figure 12.2 that I use when I switch between English and Polish). Of course I know that Chomsky knows that there is more grammatically at stake in multiple negation grammars than in an obviously single-grammar internal fact; I just wish he would say so and not make such claims as the one cited. When he does, he misleads his followers.

For example, Gregg flatly states that a "variable competence model is a rejection of the principles of generative grammar and of SLA theories based on generative theories of language" (1991: 367). Level I variable competence is no such thing. Speakers have two (or more) forms available in their linguistic competence (Figure 12.1) or competences (Figure 12.2), and another device (some sort of sociocultural one) tells them which to choose. Of course, there are more "devices" than sociocultural ones involved in those choices, but of that more later.

There is one more sophistication needed in Level I psycholinguistic representations. A selection device might be seen as one that peers into a grammar and chooses between one form or another, sometimes selecting one, sometimes another, and it might also be understood that that selection is based on the "knowledge" of an overall rate. That interpretation caused Bickerton (1971) to argue that such behavior requires a speaker to keep a tally of occurrences so that he or she may modify selection of one item or the other up or down to keep the proportion right. Even if this is a representation of nonconscious mechanisms at work (and surely it is), Bickerton imagines much too difficult a task. In a number of places (e.g., Preston 1989, 1991a, 1991b, 1991c, 1996a, 1996b) I have suggested that variation in general (and, in several of those, variation in SLA in particular) ought to be considered from the point of view of a probabilistic device, one applied *each time* a variant is selected.

For a two-way variable, a speaker (and I operate on a speaker- rather than hearer-focused model) is equipped with a coin, the two sides of which represent the options for that variable; it is flipped before the product appears. Since normal coins are fair, the one proposed here is as likely to turn up heads as tails (i.e., the two sides are in "free variation"), but, when I was a kid, we believed that unfair coins could be made. We thought that if you added weight to the tails side of a coin and flipped it, it was more likely to come up heads (and vice versa); the more weight you added to one side, the greater the probability it would come up on the other side. Although this theory may be physically suspect, we believed it as kids (and suspected kids who won a lot of money of knowing how to do it); let's also naively believe here that it is true so that we may make this coin responsive to various influences. A great deal of sociolinguistic research has shown that social factors influence the probability of "form selection"—the result of "unfair coin" tosses, and checks of the actual performance of individuals (where data are sufficient) have shown that such statistical modeling is accurate (e.g., Macaulay 1978).

Such a model is psycholinguistically plausible and, I believe, shows how Bickerton's objection to variability may be set aside. When respondents issue 20, 40, or 60 percent of one form of a variable, they are not monitoring their overall performance with some tallying device. They are providing evidence of the influence of a set of probabilistic weights that come to bear on each occurrence, a cognitively plausible (rather simple) operation. Note that, so far, the model I have proposed is also compatible with the claim that variation is the result of moving back and forth between alternative grammars (or "lects"), although Bickerton regards these fluctuations as due to unstudiable social factors. As much sociolinguistic work has shown, however, the influences of such social factors are not unstudiable at all.

Level II

In Level II sociolinguistic studies, variationists tease out the influence of one linguistic (not social) factor on another. Just as in Level I studies, the choice of alternatives is "guided," but a great deal of work has shown that linguistic facts are also guilty of influencing the choices—the specificity of subjects, morpheme boundaries, consonant clusters, and so on.

Level II studies seek reasons for such linguistic influences, just as Level I studies try to provide sociocultural explanations for why certain identities and relationships distinguish themselves linguistically. This search for influencing factors within (not outside) the components of a grammar characterizes Level II sociolinguistic research, and such work is not unusual; it is, in fact, the rule among sociolinguists. For example, the leading journal in the variationist enterprise, *Language Variation and Change*, volume 9 (1997), contained fifteen articles in all; two were Level I–only studies; six were Level II only; the remainder combined Level I and II observations. That is not surprising to me, for linguistic (not sociocultural) motives for variation are usually strongest. In an extensive review of the literature (Preston 1991a, 1991b), I found that linguistic influences were so much stronger than sociocultural ones that I formulated this relationship as the "Status Axiom" (by analogy with Bell"s 1984 "Style Axiom"). My observation suggests that variability determined by linguistic forces is available to lower level sociocultural (or "status") variability but that such linguistic influences are nearly always probabilistically heavier than sociocultural influences. Why would that be so? When some part of the sociocultural world (whether one that reflects identity or relationship) wants to symbolize itself linguistically, it does so by "creating" a preference for one form or another. Where will it find such alternative modes of expression? The sociocultural world itself is not prepared to provide the sort of variation described in Level II studies, for the sociocultural world is not made up of such things as passive versus unaccusative subjects, morpheme boundaries, or consonant clusters. If there are already options in the grammar, however, ones based primarily on accompanying linguistic forces, they may be reweighted by sociocultural ones to carry part of the burden of the presentation of identity and the manipulation of interactional stances. For most of their "lives," however, such variable elements will show that the strongest selection device is the earlier, linguistic one.

What sort of psycholinguistic device have we made for ourselves now? Figure 12.3 shows us two possibilities, both of which I suspect exist. In the first possibility, shown entirely inside Grammar 1, one "linguistic fact" ("c") has an influence on the selection of another ("a"). A second possibility is that the occurrence of one feature in the grammar (in this case, "c") refers to an "extragrammatical feature," "d" (e.g., information status).

When variationists seek to explain such internal grammatical variability in Level II studies, they seek for the same sorts of explanatory evidence general linguists do. They are, admittedly, less likely (perhaps, like old Occam and his razor, even reluctant) to believe that every such piece of variation requires a new grammar, suspecting, instead, that inherent variability exists where grammatical

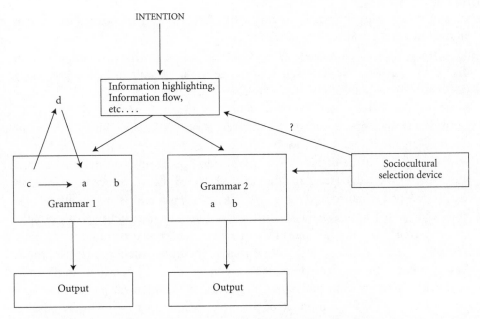

Fig. 12.3. A Level II psycholinguistic model (Preston 2000)

systems permit it (a question for grammatical theory itself) and that a 'different grammars' interpretation is a rather radical requirement.

The various linguistic features that have an influence on one another might belong to different modules of linguistic competence (or even lie outside competence), but I know of no serious theoretical proposal that suggests that these modules are not in communication with one another. In short, that we have not yet arrived at a more definitive theoretical proposal concerning the exact shape of linguistic competence (and its relation to modules outside it) will not hurt the model proposed here.

In summary, then, if we do not pay attention to the variation in language that is internal—that is, variation caused by other linguistic (not sociocultural) elements—we will miss the kinds of effects we have seen in such studies as we apply this paradigm to SLA.

LEVEL III

Finally we come to whatever it is sociolinguists could be doing at Level III; in fact, sociolinguists are particularly concerned with ongoing linguistic change, and they seek to relate patterns of linguistic change to both the sociocultural forces studied in Level I and the linguistic forces of Level II.

Variationists use the category "generation" or "age," but it is important to distinguish age as a social category from age as an attempt to look at emerging (and receding) linguistic practices (and, presumably, the grammars that underlie those practices). Teenagers use slang items that they will not use when they become adults; they are, therefore, not indicators of cutting-edge forms in the language. They are, instead, generationally distributed features, ones that indicate a speaker's age by virtue of his or her use but do not point us in the direction of the future of the language. It is often difficult to tell the difference between such age-related performance and actual change, but variationists have developed a number of tests that make the distinction less difficult to establish. For example, in many cases, the younger and older members of a speech community agree in being the most frequent users of a nonstandard feature, for they are the groups least influenced by the daily pressure of the linguistic marketplace to conform to more overt community norms (e.g., Chambers and Trudgill 1998: 78–79, who show such a distribution for a number of features, including -in versus -ing variation in English). That is, however, clearly not the case in a large number of cases. The youngest speakers are the principal users of emerging forms, and the oldest use them least, with the generations between balanced between them. Sociolinguists suspect this is an indication of linguistic change in progress.

Of course, all the work done in Level I and Level II studies should be done in Level III studies, as well as the "historical" interpretation (and its relation to the Level I and Level II factors). But I assume that you understand that it should be done and that grammatical or other cognitive interpretations of the effects are also a part of the variationists' obligation in such a study. If you grant that, on the basis of such suggestions given earlier, I will move on.

What has Level III work done to the psycholinguistic model? I am afraid that, since it addresses linguistic features that are coming in and going out, it will introduce an element not to everybody's liking. Figure 12.4 shows a shaded area in Grammar 1, while all of Grammar 2 is shaded differently. Those shadings represent "weaker" areas of the grammar (in one grammar) or weaker grammars (when two are present). What is the source of grammatical "weakness"? Gregg (1991) and Chomsky surely believe that the elements of linguistic competence are either "there" or "not there." How might they be "less there"?

From a sociolinguistic perspective, I believe one approach to this difficulty is to note that native speakers typically learn a "vernacular"—the first-learned form of their language. Needless to say, it is shaped on the basis of interaction with parents, siblings, and other children in contexts that are relatively free from formal constructions. Whatever else we learn (whether native or nonnative, in fact) is postvernacular, and it will not, no matter how good we get at it, have the deeply

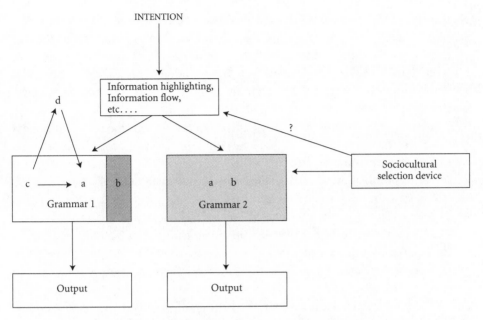

Fig. 12.4. A Level III psycholinguistic model (Preston 2000)

embedded status of our vernacular. The result is that we will not be as "fluent" in our postvernacular. Consider the following:

(a) If I had more money, I'd buy a BMW.
(b) Had I more money, I'd buy a BMW.

In my case, (a) belongs to my vernacular. If I want to express the idea contained in (a) and (b) (which I take to be the same), I will with the greatest of ease go to my vernacularly embedded choice—namely (a). I don't know when I learned (b), certainly not while growing up in Southern Indiana, but I eventually learned it, first, no doubt to process it and later to produce it, although I am fairly certain that my production is still "imitative," rather than productive. That is, I cannot imagine any circumstance in which I would use it (spoken or written) except to imitate (probably sarcastically) a high-falutin' style (or, more likely, to mock such a speaker). More important, I also have no doubt that you could find some weaknesses in my grammaticality judgments of sentences constructed along the lines of (b), but that you would find me rock-solid in the (a) territory.

This outrageous claim means, of course, that any real speaker who could hope to be an ideal native speaker-hearer for the moment (with the sorts of judgments we would want to elicit when we attempt to confirm claims about competence) would have to be one questioned about the linguistic competence of his or her pre-postvernacular period (i.e., about his or her vernacular). The further afield (or "later learned") any postvernacular constructions are from the grammatical settings of the vernacular, the weaker the grammar at those points and the less reliable respondent judgments about that territory will be (exactly as we have discovered in SLA "incompleteness" or "fossilization" studies, e.g., Coppieters 1987; Johnson and Newport 1989). Doubtless, those judgments reflect facts about performance.

When we refer to adult grammars, therefore, we refer inevitably to grammars that look like Grammar 1 in Figure 12.4—grammars that have postvernacular areas in which the constructions are "there" in competence but "weaker." In short, adult learners of their own language encounter syntactic (and other) characteristics that they learn in no substantially different way than the second or foreign language learner learns things (the shaded area of Grammar 2 in Figure 12.4), and I have no reason to assume that they end up embedded in the underlying grammars in any significantly different way.

At a different level of representation, the notions of strength outlined earlier seem to me to relate to the mysterious factor that lurks behind what has been called "style" in general throughout the history of quantitative sociolinguistics. Perhaps the major psycholinguistic upshot of such factors is, as Labov has suggested (e.g., 1972), "monitoring" or "attention to speech." Although "style" is, I suspect, a cover term for a much larger number of sociocultural functions that need to be teased out in greater detail, the psycholinguistic upshot of some items being sought by more careful monitoring may be conveniently related to the notion of the postvernacular. One must look more carefully for such items, and even such a "search" will not insure that they will be retrieved (or retrieved "correctly"). That fact suggests that the model provided so far, although based on "internal" and "external" factors that are required for a general psycholinguistic account of competence and performance, overlooks the component that contains the abilities most often addressed in psycholinguistic accounts—memory, accessibility, processing, and the like.[3] Figure 12.5 repairs that oversight, admittedly without detail.

AN ELABORATED PSYCHOLINGUISTIC MODEL

SLA researchers have paid a great deal more attention to what makes parts of a grammar weak, for they are interested in rather rapid linguistic change (although I believe it would surprise many to look at variationist results over the years that

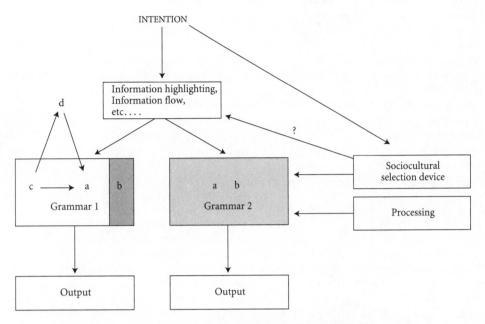

Fig. 12.5. An elaborated Level III psycholinguistic model (Preston 2000)

report ongoing change in a much more reduced time frame than one might have assumed after taking an introductory course in, say, the History of English). I will try to establish the relationship between the psycholinguistically viable picture of language variation I have provided so far (hoping to provide more evidence for what I have called 'grammatical weakness') and the more comprehensive view of psycholinguistic factors taken by SLA practitioners. Figure 12.6 shows one such SLA attempt.

I cannot provide the detail for all the components shown in Figure 12.6, but I believe (in terms I have already suggested) that the box called "THE FIRST LANGUAGE" represents my "Grammar" (as in, e.g., Figure 12.1) or "Grammar 1" (e.g., as in Figure 12.2). The entire diagram appears to represent a second or foreign language (e.g., what might be represented by "Grammar 2" in Figure 12.2). It has components from "THE FIRST LANGUAGE" and from "UNIVERSAL GRAMMAR" (from the latter, both directly and mediated by "THE FIRST LANGUAGE"), but it is also based on long- and short-term "memories," the first divided into a "Declarative" and a "Procedural," the homes of relatively "monitored" (though clearly not "conscious") representations and "automatic" ones, respectively.

Although a "dwelling place" for grammatical representations in the second language is not shown here, I assume that, from another perspective, it might be drawn in a "box" just like that provided for the first language. Since the authors want to show how grammatical representations "get there," that oversight is perhaps not serious, although first language acquisition scholars may be surprised to

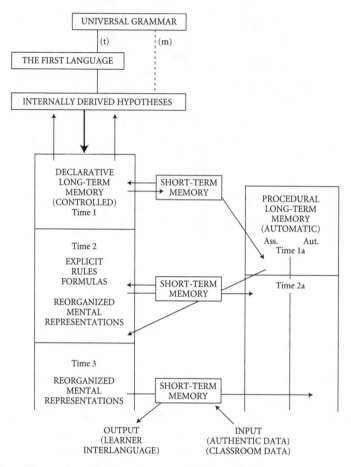

Fig. 12.6. An elaborated psycholinguistic model of SLA (Towell and Hawkins 1994: 249)

learn that "UNIVERSAL GRAMMAR" is the only input into "THE FIRST LAN-
GUAGE." For example, children learning some varieties of British (as opposed to
American) English need to learn that the main verb 'have' patterns like 'be,' not
like most other verbs; that is, they must learn to say "Has he a dollar?" (not "Does
he have a dollar?"). "Input," not UG, determines this distinction, which, by the
way, is a sort of "language variation" that does not, in my opinion, require a
"different grammar," since the "grammars" for 'be' and 'other verbs' are available
in both varieties, but that argument, essentially a minimalist one, is given in
greater detail in Preston (2000).

     In general, however, since the emphasis is on SLA, one might be inclined to
overlook a representation that suggested that "THE FIRST LANGUAGE" was a fixed
star, unless, of course, one dealt with language variation and assumed that a great
deal of "monolingual" variation is surely due to forces (and I mean psycholinguistic ones) very much like those shown here for SLA. I suggest, therefore, that

a great deal of first language variation, perhaps particularly that which is sensitive to the "stylistic continuum" (the variation from most casual to most formal) is the result of variation "imposed" by the "weaker" access speakers have to the postvernacular constructions they have learned.

I notice, for example, that the sentences of the generative enterprise that are neither "starred" (indicating ungrammatical sentences) nor "nonstarred" (indicating grammatical ones) are often those which involve what for many speakers could be characterized as postvernacular constructions. Choosing at random from current theoretical work in syntax, for example, I find the following sentence:

??John took advantage of Bill, who Mary did as well (Lasnik 1999: 172)

It is marked with a ?? to indicate that the researcher is not sure of the grammatical status of the sentence. Notice that the more vernacular the sentence is made, the more grammatical it becomes. For example:

?John took advantage of Bill, who Mary did too

Although it does not affect the grammatical point being considered here at all, I like this much better (and, of course, everybody likes "John took advantage of Bill, and Mary did too," but, from one point of view at least, that would be unfair to the syntacticians who care about the construction, not alternative ways of "saying the same thing").

I am sure that 'as well' is not as deeply embedded (or accessible") as 'too,' and I am also certain that subordinate constructions ('who'-clauses) are not as "vernacular" as paratactic 'and' constructions. In short, although I believe I have moved both of these constructions to my procedural side, I certainly have not put "Had I . . ." or "Lest I . . ." constructions there, and I see no reason to distinguish between that postvernacular first language acquisition fact and many SLA facts (including even influence from the so-called first language, since I would count such influence from my vernacular as just that as I went about acquiring my postvernacular).

Let me offer some recent work in the acquisition of Japanese English loanword phonology (by native speakers of English) to display what I take to be a reasonable trip through the mechanisms I have suggested. For example, monosyllabic words of CVC syllable structure with a lax vowel are systematically realized with gemination of the coda consonant (e.g., *cat* [kyatto]). Motivation for this is straightforward and derives from the differences in coda types in English and Japanese.

Japanese	*English*
Japanese	English
μ	μ
|/		
Obs	Obs

Codas in Japanese license obstruents only if they are doubly linked, as they are in gemination (Itô 1986), but English has no such requirement. Although native speakers of Japanese invariably produce, for example, *putto* for *put*, they could produce **puto*, a two-syllable form that obeys the phonological structure of Japanese and includes all the elements of the English input. What they prefer, however, is the form that recognizes the coda status of the English consonant and allows it to be incorporated as such into Japanese structure (through gemination). They prefer that realization over one that would, although faithful to Japanese structure, realize the consonant only as an onset in the syllable produced by the epenthetic final vowel (Broselow and Park 1995: 1167).

Yamagata and Preston (1999) studied the degree to which native speakers of English (students of Japanese) were successful in acquiring this rule (by asking them to provide a *katakana* spelling representation of the word). The items presented were *tap, cot, put, tick, peck, sup* (and a native speaker control group geminated the consonants of these test words, which, as best as we could determine, have not been borrowed into Japanese, at the .99 rate, nearly categorical, as shown in Table 12.1). Since Japanese native speaker performance in this area is nearly categorical, we did not build that variation into the representation of learner variation. Table 12.2 shows the results (for significant factors only) of a logistic regression analysis of the performance of native speakers of English in their first, second, third, and fourth year of study of Japanese in several U.S. universities.[4]

The first notable fact in these data is that speakers "improve" from first, to second, to third and fourth year. In variationist terms, such an "apparent time" study suggests that "change" is going on, and that that change is in the direction of the target-language norm (a Level III study). The statistical program, however, noted a much stronger "linguistic" influence on the selection of geminates by

Table 12.1. Gemination of monosyllables by native
speakers (Yamagata and Preston 1999)

Item	No. geminated	Percent geminated
tap (*n* = 101)	101	1.00
cot (*n* = 101)	100	.99
put (*n* = 101)	100	.99
tick (*n* = 101)	100	.99
peck (*n* = 101)	100	.99
sup (*n* = 99)	95	.96
Total (*n* = 604)	596	.99

Table 12.2. Frequency, percentage, and weight of gemination in monosyllables among nonnative speakers (Yamagata and Preston 1999)

Group	N	No. geminated	Percent geminated	Weight
Level				
1st year	217	27	.12	.25
2nd year	201	55	.27	.47
3rd and 4th years	286	142	.50	.72
Vowel length				
Short	588	220	.37	.62
Long	112	4	.03	.08
Total/Input	704	224	.32	.25

Total chi-square = 8.41; chi-square per cell = 1.40; fit: chi-square = 5.47, P = 0.15, ns

these speakers—whether or not the test word had been represented with a long vowel. Table 12.3 shows that long vowels were never represented by native speakers, but learners used this strategy in representing this word between 13 and 19 percent of the time. More importantly, however, as Table 12.2 shows, when learners did select long vowels, they almost never geminated (as the extremely low .08 probability shows in Table 12.2). This Level II result (the "selection" of one linguistic fact—gemination—by another, vowel length) may be seen as a more powerful constraint on gemination (than the gain made by more advanced students) by simply subtracting the highest and lowest probabilities in the two groups of independent variables. For years-of-study groups the range is 47 (.72–.25) but for vowel length the range is 54 (.62–.08), confirming that the linguistic variable is an even more powerful one than the developmental one (as suggested earlier and in Preston 1991a, 1991b).

Table 12.3 shows an even more peculiar aspect of these data. Although native speakers never use the long vowel strategy in realizing such loan words (e.g., *kyaato* for "cat"), it is not only a fairly frequent strategy for English speakers but one that does not improve with study. In fact, the .19 rate is the same for first- and fourth-year students. Although these learners of Japanese get more target-like in their use of gemination, they do not give up the nonnativelike use of long vowels to represent these words, although they rarely combine the vowel-lengthening and gemination strategies.

How can we place these findings in a psycholinguistically feasible sociolinguistics? First, let us note native language "sources" for whatever grammars are involved here.

Table 12.3. Frequency and percentage of long vowels in monosyllables (and the number that co-occur with gemination) (Yamagata and Preston 1999)

Long vowels	Native speakers	4th year	3rd year	2nd year	1st year
Frequency	0	24	21	30	41
Percentage	0	.19	.13	.15	.19
Co-occurrence	0	1	1	0	2
Total	604	124	162	201	217

Gemination—Japanese (English gemination is "accidental," e.g., 'hot time')
Long and short vowels—Japanese and English (although distributed differently)

Therefore, in my terms, the "Grammar 2" of these English learners takes some of its shape ("no gemination") from their "Grammar 1" (English). This is very clearly one of the "INTERNALLY DERIVED HYPOTHESES" of Figure 12.6. This declines over time, and third- and fourth-year students geminate at a rate much closer to that of native speakers, but it should be clear that the interlanguage grammar of these learners ("Grammar 2") contains a "geminate" and "don't geminate" potential, and, as I have suggested, I believe it would be uneconomical to suggest that realization and nonrealization of a geminate involves two different grammars. Since the "don't geminate" stipulation comes from L1, it reflects, in terms of Figure 12.6, automatic processes that are likely to "win" until such time as the input data have established a competing automatic (long-term) memory alternative ("do geminate"). In short, the "weakness" of Grammar 2 can be specifically related to the type of "retrieval" mechanisms at work.

I suppose that, in an epistemological sense, one might want to say that the weakness lies not in the grammar(s). The "facts" (the licensing of constructions and the grammatical configurations borne by the lexical items that enter into their combinations) are either there or not there, but to regard the inherent variability within, as well as among, these grammars (conditioned by linguistic as well as social factors) as irrelevant to the SLA process (or to the grammatical status of the vernacular and postvernacular competence of a real speaker, whether multilingual or not) fails to deal with both the facts of the data themselves and the most parsimonious account of them.

Readers who are interested in Level I variationist studies may have been disappointed so far by the account of the acquisition of English loanwords in Japanese by native speakers of English, for, although Level III was nicely represented by the apparent time construct based on years of study and a strong linguistic influence was shown (Level II), no social facts emerged. Of course, the study of classroom-learned languages may indeed be less open to the research sociolinguists are most comfortable with (in the wilds of the speech community), but, as Table 12.4 shows, social facts are not irrelevant here. When we turn to slightly more complex gemination in bi- and trisyllabic words, although native speakers again behave almost categorically, geminating the final consonant in such words as "trinket" and "dyspeptic," we see that learners are again considerably more variable. Although the class level variable is very much like that for the monosyllables (and although there is linguistic differentiation among the items themselves, which I will not discuss here), it is also the case that male respondents behaved significantly more native-speaker like than females (.58 as opposed to .38).

Of course, I would not want to leave Level I enthusiasts hanging. I believe we understand why men may outperform women in general in university-level Japanese courses. Japanese is a "hard" language, and it apparently does not attract male participants who would be most influenced by the well-recognized peer pressure for covertly prestigious behavior that many young males carry over into even their college years. Pronunciation (which this study touches on) is a particularly face-threatening behavior in foreign language classes, for it makes the per-

Table 12.4. Frequency, percentage, and weight of gemination in bi- and trisyllabics among nonnative speakers (Yamagata and Preston 1999)

Group	N	No. geminated	Percent geminated	Weight
Level				
1st year	142	8	.06	.25
2nd year	131	22	.17	.49
3rd and 4th years	187	58	.31	.71
Sex				
Male	281	68	.24	.58
Female	179	20	.11	.37
Item				
terrific	116	25	.22	.55
trinket	116	31	.27	.63
stupid	116	13	.11	.35
dyspeptic	112	19	.17	.47
Total/Input	460	88	.19	.15

Total chi-square = 6.45; chi-square per cell = 0.27; fit: chi-square = 6.92 (18 df), p = 0.96, ns

former look "foolish." Young women apparently can gain prestige from overtly prestigious linguistic behavior (this assertion is based on any number of models of gender-related sociolinguistic research, e.g., Lakoff 1975; Trudgill 1972), but young men in typically "easy"[5] foreign language classes are well known for their strong overlay of native-language phonology in their oral performances, a direct appeal to the covertly prestigious "anti-intellectual" identity such performance allows.

I hope, however, to have persuaded you that a variationist approach to SLA is not only a productive one (as I believe has already been shown in the large number of studies, many cited here) but also one that has considerable psycho-linguistic plausibility. More important, I hope to have shown that the variationist approach's sensitivity to multiple influences (from within and without) actually contributes to a more plausible psycholinguistic account of SLA (as well as variation in monolingual settings) than those that attempt "unified accounts," ones that fly flatly in the face of the data of performance, as well as our current best guess of the shape of competence.

NOTES

1. I have covered this "preliminary" territory more fully in Preston (2000).

2. Of course, I know that these two grammars may have "overlapping" territory (and that that is a very important factor in bilingual grammars), but, for simplicity of representation, I do not show that fact here.

3. I am grateful to Richard Young, who pointed out both the deterministic nature of variable rule probabilities and the failure of the model (through Figure 12.5) to engage such "real" psycholinguistic factors as memory, attention, access, processing, and the like. Both these objections are addressed in Figure 12.6, the first, diminished, I hope, by the connection between "intention" and the "sociocultural selection device" and the second at least represented by the introduction of a "processing" component. I am also grateful to Dan Douglas and Jeanette Gundel, whose questions after the oral presentation of this paper at SLRF made me elaborate parts of this considerably.

4. GoldVarb, the statistical program used here, is a version of logistic regression that includes identification of significant groups by a step-up step-down regression procedure and a combination of insignificantly different groups within a single group by the comparison of log-likelihood scores in different runs of the data (which allowed conflation of the third and fourth years, for example, in these data). The "weights" show the probability of the dependent variable's occurrence under the independent (i.e., non-interactive) influence of the specific factor under consideration. Here, for example, first-year students realize monosyllabic gemination with a probability of only .25 compared to third- and fourth-year students' .72. Generally speaking, probabilities over .50 are "promoters" of the rule, and those under .50 are "demoters"; here, the rule is construed as "gemination." The "input" is the overall probability, or the degree to which this rule

would "work" if the independent variables were not teased out. The overall insignificant chi-square ensures that the independent variables do not themselves interact. Preston (1989: 14–18) discusses the operation of this statistical program, and Young and Bayley (1996) outline procedures for using it.

5. Of course, the language selected for "easy" fulfillment of any foreign language requirement is Spanish, but, like all linguists, I know that it is not "easy." I report here only widely held folk belief (which, of course, has had a powerful influence on enrollment patterns).

CHAPTER 13

SOCIAL PSYCHOLOGICAL PERSPECTIVE ON SECOND LANGUAGE ACQUISITION

ROBERT C. GARDNER

THE basic premise underlying the social psychological perspective of second language acquisition[1] is that language is a major defining attribute of a group of people, and, thus, to learn a language involves some degree of identification with the group that speaks it. That is, the language is more than a symbolic system that facilitates communication. Language is a defining behavioral feature of a cultural group, and thus acquiring the language involves taking on patterns of behavior of that group. As a consequence, an individual's attitudes toward that group and toward other cultural groups in general will influence his or her motivation to learn the language, and thus the degree of proficiency attained.

A related issue that must be considered from this perspective is what constitutes learning a language. As initially formulated, the social psychological perspective viewed second language learning in terms of bilingual skill (and that is the stance adopted here). Taking a few courses or being able to make oneself understood in the language in a halting fashion was not the criterion. The criterion was the development of a free-flowing and automatic use of the language comparable to that of native speakers. Thus, the social psychological perspective is concerned with the development of bilingualism, not the achievement of an A grade in the course or a high mark on a test. These might represent stages along the way to the development of bilingual skill, but they are not the ultimate goals in the social psychological perspective. Having said this, however, it must be confessed that much, if not all, of the research in this field has used grades in courses, scores on tests, ratings of oral proficiency, and so on as criteria, and it is a testament to the validity of the social psychological perspective that it is able even to explain proficiency defined in terms of these types of criteria.

Prior to the 1950s, the main determinants of success in learning a second language were thought to be intelligence and language aptitude. In his review of research on bilingualism, however, Arsenian (1945) devoted a section to the social psychology of language and bilingualism, in which he raised questions about the relation between language and acculturation, the role of affective factors in second language acquisition, intergroup relations and language learning, and so on. Then, in the lead article of the inaugural issue of *Language Learning,* Marckwardt (1948/ 1988) identified five motives that were influential in promoting the acquisition of another language. He described three of them as practical (assimilation of an ethnic minority, promotion of trade, and scientific utility), and two as nonutilitarian (self-cultural development and the maintenance of ethnic identity of a minority group). Later, Nida (1956) reported a case study of a missionary who was unable to learn the language of the group with which he was to work. He noted that the individual, who was the son of immigrant parents, had identified strongly with English-speaking America. Nida claimed that this extreme identification and an emotional block against anything 'foreign' interfered with his being able to learn another language. The social psychological perspective of second language acquisition grew out of this background.

Lambert's Early Work

The initial empirical studies with a social psychological perspective were conducted by Lambert (1955, 1956a, 1956b, 1956c). His research was concerned with the assessment of bilingual dominance and the development of bilingualism. He investigated developmental changes in French and English among students differing in terms of language training—undergraduate students majoring in French, graduate students majoring in French, and native French speakers who had lived in an English-speaking country for an average of seven years. Two of his observations are noteworthy here (Lambert 1955). One was that two of the graduate students measured dominant in French. In both cases, these students could be described as particularly motivated—one because of her career as a French teacher, and the other because of his extreme identification with France. We can note here the foundation of the integrative and instrumental dichotomy that still pervades much of the research in this field today.

The second observation was that the developmental changes in second language acquisition appeared to involve at least two plateaus. Lambert (1956c) described the first plateau as reflecting a "vocabulary" cluster because those measures that involved vocabulary strength distinguished the undergraduate students from the other two groups. He defined the second plateau as reflecting a "cultural" cluster because these measures differentiated the undergraduate and graduate groups from the native speakers and involved such features as habitual word order and stereotypy of response. He proposed, therefore, that second language acquisition entails a series of barriers to overcome, with the vocabulary barrier being the easiest and the cultural barrier the most difficult. Although he did not discuss other barriers, it is possible to conceptualize a number of phases through which an individual must pass before he or she can be said to be a truly proficient user of a language. In this sense, the true acquisition of a second language can be seen to involve the development of expert performance in that language.

Expert Performance

Conceptualizing second language acquisition in terms of the development of expert performance has important implications. Ericsson, Krampe, and Tesch-Römer (1993) reviewed the literature on expert performance in many facets of human behavior and concluded that it is not dependent primarily on innate talent or ability, as is commonly believed. They reviewed many studies on such diverse topics as typing speed, artistic prowess, and chess mastery and found that expert performance results from repeated practice (i.e., from consistent and persistent motivated behavior). They concluded that it requires approximately ten years of sustained practice to develop expertise and noted (p. 366) that it takes about this long to acquire the vocabulary of a normal adult. If, therefore, we view second language acquisition as equivalent to the development of expert behavior, it follows that the motivation to learn the second language must be long-standing. From the social psychological perspective, learning a second language means the acquisition of near-native facility with the content and structure of the language and near-automaticity in its use both conceptually and behaviorally. This takes time and dedicated effort for an adult to achieve! Thus, when we speak of motivation to learn a second language, we are not speaking about some transient motivation but, instead, a long-term commitment to the task (with the associated effort, desire, and affective satisfaction).

Second Language Acquisition from the Social Psychological Perspective

The first investigation of individual differences in second language acquisition from the social psychological perspective was conducted by Gardner and Lambert (1959). They studied high school students learning French as a second language in Montreal and found that two factors were associated with achievement in French. One was aptitude; the other was motivation. They concluded that the motivation was *"characterized by a willingness to be like valued members of the language community"* (p. 271 [italics in the original]). Since then, there have been numerous studies of the relation between attitudes and motivation and achievement (e.g., Gardner 1985; Gardner and Lambert 1972). Clément and Gardner (2001) present a graph, based on an unpublished survey[2] of three databases (*PsycLit, ERIC,* and *Linguistics and Language Behavior Abstracts*), of the number of investigations published between 1985 and 1994 that dealt with individual difference variables in second language acquisition. In this ten-year period, 496 studies dealt with attitudes and 218 with motivation. Obviously, some articles referred to both attributes, and not all of them referred just to attitudes directly related to the social psychological perspective, but it is clear that there has been an active interest in the field.

The initial social psychological model was outlined by Lambert (1967, 1974), who proposed that aptitude, attitudes, orientation, and motivation promote the development of bilingual proficiency and that this can have an effect on one's self-identity. Lambert (1974) distinguished between two types of bilingualism, additive and subtractive, that reflect the effect of second language acquisition on self-identity and linked them to different language contexts. Additive bilingualism was seen to apply to members of the majority who learn the language of a minority, who do not lose any of their own ethnic identity but develop proficiency in the other language. Subtractive bilingualism, on the other hand, is more characteristic of minority group members who, in learning the language of the majority, run the risk of losing some of their own cultural identity.

Since then, there have been a number of models proposed, each of them changing the focus slightly and adding and subtracting elements. Gardner and Smythe (1975) proposed a model that retained the elements of Lambert's social psychological model but expanded it to take into account the language learning situation, distinguishing between formal and informal language learning contexts. This model, now referred to as the socioeducational model, has evolved since then (Gardner 1985, 2000) and has become much more formal, operationalizing the concepts in terms of measures of specific attributes. Currently, it focuses on six latent constructs: language aptitude, attitudes toward the learning situation, integrativeness, motivation, language anxiety, and language achievement (characterized in terms of linguistic and non-linguistic outcomes), though language anxiety plays a minor role in the theoretical model. Gardner and Smythe also developed and standardized the Attitude/Motivation Test Battery [AMTB], which assesses the eleven variables in their model. The concept of the integrative motive is hypothesized to comprise the three constructs: attitudes toward the learning situation, integrativeness, and motivation; it can be assessed by aggregating scores on eight of the variables assessed by the AMTB. A measure of instrumental orientation is included in the measures but is not a construct emphasized in the model. With the exception of attitudes toward the learning situation and language anxiety, this model shares constructs with Lambert's model, and, though self-identity is not explicitly identified in it, the concept of integrativeness involves the willingness to identify with the other language community.

A third model in this tradition is the social context model (Clément 1980). It has many constructs that are similar to those in Gardner's model, with the exception of attitudes toward the learning situation, but sometimes conceptualizes and measures them differently. A major feature of this model is that it focuses on the linguistic nature of the community, distinguishing between unicultural and multicultural communities. Moreover, it contains additional constructs such as fear of assimilation, contact with the language (which is influenced in part by the linguistic nature of the community), and self-confidence with the language. Later developments (Clément, Dörnyei, and Noels 1994) added appraisal of the classroom environment (similar conceptually to attitudes toward the learning situation in the socioeducational model but not considered by them to be part of integrative motivation).

A fourth model was proposed by Dörnyei (1994) to place more emphasis on an educational perspective of motivation and formally including both integrative and instrumental motivational subsystems. This model identifies three components of motivation, distinguishing among the language level, the learner level, and the learning situation level, and compromising seventeen constructs, some of which involve more than one measure. Many of the constructs associated with the latter level are different from those proposed in the preceding models, but those in the first two levels are comparable to those in at least one of the Lambert, Gardner, or Clément models.

There are other models that could be discussed but these four are most representative of the social psychological perspective because each involves the concept of motivation, identification with the other cultural community, and the development of near-native proficiency. MacIntyre, Clément, Dörnyei, and Noels (1998) have proposed a formal model that comprises six levels, with "communication behavior" at the top and "social and individual context" at the bottom. Twelve major constructs, many assessed by more than one measure, form the elements of these levels, but the major criterion is the willingness to communicate in the second language, not second language achievement. One thing that is obvious from these five models is that each time a new model is proposed, it is more complex than its predecessor in that it encompasses more variables. This is valuable in that it focuses attention on more variables that might be important, but it has drawbacks, too, in that with greater complexity comes less parsimony, making empirical verification more difficult.

CURRENT RESEARCH ISSUES

Currently, this is a very active research field, with many different issues under consideration. First, there is some controversy as to whether this approach is the only one that applies to second language learning. A call for a new approach to the investigation of motivation was made by Crookes and Schmidt (1991), and this was augmented by a lively exchange in the 1994/1995 issues of the *Modern Language Journal*. There have been a number of models and approaches proposed since then, but each of them seem to be more focused on classroom performance than on the development of bilingual skill.

Second, there is some disagreement about which is the more important for second language acquisition, integrative or instrumental orientations, and/or whether there are other forms of orientation (e. g., Clément and Kruidenier 1983). This can be linked to a third issue, namely the distinction between foreign and second language environments. For example, Oxford (1996b) proposes that a foreign language is typically learned in an environment where the language is seldom used or experienced, while a second language is learned in a setting where that language is typically used by the majority of individuals for everyday communication. This distinction has been made by many others, and it has even been suggested that the motivations of individuals in the two different environments would be quite different. Thus, Dörnyei (1990) proposes that instrumental motivation may be more important for foreign language learners than for second language learners, for whom integrative motivation may be the more influential. This is a compelling hypothesis, and it is certainly reasonable to assume that the language context influences the dynamics of language acquisition (cf. Clément 1980); however, it is unwise to tie this distinction to the labels "foreign" and "second language" acquisition. Instead, it should be associated with an analysis of the ethnolinguistic vitality of the language in the community in terms of the relevant demographics (Giles, Bourhis, and Taylor 1977). Simply using the label "foreign" and "second language" as indicators of this vitality can be very misleading. For example, French and English are both considered second languages in Canada, but this is simply because they are the official languages. Some parts of Canada are relatively French/English bilingual, but many are not. For example, according to the 1996 Canada census, only 12 percent of the population in the province of Ontario knows French. Interestingly, this is where much of the research by Gardner has been conducted, and his research is often referred to by others as demonstrating why integrative motivation is important for the learning of a second language. Sometimes the added meaning associated with foreign and second language simply does not apply. Thus, based on these types of numbers, much of Gardner's research would be characterized as taking place in a foreign language environment.

A fourth issue concerns the role of the classroom in motivation. One way of considering this issue from the social psychological perspective is to distinguish between trait motivation, as an ongoing relatively stable attribute, and state motivation, which is viewed as less stable and more susceptible to environmental characteristics (cf. Boekaerts 1986). Since the social psychological perspective focuses on the development of bilingual skill, the motivational attributes are viewed as relatively long-lasting. Those models that focus attention on motivation generated in the classroom (see, e.g., Williams and Burden 1997) are concerned with more situationally relevant elements of motivation. It is true that they might endure for the length of the course, and perhaps beyond, but the focus in the models and associated research is the effect of the classroom environment. Thus, this type of approach seems to have more implications for state motivation in the immediate situation, with longer range implications later on. Whether or not continued high levels of state motivation would eventuate in changes in trait motivation is an open empirical question.

FUTURE DIRECTIONS

There are many likely directions that this field might take in the future. Rather than speculate on what they might be, I propose here what I consider to be five profitable next steps. First, I see great value in a series of meta-analyses focusing attention on attributes believed to be important from the social psychological perspective. For example, it would be valuable to summarize all the findings with respect to the integrative and instrumental orientations, and other orientations, and to study how these orientations relate to various measures of language achievement. I suspect that there are enough studies so that one might assess not only whether the orientations differ in terms of their predictability of achievement but whether predictability differs depending on the measure of achievement (e.g., oral proficiency, vocabulary knowledge, grades), the sociocultural setting, the language under investigation, and so on. Moreover, it would be valuable to assess what the general level of predictability is so that one could characterize the effects as weak, medium, or strong, in the sense that Cohen (1988) uses the terms. Of course, comparable studies could be done focusing on motivation, or integrativeness, or attitudes toward the learning situation, or self-confidence, or instrumental motivation. Again, to the extent that there are enough studies in sufficiently different contexts, this type of research could put more of an empirical face on discussions concerning the role of context in second language learning, as in the relative roles of integrative and instrumental orientations discussed earlier.

A second new direction that could be valuable is the use of laboratory studies to test, in analogue settings where greater control is possible, hypotheses associated with the different models. It is doubtful whether conclusive studies could ever be done that pit one model against another, but it should be possible to test some hypotheses in laboratory settings that cannot be done easily in classroom contexts. For example, Gardner and MacIntyre (1991) conducted one study in which they contrasted integrative and instrumental motivation where students learned a series of English-French pairs of words. That study showed that both forms of motivation facilitated the learning of the pairs and that the effect of instrumental motivation was greater than that for integrative motivation. It was also demonstrated, however, that, once the basis of the instrumental motivation no longer applied, the "instrumentally motivated" students simply stopped trying, while those who were integratively motivated maintained their level of motivation to the end of the experiment. That is, an instrumental motive may not be as long-lasting as an integrative motive.

A third new direction that has great potential is the investigation of immigrants who acquire the language of the host community. There are a number of interesting possibilities here. For example, one barrier facing the immigrant is the need to adapt to the new cultural setting. Clearly, there are both instrumental and integrative reasons for learning the new language, but there is also a very definite need to adapt to the cultural setting. Research has indicated that adjustment defined in terms of life satisfaction, stress, and so on is related to competence, or at least perceived competence, in the host language (Masgoret and Gardner 1999; Noels, Pon, and Clément 1996). It is arguable, however, whether language competence promotes adjustment (Noels, Pon, and Clément 1996), whether adjustment promotes language competence, or whether both are influenced by other factors, such as the mode of acculturation (Masgoret and Gardner 1999).

A fourth potentially profitable direction, and one that is rather broad in scope, would be to direct attention to environmental factors that influence second language acquisition. This emphasis on environmental factors could include such characteristics of the cultural milieu as the ethnolinguistic vitality of the language (Giles, Bourhis, and Taylor 1977) and the perceived value of second language acquisition in the community. On the other hand, it could refer to the immediate home environment. Or it could refer to characteristics in the language classroom (Williams and Burden 1997). Each of these environmental factors could have an influence on the dynamics of the language learning process in different ways. Characteristics of the cultural milieu can affect the opportunities to use and experience the language, as well as to know and have personal experiences with members of the other language community. Home background characteristics provide the foundation for many affective reactions that the student brings to the classroom and to the whole experience of learning and using the second language. The classroom environment provides organized instruction in the language and motivationally relevant experiences that are specific to the situation (i.e., state motivation) that also might have effects on the more traitlike attributes that are referred to in social psychological models of second language acquisition.

The fifth direction involves the need for further research to assess the validity of the various models that have been, and are continuing to be, proposed. There is some research that has been done, of course, that is relevant to the different models but, as Crookes and Schmidt (1991) point out, much of the research has been conducted from the point of view of the socioeducational model. The various models do not make predictions that are in disagreement, so to some extent the results of many studies can be seen to apply to all the models. However, it is necessary to obtain more information that makes use of measures that are specific to the various models. It is unlikely that discrepant results will be obtained, but clarifying the role of these other variables would be an important advance. To elaborate, a study by Tremblay and Gardner (1995) included measures of attributions and goal salience, along with many of the measures generally used in the context of the socioeducational model. The results indicated how these variables could be incorporated into the model, but there was no indication that they appreciably improved prediction of measures of achievement.

As can be seen, this is an active area of research with great potential. The future looks bright, but continued research focusing on empirical findings to support or clarify theoretical models and hypotheses represents its greatest strength.

NOTES

Preparation of this article was facilitated by a grant (410–99–0147) from the Social Sciences and Humanities Research Council of Canada. I would like to express my appreciation to Paul Tremblay, Anne-Marie Masgoret, Ljiljana Mihic, Eunice Lee, and Jennifer Stubbs for their assistance and comments on this manuscript.

1. The terms "acquisition" and "learning" are used interchangeably in this chapter, as are the terms "foreign" and "second" language (except where stated otherwise).

2. This research was conducted with the assistance of Paul F. Tremblay and E. Joy Bergshoeff, at the University of Western Ontario.

CHAPTER 14

AN INTERACTIONIST PERSPECTIVE ON SECOND LANGUAGE ACQUISITION

SUSAN GASS

THE field of second language acquisition (SLA) has been studied from many angles. This is a result in part of the myriad disciplinary backgrounds of scholars in the field. This chapter deals with the interactionist perspective and, as such, is primarily concerned with the environment in which second language learning takes place. It is important to note from the outset that this perspective is by and large neutral as to the role of innateness. In other words, it is compatible with a view of SLA that posits an innate learning mechanism (e.g., Universal Grammar [UG]); it is also compatible with a model of learning that posits no such mechanism. A word of caution is in order, however, as the situation is far more complex than these few terse statements suggest. It is not the case that interaction does not relate to issues of UG. Rather, what is intended is that the relationship of interaction to acquisition per se does not depend on whether there is or is not an innate mechanism that guides the learning of a second language. To provide an example of what the relationship between interaction and a UG account of learning might be, one notes that there are two kinds of evidence that are available to learners,[1] positive evidence and negative evidence. Positive evidence refers to the language that a learner hears or reads and is clearly available through the linguistic environment; negative evidence is more complex. Negative evidence refers to information about what is incorrect in the language produced by a learner and what is needed to make a correction to align the learner's language with the target language. Thus, overt correction is a form of negative evidence. It may be that, for complex syntax, negative evidence is necessary; it may also be that negative evidence is difficult to provide in other than an explicit (pedagogical) format. In other words, issues that form part of learnability theory (e.g., UG) may find answers in the conversational interactions in which learners engage in that these interactions provide the forum for both positive and negative evidence.

I have argued elsewhere (Gass 1997) that the dichotomy between innatist and environmental approaches is ill conceived in the sense that a presumed dichotomy leads only to a discussion of "which is correct," instead of "how do they complement one another." But the goal of second language research must be the determination of how these approaches are intertwined, assuming that both are indeed relevant, even though they provide different sorts of explanations (cf. also Pinker 1994). This chapter deals with interactionist approaches that focus on how learners use their linguistic environment (in particular, conversational interactions) to build their knowledge of the second language.

INPUT

Researchers in SLA who investigate learning from an interactionist perspective look at two main issues: (1) input and (2) the conversational interactions in which learners engage, the second being an outgrowth of the first. Input has had an uneven history in the history of (second) language research. In behaviorist views of language learning, input was central to an understanding of how learners acquired a language, first or second. Imitation and habit formation were primary concepts in this process. If habits were formed through imitation, then it was necessary to examine the input to learners to determine what they were imitating. It was also necessary to examine the relationship between the input (what was to be imitated) and production (the product of imitation).

From the mid-1950s on, behaviorism was on the wane, and, as a consequence, so, too, was the importance ascribed to input. A new era of language research in general emerged, and acquisition research followed, deemphasizing the significance of input and turning its attention to the nature of the internal linguistic resources with which a learner comes to the learning task.

By the early 1970s, scholars began to take a more balanced view on what was relevant and not relevant to the study of second language learning. With specific regard to input, Ferguson (1971, 1975) began to investigate the nature of input to nonproficient speakers of a language. In particular, he considered special registers such as "baby talk" (language addressed to young children) and "foreigner talk" (language addressed to nonnative speakers of a language). His focus was on the similarities between these language systems, with an ultimate goal of understanding the nature of human language. With regard to foreigner talk, the system of greatest interest to researchers in second language acquisition, certain common features became apparent. Speech directed toward nonproficient nonnative speakers was found to include modification of features, ranging from the phonological to the syntactic. For example, speech tends to be slower, more clearly enunciated, and even louder. In terms of the lexicon, vocabulary tends to have a preponderance of common words. Syntax is simple, often including two sentences where one might normally expect to find one complex sentence. These characteristics are commonly found in speech to learners, although clearly there is variation among individuals.[2]

What function does modified speech serve? A lengthier discussion and exposé on this topic is found in Gass (1997). For present purposes, it is important to point out that there are two perspectives from which one can answer this question. First is the perspective of the fluent speaker of the target language. It is likely that the purpose is to aid comprehension. One does what one can to ensure that one's conversational partner is able to understand minimally the general meaning and to be in a position to respond appropriately. The example that follows shows how a native speaker (NS), upon realizing that an original question may have been too difficult for a learner (NNS), modifies her speech to give the learner a greater opportunity to comprehend.

(1)   From Gass and Varonis (1985: 51)
    NNS: How have increasing food costs changed your eating habits?
    NS: Uh well that would I don't think they've changed 'em much right
           now, but the pressure's on.
    NNS: Pardon me?
    NS: I don't think they've changed our eating habits much as of now.
        ...

In this example the reduced pronoun ('em them) is modified to include full information (our eating habits).

A second way to consider the function of modified speech is to examine the question from the perspective of the learner. All participants in a conversation need to be true participants. Modified speech contributes to the likelihood that the learner can understand and can, therefore, get through what is essentially a social interaction. In other words, modified speech helps the learner participate in a conversation as fully as possible. Assuming that a learner is able to participate in a conversation, she or he is ensured of receiving a greater quantity of input. This in turn bears on what the learner is able to take from a conversation, a point I will return to later.

INTERACTION

Using a second language in a conversation with a native speaker or fluent non-native speaker has traditionally been viewed as a means to practice what has already been learned. The interactionist hypothesis, which was given initial prominence by Wagner-Gough and Hatch (1975) and refined by Long (1980, 1981, 1983) and others (Gass and Varonis 1985, 1989; Mackey 1999; Pica 1987, 1988; Pica and Doughty 1985; Pica, Doughty, and Young 1986; Pica, Young, and Doughty 1987; Schmidt and Frota 1986; Varonis and Gass 1985a), has as its main claim that one route to second language learning is through conversational interaction (Gass 1997; Long 1996; Pica 1994).

In Wagner-Gough and Hatch's original work (1975), the role of conversation was valued not just as a means for providing opportunities to practice previously learned language but as a locus of learning itself. Long, in his early work (1980, 1981, 1983), showed how conversations involving nonfluent nonnative speakers of a language were quantitatively different from conversations in which both parties (assuming dyadic conversation) were equal and fluent participants. Wagner-Gough and Hatch and Long went beyond modified speech (e.g., simpler syntactic structures, easier vocabulary) to consider the structure of conversation itself. I present examples of typical patterns found in conversations involving nonfluent nonnative speakers of a language. This is not to say that these patterns do not exist in conversations involving fluent speakers, only that they are more frequent in nonnative learner speech.

(2)   Confirmation check (from Mackey, Gass, and McDonough 2000):
      NNS: *c'è una verdi, uh* . . .
             there is a green, uh
      NS: *una verdi?*
             a green?

In this example, the NS's questioning of the word *verdi*, which in fact is inappropriate in Italian, resulted in a subsequent negotiation until the correct word *pianta* (plant) was recognized later in the exchange.

(3) Comprehension check (from Varonis and Gass 1985a):
     NNS1:   And your family have some ingress.
     NNS2:   yes ah, OK, OK?
     NNS1:   more or less OK?

(4) Clarification request (from Mackey and Philp 1998);
     NS: there's there's just a couple more things
     NNS: a sorry? Couple?
     NS: couple more things in the room only just a couple
     NNS: couple? What does it mean couple?

(5) Or-choice:
     NS: Where did you go yesterday?
     NNS: What?
     NS: Did you go to the zoo or to the garden?

(6) Topic-focused:
     NS: Did your friend travel with you to Italy and Switzerland?
     NNS: What?
     NS: Your friend, did she travel with you?

(7) Elaboration (from Gass and Varonis 1985):
     NNS: How have increasing food costs changed your eating habits?
     NS: Well, we don't eat as much beef as we used to. We eat more
             chicken and uh, pork, and uh, fish, things like that.
     NNS: Pardon me?
     NS: We don't eat as much beef as we used to. We eat more chicken
             and uh, uh pork and fish. . . . We don't eat beef very often. We
             don't have steak like we used to.

Examples 3–7 are crucial to an understanding of the interaction hypothesis and to an understanding of how modified interactions contribute to learning. Long defined the interaction hypothesis as follows: "*Negotiation for meaning*, and especially negotiation work that triggers *interactional* adjustments by the NS or more competent interlocutor, facilitates acquisition because it connects input, internal learner capacities, particularly selective attention, and output in productive ways" (1996: 451–452; italics in the original). He also said:

> It is proposed that environmental contributions to acquisition are mediated by selective attention and the learner's developing L2 processing capacity, and that these resources are brought together most usefully, although not exclusively, during *negotiation for meaning*. Negative feedback obtained during negotiation work or elsewhere may be facilitative of L2 development, at least for vocabulary, morphology, and language-specific syntax, and essential for learning certain specifiable L1–L2 contrasts. (Long 1996: 414; italics in the original)

It is through negotiation work (e.g., asking for clarification) that the learner may direct attention to an area of the target language (1) about which she or he may be entertaining a hypothesis (or about which she or he is trying to formulate a hypothesis), or (2) about which she or he has no information. This is not to say that learning necessarily takes place during a conversation; the interaction itself may only be the first step in recognizing that there is something to learn. Interaction may be a priming device representing the setting of the stage for learning. The following examples represent two ways in which conversation can lead to learning: (1) on the spot learning, and (2) delayed learning.

Example 8 comes from a study (Gass and Mackey 2000) that used stimulated recall to determine what a learner was thinking during a prior interaction. The relevant part of the interaction is provided, followed by the learner's comments on the interaction. The comments were made immediately following the interaction.

(8) On the spot learning (from Mackey, Gass, and McDonough 2000):
     NNS: so the people make a line in front of the place
     NS: they are standing in line?
     NNS: ahh, they are standing in line
     (Twelve turns later)
     NNS: Beside the people standing in line

     Retrospective comment:
     Make a line is the same meaning as *stand in line,* actually I thought of this
     situation as "make a line" but after she said "standing in line," her
     expression is better than mine so I changed mine.

The learner in this instance used the conversation as a way of obtaining new linguistic information, as is evidenced by her retrospective comments. She then tried out her newly learned information later in the conversation.

But sometimes learning does not take place immediately; some time to "digest" the new linguistic input is often needed. This is illustrated in example 9, which took place over the time period of a class.

(9) Delayed learning (from Ohta, 2001)
     NNS1:   Kutsu o shiroi no kutsu o *hamete imasu* ka?
             Shoes ACC white (GEN ((*sic*)) shoes ACC wearing ((*sic*)) INT?
             Is the person wearing white shoes" ((wrong verb for "wear," ital-
             icized))
     NNS2:   Iie *haite imasen.* Ano:::
             No, he's not. Uh:: (correct verb for "wear," italicized)

NNS1: Ano: ano: kuroi no kutsu o *hai- hamete imasu ka?*
U:h u:h black (GEN ((*sic*)) shoes ACC wea-wearing ((*sic*)) INT?
U'h u'h is the person wearing black shoes ((wrong word for
"wear," italicized))

NNS2: Hai *haite* imasu
Yes, he is ((correct verb for "wear," italicized))
(*Later in the class*)

NNS1: Anoo uh jiinzu o::: jeans? Jinzu o ha uh::::: *haite imasu* ka?
U:h uh: you're um jeans? Are you u:::h wearing Jeans?

NNS1: Sorekara shiroi no kutsu ga kutsu o how do you say it? Kutso o:::
And white shoes shoes how do you say it for shoes?

NNS3: haitemasu. haki-
Wearing. Wear-

NNS1: what? *Haite imasu* ka?
What? Is it "haite imasu?"
(Later in the class)

NNS1: Hanjiinzu o:: um oh what is it? Hare- *haite imasu* ka?
Shorts ((*sic*)) ACC um oh what is it? Do you we-wear shorts?

NNS4: (inaudible)

NNS1: Sorekara::: kiroi to shiroi no kutsu g- o::: yeah. *Haite imasu* ka?
And::: are you wearing yellow and white shoes?

In this example, the learner (in a classroom context) initially uses the incorrect form for the verb 'wear', *haimete,* rather than the correct form, *haite.* She begins to receive input with the correct form and eventually asks about the correct form, but it is not until quite a bit later in the class that she finally, presumably as a result of the interaction, begins to use the correct form.

Learners do not always use a conversation to obtain new information; there are times when she or he uses it to try out certain hypotheses about the second language and to receive feedback on production. Example 10 shows how a learner uses a conversation to test an hypothesis.

(10) From research reported on in Mackey, Gass, and McDonough 2000
NNS: *poi un bicchiere*
then a glass
INT: *un che, come*
a what, what?
NNS: *bicchiere*
glass

Retrospective comment:
I was drawing a blank. Then I thought of a vase, but then I thought that
since there was no flowers, maybe it was just a big glass. So, then I
thought I'll say it and see. Then, when she said "come" [what], I knew
that it was completely wrong.

In this instance, the learner is throwing out a word to see where it gets her.

Recasts

Feedback to learners can be explicit (e.g., an overt correction) or implicit, as often
seen through negotiation work. Perhaps the most subtle type of feedback comes
in the form of a recast, as in this example, in which the native speaker recasts the
nonnative speaker's incorrect question.

(11)   From Mackey and Philp (1998):
       NNS: I think some this girl have birthday and and its big celebrate
       NS: big celebration
       NNS: oh

A question arises as to the effectiveness of recasts. Are they noticed, and, if
so, are they taken as a form of correction? Lyster and Ranta (1997) collected data
from grades 4–6 children in French immersion programs. They were primarily
concerned with the reaction by the student immediately following a recast, inasmuch as this reveals what the student does with the feedback. Despite the preponderance of recasts in their database, recasts were not found to have an impact
on subsequent production. Using the same database, Lyster (1998) found that there
was some confusion between the corrective and the approval functions of recasts,
thereby questioning their usefulness in terms of corrective feedback.
    Other studies, however, do show a positive effect for recasts. Mackey and Philp
(1998) argue that using the production immediately following a recast may not
be the most appropriate way to determine effectiveness. They make the point (cf.
Gass 1997; Gass and Varonis 1994; Lightbown 1998) that, if one is to consider
effectiveness (i.e., development/acquisition), then one should more appropriately
measure delayed effects. Their study on the acquisition of English questions
showed that, for more advanced learners, recasts plus negotiation were more beneficial than negotiation alone. This was the case even though there was not always
evidence for a reaction by the learner in the subsequent turn (see Oliver 1995).

Another study that attempts to determine the role of recasts (in this case, as opposed to models) is a 1998 study by Long, Inagaki, and Ortega, who analyzed data from English learners of Japanese and of Spanish. Their results were mixed inasmuch as only one of the learner groups (Spanish) showed greater learning following recasts as opposed to models, and their findings were not valid for all grammatical structures investigated.

Does Interaction Contribute to Learning?

In recent years, the question has moved from the arena of speculation to a serious investigation of the effects of interaction. Loschky (1994), in an investigation of English learners of Japanese, found that interaction had a positive effect on comprehension but did not find an effect on the acquisition of vocabulary or on the acquisition of morphosyntax (locative expressions) (cf. Ellis, Tanaka, and Yamazaki 1994). Gass and Varonis (1994) did show that the effects of interaction went beyond a subsequent turn. As in previous studies, vocabulary did not appear to be affected, although general discourse organizational strategies were affected. Mackey (1999) provides the most detailed support in favor of the effects of interaction. In her investigation of a single grammatical structure, question formation, she found a relationship between conversational interaction and development in that those who were involved in structure-focused interaction moved along a developmental continuum more rapidly than those who did not. Mackey's study supports the notion that interaction is not necessarily (or not always) the locus of immediate learning but often may be the catalyst for later learning. She found that, for the developmentally advanced structures, the effects of interaction were noted in delayed posttests rather than immediately.[3]

ATTENTION

Central to the interaction hypothesis is the concept of attention or noticing. If interaction is to have an effect (either through negotiation or recast), the learner must notice that his or her conversational partner is explicitly or implicitly making a correction.[4] If there is no attention to a particular part of language during an interaction, then it is difficult to attribute the source of change to the interaction itself. Example 12 illustrates how the direct questioning of an utterance makes the learner notice the discrepancy between her pronunciation of *yellow* and the native speaker interviewer's pronunciation.

(12)   From Mackey, Gass, and McDonough 2000
      NNS: The color is /**wellow**/
      NS: Is what?
      NNS: /wellow/ /wellow/ color
      NS: Yellow?
      NNS: Yellow.

      Retrospective comment:
      My pronounce is different. I say /wellow/ but yellow is the exact
      pronounce. Yellow, yellow.

The question remains as to what learners do notice. Williams (1999) considered learner-generated attention to form. She points out that most of the focus on form research within a classroom context focuses on teacher-generated attention (cf. Sharwood Smith's [1991, 1993] discussion of enhanced input and internally and externally induced salience). She found that learners are indeed capable of focusing attention to language form but that there is variation according to proficiency level and even activity types.

Mackey, Gass, and McDonough (2000) also investigated what learners notice in an interaction. Their investigation differed from that of Williams in that they were concerned with interactional feedback and how learners actually interpreted that feedback. Through a postinteraction stimulated recall of learners of English and learners of Italian, they found that learners do notice interactional feedback, but they do not do so in a uniform manner. Lexis and phonology are more likely to be noticed than aspects of morphosyntax. The results also suggest that the manner of feedback (e.g., recasts or negotiation) have different effects alone or in combination. Neither of these studies investigated the next step, which is to determine what happens after learners notice a gap between their knowledge of the second language and the second language itself. In other words, the crucial step of actual learning stemming from interaction needs to be taken (cf. Swain and Lapkin 1998).

OUTPUT

In preceding sections, I have considered the nature of language that is directed toward learners and the function of modified language and/or modified conversational structure. However, in any discussion of the interaction hypothesis, there is a third prong to examine, and that is the role of output. In earlier conceptualizations of second language acquisition, output served little learning purpose, other than, perhaps, to reinforce previously learned linguistic knowledge. Swain's (1985) pioneering work in this area came from observations of immersion programs in Canada (see also Kowal and Swain 1997; Swain 1995; Swain and Lapkin 1995, 1998). She noted that children who had spent many years in immersion programs were still lagging in targetlike abilities. In looking more carefully at the classroom context in which the target language was used and that was the prime source of information about the target language for these children, she noted that what was lacking was consistent and frequent use of the second language. She proposed that one needed more than input, learning a second language required a significant amount of output. Output, or language production, forces learners to focus on the syntax of an utterance and, consequently, on formulating hypotheses about how the target language works. This is different from receiving input, because input involves only comprehension, and comprehension often requires little syntactic organization.

THEORY OF CONTRAST

What sort of mechanism allows for learning to take place as a result of negative evidence derived from conversational interaction? One possibility to account for learning through conversation is the direct contrast hypothesis (Saxton 1997), defined within the context of child language acquisition as follows:

> When the child produces an utterance containing an erroneous form, which is responded to immediately with an utterance containing the correct adult alternative to the erroneous form (i. e., when negative evidence is supplied), the child may perceive the adult form as being in *contrast* with the equivalent child form. Cognizance of a relevant contrast can then form the basis for perceiving the adult form as a correct alternative to the child form (Saxton 1997: 155; emphasis in original)

Attention alone is not sufficient. A contrast must be attended to, or, in SLA parlance, a gap must be noticed. And conversation provides a forum for the contrast to be detected, especially when the erroneous form and a correct one are in immediate juxtaposition.

However, many problems remain, as Doughty (in press) points out. Issues of memory structures and analysis must be dealt with. Why is one exposure sometimes sufficient and sometimes not? What are the sources that draw learners' attention to some parts of language and not others at any given moment?

It is likely that there are limitations to what can and cannot be learned through the provision of negative evidence through conversation. One possibility is that surface-level phenomena can be learned, but abstractions cannot. This is consistent with Truscott's (1998) claim that competence is not affected by noticing. Negative evidence can probably not apply to long stretches of speech, given memory limitations (see Philp 1999). But, it may be effective with low-level phenomena, such as pronunciation, or as the basic meanings of lexical items. In fact, these are precisely the areas that Mackey, Gass, and McDonough (2000) have isolated as those that are sensitive to feedback. Future research will need to determine the long term effects of interaction on different parts of language (see Gass, Svetics, and Lemelin, forthcoming).

NOTES

1. There is a third type of evidence, indirect negative evidence (see Plough 1994, 1995). To simplify matters, we do not deal with this complex type of evidence.

2. It is beyond the scope of this chapter to comment on whether or not these systems are learned. It is important to note, however, that the extent to which an individual adopts foreigner talk characteristics in her speech may depend on an individual's experience with nonnative speakers. Varonis and Gass (1985b) describe an interaction in which a salesperson adopts very few foreigner-talk features (she speaks rapidly, uses idioms, uses anaphoric pronouns with no obvious referent). It was speculated that this is so precisely because of her lack of experience with noncomprehending individuals.

3. Preliminary analysis of data by Alvarez-Torres and Gass (forthcoming) suggests that, when learners are allowed to interact (either with or without prior input), they are more likely to demonstrate increased knowledge than when they only have input or when input follows interaction.

4. This is not to say that attention cannot come from a learner's noticing a new form on her own (i.e., without an interlocutor's correction).

CHAPTER 15

PRAGMATICS AND SECOND LANGUAGE ACQUISITION

KATHLEEN BARDOVI-HARLIG

THE study of pragmatics is traditionally held to encompass at least five main areas: deixis, conversational implicature, presupposition, speech acts, and conversational structure (Levinson 1983). Within second language studies, work in pragmatics is narrower than in the field of pragmatics at large, including the investigation of speech acts and, to a lesser extent, conversational structure and conversational implicature. It is also broader, investigating areas traditionally considered to be sociolinguistics (Stalnaker 1972). For example, Kasper and Dahl (1991: 216) included speech acts, conversational management, discourse organization, and sociolinguistic aspects of language use, such as choice of address forms, as part of pragmatics. In the intersection of second language studies and pragmatics, research is best characterized by Stalnaker's definition of pragmatics as "the study of linguistic acts and the contexts in which they are performed" (Stalnaker 1972: 383).

The most dominant area of pragmatics in second language studies is the study of speech acts (Searle 1969, 1976). Speech act theory views utterances not just as stating propositions but as a way of *doing* things with words; hence the concept of *act*. Speech acts include five categories: representatives (asserting, explaining), directives (requesting, advising), commissives (promising, threatening), expressives (apologizing, complimenting), and declarations (declaring war, hiring/firing someone from a job). Every speech act has two forces: the intended force of an utterance (the illocutionary force) and the actual effect on the hearer (the perlocutionary force). As an illustration, by arguing (the intended illocutionary force) I may convince or persuade someone (the perlocutionary force). Second language studies have typically investigated illocutionary force, although perlocutionary force, the effect of learners' utterances, would be relevant in second language research and represents an area for future investigation.

The second area of pragmatics addressed in second language studies is conversational structure. The study of conversational structure includes the investigation of turn taking, how turns are constructed, back channeling (signaling comprehension or lack thereof without claiming the floor), adjacency pairs (e.g., question and answers), and conversational boundaries (such as opening and closing conversations) (Schegloff and Sacks 1973).

The third and least investigated area in second language pragmatics is conversational implicature. Often referred to as simply "implicature," conversational implicature is one of the most important concepts in pragmatics (Levinson 1983). The identification of an implicature allows speakers to comprehend the message behind an illocutionary act. Implicature plays a significant role in the interpretation of indirect speech acts. To account for conversational implicature, Grice (1975) introduced the cooperative principle and four related maxims: quantity, quality, relation, and manner (Grice 1975: 45–46):

- The cooperative principle: Make your contribution such as is required, at that stage at which it occurs, by the accepted purpose or direction of the talk exchange in which you are engaged.
- Quantity: (1) Make your contribution as informative as is required for the current purposes of the exchange; (2) do not make your contribution more informative than is required.
- Quality: Try to make your contribution one that is true. (1) Do not say that which you believe to be false, and (2) do not say that for which you lack adequate evidence.
- Relation: Make your contributions relevant.
- Manner: (1) Avoid obscurity; (2) avoid ambiguity; (3) be brief; (4) be orderly.

TRANSITION TO SLA STUDIES: INTERLANGUAGE PRAGMATICS

The study of L2 pragmatics has come to be known as *interlanguage pragmatics,* and more recently simply as *ILP* (Kasper and Schmidt 1996). Interlanguage pragmatics has developed two strands of research: Comparative-sociolinguistic and acquisitional. In interlanguage pragmatics research, the comparative and sociolinguistic studies dominate the field. As Kasper observed:

> The bulk of interlanguage pragmatics research derived its research questions and methods from empirical, and particularly cross-cultural, pragmatics. Typical issues addressed in data-based studies are whether NNS differ from NS in the (1) range and (2) contextual distribution of (3) strategies and (4) linguistic forms used to convey (5) illocutionary meaning and (6) politeness—precisely the kinds of issues raised in comparative studies of different communities. . . . Interlanguage pragmatics has predominantly been the sociolinguistic, and to a much lesser extent a psycholinguistic study of NNS' linguistic action. (1992: 205)

Comparative studies have resulted in a significant body of research in four main areas: (1) development and refinement of elicitation tasks, (2) description of L1 speech acts, (3) description of L2 speech acts (especially by advanced NNS), and (4) the comparison of L1 and L2 production by native and nonnative speakers.

In applied linguistics, the face of pragmatics was forever changed by the introduction of the discourse completion task (DCT) to study speech acts (Blum-Kulka 1982) and the subsequent publication of the results of the Cross Cultural Speech Act Realization Project (Blum-Kulka and Olshtain 1984; Blum-Kulka, House, and Kasper 1989). The DCT introduced a means by which the performance of speech acts could be compared cross-linguistically and cross-culturally, thus offering a methodology that was understandably absent from a tradition derived from philosophy. The use of the DCT surpassed even the collection of natural conversation in the decade that followed. Discourse completion tasks take at least three formats: (1) dialogue completion tasks with rejoinders (such as Larry's reply in 1); (2) dialogue completion tasks without rejoinders; and (3) open questionnaires in which only the scenario is provided but no turns.

(1)   At a student's apartment.
      Larry, John's roommate, had a party the night before and left the kitchen in a mess.
      John: Larry, Ellen and Tom are coming over for dinner tonight and I'll have to start cooking soon; ____
      Larry: OK, I'll have a go at it right away.

Additional elicitation tasks continue to be developed, including multiple-choice questionnaires, video elicitation tasks, and picture-prompted tasks, among many others (see Bardovi-Harlig 1999b).

Through its comparative studies, ILP has contributed significantly by describing the realization of a range of speech acts by native speakers in a number of languages. ILP has also yielded a description of speech acts in a variety of second languages. More important, it has resulted in a number of comparisons of native-speaker and nonnative speaker production.

Nonnative speakers can differ from native speakers in the production of speech acts in at least four ways. Native and nonnative speakers may use different speech acts, or, where the same speech acts are used, these may differ in semantic formula, content, or form (Bardovi-Harlig 1996):

1. Native and nonnative speakers may perform different speech acts in the same contexts, or one group may not perform any speech act.
2. Speakers may use different semantic formulas. Semantic formulas represent the primary content of the parts of an utterance. An apology may contain the head act "I'm sorry" as well as an explanation or an offer to restore the damage.
3. The content of semantic formulas may also differ, even when speakers use the same semantic formulas. "My printer is jammed" and "I didn't feel like doing the assignment" are both explanations for why an assignment is late, but the content is significantly different.
4. The form of a speech act may also differ. In a study of requests, S. Takahashi (1996) found that learners of English favored monoclausal request formulas, "Would you verb?" or "Could you verb?" whereas NS preferred biclausal request formulas, "Would it be possible for you to verb?" or "I was wondering if you could verb."

The comparisons serve a number of functions: as primary research into L2 pragmatics, as a type of pragmatic error analysis, as a needs assessment for the development of pedagogical methods and materials for teaching pragmatics, and as models for pedagogical materials. They may also serve to define research areas for acquisitional ILP studies.

The Study of Pragmatics within SLA

The second, smaller area of investigation within ILP concerns the acquisition of second language pragmatics. Kasper and Dahl (1991: 216) defined interlanguage pragmatics as referring to nonnative speakers' comprehension and production of pragmatics and how that L2-related knowledge is acquired. This is not a new area, just an underdeveloped one. This claim was made first by Kasper (1992) and has been addressed more recently by others (Bardovi-Harlig 1999a; Kasper and Rose 1999; Kasper Schmidt 1996; Rose 2000). The crucial distinction between comparative and acquisitional studies is the concern for the *development* of pragmatic knowledge. The central question driving SLA pragmatics research must be "How does L2 pragmatic competence develop?"

As with other areas of SLA research, the investigation of development is carried out through cross-sectional or longitudinal studies and ideally includes beginners through advanced learners. In contrast, the comparative studies are often single-moment studies (Rose 2000). Early longitudinal studies include Schmidt's (1983) well-known report on Wes, a learner of English, Schmidt and Frota's (1986) study of a beginning learner of Brazilian Portuguese, and Billmyer's (1990) study of instructed learners of English. Later studies include Ellis's (1992) longitudinal study of two children's untutored acquisition of English requests and Sawyer's (1992) study of the acquisition of the sentence-final particle *ne* by American learners of Japanese. Bouton (1994) investigated the development of comprehension as related to implicature, and Bardovi-Harlig and Hartford (1993) studied the changes in the speech acts of advanced nonnative speakers during their first year of graduate school. Siegel's (1996) ethnographic longitudinal study followed the acquisition of sociolinguistic aspects of Japanese by four Western women in Japan, and Cohen (1997) reported on his own acquisition of Japanese in a foreign environment by means of a diary study. Kanagy and Igarashi (1997) studied the acquisition of pragmatic routines in a Japanese immersion kindergarten by L1 speakers of English. Churchill (1999) investigated the acquisition of requests by Japanese enrolled in a partial immersion content-based English program in Japan.

The number of longitudinal studies compares favorably to the number of cross-sectional studies done in the same period. The emphasis on speech acts reflects the importance of the framework in ILP. A number of cross-sectional studies of requests were carried out in a range of target languages and included Blum-Kulka and Olshtain (1986, Hebrew), Takahashi and DuFon (1989, English), Svanes (1992, Norwegian), Takahashi (1996, English), Hassall (1997, Bahasa Indonesian), and Hill (1997, English). Studies of refusals in English were carried out by Takahashi and Beebe (1987), Robinson (1992), and Houck and Gass (1996). Apologies in English were studied by Trosborg (1987) and Maeshiba, Yoshinaga, Kasper, and Ross (1996). Omar (1992) studied greetings and leave takings in Kiswahili. Takenoya (1995) studied the acquisition of Japanese address terms by Americans. Multiple speech acts were investigated by Scarcella (1979, English), Olshtain and Blum-Kulka (1985, Hebrew), Trosborg (1995, English), Koike (1996, Spanish), and Rose (2000, English). The assessment of assertiveness was studied by Kerekes (1992, English), and pragmatic and grammatical awareness was studied by Bardovi-Harlig and Dörnyei (1998). For a review of the longitudinal and cross-sectional studies, see Kasper and Rose (1999).

Framing the Questions of Acquisition

M. Long (1990) distinguished description and explanation as dual goals for a theory of second language acquisition, stating that a theory of SLA needs to account for the accepted findings. As a starting point, investigations of the acquisition of interlanguage pragmatics would provide a description of the development of L2 pragmatics, which would constitute the body of "accepted findings." Because the overarching question of acquisitional ILP research ("How does L2 pragmatics develop?") has such a broad scope, specific questions of smaller scope are also necessary. Kasper and Schmidt (1996) posed fourteen guiding questions, which I have arranged below by topic.

Measurement

1. How can approximation to target language norms be measured? Kasper and Schmidt (1996) identify the fact that there is a lack of a common means to measure pragmatic development as one factor that has contributed to the underrepresentation of acquisitional studies.

Development

What are the stages of L2 pragmatic development?

2. Is there a natural route of development as evidenced by difficulty, accuracy, or acquisition orders or discrete stages of development?
3. Does (must) perception or comprehension precede production in acquisition?
4. Does chunk learning (formulaic speech) play a role in acquisition?
5. Does L1 influence L2 pragmatics?

Comparisons

Comparisons between L1 and L2 pragmatics lead to distinguishing the universals of acquisition of pragmatics from the particulars of (adult) second language acquisition. Kasper and Schmidt (1996) pose these questions:

6. Is the development of L2 pragmatics similar to learning a first language?
7. Are there universals of pragmatics and do they play a role in interlanguage pragmatics?

Variables

Research in comparative ILP, acquisitional ILP, and SLA more generally suggest the following variables and corresponding research questions:

8. Do children enjoy an advantage over adults in learning a second language?
9. Does foreign versus second language input make a difference?
10. Does instruction make a difference?
11. Do motivation and attitudes influence level of acquisition?
12. Does personality play a role?
13. Does a learner's gender play a role?

Among these questions, the most broadly investigated is the influence of the first language but, as Rose (2000) has pointed out, the results from comparative studies on transfer may have to be reassessed when more acquisitional studies have been completed. Acquisitional studies on the influence of instruction represent a growing area of investigation (Billmyer 1990; Bouton 1994; House 1996; and the many empirical studies included in Rose and Kasper in press). As M. Long (1990) said, the seed of explanation often lies in the description itself, and any of the variables mentioned may potentially play a part in an explanation of how or why L2 pragmatics is or is not acquired.

Mechanisms of Change

As part of an explanation, a theory of (pragmatics in) SLA must also be able to account for the mechanisms of change and to explain how learners move from one pragmatic stage to another.

14. What mechanisms drive development from stage to stage?

This is the least researched area in ILP, although Schmidt (1993) and Bialystok (1993) address this issue. Kasper and Schmidt (1996) point out that there should be overlap in the mechanisms that drive change in other areas of SLA.

INVESTIGATING THE PRAGMATICS OF GRAMMATICALLY LOWER PROFICIENCY LEARNERS

This final section explores some of the issues that arise in studies of beginning language learners. Although definitions of pragmatic competence necessarily include a linguistic component, it seems that they are not geared to acquisition studies. (Note that definitions in this area often refer to deviations from the target.) Blum-Kulka posits a three-way division among social acceptability (this determines when to perform a speech act, sequencing and appropriacy, and degree of directness), linguistic acceptability (deviations from which result in utterances that are "perfectly grammatical, but fail to conform to the target language in terms of what is considered an 'idiomatic' speech act realization"; 1982: 52), and pragmatic acceptability (whether an utterance has the intended illocutionary force). Blum-Kulka identifies unintended shifts in illocutionary force as the most serious consequence of nonnative speech act realization. Such shifts can occur with both linguistically acceptable and unacceptable utterances. Thomas (1983) identified sociopragmatic failure (inappropriate utterances caused by a misunderstanding of social standards) and pragmalinguistic failure (utterances that convey unintended illocutionary force). Cohen suggests a third division, between sociocultural and sociolinguistic ability. Sociocultural ability refers to a speaker's ability "to determine whether it is acceptable to perform the speech act at all in the given situation and, if so, to select one or more semantic formulas that would be appropriate in the realization of the given speech act" (1996: 254). In contrast, sociolinguistic ability consists of speakers' control over their selection of language forms used to realize a speech act (e.g., *sorry* versus. *excuse me*).

None of these distinctions is explicitly designed to deal with emergent interlanguage grammar. In fact, the practice of separating grammatical development (stated in terms of errors) from pragmatic development is well established:

> Very often, of course, it is not pragmatic failure which leads non-native speakers to misinterpret or cause to be misinterpreted the pragmatic force of an utterance, but an imperfect command of the lower-level grammar. . . . I do not in any way underestimate the importance of these factors [grammatical error and covert grammatical error], but they have already been dealt with extensively. (Thomas 1983: 94)

Although such a separation between grammar and pragmatics has been productive in the analysis of language samples of relatively proficient learners—whose grammaticality was no doubt enhanced by the use of written elicitation tasks—with low-level learners linguistic and pragmatic development are intertwined (Bardovi-Harlig 1999a). It may not be possible to make a clear distinction, as the following four studies of low level learners show.

Rose's (2000) cross-sectional study of oral elicited requests by second- to sixth-grade children learning English in Hong Kong reveals an early development of a conventionally indirect request formula, *can you/I*, and subsequent development of grammar.

(2)   Can you McDonald, please? (second grade)

(3)   Can I eat lunch in McDonald? (fourth grade)

(4)   Can you take me to McDonald's for lunch? (sixth grade)

Data from spontaneous requests show a closer relationship between the linguistic and the pragmatic (Churchill 1999; Ellis 1992). Ellis (1992) investigated the classroom requests of two boys, ages ten and eleven, who were enrolled in an ESL language unit designed to help primary school children learn enough communicative English to join appropriate content classes. As example (5) shows, the use of nominal utterances, an early stage of language development, corresponds to the pragmatic request strategy of naming the desired item. The "give me" strategy in (6) and the "want" strategy (softened with "Miss") in (7) emerge before the learner produces a direct object.

(5)   Big Circle (R wanted to staple his card, a cutout of a big circle) (Term 1)

(6)   Give me (R wanted a ruler from another student) (Term 2)

(7)   Miss I want [the stapler] (Term 3)

(8)   Tasleem, have you got glue? (Term 4)

(9)   Can I take my book with me? / Can you pass me my pencil? (Term 5)

Churchill's (1999) year-long study of thirty-seven teenage learners of English (immediate to high beginners on the ACTFL OPI) enrolled in a partial immersion content-based high school EFL language program shows similar interdependence of pragmatics and linguistic development.

(10) Tomomi: File . . . Return . . .
      NS: Huh? What do you want?
      Tomomi: Return to me.

(11) Reiko: Please . . . Colored pencils. . . .
      NS: no response
      Tomoko: Lend us.

The requests in (10) and (11) (which is constructed cooperatively by two learners) are quite direct, at least in part because of the low level of language development. In spite of the form of the early requests, the learners in the two observational studies demonstrate competence at the social level. As students they are expected to ask for what they need so that they can go about the business of being students, whether they are in primary school or high school. These learners' production of requests shows social acceptability (Blum-Kulka 1982) or sociocultural ability (Cohen 1996) in the appropriacy of performing the act. The second part of the social component—degree of directness and/or selection of semantic formulas—depends on grammatical development.

As a final exploration of the relation of pragmatic and grammatical development, consider a pair of spontaneous disagreements by adult learners during conversational interviews collected over a period of a year (Salsbury and Bardovi-Harlig 2000). Compare the linguistic mitigation in (12) used by Mousa, an adult learner in an intensive English program in his ninth month of study, with the lack of mitigation in (13), recorded in his tenth month. In (12), Mousa disagrees with the interviewer over the use of the term *test anxiety* to characterize his feelings. Mousa mitigates his disagreement with the hedge *quite* and a partial agreement *I have a little*.

(12)   Mousa (age 21, male); Interviewer (age 32, male, Ph.D. candidate)
        M: I don't know, maybe when ah, I'm taking like TOEFL, I have, a kind
              of feeling, sometimes I don't see, I don't—
        I: It's called *test anxiety*.
        M: *I don't have quite like this, but I have a little, but not quite like this.*
              . . .

In (13) Mousa disagrees with a classmate's opinion on polygamy, a topic that Mousa introduced. In the final line, Mousa goes bald on record with his disagreement saying *no, no, no, you care!*

(13)   Mousa (age 21, male); Takako (age 19, female, classmate)
        M: You said like, if your, you don't care if your, your, your husband has
              other wife?
        T: I don't know.
        M: You don't care about that?
        T: Like, now, I'm a little bit thinking, before I didn't like it, but now
        M: If you say that, I will say no, no
        T: I don't care
        M: *No, no, no, you care!*

On the one hand, Mousa's disagreement in (12) might be seen as more pragmatically successful than his disagreement in (13)—especially if we take a targetlike perspective. His disagreement in (12) is mitigated and shows a higher degree of grammaticalization than that in (13). The difference between (12) and (13) could result from a topic effect that prevents monitoring. On the other hand, the difference between (12) and (13) could be viewed as an indication of Mousa's developing L2 pragmatic competence.

Consider the structure of the disagreement. In the first two adjacency pairs, Mousa asks for clarification, a turn that is associated with dispreferred turns such as disagreement. Mousa then warns his classmate (using an emergent conditional) that he will disagree. At this point, it is still possible for the disagreement to be withheld, but his classmate again repeats that she does not care, and Mousa disagrees. Mousa has a well-estabished pragmatic sense of the turns that constitute oppositional talk and their sequencing (part of Blum-Kulka's social acceptability). Mousa also uses greater mitigation with the male interviewer, eleven years his senior, than with his female classmate, two years his junior. Mousa shows what Cohen called sociolinguistic ability, the ability to control the selection of forms for pragmatic purposes; in Mousa's case, he selects among the forms in his interlanguage inventory. Note that Takako, too, uses her emergent skills to mitigate her contribution: "I'm a little bit thinking." Although her turn is not grammatical, she clearly uses linguistic forms for pragmatic purposes. Cohen's definition of sociolinguistic ability seems to be the definition of linguistic ability that is most compatible with developmental aspects of L2 pragmatics. As in other areas of SLA, it is important to develop frameworks that encourage and support the investigation of acquisitional stages—the process of second language acquisition—rather than the final outcome alone. The research in pragmatics and SLA of the future promises not only to describe and explain development of L2 pragmatics but also to contribute to our fundamental knowledge of what constitutes pragmatic competence.

PART V

THE STUDY OF SECOND LANGUAGE TEACHING

CHAPTER 16

....

CURRICULUM DEVELOPMENT: THE INTERFACE BETWEEN POLITICAL AND PROFESSIONAL DECISIONS

....

PÉTER MEDGYES

MARIANNE NIKOLOV

THIS chapter falls into two main parts. The first part is concerned with general aspects of curriculum development and innovation. It sets out to define the curriculum in relation to its twin concept, to define the syllabus, and it examines the connection between theoretical and practical aspects of curriculum development. The chapter goes on to address the issue of curriculum innovation, an undertaking aimed at resolving the conflict between what is desirable and what is acceptable and feasible. In view of pressing needs, this contradiction has become more acute in recent years, giving rise to various kinds of friction between curriculum designers and teachers on the one hand and specialists and policymakers on the other. Among the conditions supposed to ensure the success of curriculum reforms, the primary one requires concerted efforts between all participants in education. Turning to language education in particular, the first part of the study concludes by taking stock of the major curriculum models adopted in the past thirty years.

The second part is devoted to illustrating the main aspects of curriculum design postulated in the first part. The country chosen to exemplify these assumptions is Hungary, a country in which curriculum reforms were necessitated by pervasive political, economic, and social changes in the last decade of the twentieth century. Through an analysis of interim versions of the National Core Curriculum, it is shown how political decisions are brought to bear on curriculum reform in general and on the development of the foreign language syllabus in particular.

WHAT IS THE CURRICULUM?

Issues relating to the curriculum have been of interest to philosophers and educators since the time of Plato, but its formal study began in the twentieth century. However, as in the case of many other new disciplines, there was no consensus over the meaning and scope of curriculum studies, and definitions varied according to academic allegiance and geographic location.

It was not until the last quarter of the century that debates over definition had subsided and the term *curriculum* had come to refer to the whole educational process, to "the totality of content to be taught and aims to be realised within one school or educational system" (White 1988: 4), including methods and approaches, measures of evaluation, teaching materials and equipment, and even teacher education (Stern 1983). In contrast, the *syllabus* is a more circumscribed document generally taken to refer to the content of an individual subject, such as history, physics, or English as a second or foreign language (Dubin and Olshtain 1986; Yalden 1987).

Curriculum studies is an umbrella term covering both theoretical and practical issues, and in fact researchers differ mainly in their choice either to move toward deeper immersion in academic scholarship, with only an indirect or tangential interest in practical issues, or to become more closely involved with school affairs and the mechanics of curriculum innovation (Jackson 1992). In this regard, Pratt and Short complained that although "a considerable body of knowledge concerning curriculum [studies] has emerged in the course of the twentieth century, so far its impact on actual school practice has been minimal" (1994: 1325). This outcome is not only a result of the lack of a widely accepted and explicitly formulated theoretical paradigm (Johnson 1989) but also of the adoption of a top-down model of curriculum development. According to this model, the theorists' job is to articulate well-defined general educational aims and behavioral objectives, design detailed content specifications, and set valid and reliable assessment criteria, whereas practitioners are relegated to the task of implementation.

Challenging this distribution of work, Stenhouse (1975) argued that it forces teachers to adopt a *hidden curriculum*, that is, an alternative teaching program in the face of official dictates. This contradiction can be resolved only by offering teachers the chance to subject their professional skills and attitudes to critical scrutiny through continuous and active involvement in curriculum research and development. The underlying images in Stenhouse's line of argument are those of the *reflective teacher* (Schön 1983) and the *teacher researcher* (Freeman 1998), which have become catchphrases in educational literature.

What Is Curriculum Innovation?

Attempts at innovation are spurred and justified by human needs, which, for the purpose of this discussion, may be defined as "a discrepancy between an actual and a preferred state" (Pratt and Short 1994: 1321).[1] The key attributes of innovation are that (a) it is change that involves human intervention and (b) it is aimed at bringing about improvement (White 1993). Obviously, certain needs specifically call for innovation in education, even though sociologists seem to agree that education basically serves a socially and culturally reproductive function and is therefore conservative and resistant to change.

Until the 1970s, educational and curriculum reforms followed one another at a steady pace, and most of them were limited to the institution of minor modifications. In the final decades of the century, however, the pace of curriculum reforms accelerated, and their scope widened in response to the demands of a rapidly changing world. Fundamental measures were taken to reform and centralize the curriculum even in such countries as the United Kingdom, the United States, and Australia, which earlier had taken little interest in curriculum issues (Skilbeck 1994).

Curriculum reform, like any other innovation, involves several categories of participants, each assigned distinct roles. Five main types of role may be distinguished:

1. *Policymakers*, who take the major decisions (politicians, ministry officials, deans, heads of departments)

2. *Specialists*, who provide the necessary resources (curriculum and syllabus designers, materials writers, methodologists, teacher trainers)
3. *Teachers*, who deliver the services
4. *Students*, who receive the services
5. *Mediators*, who liaise among all the participants (government agencies, such as the British Council, the United States Information Agency, and the Goethe Institut, or nongovernmental organizations such as the Soros Foundation).

POLICY CONSTRAINTS

In theory, any participant may initiate action, but in practice teachers (not to speak of students) can seldom make their voices heard beyond their classrooms or schools. Specialists, but especially curriculum and syllabus designers, are usually in a better position to influence policymakers (Kaplan 1992). However, the right of policymakers to act at their own discretion is rarely challenged, in recognition of the responsibility they assume for their decisions. Judicious specialists are willing to admit that a policy decision may be beneficial even when it runs contrary to current educational or research wisdom (Judd 1992). After a decision has been made, it is the professional and moral duty of specialists to state their views on feasibility, costing, and other aspects of implementation; again, it is up to policymakers whether or not to seek expert advice.

Despite vigorous efforts, it appears that curriculum innovation is suffering from what the American sociologist Ogburn (cited in Skilbeck 1994) once defined as *social lag*. Driven by economic, financial, and social constraints, policymakers often find the speed at which educational reforms are being introduced too slow. In Pratt and Short's view, "curriculum is not successfully developed and installed until political pressure is strong enough to overcome the forces of tradition, inertia, and vested interest that work against change in educational institutions" (1994: 1320). To make matters worse, there is growing dissatisfaction with the quality of education delivered, from which policymakers conclude that "the curriculum should no longer be considered the "secret garden" for the professionals to tend and enjoy. . . . The content of schooling and methods of teaching are held to be too important to be left in the hands of teachers and other educational professionals. They must be brought into line with the overall objectives of society." (Skilbeck 1994: 1339, 1341).

CONDITIONS FOR SUCCESS

Curriculum development is a complex activity, and its products usually have slim chances of long-term survival: in Adams and Chen's estimate (1981, cited in Markee 1997), 75 percent of all innovations fail to take root. However, if certain preliminary measures are not spared before designing the curriculum, the chance of success may be greatly enhanced. The first question to be asked is whether the reform is necessary, timely, and feasible. The continuation of a program that has lost steam usually causes less damage than the introduction of a reform that is unjustifiable, premature, or short of financial support and human resources. The second issue is that campaignlike reforms urged by agents with vested personal interests in its realization are dangerous. In general, evolution is a far more desirable goal than revolution in curriculum development (Johnson 1989; Stenhouse 1975). The third consideration is that curriculum design should be conducted with methodological rigor (Markee 1997). Fullan is right in saying that "large plans and vague ideas make a lethal combination" (1982: 102). Finally, any innovative idea is bound to hurt those whose psychological and occupational security rests on the survival of the old system. Therefore, efforts should be made to convince opponents about the benefit that the new curriculum will bring them (Kaplan 1992).

Once the decision has been made to get the curriculum reform off the ground, a team of specialists is invited to set to work. Experienced specialists are aware that curriculum development, like most human endeavor, is a hopelessly untidy business, rife with mismatches, uncertainties, and redundancies. It cannot be expected to work merely by legislation, decree, white papers, and centrally issued directives (Skilbeck 1994). This being the case, every participant involved in the undertaking should be prepared to engage in continuous communication with every other agent. Only by dint of close collaboration can problems be identified, precluded, and remedied.

CURRICULUM MODELS IN LANGUAGE EDUCATION

Let us now turn to issues that specifically relate to second and foreign language education. In analyzing the relationship between general curriculum theory and curriculum theory in language teaching, Stern noted that, in fact, "very little movement of thought across these two trends has taken place" (1983: 442). The two exceptions he referred to are Halliday, McIntosh, and Strevens (1964) and Mackey (1965), who had made elaborate attempts at designing a language curriculum based on theoretical underpinnings. With reference to language projects, Kennedy (1988) also complained that, whereas the literature in other fields of education was rich, there was a scarcity of research relating to language education. In a similar vein, Fettes wrote that "the exclusion of education research from the field of language planning . . . appears decidedly unhelpful" (1997:17).

Investigating innovative language syllabuses in the last third of the twentieth century, one is dazzled by the variety of directions and models. After the eclipse of the audiolingual method in the late 1960s, Stern (1983) advocated the need to break away from the method concept; indeed, *method* became a taboo word, as testified by the names of the most quoted language teaching models of the 1970s, including silent way, community language learning, suggestopedia, and total physical response (Richards and Rodgers 1986; Stevick 1980).[2]

However, the real breakthrough in language education came with the advent of communicative language teaching (CLT), a paradigm that has permeated the language teaching scene since the 1970s. Originally called the communicative approach, it had gone a long way before it shed the capital letters and metamorphosed from a method through a syllabus (cf. the functional-notional syllabus; Munby 1978; van Ek 1977; Wilkins 1976) to an all-encompassing humanistic philosophy of language education (Moskowitz 1978; Rogers 1969; Stevick 1990), begetting a plethora of syllabuses and methodologies, as well as classroom procedures and techniques (Breen and Candlin 1980; Brumfit and Johnson 1979; Krashen and Terrell 1983; Littlewood 1981). Among the best-known syllabuses are the procedural syllabus (Prabhu 1987), the content-based syllabus (Snow, Met, and Genessee 1989), the negotiated syllabus (Clarke 1991), the task-based syllabus (Crookes and Gass 1993; Skehan 1996), the learner-centered syllabus (Tudor 1997), and syllabuses initiated by the Council of Europe (1998).

Nevertheless, two caveats may well be in place. One concerns critiques that have found fault with CLT on both theoretical and pragmatic grounds (Medgyes 1986; Swan 1985). The other has to do with the imposition of CLT under all circumstances, even in countries whose educational ideologies and cultural traditions are not in harmony with learner-centeredness and humanistic education as defined by the leading theoreticians and ambassadors of CLT (Holliday 1994, Phillipson 1992). While CLT has become a buzzword, there is reason to believe that teachers have continued to follow more structural lines in their classroom practices (Karavas-Doukas 1996).

HUNGARY–A CASE STUDY

To illustrate the process of curriculum development and the nature of curriculum innovation, the rest of the chapter presents a case study. The country chosen to exemplify the assumptions made in the previous sections is Hungary, the authors' country of origin.[3] After a discussion of how political changes have influenced educational policy in the past decade, the investigation will focus on the processes that have interacted in the development of a new national core curriculum (NCC) in general and the foreign language syllabus in particular, as well as the degree of impact these processes have had on classroom practice.

The Political and Educational Context of Curriculum Innovation

By the mid-1980s, it had become obvious in Hungary, as in all the other countries of Central and Eastern Europe, that the communist system was not going to improve unless the entire political and economic structure underwent change. As a herald of an imminent cataclysm, the Education Act of 1985 undermined the communist educational system, while the 1990 Amendment, passed by the last communist government, gave it the coup de grace. By reducing heavy administrative and political control over education, these two acts gave more autonomy to individual schools, canceled the prescriptive control of the curriculum, and restored teachers' pedagogical sovereignty, offering them a free choice of methodology and teaching materials (Medgyes and Miklósy 2000).

Communism imploded in 1989. The first free election, held in 1990, brought a conservative government to power, which, oddly enough, condoned a model of education more centralized than the one adopted by its reform-minded communist predecessors. Whereas the socialist-liberal government formed in 1994 was committed to liberalizing the education system, four years later the pendulum swung back at the push of another conservative government.

There are at least two lessons to learn from this political tug-of-war. One has to do with the limited impact policy decisions taken by consecutive governments with differing ideologies seem to have had on classroom life; apart from a growing feeling of insecurity among teachers, aggravated by a dramatic drop in their standard of living, no significant changes can be registered in their teaching practices. The second point relates to the academic performance of Hungarian students in the light of international comparative studies. Whereas Hungarian students used to do extremely well in the 1970s and 1980s, their results have gradually declined since the late 1980s (Csapó 1998), and no government or political will has proven capable of reversing this downward trend. In addition, these two points are in-dications of the "social lag," referred to earlier, with which education responds to political, social, and economic changes.

Educational Policy and the National Core Curriculum

These ups and downs in Hungarian politics are reflected in curricular innovation and can be traced through the development of the NCC. The need to design a new curriculum had already been recognized by the last communist government. Then, in the early 1990s, several versions followed one another in quick succession, three of which are be analyzed in some detail: Version 1 (National Core Curric-ulum: First draft 1990), Version 2 (Hungarian Ministry of Education 1992), and Version 3 (Hungarian Ministry of Education 1995), this last being the current NCC.

The curriculum designers involved in developing the NCC had been randomly selected, and it was at the whim of policymakers that their services were, in fact, retained throughout the process or dispensed with at a certain stage. In accordance with the consensus-seeking ethos of postcommunist democracies, other specialists, including designers of local curricula, materials writers, and examination experts, were also invited to comment on the different versions of the NCC. Their sug-gestions, however, were often considered not so much on the basis of their in-trinsic professional value as on the strength of the political message they were judged to carry. Furthermore, many schools, pedagogical institutes, and university departments were also invited to provide feedback, but it is unclear what actually happened to this feedback. As for teacher feedback, since teachers had not been asked to express views on curricular matters, the scope of their responses was rather limited, and their voices could hardly be heard in the NCC.

Version 3 (Hungarian Ministry of Education 1995) may be considered inno-vative on several counts. To give an example, traditional subject areas were ar-ranged in integrated cultural domains, in an attempt to loosen up subject bound-aries across the curriculum. This approach came under heavy criticism on the grounds that on the one hand it was alien to Hungarian educational traditions and on the other hand that there were no teachers available to teach such inte-grated content areas. To make matters worse, the idea of introducing cultural domains was not carried beyond the confines of the NCC, and the subsequent examination reform still structured its requirements around traditional school subjects, rather than around cultural domains. In other areas, too, while the NCC broke new ground, it was fraught with contradictions, which, combined with protests from specialists professing conservative views, rendered implementation a daunting task. Confronted with both pragmatic and ideological constraints, the present conservative government decided to slow down the process of introducing the NCC and, simultaneously, to subject the NCC to thorough revision.

Another controversy concerned the two-tier versus the three-tier curriculum hierarchy. According to the original two-tier idea, local educational bodies, particularly schools, were urged to develop (on the basis of the NCC) their own local curricula, which were intended to give schools the opportunity to meet local needs and to involve teachers in a worthwhile professional activity besides classroom teaching. As a result, hundreds of local curricula were devised and implemented all over the country. However, when the new conservative government took over, it decided to insert the centrally prepared *frame curricula* between the NCC and the local curricula. Partly according to one's political allegiance, a frame curriculum may be regarded either as a helpful device intended to exempt schools and teachers from the burden of extra work or, conversely, as a pretext to curb their administrative and professional autonomy.

Foreign Languages in the National Core Curriculum

Modern languages, which represent one of the ten cultural domains, may be perceived as a primary conveyor of innovation in the NCC. On the one hand, the most spectacular curricular change in 1989 ended the monopoly of Russian with the result that the study of other foreign languages became accessible on a large scale (Enyedi and Medgyes 1998; Nikolov 1999a). On the other hand, the entry of Hungary into the European Union in the foreseeable future has increased the need to speak foreign languages and adopt European norms. All the documents relating to foreign-language education since 1989 have been designed to be "euroconform"; more specifically, they have adopted the functional-notional syllabus and have advocated humanistic and communicative principles of education.

Although the three major versions of the NCC address essentially the same political, linguistic, and pedagogical concerns, they exhibit differences in language policy and specialist opinion. To illustrate these differences, five issues are examined briefly.

1. *Native language versus foreign languages.* Versions 1 and 2 emphasize the isolation of Hungarian among Indo-European languages and elaborate on the role of foreign-language study in the learners' native language development. Whereas Version 1 explicitly states that teaching should shed light on similarities and differences between the first and the foreign language, this contrastive principle has been softened into "awareness raising" in Version 2, only to be pushed into the appendix in Version 3.

These alterations testify to shifts of focus both in linguistic attitudes and in the political agenda.

2. *Choice of languages.* It is interesting to examine how the role of Latin in relation to other foreign languages has changed over time. While in Version 1 only English and German are listed as examples of modern languages and Latin is referred to only indirectly, Version 2 avoids specifying any languages. Perhaps with the purpose of making concessions to conservative policymakers, Version 3 mentions Latin as a second foreign language in the introduction but then supplies examples only for English, French, German, and Russian.

3. *Starting age.* Before 1989, students started learning Russian in grade 4 (age 9), but as the regime became more liberal, so the opportunity for learning other foreign languages improved. Despite pressing social and individual demands for foreign language instruction after 1989, neither Version 1 nor Version 2 specifies the starting age. To aggravate the situation, Version 3 pushes the compulsory starting age back to grade 5 (age 10), that is, a year later than stipulated in the 1980s.

4. *Proficiency levels.* While Version 1 includes three levels of language proficiency—minimal, basic, and intermediate—Version 2 focuses on the first two levels and relegates the third to the appendix. In contrast, Version 3 maintains only the first two levels, in order to conform to the Council of Europe specifications (Council of Europe 1998).

5. *Specification of skills.* Version 1 reflects teaching and testing traditions by including *Landeskunde* (i.e., the life and institutions of target cultures), as well as translation beside the four language skills (i.e., listening, speaking, reading, writing). These areas are excluded from later versions: *Landeskunde* disappears without trace and requirements have been set only for the four skills found in the Council of Europe documents.

Foreign Language Classrooms

While the NCC underwent several changes before completion, teachers kept teaching according to their own hidden curriculum, scarcely affected by official dictates. A classroom observation study involving 118 English classes for students from disadvantaged backgrounds (Nikolov 1999b) looked into what teachers and students were actually doing in the classroom. This study reveals that the approach adopted by the language teachers under examination is rather eclectic. Techniques of the grammar-translation and the audiolingual methods mingle with ones more characteristic of the communicative classroom. While the majority of teachers use communicative coursebooks imported from Britain, these coursebooks are exploited in a traditional way. Although other studies that surveyed classes working in more auspicious conditions described a more reassuring picture of language teaching in Hungary (Dörnyei, Nyilasi, and Clément 1996; Terestyéni 1996), both types of study seem to confirm that most language teachers in Hungary use the coursebook as a syllabus and supplement it with test-preparation materials. In view of this, it is little wonder that the lack of a stable NCC has caused little trouble in the school life of postcommunist Hungary.

CONCLUSION

This study attempted to show curriculum development as a process furthered by agents who subscribe to different philosophies of education. Decisions made at policy and specialist levels are seldom based on consensus, and changes are often instituted over the heads of teachers and learners. The Hungarian national core curriculum may be considered as a typical example of a reform curriculum: While extolling the merits of communicative language teaching and setting "euroconform" requirements, it disregards the genuine needs of classroom participants and connives at the use of outdated classroom methods. In some sense, perplexed by the ever-changing and often contradictory expectations of curriculum dictates, teachers in Hungary and elsewhere are right in pursuing their own hidden agendas, instead of jumping on the bandwagon. For most of them, a gentle breeze in the form of a new technique is more refreshing than a gale of disparate ideas formulated in a reform curriculum.

On a more general plane, it was argued that if there is a gap between policymakers and specialists, the gap between either group and teachers is far wider. Hence, it is usually a long time before curriculum innovation, even at its best, permeates the thinking of those at the chalk-face and in turn alters their daily practice.

NOTES

We thank József Horváth and Christopher Ryan for their comments.

1. Such a need may be manifested, for example, in a language problem, which "occurs whenever there is linguistic discontinuity between segments of a population that are in contact" (Kaplan 1992: 144).

2. Despite the originality underlying their philosophies and practices, these models had in fact limited currency in language classrooms.

3. Markee (1997) warns that case studies may prompt some readers to ask, "What does this project have to do with me?" This is a legitimate criticism, but only if the case study fails to demonstrate the issues raised or exhibit their relevance to the readers' own concerns and environments. The authors hope to have avoided both pitfalls.

CHAPTER 17

COMMUNICATIVE, TASK-BASED, AND CONTENT-BASED LANGUAGE INSTRUCTION

MARJORIE BINGHAM WESCHE

PETER SKEHAN

IN this chapter we first review current approaches to communicative language teaching (CLT), with reference to the role of research in effecting changes in CLT emphases over time. We then present in greater depth two relatively recent trends in curriculum design that conform to CLT principles: task-based instruction, which targets explicit language learning objectives within communicative activities, and content-based instruction, which integrates language learning with subject matter learning.

COMMUNICATIVE LANGUAGE TEACHING

Communicative language teaching has evolved over the past several decades in response to changing views on the nature of communicative language use and the abilities that underlie it, research findings from interdisciplinary perspectives on how additional languages are acquired, and insights of teachers as they reflect upon their attempts to implement CLT principles in diverse instructional settings. There is now some degree of consensus regarding the qualities required to justify the label "CLT." Communicative classrooms generally feature:

- Activities that require frequent interaction among learners or with other interlocutors to exchange information and solve problems
- Use of authentic (nonpedagogic) texts and communication activities linked to "real-world" contexts, often emphasizing links across written and spoken modes and channels
- Approaches that are learner centered in that they take into account learners' backgrounds, language needs, and goals and generally allow learners some creativity and role in instructional decisions.

To support these features, CLT may be organized around or include:

- Instruction that emphasizes cooperative learning such as group and pair work
- Opportunities for learners to focus on the learning process with the goal of improving their ability to learn language in context
- Communicative tasks linked to curricular goals as the basic organizing unit for language instruction
- Substantive content, often school subject matter from nonlanguage disciplines, that is learned as a vehicle for language development, as well as for its inherent value.

Influences on the Development of Communicative Language Teaching

Methodological Preliminaries

To understand the nature of communicative language teaching in its various forms, it is helpful to consider certain characteristics of the methodologies that immediately preceded CLT, particularly grammar translation and the method that largely replaced it—in North America beginning in the 1960s, audiolingualism. While grammar-translation and audiolingualism were in many ways quite different from one another, they nonetheless shared a view of language as a formal system of rules or structures to be mastered and of language learning as the inculcation of habits—in the first case along with metalinguistic knowledge. These respective views were (and in many places still are) represented in textbooks and syllabi organized around particular language features, with minimal emphasis on meaningful language use. It was assumed that the learning of sentence-level grammar, through the study and exemplification of rules or, in audiolingualism, through the practice of patterns, would be efficient as a basis for eventual use of the language outside the classroom. Tight instructional control, reliance on exercises and practice, and avoidance of error were all presumed to help ensure progress.

Linguistic Influences

Both these views of language teaching were coming under increasing pressure by the early 1970s, particularly in the English-speaking world and in western Europe. One source of discontent was the failure of both traditional and audiolingual instruction to prepare learners for spontaneous, contextualized language use. The theoretical bases of the audiolingual method, American structural linguistics and behaviorism, had been largely discredited as a viable explanation of language learning (Chomsky 1959). In Britain, linguists such as Halliday (1978) working in the neo-Firthian tradition of systemic or functional linguistics, conducted empirical work that demonstrated patterns of language use well beyond the sentence level. Their work continued to underscore the crucial importance of context of situation in the description of language systems. Some American sociolinguists, interested in language as social behavior, were involved in related work. Hymes and others observed that the scope of Chomskyan concern with syntax, like structural linguistics before it, covered only a part of what language users needed to know in order to communicate effectively. For Hymes (1967, 1971a), what was needed was a characterization of "communicative competence," which included knowledge of appropriate and effective, as well as correct, language behavior for given communicative goals. Widdowson (1978) was to later coin the related terms *usage* and *use,* influential in language teaching, to refer to the distinction between language as a formal system and language use within communicative events.

In Europe, there were attempts to use developments in discourse linguistics to explore different methods of teaching languages. Speech act theory (Austin 1962; Searle 1969), as well as discourse analysis (Sinclair and Coulthard 1975; see review in Hatch 1992) were influential. These developments signaled that it was fundamental to consider what language users wanted to accomplish by their utterances and that if one approached the elements of language by trying to classify units of meaning rather than structures, a very different teaching inventory would result. Wilkins, for example, in his influential notional syllabuses (1976), outlined how learners might be instructed in such language functions as greeting, describing, or apologizing or in such notions as size, color, proximity, and time. Related efforts led to discourse-based pedagogical grammars for teachers (e.g., Edmondson and House 1981) and to the "threshold-level" Council of Europe syllabus specifications of language activities, functions, and notions organized by situational contexts, which was applied to a number of European languages (Trim 1980; van Ek 1975). A related but distinct influence on the emergence of CLT in the 1970s was the increasing interest of researchers in analysis of the discourse typical of given contexts and by given communities of speakers and the application of these insights to development of courses in English for Specific Purposes (ESP) or in other languages (see Munby 1978; Uber Gross and Voght 1991). The pedagogical assumption in syllabi based on relevant notions and functions was that such elements would be more acceptable and meaningful to learners and thus be more motivating. It was also proposed that teaching learners to perform communicative functions would have more immediate "payoff," in that the notions and functions so encoded by language could then be used by learners to express personal meanings. This contrasted markedly with the delayed gratification required by grammar-based approaches, where meaningful language use had to await comprehensive exposure to the grammar.

Second Language Acquisition Influences

It was also in the 1970s and early 1980s that the new field of second language acquisition (SLA) was taking shape, inspired by empirical research on first language acquisition in children and cross-Atlantic developments in linguistics. The new field was served with living laboratories by the bilingual education movement for non-English speaking children in the United States, the massive influx of immigrants and guest workers to North America and western Europe—particularly Germany and France—and by Canada's national effort to find more effective ways of teaching French to anglophone children through "immersion," that is, use of the L2 as the medium of school instruction for language-majority children. By the middle of the 1980s, a number of studies had reported evidence of developmental sequences and stages in the acquisition of certain grammatical morphemes and syntactic structures in English and several other languages by learners of different ages. These patterns partially matched those found in first language acquisition and were largely independent of classroom syllabi, showing strong similarities between instructed and naturalistic learners (see reviews in Larsen-Freeman and Long 1991; Long 1983). Although subsequent work would point out problems with the research methodology and limitations regarding its applicability, the evidence for an internal acquisition syllabus in these areas of language was indeed dramatic. For some, the findings threw into doubt the value of language instruction itself (Macnamara 1973; Newmark and Reibel 1968), while for others they spurred efforts to ensure that instruction supported the internal acquisition syllabus of learners (Dulay, Burt, and Krashen 1982).

Second language researchers developed these insights in the 1970s and 1980s, directing attention to the nature of the linguistic environment available to learners and its possible role in acquisition. They focused particularly on the language input directed to learners and on modifications from native-speaker norms to input features and interactional moves at different levels of language use. The importance of well-formed models, message comprehensibility, and salience of formal features, among other L2 input characteristics, was examined in terms of input processing frameworks (Chaudron 1985; Gass 1988) and acquisition outcomes (see reviews by Hatch 1983; Larsen-Freeman and Long 1991; and Wesche 1994). This work led to a widely held view of the role of input, best articulated by Krashen (1985), which underlies North American CLT approaches. In this view much "acquisition" takes place incidentally through motivated receptive language use in meaningful contexts. This occurs as learners at some level notice formal language features while simultaneously understanding—with the help of contextual cues—the intended meanings of the unfamiliar language forms and patterns they hear or read. As long as rich language input that is comprehensible to the learner yet contains novel language elements is provided and the learner is open to it, internalization of the target language grammar proceeds according to the internal syllabus. This viewpoint complemented the moves toward CLT based on social linguistic theory.

By the late 1970s, Canadian researchers were beginning to record consistent patterns in immersion learners' developing interlanguage that were quite positive relative to the results of other language teaching methods. Immersion instruction produced high-level listening and reading proficiency and fluency in oral and written expression, providing support for use of the second language as a vehicle rather than an object of study (Swain and Lapkin 1982). However, persistent nonnative usage by immersion students in speaking and writing was also noted, particularly errors that did not impede communication (Harley 1984), in spite of supplementary French grammar instruction in the upper elementary grades. Such instruction tended to emphasize manipulation of language forms themselves rather than "relating forms to their meaningful use in communicative events" (Allen et al. 1990). Descriptive research of immersion and core French classrooms using the Communicative Orientation of Language Teaching Observation Scheme (COLT) (Allen 1989; Allen et al. 1990; Spada and Fröhlich 1995) suggested that, in classrooms that included language analysis as an integral part of communicative activities, learners achieved higher accuracy in speaking and writing. Swain (1985) posited a role for "pushed" output, with importance given to precision and accuracy. Subsequent research in diverse CLT contexts suggests that focus on form is most effective when it is directly related to meaningful communication, whether it be through manipulation of materials and tasks to highlight given language features, communicative feedback to the learner, practice of given components, emphasis on planned production, or explanation when communicative problems arise (see review in Spada 1997).

During the same period, other researchers increasingly noted the central role of social relations in SLA (Beebe 1985; Hatch 1978, 1983; Long 1983; Wong Fillmore

1979). The relationships between and among interlocutors were seen as the basis for consequential communicative exchanges that could provide input for acquisition. For example, proficient speakers tended to provide richer, more grammatical, and more persistent input to L2-speaking social equals in ongoing relationships than to subordinates in temporary relationships (Long 1983), while extroverted learners were better at getting input from native speakers than were shy ones (Wong Fillmore 1979). Hatch was perhaps the first to propose that interactive communication itself might play a central role in acquisition: "One learns how to do conversations, one learns how to interact verbally, and out of this interaction syntactic structures are developed" (1978: 404). Research on input and acquisition has since highlighted the particular value for interlanguage restructuring of purposeful interaction, especially that involving negotiation, recasts, and other feedback, and to relate this to the CLT classroom (see reviews in Larsen-Freeman and Long 1991; Pica 1994). When learners are involved in communication, motivation to understand and express meanings is high; furthermore, such interaction may provide highly specific feedback, appropriate models, and other pertinent information at the very moment when the learner is attentive and aware of a problem. The body of research on input and interaction has provided empirical support for teaching language through communication and information on optimal supporting conditions (Wesche 1994).

Practical Developments

Each of the developments discussed focused on language beyond the level of the sentence and explored how an understanding of the organization of larger units of spoken or written language is essential to effective communication. Amid all this ferment, contextualized material increasingly found its way into mainstream language teaching textbooks, even though the fundamental organizing principle tended to remain a sequence of rules or structures (e.g., the passive), so that there was not yet a fundamental shift. An early example from Britain of a more substantial influence on general language teaching of these developments was the appearance of the *Strategies* series of course books during the 1970s (Abbs and Freebairn 1975). Such course books took a functional approach to syllabus design. The focus became the use of structural elements to achieve the communicative purposes required by different language functions, rather than their presentation out-of-context as systems in their own right. While functions as the unit of syllabus organization represented a major change, the difference between learning about communication using an analytical approach and learning through communication (i.e., experiential learning) was still at issue (Stern 1981). A curriculum model proposed in a widely read article by Allen (1983) clarified the difference, distinguishing three components: structural analytic (grammar teaching), functional analytic (description and explanation of language functions), and experiential (purposeful language use). In a 1989 article, Stern again detailed the distinction between analytical and experiential teaching/learning at all levels of the language system, calling for complementarity and balance, in a paper that had considerable influence on language curriculum development in Canada. This was a period of great excitement in language teaching, which brought new vitality through learner-oriented and meaning-based materials. Communicative approaches began to penetrate more widely, not simply appearing in course book series for traditional EFL markets but also influencing courses developed for particular countries and contexts and for languages other than English.

There were also developments in methodology. A wide variety of communication games and other activities was popularized during this period. Teachers and materials writers were inventive in finding plausible reasons for learners to use the L2, and information gap activities became commonplace in language classrooms. But these precepts produced a rather curious situation in which apparent acceptance of CLT masked widespread confusion about what it entailed. By the early 1980s, particularly with newly trained teachers in an EFL context, communicative language teaching had become widely accepted. Yet its heavy demands in terms of teacher ability and materials, disagreement about how one best achieved the end goal of communicative language use ability, and the lack of progress in clarifying what the term *syllabus* might mean in a communicative context meant that its practice remained quite varied. Perhaps as a result of this, while the main coursebook series that emerged all claimed to be communicative, the most exciting developments during this period were associated with supplementary materials. These materials generally presumed a main coursebook that provided a syllabus but lacked engaging communicative activities. The supplementary materials then embodied the sorts of criteria outlined at the beginning of this chapter and enabled the teacher to address the limitations of the core materials through judiciously chosen activities. For example, the Module Project of the Modern Language Centre at the Ontario Institute for Studies in Education (OISE) (Allen, Howard, and Ullmann 1984) provided theme-based activities that required varied language modes and skills. *Listening links*, by Geddes and Sturtridge (1979), and *Task listening* (Blundell 1983) allowed teachers to draw upon a range of activities that were entertaining and that developed one particular skill area in a communicative manner. Comparable materials abounded in other domains.

These developments on both sides of the Atlantic created an important climate within language teaching by demonstrating the limitations of conventional approaches and by offering alternatives. In Britain and North America, Widdowson's *Teaching Language as Communication* (1978), and his *Explorations in Applied Linguistics* (1979), had great impact, particularly in clarifying what communicative language teaching was trying to achieve. Canale and Swain's (1980) "Theoretical

Bases of Communicative Approaches to Second Language Teaching and Testing," in the inaugural issue of *Applied Linguistics,* synthesized recent work on the nature of Communicative language knowledge and proposed a descriptive framework to guide both language teaching and language testing. It should be noted in this context that a ferment in language testing concepts and practice had paralleled the developments in linguistics and language teaching, and each provided considerable cross-influence. The significant, ongoing contributions of language testing specialists to CLT should be noted here, particularly as regards redefinition of communicative language ability and how such ability can be elicited and measured through test performance (Bachman 1990; Canale and Swain 1980; Carroll 1980; McNamara 1995, 1996; Morrow 1979; Oller 1979; Shohamy 1985; Skehan 1984; Spolsky 1973, 1989; Weir 1983; Wesche 1987).

Against the background of such influences, coursebooks from the 1980s on have increasingly attempted to embrace communicative approaches, with each unit likely to contain some sort of communicative or quasi-communicative activity. However, this again raises the central issue for communicative materials: What is the relationship between form and language use? At an earlier stage with materials called "communicative," the activity came first, and concern for form was secondary. With contemporary "complete package" coursebooks, the underlying organization and syllabus, particularly in Britain and in EFL contexts, have largely returned to an analytic approach, with sentence structures retaining central importance. Overall, the quality of the communicative materials, and their relationship with whatever language patterns are being taught in a particular unit, have improved considerably. But, in the final analysis, current materials tend to reflect a version of the "3Ps" approach to instruction: presentation, practice, and production. The essential difference, therefore, is that the production stage of instruction is more likely to use engaging communicative activities, drawing upon authentic or at least more lively materials, with some scope for spontaneity. Coursebook authors have also become more adept at "braiding" communicative activities around the underlying structural syllabus. The result is that "the communicative approach" has in many cases been appropriated by a relatively conservative perspective to language teaching. In North America, however, there continues to be a far greater emphasis on experiential language learning. (See, e.g., Lee and VanPatten 1995; Savignon 1991).

Strong and Weak Forms of Communicative Language Teaching

In concluding this discussion of CLT, we return to the connection between communicative language teaching and terms such as *syllabus, methodology,* and *ap-*

proach. From the beginnings of communicative language teaching to the present, it has been possible to distinguish what Howatt (1984) has called "weak" and "strong" versions, sharing the same objectives but reflecting different assumptions about how second languages are learned. Whereas both weak and strong forms of CLT provide opportunities for learners to use the target language for communicative purposes, weaker forms tend to view spontaneous communication as an end rather than a means and to incorporate practice based upon description of communicative language features, such as appropriate forms for expressing given language functions. The weak form essentially implies that there is a set of classroom practices that describes and exemplifies relationships between form and meaning. The capacity to express meanings is seen as the fundamental goal of language instruction, with the result that form-based activities for the sake of extending the formal system in itself are not favored. But, equally, in weak versions of CLT, formal properties of language may come into focus explicitly with a concern for specific forms or form-function-meaning relationships. CLT of this sort is closer to a methodology-specification than a syllabus-specification, although it does not comprehensively achieve such a status. It seems more appropriate, therefore, to continue to use the term *approach* to characterize weak versions of CLT.

But there are stronger versions of communicative language teaching, as enshrined in immersion and in other content-based language instruction, and some forms of task-based learning, which we explore later. In these stronger forms, the syllabus dimension is addressed slightly differently, with a tacit acceptance of the "acquisition hypothesis": that engaging in language use will drive forward structural development and that—at least for certain structures—a "natural" syllabus will emerge through interactions in the language, as is the case in first language development. The strong version rests on the assumption that communicative language ability is, in large part, acquired through communication; thus, instruction is organized around situations, oral and written texts, skill or knowledge domains, or tasks that require communicative language use of various kinds. While quite diverse content may assure acquisition of underlying systems (e.g., phonology, word order, function words), content that is highly relevant to learners' interests and postlanguage needs will be most effective. This is so not only because it will be more motivating to learners but more important, because much of what is learned is context specific (e.g., content vocabulary that includes lexical phrases, usage that respects given discourse communities). Taking such a viewpoint to its logical extension, the distinction between language syllabus and methodology disappears: Engaging in contextualized language use (the strong CLT interpretation) drags with it an inevitable syllabus specification. We shall see that content-based instruction (CBI) and task-based instruction (TBI) have each dealt with this issue, the syllabus-methodology relationship, but in slightly different ways.

The current situation of CLT is complex, as the weak forms have increasingly appropriated elements of communicative language use into the classroom, and the strong forms have, spurred by research findings that reveal their inability to promote levels of accuracy matching their success in development of fluency, increasingly sought ways to incorporate a focus on form and language awareness into classroom practice. The tension between analytical and experiential approaches to CLT may be gradually resolving itself through this recognition of their complementarity and, at the same time, of the need to tailor solutions for particular CLT contexts both to the learners' characteristics and to their given language objectives. As we have seen, there is an emerging consensus that CLT is best understood as a general approach rather than a specific teaching method. Indeed, Celce-Murcia (1997: 148) questions "whether it makes any sense to talk about CLT at all," but also notes, citing Thompson (1996), that the term retains utility as a well-established label that reminds teachers and teacher trainers of "the primary goal of language instruction, namely, to . . . develop the learner's communicative competence." For his part, Kumaravadivelu has proposed the concept of "macrostrategies" for L2 teaching. In place of an integrated method, a set of guiding strategies such as "facilitate negotiated interaction," "contextualize linguistic input" or "foster language awareness" can be formulated to guide practitioners in working out appropriate "microstrategies" for their own teaching contexts (1994: 33–37).

Beyond such concerns within what might be termed "favored" teaching circumstances, there is also the issue of the generalizability of CLT to ethnocultural situations where the culture of formal instruction and the norms that govern communicative interaction among nonintimates or teachers and students run counter to CLT principles. For example, Li (1998), in a study of attitudes of Korean EFL teachers toward CLT, enumerates serious barriers to its transfer to EFL contexts, even where communicative language ability is the stated instructional objective. Teachers themselves often perceive that CLT will not work in their context for cultural reasons, such as lack of fit with traditional teacher/student roles or established evaluation methods, and for practical reasons, such as teachers' deficiencies in productive English, poor teaching conditions, and lack of training. He concludes that there is a conflict in many countries "between what CLT demands and what the EFL situation . . . allows" (1998: 695) and suggests that "implementation should be gradual and grounded in the countries' own EFL situations" (677). Positive teachers' perceptions must be developed. Goals must also be adapted to the local situation (such as greater emphasis on reading for meaning). Holliday (1994) likewise argues for the promotion of appropriate methodologies, which match cultural expectations and educational traditions.

Despite these criticisms, there have been attempts to develop the strong form of CLT within its own terms. We turn to these next.

TASK-BASED INSTRUCTION

Task-based language learning was defined by Breen (1987: 23) as "any structured language learning endeavour which has a particular objective, appropriate content, a specified working procedure, and a range of outcomes for those who undertake the task." "Task" is, in this view, assumed to refer to a range of work plans that have the overall purpose of facilitating language learning—from the simple and brief exercise type, to more complex and lengthy activities such as group problem solving or simulations and decision making. Within a CLT approach, more restricted definition is necessary for task-based instruction approach. Candlin notes that, among other things, communicative tasks must provide "comprehensible input and procedures for engaging that input" (1987: 8). Useful tasks for language learning should "promote attention to meaning . . . [and] to relevant data; should be challenging but not threatening; should involve language use in the solving of the task" (9), and involve affective, communicative and social factors. Skehan (1998d), following Nunan (1989), suggests that a task is an activity in which:

- Meaning is primary
- There is some communication problem to solve
- There is some sort of relationship with real-world activities
- Task completion has some priority
- The assessment of the task is in terms of outcomes.

These criteria in operation can be exemplified by sample tasks where:

- Learners, in pairs, try to identify which objects-in-common they each have about their person (Willis and Willis 1987)
- Learners, in pairs or groups, try to agree on the advice that could be given to the writers of letters to an Agony Aunt (Skehan and Foster 1997).

Task-based instruction (TBI), in other words, places the task centrally, as the unit of syllabus design (Long and Crookes 1992), with language use during tasks as the driving force for language development (Long 1989; Prabhu 1987). This interpretation is linked to second language acquisition research that suggests that interlanguage development is internally influenced and not open simply to teacher control of input. Such a view of how tasks should be used in language instruction was very influential by 1990 and reflected optimism that interaction-driven language development was possible. We briefly review related research before going on to consider the different pedagogic approaches to implementing TBI.

Research Findings

Two issues have some prominence in task-based research: research into the effects of task characteristics and task implementation conditions.

Features

A major contribution of task-linked research is that it does not assume that the qualities of tasks are self-evident but instead gathers empirical data to establish whether there are systematic influences on performance that follow from the choice of a task with a particular set of characteristics. In practice, this has meant research into task difficulty issues and research to establish whether particular task characteristics are associated with particular patterns of language use. (See Skehan 1998d for review.) The research has shown that characteristics such as type and familiarity of information, structure of task, and nature of outcome systematically influence performance on different aspects of language (Skehan 2001).

Task Conditions

The bulk of the research into task conditions has focused on what happens before a task and what happens after it. In the former category, there has been considerable research into the effects of pretask planning. Virtually all studies demonstrate that planning is associated with more complex and more fluent language (e.g., Crookes 1989; Foster and Skehan 1996; Mehnert 1998; Ortega 1999; Wigglesworth 1997). Some studies also suggest that planning is associated with greater accuracy (Foster and Skehan 1996; Mehnert 1998; Skehan and Foster 1997; Wigglesworth 1997). There have also been studies of posttask influences on task performance. Bygate (1996, 2001) and Lynch and MacLean (2001) have shown that providing the opportunity for learners to repeat a task produces beneficial results and more form-focused performance. Skehan and Foster (1997, in preparation) show that giving learners a posttask to do that focuses their attention on language can lead, fairly selectively, to an increase in the accuracy of the task performance.

Practical Perspectives

Task-based instruction is particularly interesting because it is associated on the one hand with considerable research activity and on the other with active pedagogic investigation and materials preparation. Many of the studies reported in the previous section were field experiments; that is, they were set in actual classrooms. As a result, compared to other research literatures, the ecological validity of the work enables the relationship between findings and actual teaching to be argued more strongly, and so teachers might take them into account when choosing tasks for particular purposes or when thinking about how best to implement tasks.

Interest in using tasks in language teaching has grown considerably over the past twenty-five years. Initially, tasks were largely used as adjunct activities, often taken from supplementary materials. Subsequently, a number of textbook series that claim to be task based have appeared. In the United Kingdom, *Cobuild* (Willis and Willis 1987) was perhaps the first, and more recently there has been *Cutting Edge* (Cunningham and Moor 1998). In the United States, *Pyramid* (Madden and Reinhart 1987) takes a task-based approach, as does *Atlas* (Nunan 1995) on a more international basis.

Advocates of a task-based approach have rejected the conventional, rule-focused presentation-practice-production sequence, claiming that, if task is the primary unit for pedagogic development (e.g., Long and Crookes 1992), then tasks themselves (not structures) should be the building blocks that underlie pedagogy. A different methodology will be needed, and pedagogic sequencing will have to be achieved following some new criteria.

Three broad approaches to pedagogy can be distinguished, all of them having slightly different perspectives to the relationship between form and meaning.

First, Samuda (2001) proposes that there need not be an overt tension between an artificially focus on a particular structure and a desire to use convincing tasks. She argues that it is possible to "seed" tasks with particular structures, and that, provided that the teacher is sufficiently skillful, the naturalness of the task need not be compromised. The key feature for her is a teacher who can adapt to an unfolding task so that she or he can exploit, in an opportunistic manner, openings for work on the structure which the teacher has chosen as suitable.

The second approach is that of Skehan (1998d), who argues that one cannot be so confident that reactive teaching of this sort is feasible and that a focus on a particular structure will not compromise naturalness of communication. He suggests that teachers should be able to draw upon findings from the task literature to choose and use tasks to maximize the chances that pedagogically desired lines of progress will occur; teachers should choose tasks to make it more likely that restructuring and interlanguage change can occur or select task conditions to promote the development of fluency. Teachers, then, need explicitly to use periodic cycles of accountability, with learners, to plan future teaching.

Finally, there are two versions of the third, thoroughgoing, task-driven approach. Long (1989) argues that tasks that promote interaction will bring with them negotiation for meaning and that this negotiation will generate the focus-on-form and feedback that learners require to make progress. Willis (1996) proposes a task-based methodology that (a) primes a topic area, (b) requires task-based language use, and then (c) provides learners with opportunities to reflect upon the language that completing the task has made salient. (Learners will have been induced to "notice a gap" [Swain 1995]; and then consolidate it.)

Task-based instruction has been a very interesting development of CLT. Its early and over-optimistic promise is now tempered with greater realism concerning its limitations. The cumulative richness of research findings and pedagogic experiences has enabled us to see its strengths and weaknesses more clearly. In particular, a realization that a focus-on-form by learners cannot be guaranteed but has to be "designed into" TBI is an important pointer to future developments. Perhaps Spada's (1997) conclusion that form-based and meaning-based approaches need not be in opposition to each other but can operate synergistically is the most realistic current judgment.

CONTENT-BASED INSTRUCTION

Content-based language instruction (CBI) refers to the integration of school or academic content with language-teaching objectives. A primary advantage of CBI over other CLT approaches is that using subject matter as the content for language learning maximizes learners' exposure to the second language. Furthermore, this exposure is to a highly contextualized and particularly relevant subset of the language. In successful CBI, learners master both language and content through a reciprocal process as they understand and convey varied concepts through their second language. Language development progresses alongside study of a given topic or texts through repeated communicative encounters with given language forms and patterns. Content learning—like other meaningful language use—involves comprehending meaning and associating language forms, meanings, and functions in different contexts. Repeated use of new language ensures ongoing mental elaboration and practice, increasing its availability for new encounters and long-term retention. For these reasons, CBI can be very effective for both language and content learning. However, ensuring the necessary conditions to achieve this presents an ongoing challenge.

Features

All forms of successful CBI share certain features, because the most essential element of each is the same—students struggling to master new concepts and conceptual skills through a language in which they have limited proficiency. Because academic language proficiency is crucial to school success, CBI may be seen as particularly relevant to learners who are preparing for full-time study through their second (or weaker) language, at any level of education. Contextual and pedegogical features shared by different forms of CBI include:

- *The premise that learners in some sense receive "two for one," that is, content knowledge and increased language proficiency.* Motivation to understand and learn is promoted through the social environment of the school, which provides learners with opportunities for consequential engagement with both interlocutors and significant texts. The learning of both content and language rests on the premise that learners will be able successfully to access and learn subject matter texts and concepts through their L2.
- *A language curriculum in which expository texts and discourse are central.* Most often these are "authentic" written texts for native speakers with a purpose other than teaching language, which represent L1 norms of usage. For nonnative speakers, these texts, instructor explanations, and attendant activities and assignments are the main source not only of content knowledge but of new language forms, patterns, functions and meanings to be understood and internalized.
- *Orientation into a new culture or "discourse community" (Kramsch 1993).* The instructional situation itself may require considerable socialization, even for native speakers (e.g., into school roles and routines in early immersion, kindergarden, or into academic life and a specialized discipline for postsecondary students), but the gap will be greatly compounded for L2 speakers by a learning context and discourse that represent assumptions, roles, and customs very different from those they know.
- *Adaptation of language input, interactional moves, and context to accommodate learners' limited language proficiency.* The linguistic and conceptual complexity and the novelty of texts and learning activities largely determine their difficulty for L2 learners and, likewise, the support learners will need. This can be provided through modifications to L2 students' workload, adapted language use in instruction and evaluation, greater contextual support, and increased time or modifications to the amount, form, or complexity of the content presented. Support can also be provided through explicit language instruction related to the content being learned.
- *Focus on academic language proficiency.* The second language abilities emphasized in CBI—again in contrast to most other CLT—are primarily those needed for dealing with instructional discourse: that is, what Cummins (1984) has characterized as "context reduced" and "cognitively demanding" dimensions of language use. These contrast with context-embedded, cognitively undemanding dimensions, such as conversations with intimates about familiar events. Reading, writing, listening, speaking, and various kinds of interaction all have an important place in school lan-

guage. Mohan and his colleagues have further characterized school discourse in terms of the forms and patterns in expository prose that correspond to basic human knowledge structures common in school curricula (Mohan 1986). They have also shown how key graphics that reflect the way information is organized in discourse can aid in the learning of both language and content (Early, Mohan, and Hooper 1989; Tang 1992). Thus certain language forms are typically used to describe hierarchical classification systems, be they for business, biology, or library science, and their structure can be represented graphically, such as through classification trees. Likewise, cyclic or linear sequencing of events can be represented in cyclical or linear diagrams and generally evoke certain discourse markers to show time relationships among events.

Strong and Weak Forms of CBI

Content-based instruction is, by definition, a "strong" form of communicative language teaching, but it also has its own "weaker" and "stronger" forms. Weaker forms include language courses whose main aim is to develop learners' communicative proficiency in the second language through a curriculum organized around the learning of substantive information and skills (Brinton and Master 1997; Brinton, Snow, and Wesche 1989). The course syllabus may be theme-based or organized around specific texts, or it may be based on the content of a regular school or university course in another discipline and serve as a language support course for L2 speakers enrolled in that course. At the "strong" end of the scale are "language-sensitive" content courses for L2 speakers in nonlanguage disciplines, in which the primary goal is mastery of the subject matter (Brinton, Snow, and Wesche 1989). Successful CBI contexts for both content mastery and language development must systematically take into account learners' limited language proficiency. Examples of strong forms include mainstreaming of second language speakers in classes for native speakers, with some individualized adaptation for their language level. "Sheltered" formats group second language speakers in a content course taught in the language they are learning. Examples include foreign language "immersion" programs, in which the school curriculum is taught through the foreign language—generally by native speakers (Genesee 1987; Harley 1993; Met and Lorenz 1997). Postsecondary study of a nonlanguage discipline taught through a second or foreign language is another example—a popular form of "languages across the curriculum" (LAC). (See, for example, Anderson, Allen, and Narváez 1993; Krueger and Ryan 1993; Stryker and Leaver 1997.) Mixed forms may involve both language and content-oriented CBI. For example, two-way bilingual or multilingual school instruction involves two or more instructional languages, with native speakers of each taking some classes with second language speakers, plus separate L2 language arts classes (Baetens-Beardsmore 1993; Rhodes, Christian, and Barfield 1997). The concepts underlying CBI apply to occupational training as well—for example, college diploma programs that serve adult immigrant students with a language component (Wesche 2000). CBI also underlies school-based efforts to revive or support declining indigenous languages, modern examples of which include Hawaiian (Slaughter 1997), Welsh (Dodson and Thomas 1988), Catalan (Artigal 1997), and Inuktituk (Fettes 1998).

At the postsecondary level, CBI makes a special contribution to advanced language learners who are seeking not only language mastery but cultural insights as they prepare for academic study and professional careers that require highly functional L2 ability. North American college and university ESL programs, with their mission of preparing speakers of other languages for academic study, have been pioneers in developing content-based methodologies. (See, e.g., Burger, Wesche, and Migneron 1997, Snow 1998, Snow and Brinton 1997.) Initiatives in other languages have involved French as a second language in Canada, where concerted efforts were made in the mid-1980s and early 1990s by English-language universities to offer courses in different disciplines in French for entering graduates of French immersion secondary school programs. (It should be noted that similar opportunities have long been available to some through Canada's bilingual universities [Wesche 1985, 2000]). American university foreign language programs undertook a wide range of cross-curricular language (LAC) program initiatives in the 1990s to enhance language learning and use in academic life, in many cases supported by government educational funding agencies or private foundations. (See examples in Krueger and Ryan 1993; Stryker and Leaver 1997.) During the same period, Australia also spawned diverse CBI programs at the postsecondary level in a number of languages, including the use of CBI in language-teacher training. (See, e.g., Chapell and De Courcy 1993.)

Whereas all forms of CBI share the features we have described, they do not all share a pedagogical focus on formal aspects of the code, or "language analysis" (Stern 1989). Research findings indicate an important role for attention to form as part of communicative activity in the development of accuracy and more nativelike language usage, particularly with respect to learner errors that do not impede communication and thus bring little natural feedback (Allen et al. 1990; Harley 1993). Although CBI in its stronger forms has often proceeded without instructional emphasis on language analysis, its contexts provide rich opportunities, such as preparation of complex oral and written texts, for an emphasis on accurate and culturally appropriate language. Accuracy in language use is an important educational goal, and, in recent years, realization of the need for more attention to formal properties of language and discourse has brought change to many CBI contexts (see review in Spada 1997). Methods for ensuring such a focus within purposeful communicative activity include careful curricular formulation of specific language objectives for content units (Snow, Met, and Genesee 1989), an emphasis on accuracy as well as fluency in language production (Swain 1985, 1995), the systematic incorporation of tasks focused on formal aspects of language into the curriculum (see previous discussion), and explicit language instruction.

Most forms of CBI for L2 speakers can provide neither regular contact with peers who are native speakers of the target language nor, with the exception of ESL, broad exposure to out-of-class language use. Learners in classes limited to L2 speakers, even when all instruction is in the instructional language, tend to develop classroom "dialects" that may slow their progress toward target language performance. In classes where native speaker peers are present, learners achieve higher levels of spoken fluency, greater ease in social situations, and more of what some have called "cultural literacy" regarding the target language community. Some notable examples of the relatively rare CBI situations that involve significant contact with native speaker peers are:

- Two-way immersion, in which peers from two different L1s each separately study the other language as an L1 and L2 and attend certain school classes together in both languages (Rhodes, Christian, and Barfield 1997)
- European schools, established primarily for children of European Community employees, that aim to develop each learner's home language and culture and a "European" identity with native speaker teachers and peers in at least three languages by graduation (Baetens-Beardsmore 1993)
- The LAC graduate program at the Monterrey Institute of International Studies (MIIS), in which mixed classes of American and international students take courses together through different languages, including English (Shaw 1996).

A further, well-proven approach to complementing CBI instruction with contact experiences lies in organized, out-of-class language activities, exchanges, and study abroad (Freed 1995; MacFarlane and Wesche 1995.) MacFarlane (1997), for example, in her study of school group exchanges in Canada, demonstrated the kinds of classroom-complementary language development that can occur during extended contact experiences.

Research Findings

As with task-based instruction, an abundant and continually evolving literature on content-based instruction now exists. It includes three decades of documentation on school immersion (for reviews see Calvé 1991; Genesee 1987; Johnson and Swain 1997; Snow 1998; Swain and Lapkin 1982), and a similarly vast literature on bilingual education provides many pertinent studies (see Baker 1996). Excellent reviews and collections also cover school level CBI for mainstreamed second language learners (see, e.g., Faltis and Hudelson 1998; Genesee 1994) and postsecondary CBI and LAC (Rosenthal 2000, and previously listed references). Discussion of common implementation issues for CBI programs at different levels may be found in program handbooks, manuals, research reports, and web sites.

Since studies have most often been undertaken to evaluate existing program initiatives, theory development has drawn heavily from the interpretation of patterns of program success and failure and research in related fields (Grabe and Stoller 1997). Over time, program descriptions and data on learner outcomes have yielded to more detailed analysis of classroom processes. The development of shared concepts and models has led to comparisons within and across programs. The resulting literature provides guidance for diverse CBI initiatives. Several points are notable: First, successful programs respect the particularities of each context; second, shared issues arise in implementing and maintaining CBI programs over quite diverse contexts.

Overall, the research findings on a broad range of CBI programs are highly consistent, showing that successful subject matter learning, second/foreign language development superior to that achieved otherwise in school or academia, and positive attitude changes (by both learners and instructional staff) can all be achieved–with willing learners–through CBI approaches. Such programs tend to be highly appreciated by students for their relevance and by participating staff for the satisfaction of effectively helping students to prepare for life after language instruction (Grabe and Stoller 1997; Snow 1997, 1998; Wesche 1993a, 1993b).

Stronger forms of CBI nonetheless face significant obstacles, and their existence can usually be traced to highly committed individuals and groups. Significant shared issues confronting such programs include (among others) lack of specific teacher preparation (content-teachers for L2 learners or language teachers for content instruction), inadequate or non-existent curricular definition to integrate language and content objectives, and related problems, such as unrealistic expectations and inappropriate assessment practices. CBI initiatives often suffer from lack of administrative support and may face daunting obstacles to cross-disciplinary collaboration, in itself an extremely complex issue at secondary and postsecondary levels.

LANGUAGE AND CONTENT INTERFACE

The most important pedagogical issue for CBI at all program levels is almost certainly the interface of language and content. Learners tend to be highly motivated in CBI contexts, particularly if they are there by choice. However, a serious mismatch between course demands and learners' language and subject matter capabilities easily leads to frustration, lack of progress, and loss of motivation. (See examples in Johnson 1979; Shaw 1996.) Mohan (1986) referred to "the language factor in content" that slows learners in accessing content in their L2 and may prevent full understanding. In assessment, high language demands (such as essay tests) may furthermore mean that L2 learners are unable to demonstrate the content knowledge they do have (Brinton, Snow and Wesche 1989; Klee and Tedick 1997). The "content factor in language" is also at work, in that learners who are overwhelmed with content learning demands cannot adequately attend to the language they are exposed to or produce. (See examples in Johnson 1979; Ready and Wesche 1992.) Whereas interface problems are present in all forms of CBI, managing them is particularly critical in late-secondary and postsecondary programs, because of the complexity of disciplinary content, sophisticated language demands, and the high stakes for students. Heavy reading loads and complex written texts raise difficulties with both content learning and language development and are a persistent issue in most postsecondary programs. Concern of content instructors that adaptations for L2 speakers may "water down" content is not new. Neither is the solution. In the words of the Moravian bishop Jan Amos Comenius (1638): "If students do not understand the subject-matter, how can they master the various devices for expressing it forcibly? The time is more usefully spent on less ambitious efforts, so devised that knowledge of the language and the general intelligence may advance together step by step" (*The Great Didactic* [1638], tr. Keatinge, 1920/1967: 204–205).

Confirmation of this wisdom in modern formats is found in reports of well-researched programs that represent strong forms of CBI: linked language and discipline courses in French and English at the University of Ottawa (Burger, Wesche and Migneron 1997); an "immersion semester" load of sheltered discipline courses in Spanish, German, or French at the University of Minnesota (Klee and Tedick 1997), and language-sensitive mainstream instruction for students with a non-English home language in courses at California State University at Los Angeles (Snow 1997). All point to the crucial need for attention to the pedagogical and other conditions that can ensure that learners arrive at an in-depth understanding of the content and are able to reformulate it appropriately in their L2 for relevant purposes. Through these efforts and those of the students themselves, the learning of both will "advance together step by step."

CONCLUSION

CBI, particularly its strong forms, involves relatively intensive exposure to highly contextualized new language of particular relevance to the learners. It can provide the motivating purpose for language learning, a naturalistic learning context that includes social and other pragmatic dimensions, and the possibility of form-focused activity. Together, these perhaps offer as close to a comprehensive environment for second language development as is possible in the classroom. CBI appears to be particularly advantageous for two clienteles. The first is young school learners (e.g., in kindergarten immersion) who are preliterate and who accept a native-speaker teacher as a language model to be imitated, thus minimizing the accuracy problem. It also works well with older learners who have had some previous language instruction that prepares them to cope with academic content at a higher level. In this case the CBI approach can draw upon existing grammatical knowledge while focusing on content, playing an "activating" role for known language while supporting ongoing acquisition of context-related elements. Finally, it should be noted that, while CBI is founded upon sound principles, the outcomes depend upon the details of its implementation.

Communicative language teaching in the broad sense undoubtedly represents the most interesting development in language teaching that has occurred over the past twenty-five years. Yet its worth and applicability are still in question, perhaps for two reasons. One is that CLT by its nature cannot solve the syllabus problem and so cannot lend itself to organized, accountable, easy-to-teach coursebooks and evaluative tools in the way that other syllabi and methodologies may. It encompasses a wide range of formats, serving different clienteles and purposes, none of which can claim to be a complete solution to how language should be taught. The second reason for doubt about CLT's effectiveness concerns the role of formal instruction. Early, strong versions of CLT, which assumed that "talking to learn" would be sufficient, have been disappointing. In spite of their success in developing highly functional L2 skills in learners, they have not led to matching accuracy in production. It is clear that merely engaging in language use is not enough; some degree of focus on form is needed. But it is also clear that this is best done within communicative activities, rather than independently.

As a development grounded in language description and empirical research, the communicative approach has continually had to measure itself with evidence. What we have learned is that CLT is not a panacea that can achieve success whatever the circumstances. It has to be carefully introduced and implemented and requires appropriate teacher training and adaption to local conditions. Even so, we now have a much clearer idea of what can be achieved with CLT and the conditions for its success.

Communicative language teaching as we know it may be increasingly super-ceded in some contexts by approaches comparable in principle but different in degree or in contextualization. Task-based instruction, for example, could be considered simply a more thoroughgoing version of CLT. It may be that versions of TBI with clear provision for focus on form will show that continued progress is possible in promoting accuracy and complexity, as well as fluency. A distinguishing feature of TBI has been how integrally it is connected with empirical research. It may be that this connection will demonstrate that TBI can meet challenges that other methodologies do not and that the empirical basis for the approach will lead to its wider adoption.

Content-based instruction is distinguished by its application in specific contexts, which, while they may offer good conditions for language development, also constrain the language syllabus, and generally require "tailor-made" programs. It is nonetheless attractive because it offers simultaneous content and language development, often employing content that would have to be addressed anyway, and because it emphasizes academic language skills. CBI is likely to continue to flourish in contexts where learners have the clear and present need to develop their academic second language skills. It is also likely increasingly to incorporate form-focused activities.

It is difficult to predict how communicative language teaching, task-based instruction, and content-based instruction will develop in the future. The manner in which each links with research perspectives means that they will not be easy to ignore; they already influence standards for the ways in which methodologies and syllabuses should be evaluated. Each has limits to its application, but all have been shown to be effective under favorable circumstances. It is likely that each will continue to evolve and become even more effective as the underlying SLA principles become better understood and are incorporated into teaching

CHAPTER 18

BILINGUAL EDUCATION

COLIN BAKER

THIS chapter suggests that an international understanding of bilingual education requires a series of multidisciplinary perspectives. Bilingual education is not just dual language policy, provision, and classroom practice in schools. Bilingual education is also part of manifest and latent national or regional language planning that sometimes seeks to assimilate indigenous and immigrant minorities or to integrate newcomers or minority groups. Other times, bilingual education is a major plank in language revitalization, language reversal, and language activism.

Tensions exist between demands for assimilation and pleas for the reversal of language shift. This ensures that politics is rarely absent from debates about bilingual education. Indeed, there is no understanding of international bilingual education without contextualizing it within the politics of a country (e.g., Canada) or a region (e.g., the Basques region of Spain) or a state (e.g., California). Bilingual education can be fully understood only in relation to political ideology, movements in political ideas and political opportunism. The increasing politicization of bilingual education has recently led to key economic questions, such as whether the bilingual education option is expensive, cost efficient, or cost effective.

The pedagogic, language planning, political, and economic perspectives are not the only perspectives on bilingual education. There are public (opinion) perspectives (see Krashen 1999) and sociolinguistic perspectives (e.g., McKay and Hornberger 1996), psychological perspectives (e.g., Baker 1996), historical perspectives (e.g., Kloss 1998; Lewis 1981), and important national perspectives (see Cummins and Corson 1997). Also, the four perspectives presented here are capable of extension into components (e.g., pedagogy into teaching methodology, learning strategies, curriculum resourcing, teacher training, and school organization) and overlap and interact (e.g., language planning and economics interact with politics).

Four perspectives on bilingual education are now presented. The conclusion will centers on the issue of whether these perspectives can be integrated or whether they must remain separate and in conflict.

BILINGUAL EDUCATION AS LANGUAGE PLANNING

The first perspective is the viewpoint of language planners (e.g., in Wales, Ireland, Catalonia, and the Basque country) who believe that bilingual education is one essential means of language maintenance, language revitalization, and reversal of language shift. In this perspective, bilingual education needs to be embedded within a framework for language revitalization, and this is now our focus.

For a language to survive and revive, it has to be lived and loved. Daily language use and a consistently favorable attitude toward a language are all important. While it is implausible, imagine a minority language with rights to use enshrined in law, with radio and television, CDs and computer programs available in that minority language, bilingual signage, but with everyone using the majority language at home, when experiencing the mass media, in leisure and religious activities, in employment, and in all daily social interaction. It is theoretically possible to have many support systems for a language but for the language to be dying because it is not used in families and communities. Therefore, at the heart of language planning is planning for reproduction and usage. This suggests that language rights, mass media, signposts, and many other strategies and actions are not of first-order importance in themselves. While each contributes to the status and institutionalization of a language, each is ultimately important to the extent to which it contributes to the four priorities to be discussed.

It has been argued by a premier European language planning government institution (see Welsh Language Board 1999) that there are four major priorities that directly relate to the survival and strengthening of a minority language:

1. Language reproduction in the family
2. Language production from preschool education through formal schooling to adult education
3. Using the minority language for economic purpose
4. Social, cultural, and leisure participation through the minority language.

Minority languages decline when families fail to reproduce the language in their children. One basic performance indicator of the future of a language is age trends. Where and when much higher proportions of older people speak a minority language than younger age groups, the language is imperiled. Where and when younger age groups are a larger proportion of the population than older speakers of the language, a positive sign for the future of the language is present. Thus, family language planning is a top priority, quintessential but insufficient by itself. The family plants the seed and ensures its early growth. The blossoming requires cultivation in bilingual education, the employment market, and social/cultural life.

No minority language has a secure future unless parents raise their children through that language. For example, in Wales, nearly one in ten Welsh-speaking parents raises his or her children through the medium of English (Welsh Language Board 1999). Language reproduction and production via bilingual education are thus essential to make up the shortfall in language transmission at the family level and to increase the stock of minority-language speakers. Language acquisition in preschool education, in elementary and high schools, at higher education levels, and in adult language learning classes becomes essential to increase the supply of minority-language speakers.

Language planning through bilingual education has succeeded in the Basque country, Canada, Catalonia, and Wales, for example, and becomes a necessary but insufficient foundation, by itself, for language revitalization.

The case of Ireland signals a warning. The creation of the Irish Free State in 1922 made Irish the first official language of the country, and Irish was made compulsory in schools, compulsory to pass as a subject in order to matriculate from school, and compulsory for entrance to much public sector employment and to university. Despite constant state intervention and schemes to support the Irish language, the Irish language has continued to decline in daily usage.

One reason for the decline in the Irish language, despite language rights and language planning, has been a lack of a strong economic dimension to the Irish language. After leaving school, children found that the Irish language was of little real value in the employment market. For many jobs, Irish was practically irrelevant. Instead, schoolchildren, their parents, and students in Ireland have become increasingly aware of the economic advantages of the European Union languages, particularly French, German, Spanish, and English. The economic value of a language is not the only determinant of its value and usefulness, but it is a crucial factor.

The more a minority language can be tied in with employment, promotion in employment, and increasing affluence, the greater the perceived value of that language. The greater the number of jobs that require bilingualism (and often biliteracy), the more importance a minority language will have in the curriculum. That is, an economic value to a minority language provides needed instrumental motivation for children to become proficient in that language in school.

The more a minority language is aligned with employment and economy, the more parents may become motivated and encouraged to reproduce that language among their children. A strong economic value to a language gives added momentum for language reproduction in the family. It also gives momentum to preschool efforts for language acquisition—that is, inculcation of the language in the very young in an informal, subconscious, and enjoyable fashion.

The danger of promoting only the economic value of a minority language is that it may have only short-term monetary associations. There is a possibility of doing the right thing for a temporary reason. Once the economic needs are fulfilled, the individual may not use the minority language. For a language to be of increased value and to be used daily, it has to capture also particular contexts or domains where people's noneconomic activity occurs; for a language to survive and multiply, it has to be used regularly in everyday interaction and relationships. Languages live when they are continually and consistently used in everyday life.

A language thus needs to be associated with all the positive aspects of cultural, leisure, and community life. The widest form of cultural participation needs to be encouraged:

- From the fun of festivities to the dancing of discos
- From the rites and rituals of religion to the rhythms of rock music
- From the cheering at sports events to quiet group hobbies and pastimes.

Where there is valued cultural and leisure use of a minority language, language reproduction in the family becomes more encouraged and motivated. In the same way, language production through education becomes more meaningful when it is seen that a minority language has an enjoyable use in cultural and leisure activity.

Any language without literacy in this century may be in grave danger of dying out. Literacy in a minority language gives many more uses and functions to that language (e.g., in employment and in leisure reading). A language without literacy is like a colonized language. When the British colonized areas of Africa and India, they frequently allowed literacy solely in the English language. The indigenous languages were relegated to lower status, noneconomic uses; English was the key to educational wisdom, employment, and wealth. A language without literacy has many fewer functions and much less status. Bilingual education has a crucial function in promoting biliteracy (except where there is a strong religious promotion of literacy).

The language planner's view of bilingual education necessarily focuses on the importance of producing more speakers of a minority language than are generated through the home. A language planner's view of bilingual education necessarily focuses on strengthening the minority language among first language speakers, majority-language children learning a minority language as a second language as early as possible and becoming fluent in that minority language so as to operate in the curriculum of the primary and secondary school. Also, in a language planner's view, it is important to have the minority language culture infused throughout the curriculum. Thus, a "minority language" cultural dimension added to every curriculum area becomes important to a language planner in giving a language rootedness, identity, and connectedness at a cognitive and affective level with the kaleidoscopic colors of a minority-language culture.

However, there are three particular limitations to the language planning perspective of bilingual education that need to be briefly mentioned. First, there is a danger in the language planner's regarding bilingual education as existing for the sake of the language and not necessarily for the sake of the child. Bilingual education can be seen as a salvation for the language, whereas an alternative (but not contradictory) viewpoint is that a minority language is taught for the sake of the child. A humanistic educationalist may argue that bilingual education needs to be defended for its value and for its contribution to the development of the child, rather than for its support of the language. Second, the language planning perspective on bilingual education tends to have a limited view of the functions and purposes of education. There are occasionally arguments between the supporters and the critics of bilingual education that separate and artificially disassociate debates about language and debates about effective education. We return to this theme later in this chapter when the politics of bilingual education are considered. Third, there is sometimes overoptimism among language planners about what can be expected from, and delivered by, bilingual education in revitalizing a language. When a language fails to be reproduced in the family, and when there are insufficient support mechanisms (e.g., language rights, mass media) outside schools, it is not uncommon to hold too high expectations of language reversal via bilingual education. While bilingual education has an important role in language reproduction, and while probably without bilingual education a minority language cannot survive except through intense religious usage, bilingual education cannot deliver language maintenance by itself.

BILINGUAL EDUCATION AS PEDAGOGY

Over the past few decades, a growing number of educationalists throughout many countries of the world have supported and promoted different forms of bilingual education. While bilingual education takes many different forms (see Baker and S. P. Jones 1998), the foundational perspective of such people is that bilingual education is typically superior to monolingual education. While one must not underestimate the critics of bilingual education (e.g., the anti-Latino lobby in the United States and the assimilationists in the United Kingdom), the philosophy, principles, policies, and practices of bilingual education have grown remarkably in recent decades. Educationalists have increasingly considered the value of two or three majority languages in schools, not just taught as languages but as means for the transmission of curriculum content. For example, Scandinavia, as well as Japan and other Far East countries, is increasingly seeing the importance of languages in the global market, in intercontinental communication, and in information exchange, while educators interested in minority languages argue for the benefits of bilingual education as standard raising, child centered, and responsive to parents and pupils as clients.

Among educationalists, arguments for bilingual education vary according to local politics and the status and power of majority and minority languages, but they tend to revolve around eight particular advantages of bilingual education. These are briefly outlined (see Baker and S. P. Jones 1998 for more detail).

1. Bilingual education allows both languages (sometimes three languages) to develop fully. Rather than engaging in token second language learning, children develop proficiency two or more languages. This allows them to engage in wider communication and to have more options in patterns of communication across generations, regions and cultural groups.

2. Bilingual education develops a broader enculturation and a wider and a more sympathetic view of different creeds and cultures. Rather than token multicultural lessons, bilingual education gives deep insights into the cultures associated with the languages, fosters a broader understanding of differences, and, at its best, avoids the tight compartmentalization of racism—the stereotyping of different social groups—and fosters a more multiperspective viewpoint that is sensitive to differences.

3. Bilingual education can easily lead to biliteracy. Being able to read and write in two or more languages allows more possibilities in uses of literacy (e.g., in employment), widens the choice of literature for pleasure, gives more opportunities for different perspectives and viewpoints, and leads to a deeper understanding of history and heritage, of traditions and territory.

4. Research suggests that when children have two well-developed languages, they enjoy certain cognitive benefits. Schools are often important in developing a child's two languages to the point where the children may be more creative in thinking because of their bilingualism and more sensitive in communication as they become interpersonally aware, for example, about the need to codeswitch and to inspect their languages more (that is, they have metalinguistic advantages).

5. Heritage language education (developmental maintenance bilingual education) may raise children's self-esteem. When a child's home language is replaced by the majority language, the child, the parents, and the child's community may seem to be rejected. When the home language is used in school, then children may feel themselves, their home, and community to be accepted, thus maintaining or raising their self-esteem. Self-esteem, a confidence in one's own ability and potential, interacts in an important way with achievement and curriculum success.

6. Not only Canadian immersion studies but also studies of developmental maintenance bilingual education suggest that curriculum achievement is increased through such education. The precise way that bilingual education raises standards is neither simple nor straightforward (August and Hakuta 1997). There is likely to be a complex equation involving the support of the home, the enthusiasm and commitment of teachers in school, children's feeling of acceptance and security, and the relationship between language and cognitive development.

7. The role of bilingual education in establishing security of identity at a local, regional, and national level may be important. As a basic psychological need, security and status in self-identity may be important. For example, bilingual education has aided the establishment of a Welsh identity in children (Baker and M. P. Jones 1999).

8. Economic advantages of bilingual education are increasingly being advanced. Bilingualism can be important in securing employment in many public services and sometimes in private companies, as well. To secure a job as a teacher, to work in the mass media, to work in local government, and increasingly, to work in the civil service in areas such as Canada, Wales, and the Basque country, bilingualism is increasingly important. Thus, bilingual education is increasingly seen as delivering relatively more marketable employees than monolingual education.

While bilingual education worldwide has an increasing number of supporters (though it is not without some virulent critics, especially in the United States—see Cummins [2000b]—there are limitations in the pedagogical view of bilingual education. For example, bilingual education does not guarantee effective schooling. Occasionally, there is a naiveté among those who support bilingual education in their assumption that the use of two or more languages in the school curriculum automatically leads to a raising of standards, more effective outcomes, and a more child-centered education. In reality, the languages used in a school are but part of a wider matrix of variables that interact in complex ways to make schooling more or less effective. Among bilingual schools in every country, there appears to be a mixture of the outstanding and the ordinary, those that are enhancing their quality and those that depend on past glories, rather than current successes. The school effectiveness research movement has determined many of the important factors that make schools more or less effective (August and Hakuta 1997). Bilingual education is only one ingredient among many. Indeed, there is sometimes a lack of clarity of the aims and objectives of bilingual education. In Wales, the educators have articulated four aims of bilingual education for all children (Welsh Language Board 1999: 30):

1. To develop communicative fluency in Welsh and English languages
2. To develop biliteracy in Welsh and English languages
3. To become multicultural and increasingly multilingual
4. To have an entitlement to an equal access to the potential economic and employment benefits of bilingualism.

Bilingual schools also need to emphasize specifics in the value-addedness of bilingual education, other than in generality. Specific valued-added attributes of bilingual education need to be clearly articulated and then monitored, with qualitative and quantitative evidence developed to show that the extra aims and objectives of bilingual education are being delivered.

Another limitation of the pedagogical perspective on bilingual education is the type and use of language learned at school. Canadian research suggests that the language register of formal education does not necessarily prepare children for language use outside the school (Cummins 2000b). The language of the curriculum is often complex and specialized. The vernacular of the street may be different. Canadian children from English-speaking homes who have been to immersion schools and learned through the medium of French and English sometimes report difficulty in communicating appropriately with French speakers in local communities. Local French speakers may find their French too formal, inappropriate, even off-putting.

A further concern about bilingual education is that language learning may stop at the school gates. The minority language may be effectively transmitted and competently learned in the classroom. Once outside the school gates, however, children may switch into the majority language. Thus, the danger of bilingual education in a minority language is that the language may become a language of school but not of play, a language for the delivery of the curriculum content but not of the peer culture. Even when children are taught through the medium of a minority language at school, the common denominator language of the peer group in the street is often the majority language. When one child turns to English, often so does everyone else. The language of the screen, shop, or street may be different from the language of the school. Extending a minority language learned at school to use in the community is something that is difficult to engineer and difficult to plan but nevertheless vital if the language is to live outside the school gates.

BILINGUAL EDUCATION AS POLITICS

Wherever bilingual education exists, politics is close by. To assume that bilingual education is educationally justified and therefore, ipso facto, will enjoy strong support is naive. Bilingual education is not simply an educational issue. Behind bilingual education there are always expressions of political ideology, tides of political change, and political initiative. To argue for bilingual education solely as a strong plank of language planning and language revitalization is simplistic. Language planning itself is predicated on language politics. What might be presented as pure motives—the preservation and conservation of the dying languages of the world—may hide basic political assumptions and ideologies. Surrounding bilingual education are usually political debates about national identity, dominance, and control by elites in power, power relationships among politicians and civil servants, questions about social order, and the perceived potential subversiveness of language minorities.

The case of Proposition 227 in California is perhaps the most compelling example of powerfulness of political will (Crawford 1999). Between 1978 and 2000, the number of students designated as having limited English proficiency (LEP) in California rose from approximately a quarter of a million to 1.4 million. While Spanish is the language most often spoken by such bilingual students, there are also significant populations of Armenian, Cantonese, Hindi, Hmong, Khmer, Korean, Mandarin, Panjabi, Russian, Serbo-Croatian, Tagalog, Ukrainian, Urdu, and Vietnamese students, for example. With its multilingual population, California had become a state where both experimentation and experience with bilingual education had blossomed. A symbol of this status is the California Association for Bilingual Education, which draws some ten thousand educationalists to its annual conference and has an established place both inside and outside the United States for being at the cutting edge of practice in bilingual schools.

In early 1996, the *Los Angeles Times* gave extensive coverage to the political activism of a small group of Spanish-speaking parents who were pulling their children out of the Ninth Street Elementary School. A Silicon Valley businessman, Ron Unz, having failed to win the Republican nomination for a congressional seat three years earlier, saw this as his political opportunity. Relying on a personal philosophy in favor of assimilation of immigrants, he denounced bilingual education, multiculturalism, and ethnic separatism. But, rather than focusing on the English language and the unification of American identity, his arguments were targeted at the educational ineffectiveness of bilingual schools in California. The press was delighted to add heat to the debate with mostly one-sided, personality-based, template reporting that cultivated controversy (Crawford 1999).

In July 1997, petitions for Proposition 227 began circulating, seeing 433,000 signatures from registered voters to qualify for inclusion as an initiative statute on the November ballot. The proposition was presented as an effort to improve English language instruction for children who needed to learn the language in order to take advantage of economic and employment opportunities. In effect, Proposition 227 aimed at outlawing bilingual education in California, allowing temporary sheltered English immersion. "Therefore," says the text of Proposition 227, "it is resolved that: All children in California public schools shall be taught English as rapidly and effectively as possible" and that such children "shall be taught English by being taught in English."

Proposition 227 was passed in a public ballot by a margin of 61 to 39 percent. Analysis of the voting and subsequent surveys found that Latinos were clearly against the proposition, but, nevertheless, bilingual education had become virtually illegal. With the sweet scent of victory in California, Ron Unz proceeded to Arizona and elsewhere across the United States.

On April 28, 1998, the U.S. secretary of education, Richard W. Riley, declared his nonsupport for Proposition 227. He stated that the Unz initiative "would lead to fewer children learning English and would leave many children lagging behind in their academic studies." In arguing that the initiative would be counterproductive, Secretary Riley (1998) asserted that a one-size-fits-all approach to learning English "is not supported by years of research," deprofessionalizes teachers, "is punitive and threatening," since it allows liability in litigation, and is a direct attack on local control of education. Instead, he affirmed "the economic, cultural, and political importance of being bilingual in our global culture."

Those teachers and administrators who willfully and repeatedly violate Proposition 227 are left open to lawsuits from parents and may be found personally liable for financial damages and legal fees. However, there is a minor provision for parental waivers and exceptions. This provision has been effective in preserving bilingual education in school districts where there is strong parental support and a history of effective bilingual programs.

The almost overnight outlawing of bilingual education in California has three lessons of international relevance:

1. A failure to disseminate research backing for strong forms of bilingual education can be fatal. Dissemination of research is needed not just to teachers but also to parents and the general public. It is essential that the

public image of bilingual education be based on fact, rather than fiction, evidence, rather than prejudice.

2. Bilingual education is not simply about politics. Despite the call for de-politicizing bilingual education (August and Hakuta 1997), the reality is that opponents of bilingual education would win more ground if supporters stopped arguing for bilingual education. Claims for the advantages of bilingualism and bilingual education must be part of a marketing campaign that reaches the mass media, parents, the public, and, particularly, politicians.

3. Compelling evidence is needed, not just from individual case studies, studies of outstanding schools, or examples of effective practice. In a culture of accountability, higher standards for all students in all schools are needed. Bilingual education has to provide evidence across the board for high standards, high achievements, and those outputs and outcomes of schooling that parents, the public, and politicians regard as important.

Cummins (1999, 2000b) has argued that research on bilingual education has become so unfocused, has sent out so many mixed messages, and is particularly so ignorant of underlying theory that politicians can selectively use research to fit and support their ideology. He contends that the much publicized research reviews and meta-analyses of August and Hakuta (1997), Baker and de Kanter (1983), Greene (1998), Rossell and Baker (1996), and Willig (1985) all assume that research reviews can directly inform policy making. Cummins sees this assumption as naive because of the "myriad human, administrative, and political influences that impact the implementation of programs over time" (Cummins 1999: 26). There are hundreds of variables that affect program outcomes, so research cannot, by itself, directly guide policy, provision, and practice. Rather, Cummins (1999, 2000) argues that it is tested theory that should drive policy making: "In complex educational and other human organizational contexts, data or 'facts' become relevant for policy purposes only in the context of a coherent theory. It is the theory rather than the individual research findings that permits the generation of predictions about program outcomes under different conditions." (Cummins, 1999: 26). That is, research should commence from theoretical propositions, testing, refining, and sometimes refuting those propositions. When theory is firmly supported by research, and if the theory accounts for findings from a variety of contexts, theory will explicitly inform policy making. Thus, Cummins (1999, 2000b) is critical of the U.S. National Research Council report (August and Hakuta 1997), since it comprehensively summarizes research but virtually ignores theories that address policy-relevant issues. Cummins (1999, 2000) asserts that theories such as thresholds, interdependence, and conversational and academic language proficiency (see Cummins 2000b) are supported by research and answer a range of policy issues. Such theories are a more important focus than reviews of research.

However comprehensive and elaborate the theoretical foundations of bilingual education, however strong the educational arguments for bilingual education, and however strong the arguments for the preservation of dying languages in the world, it is the politics of power, status, assimilation, and social order that can readily put an end to bilingual education.

THE ECONOMIC PERSPECTIVE ON BILINGUAL EDUCATION

A highly original and essential economic perspective comes from Dutcher (1995), who analyzes the cost-effectiveness and cost-efficiency of developmental maintenance bilingual education. In a World Bank paper on the use of first and second languages in elementary education, Dutcher examines international evidence from Haiti, Nigeria, the Philippines, Guatemala, Canada, New Zealand, the United States (the Navajo), Fiji, the Solomon Islands, Vanuatu, and Western Samoa. She concludes that development of the mother tongue is critical for cognitive development and as a foundation for learning a second language. That is, submersion and transitional models of bilingual education are universally less effective in developing a child's thinking abilities. When such development is slowed considerably by learning in a second language (e.g., submersion), then the second language will itself be learned more slowly.

This finding, well replicated internationally (see Baker and S. P. Jones 1998), clearly relates to the economics of bilingual education. Dutcher (1995) concludes that the recurrent costs for bilingual education are approximately the same as those for traditional programs. Bilingual education is not an expensive option and entails costs similar to those of mainstream programs. However, the most important conclusion is that developmental maintenance bilingual education creates cost savings for the education system and for society. For example, such bilingual education provides higher levels of achievement in fewer years of study. Student progress is faster, and higher achievement benefits society by leading to less unemployment and a more skilled workforce.

In submersion and transitional models of bilingual education, there may be costs to a national economy due to slower rates of progress at school, lower levels of final achievement, and sometimes the need for special or compensatory education. Higher dropout rates mean lower potential for future employment, and the economy suffers because of the lower skill level of the workforce and higher unemployment rates. In economic terms, students need to gain productive characteristics through education, and Dutcher (1995) indicates that this is achieved through early use of the native language.

Such cost-efficiency of developmental maintenance bilingual education is exemplified in a World Bank cost-effectiveness study on Guatemala, where Dutcher (1995) found that bilingual education was a prudent policy. Repetition and dropout rates were decreased through a bilingual education intervention program, and standards of achievement rose (including in Spanish). It was estimated that education cost savings due to bilingual education were US$5.6 million per year, while cost benefits were in the order of US$33.8 million per year. Also, individual earnings rose by approximately 50 percent. In Guatemala, developmental maintenance bilingual education made economic sense as it produced a more skilled, better trained, and more employable workforce. Submersion and transitional forms of bilingual education, in comparison, tend to lead to higher dropout rates and lower levels of achievement and thus have less chance of serving and stimulating the economy through provision of a skilled workforce.

CONCLUSION

This chapter has suggested that bilingual education derives its raison d'être not only from a concern for language maintenance and revitalization but also from a variety of educational, economic, social, cultural, and political concerns.

An idealistic conclusion would be to suggest the possibility of integrating the four perspectives discussed. When there is an integration of the four perspectives in language planners, bilingual educationalists, and the politicians who influence the growth of bilingual education, then a mature, logical, rational, and smooth evolution in bilingual education is possible. However, it is apparent that, more often than not, there is a separation between the perspectives. Each offers a partial view, a view that could be expanded by incorporation of the other perspectives. All four perspectives are included in international bilingual education.

In particular, educationalists who support bilingual education need to understand the politics behind, and sometimes against, bilingual education if there is to be movement forward. The defense and expansion of bilingual education cannot come suddenly from language planning perspectives (language planning acquisition) or through a statement of the many and real advantages of bilingual education. Bilingual education may flourish or otherwise through the locus of political power, the movement of political ideology, and political influence. This is where language planners and educationalists in support of bilingual education can join forces. The future fortunes of bilingual education are open to political influence. The benefits of bilingual education are neither self-apparent nor intrinsically obvious. Therefore, the notion of bilingual education has to be marketed in order for both the public and politicians to be persuaded and convinced. That is, undoubtedly, the task for the coming decades.

PART VI

VARIATION IN
LANGUAGE USE AND
LANGUAGE
PERFORMANCE

CHAPTER 19

SOURCES OF VARIATION IN LANGUAGE LEARNING

REBECCA L. OXFORD

THIS chapter synthesizes research on sources of variation in language learning. It answers the question "What factors influence the way people learn languages?" One key set of factors influencing variation in language learning is *contextual,* including: (a) "large culture," (b) "small culture," and (c) second versus foreign language environments. Other influential variables include three categories of *individual student characteristics:* (a) stylistic, (b) cognitive and affective, and (c) demographic. Student characteristics can be influenced by contextual variables, so overlap exists among the categories.

CONTEXTUAL SOURCES OF VARIATION IN LANGUAGE LEARNING

This section includes ethnic, national, or international background (large culture) and any cohesive social grouping, however small (small culture) (Holliday 1999). It also concerns second and foreign language learning environments. Other contextual variables, such as teacher and student roles and discourse practices, are beyond the scope of this brief chapter.

Large Culture

In this section, large culture is generally known by the simple label *culture*. "Studying culture does not mean looking only at customs, institutions, and artifacts . . . , but also studying people's values, beliefs and attitudes and how they influence or are influenced by interactions among people" (Steinmetz, Bush, and Joseph-Goldfarb 1994: 12). According to Kramsch (1998: 6), culture "refers to that which has been grown and groomed (from the Latin *colere*: 'to cultivate')" and includes social, historical, and imaginative aspects. Any cultural generalizations found in this chapter are intended not as stereotypes but instead as starting points for further discussion and research.

Culture plays a vital role in the formation of the individual's personality and learning processes (Banks 1991; Oxford 1996a, 1996c; Oxford and Anderson 1995). Saleh (1997), using results from a university study of language learners, asserted that individualism/collectivism (I/C) and cultural tolerance of ambiguity (TOA) affect language learning, mediated by personality types. *Individualistic* cultures— for example, the United States and Western Europe—emphasize loose social ties, autonomy, confrontation, right to privacy, and personal goals, while *collectivist* cultures—for example, the People's Republic of China—create strong, cohesive in-groups with group norms, that value nonconfrontation, collaboration, and strong hierarchies and rules (Hofstede 1980, 1986; Saleh 1997; Triandis 1989). *Low-TOA* cultures use rules and regulations to avoid uncertainty, while *high-TOA* cultures are open to change and take risks (Saleh 1997).

Large culture and small culture frequently intersect. Students' large-cultural beliefs influence and sometimes limit language achievement in small-cultural university classrooms (Yang 1992). Culturally influenced teacher beliefs influence learner beliefs and language learning strategy use (Takeuchi 1999). Unspoken or misunderstood differences between teacher beliefs and learner beliefs in a specific classroom can cause difficulties and frustration (Barcelos 2000). Fortunately, culturally influenced beliefs of teachers and learners can be modified through in-depth discussion and other activities, and such alterations can change behavior in the language classroom (Nyikos 1996; Yang 1992).

Small Culture

Voices from the language classroom (Bailey and Nunan 1996) reveal the importance of the classroom as a small culture. Other small cultures for language development might include informal or "street" learning and self-access centers. Learners from many countries described their language teachers in dramatic, often metaphoric ways, with categories of metaphors such as Teacher as Hanging Judge,

Entertainer, Co-learner, Prophet, Babysitter, and Absentee (Oxford in press). Analysis according to intimacy and power themes produced three general teaching approaches (autocratic, democratic/participatory, and laissez-faire). Narratives showed rejection of the first and third approaches and pleasure with the second.

Kjisik and Nordlund (2000) described a Finnish university's language learning culture, in which students received training in learner autonomy, with support groups on student-chosen topics (e.g., sports, cooking, letter writing, negotiations). Results showed enhanced motivation, strategy use, satisfaction, and autonomy. For more on language learning autonomy, see Benson and Voller (1997) and Wenden (1995).

Second Versus Foreign Language Learning Environments

A *second language* (SL) environment is a setting where the target language is the primary mode of ordinary communication for the majority of people and where abundant target language input occurs naturally (e.g., English learning in the United Kingdom or French learning in Côte d'Ivoire). A *foreign language* (FL) environment is a location where the target language is not the main vehicle of ordinary communication and where input in this language is consequently limited (e.g., English learning in Egypt or Japanese learning in Venezuela). In FL settings, the target language is often taught "academically," as a subject to be memorized for tests, rather than as a communication tool, and therefore many FL learners, though certainly not all, have lower motivation and poorer performance than SL students (Dörnyei 1990; Green and Oxford 1995). Some locations, such as Puerto Rico, are hybrid (EFL/ESL) environments (see Blau and Dayton 1992; Bliss 1993; Green and Oxford 1995).

Contextual factors in language learning have just been presented. The next section concerns individual student characteristics.

INDIVIDUAL STUDENT CHARACTERISTICS RELATED TO VARIATION IN LANGUAGE LEARNING

This section focuses on three sets of individual-difference variables associated with language learning (Ehrman and Oxford 1995; Skehan 1989): stylistic, cognitive and affective, and demographic factors. These are influenced by the contextual factors discussed earlier. Other individual student characteristics, such as aptitude, attention, and metalinguistic awareness, are not explored here due to space restrictions.

Stylistic Factors

The term *styles* refers to general approaches to learning or problem solving, as part of the larger issue of coping with everyday life. Brain hemisphericity, learning styles, and personality types are in this category.

Brain hemisphericity (brain dominance) is the tendency of an individual to process information mainly through either the left hemisphere or the right hemisphere of the brain (Torrance, Taggart, and Taggart 1984). Brain activity within and across the two hemispheres is complex, because (a) one hemisphere can sometimes take over certain functions if the other hemisphere is damaged, and (b) gender differences exist in overall brain lateralization (women are more bilateral) and in the corpus callosum, the connective, hemisphere-linking brain tissue (which is thicker in women, allowing greater information transfer across hemispheres) (Green 1994; Kalat 1995; Springer and Deutsch 1989; Temple 1993).

However, some generalizations are possible. Both hemispheres carry out the same tasks in different styles: sequential for the left hemisphere and parallel for the right hemisphere. Left-hemispheric dominant individuals are more analytic, verbal, linear, logical, and rational learners, whereas right-hemispheric dominant individuals are more integrative, imagistic (through the visual, tactile, kinesthetic, and auditory senses), nonlinear, intuitive, and emotional learners (Torrance 1988). Brain hemisphericity greatly influences learning styles, academic achievement, and choice of academic major and career path (Iaccino 1993; Saleh 1997). Kinsella and Sherak (1998) explored ways to address the different needs of right-brained and left-brained language learners.

Learning styles, such as sensory preferences and field independence (FI) versus field dependence (FD), are the general approaches students use to learn any subject, including another language (Oxford and Ehrman 1993). "Learning style consists of distinctive behaviors which serve as indicators of how a person learns from and interacts with his [or her] environment" (Gregorc 1979: 234). Taking learning styles into consideration can increase language achievement (Reid 1995, 1998). Learning styles correlate with personality types, brain hemisphericity, and choice of learning strategies (Ehrman 1996; Ehrman and Oxford 1989, 1990, 1995; Lawrence 1984; Oxford 1990, 1996a; Reid 1995; Schmeck 1988).

Sensory preferences include visual, auditory, kinesthetic, and tactile, the last two of which are sometimes clustered into the haptic or hands-on style (Dreyer 1998; Ehrman 1996; Reid 1995, 1998). *Visual* students enjoy reading, video, computers, pictures, and written classroom instructions and dislike lectures that lack visual support. *Auditory* students enjoy purely oral directions, lectures, conversations, and debates. *Hands-on* or *haptic* learners like movement, tangible objects, collages, and physical models. ESL students from different cultures varied significantly in their sensory preferences (Reid 1987, 1995, 1998).

The distinction between *FI* and *FD* refers to the degree of ability, ordinarily stable, to distinguish key elements from a confusing or distracting background (field) (Dreyer 1998; Stansfield and Hansen 1983; Witkin et al. 1977). Learners with FI rely on internal points of reference, are analytic, reflective, task oriented, and able to detach from the context, and prefer factual, impersonal materials for learning, while learners with FD have opposite features. FI helps develop analytic language learning skills (Chapelle 1995), but social language skills relate to FD (Dreyer 1998). Ehrman (1996) has modified the FI/FD distinction somewhat by adding the concept of field sensitivity.

The best-known system of *personality types* is found in the Myers-Briggs Type Indicator, or MBTI (see Myers and McCaulley 1985), which contains four dimensions: extroverted/introverted, sensing/intuition, thinking/feeling, and judging/perceiving. The resulting matrix categorizes individuals into sixteen types. *Extroverts* gain energy from working with others, while *introverts* gain energy from working alone or with a trusted friend. *Sensing-oriented* individuals are realistic, practical, and fact oriented, whereas *intuitive* individuals are imaginative, futuristic, and theory oriented. *Thinking-oriented* individuals concern themselves with impersonal analysis and logic, while *feeling-oriented* individuals are more emotional and overtly compassionate. *Judging-oriented* people like structure and rapid judgments, while *perceiving-oriented* individuals are spontaneous and dislike quick decisions. Personality type influenced adult language achievement in intensive programs (Ehrman and Oxford 1989, 1990), and personality-type conflicts between teachers and students harmed achievement (Oxford 1996c; Oxford, Ehrman, and Lavine 1991; Wallace and Oxford 1992).

Cognitive and Affective Factors

This set of factors includes motivation, self-referential judgments, anxiety, and language learning strategies. Each of these is a clear source of variation in language learning.

Language learning motivation is "the extent to which the individual works or strives to learn the language because of a desire to do so and the satisfaction experienced in this activity" (Gardner 1985: 10). *Motivational orientation* refers to the reason(s) that a person has decided to learn a language (Oxford 1996b, 1996d). Early Canadian work on motivational orientations showed that SL learners who wanted to integrate to some degree into the target culture (integrative orientation) were more proficient than those who learned the language for career or academic purposes (instrumental orientation) (Gardner 1985; Gardner and Lambert 1972). Crookes and Schmidt (1991) and Dörnyei (1990, 1994) argued that the instrumental orientation is more important to FL proficiency.

Clément, Dörnyei, and Noels (1994) identified five EFL motivational orientations:

1. To make friends and travel
2. To identify with the target language group
3. To know various peoples, cultures, and world events
4. To advance academically or professionally
5. To understand English-language media.

Students strongly supported all except the second factor; they were not particularly interested in integrating into Anglophone cultures.

In the 1990s, researchers proposed new models of language learning motivation. For instance, Dörnyei's (1994) model contains three levels. The *language level* reflects cultural-affective, intellectual, and pragmatic values associated with the target language and has two subsystems: integrative and instrumental. The *learner level* concerns fairly stable personality traits of the learner, such as linguistic self-confidence and need for achievement. The *learning situation level* reflects situation-specific motives and includes course-, teacher-, and group-specific components. A model by Crookes and Schmidt (1991) contains the following: (a) interest, (b) relevance, (c) expectancy of success, (d) outcomes, (e) decision to engage in learning, (f) persistence, and (g) high activity level. Schmidt, Kassabgy, Boraie, Jacques, and Moody (1996) empirically created a model of motivation (value, expectancy, and motivational strength), instructional preferences, and learning strategies. Tremblay and Gardner (1995) developed a highly complex, empirically derived model of language learning motivation.

Self-referential judgments, such as self-esteem and self-efficacy, are judgments the learner makes about herself or himself, as discussed later. Attributions (Weiner 1986) and locus of control (Rotter 1966) are also important but have not been studied sufficiently in the language learning field.

Self-esteem is a judgment of one's own personal worth or value. *Global self-esteem* arises when the person is around the mental age of eight and is based on two factors: (a) self-perceptions of competence in broad areas, such as academics, sports, social interaction, or physical appearance, and (b) a personal assessment of the importance of these areas. *Situational self-esteem* relates to a specific setting, event, or activity type. A language student can feel generally good about himself or herself (global self-esteem) but simultaneously experience low situational self-esteem in a negative language learning environment (Scarcella and Oxford 1992).

Self-efficacy refers to one's judgments about one's own ability to succeed on a task or long-term effort. Individuals who doubt their capabilities might slacken their efforts when facing serious difficulties, but those with strong self-efficacy make greater efforts to master challenges (Bandura 1982; Pintrich and Schunk 1996). Self-efficacy was enhanced by instruction in language learning strategies in a study by Chamot et al. (1996).

Anxiety can either be a state or a permanent trait of fear or apprehension (Horwitz and Young 1991; Young 1998). With *debilitating anxiety*, motivation suffers, poor performance occurs, and still greater anxiety is aroused, but *facilitating anxiety* stimulates the learner to try harder and perform better. Certain language activities, such as speaking in front of others or writing a paper, can generate anxiety about performance. Other anxiety-causing variables are certain classroom structures, perceived irrelevance of the target language, and culture shock. Language anxiety can be reduced through relaxation, humor, discussion, support groups, and other means (Young 1998).

Learning strategies are steps or operations used by learners to learn more effectively, that is, to facilitate acquisition, storage, retrieval, and use of information (Rubin 1987). Learning strategies are linked to learning styles, personality, gender, and culture (Cohen 1998; Ehrman and Oxford 1995). Cohen (1998) differentiated between language learning strategies and language-use strategies, while O'Malley and Chamot (1990) and Oxford (1990) presented two detailed taxonomies of language learning strategies. The O'Malley-Chamot taxonomy contained two major sets of strategies, cognitive (e.g., taking notes, outlining, linking new with old material) and metacognitive (e.g., planning, organizing, evaluating), and a smaller third set, socioaffective (e.g., asking questions for clarification or verification). Oxford's taxonomy included cognitive, metacognitive, memory-related, social, affective, and compensatory strategies.

Relationships between strategy use and language proficiency were initially examined through the "good language learner" investigations (Naiman et al. 1978; Rubin 1975), which resulted in general profiles of successful language learners and identified specific patterns of strategy use as success markers. Later studies showed no uniform pattern of specific strategies among successful language students. Less able learners used strategies in a random, unconnected, and uncontrolled manner (Vann and Abraham 1990). In the 1990s, strategy use was linked to language proficiency in more than thirty studies around the world (e.g., Dreyer and Oxford 1996; O'Malley and Chamot 1990; Park 1994; Rost and Ross 1991; Takeuchi 1993, 1999), but the relationships were sometimes highly complex. Effects of learning strategy instruction on both proficiency and self-efficacy are the focus of much research (Chamot et al. 1996; Rost and Ross 1991).

Demographic Factors

Many demographic factors affect language learning. Two of these, gender and age, stand out as particularly important and are addressed here, but others that are not addressed include home language, foreign travel experience, and (in SL settings) length of time in the country where the target language is used.

Gender makes a difference at all reference, hence females are superior in verbal skills, while males are superior in spatial skills, and these findings relate to brain functioning (Burstein, Bank, and Jarvik 1980; Kimura 1992). In general, females are slightly more feeling oriented, while males are slightly more thinking oriented (Myers and McCaulley 1985). In several studies (e.g., Kahle and Lakes 1983), females enjoyed cooperative and social learning, while males preferred individual, independent learning. Most studies (e.g., Bacon 1992; Green and Oxford 1995; Oxford and Nyikos 1989; Politzer 1983; Saleh 1997; Yang 1992) found that females use language learning strategies more frequently than males.

Age is also significant. Singleton and Lengyel (1995) attacked the critical period hypothesis, which suggests that learning a language at an early age is sufficient or necessary to attain nativelike proficiency and that there is an age beyond which learning another language is not fully possible. Although younger learners do have some advantages (fluency and pronunciation), older learners have other advantages (syntax and morphology) (Scarcella and Oxford 1992). However, many adults and children can become proficient in the target language under the right conditions, perhaps by following different routes.

CONCLUSION

The information in this chapter points to an urgent need to know more about our diverse students: their cultures, motivations, styles, strategies, anxiety, and other factors. The research synthesized here can enable educators to develop new instructional techniques, curricula, and lesson plans to accommodate these variations. Language instruction should begin with an understanding of the ways students learn, and language researchers should continue to promote this understanding through well-designed studies.

....

CHAPTER 20

LANGUAGE TRANSFER AND CROSS-LINGUISTIC STUDIES: RELATIVISM, UNIVERSALISM, AND THE NATIVE LANGUAGE

....

TERENCE ODLIN

LANGUAGE transfer, or cross-linguistic influence, has long been a topic that many in applied linguistics have pondered, even though some have doubted its importance (e.g., Dulay, Burt, and Krashen 1982). In recent work on transfer, two different orientations have been prominent—one universalist and the other relativist. Although these orientations are opposed to each other in certain ways, research on both relativism and universalism intersects with the study of cross-linguistic influence. This chapter emphasizes the significance of the relativist orientation, but it also contends that any thorough understanding of transfer and universals necessitates a broad view of what characterizes all human languages.

TRANSFER AS A RELATIVIST CONCERN

Nonlinguists occasionally ask the question "What is the hardest language in the world?" The usual response of professionals is, of course, that children do not have any advantage in learning English, for example, as opposed to Swedish, Finnish, or Estonian. On the other hand linguists will normally acknowledge that adult language learning does not allow for such a categorical response. "It all depends" is one possible answer, even though this may not satisfy the person asking the question. However much or little linguists have thought about the issue of cross-linguistic influence, most would probably acknowledge that Swedish, a Germanic language like English, will take less time than Finnish for English-speaking adults to learn, even bearing in mind all the meanings that "learn" can have (cf. Ringbom 1987). On the other hand Finnish will prove relatively easy for Estonians (whose language is, like Finnish, Uralic), whereas these same learners will encounter much of the difficulty that Finns do when it comes to learning English. This point is perhaps so obvious to linguists as to seem uninteresting. However, ignoring it has resulted in surprisingly little discussion of the fact that language transfer entails a relativist approach to second language acquisition.

The link between relativism and transfer has recently received increased attention (e.g., Kellerman 1995; Jarvis 1998; Odlin 1998), but earlier research also considered that possibility. For example, Kaplan argued that "Logic (in the popular rather than the logician's sense of the word), which is the basis of rhetoric, is evolved out of a culture; it is not universal" (1966/1984: 44). From that position, Kaplan asserted that the difficulty encountered by speakers of other languages with English writing stems from rhetorical differences. The consequences of discourse differences have gotten considerable attention in subsequent work on contrastive rhetoric (e.g., Connor 1996) and also in the related field of contrastive pragmatics (e.g., Kasper 1992). Nevertheless, the issue of relativism remains controversial largely because of the complexities of the relation between linguistic relativity and linguistic universals. Much of the difficulty is evident in the hedge that Kaplan used to characterize "logic": "in the popular rather than the logician's sense. . . ." The popular sense of the term can in fact mean *all* the ways of structuring arguments, not only emotional and ethical arguments but also rational ones (whether or not Aristotle offers the most reliable guide to understanding rhetoric). Accordingly, there exists an important overlap between the logic of rational arguments and the logic of logicians.

How much of an overlap there is remains controversial. Few if any philosophers nowadays would equate the logical systems they have developed with a general cognitive code, but there are widely varying opinions on the fit between invented logical systems and mental capacities. Some thinkers even deny the usefulness of positing a universal semantic code. Quine (1960), for example, has contended that logic is much less independent of the language spoken by the logician—even when the logician employs a modern calculus that supposedly eliminates the problems that ensue when syllogisms are formulated in English, Greek, or any other natural language. Moreover, he argues against the notion of semantic equivalence as a neutral baseline to compare languages or to verify the accuracy of translations. Interestingly, he speculates on the difficulties encountered by an English-speaking linguist attempting to learn a very different kind of language and appeals to the notion of native language "habits" (1960: 70). The behaviorist stance on transfer here is, of course, widely challenged now (e.g., Sharwood Smith 1979). More telling, however, is the fact that Quine has little to say about the interlingual identifications made by bilinguals who have known two languages from early childhood, and so he cannot really account for the intuitions of ordinary child or adult bilinguals (cf. Fishman 1977a; Lyons 1977: 236).

However bilinguals establish their interlingual identifications, the process must rely on a calculus more or less independent of the two languages, a calculus providing something akin to "logic in the logician's sense." The cognitive basis for such a calculus is perhaps best understood as "the language of thought," a system flexible enough to allow children to acquire any language and also to accommodate other mental phenomena such as imagery. While Fodor (1975) allows for the possibility that a language of thought can coexist with language-specific schemata that might affect processing, Pinker has been more skeptical about linguistic relativism: "People do not think in English, Chinese, or Apache; they think in a language of thought. This language of thought probably looks a bit like all of those languages" (1994: 81).

Among linguists engaged in cognitivist or generativist research, Pinker's position probably has more adherents than Fodor's. However, recent work on linguistic relativity suggests that the latter position is more tenable. Lucy (1992) reports a highly detailed study of cognitive consequences of contrasting noun phrase patterns in English and Yucatec Maya, and the results were consonant with his general expectation that "language influences . . . do not affect a speaker's potential ability to see a referent at all or in a certain way, but rather affect a speaker's habitual dispositions towards, or ways of responding to, a referent" (1992: 91). Another recent study (Pederson et al. 1998) focused on the relation between linguistic structure and spatial memory. Like Lucy, the investigators obtained results that support the notion that linguistic structure can affect habitual thought. The investigations just described suggest that relativist approaches to language need to be taken seriously even by linguists who have questioned the significance of "Whorfian" ideas (a somewhat misleading term in view of the long history of linguistic relativism described by Janney and Arndt 1993). If the structural peculiarities of any language affect memory and other cognitive capacities, certain questions about bilingualism call for greater attention including these:

- Does acquiring a second language offer the possibility of new modes of habitual thinking?
- Can habitual thought patterns from L1 interfere with the acquisition of the new modes?

Wilhelm von Humboldt (1836/1988: 60) took an affirmative position on both questions, and he was probably right. Some research does support him on the first question, such as work by Bloom (1981) suggesting that bilinguals sometimes show a wider range of habitual thought patterns, though it must be noted that the Bloom study has proven very controversial (cf. Odlin 1989; Pinker 1994). The second question invites speculation about the conceptual roots of language transfer. The implications of Lucy's research, for example, may or may not be straightforward for second language research. Yucatec is a language where the count/noncount distinction matters little because of the absence of obligatory marking of plurality. Many other languages (e.g., Chinese) likewise show significant differences from English in their nominal systems, and even a language as similar to English as Spanish shows important contrasts with regard to noncount nouns. Such differences may well have consequences for the acquisition of grammatical targets such as the English article system. Master (1987) compared speakers of languages with no articles (e.g., Chinese) with speakers of languages with articles (e.g., Spanish). As with several other studies, Master's investigation showed that the presence of articles in the native language facilitates the acquisition of articles in English (cf. Odlin 1989). Even so, he noted that Spanish speakers did encounter difficulties that seemed to arise from an unclear sense of how noncount nouns function in English. Although problems with areas such as pluralization no doubt have other sources as well (e.g., word-final consonant clusters), differences in habitual thought may contribute to difficulties.

The study by Pederson et al. likewise invites speculation about how speakers of different languages might compare in the ways they tackle spatial relations in a second language. Tasks similar to those in the Pederson study have been used in second language research, as in work by Bongaerts, Kellerman, and Bentlage (1987) comparing how speakers of Dutch perform in their L1 and in L2 English, and the results indicate some influence from Dutch, although much of it may stem simply from inadequate lexical knowledge. In other types of spatial reference, however, there is strong evidence for conceptual transfer. Ijaz (1986) reports differences in the use of English prepositions by speakers of German and Urdu on items on a cloze test such as *The keys are hanging ___ the hooks.* The German speakers who did not supply the target language form *on* typically used *at* (corresponding to German *an*, 'at'), while Urdu speakers often chose *with* (corresponding to Urdu /say/, 'with').

Prepositional choices often depend not only on conceptions of static space but also on conceptions of motion. Jarvis (1998) discusses a frequent difference in the way that speakers of Finnish and speakers of Swedish described the part of the film *Modern Times* in which Charlie Chaplin and Paulette Goddard accidentally collide in the street. The Swedes often chose *ran on*, which corresponds to Swedish *springa på* ('run on'), while the Finns often chose *crash to*, which corresponds to Finnish *törmätä* ('crash') plus an illative case ending equivalent to English *to*. It is also significant that a Finnish control group describing the same film almost always used a verb denoting a crash (i.e., *törmätä*), whereas a Swedish group chose either a verb normally used to denote running (i.e., *springa*) or one to denote a crash (*krocka*). Accordingly, the differences in the Finnish and Swedish interlanguages may reflect not only structural differences but also the way that the two groups cognized the event seen in the film. Further evidence for differences in spatial cognition is evident in a recent study by Jarvis and Odlin (2000).

Other studies have also considered native language influence on choices of prepositions and/or verbs of motion (e.g., Harley 1989), and it seems quite clear that L1 patterns of spatial reference frequently find their way into interlanguage. Kellerman (1995) and Slobin (1993) note still other cases of such influence which involve temporal reference. As with space, time often shows language-specific mappings in tense, modality, and aspect (TMA) systems, and several studies indicate that the native language can affect TMA choices in the interlanguage (e.g., Ho and Platt 1993; Klee and Ocampo 1995; Sabban 1982; Wenzell 1989). If native language conceptions of space and time play an important role in structuring learners' adaptations of target language patterns, there is good reason to believe that semantic transfer should be considered an extension of linguistic relativity into second language acquisition.

On the Varied Bases for Language Universals

The growing importance of relativist approaches does not vitiate universalist insights, and if research in applied linguistics shifts toward a relativist framework, there will still be a need to look for the common thread (or threads) running through human languages. Even while there exist language-specific forms best interpreted within a relativist framework (as discussed earlier), panlinguistic patterns still inform human languages. Hockett (1961/1966) contends that all languages have deictic elements, and Anderson and Keenan (1985) consider spatial deixis to be a universal. With regard to temporal deixis, not all languages grammaticalize the notion of tense (Comrie 1985). On the other hand, aspect is probably a grammatical category applicable to all human languages, and Comrie (1976) argues that the perfective/imperfective semantic contrast is relevant to any language that codes aspect. Along with certain conceptions involving space and time, some other notions seem likely universals aiding all learners in their attempts to make interlingual identifications. Ijaz (1986), Jarvis (1998), and others have relied on conceptions of categories in terms of core and periphery, that is, prototype theory as developed by Rosch (1974) and others. Thus, for example, the prepositions and postpositions of many languages often show a core meaning that will match core meanings in other languages, even though there can be great cross-linguistic variation in the peripheral meanings, as well as in the patterns of morphological realization.

If semantic universals aid in making both first and second languages learnable, the problem of ascertaining the specific principles that assure learnability remains. The conceptions of Chomsky (1995) and others of such principles, often termed Universal Grammar (UG), have prompted numerous studies in second as well as first language acquisition, though there do exist other approaches to universals and acquisition (e.g., Greenberg 1991; Wolfe-Quintero 1996). Within the Chomskyan framework, transfer has attracted considerable attention, much of it in the context of arguments made by Bley-Vroman (1989). As he observes, adult learners may have no access to UG (and, of course, it is also possible that UG itself is simply nonexistent). On the other hand, there are two possible affirmative answers to the access question. Bley-Vroman notes that adults may have direct access, sharing with children some sense of what a language must look like (as this might be identified in the principles and parameters of UG); alternatively, whatever access adults have might be channeled through their native language. The logic of the second approach runs as follows: Like every other human language, the learner's native language instantiates UG principles and thus serves as a reference point for deciding what can or cannot be characteristic of any other language. Bley-Vroman acknowledges, of course, that not all learner intuitions are accurate and that they may often reflect only some language-specific characteristic (in which case negative transfer can occur). The access question has led to numerous studies, many of them reviewed by White (2000a), but no consensus has yet developed. Whatever the verdict on the access issue, both of the following points remain valid:

- The importance of transfer to second language acquisition does not stand or fall on the answer to the access question.
- UG research focuses on a subset of possible language universals, and accordingly there remains a need for universalist research that looks beyond the issues raised by UG theorists.

With regard to the first point, it will help to list just a few of the questions that have proved important to transfer researchers, even though they have gotten little attention in UG debates:

- What kind of cognate vocabulary can trigger interlingual identifications (e. g., Schweers 1993)?
- What ways do listening and reading comprehension interact with transfer to promote acquisition (Ringbom 1992)?
- How much do learners rely on genre conventions in their native language when writing, for example, a business letter or a résumé (e.g., Connor 1996)?

With regard to the second point, concerning universals, some linguists have opted for approaches outside the UG framework, as the following questions indicate:

- How may universals of language change and second language acquisition be related (Greenberg 1991)?
- Is the Topic/Comment category the basis for interlingual identifications made by speakers of English learning Chinese (Jin 1994)?
- Does the semantic similarity between existential and possessive constructions have any effects on acquisition (Duff 1993)?

While UG research has focused on a small number of principles that may or may not characterize human language generally, the examples just given indicate that the sources for language universals are highly varied. Gass and Ard (1984) identify six different sources: a physical, a perceptual/cognitive, a neurological, a diachronic, and an interactional, plus one possibly available only to children, a language acquisition device (LAD). The LAD (which has also gone by other names) is often hypothesized to work according to a genetic timetable that children apparently follow despite the fact that they acquire language in highly diverse circumstances. As Gass and Ard suggest, the six bases for universals may overlap considerably, though the possible uniqueness of the LAD to child language makes its status problematic for many issues, including transfer (cf. Selinker and Lakshmanan 1992; Singleton 1989). In any case, the clear diversity of the sources certainly argues against any reductionist approach to universals.

Chomsky and many others have foregrounded what they consider to be uniquely human cognitive capacities, and UG theorists in second language research have naturally maintained the same focus. Even so, it would be mistaken to conclude that the human race is the only species possessing any of the capacities involved in language, even if researchers finally agree that chimpanzees and other primates lack the capacity for syntax (cf. Bickerton 1990). However unique human syntactic capacities may be, it is no doubt true that human language can communicate notions that are, as best we can tell, unknown to other species, such as arguments about the constitutionality of laws. Nevertheless, humans, along with other mammals, communicate emotions, and, as Darwin (1872/1979), Lazarus (1991), and others have contended, affect is an area likely to show evolutionary continuity between other mammals and the human species. If emotional displays and language never interacted, the role of affect would hold little interest for linguists. However, one likely universal is that all languages can express affective states, and it is natural to wonder if there are any other universals involving emotion and language. On the other hand, considerable evidence indicates that language-specific patterns can have affective consequences, in which case transfer seems inevitable.

One instance noted by Schweers (1993) offers an intriguing example of how a semantic difference in cognate words has affective consequences. The English form *pregnant* and the Spanish *preñada* are transparently similar, but the latter has a restriction not found in English: *preñada* normally does not indicate the state of a *human* female. From this restriction, *preñada* may often seem to Spanish speakers to be the wrong word to guide them in their search for an appropriate English form. In fact, Schweers describes in detail the reluctance of one Spanish speaker to use *pregnant* to describe (in English) a picture of an expecting mother in a clinic. Although this evidence is anecdotal, it nevertheless has crucial implications for contrastive analysis. The actual similarity or dissimilarity of forms and meanings is only one factor at work in transfer; the *judgment* of each individual learner matters just as much. Kellerman (1977) emphasized the importance of judgments in the area of idioms a quarter of a century ago, and even though there are problems with his original claim, subsequent work has shown the value of considering learner perceptions of language distance (e.g., Odlin 1991; Sjöholm 1983).

Learners' subjective positions can lead to interlingual identifications in other areas of language besides lexis. Odlin (1998) discusses euphemistic and dysphemistic (i.e., strong) forms of negation in relation to learners' social perceptions. Along with the neutral *no one*, a dysphemistic choice, *devil a one*, was available to speakers of Irish and Scottish Gaelic learning English in the nineteenth century, as well as a euphemistic choice, *sorrow a one*. Both the dysphemistic and the euphemistic forms have parallels in Gaelic, and it appears that learners in the nineteenth century (and earlier times) made interlingual identifications with the affective loadings in mind. The transfer here involves syntax as well as lexis, since the negation patterns in Gaelic are realized in focusing constructions. Even when they do not involve negation, moreover, focusing structures interact with affective factors not only in the Celtic languages but in others as well (Irvine 1982; Odlin 1998). It is worth noting that the contrastive pragmatics of negation has also been investigated with actual learners, including a study of refusals in Japanese and

English that indicates the influence of Japanese on learners' formulas in English (Beebe, Takahashi, and Uliss-Weltz 1990).

Conclusion

As noted, there is reason to believe, with Darwin, in the existence of pancultural emotions. On the other hand, relativists (e.g., Lutz and White 1986) have noted problems with a universalist position, and many empirical questions remain to be resolved. Beebe, Takahashi, and Uliss-Weltz (1990) argue that speech acts, such as refusals, reflect language-specific cultural values not readily given up when learners attempt a new language. The affective burdens that learners may thus experience are, as these researchers suggest, a crucial area for investigation. The growing interest of second language researchers in emotion (e.g., Rintell 1989; Schumann 1994) may lead to a wider discussion of language universals and relativism in the years to come. If so, studies of cross-linguistic influence may attract the interest of anyone concerned with how human beings share a common heritage yet differ in crucial ways.

C H A P T E R   2 1

....

LANGUAGE USES IN PROFESSIONAL CONTEXTS

....

MARY MCGROARTY

SCHOLARS in several disciplines have studied the language used in professional contexts for many different reasons, so this topic represents an unusually interdisciplinary panorama. Here I review some current work that constitutes the study of language in professional contexts, with the dual goals of illustrating representative approaches taken to date and suggesting where additional efforts by applied linguists could be most productive. The discussion concentrates on areas not discussed elsewhere in this *Handbook*. Hence, I do not comment in depth on language use in schools, or on the implications of research on workplace language for societal multilingualism, or on language policy and planning, or on translation and interpretation (all specifically addressed elsewhere in this volume), or on language use in religion. These disclaimers reveal the extreme multidisciplinarity of academic attention to language employed in professional settings; it implicates many possible avenues of scholarship related to applied linguistics (see, e.g., Gunnarsson, Linell, and Nordberg 1997) and thus typifies the richness of the field.

The study of language in professional contexts overlaps an area more widely recognized within applied linguistics, namely Language for Specific Purposes (LSP, or English for Specific Purposes, ESP), a subfield recognized at least since 1964 (Swales 2000). As Swales notes, early LSP work relied on two straightforward assumptions:

1. Descriptive structural analysis of language used in work settings would provide an adequate basis for the development of teaching materials.

2. Those engaged in teaching languages (most often, but not always, English) for defined groups of adult learners would be capable of conducting at least basic required descriptive research on which design of teaching materials would be based.

From the start, LSP has had a strongly pedagogical impetus.

During this same nearly forty-year span, investigators in other disciplines looked to the study of language used in specific professional or occupational settings as data germane to a gamut of theoretical and empirical questions, ranging from issues of occupational socialization to the expression and constitution of social relationships. The social relationships highlighted in such research were usually those that illustrated particular identities crucial to the occupational settings at hand: experts versus nonexperts, doctors versus patients, judges versus attorneys versus clients, teachers versus students, supervisors versus workers. Various projects have, at times, included consideration of other demographic categories, such as men versus women, native speakers versus nonnative speakers, and native residents versus immigrants to a country, all of which co-exist with standard occupational hierarchies. Individuals can be part of many of these categories, with the relevance of each aspect of identity determined according to past history and present communicative situation (see Norton elsewhere in this volume). The methodology used in these investigations has generally been that of discourse or conversation analysis (see Johnstone 2000). In the past twenty years, propelled by more explicit theorizing of concerns related to gender (Kendall and Tannen 1997; Leidner 1993; Wodak 1997) and political power (Benhabib 1997, 1999) that have marked all social sciences, academic discussion of workplace language has produced more differentiated and often more subtle renderings and interpretations of the language used in various occupational settings. Thus, a survey of language uses in professional contexts must include more and less than LSP: more in that one of its goals is to illuminate not only language but also aspects of social structure, less in that it does not aim, necessarily, to serve as the basis for pedagogical methods and materials.

Because research in this area has generally been motivated by an interest in social relations, much of the foundational research on language uses in professional contexts has been done by social scientists in sociology, anthropology, or political science. Given these distinct disciplinary foci and research methods, there is considerable variation in the type and amount of language data gathered and in the nature, systematicity, level of detail, and sophistication of the linguistic analyses applied. Schegloff has remarked on the need to balance the focus on social structure with a focus on conversational interaction in conversation analytic approaches, noting that "each makes its own claims in organizing observation and analysis of the data, and one can preempt the other" (1991: 57). Moreover, research done since the 1980s has emphasized the interconnectedness of oral and written language in any workplace setting (see, e.g., Spilka 1993), presaging the interests in intertextuality and historicity now prevalent in critical theoretical discussions in many fields. Hence, there is considerable opportunity for applied linguists to supplement the research summarized here either for the specific aim of developing pedagogical tasks and materials, the usual mandate of LSP, or for the more general goal of expanding knowledge of the relation between language use and social setting, the lodestar of contemporary sociolinguistics.

Language Uses in Traditional Status-Differentiated Professions

Social scientists have examined the language used in the traditional high-status professions of law and medicine and in the similarly status-sensitive fields of education and social work for decades; consequently, applied linguists find a substantial foundation for related work. More recent trends in these fields incorporate theory and scholarship related to expression and realization of gender and ethnicity and aspects of technological change as all these interact with occupational and institutional authority.

Law

Law is the professional arena in which the study of language has been preeminent, both because the practice of law is driven by verbal and textual exchange (scholars have asserted that "language *is* legal power"; Conley and O'Barr 1998: 14) and because, for centuries, legal proceedings have been described and recorded, sometimes verbatim, yielding an enormous amount of publicly accessible material for analysis. Current investigators (e.g., Shuy 1998) have complemented the study of legal records with many of the tools of contemporary social scientific and applied linguistic analysis, such as ethnographic interviews and detailed discourse analysis of court transcripts.

Contemporary research on actual language use in legal settings reflects concern for both the expressive and constitutive role of language in pertinent relationships.[1] Furthermore, many contemporary studies of legal language address not simply a two party (that is, attorney-client) interaction but language used in the courtroom, a highly ritualized setting where at least three different status positions—judge, attorney, and members of the public (sometimes considered separately as members of a jury versus lay litigants, plaintiffs, or defendants versus onlookers)—affect the nature of communication. Often when the profiles of relevant interlocutors include differences in gender or cultural or ethnic group membership as well as in their role in legal interactions, such dual identities are foregrounded in the study of legal discourse (e.g., Eades 1994; Walsh 1994).

Where early studies of language uses in legal settings sought generally to characterize the role-related discourse used by various parties, more contemporary work (e.g., Conley and O'Barr 1990, 1998; O'Barr and Conley 1996) seeks to determine the development of, and differences between, the evolution of legal meanings for lay people involved in legal proceedings compared to legal professionals. An extension of such work is the explication of legal language as the expression of a particular ideology, with judges, in their roles of substantive legal authorities and arbiters of courtroom procedure, as its principal exponents (Harris 1994). Philips (1998) examines the interplay among three different ideological frameworks—due process, state policy, and courtroom control—manifested in the discourse of judges and shows that the connections perceived by the judges across the three areas are usually invisible to outsiders, rendering judicial conduct at worst unpredictable and at least mysterious. Her work, as well as that of O'Barr and Conley (1996) on the contrasting understandings of individuals in small claims courts and of Matoesian (1999) on the development of expert witness identity through court testimony, exemplifies the trend toward documenting the multivalent nature of discourse in multiparty legal settings.

Another important development in the study of language use in legal settings is the attention to effects of new technologies for communication and analysis within the legal system, in, for example, the use of videotaped depositions (Pearson and Berch 1994), voice recognition technology (Jones 1994; Nolan 1994), and use of computerized linguistic analysis to establish or disprove authorship of a text (Eagleson 1994; Smith 1994). The latter two uses are particularly common in the subfield known as *forensic linguistics*. With the development of increasingly sophisticated technologies for language recording and analysis and concomitant application of the analytical approaches stimulated, in part, by advances in corpus linguistics (see Burstein and Chodorow elsewhere in this volume), there is tremendous potential for applied linguistic research here.

Medicine

Interest in more- and less-authoritative social roles enacted through the discourse between health professionals and lay patients parallels work on legal discourse in many ways. However, the context of most medical interactions, unlike much interaction in legal settings, does not regularly include public discourse. Many crucial interactions take place between doctors and patients or across several different parties (doctors, nurses, pharmacists, nurses' aides, housekeepers, patients, relatives of patients) and, unlike court proceedings, are not routinely recorded verbatim, although conventions of clinical practice often include generation of and reliance on practictioners' dictated or written notes about patient care. Compared to law, then, the nature and amount of data from medical settings available for analysis has been somewhat more limited. Early work (see, e.g., Fisher and Todd 1983; Mishler 1984) documented the ways physicians managed communication with patients to provide technical information in what they believed to be understandable language, direct the interactions efficiently, and minimize emotional responses. Related research (Engeström 1993) used the discourse of medical consultations to explore whether reorganization of government-funded medical care had any impact on physicians' communication styles or typical modes of activity. More recent discussion of these topics (Todd and Fisher 1993) adds documentation of various realizations of power and resistance through specific discoursal strategies used by providers and patients.

The role of language in the occupational socialization of doctors has attracted analytic attention from several social scientists and medical educators.[2] Current work has examined the functions of language used by experts to induct novices into the profession, thus documenting developmental constraints on discourse. During formal medical education, senior physicians' knowledge of the content of the lectures and lab sessions medical students would have completed up to a certain point determined whether they referred to patients' problems in more or less technical terms (Cicourel 1992), documenting developmental constraints on discourse. Becoming a member of any profession, not only medicine, requires novices not only to know technical terms but also to be able to reproduce the decision processes that lead to designation as a competent member of the profession. Discourse analytic methods have been used to track the socialization of medical students and to explore the effectiveness of less teacher-dominated, more discussion-oriented modes of medical training, the topic of a special issue of *Discourse Processes* in which several scholars analyze a segment of videotaped discussion of a clinical case by medical students and their faculty tutor (Koschmann 1999).

Feminist theory and scholarship have increased attention to the relationships between gender and communication in medical practice. Because women use medical care more than men do, both for themselves and as mothers, communication between women patients or parents and male health care providers has frequently been investigated (e.g., Maynard 1992; Tannen and Wallat 1993; Todd 1993). In the United States, most physicians have been male and many other health providers, such as nurses, female (though proportions are changing), so the dynamics of communication between providers in different occupational categories has inspired research; Fisher's (1995) exploration of the differences in social psychological dimensions of health care received from doctors versus nurse practitioners is one such example.

The study of language in "language-intensive" branches of medicine such as psychiatry and psychotherapy has been a favorite site of investigations using discourse analytic methods. Although it would be misleading to pose a dichotomy between these specialties and other branches of medicine, the former areas often rely relatively more heavily on procedures such as physical examinations, lab tests, and visual representations (x-rays, sonograms, other forms of physical imaging) as routine components of professional research and clinical practice.[3] Labov and Fanshel's pioneering work (1977) showed that conversational analysis methods could be productively applied to psychotherapy, a line of inquiry that continues active (Ferrara 1994).

The impact of new technologies on the nature and frequency of medical communication between patients and caregivers and between various groups of health care providers represents another central area for research and theory. Multiple types of computerized equipment are now commonplace in many hospitals and medical offices, requiring that nurses and other providers learn to manage communication with and through such devices in addition to the older channels of handwritten notes or telephone conversations. These technological changes interact with considerations of typical gender roles in emerging occupational identities within health care (Cook-Gumperz and Hanna 1997). Material constraints on electronic communication represent another current issue. Vaik's (1992) study of the discourse of radio call-in therapy shows that such talk alternates between a nondirective therapeutic and more directive counseling tenor and that commercial constraints of time and the necessity to state problems publicly (though without full names) affect the framing and disposition of problems.

Education

Whether education and social work qualify as high-status professions has long been debated (Etzioni 1969; Freidson 1973), but both the strong institutional structures and the status differential between teachers and students or social service providers and clients suggest that they merit inclusion in a general overview of language uses in professional settings. I mention education only briefly here because other chapters in this volume provide more detail, on, for example, the study of classroom discourse (see contributions by Poole, Lantolf, and Gass elsewhere in this volume). Investigators have used the conversation analytic approaches employed in the legal and medical arenas to examine processes of student classification and advising in special education placement conferences (Mehan

1986) and in language proficiency interviews (Young and He 1998). Such work illuminates the gatekeeping function of language use in educational institutions.

Social Services

The nature and types of social services available in different national contexts and the types of bureacracies established to deliver them are highly context-specific. However, wherever services exist, determinations of eligibility and benefits must be made, often through the mechanism of individual interviews; hence, the relevance of language as gatekeeper in this sphere as well (McGroarty 1996). As in all professional uses of language addressed here, the problematics of status-differentiated interviews increase when populations to be served differ in native language and communicative orientation from service providers. Britain's Industrial Language Training Project, established to address conflicts around the nature of communication in workplaces and in provision of social services, represented a wide-ranging and influential research program in this area; it was one of the first efforts that drew on large-observations and discourse samples to suggest that related language training be developed not only for minority language background workers but also for those who interacted with them (Jupp, Roberts, and Cook-Gumperz 1982; Roberts, Davies, and Jupp 1992). Some similar methods have been used to document the second language acquisition of "guest workers" in their interactions with social service providers or employers in several European countries (Bremer, Roberts, Vasseur, Simonot, and Broeder 1996).

Language Uses in Other Professional Arenas

The discourse analytic methods applied to interactions in high-status professions have also been employed in other occupational settings in which hierarchical role differentiation, though still present, is less marked. From a research perspective, it is particularly provocative to examine language use in organizations aspiring to the "transformative," or "best-practices," ethos touted by many commentators; in such settings, language becomes one of the principal modes of instrumental activity between presumably coequal participants (Deetz 1995). Related studies have documented how workers engaged in verbal interaction mediated through speech, print, or both seek to influence each other during transactions such as fixing a machine, arranging schedules, negotiating future business arrangements, or making purchases. Given the trends toward flattened hierarchies in many workplaces and less adversarial attitudes toward customers, understanding the complexities of workplace language use in such settings is even more crucial than it might be in status-differentiated settings, for participants' effectiveness may depend less on hierarchical authority and more on their communicative abilities (Deetz 1995). Indeed, much postmodernist scholarship on language use in the workplace forges explicit connections between language use and the kind of individual identity promoted by employers, especially large corporations. In an ironic extension of Goffman's (1959, 1961) theories of self-presentation in the context of total institutions, the total institutions of note in contemporary scholarship on workplace language use are not those to which individuals are consigned because of deviance or disease but rather those with which interlocutors freely seek affiliation because of economic and emotional rewards.

Manufacturing/Engineering

Current studies of the nature of work in manufacturing settings offers insights into language as one form of activity that represents and contributes to accomplishment of corporate goals and, at the same time, contradicts some commonsense notions about the skills and language abilities needed to be a competent worker. Ethnographic work at a successful U.S. wire manufacturing plant has shown that rhetoric about the need for a highly skilled workforce (Hull 1997) misrepresents the idiosyncratic but efficacious approaches to production job performance, including various combinations of using talk and referring to written job procedures and specifications, and the possibility of decontextualizing supposedly prerequisite skills from contexts of use (Darrah 1990, 1997). In another U.S. manufacturing plant, growing emphasis on an incentive system based on pay for knowledge and teamwork led to some new literacy demands, but workers did not always see these as useful, nor did they value the company's concomitant requirement to learn about additional jobs or of offers of related training (Hart-Landsberg and Reder 1997). Both studies suggest that effective language use is embedded in additional understandings of the physical requirements and social relationships that govern production work and cannot be defined in the abstract.

In many English-speaking countries, changes in the manufacturing process have coincided with demographic changes in the workforce such that many worksites include employees from extremely varied linguistic and cultural backgrounds. Applied linguists have documented some of the ways workers and supervisors succeed or fail at managing both the production processes and social relationships in multilingual, multicultural work sites. Their work has enhanced the understanding of the multiple functions of language at work, as well as the connections across different language communities outside work. Clyne's (1994) study of multicultural workplaces in Melbourne showed that various cultural groups favored relatively different patterns of speech act sets in talk and that these patterns interacted with turn-taking behavior to shape communication; further, members of different linguistic and cultural groups tended to employ characteristic discourse styles based on their native languages even when communicating entirely in English. Goldstein's (1997) data on the language choices made by Portuguese-speaking women workers at a Toronto factory indicated that, because of the women's participation in dense and active social networks, they found mastery of English often unnecessary for meeting their workplace responsibilities, although many desired it for other personally significant purposes, such as communicating with children's teachers. Both projects provide ample evidence that good communicators in the workplaces are those who can grasp and convey comprehension of the material, historical, social, and cultural presuppositions that shape their work duties and that such understandings need not be achieved or communicated mainly or exclusively in English, even when that is the language of the surrounding society.[4]

Studies of workplace language in many industries attest that language, like other aspects of workplace activity, can reveal tensions. Kunda's ethnography of a U.S. high-tech company (1992) foregrounded (1) the company's language practices as exemplified in written documents, (2) the constant stream of e-mail, and (3) often ritualized presentations of work groups to each other as powerful normative influences on members of the organization. In exploring relationships between workers' experiences and attitudes and corporate success in an industry known for dramatic shifts in products and organization, the study documented an atmosphere of "high pressure ambiguity" (1992: 234) that coupled high expectations with lack of clear directives on how to achieve them. While documenting the experience of nonnative speakers of English working at professional jobs in Australia, Willing and collaborators (1992) found that meetings generally posed much more complex linguistic and interactional demands than moment-to-moment performance of other job duties. In a study of a British manufacturing plant adjusting to a change in management after a takeover, T. J. Watson (1997) showed that the talk among the production managers revealed ongoing tensions between the bottom-line-oriented new ownership and the original owners' empowerment philosophy, even as the managers sought to reconcile them.

Technology-oriented companies have been on the forefront of computer use for internal employee communication, as well as for regulation of production, and they have thus been settings for much work that explores the multiple and reciprocal influences of technology, language, and social groups on each other. Murray's (1995) study of computer usage for management and internal communication at a U.S. high-tech company showed that, like earlier communications technologies, computer "technology both transforms and is itself transformed by society" (1995: 5); this study documented the now widely recognized attributes of a simplified register found in computer-mediated communications and illustrated some of the context- and topic-sensitive reasons for choosing among a variety of communication modes (fax, e-mail, phone call, personal conversation). The interface between people and technology is attracting considerable innovative theorizing (Devlin and Rosenberg 1996). Empirical research that uses the many techniques available in applied linguistics has a central role in further specification of the reciprocal influences of technology and human communication on each other.

Language in Business and Sales-Related Positions

The past fifteen years have witnessed an explosion of interest in the language used to conduct business negotiations within and across various linguistic and cultural borders because of the economic shifts resulting from the demise of command economies and the increasing internationalization of business (Harris and Bargiela-Chiappini 1997). While there are literally hundreds of manuals and how-to guides aimed at sharing techniques for successful negotiation and sales, relatively few are based on real language data derived from relevant settings. Within the past ten years, scholars in applied linguistics and related areas have begun to fill this gap through empirical analyses of intercultural and interlingual negotiations; chapters in Bargiela-Chiappini and Harris (1997) provide several relevant comparisons of the discourse of negotiations and service encounters within and across diverse linguistic and cultural groups.

The role of the job interview in attaining initial employment is another area where prescriptive recommendation abounds but actual data are comparatively scant. Applicants are often urged to "sell themselves" in interviews, and current applied linguistic scholarship shows this is by no means a simple injunction; White's (1994) study of the language used in eighty genuine job interviews indicated the successful interviews (defined as those where the applicant got the job) could be described on the basis of a set of linguistic dimensions and, further, that the relevant dimensions differed somewhat according to type of job (professional versus no degree requirements) and gender of applicant.

The growth of the service sector characteristic of most developed economies has led to greater interest in related language issues, particularly the role of sales

in shaping and meeting consumer demands. Contemporary social science scholarship offers many important insights into the contradictory impulses that, in the
spirit of "best-practice" companies and Total Quality Management, promote personal, individual engagement in job-related interactions while, at the same time,
aiming for greater efficiency and standardization of outcome. These tensions are
tellingly explored in Leidner's (1993) ethnography of the recruitment, training,
and occupational experiences used by a McDonald's restaurant and by a life in-
surance company that depended on door-to-door sales calls. In both enterprises,
trainees were exposed to the language forms and uses deemed appropriate by the
companies with videos and actual scripts, which they had to rehearse, and successful performance of scripted language on the job was reinforced by supervisor
comments and, eventually, by some employees' own self-monitoring. Leidner argues that the ubiquitous and routinized service encounters characteristic of much
contemporary life are actually changing norms of language use and interpretation:
"Scripted service work accustoms both workers and service-recipients to participation in interaction that violates basic norms" (1993: 215) of genuineness, authenticity, and individuality to which most North Americans adhere, and
employees become habituated to these new interactional norms and carry them
into areas outside the job. Empirical research in applied linguistics could assess
the changes in language behaviors and attitudes suggested in this work. Anthropologists have already documented innovations in local styles of social interaction
and communication brought about by the establishment of fast food outlets in
parts of Asia (J. L. Watson 1997); applied linguistic research can be used to gauge
the impact of new forms of commercial transaction on language norms and attitudes, discourse conventions, and the politeness formulas and vocabulary items
that pertain to interactions between employees and consumers in a service economy.

Symbolic Language: Media and Advertising

Many of the developments related to recognition of the links between language
use and creation and manipulation of power relationships that mark the study
of language use in various professional contexts also apply to the study of language
used in mass media (see, e.g., Bell 1991; Fairclough 1995), though these are not
explored in detail here. As with other aspects of language use in professional
contexts, studies of media language also demonstrate trends toward a critical
perspective on the contents of messages, as well as the language used, particularly
as implicated in crosscultural references (Riggins 1997), and the reciprocal influences of various technological forms on media content and language (see Myers
1999).

CONCLUSION

Scholarship on the language used in professional and occupational settings has been sponsored by a variety of institutions and agencies whose agendas affect the research purpose and phenomena chosen for study, the accessibility of data, and the ultimate use and dissemination of the results. Research has been conducted from a descriptive, a confirmatory, or a critical stance. Whatever the occupational focus or analytic stance, current scholarship on language and work is now more sensitized to issues of the way people construct and maintain their work worlds through talk and, frequently, through the generation, consultation, and interpretation of related print materials and electronic technologies. Social changes that affect the economic opportunities available to men and women have made gender an important variable in the study of workplace language. Demographic changes leading to more multiethnic and multicultural workplaces mean that applied linguistic research can be used to identify relevant communication issues, whether worksite communication takes place in several languages or only in one. Finally, technological changes related to the integration of computer technologies into many workplaces coincide with other social and demographic developments, affecting many aspects of communication. Language used in the workplace is never only about work; it expresses and shapes the social realities experienced by workers and spills over into the understandings about work, life, and people that carry over into other realms of individual and social experience. Hence, ongoing research on language uses in professional and occupational activities belongs in the mainstream of contemporary applied linguistics. Without it, theorists, researchers, and policymakers are likely to oversimplify the complexities and contradictions that connect the study of language and society.

NOTES

1. The historical provenance of legal language, a line of research related to philology, has interested attorneys and legal scholars for decades; see, for example, Melinkoff's classic *The Language of the Law* (1963), which characterizes legal language as "wordy, unclear, pompous, and dull," and a more recent exemplar, Tiersma's *Legal Language* (1999). I do not discuss these works further here because they deal mainly with written language and word-level phenomena, rather than with the actual language used by participants in legal proceedings. Still, they represent a genre worth noting by applied linguists. Both books provide the historical pedigree (going back, in some cases, more than two millennia to Celtic Britain) of technical legal terminology used most often in writing, and both admonish attorneys to eschew obfuscation and communicate clearly in

"plain language." Melinkoff observes that, even before the seventeenth century, lawyers and even judges made money in part on the basis of the lengths of documents they prepared and filed, a strong incentive for wordiness (pp. 186 ff.). Tiersma's treatment begins to address the conflicting motivations for uses of language in legal settings (establishing and maintaining authority versus communicating with outsiders, be they clients or jury members) and the economic practices that promote relative wordiness (charging by the page or the hour) versus concision (charging based on contingencies or recovery). Though the latter observation is based on the writer's experience rather than a particular research study, it is one of many areas of language use in the law where applied linguistic research using contemporary empirical methods would be well warranted.

2. A classic in this genre is Becker et al., *Boys in White* (1961), an account of medical school life at the University of Kansas in 1956–1957. While it is enlightening to read the book as a portrait of the social divisions that affected student experience at the time—one of the most important of which was whether or not the students were members of fraternities or "independents," a second was whether students were married or single—it contains little explicit attention to language, defined either as number and type of technical vocabulary items to learn or as communication skills students needed to acquire. Instead, investigators represent students as overwhelmingly engaged in figuring out what the faculty members would select for the frequent quizzes, tests, and practical laboratory exams, a preoccupation certainly not limited to medical students, though it was, apparently, characteristic of them.

3. Because of the necessarily embodied nature of medicine and medical practice, studies of medical communication routinely include much greater attention to nonverbal behavior than do studies of language use in legal settings or in most other professional or occupational arenas; see, for example, Robinson (1998) for a careful explication of the simultaneous functions of verbal and nonverbal elements in the initial moments of medical office visits. In this chapter, for reasons of length, I restrict discussion to studies that emphasize the linguistic aspect of medical communication but note that any overall consideration of communication in the provision of health care must reckon with the physicality of interactions between providers and patients.

4. These studies also suggest that the performance of successful bilinguals deserves reconceptualization on a theoretical level, a principal contention of Woolard (1999). Additional applied linguistic research on dimensions of language contact in the workplace could advance theoretical developments here besides providing data valuable for a wide range of practical decisions.

PART VII

BILINGUALISM AND THE INDIVIDUAL LEARNER

CHAPTER 22

CONTEXTS FOR BECOMING BILINGUAL LEARNERS IN SCHOOL SETTINGS

CHRISTIAN FALTIS

THERE are a number of ways that researchers and educators have positioned themselves theoretically with respect to how context figures into becoming bilingual (and biliterate) in school settings. For some, context is defined not only as an "interactionally constituted environment" (Díaz, Moll, and Mehan 1986: 193) that influences how students and teachers participate and make meaning in two languages but also as an outcome of joint efforts to share or create contexts for participating in interaction at any given time and place (Auer 1992). In other words, not only is what happens during classroom interactions influenced by immediate context but what happens is in itself also responsible for the availability of the very context that is necessary to make meaning during interactions. This is what I refer to as a "discourse perspective" for studying context, because the analytic focus is on how particular local contexts influence classroom oral and written discourse, as well as on the contexts they create as a result of that discourse (Díaz, Moll, and Mehan 1986; Gutiérrez 1993; Gutiérrez and Larson 1994; Wolfe 1999).

For others who study learners who are becoming bilingual in school, context refers to societal, community, and pedagogical forces or texts that influence how learners become bilingual in school settings as well as how bilingual they become (Cortés 1986; Gersten and Faltis 2000; Ogbu and Simons 1998; Valdés 1998; Wolfe and Faltis 1999). Often, research from this "intertextual perspective" relies on particular instances of classroom discourse as evidence for the relationship between contextual forces and the creation of certain texts in bilingual classroom settings by teachers and students alike. From this perspective, meanings that students and teachers share, don't share, or create through joint interactions are necessarily dependent on other texts (contexts) that are relevant for the interpretation of classroom texts. (See Lemke 1992.)

In this chapter, I intend to focus on societal, community, and pedagogical contexts that come into play when learners become bilingual in school settings, drawing from studies that use both discourse and intertextual perspectives. Note that while the presentation is linear and may imply a social-to-individual direction, this is not my intention. Nor should the presentation imply a concentric circle model where each interaction is embedded in a larger context and so on ad infinitum. From my perspective, context moves in and out of focus in no predictable way, because participants in interaction have as much to do with creating contexts that give meaning to their interaction as context has on influencing their interaction and meaning.

SOCIETAL FORCES AS CONTEXT

National as well as local views on the use of more than one language in school and society have a powerful influence on the ways the two language are distributed and used for learning, which has an impact on how and how well students become bilingual (Jacobson and Faltis 1990). For example, throughout the history of the United States, attitudes toward the use of languages other than English in schools have ranged from supportive to disapproving. During supportive times, when bilingualism is considered to be a national and cultural resource, teachers and students use more of the non-English language across the grades regardless of how well students acquire English, and students typically become highly fluent bilinguals (Fishman 1989). However, when the use of non-English languages in schools is viewed as a hindrance to becoming American, there is tremendous pressure placed on teachers and students to curtail non-English language use for any educational purposes (save for foreign language learning in secondary schools). In this context, most students who begin school as non-English speakers end up as monolingual English speakers by adulthood (Pease-Alvarez 1993; Wong

Fillmore 1991). At the present time, most bilingual education programs in the United States are transitional in nature, with the goal of moving students out of their native language and into English as quickly as possible, typically in three academic years or less (Faltis and Hudelson 1998; Ramírez and Merino 1990).

An alternative approach to bilingual education that emerged in the 1990s on a small scale and the appears to have the support of mainstream politicians and parents alike across the United States is called "dual language bilingual education" (Lindholm and Molina 2000). This mainly elementary-level approach to bilingual education enrolls children from two different language groups (usually Spanish and English) to learn through each others' native language. Dual language programs are sometimes referred to as two-way immersion or maintenance bilingual programs (Faltis and Hudelson 1998). The goals of the approach are that speakers of each language will:

1. Learn the language of the others
2. Achieve academically in both languages
3. Come to appreciate each others' languages and cultures (Lindholm 1994).

Dual language bilingual education is attractive to parents, educators, and researchers in the dominant society ostensibly because minority students are no longer segregated from mainstream students. It offers a viable solution to America's struggle with monolingualism, and achievement levels in language and academics of both minority and mainstream children have shown a steady increase (Lindholm and Molina 2000).

Dual language bilingual programs in the United States and elsewhere are partially modeled after the French immersion schools that began in the French-speaking provinces of Canada in the early 1960s. In immersion schools, mainly middle-class English-speaking children of educated families enroll in French-medium classrooms and achieve high levels of academic listening and reading comprehension in French without any loss of academic ability in English (Genesee 1987; see also Cenoz and Genesee 1998; Cummins and Corson 1997; Gersten and Faltis 2000 for writings about dual language programs in Africa, Hong Kong, Ireland, the Philippines, Slovakia, and Spain). Immersion schools have the support of parents and the English-speaking community, reflecting a societal context (at least in eastern Canada) in which bilingualism is considered an economic resource.

Despite the promise of dual language programs worldwide and of Canadian French immersion schools for producing high-level balanced bilingual learners, it is important to emphasize that the languages used in these programs and schools to promote bilingualism are not neutral; each carries with it sociohistorical dimensions of power and utility for society (Edelsky 1991). Both dual language programs and immersion schools exist in societies that differentiate the significance of acquiring a second language and the language being acquired (Valdés

1997). In the United States, minority children in dual language programs are expected to acquire high levels of English, the language of power, business, and education. Likewise, in Spain and Slovakia, minority-language children and their communities (Basque and Hungarian, respectively) are pressured to acquire high levels of the dominant language because, in their respective societies, only one language counts, and the children know this (Cenoz 1998; Gersten and Faltis 2000).

In contrast, for children of the dominant groups in these programs and schools, parents and teachers enthusiastically applaud any acquisition of a non-dominant language. In French immersion schools, for example, English-speaking children acquire listening and reading abilities comparable to those of their French-speaking peers, but in no way do they advance to nativelike abilities in speaking and writing (Baker 1996). Nonetheless, their efforts are praised. Outside school, English-speaking children and their families have virtually no contact with the French-speaking community. Gaining proficiency in French is not a social goal but rather an instrumental one, and French is still considered by English-speaking and many French Canadians as a language that is less valuable than English (Baker 1996). Students who are becoming bilingual under these societal forces are not easily tricked into believing that a language that society considers to be instrumental for what is really valued is in any way equal to their native language.

COMMUNITY FORCES AS CONTEXT

The ways that minority-language and bilingual communities perceive and respond to their past and present treatment in schools constitute what Ogbu (1983; Ogbu and Simons 1998) refers to as "community forces" that interact with and have an impact on the extent to which children of these communities become bilingual and succeed in school. (See Richards 1987 for a specific application of Ogbu's work to a Mayan-Spanish bilingual community in Guatemala.) According to Ogbu, community forces are a consequence of societal attitudes toward, and the dominant group's treatment of, language-minority groups, especially in school and in the workforce. Ogbu argues that language-minority groups who were originally conquered, colonized, or enslaved (and many of their direct descendants) develop cultural models or belief systems to form their identities and guide their actions in society. For Ogbu, these belief systems stem from a language-minority group's frames of reference, their folk theories of making it, their degree of trust in the dominant society and its institutions, and the beliefs they have about the effect of adopting dominant societal ways on minority identity.

Community beliefs about how well their children are doing in comparison to children from the dominant society serves as an important frame of reference. For example, the community may question whether the bilingual programs that serve their children are offering the same quality of education as that received by the children of dominant groups. Are bilingual teachers as well prepared as English-medium teachers? Do schools with high numbers of non-English language children have the same quality literacy programs and reading materials as schools filled with children from the dominant society? When beliefs about who is getting a better education are coupled with folk theories about the chances of making it in mainstream society and the value of school credentials (e.g., a high school diploma, a college degree), community members begin to form belief systems about the value of their ways of doing things, including language learning and use, as compared to the dominant ways of behaving.

Ogbu (1983) also brings up the value of having role models within a community for forming folk belief systems about language and schools and about what role school has in determining success in later life. With respect to bilingualism, language-minority children and their families may ask themselves who the people are in, as well as outside, their community that they would most like to resemble, and how their home language figures into that image. On the basis of answers from multiple sources, communities form folk theories about what needs to be given up or added on to become like their role models. For some, losing ties with their native language is viewed as necessary in order to reach their goals for being successful (Wong Fillmore 1991; Pease-Alvarez 1993); for others, who don't see a connection between school and success in the dominant society, not fully learning the dominant ways, including language, is seen as a way to preserve their collective identity (Ogbu and Matute-Bianchi 1986).

The degree to which language-minority communities trust the school and school personnel to provide the best possible education for their children also contributes to community forces as context for how, and how well, students become bilingual in school settings. According to Ogbu (1983), recent immigrant minorities, especially those from poor countries, usually carry with them optimistic attitudes toward schooling, resulting in an initial faith in public schools controlled by the dominant group in the host society. However, over time, and through contact with established minority group members who are functionally bilingual and who share experiences about racism, discrimination, and conflict with them, this trust may wane. As a result, these immigrants, no longer newcomers to host country schools, begin to treat schools and programs for their children with suspicion, especially if they believe that schools favor the dominant group and, at the same time, deprive their children of language and cultural identities. This group-level suspicion can lead the children of immigrants who stay in the school system to develop, over time, what Ogbu refers to as "oppositional collective or group identities" (Ogbu and Simons 1998: 177). When this happens, although native language use may be maintained, academic achievement as measured through the dominant language and culture may suffer.

Pedagogical Orientations and Teacher Abilities as Context

Pedagogical orientations of keys players in all levels of education not only reflect societal and community forces but also create contexts for how children who are becoming bilingual are prepared for society in school (Edelsky 1991). Administrators, school board members, and teachers are, after all, primarily members of the dominant society, and their orientations toward pedagogy and the goals of schooling influence the distribution and use of languages other than the dominant one in school (Kjolseth 1970).

Administrators and classroom teachers who view the alienation of language-minority students from their native language and culture as an essential function of schooling more than likely adhere to a "time on task" perspective of bilingualism (Cummins 1986). From this perspective, since learning the dominant language and culture is paramount, the more experience and practice (time) in and through the dominant language (task), the more students will learn it. This stance derives from a common-sense belief that learners have two separate and independent languages that operate separately (Cummins 1986). Accordingly, providing students with too much exposure to their native language will ultimately be a waste of their time and energy, since the way to develop bilingualism is to provide learners as much exposure to the dominant language and culture as possible. In this context, learners have minimal support in their native language and are moved into the dominant language as soon as possible.

Schools that operate from this assimilationist perspective typically have very few literacy materials available in the bilingual learners' native languages, and teachers tend to have low levels of proficiency in the students' native languages (Cazden 1992). In the United States, the national average is eighteen English-language children's books per child (White 1990). In California schools with high numbers of bilingual learners (85 percent or greater), the average number of children's books in the learners' native language is less than two per child (Pucci 1994). In one maintenance bilingual classroom in a Texas school, the situation was only slightly better (Smith 1999); there was at total of eighty books, thirteen of which were in Spanish. He noted: "The books in English were all colorful, fully illustrated and of various sizes, shapes and themes. Of the books in Spanish, two were tattered with pages missing and another was a basal social studies text nearly 10 years old" (Smith 1999: 277). This lack of support for the student's native language sends a powerful message to the students about the value of their language and culture.

Conversely, administrators, school boards, and teachers in favor of cultural pluralism strive for an additive approach to bilingualism, that is, to enable students to become highly biliterate and bilingual by providing quality educational experiences in two languages (Krashen 1996). Moreover, schools and bilingual teachers who support cultural pluralism believe that children have the right to maintain and develop their mother tongue (the language they learned first), identify with it, and use it to communicate across time and space (Kjolseth 1970). Children who become bilingual in schools and classrooms built around these perspective are in an optimal position to develop high levels of academic literacy and content knowledge in both their native language and the dominant language. There are usually high numbers of high-quality literacy materials available in the bilingual learners' native languages (Krashen 1996; Shannnon 1995), and teachers tend to be more proficient in their students' native language than do teachers in transitional, assimilationist bilingual programs (Cazden 1992).

Within both assimilation- and cultural pluralist–oriented bilingual classroom settings, however, a teacher's pedagogical orientation and the way he or she uses language in the classroom can also have a bearing on how, and how well, learners become bilingual. Pedagogical orientation refers to how a teacher understands the nature of teaching and learning and his or her theoretical commitments to practice (Edelsky 1993). To simplify matters, following Wolfe (1999), bilingual teachers can be transactional- or transmission-oriented in their pedagogical stance toward teaching and learning. Broadly speaking, transactional-oriented bilingual teachers rely on a holistic approach to teaching and learning. Teaching is a matter of moving students from literacy practices valued through their own histories to multiple literacy practices, including knowledge about how language works (Hudelson 2000; Wolfe 1999). From this stance, language acquisition and learning depend on access to and participation in legitimate social activities in which learners use many forms and functions of language with the goal of understanding and using new literacies to accomplish their purpose (Faltis and Hudelson 1998). In bilingual classrooms, this means that learners become bilingual by using both their native language and the dominant language for multiple academic purposes. Moreover, learners may continue using their native language even though they are academically proficient in the dominant language. Learner are not pushed into the dominant language; rather, because they see themselves as language users, they often choose to experiment with their new language on their own (Edelsky 1986; Hudelson and Serna 1994).

In contrast, transmission-oriented bilingual teachers generally view teaching and learning as a matter of giving learners the language and knowledge they need to succeed on tests (Edelsky 1991). An assumption behind this approach to teaching and learning is that learners need to have language and content information broken down into, and presented to them in, bits and pieces they need to master. Learners who become bilingual in transmission-oriented classrooms are taught that learning is a matter of doing well on worksheets, homework, and standardized tests. Likewise, biliteracy is presented as a set of skills in two languages, but the native language skills are valued only to the extent that they enable students to perform well on dominant-language standardized tests (Cummins 2000a).

A teacher's pedagogical orientation also includes how the learners' two languages are used for instruction during classroom interaction with learners and for literacy purposes. Many teachers in bilingual classrooms translate much of what they say and write from one language to the other to ensure that all learners understand and to move the lesson along. This gives the appearance that the two languages are being used more or less equally. It has been well documented, however, that bilingual learners do not attend to teacher talk or writing in their developing language when the teacher consistently translates into their native language (Wong Fillmore and Valadez 1986). Accordingly, in bilingual classrooms where the teacher translates most of what she says or writes, bilingual learners have fewer opportunities to discuss academic topics at length in their second language than they do in their native language. Obviously, this strategy does not facilitate learning in and through the second language.

Some bilingual teachers also switch from one language to the other without translating, using both languages concurrently to interact with students (Jacobson and Faltis 1990). Again, however, as was mentioned, languages in bilingual classrooms are never neutral. For example, a study of classroom language use in a bilingual high school civics class taught by a teacher who was highly supportive of additive bilingualism revealed that the teacher unwittingly used the dominant language (English) to convey essential concepts twice as often as he used the students' native language (Spanish), and he used the dominant language almost exclusively to maintain classroom control (Sapiens 1982). The message for students, even in this language-minority-friendly classroom, is that the dominant language matters and the learners' native language serves no purpose other than as a bridge to English. (See also Escamilla [1994] for similar findings in an elementary school bilingual program and Shannon [1995] for a study of how one bilingual teacher resists the hegemony of the dominant language.)

A final, but nonetheless highly important, aspect of pedagogical orientation as context is how well prepared bilingual teachers are for teaching in the non-dominant language of the classroom. Christian, Montone, Lindholm, and Carranza (1997) claim that the majority of teachers in dual language bilingual programs have native or near-native ability in the nondominant languages in which they teach. However, as Guerrero (1997) and August and Hakuta (1997) point out, dual language bilingual programs are very rare, and there is no research to substantiate Christian et al.'s (1997) claim. Moreover, the overwhelming majority of bilingual teachers work in transitional bilingual programs where the goal is to get learners into the dominant language as quickly as possible. Very few of these teachers have ever taken academic work in their students' language or studied teaching methods courses through that language (Calderón and Díaz 1993).

Even in bilingual programs that profess to be native-language maintenance programs, teachers are often incapable of teaching entire lessons in the learners' native language, especially in the upper elementary grades (Escamilla 1992). In secondary school bilingual programs, the situation is even worst. Bilingual learners are placed with teachers who have difficulty expressing complex ideas and using specialized academic vocabulary in the learners' native language (McCollum 1994). Bilingual learners with bilingual teachers who are more proficient in the dominant language and in their students' native language create telling contexts for learners to understand the role of their language in school and society.

CONCLUSION

Understanding the nature and role of context for bilingual learners is complex and remains understudied. Although it is certain that context influences how, and how well, learners become bilingual and that what happens to learners results in the creation of new contexts, very little is known about the kinds of contexts bilingual learners create for themselves or what it means when a bilingual learner says, "Teacher, there are no books in Spanish" (Smith 1999: 277), or, "We're a really lucky class because Mrs. D gots us the Spanish books and the English books . . . like for Alicia she could have the English book and like we could . . . whoever needs to learn Spanish they could have a Spanish book" (Shannon 1995: 190).

In this short chapter, I have touched upon what I consider to be three major contexts that contribute to how, and how well, learners become bilingual in school settings. The key points that I have attempted to make are these:

- The effect of various contexts on bilingual learners is also responsible for creating contexts that learners rely on for making sense of their language and its role in learning.
- The languages of bilingual learners are not neutral. Societal and community forces, as well as teachers' ideologies about language and learning,

carry with them sociohistorical dimensions about the usefulness and power of a bilingual learner's two languages.

- A language-minority community relies on past and present treatment by, and attitudes toward, the dominant society for supporting or questioning bilingual education.
- How, and how well, bilingual teachers use bilingual learners' native language creates a powerful context for becoming bilingual in school settings.

My hope is that this discussion of context will stimulate a reexamination of the forces that enter into the lives of bilingual learners on a daily basis.

CHAPTER 23

COGNITIVE PROCESSING IN BILINGUALS: LANGUAGE CHOICE AND CODE-SWITCHING

KEES DE BOT

THE main questions related to cognitive processing are:

- How do we go from a communicative intention to articulation in language production?
- How do we go from auditory or visual input to message interpretation in perception in terms of the psycholinguistic processes involved?

For cognitive processing in bilinguals,[1] the same questions are relevant, and an additional question is: What specific mechanisms are needed to deal with more than one language?

Since not all aspects of cognitive processing can be dealt with here, this chapter focuses on one very central issue: the mechanisms of language selection and language separation in bilingual language use. This is a crucial issue for our understanding of the processes of bilingual language use, not just in full bilinguals but also in incipient learners of a second language. Through a componential analysis of learners' language, we may get a better understanding of the locus of problems. (See de Bot, Paribakht, and Wesche 1997 for a similar study on lexical knowledge.) In the present chapter the focus is on the processes that are needed to keep languages apart in language production.

In the study of cognitive processing in bilinguals, there are various sources of data. As in monolingual processing, spontaneous speech data and various experimental paradigms can be used, both with healthy and with aphasic language users. One source of data is unique to bilinguals: data from code-switching.[2] In bilingual experiments, the processing of more than one language is typically induced by the experimental conditions and therefore is not really natural. In many societies, code-switching (henceforth CS) and the use of more than one language is the normal way of expressing oneself and is not different from other types of spontaneous speech in that sense. The study of code-switching provides us with a unique window on the ways languages can interact in language processing, and the way the various languages are used together can help us understand the cognition of bilingualism. In the same vein, the perception of CS is a unique process in which various layers of processing of more than one language are involved. Obviously the study of CS phenomena in production is much easier than tracking the role of different languages in perception. Though the latter has been done, and should be done (cf. Grosjean 1988), the emphasis in the present article is on the production side. The main objective is to show how language selection may take place and to show that simple language assignment to higher linguistic units is too simple an explanation for many forms of CS presented in the literature. It is proposed that in language production there are many "switching sites" and that, in the planning and execution of utterances, language assignment has to be coded for these sites.

Within this context, the notion of "a language" as an entity, which is central to much linguistic research, may be irrelevant from the perspective of the individual speaker who doesn't get all the linguistic input labeled for language and who has to set up a system of distributional properties of grammatical rules and lexical items; this system may end up as one that is similar to what we find in descriptive grammar books and dictionaries for specific languages and may be described as a coherent system by grammatical or lexical entities. It is, however, likely to be highly idiosyncratic and far removed from the idealized native speaker who figures in the study of linguistic theory.

A second implication of a processing approach implies, in particular, that, with respect to output (i.e., speech production), all utterances are real data in the sense that the model used should be able to explain how this could happen. We have to be able to explain not just the typical but also the atypical, which is often most revealing. The aim of this chapter is to show on the one hand that CS as language production is not basically different from producing monolingual speech and on the other hand, that all CS can be explained within a model that defines the different steps in the production process.

LANGUAGE PRODUCTION IN BILINGUALS

For the discussion of language production and code-switching, Levelt's "speaking" model (1989) is taken as a starting point. This is arguably the most established psycholinguistic model available, and various researchers have shown its relevance for bilingual processing (e.g., de Bot 1992; de Bot and Schreuder 1993; Green 1993; Myers-Scotton 1995; Poulisse 1997). The Levelt model is discussed briefly here in order to give the reader an idea of the main line of argumentation. More elaborate versions of the model are described in Levelt 1989, 1993; Levelt, Roelofs, and Meyer 1999).

In the speaking model, different modules are distinguished:

- The conceptualizer
- The formulator
- The articulator.

Lexical items are stored in the lexicon in separate stores for lemmas and lexemes. The different parts can be described briefly as follows:

- *The conceptualizer.* In this module, communicative intentions are translated into messages that can function as input to the speech production system. Levelt distinguishes "macroplanning," which involves the planning of a speech act, the selection of information to be expressed, and the linearization of that information, from 'microplanning," which involves the propositionalization of the event to be expressed, the perspective taken, and certain language-specific decisions that have an effect on the form of the message to be conveyed. The output of the conceptualizer is a preverbal message, which consists of all the information needed by the next component, the formulator, to convert the communicative intention into speech. Crucial aspects of the model are:

  That there is no external unit controlling the various components
  That there is no feedback from the formulator to the conceptualizer
  That there is no feedforward from the conceptualizer to the other components of the model.

This means that all the information that is relevant to the "lower" components has to be included in the preverbal message.

- *The formulator.* In this module, the preverbal message is converted into a speech plan (phonetic plan) by the selection of lexical items and the application of grammatical and phonological rules. Lexical items consist of two parts, the lemma and the morphophonological form, or lexeme. In the lemma, the lexical entry's meaning and syntax are represented, while morphological and phonological properties are represented in the lexeme. In production, lexical items are activated by matching the meaning part of the lemma with the semantic information in the preverbal message. Accordingly, the information from the lexicon is made available in two phases; semantic activation precedes from activation (Schriefers, Meyer, and Levelt 1990). The lemma information of a lexical item concerns both conceptual specifications of its use, such as pragmatic and stylistic conditions, and (morpho-)syntactic information, including the lemma's syntactic category and its grammatical functions, as well as information that is needed for its syntactic encoding (in particular, number, tense, aspect, mood, case, and pitch accent). Activation of the lemma immediately provides the relevant syntactic information, which in turn activates syntactic procedures. The selection of the lemmas and the relevant syntactic information leads to the formation of a surface structure. While the surface structure is being formed, the morphophonological information in the lexeme is activated and encoded. The phonological encoding provides the input for the articulator in the form of a phonetic plan. This phonetic plan can be scanned internally by the speaker via the speech-comprehension system, which provides the first possibility for feedback.

- *The articulator.* This module converts the speech plan into actual speech. The output from the formulator is processed and temporarily stored in such a way that the phonetic plan can be fed back to the speech-comprehension system and the speech can be produced at normal speed.
- *A speech-comprehension system connected with an auditory system.* This module plays a role in the two ways in which feedback takes place within the model: The phonetic plan, as well as the overt speech, is passed on to the speech-comprehension system, where mistakes that may have crept in can be traced. Speech understanding is modeled as the mirror image of language production, and the lexicon is assumed to be shared by the two systems.

SPEECH PRODUCTION IN BILINGUAL SPEAKERS

The Levelt model has been developed as a monolingual model, and, if we want to apply it to CS and other bilingual phenomena, we need to clarify to what extent the present model is capable of handling bilingual speech.

In her discussion of learners of a foreign language as bilingual speakers, Poulisse (1997) mentions the following factors that have to be taken into account in a bilingual model:

1. L2 knowledge is typically incomplete. L2 speakers generally have fewer words and rules at their disposal than L1 speakers. This may keep them from expressing messages they had originally intended to convey, may lead them to use compensatory strategies, or may lead them to avoid words or structures about which they feel uncertain.
2. L2 speech is more hesitant and contains more errors and slips, depending on the level of proficiency of the learners. Cognitive skill theories such as Schneider and Shiffrin's (1977) or Anderson's ACT* (1982) stress the importance of the development of automatic processes that are difficult to acquire and hard to unlearn. Less automaticity means that more attention has to be paid to the execution of specific lower level tasks, which leads to a slowing down of the production process and to a greater number of slips because limited attention resources have to be expended on lower level processing.
3. L2 speech often carries traces of the L1. L2 speakers have a fully developed L1 system at their disposal and may switch to their L1 either deliberately ("motivated" switches) or unintentionally ("performance" switches). Switches to the L1 may, for example, be motivated by a desire to express group membership in conversations in which other bilinguals with the same L1 background participate, or they may occur unintentionally, for example, when an L1 word is accidentally accessed instead of an intended L2 word. Poulisse and Bongaerts (1994) argue that such accidental switches to the L1 are very similar to substitutions and slips in monolingual speech.

Poulisse (1997) argues that the incomplete L2 knowledge base and the lack of automaticity of L2 speakers can be adequately handled by existing monolingual production models but that the occurrence of L1 traces in L2 speech pose problems for such models. Paradis (1998), on the other hand, claims that neither switches to the L1 nor cross-linguistic influence (CLI) phenomena call for adaptations in existing models. In terms of processing, Paradis argues, CLI-phenomena cannot be distinguished clearly from CS-phenomena: Both result from the working of the production system in an individual speaker, and the fact that CLI may sometimes be undesirable in terms of an external model of the target language is not relevant here. Though in this chapter the main focus is on CS, the same kind of argumentation can be used in various aspects of CLI, and it would certainly be worth while to review the literature and data on CLI from the perspective given.

In dealing with bilingual speakers there are two aspects that have to be accounted for: How do those speakers keep their languages apart? How do they implement language choice?

KEEPING LANGUAGES APART

Psycholinguistically, CS and keeping languages apart are different aspects of the same phenomenon. In the literature, a number of proposals have been made on how bilingual speakers keep their languages apart. Earlier proposals involving input and output switches for languages have been abandoned for models based on activation spreading.

On the basis of research on bilingual aphasia, Paradis (1981) has proposed the subset hypothesis, which, it is claimed, can account for most of the data found. According to Paradis, words (but also syntactic rules or phonemes) from a given language form a subset of the total inventory. Each subset can be activated independently. Some subsets (e.g., from typologically related languages) may show considerable overlap in the form of cognate words. The subsets are formed and maintained by the use of words in specific settings: Words from a given language will be used together in most settings, but, in settings in which code-switching is the norm, speakers may develop a subset in which words from more than one language can be used together. The idea of a subset in the lexicon is highly compatible with current ideas on connectionistic relations in the mental lexicon (cf. Roelofs 1992).

A major advantage of the subset hypothesis is that the set of lexical and syntactic rules or phonological elements from which a selection has to be made is reduced dramatically as a result of the fact that a particular language/subset has been chosen. Our claim is that the subset hypothesis can explain how languages in bilinguals may be kept apart, but not how the choice for a given language is made. The activation of a language specific subset enhances the likelihood of elements of that subset being selected, but it is no guarantee for the selection of elements from that language only.

According to the subset hypothesis, bilingual speakers have stores for lemmas, lexemes, syntactic rules, morphophonological rules and elements, and articulatory elements that are not fundamentally different from those of monolingual speakers. Within each of these stores there are subsets for different languages, but also for different varieties, styles, and registers. There are probably relations between subsets in different stores; that is lemmas that form a subset in a given language will be related to both lexemes and syntactic rules from that same language, and phonological rules from that language will be connected with articulatory elements from that language. The way these types of vertical connections are made is in principle similar to the way in which connections between elements on the lemma level develop.

LANGUAGE CHOICE AND CS

A distinction needs to be made between CS that is used as a meaningful discourse strategy and CS that results from lack of knowledge, because, as will be shown later on, the mechanics of these two types of CS in terms of the proposed model are totally different.

How is language choice implemented? In speaking, the step that is probably most crucial is the matching of chunks from the preverbal message with the meaning part of lemmas, because here the transition from (largely language-independent) conceptualization to language-specific coding takes place. In Levelt's description, the lemma consists basically of three parts: semantic specification, syntactic information, and pointer to a particular lexeme. The semantic specification is "the set of conceptual conditions under which the lemma can be appropriately used" (Levelt 1993: 4), which is matched with a chunk from a preverbal message. It is likely that, in lexical retrieval, a single concept can temporarily activate more than one semantically related lemma, which suggests that the lemma store is organized according to semantic principles. The syntactic information refers to the syntactic category of a lemma and its grammatical functions. When a lemma is activated, its particular syntactic environment is defined as well; for example, the verb 'sell' will involve a subject, an object, and a prepositional phrase. Other lemmas will be labeled as "recipient" or "agent." The lemmas that have been activated will "search" for other lemmas that fit; that is, the verb will "search" for a subject (and, according to its valence, sometimes a direct object/indirect object). "Grammatical encoding is like solving a set of simultaneous equations: The surface structure must be such that for all lemmas the required syntactic environments are realized" (Levelt 1993: 4).

The third type of information in the lemma is a pointer to a lexeme. Lexemes contain the phonological specifications of a lemma and the morphological makeup. The exact relation between the lemma and the lexeme is not entirely clear. Data from tip-of-the-tongue research have shown that occasionally speakers, while having retrieved a lemma, cannot find the lexeme connected with it. In most cases, the speaker has some information on the lemma, such as the first letter or the number of syllables (cf. Meyer and Bock 1992). In phonological encoding, different types of information come together, in particular prosodic, metrical, and segmental information. In this process, the development of metrical frames precedes the insertion of segmental information.

For our discussion of the process of language production in bilinguals, the relevant point is that there are a number of steps in the process of lexical access where choices have to be made. De Bot and Schreuder (1993) and Poulisse and Bongaerts (1994) argue that "language" is one of the features used in lemma selection. So, for the selection of the lemma 'boy,' not only do the semantic features 'male' and 'young' have to match relevant conceptual information in the preverbal message, but, for a bilingual speaker who has English as one of his languages, the lemma 'boy,' for it to be selected, will also need to contain information on which language it belongs to, and this information will have to match the language cue in the preverbal message. Translation equivalents such as 'boy' and 'jongen' show considerable overlap in their semantic specifications but differ mainly with respect to the "language" feature. Here we assume that there is no real contrast between a view of networks versus tagging since, in both views, "language" is part of the conceptual specifications that play a role in lemma selection. So, the communicative intention as expressed in the preverbal message also has to contain information about the language to be used.

One of the crucial points of the model proposed here is that there is no possibility of conveying information from the conceptualizer to the formulator other than through the preverbal message. In other words, all information about language choice has to be included in some form in the preverbal message. One way to do this is to label parts of the message for language. A number of arguments speak against a solution that implies that either "language A" or "language B" is selected and in which such a selection defines the language choice for the remaining steps in the production process. "Language" is part of the conceptual specification and, therefore, one of the characteristics of a lexical element used in the retrieval process. In this process, semantic cues of the lexical elements are matched with semantic information in the preverbal message. The cues to an element can have certain values; some cues are more important than others. Depending on the setting, some cues attached to the lexical element will have more value or weight than others; if the size of an entity is relevant, size information must be expressed: The "size" cue has a high value. The selection of one of the French words corresponding with the English word 'ball' can serve as an example (Paradis personal communication): If the "size" cue is important, a selection has to be made between an item with the characteristic "small" (which would be *balle* in French) or with the characteristic "big" (which would lead to the selection of *ballon*). If the size cue is not important, either of the two can be chosen. Accordingly, if language choice is a pertinent condition, the value of this cue will be expressed appropriately: In some settings, the lemma to be activated must have the characteristic L_a (language a) or L_b, while in other settings the value of this language cue is low, which means that lexical items from either L_a or L_b are equally appropriate. This implies that there may be more or less random CS and that not every single switch has to be initiated and controlled by some higher level process.

Research on CS has shown that, in specific settings, words from two languages can be mixed almost at random (e.g., Swigart 1992). In such cases it is highly unlikely that each individual word will be labeled specifically for the language in which it appears. Scotton and Ury (1977) mention cases of extensive code-switching as resulting from the adoption of a neutrality strategy when the choice of one of the languages would be "marked" or when there is ambiguity as to which language is the more appropriate one in a given setting: In such a case, the cue values for both languages are high, because both have to get about equal access to the output system. In some cases, language turns out to be a less important cue than other semantic cues. The following examples show that a word from another language is sometimes selected because that word meets the conceptual conditions better than a word from the cued language. In this case the language cue is suppressed because of semantic considerations:

(1) *Je moet niet 's avonds naar buiten gaan omdat je anders* znun *tegenkomt, snap je?*
     'You must not go out at night, because you may come across *ghosts*. (Nortier personal commumication)

Apparently, the Dutch word for 'ghosts,' *geesten,* is not adequate here in the eyes of this speaker (who is highly proficient in Dutch) to express the specific semantics of Moroccan Arabic (MA) *znun*; therefore, the Moroccan-Arabic word is preferred to the Dutch word *geesten*.

Similar examples are derived from Backus's work on Dutch/Turkish CS (1992):

(2) *Wij zijn gewoon hetzelfde als <u>babamiz, annemiz.</u>*
     We're just the same as <u>our parents.</u>

(3) *Maar dat is toch weer <u>köy,</u> hè.*
     But that is again backwardish, boorish.

In example (2) the speakers knew the Dutch word for 'parents,' but this may not, for them, express the same emotional value, and therefore they used the Turkish labels. In (3) there are various ways to express this in Dutch, but the speaker preferred to use a probably more precise Turkish expression than the Dutch one.

The language cues in the preverbal message define what the system aims at. This may not be the same as what the production system (i.e., the formulator) can actually deliver. In speaking, the number of words produced in a given period of time can be very high: According to Levelt (1989), this amounts to a rate of two to five words per second. Consequently, the speaker is in constant need of words. Bilinguals, even very proficient ones, reportedly need more time to retrieve words from memory than monolinguals: Mack (1986) reports differences up to 150ms in word recognition tasks. Similar figures are presented by Hermans (2000) on L2 production. This means that there is hardly any time for the selection of the right lexical item. The nonnative speaker of a language in particular has to find a balance between the time needed to find the right word and the character-istics of the lexical element he is looking for. Depending on the value of the various cues in the preverbal message, the speaker tries to find words that, in any case, correspond to the cues with a high value, ignoring less important values when running out of time. It is a well-known strategy of language learners to hope that an L1-word "will do" when the L2 word cannot be found (Poulisse and Bongaerts 1994).

The preverbal message may (or, rather, has to) contain information on cue values for different subcomponents of the production system. It is very likely that there is a hierarchical order in the sense that language selection at the highest level (i.e., the selection of lemmas on the basis of conceptual information in the preverbal message) will have an effect on later selection processes: There may be a preferential choice based on information from the preverbal message. According to the speaking model, activation of a lemma leads to the activation of gram-matical procedures; or, to use Levelt's words, "encoding operations are largely controlled by the grammatical properties of the lemmas retrieved. . . . The gram-matical encoding procedures of the Formulator will be guided by the information the lemmas make available" (1989: 236).

In his description of the grammatical encoding process, Levelt makes use of Kempen and Hoenkamp's (1987) proposals for "procedural packages" for building the syntactic environment around major category lemmas. The lemma categories are N, V, A, and P, and their categorical procedures NP, VP, AP, and PP, re-spectively. S as a procedure is activated by the first categorical procedure that was activated by the first lemma that became available. It is therefore conceivable that the language of the first selected lemma has a major impact on the choice of the lemmas that follow.

The setting of the language cue at the sentence or clause level may work out differently on successive levels. It may be that the relative contribution of the two languages is different on different levels but complementary in the sense that the overall ratio for the two languages (i.e., the frequency of CS into one or the other language) remains constant. There is substantial evidence that the value of the language cue has an effect on the relative frequency of code-switching; for example, Poplack (1985) reports on a study of French/English code-switching in Ottawa, where French is the minority language, and in Hull, where English is the minority language. Speakers of French tended to switch three to four times more frequently in Ottawa than in Hull, which reflects the norms/values for the use of the two languages in these two settings.

LANGUAGE PRODUCTION AND SWITCHING SITES

It has been argued in the first part of this chapter that the setting of the language cue more or less defines language choice. In this section, it is shown that there are several "switching sites" during the production process. In order to do this, we have to look at the various steps in the process. For the generation of a sentence, the steps—presented in figure 23.1—can be distinguished. The figures refer to those sites at which elements have to be selected and at which accordingly elements from different languages can in principle be selected.

At all those switching sites, a choice has to be made, or an element from a particular language can be selected. The idea that there are choices to be made at lower levels of the production system is basically absent in the literature on CS. Most research on CS is concerned with syntactic and morphological constraints, and very few studies look at switching phenomena at other levels in the process. Here the switching sites are mentioned and discussed briefly. It would be a useful enterprise to look at various sources of CS data and theories on CS to see how these findings and models fit in with this idea of a cascade of switching sites, but that would take somewhat more space than is available for the present essay.

1. *The selection of lemmas.* As mentioned in examples 1–3, a mismatch at the conceptual level may lead to the selection of a word from another language.
2. *The activation of syntactic structures.* In her discussion on syntactic constraints on code-switching, Nortier (1989) reports a rank order of CS sites. These rank orders show that CS is most likely between coordinated Ss and around adverbs/APs, and less likely between subordinated and main Ss, and far less likely between subject NP and the rest of the sentence or inside PPs. In terms of Levelt's model, this may have to do with variation in linearization problems for these different CS sites, but a discussion of this (complicated) matter is beyond the scope of the present

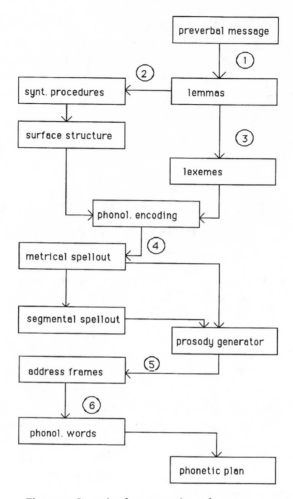

Fig. 23.1. Steps in the generation of a sentence

chapter. In the CS literature, there are numerous examples in which the syntactic procedure and the words that fill it are from different languages. Item (4) (Schatz, personal communication) is an example of this:

(4)   Dutch/English:
      And then wij waren daar *in between*
      '*And then* we were there *in between*.'

3. *The selection of lexemes.* In the selection of the lexeme, morphemes have to be combined; for example, a verb stem with a tense or aspect marker. An example of the combination of a stem from one language and a bound morpheme from another language is the use of '*climbden*' by

Dutch migrants in Australia. Here an English verb stem is combined with a Dutch marker (Clyne 1987).

4. *The output of the phonological encoding into the metrical spell-out.* An example of this is presented by Hulsen (2000). In her study on Dutch migrants in New Zealand, she mentions the use of the word *'Vi-oolin'* to name a picture of a violin in Dutch. Here the metrical spell-out of the English word is filled with phonemes from Dutch.

5. *The output of the prosody generator as input for the address frames.* Morimoto (1999) reports various examples in a study on word-internal code-switching with lexemes from one language combined with affixlike elements from another language. Data on Japanese-English code-switching show that the prosodic nature and selectional restrictions determine the acceptability of certain combinations of stems and affixes. If affixes are morphologically and prosodically bound, as Morimoto suggests, then this information has to be available fairly early in the production planning process, because such information is needed in order to allow language assignment at those lower levels.

6. *The transition from address frames to phonological words.* Here again there are many examples of bilinguals using sounds and elements from one language in a phonological structure from another language. One example is the use of an (English) bilabial /W/ rather than (Dutch) labiodental /W/ by Dutch migrants in Australia (de Bot and Clyne 1994).

CONCLUSION

In this chapter, an attempt has been made to show how recent findings and psycholinguistic models based on these findings can be used to gain a better understanding of cognitive processing in bilinguals. The production process has attracted a lot of attention in psycholinguistics in recent years, and several proposals to adapt monolingual models for bilingual language use have been made. The main points with respect to bilingual processing are how languages are selected for production and how languages are kept separate in situations in which switching is not an option. One way to study these points is to look at what happens in CS. As in monolingual speech, bilingual or CS speech is the result of a large number of interlocking subprocesses. It is argued here that, in a number of these subprocesses, language choice plays a role; research on CS should look more at those processes rather than restrict itself to word-order problems or morphology. CS on other, lower, levels can be evidenced as well, and more thorough studies of these "lower level" processes may further our understanding of cognitive processing in bilinguals and, consequently, our understanding of that special group of speakers who have only one language at their command.

It would be worthwhile to extend the present analysis to learner language. Cross-linguistic influence is one of the key issues in research in second language acquisition, but as yet there is hardly any research that attempts to relate the wide range of transfers from one language to another to a psycholinguistically based processing model. In such an analysis the different layers in language use—down from articulatory features up to conceptual components—should be looked at in an integrative way, since, as was pointed out in this chapter, there are choices at different levels, but these choices interact, and therefore isolating aspects of language in the analysis of CLI is likely to blur the picture.

NOTES

1. *Bilingual* is used as a term to refer to "more than one language" here.

2. Register shift and style shift in monolinguals are in fact similar to code-switching in bilinguals, which shows that the border between monolingualism and bilingualism in terms of the processes involved is vague.

CHAPTER 24

THE BILINGUAL LEXICON

JUDITH F. KROLL
TON DIJKSTRA

How do bilinguals recognize and speak words in each of their two languages? Past research on the bilingual lexicon focused on the questions of whether bilinguals represent words in each language in a single lexicon or in separate lexicons and whether access to the lexicon is selective or not.

These questions endured because they constitute a set of correlated assumptions that have only recently been teased apart. One concerns the relation between representation and process. As Van Heuven, Dijkstra, and Grainger (1998) note, it is not logically necessary to identify selective access with segregated lexical representations and nonselective access with an integrated lexicon; the form of representation and the manner of access can be treated as independent dimensions. Another issue concerns the way in which the lexicon itself has been operationalized. Different assumptions about the information required to recognize and speak a word in the first (L1) or second (L2) language have led to models of the bilingual lexicon that differ in the types and levels of codes that are represented. (See Francis 1999 and Pavlenko 1999 for a discussion with respect to semantic and conceptual representation.)

In this chapter we review the way in which models of the bilingual lexicon reflect different assumptions about the architecture and processing of words in two languages and then consider three central questions about lexical access:

1. What codes are activated?
2. When are these codes activated?
3. What are the critical factors that affect lexical selection?

We examine the answers to these questions first for comprehension and then for production. Because we assume that comprehension and production rely on a common representational system but differ in the problems that they pose for the system, we finally consider the implications of the comparison for reaching general conclusions about the nature of the bilingual lexicon.

Models of the Bilingual Lexicon

The Revised Hierarchical Model

Initial attempts to model the bilingual lexicon proposed a hierarchical arrangement to represent word forms and word meaning (e.g., Potter, So, Von Eckhardt, and Feldman 1984). These models solved the problem of whether there were integrated or separate lexicons by assuming that both alternatives were accurate but that they described different levels of representation; at the level of word form, they proposed independent lexical representations for each language, but at the level of meaning they assumed a single conceptual system. The empirical basis for these assumptions has been reviewed extensively in the recent literature, so we will not describe it here. (See Chen 1992; De Groot 1993, 1995; Kroll 1993; Kroll and De Groot 1997; Kroll, Michael, and Sankaranarayanan 1998; Smith 1997.) With these assumptions in place, the focus shifted to consider whether words in the bilingual's two languages are connected via the lexical representations or by direct access to the conceptual representations. Initial evidence suggested that the connections between lexical forms in L1 and L2 might be active early in L2 acquisition but that, by the time the bilingual achieved proficiency in L2, words in each language could access concepts directly (e.g., Chen and Leung 1989; Kroll and Curley 1988).

Kroll and Stewart (1994) proposed the revised hierarchical model (RHM) (Figure 24.1) to capture the developmental consequences of a shift from lexical to conceptual processing with increasing L2 proficiency. They argued that, early in acquisition, the reliance on lexical-level connections between words in the two languages provided a means for transfer; L1 could provide the meaning for an L2 word if L2 activated its respective translation equivalent. However, unlike other models, the RHM assumed that the lexical level links remained even after conceptual processing was established for L2. The implication of the sequential acquisition of these links was a set of hypothesized asymmetries. Lexical links were assumed to be stronger from L2 to L1 than the reverse, as this was the initial

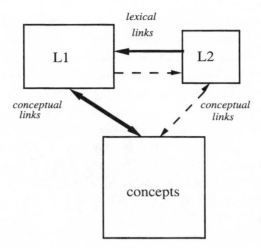

Fig. 24.1. Revised hierarchical model (adapted from Kroll and Stewart 1994)

direction of transfer during acquisition, and L1 was assumed to have stronger connections to concepts than L2.

To test the predicted asymmetries between lexical and conceptual representations, Kroll and Stewart (1994) examined translation performance in a group of highly fluent Dutch-English bilinguals. In one condition, the words to be translated were presented in a semantically categorized list. In another, the words were randomly mixed. Under these conditions forward translation, from L1 to L2, was slower than backward translation, from L2 to L1, and only forward translation was affected by the semantic list manipulation, suggesting that only in that direction of translation was performance conceptually mediated. The absence of semantic processing for backward translation suggested that the task could be performed on the basis of lexical-level connections between words in the two languages.

Subsequent research provided mixed support for the RHM. On one hand, a set of studies showed that forward translation is more sensitive to semantic factors than backward translation (e.g., De Groot, Dannenburg, and Van Hell 1994; Sholl, Sankaranarayanan, and Kroll 1995) and that more semantic processing is observed in priming tasks from L1 to L2 than the reverse (e.g., Fox 1996; Keatley, Spinks, and De Gelder 1994), even when primes are masked and participants are unaware of the bilingual nature of the experiment (Gollan, Forster, and Frost 1997; Jiang 1999). However, other studies reported semantic effects in both directions of translation (e.g., De Groot and Poot 1997; La Heij, Kerling, and Van der Velden 1996) and also questioned the reliance on lexical links during early stages of acquisition (e.g., Altarriba and Mathis 1997; Frenck-Mestre and Prince 1997). (See Kroll and De Groot [1997] and Kroll and Tokowicz [2001] for a discussion of how these apparent discrepancies may be resolved.)

The RHM assumed independent lexical representations for words in each language. As we will see in the sections that follow, more recent studies on comprehension and production of words in two languages suggest that the assumption of independence at the lexical level was incorrect. (See also Brysbaert 1998; Van Heuven et al. 1998.) However, even models of the bilingual lexicon that assume an integrated lexicon and parallel access must address asymmetries in the way in which words in the two languages are processed by virtue of the relative dominance of one language over the other and the context in which they occur. In comprehension, these asymmetries may be revealed in greater or faster activation of orthography and/or phonology associated with L1. In production, there may be a bias to activate and select lexical candidates in L1 even when the task requires that words are spoken in L2.

The Bilingual Interactive Activation Model (BIA)

Which mechanisms should be incorporated in a processing model to implement the assumptions of an integrated lexicon and parallel access and at the same time allow simulation of asymmetric L1/L2 processing and context effects? In the domain of language comprehension, Van Heuven, Dijkstra, and Grainger (1998; Dijkstra and Van Heuven 1998; Dijkstra, Van Heuven, and Grainger 1998) have developed a computer model for bilingual visual word recognition that incorporates one possible proposal. The bilingual interactive activation (BIA) model (Figure 24.2) is a bilingual extension of the well-known interactive activation (IA) model for monolingual visual word recognition (McClelland and Rumelhart 1981).

It consists of a network of hierarchically organized representational units of different kinds: features, letters, words, and language nodes. The model differs from the original IA model in two main respects: First, it incorporates an integrated lexicon with words from two different languages rather than one, and, second, it includes an extra layer of two language nodes that can be considered as language labels (tags) that indicate the language membership of each word.

According to the model, presentation of an input letter string leads to parallel activation of several possible words (the "neighborhood") irrespective of language. Next, activated lexical candidates compete and suppress each other's activation until one item surpasses its activation threshold and is recognized. Competition takes place between items from the same and different languages through the mechanism of lateral inhibition. By means of this mechanism, the model simulates the results of several studies that showed both within- and between-language effects of the number of lexical competitors (Dijkstra, Van Heuven et al. 1998; Van Heuven, and Grainger 1998).

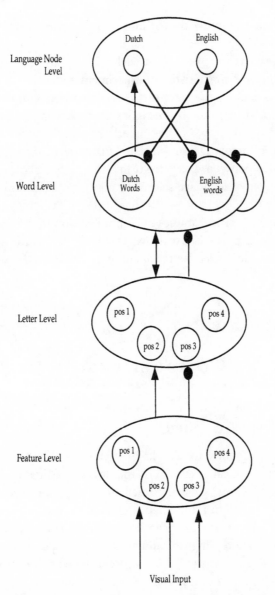

Fig. 24.2. Bilingual interaction activation model (adapted from Dijkstra, Van Heuven, and Grainger 1998)

The BIA model accounts for asymmetries observed in unbalanced bilinguals (stronger effects from L1 on L2 than vice versa) by assuming that, relative to L1 words, the subjective frequency of L2 words is lower for participants with lower L2 proficiency. This is implemented in terms of the model's resting level activations, which are generally lower for words in L2 than L1. As a consequence, L2 words on the whole become activated more slowly and to a lesser extent than L1 words.

The language nodes in the BIA model account for context effects that are dependent on specific characteristics of experiment and task. (Such context effects are discussed in detail in the next section.) These nodes modulate the relative activity in the L1 and L2 lexicons during lexical processing by exerting top-down inhibitory effects on all words of the other language (e.g., the English language node suppresses all active Dutch words). This mechanism induces stronger or weaker interactions between words from L1 and L2, thus allowing the simulation of the relative degree of language selectivity observed under various experimental circumstances.

We now review empirical studies in comprehension that support the language nonselective access hypothesis. Next, we specify under which experimental circumstances more or less selective results have been observed.

COMPREHENSION

What Codes Are Activated?

One of the most frequently used tasks in monolingual and bilingual word recognition research is lexical decision. In this task, participants decide as quickly and accurately as possible whether presented letter strings are words in a prespecified target language. In monolingual lexical decision, response times are usually in the order of 500–550 ms. The same experiments performed in L2 with relatively proficient Dutch-English bilinguals led to response times of about 600 ms in L2, but for less proficient participants considerably longer latencies may be obtained (e.g., Dijkstra, Grainger, and Van Heuven 1999).

It has been shown that presentation of a word to monolinguals induces activation not only of orthographic codes but of phonological and semantic codes, as well (e.g., Frost 1998; James 1975). Furthermore, monolingual studies involving ambiguous words (e.g., 'bug,' referring to an insect, a spy, or a programming error) suggest that different meanings of these words are initially activated during recognition (e.g., Kawamoto and Zembldige 1992; Simpson 1984). In a study on word naming, Gottlob, Goldinger, Stone, and Van Orden (1999) found that English homographs (words with separate pronunciations and meanings, such as 'lead') were read slower than homonyms (with a single pronunciation but separate meanings, such as 'spring') and control words (e.g., 'clock'). Thus, during monolingual word recognition there is *intra*lingual coactivation of lexical candidates with overlap in meaning or form.

According to a nonselective access view, it should not matter very much whether the coactivated lexical candidates belong to the same language or to another. In other words, this view predicts that there will be *inter*lingual activation of similar words during bilingual word recognition as well. In contrast, according to a language-selective access view, a presented word will activate the form and meaning representations only from the language that is currently selected.

A study by Dijkstra et al. (1999) indicates that cross-linguistic competition between form-similar and meaning-similar words does indeed occur. In a series of experiments, Dutch-English bilinguals were tested with English words varying in their degree of orthographic (O), phonological (P), and semantic (S) overlap with Dutch words. Thus, an English word target could be spelled the same as a Dutch word and/or could be a near-homophone of a Dutch word. Whether such form similarity was accompanied with semantic identity (translation equivalence) was also varied. This led to six different test conditions, exemplified by the following words: 'hotel' (overlap in S, O, and P codes), 'type' (S, O), 'news' (S, P), 'step' (O, P), 'stage' (O), and 'note' (P). The first three conditions are what are usually called "cognates," while the last three conditions contain "interlingual homographs" or "interlingual homophones." Lexical decisions were facilitated by cross-linguistic orthographic and semantic similarity relative to control words that belonged only to English. However, phonological overlap produced inhibitory effects. This study indicates that (at least for L2) a presented word form leads to the activation of all representations that it is associated with, irrespective of the target language.

When Are These Codes Activated?

The empirical evidence just discussed indicates that, under particular experimental circumstances, form and meaning representations of lexical candidates that belong to different languages become activated and may affect the pattern of results. A further question concerns the time course of such effects. At which moment in time is the necessary lexical candidate selected? Given that all three types of representations (S, O, and P) may affect the response, earlier views that assume that lexical selection always occurs at the orthographical level clearly cannot be correct.

A recent study by Dijkstra, Timmermans and Schriefers (2000) suggests that coactivation of lexical candidates from different languages occurs until relatively late in the word recognition process. In three experiments, bilingual participants processed the same set of interlingual homographs embedded in identical mixed-language lists, but each experiment had different instructions. Homographs of three types were used: High-frequent in English and low-frequent in Dutch (HFE-LFD); low-frequent in English and high-frequent in Dutch (LFE-HFD); and low-frequent in both languages (LFE-LFD). In the first experiment (involving language decision), one button was pressed when an English word was presented and another button for a Dutch word. In the second and third experiments, participants reacted only when they identified either an English word (English go/no-go) or a Dutch word (Dutch go/no-go). It turned out that participants were able to exclude effects from the nontarget language on homograph identification only to a limited degree. Target-language homographs were often "overlooked," especially if the frequency of their other-language competitor was high. The results suggest that the two readings of a presented homograph are involved in a "race to recognition" that is won by the fastest candidate. Even more interesting, it appeared that a slowing down of the response occurred if two candidates were relatively close to the "finish," that is, their recognition activation threshold. For instance, in the Dutch go/no-go task, responses to homographs were much slower in the HFE-LFD condition than in the LFE-LFD condition, although the proportion of responses did not differ between the two conditions. This suggests that selection takes place relatively late, implying coactivation of lexical candidates from different languages over a considerable period of time.

The observed effects were dependent on the relative word frequency of the two readings of the interlingual homograph. This factor, of course, is an approximation of the participants' subjective frequency, that is, the number of times they have encountered or used the word in question. For bilinguals, this subjective frequency is lower for items that belong to their L2 than to their L1, it being correlated to their L2-proficiency. If the subjective frequency of the L2-reading is negligible relative to its L1 frequency, the L2 reading will not be able to affect the lexical processing to any considerable extent. In other words, low proficiency bilinguals might show relatively weak effects from their L2 on their L1 lexicon (but strong effects from their L1 on their L2 lexicon). This point brings us to a consideration of critical factors that may affect the selection of lexical candidates during the bilingual word recognition process.

Critical Factors That Affect Lexical Selection

We have seen that different codes are activated and competition may occur even during response selection. However, we have already suggested, as well, that observed result patterns may not be a direct reflection of an underlying architecture. They may have been "changed" by processing or decision strategies from the participant that relate to task demands and stimulus presentation conditions. In other words, even though the bilingual word recognition system may be basically

nonselective in nature, seemingly selective results may be obtained under particular experimental circumstances. A number of influential factors have been identified in earlier studies (e.g., Grosjean 1998), including L2-proficiency, language
intermixing, task demands, and instruction. Apart from proficiency, which we
referred to earlier, we now discuss these factors and their relative effect on the
(non)selectivity of bilingual word recognition in more detail by summarizing a
few recent studies that examined them.

Language Intermixing and Task Demands

Language intermixing refers to whether an experiment contains exclusively items
that belong to one language (blocked presentation) or items from two languages
(mixed presentation). The term thus refers to one aspect of "stimulus list composition." In a series of three lexical decision experiments, Dijkstra, Van Jaarsveld,
and Ten Brinke (1998) showed that interlingual homographs may be recognized
faster than, slower than, or as fast as single language control words, depending
on language intermixing and task demands. In Experiment 1, Dutch bilingual
participants performed an English lexical decision task on a list that included
English/Dutch homographs, cognates, and purely English control words. Response
times to interlingual homographs were unaffected by the frequency of the Dutch
reading and did not differ from monolingual controls. In contrast, cognates were
recognized faster than controls. The first result seems to be in support of selective
access models, while the second result favors nonselective access. In Experiment
2, Dutch participants again performed an English lexical decision task on homographs, but, apart from nonwords, Dutch words were included that required a
"no" response. Strong inhibition effects were obtained that depended on the relative frequency difference of the two readings of the homograph (as in the study
by Dijkstra, Timmermans, and Schriefers 2000, discussed earlier).

In retrospect, the different pattern of results in Experiments 1 and 2 may be
due to differences in language intermixing in the two experiments. The selective
access view of bilingual word recognition is evidently rejected by the results of
Experiment 2; therefore it must be that Experiment 1 created experimental circumstances in which null results for interlingual homographs arose in a language
nonselective access system. Other studies have confirmed the importance of language intermixing for performance and have proposed accounts to explain the
null effects (De Groot, Delmaar, and Lupker 2000; Dijkstra et al. 1999).

In Experiment 3, Dijkstra, Van Jaarsveld, and Ten Brinke (1998) used the same
stimulus materials but changed the task demands. Participants now performed a
general lexical decision task, responding "yes" if a word of either language was
presented (rather than saying "no" to Dutch words). In this experiment,
frequency-dependent facilitation effects were found for the interlingual homographs. Dijkstra et al. explain these results by pointing out that the task in Ex-

periment 2 required the participants to make a distinction between the two readings of interlingual homographs, while they were able to use either reading in Experiment 3. Thus, the same underlying architecture (involving representations for homographs in different languages) could lead to both inhibition and facilitation effects.

Effect of Instruction

We have seen that several factors (proficiency, language intermixing, task demands) may affect the (non)selectivity of the result patterns in bilingual word recognition experiments. In this context, the question arises to which extent top-down factors, such as participant expectancies based on the instructions of the experimenter, may affect the observed result patterns.

While adequate evaluation of this issue will require additional empirical evidence, it appears that bottom-up factors, such as language intermixing and stimulus characteristics (e.g., frequency, code similarity), are the more important ones. Dijkstra, De Bruijn, Schriefers, and Ten Brinke (2000) contrasted the effect of instruction-induced expectancies and language intermixing in an English lexical decision task performed by Dutch-English bilinguals. At the start of the experiment, participants were explicitly instructed to respond "yes" to interlingual homographs and exclusively English words and "no" to English nonwords and to exclusively Dutch words. In the first part of the experiment the stimulus list did not contain any Dutch words. In the second part of the experiment, Dutch items were introduced. No significant differences were found between interlingual homographs and controls in the first part of the experiment, while strong inhibition was obtained for interlingual homographs in the second part. This effect is demonstrated for words with a low-frequency reading in Dutch and a high-frequency reading in English, as shown in Figure 24.3.

The reader will note that these results converge with those of Experiments 1 and 2 by Dijkstra, Van Jaarsveld, and Ten Brinke (1998), discussed earlier. They suggest that language intermixing, rather than instruction-based expectancies, drives the bilingual participants' performance. However, the issue is still not decided, because a study by Von Studnitz and Green (submitted) suggests that the result patterns may yet be modulated by participant strategies.

To summarize this section on bilingual comprehension studies, it appears that:

1. Lexical codes from different languages are activated in parallel on the basis of an input string.
2. Selection of the lexical candidate that is identified appears to take place rather late in the recognition process.
3. Several factors affect the ultimately arising result patterns, the most important of which are a participant's L2-proficiency level, the requirements

Homographs

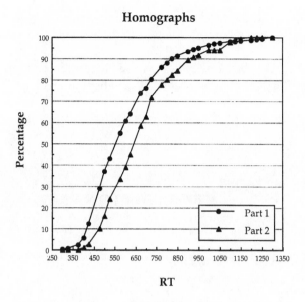

Controls

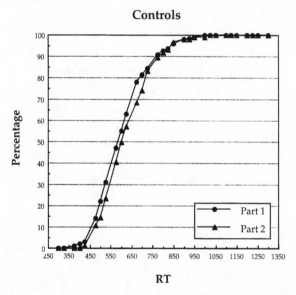

Fig. 24.3. Cumulative response distributions to interlingual homographs and matched exclusively English controls. Data are from the first and second parts of the English visual lexical decision by Dijkstra, De Bruijn, Schriefers, and Ten Brinke (2000).
Note: Homographs had low-frequency Dutch and high frequency English readings. Exclusively Dutch words, which required a "no" response, occurred only in the second part.

of the task, and the blocked or mixed presentation of items from different languages.

We now examine the same issues on code activation and factors that affect lexical selection for the bilingual's language production process.

PRODUCTION

What Codes Are Activated?

To speak a word in order to express a thought or to name a picture, the speaker must engage a sequence of processes to map the meaning of the intended utterance onto the phonology of the appropriate word. Even within a single language, the hypothesized process is quite complex (Bock and Levelt 1994; Dell 1988; Levelt 1989; Levelt, Roelofs, and Meyer 1999). An initial debate concerned the seriality of this process. Some researchers argued that phonology becomes specified only after a single meaning is identified (e.g., Levelt et al. 1991), and others claimed that as soon as meanings are activated, but before a single meaning is selected, there is corresponding activation of phonology (e.g., Dell and O'Seaghdha 1991; Starreveld and La Heij 1995). Recent evidence favors the view that language production is a cascaded process whereby some, but not all, close competitors may engage their associated phonology in overlapping stages (e.g., Cutting and Ferreira 1999; Damian and Martin 1999; Jescheniak and Schriefers 1998; Peterson and Savoy 1998).

For a bilingual, there is the additional matter of selecting the language in which a word should be spoken. It might seem that simply intending to speak in one language rather than the other would be sufficient. Unlike perception, which is to a large degree driven by the properties of the stimulus input, production, even of a single word, is a top-down process, initiated by conceptual activity. The language to be spoken could plausibly be selected from among other conceptual constraints prior to lexical access. (See de Bot and Schreuder 1993; Poulisse 1997). It is, therefore, surprising to discover that words in both of a bilingual's languages appear to be active well into the process of lexicalizing a concept into a single spoken word. The evidence that we will review suggests that, like perception, lexical access in production is nonselective. However, because production is conceptually driven and typically unfolds over a longer time than perception, the answer to the question of what is activated is not necessarily the same.

In past research, the primary task that has been used to investigate the form of the codes active during lexical access is picture-word interference, a variant of the Stroop (1935) task. In this paradigm, a picture is presented, and its name must be spoken aloud as quickly as possible. At some point before, during, or after the onset of the picture, a word distractor is presented visually or auditorily. By observing the consequences of the relation of the word to the name of the picture and the timing of its presentation, it is theoretically possible to infer the nature of the activated information at any given point during the process. The general pattern of results is clear: Semantically related words produce interference, form-related words (by orthography, phonology, or both) produce facilitation, and identical words (i.e., the picture's name) produce facilitation relative to unrelated controls (e.g., La Heij 1988; Schriefers, Meyer, and Levelt 1990). However, the goal of assigning a given code to a specific component stage of production has been only partly successful (e.g., Damian and Martin 1999; Starreveld 2000).

Two recent studies used the picture-word interference paradigm to investigate the activity of the nontarget language when words in only one of the bilingual's two languages are to be spoken. Hermans, Bongaerts, de Bot, and Schreuder (1998) had fluent Dutch-English bilinguals name pictures in English, their L2, with distractor words presented auditorily following a variable stimulus onset asynchrony (SOA). The main question was whether the name of the picture in L1 would be activated when the task required naming in L2. For example, if a picture of a mountain was to be named 'mountain' in English, would the Dutch word 'berg' be active? Distractors that were semantically and phonologically related or unrelated to the picture's name were presented in L1 or in L2. In the critical condition, the distractor was a word that sounded like the L1 name of the picture (e.g., 'berm' or 'bench' instead of 'berg'). The results for these "phono-Dutch" words were more like those for the semantic distractors than for the phonological distractors (i.e., they followed a similar time course), suggesting that the translation equivalent is active through the stage of selecting an initial lexical candidate but one not yet phonologically specified. Furthermore, semantically related distractors produced similar interferences regardless of the language in which they were presented, a result that also converges on the conclusion that lexical access is nonselective with respect to language, at least during the initial stages of production.

Similar studies by Costa, Miozzo, and Caramazza (1999) and Costa and Caramazza (1999), but using visual distractors, also revealed cross-language effects and demonstrated that even L2 distractors can influence L1 naming performance. However, Costa et al. also found some limits on the degree to which the phonology of translation equivalents was activated and argued that ultimately production proceeds on the basis of a selective process that favors lexical candidates in the language in which the bilingual intends to speak.

These studies provide evidence that lexical alternatives are available in both languages, at least during the early stages of production, when abstract lexical representations corresponding to the intended meaning of the utterance (some-times called "lemmas") are activated. However, unlike evidence on monolingual production, which shows that close lexical competitors may be phonologically specified (e.g., Jescheniak and Schriefers 1998; Peterson and Savoy 1998), there is no indication from bilingual picture-word experiments that non target competi-tors are phonologically encoded.

When Are These Codes Activated?

Examining the time course of picture-word interference effects is one way to investigate the availability of meaning and phonology during production. How-ever, because the distractor word itself is recognized, a process that cannot be viewed independently of the primary picture-naming task, the paradigm does not provide a pure window into the time course of production.

Kroll and Peck (1998) developed a new task, cued picture naming, to obtain a more direct measure of L1 activity during L2 production. Participants are pre-sented with a pictured object and told to produce the object's name when they hear a tone cue. The cue is presented following a variable SOA. In pure conditions, the subjects are instructed to name the picture in their L1 or L2 when they hear the cue. In mixed conditions, they are instructed to name the picture in one language if the cue is a high tone and in the other if the cue is a low tone (Figure 24.4). Thus, in pure conditions, the language of naming is certain; only the onset of production depends on the presentation of the cue. In mixed conditions, the language of naming is uncertain until the cue has been processed.

Kroll and Peck (1998) investigated the time course of picture naming in the cued task for English-Spanish bilinguals. As expected, naming latencies decreased with increasing SOA, reflecting a general effect of preparation, and the time to name pictures was faster for L1 than L2, also expected because L1 is the first and dominant language. However, the results also suggested an asymmetry in the time course of activation of cross-language competitors, with greater cost to L1 than L2 under the mixed conditions. When the language of naming is uncertain, both languages must be simultaneously active. If L2 picture naming normally involves the activation and subsequent inhibition of L1, then mixing L1 and L2 should have little effect on L2 performance. However, if the more dominant L1 does not nor-mally involve the activation and inhibition of L2, then mixing languages should have particularly deleterious effects for L1 picture naming, as these results suggest.

Furthermore, there was an indication that in the blocked condition there was a steeper decline in L2 than L1 naming latencies at the long SOAs. If L2 cannot be prepared until the activation of L1 has decayed or been inhibited, then L2 naming will be slow relative to L1 and relative to conditions in which L1 is not

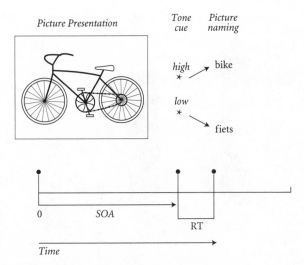

Fig. 24.4. Illustration of the mixed cued picture naming task
Note: In the example shown, a Dutch-English bilingual is shown a picture of a bicycle. When a high tone is presented, the picture is to be named "bike" in English. When a low tone is presented, the picture is to be named "fiets" in Dutch.

active. The pattern of results is consistent with the claim that additional time is needed to resolve competition from activated lexical candidates in L1 before L2 naming can proceed. The picture-word interference results also suggest that this is the case.

Kroll, Dijkstra, Janssen, and Schriefers (1999) examined performance in the cued picture naming task using conditions aimed at identifying the locus and form of these effects more precisely. Two sets of experiments were designed, one with Dutch-English bilinguals and the other with English-French bilinguals. In each experiment, the mixed task was performed with the tone cue presented at an SOA of 0, 500, or 1000 ms. The critical materials were pictures whose names were cognates, translation equivalents that share identical or similar word form (e.g., 'bed'-'bed' or 'tomaat'-'tomato' in Dutch and English).

If both language alternatives are active to the level of the phonology, then we might predict an effect of cognate status because of the high degree of phonological overlap between the L1 and L2 names. Results for both bilingual groups were similar. In each case there was facilitation for pictures with cognate names relative to controls for both L1 and L2 (Figure 24.5). A monolingual control group naming pictures in English only produced no effect of cognate status. For bilinguals, the time course data for L1 revealed a benefit for cognate pictures across all SOAs. For L2, the effects were present only at short SOAs; by 1000 ms the cognate facilitation was absent. The inhibitory process for L1 may have been complete by the time of the longest SOA, and thus no effect of cognate status was observed for L2. For

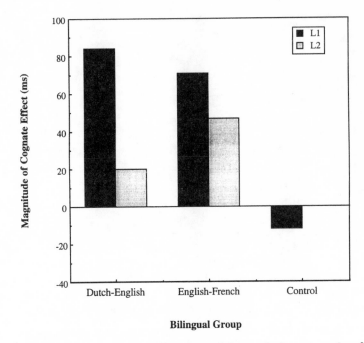

Fig. 24.5. Magnitude of the cognate effect (in ms) in cued picture naming for Dutch-English and English-French bilinguals naming pictures in their L1 and L2
Note: Control data for native English speakers naming English-French cognate pictures in L1. Bars above the line indicate facilitation.

both bilingual groups there was also a reversal of L1 and L2, with faster picture naming latencies for L2 than for L1. The finding of slower RTs for L1 than L2 (a result also reported by Meuter and Allport [1999] following a language switch) suggests that L1 was inhibited when L2 responses were required to be prepared.

To summarize, the data from the cued picture naming experiments show that when picture naming is performed in L1, there is not normally an influence of L2 unless the task requires that L2 be active, as in the mixed conditions. For L2, however, there is a persistent effect of L1 that appears well into the lexicalization process and regardless of whether or not the task requires L1 to be active. Whether lexical alternatives are specified to the level of the phonology appears to depend in these experiments on the nature of the task. It remains for future research to specify the conditions that determine the locus of language selection.

Critical Factors That Affect Lexical Selection

If lexical access is nonselective during production and the language to be spoken is not determined until a relatively late point in the process, then the factors that influence selection will play an important role in constraining the nature of the resulting utterances. For example, one might expect that the later in time that language is selected, the more likely we are to observe errors of language, with substitutions of words from the unintended language. These errors occur (Poulisse 1999), but they are relatively rare unless the bilingual is in a context in which code switching is likely—see de Bot, this volume, for a related discussion—or unless the speaker is less proficient in L2. Particularly for L2, for which the evidence reviewed suggests that L1 competitors are active well into the lexicalization process, we need to consider what mechanisms may be in place to control the consequences of unintended activation of L1.

Inhibitory Control

The issue of how bilinguals resolve competition across their two languages has been addressed at a theoretical level in terms of language mode (e.g., Grosjean 1997a, 1998, 2001) and by models that propose inhibitory control mechanisms (e.g., Green 1986, 1993, 1998). In the section on perception, we considered factors (e.g., list composition, instruction) that are thought to influence the relative activation of words in the two languages. Here we consider another factor, the recruitment of externally driven attentional resources, that may selectively bias the way in which the activation within the lexical system is utilized.

Green (1998) proposed the inhibitory control model to provide a mechanism that would allow the bilingual effectively to suppress activity in the nontarget language and thereby to avoid speaking words in the unintended language. For example, when translating from L1 to L2, the bilingual must avoid inadvertently naming the L1 target word itself. According to the model, before any task can be performed, a task schema must be engaged (e.g., for naming a picture in L1 or L2, for translating a word, or for making a lexical decision). The more resources that need to be allocated to inhibiting nontarget responses, the greater the predicted processing costs.

The effects of an inhibitory control mechanism have been examined in experiments on language switching in which bilinguals change the language of production over a predictable sequence of trials (e.g., Loasby 1998; Meuter and Allport 1999). The typical result is that larger switch costs are observed when bilinguals switch into their more dominant language (L1) than when they switch into the weaker language (L2). The interpretation of the asymmetric switch costs for the two languages is that L1 is more likely to be active, and therefore more likely to be suppressed during the processing of L2, than L2 is during the processing of L1.

A curious aspect of the language switching results is that the asymmetric pattern of switch costs occurs even when successive items are not related to one another, suggesting that this inhibitory mechanism is global rather than local. A related question is whether, in the presence of cues to the language of production, the relative activation of nontarget competitors can be reduced, thereby reducing the inhibitory control requirements. We consider this issue next.

Cues to Language Selection

If the goal of language production is to accomplish the task of lexical selection as quickly as possible, then the longer the language of speaking remains open, the longer selection will be delayed. One way to achieve early language selection is to rely on cues that signal one language. In picture naming, the drawings used as stimuli typically contain little information that biases them toward one language. In contrast, tasks such as translation provide clear cues to the language to be spoken. When a word is presented for translation it is, in a sense, the very competitor that the speaker must avoid producing. Having a specific cue (don't name that word, and, more generally, don't name a word in that language) may enable selection to occur earlier.

Two recent studies provide some evidence for the hypothesis that language cues available in the translation task permit language selection to occur earlier than in picture naming. Kroll, Dietz, and Green (in preparation) tested the hypothesis that switch costs would be greater in the picture-naming task than in translation, even though the actual spoken production in the two languages was identical. The results supported the predictions. Performance in the picture-naming task replicated the pattern of switch costs reported by Meuter and Allport (1999) for numeral naming. There were large costs to switch into the more dominant L1, but smaller costs to switch into L2. However, the same pattern was not observed in the translation task where the switch costs were not significant for either language.

A second source of evidence for the claim that the translation task provides cues that enable earlier language selection than picture naming comes from a recent Stroop translation study (Miller 1997). This version of the Stroop task is similar to picture-word interference, but with translation rather than picture naming as the primary task. When distractor words appeared in the language of production, Miller replicated the pattern of semantic interference and form facilitation that has been reported previously for the translation Stroop task (La Heij et al. 1990) and in bilingual picture-word interference (Costa, Miozzo, and Caramazza 1999; Hermans et al. 1998). However, Miller's study also included a condition in which distractor words were related to the language of the word to be translated, rather than to the language of production. In this condition, semantic interference and form facilitation were significantly reduced. Of interest is that both Costa, Miozzo, and Caramazza (1999) and Hermans et al. (1998) reported semantic interference in picture naming, regardless of the match between the language of the distractor and the language of production. The difference between picture naming and translation in these Stroop-type tasks mirrors the difference observed in the language switching tasks. In both cases, it appears that language selection may occur earlier in translation than in picture naming by virtue of the presence of the language cue contained within the input itself.

DISCUSSION: SIMILARITIES AND DIFFERENCES BETWEEN COMPREHENSION AND PRODUCTION

In this chapter, we have contrasted comprehension and production to reveal those aspects of bilingual lexical representation and processing that are common to both modes of language use. We now evaluate the outcome of this comparison. It is important to note that some of our conclusions will necessarily be influenced by the fact that most of the research on bilingual word recognition and comprehension has been in the visual domain. The small number of studies on the recognition of spoken words in bilinguals (e.g., Grosjean 1988; Li 1996; Spivey and Marian 1999) makes it difficult to compare the comprehension and production of spoken language alone.

Perhaps the most striking similarity between comprehension and production in bilinguals is the overwhelming evidence for nonselective access to words in both languages, regardless of whether the task logically permits the language of processing to be selected in advance. Comprehension and production also share the consequences of the lower L2 than L1 proficiency in unbalanced bilinguals. In both modes of language use, there appears to be more evidence for effects of L1 on L2 than the reverse, and a suggestion that the relative asymmetry in the magnitude of these cross-language influences may be larger for less fluent bilinguals.

Though the two domains share the aspect of language nonselective access, this does not imply that orthographic, phonological, and semantic codes are used in the same way or at the same moment in processing. For example, the bottom-up nature of comprehension requires that orthographic codes play a larger and earlier role in word recognition than they do in word production, although little is known about the activation of orthography during production. Likewise, the role of phonology is likely to be more critical in production than in comprehension, although, as we have seen, there is overwhelming evidence to suggest that phonology is involved in bilingual word recognition and that it determines, at least in part, the magnitude of cross-language influences. In both domains, there is evidence for semantic processing, but again the contribution of meaning is generally more reliable in production than in comprehension. In comprehension, semantics appear to play a role when there is a consistent correspondence between lexical form and meaning, as in the case of cognates, suggesting that semantic codes are activated even when they are not required by the task.

The time course over which these lexical codes are activated must also be different for comprehension and production. Because the longer time course associated with production provides additional opportunities for feedback and interaction between codes, there is the possibility that the cohort of activated lexical competitors will differ from those available in comprehension. The different nature of orthographic and conceptual representations makes such a difference all the more likely. For instance, it may be that more lexical alternatives are initially activated in comprehension than in production because there are simply more orthographic neighbors of the input word than semantic alternatives for the output concept.

The inherent different nature of comprehension and production also has its effects for factors that may potentially affect lexical selection. There are a large number of variables (e.g., stimulus list composition, language mixing, instructions, language cues, and aspects of attentional control) that may influence lexical selection in each domain. Because comprehension and production differ in the cognitive resources that they require, and because we know that the ability to understand precedes the ability to speak, it seems likely that the role that external factors play in moderating the relative activation of alternatives in each language and in potentially inhibiting the unintended language, will be different.

Furthermore, in production, the language of speaking can and must be determined by the language user; in comprehension the requirement to determine the language in which the task is performed depends in a more complex way on the nature of the task itself. For example, to perform a generalized lexical decision task, it is logically not necessary to specify the language of the activated lexical form. But, to speak a word in order to name a pictured object, it is mandatory that language be specified. Even in the case of highly similar cognate translations, words in two languages rarely have an identical pronunciation, so language must be known if performance is to be error-free.

CONCLUSION

The answers to the questions that we have posed about the bilingual lexicon are, of course, preliminary. As noted earlier, we have said nothing about the comprehension of spoken language in the bilingual, nor have we considered how these questions might be answered for bilinguals for whom the two languages do not share the same alphabet. Rather, our discussion reflects the fact that we are just beginning to develop a theoretical framework for how words in the bilingual's two languages are represented and processed. The current issue driving experimental research is no longer simply whether or not there are two lexical representations, or whether or not processing is language selective. Research has gone beyond that point and now focuses on investigating how the output of activity from the representational system interacts with the processing goals and context in which the languages are used.

PART VIII

MULTILINGUALISM IN SOCIETY

CHAPTER 25

LANGUAGE CONTACT

PETER HANS NELDE

In the past forty years, scientific research on multilingualism has experienced numerous stimuli, the majority of which can be attributed to language contact research in the Weinreich tradition, going back to his famous *Languages in Contact* (1953). Weinreich's work is based on the fact that speakers or language communities, rather than languages on an abstract level, are in contact with each other and that any analysis of multilingual behavior is useless without consideration of the linguistic and cultural roots of the given situation. Today, research into language contact is manifest in two volumes of an International Handbook (*Contact Linguistics*), which appeared for the first time in Dirven and Pütz in 1996 and 1997. The interest of applied linguistics in language contact research or contact linguistics—a term used since the Brussels "Contact and Conflict" congress in 1979—begins with the recognition that the majority of the world's population is multilingual, so multilingualism is to be regarded as the norm, rather than the exception. Although multilingualism and language contact between individuals and groups are as old as the Babylonian confusion of tongues, language contact research first obtained a secure position in applied linguistics in the 1970s through the development of the social sciences. The great significance of multilingualism in the future of Europe and North America and its greater importance in many other parts of the world led to an interdisciplinary interest in contact linguistics, whose relation to multilingualism can be portrayed graphically; see figure 25.1.

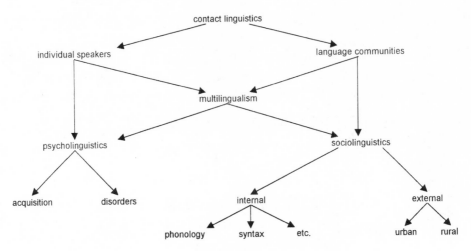

Fig. 25.1. The relation of contact liguistics to multilingualism

WHAT IS CONTACT LINGUISTICS?

As an interdisciplinary branch of multilingual research, contact linguistics incorporates three areas of inquiry: language use, language user, and language sphere.

The significant parameters of contact linguistics are linguistic levels (phonology, syntax, lexicon) and also discourse analysis, stylistics, and pragmatics. In addition there are the many external linguistic factors, such as nation, language community, language boundaries, and migration.

The type of multilingualism is also relevant, that is, whether it manifests itself as individual, institutional, or state bilingualism, as social multilingualism, as diglossia or dialect, or as natural or artificial multilingualism, for which the immediate levels—such as so-called semilingualism or interlinguistics—also must be considered. In the process it is helpful to make a basic, simplifying distinction between autochthonous (native) and allochthonous (migrant, refugee) groups, since instances of language contact can rarely be isolated as single phenomena but, rather, usually represent clusters of characteristics.

The structuring of social groups is of crucial importance to the language user. Besides the conventional differences of age, sex, and social relationship, minority status receives special attention from researchers of multilingualism.

Above and beyond these factors, all of the sectors responsible for the social interplay of a language community play an essential role. Added to traditional sectors such as religion, politics, culture, and science in the past few decades are others, including technology, industry, city and administration, and, most recently, also media, advertising, and data processing. In the educational/cultural sector, the schools occupy a special place, as they are constantly exposed to new forms and models of multilingual instruction from North America and—above all—from Canada. The question of whether bilingual and multilingual education will interfere with a child's right to use his or her mother (home, first, colloquial) tongue depends mainly on the intentions of the respective language planners, so conformity and integration, instead of language maintenance, constitute the motivating forces of multilingual instruction. To oversimplify the issue, the underprivileged must submit to "bilingual" education and thus to assimilation, while "foreign language" instruction is available to the sociological elite. Contact processes that have concerned researchers in multilingualism since the beginning are partly diachronic and partly synchronic in nature. Besides language change, borrowing processes, interference, and language mixing, there are *linguae francae*, language alternation, language maintenance and loss, code-switching, pidginization, and creolization.

The effects of such language contact processes can be registered by measuring language consciousness and attitude. Language loyalty and prestige play a decisive role in the linguistic identity of a multilingual person, and extreme care must be taken in interpreting so-called language statistics (censuses and public opinion surveys).

The language spheres in which considerations of multilingualism have become indispensable extend over numerous areas of study and are, furthermore, dependent on the respective level of development and interest. These spheres include, to name a few, language policy, language planning, language ecology, language contact in multinational industries and organizations, and language care and revitalization among minorities, as well as single development, planned languages, and the role of English as a world language, with all the concomitant effects on the respective individual languages. (For a complete list of topics see Nelde et al. 1996.)

Such a bird's-eye view shows well enough how extensive, interdisciplinary, and yet specialized the field of multilingualism is as related to contact linguistics.

CONTACT AND CONFLICT

Ethnic Contact and Conflict and Sociology

Most contact between ethnic groups does not occur in peaceful, harmoniously coexisting communities. Instead, it exhibits varying degrees of tension, resentment, and differences of opinion that are characteristic of every competitive social structure. Under certain conditions, such generally accepted competitive tensions can degenerate into intense conflicts, in the worst case ending in violence. The possibility that conflict will erupting is always present, since differences between groups create feelings of uncertainty of status, which can give rise to conflicts. Sociologists who have dealt with contact problems between ethnic groups define conflicts as contentions involving real or apparent fears, interests, and values, in which the goals of the opposing group must be opposed, or at least neutralized, to protect one's own interests (e.g., prestige, employment, political power) (Williams 1947). This type of contension often appears as a conflict of values, in which differing behavioral norms collide, since usually only one norm is considered to be valid. Conflicts between ethnic groups, however, occur only very rarely as openly waged violent conflicts and usually consist of a complex system of threats and sanctions in which the interests and values of one group are endangered. Conflicts can arise relatively easily if—as is usually the case—interests and values have an emotional basis.

The magnitude and the development of a conflict depend on a number of factors determined by level of friction between two or more ethnic groups, the presence of equalizing or mitigating elements, and the degree of uncertainty of all the participants. Thus, a one-sided explanation of the conflict, or one based on irrational prejudices, will fail. Very different factors that influence each other can reinforce and escalate to cause group conflict. This group conflict is part of normal social behavior in which different groups compete with each other and should therefore not be connoted only negatively, since in this way new—and possibly more peaceful—forms of coexistence can arise. On the other hand, tensions between ethnic groups brought about by feelings of intimidation can give rise to new conflicts at any time, conflicts that can be caused by a minority, as well as by a majority group. As long as society continues to create new fears, because of its competitive orientation, the creation of new conflicts appears unavoidable.

Political Language Contact and Conflict

Along with sociologists, political scientists also assume that language contact can cause political conflict. Language conflicts can be brought about by changes in an expanding social system when there is contact between different language groups (Inglehart and Woodward 1972). Belgium and French Canada are examples of this. The reasons for such a situation are the following: A dominant language group (French speakers in Belgium, English speakers in Canada) controls the crucial authority in the areas of administration, politics, and the economy and gives employment preference to those applicants who have command of the dominant language. The disadvantaged language group is then left with the choice of renouncing its social ambitions, assimilating, or resisting. While numerically weak or psychologically weakened language groups tend towards assimilation, in modern societies numerically stronger, more homogeneous language groups that possess traditional values, such as their own history and culture, prefer political resistance, the usual form of organized language conflict in this century. This type of conflict becomes especially salient when it occurs between population groups of differing socioeconomic structures (urban/rural, poor/wealthy, indigenous/immigrant) and when the dominant group requires its own language as a condition for the integration of the rest of the population. Although, in the case of French-speaking Canada, English appeared to be the necessary means of communication in trade and business, nearly 80 percent of the francophone population spoke only French and thus was excluded from social elevation in the political/economic sector. A small French-speaking elite, whose original goal was political opposition to the domination by English, ultimately precipitated the outbreak of the latent, socioeconomically motivated language conflict.

Most current language conflicts are the result of differing social status and preferential treatment of the dominant language on the part of the government. In these cases, the religious, social, economic, or psychological fears and frustrations of the weaker group may be responsible for the language conflict. However, a critical factor in the expansion and intensification of such conflict remains the impediment to social mobility, particularly of a disadvantaged or suppressed ethnic group (e.g., the numerous language conflicts in multiethnic Austria-Hungary).

Language problems in very different areas (politics, economics, administration, education) appear under the heading of language conflict. In such cases, politicians and economic leaders seize upon the notion of language conflict, disregarding the actual underlying causes, and thus continue to inflame "from above" the conflict arisen "from below," with the result that language assumes much more importance than it may have had at the outset of the conflict. This language-oriented "surface structure" is used to obscure the more deeply rooted, suppressed "deep structure" (social and economic problems). Furthermore, multilingual conflicts in Europe, especially in urban societies, show quite clearly that language conflicts are caused primarily by attempts on the part of the dominant group to block social mobility.

Language Conflict and Contact Linguistics

Even in contact linguistics the term conflict remains ambiguous, at least when it refers generally to social conflict that can arise in a multilingual situation. The notion appears to us essential here that neither contact nor conflict can occur between languages; each is conceivable only between speakers of languages. Oksaar (1980) correctly points out the ambiguity of the term "language conflict" as either conflict between languages within an individual or conflict by means of language(s), including processes external to the individual. Similarly, Haarmann (1980—2: 191) distinguishes between interlingual and interethnic language conflicts.

Among the founders of modern research in language contact—running parallel to the rapidly developing sociolinguistics and sociology of language (e.g., Weinreich and Fishman)—the term "conflict" rarely appears. While Weinreich views multilingualism (bilingualism) and the accompanying interference phenomena as the most important form of language contact, without regard to conflict between language communities on the basis of ethnic, religious, or cultural incompatibilities, Fishman (1972: 14) grants language conflict greater importance in connection with language planning. Haugen (1966a) was the first to make conflict presentable in language contact research with his detailed analysis of Norwegian language developments. Indeed, even linguists in multilingual countries (e.g., Yugoslavia, Switzerland, Belgium) resisted, up until the end of the 1970s, treating conflict methodically as part of language contact research, since such an "ideologicalization" of language contact appeared to them as "too touchy" (Fishman 1980: xi). One reason for the late discovery of a term indispensable in today's contact research is to be found in the history of contact linguistics itself: In traditional language contact research (as well as in dialectology and research on linguistic change), the emphasis was on closed, geographically homogeneous and easily describable socioeconomic groups, rather than on urban industrial societies, ripe for social and linguistic strife, whose demand for rapid integration laid the groundwork for conflict. However, it is precisely in modern urban society that conflicts result essentially from the normative sanctions of the more powerful, usually majority, group, which demands linguistic adaptation to the detriment of language contact and thus preprograms conflict with those speakers who are unwilling to adapt.

Despite a less than ideal research situation essentially limited to empirical case studies of language contact, the following statements can be made. Language conflict can occur anywhere there is language contact, chiefly in multilingual communities, although Mattheier (1984: 200) has also demonstrated language conflicts in so-called monolingual local communities. Language conflict arises from the confrontation of differing standards, values, and attitude structures and strongly influences self-image, upbringing, education, and group consciousness. Thus, conflict can be viewed as a form of contact or, in terms of a model, as a complementary model to the language contact model.

Contact linguists have either described conflict research as an integral part of language contact research (Nelde et al. 1996) or have dealt with special topics from the perspective of conflict. The methods used are heterogeneous and come from numerous neighboring disciplines (e.g., psycholinguistics and sociolinguistics, communication research, sociology). For lack of its own methods, research still employs predominantly empirical procedures. Along with interview and polling techniques, privileged informants and representative sampling, prejudice research and stereotype and attitude observation, the past few years have seen combined investigation models such as socioprofiles and ethnoprofiles, community and polarity profiles (Nelde 1995).

ESSENTIAL PRINCIPLES OF CONTACT LINGUISTICS

These observations on language contact and conflict situations lead to some basic premises of contact linguistic, which, despite their occasional seeming triviality, merit consideration at this juncture:

1. Language contact exists only between speakers and language communities, not between languages. Comparison of one and the same language in different contexts is therefore possible only in a quite limited way.
2. The statement that there can be no language contact without language conflict ("Nelde's Law": K. de Bot 1997: 51) may appear exaggerated, but there is in the realm of the European languages at present no imaginable contact situation that cannot also be described as language conflict.
3. Contact linguistics usually sees language as a significant secondary symbol of fundamental causes of conflict of a socioeconomic, political, religious, psychological, or historical sort. Thus, in a way, language conflict appears to be the lesser evil, since it apparently can be more easily corrected and neutralized than primary sociopolitical conflicts.
4. Contact linguistics, at the same time, makes it clear that conflicts should not be condemned as only negative; rather, it proves that new structures that are more advantageous than the foregoing ones can often result from conflicts.

Typology of Conflict

The current language conflicts in Europe, North and Central America, Southeast Asia, and parts of Africa can be viewed as situations of either *natural* or *artificial* language conflict.

Natural Language Conflict

Natural language conflicts are those situations that have traditionally existed between indigenous majorities and minorities. The extensive literature of language conflict abounds with examples of this type, particularly those of minorities pitted against official national or regional languages. Conflict has frequently arisen in these situations of language contact because the linguistic minority was not in a position to assimilate. This type of conflict can be found, for example, in Europe along the Germanic-Romance and the Slavic-Germanic linguistic boundaries and in Canada within the French-speaking minority and among a few indigenous peoples. Natural language conflicts can become problematic when ideology on either side—not only the majority but the minority, as well—is used to intensify the differences that exist, and peaceful coexistence between language communities can easily be threatened when the banner of language is hoisted as the defining symbol of a people.

The conflict between Belfast (Northern Ireland) and Connemara (North of Galway in the Irish republic), for example, involves considerably more than just language: An urban, Protestant, working environment (Belfast) in fact has little if anything in common with a rural, Catholic region of high unemployment (Connemara). The issue of language only exacerbates these differences.

A similar situation is reflected in the ideologically motivated opposition between Afrikaans and English in Namibia (and also in South Africa). The vast majority of the Namibian populace, regardless of race or social status, speaks or at least understands Afrikaans. The country's official language, however, is English, cast as the "language of freedom," though fewer than 3 percent of the population speak it as their first language. Afrikaans, the former language of instruction and administration, remains the "language of oppression."

More recently, the study of Russian has witnessed a rapid decline in the former Eastern/Bloc countries, and one can only speculate on the relationship between the sudden lack of interest in Russian and the "de-ideologicalization" of that language in the new republics. After 1992, in the Croatian part of Bosnia-Herzegovina (*Herzeg*), all mentions of the term *Serbo-Croatian* have been expunged from schoolbooks and replaced, not on linguistic but on ideological grounds, by the term "Croatian."

Artificial Language Conflict

Artificial, or self-imposed, conflict arises out of situations of compromise in which one or more language communities is disfavored. These situations have existed in every society from Babel to Brussels. Symmetric multilingualism, in which equal numbers of speakers are invested with equal rights and in which both language prestige and linguistic identities are congruent, is impossible, since one of the language groups will always be subject to stigmatization and/or discrimination, with conflict the inevitable result.

Artificial language conflict occurs especially when, motivated by the need for rapid international communication, politically influential economic powers export their languages (and their resulting socioeconomic influence) to their trading partners. Thus, Russian (before 1990) and English have become languages of great economic expansion, despite a noteworthy lack of formal educational planning. Secondary schools in Strasbourg, for example, have abandoned study of the native German dialect for English (as the first foreign language), with the result that German is being lost as a local working language. It is offered as a second "foreign" language only to students over twelve years of age, with the result that a passive knowledge of the mother tongue (a German dialect) is now all that remains.

The European Union has provided interesting examples of artificial language conflict. In the debate over which language(s) would speak for Europe, the Danes years ago, in a spirit of genuine cooperation, seemed to have opted to forgo the use of Danish. In retrospect, Denmark may appear to have resolved the issue, in the early years of the European Union, of how to reduce the number of official languages to at most two, with English and French destined to be the languages of international communication. The initial delight of London and Paris at this helpful suggestion was quickly dampened, however, since the Danes also suggested that the English should use French and the French should use English. After that suggestion, enthusiasm for the Danish solution quickly withered.

The presence of almost 4,000 translators and interpreters in Brussels suggests a return to the Tower of Babel. At the present time (the year 2000), the eleven working languages of the fifteen member states generate a total of ($10 \times 11 =$) 110 two language combinations. The enlargement of the European Union by six or more additional member-states in the coming years, with several new languages, leads to so many mathematical combinations that no assembly hall in the world would be able to accommodate meetings for all the interpreters.

These examples amply demonstrate that the language contacts and conflicts that threaten the peaceful coexistence of peoples are not always the consequence of longstanding historical contacts and conflicts among language communities. The new orders and restructurings of recent years have also led to sources of conflict that were not fully grasped just a few years ago. In any event, neither natural nor artificial conflict should be judged only negatively; rather, we should hope that out of conflict there may ensue new alliances and new solutions that will function better than any of the efforts of the past.

FUTURE PROSPECTS

There are hardly any areas of human life that do not have to do with language contact and multilingualism in some way. Since its renaissance in the 1950s and 1960s, research on multilingualism has been carried out on contact linguistic initiatives because of the inclusion of neighboring disciplines such as sociology and psychology. In the new century, younger subdisciplines will probably play a leading role because of their pronounced orientation to practical applications. The difference between the so-called internal and external linguistic criteria that was stressed in the past will be abandoned, since the interdependence and inseparability of these factors has become apparent in the most recent research results. In addition to the traditional ("hyphenated") linguistic disciplines, these areas of research will surely include ecolinguistics, which has already provided research on language contact with many new stimuli. In the area of the conflict issues mentioned before, ecolinguistic initiatives have proved to be particularly successful, so much so that the constantly changing forms of language contact and multilingualism can be described more satisfactorily. More and more new migrant groups (evacuees, asylum seekers, refugees, expatriates) are being included in the traditional autochthonous and allochthonous forms of multilingualism, in addition to the native minorities. Here, we see, at the beginning of the new century, new language contact research fields arising. One example is connected to the development of the new media and their dominant role in changing societal structures by destroying traditional fields in the society. This also has an enormous influence on the central concept of contact linguistics, which remains multilingualism. In future research, we will have to develop new forms of multilingualism that will emerge from virtual contacts and from new economic-based minorities. It is one of the chief tasks of contact linguistics to meet this challenge and to concern itself more intensively than in the past with a field that can serve as an outstanding example of applied science, the significance of which, for life and survival on an overpopulated planet with hundreds of different languages, cannot be overvalued.

CHAPTER 26

PIDGINS AND CREOLES

JEFF SIEGEL

PIDGINS and creoles are new languages that develop in language contact situations because of a need for communication among people who do not share a common language. A pidgin continues to be used primarily as a second language for intergroup communication, while a creole has become the mother tongue of a particular group of speakers. The lexicon of a pidgin or creole is derived from the various languages originally in contact, with the majority usually coming from one particular language, called the *lexifier*. However, the grammar of a pidgin or creole is different from that of the lexifier or any of the other contributing languages.

Most scholars in the field of pidgin and creole studies (or "creolistics") would agree on these characterizations of the languages they study, but on little else. A great deal of controversy has existed in the field since it became a separate (and ultimately respectable) area of linguistics in the 1960s. There are disagreements about the precise definitions of *pidgin* and *creole*, about which language varieties are actually pidgins or creoles, and about the origins of the linguistic features of these languages. Since these theoretical controversies are given excellent coverage in other overviews (e.g., Rickford and McWhorter 1997), I only outline them briefly here. Then I present some sociolinguistic background information on speakers, status and attitudes. Finally, I go on to discuss some areas of applied linguistics that concern pidgins and creoles.

The Origins and Definitions
of Pidgin and Creoles

Pidgins most often arise in situations that involve trading or large-scale population movement. An earlier "prepidgin" or "jargon," which is quite variable in structure, may later become a "stable" pidgin, which has developed its own lexical and grammatical norms. However, compared to the contributing languages in contact, the stable pidgin is formally less complex, having a much smaller total lexicon and little if any morphological marking of grammatical categories. Two examples are Russonorsk and Pidgin Fijian.[1] A stable pidgin is normally quite restricted in function, but in some cases it may later extend into wider areas. As a result, the language becomes lexically and grammatically more complex. It is then called an *expanded* pidgin. An example is Melanesian Pidgin, now spoken as three main dialects: Tok Pisin in Papua New Guinea, Pijin in the Solomon Islands, and Bislama in Vanuatu.

When a pidgin (or prepidgin) is learned by children as their first language and becomes the mother tongue of a new community, it is called a creole. Unlike pidgins, creoles are not restricted in use and are like any other vernacular language in having a full range of informal functions. Creoles are also more complex than pidgins in terms of lexicon, morphology, and grammatical rules. Some creoles seem to have arisen very quickly, perhaps even before a stable pidgin had developed—for example, among children of slaves born in the Caribbean (e.g., Jamaican Creole). Other creoles clearly developed from a pre-existing stable pidgin—for example, among Australian aboriginal children brought up at a mission station where their parents took refuge from murderous colonialists (Northern Australian Kriol).

Terminological controversies in the field result from researchers' focus on different aspects of these languages. The perfect example is Melanesian "Pidgin." For those who consider sociolinguistic criteria, some call it a pidgin because it is a second language, rather than the mother tongue for the large majority of its speakers. Others call it a creole because it has some native speakers and is used in a wide range of functions. Those who consider only linguistic criteria call it a creole because the grammatical features that it has developed are just as complex as those of clearly recognized creoles. Closely related to this controversy is the recent debate over whether or not creoles can be defined as a coherent group of languages according to purely linguistic criteria (McWhorter 1998; Mufwene 1997).

An issue that has dominated the field of pidgin and creole studies for nearly a hundred years is the origins of the grammatical features of creoles and the apparent grammatical similarities among creole languages the world over. There are basically three main camps: the substratists, the superstratists, and the universalists. The substratists (e.g., Alleyne 1980; Lefebvre 1999) believe that the features can be traced back to the substrate languages—for example, that the features of Caribbean creoles are derived from the West African languages of the slaves. The superstratists (especially Chaudenson 1992) believe that the features can be traced back to both standard and nonstandard varieties of the lexifier language. The universalists (especially Bickerton 1981, 1984) believe that creoles reflect character-istics of innate human linguistic endowment and that only this can explain the similarities between far-removed creoles.

Over the last twenty years, a lot of time and energy has been spent supporting one of these positions (and attacking others). However, most creolists these days believe in some kind of compromise among all these positions (Mufwene 1986). There are signs that, in the next twenty years, creolists will move to concentrate on the cognitive processes and constraints that may be relevant to pidgin and creole genesis—for example, by looking more closely at research in first and sec-ond language acquisition (e.g., DeGraff 1999; Siegel 1999a).

In some pidgin and creole situations, especially where English is the lexifier language as well as the language of government and education (as in Guyana, Hawai'i and Australia, for example), a continuum of varieties exists. These range from what is called the *basilect* (furthest from the lexifier) to the *acrolect* (closest to the lexifier), with intermediate varieties, the *mesolects,* in between. This kind of continuum was thought to have arisen from a process of decreolization that occurs when creole speakers come into greater contact with the lexifier language (for example, through more widespread education). In this process, the gram-matical rules of the creole supposedly change to become more like those of the standard form of the lexifier. Linguists such as Bickerton (1975) believed that synchronic variation along the continuum reflected diachronic language change.

However, several issues are being debated with regard to the notions of de-creolization and the creole continuum. First, many scholars now think that lin-guistic change in creoles does not necessarily take place in the direction of the lexifier (e.g., Bailey and Maynor 1998; LePage 1977). Second, a current view is that the continua of internal variation are not necessarily the result of decreolization but were present in many creoles from the beginning (e.g., LePage 1977; Valdman 1991). Third, the whole concept of the creole continuum has been attacked on two fronts. Scholars such as LePage and Tabouret-Keller (1985) argue against the notion that variation in the continuum occurs along a single dimension. Other researchers reject the whole notion of a continuum in some situations, favoring a model with two discrete systems, the creole and the lexifier, with code-switching between the two (Edwards 1983; Lawton 1980; Siegel 1997a). More detailed his-torical and contemporary research (such as that of Patrick 1999a) may help to settle these controversies.

Finally, there are debates about whether particular languages are (or were) pidgins or creoles. The most well-known example is African American Vernacular

English (AAVE) (see Rickford 1999; Winford 1997, 1998). Other languages with disputed "creoleness" are Afrikaans, Brazilian Portuguese, Kituba, Shaba Swahili, and various "mixed" languages, such as Michif. In order to avoid these controversies, I deal only with undisputed creoles in this article, but many of the applied issues are also relevant to varieties such as AAVE.

SOCIOLINGUISTIC BACKGROUND

The applied issues discussed in this chapter are relevant mainly to expanded pidgins and creoles, which I group together for convenience, using the abbreviation P/C (pidgin/creole). There are at least 76.8 million speakers of P/Cs—35.1 million of expanded pidgins and 41.7 million of creoles (based on figures in Grimes 1999 and in Smith, N., 1994).[2] They are spoken by indigenous populations in at least fifty countries or territories and by immigrants in many other places—for example, up to one million speakers of Haitian Creole in the United States (Joseph 1997: 281). Note that "pidgin" and "creole" are technical terms used by linguists and not necessarily by speakers of the languages. For example, speakers of Jamaican Creole call their language "Patwa" (from *patois*).

In most places where a P/C is spoken, its speakers form a majority of the population—for example, in Cape Verde, Mauritius, Papua New Guinea, and most Caribbean nations. In other places, however, P/C speakers are a minority—for example, Kriol and Torres Strait Creole speakers in Australia and Gullah and Louisiana Creole speakers in the United States. Creole-speaking immigrants are also minorities in Britain, Canada, the Netherlands, the United States, and other countries. In some places, P/C speakers are the majority in a particular state or territory, but a minority in the country as a whole—for example, in Hawai'i which is a state of the United States.

In nearly all cases, P/Cs are spoken mainly in informal contexts, while a different language—most often the standard form of a European language—is the official language of government, the law, and education. An important factor is whether this official language is the same as the lexifier language of the P/C. When the lexifier and the official language are different, as with English-lexified Sranan and Dutch in Surinam, the P/C is recognized as a separate, autonomous language (Winford 1994). When they are the same, the P/C is often perceived as nonautonomous.

Like other languages, P/Cs are valued by their speakers in the private domains of family and friendship. Speakers often have positive attitudes toward their language as a marker of solidarity and local social identity, as reported for Hawai'i Creole (Sato 1991; Watson-Gegeo 1994), Australian Kriol (Siegel 1998), and Dominica Creole French (Fontaine and Leather 1992). But, unlike other languages, P/Cs are rarely valued in public formal domains, and, as a result, they generally suffer from overall negative attitudes and low prestige (see, for example, Rickford and Traugott 1985; Winford 1994).

The stigmatization of P/Cs can in some ways be attributed to the nature of these languages and their origins as described earlier. First of all, as languages of former indentured laborers or slaves, P/Cs are associated with repression and powerlessness, and indeed to this day they are often spoken by disadvantaged sections of society. In contrast, it is the official language that has high prestige and is seen as the key to success. Second, as the new languages, of relatively recently formed speech communities, P/Cs suffer from comparison to the official languages with their long historical traditions and bodies of literature (Alleyne 1994). Third, P/Cs are often not considered to be legitimate languages but rather are seen as deviant and corrupt forms of their lexifiers. This is especially true in situations where a P/C coexists with the standard form of its lexifier. This view is reinforced by the fact that, at least superficially, the P/C and the standard share the same lexicon. The P/C is not seen to have its own grammatical rules, and so the way it is spoken is considered to be the result of performance errors, rather than of language differences. This lack of autonomy is exacerbated in countries like Jamaica and Guyana, where there is a creole continuum, as there seems to be no clear dividing line between the lexifier and the creole. In addition, in such situations, the more creole-like varieties at the basilectal end of the continuum have lower social status than the more standard-like varieties at the acrolectal end.

Hawai'i Creole, locally known as "Pidgin," is a good example of a P/C that has been denigrated over the years by teachers, administrators, and community leaders. A history of attitudes toward the language is presented in a recent position paper, "Pidgin and Education," by a group of interested staff and students at the University of Hawai'i (Da Pidgin Coup 1999: 6–8). It notes that, in publications starting from the 1920s, Pidgin was consistently labeled with negative terms such as "lazy," "ungrammatical," "faulty," "sloppy," "slothful," and "ugly." In the 1930s and 1940s, it was even considered a speech defect. In 1962, a major local newspaper compared Pidgin to the language of animals in an editorial entitled "Why Not Just Grunt?" (*Honolulu Star-Bulletin*, 13 February 1962). Such extreme statements are now getting harder to find, but the language is still commonly referred to as "bad English" or "broken English."

When the field of pidgin and creole studies emerged in the 1960s, linguists produced many studies showing that P/Cs are legitimate, rule-governed varieties of language that differ in systematic ways from recognized standard languages. These studies have had a limited effect, but they have led to more positive attitudes in some sections of P/C-speaking populations and to efforts to raise the status and extend the functions of some P/Cs. This brings us to the issues of applied linguistics.

APPLIED ISSUES

In accordance with current trends in linguistics over the past quarter century, pidgins and creoles have often been abstracted away from the populations who speak them. As Alleyne (1994), Rickford (1997), and others have pointed out, most creolists have been more interested in working on the hot theoretical issues than on the applied issues that directly affect the speakers of the languages they study. Nevertheless, some applied work has been done in the areas of language planning, language and education, and language and the law.

Language Planning

Over the years, there have been many calls to expand the use of particular P/Cs into public and official areas, such as government, the broadcast media, and education. Most of the arguments for this expansion are sociopolitical, pointing out that a large proportion of the population is disenfranchised by not knowing the established official language. The use of the P/C in government and other official domains would give people greater access and allow them to participate in decision-making processes, thus counteracting neocolonialism and elitism. (See, for example, Bebel-Gisler 1981; Devonish 1986.) Therefore, the ideology behind language planning for P/Cs has largely involved vernacularization (Cobarrubias 1983), but in most cases the planning has been initiated by religious groups or popular movements, rather than by government organizations.

With regard to status planning efforts (Haugen 1983), the aim in all cases has been to increase both the status and the functions of the P/C so that it is used in official contexts alongside the existing official language (instrumentalization). With regard to corpus planning, the major activity has been codification: choosing a variety of the P/C to be used for these wider functions and developing a writing system for it (graphization).[3]

The codification of a P/C does not involve developing a "standard" in the usual sense of the term. This is so because of two additional goals of codification in P/C contexts:

1. Developing a variety of the P/C that would be accessible to the majority of its speakers
2. Making the P/C autonomous from its lexifier so that it is perceived as a separate, legitimate language.

For other languages, a standard is developed on the basis of a prestige variety used by the social elite and found in an established literary tradition. In addition, it is often modeled on an already established standard used in the community (such as Latin in the European context). In contrast, a P/C normally has no established literary tradition. The prestige variety is the form closest to the lexifier, and the established standard is often the lexifier itself, both spoken by only a small elite class (see Sebba 1997). Obviously, the goals of accessibility and autonomy would not be accomplished by developing a standard form of the P/C on the basis of the lexifier.

Instead, codification of P/Cs has involved selecting the varieties distinct from the lexifier that would be the most efficient to use for communication within the P/C-speaking community. Where there is a creole continuum, this could mean selecting the most common intermediate or mesolectal varieties considered to be acceptable forms of the creole. While such a method has been advocated for the English-lexified creoles of the Caribbean (Devonish 1986: 115), it has not been accomplished to any degree. An alternative is to select the most widespread variety of the P/C that is furthest from the lexifier, usually the rural or basilectal variety, as opposed to the urban variety more influenced by the lexifier. This is what has occurred with Tok Pisin in Papua New Guinea (Wurm 1980). The argument there was that urban speakers would be more familiar with the more conservative rural varieties than rural speakers would be with the more innovative and anglicized urban varieties. While Tok Pisin is usually seen as a success story in P/C language planning, with the language widely used in some official functions, Romaine (1992, 1994a) sees increasing "linguistic fragmentation" in the language, with the gap between urban and rural varieties growing.

The extension of a P/C into formal domains necessarily involves its becoming a written language. The choice of an orthography is again influenced by the nature of P/Cs and people's attitudes toward them. There are basically two types of orthographies used for P/Cs: etymological and phonemic.[4] An etymological orthography is generally based on the conventional spelling of the lexifier language—for example, in Hawai'i Creole:

They wen' buy 'em las' night.
'They bought it last night.'

This type of orthography is easy to read for those literate in the lexifier, but it reinforces the view that the P/C is a deviant variety of the lexifier. On the other hand, a phonemic orthography is based on the sounds that actually occur in the P/C without any reference to the lexifier, ideally with one symbol for each sound. Here is the same Hawai'i Creole sentence in a phonemic orthography:

Dei wen bai om las nait.

This type of orthography reinforces the autonomy of the P/C, but it is not easy to read for those literate in the lexifier. Other advantages and disadvantages of each type are described by Winer (1990).

There are also two types of compromise orthographic systems. A modified etymological orthography distinguishes the salient linguistic features of the P/C and uses phonemic representation for words not from the lexifier (Winer 1990). An intermediate phonemic orthography basically has one symbol (or digraph) for one phoneme, but in some cases it uses the spelling conventions of the lexifier— for example, ⟨ou⟩ for /u/ in French-lexified creoles (Schieffelin and Doucet 1994).

Supporters of a phonemic orthography believe that it is easier for illiterate people to learn to read and that therefore, in addition to the autonomy factors, it is better suited to fulfil the libertarian goals of access and equity. Supporters of an etymological orthography believe that there will always be bilingualism and a need to become literate in the lexifier and that similar orthographies will promote this biliteracy. Sociopolitical ideologies also affect orthographic preferences. For example, Schieffelin and Doucet (1994) describe how some groups in Haiti oppose an etymological orthography because of its association with French (the language of the former colonial power), while others oppose the phonemic orthography because it looks too much like English (the language of the English-speaking Americans, who occupied Haiti from 1915 to 1934).

The first Haitian Creole orthography was developed in the 1920s, and there have been several others proposed since then, all surrounded by vigorous ideological debates. The current official system, òtograf IPN (Institute Pédagogique National), is an intermediate phonemic orthography developed in the mid-1970s and made official in 1980. This system is now widely used by the writers of Haitian Creole, although it still has its pro-etymological detractors, such as Métellus (1998). In 1976, a phonemic orthography was developed for Seselwa, the French-lexified creole of the Seychelle Islands, in the Indian Ocean (Bollée 1993), but this was later amended to be more similar to that of Haitian Creole (Baker 1991). In the Caribbean, orthographies based on the Haitian IPN model were developed for the French-lexified creoles of Guadeloupe and Martinique in the mid-1970s and for those of St. Lucia and Dominica in the early 1980s. These are in general use, although alternatives have been proposed (Hazäel-Massieux 1993).

With regard to English-lexifier P/Cs, Tok Pisin had several different orthographies in use from 1935 through the 1950s, when standardization efforts began.

A standard finally emerged from that used in the Tok Pisin translation of the New Testament, published in 1968 (Wurm 1985). Agreement on an orthography for Bislama did not occur until 1995 (Crowley 1996). An orthography for Jamaican Creole (which could be adapted for other English-lexified creoles in the Caribbean) was developed by Cassidy (1961, 1993), and one for Hawai'i Creole was developed by Odo (see Bickerton and Odo 1976). These orthographies are widely used by linguists but rarely by others. For example, nearly all literature in Hawai'i Creole and the recent translation of the New Testament use different modified etymological orthographies, rather than the phonemic Odo orthography. Sranan (Surinam) also has an official (largely) phonemic orthography that is not widely accepted. An intermediate "rule-based" orthography developed specifically for Belize Kriol in the mid-1990s seems to have won greater acceptance (Decker 1995).

Regarding other creoles, Papiamento (Netherlands Antilles) has two official orthographies, both widely used: an etymological one, used on the island of Aruba and a more phonemic one, used on Curaçao and Bonaire (Kouwenberg and Muysken 1994). Most recently, in 1998, the government of Cape Verde decided to support officially a unified orthography for Capeverdian (Gonsalves 1999).

In other aspects of corpus planning, there are at least seventeeen P/Cs that have a dictionary or a detailed grammar or both. Of course, some have more than one—for example, Haitian Creole has at least half a dozen dictionaries. However, government-sponsored language planning organizations for P/Cs are not very common. I am aware of only two: Instituto Lingwistiko Antiano for Papiamento in the Netherlands Antilles (Dijkhoff 1993) and Lenstiti Kreol in the Seychelles (Bollée 1993). Nongovernment organizations that conduct some language planning activities exist in other countries—for example, the Folk Research Centre in St. Lucia (Frank 1993) and Komité pou Etid Kwéyòl in Dominica (Stuart 1993).

With regard to instrumentalization, one of the first extensions of the use of P/Cs has been their adaptation by various Christian churches for use in religion. There are translations of the New Testament in many P/Cs—for example, all three dialects of Melanesian Pidgin, Cameroon Pidgin, Sranan, Haitian Creole, St. Lucia Creole, Papiamento, and Sango. These P/Cs are also commonly used in religious services by most denominations.

Extension into secular written literature has also occurred for nearly all P/Cs, but with different degrees of popularity. For example, in the Seychelles, short stories in Seselwa began to appear in 1979, and by the late 1980s six novels and several collections of short stories and children's stories were in print (Bollée 1993: 91). However, there was not a very good market for this literature, and by the 1990s it was not easy to find. On the other hand, literature in Haitian Creole has been more varied and more popular. The highly acclaimed novel *Dezafi* by Franketienne appeared in 1975, and a detailed historical work by Michel-Rolph Trouillot appeared in 1977 (Schieffelin and Doucet 1994: 183). Since then, a substantial body of Haitian Creole literature has developed in novels, short stories, plays, and poetry (St. Fort 2000).

Literature is one of the few areas into which most English-lexified P/Cs have extended. For example, poetry, short stories and plays have been written in Nigerian Pidgin and in Cameroon Pidgin (Todd 1990: 75–77). Throughout the Caribbean, English-lexified creoles are used in stories, especially in dialogue, and also in songs, poems, and plays (Winer 1990). Jamaican Creole is also widely used in cartoons and comics, and since the 1990s it has been used in stories as voice of first- and third-person narration. In recent years, Hawai'i Creole has also become a literary language, with the appearance of many popular short stories and poems and several novels that incorporate dialogue in the language. Romaine observes that the emergence of Hawai'i Creole as a literary medium is "a sign of the vitality of a language coming of age and gaining status" (1994b: 551).

In contrast, Mühlhäusler (1995, 1996a) and Charpentier (1997) claim that literacy in Melanesian and Australian P/Cs is something that has been imposed by Europeans on speakers of these languages and that it is basically irrelevant to their societies. However, in a rebuttal of these claims (Siegel 1998), I present evidence showing that, while the idea of literacy has been introduced from the outside, it has been adopted by speakers of Melanesian and Australian P/Cs for their own purposes and now plays an important part in their communities.

The broadcast and print media are another area of expansion for most P/Cs, except for English-lexified creoles where English is the official language. P/Cs are most common in radio broadcasting, especially for news and announcements. Haitian Creole and Seselwa are also used on television. Use in the print media is somewhat limited in comparison, but Papiamento is widely used in daily newspapers and magazines. News reports in Seselwa and Tok Pisin can also be found on the internet.

Some P/Cs are now used in politics—for example, in political speeches during election campaigns. This occurs in St. Lucia, but the creole is not used in Parliament. However, in other countries, such as Papua New Guinea, Vanuatu, and the Seychelle Islands, the P/C is frequently the language of parliamentary debate. At least three countries have declared a P/C as a national and official language: the Seychelles (1979), Vanuatu (1980), and Haiti (1987). So, certainly some P/Cs have gained a fair amount of status. But as Sebba (1997: 258) points out, no P/C has ever been the sole official language of a country. These official P/Cs share their official status with English or French (or both), which generally still have more prestige.

In summary, since the 1970s, linguists have been involved in language planning for P/Cs, particularly in instrumentalization and orthography development. In some places, especially where there is a creole continuum, their efforts have had little effect on actual language use and attitudes. But in others, the functions of P/Cs have expanded into new areas, and, as Dejean (1993: 80) notes for Haiti, at least creole voices are now being heard more often.

Language and Education

One official area into which P/Cs have been slow in expanding is education. While P/Cs are sometimes used informally in the classroom, the official language of education in almost all contexts is still a standard variety that most P/C-speaking students do not know. As a result, these students face inequities in formal education, as reported for creole speakers in the Caribbean (Devonish 1986; LePage 1968; Winer 1989) and for creole-speaking immigrants in Britain (Dalphinis 1991, Edwards 1979) and North America (Coelho 1988; Winer 1993). These inequities include:

1. Teacher's negative attitudes and ignorance (Breinberg 1986; Pratt-Johnson 1993)
2. Negative attitudes and poor self-image among the students themselves because of denigration by others of their speech and culture (Fischer 1992)
3. Repression of self-expression because of the need to use an unfamiliar form of language (Feldman, Stone, and Renderer 1990)
4. Difficulty in acquiring literacy in a second language (UNESCO 1968).

An obvious way to deal with these inequities would be to use the language of the students as a language of instruction or a subject of study. But this is rarely done. More common, in fact, are calls to ban the P/C from the schools, as has occurred in Hawai'i (Sato 1991).

The reasons for not using P/Cs in education are closely related to the nature of these languages and the prevailing attitudes toward them. First of all, many people, including educators, still believe that P/Cs are deviant forms of the standard and thus are not suitable for education. Such attitudes have been reported for many P/Cs, such as Carriacou Creole English (Kephart 1992), other varieties of creole in the Caribbean (Alleyne 1994; Winford 1994), Krio in Sierra Leone (Fyle 1994), Nigerian Pidgin (Elugbe 1994), Hawai'i Creole English (Sato 1985), Torres Strait Creole (Shnukal 1992), and Tok Pisin (Nidue 1988).

But even when P/Cs are recognized as legitimate languages, some educators, administrators, and linguists still argue that using them in education would be both "impractical" and detrimental to students. One argument concerns the lack of standardization. Especially in situations where there is a creole continuum, it is difficult to select a norm to be used in education. Another "impractical" argument is that even if P/Cs could be standardized, the cost of developing written materials would be a disadvantage. Thus, linguists such as Todd (1990) advocate only the oral use of P/Cs in the classroom to facilitate communication in the early years, but not the written use.

The "detrimental" arguments are premised on the belief that a goal of the education system should be the acquisition of the standard language of education. Thus, learning in or about a P/C is seen as a waste of time—time that would be better spent learning the standard. Closely related is the "ghettoization" argument (Snow 1990), which asserts that use of a nonstandard variety of speech in the classroom deprives children of the instruction they need to get the economic benefits that speakers of standard varieties have and condemns them to permanent underclass status. This argument has been used, for example, to oppose Torres Strait Creole as an educational language (Shnukal 1992: 4). Third is the "interference" argument, which claims that using a P/C in education will make it difficult for students to learn the standard because of negative transfer or confusion between the two closely related varieties. (See, for example, Elsasser and Irvine 1987.) Thus, according to Charpentier, using Bislama along with English in education in Vanuatu would "lead to a social, psychological and pedagogical blockage, seriously compromising any passage to literacy" (1997: 236).

The "impractical" arguments are countered by the existence of viable educational programs that use creoles as the languages of instruction and initial literacy in primary schools. One example occurs in Australia, where a bilingual program that uses Kriol has been running since 1977 at the Barunga Community Education Centre (Siegel 1993). Another occurs in the Seychelles, where Seselwa has been the primary medium of instruction in all schools since 1981 (Bollée 1993). Both programs have been successful, despite some initial problems in standardization, and the Barunga program has illustrated how materials can be produced locally at very low cost using modern desktop publishing technology (Northern Territory Department of Education 1995).

The major premise of the "detrimental" arguments is not accepted by many linguists. Devonish (1986), for example, argues that, if creoles were used in more official capacities in creole-speaking countries, speakers would not need to learn the European standard. But, even if the learning of this standard is accepted as the goal of education, there is no evidence that using a P/C in school is detrimental. On the contrary, research in Australia (Murtagh 1982), in the Seychelles (Ravel and Thomas 1985), in Carriacou (Kephart 1992), and in Papua New Guinea (Siegel 1997b) demonstrates that using a P/C in formal education has no negative effect on the subsequent acquisition of the standard language and may even be advantageous.[5]

Three types of educational programs using P/Cs are in existence: instrumental, accommodation, and awareness. Instrumental programs use a P/C as a medium of instruction to teach initial literacy and content subjects such as mathematics, science, and health. In addition to those in Australia and the Seychelles already mentioned, there are nationwide instrumental programs in primary schools using Haitian Creole (Bentolila 1987; Dejean 1993; Valdman 1989) and Papiamento (Appel and Verhoeven 1994). There are also some individual primary programs using Tok Pisin (Siegal 1996), Krio (Shrimpton 1995), Torres Strait Creole (Turner 1997), Guadeloupean Creole, and San Andres Creole. In the United States, bilingual programs exist for immigrants who speak Haitian Creole (Burtoff 1985; Joseph 1997; Zéphir 1997) and Capeverdean (Gonsalves 1996). P/Cs are also used in nonformal adult educational programs in Britain, Dominica, Mauritius, the Solomon Islands, St. Lucia, and Vanuatu (for references see Siegel 1999b).[6]

In accommodation programs, a P/C is accepted in the classroom, but it is not a medium of instruction or subject of study. In the early years of school, students are allowed to use their home varieties of language for speaking and sometimes for writing, and teachers may utilize their students' own interactional patterns and stories for teaching the standard. Individual accommodation programs of this type have existed in Hawai'i (e.g., Boggs 1985; Rynkofs 1993). At the higher levels, literature and creative writing in local P/Cs may be accommodated into the curriculum, as has been done in Trinidad and Tobago (Winer 1990).

Awareness programs make P/Cs a topic of study. The students' own varieties are put into context by teaching some basic sociolinguistics about different language varieties, standardization, and language attitudes. In some cases, the P/C's grammatical rules and pragmatics are explicitly contrasted with those of the standard variety. An objective here is to help students to acquire the standard by focusing on how its structure and use are different from their own varieties.[7] In Hawaii, two of the government-funded programs for creole speakers referred to by Watson-Gegeo (1994) have had awareness components. But the most significant awareness programs have been developed in countries where creole speakers are a minority, namely among Kriol speakers in Western Australia (Berry and Hudson 1997) and Caribbean English creole-speaking immigrants in Britain (ILEA Afro-Caribbean Language and Literacy Project in Further and Adult Education 1990), Canada (Coelho 1988, 1991), and the United States (Fischer 1992).[8]

These references for awareness programs in minority contexts are also important resources for teachers who are not creole speakers and who know little about the language of their students. In Australia, a professional development course for teachers of Kriol-speaking students also exists (Catholic Education Office 1994), and many other resources for teachers have been produced by the national and state governments (see Siegel 1999c). Other important resources for teachers, giving background information about creoles as well as suggestions for classroom activities, have been written by Pollard (1993) for Jamaican Creole; Edwards (1979) for Caribbean English creoles in Britain; Dalphinis (1985) and Nwenmely (1996) for French-lexified creoles in Britain; and Nichols (1996), Winer

(1993), and Winer and Jack (1997) for English-lexified creoles in the United States. Craig (1999) has written a detailed guide to teaching speakers of English-lexifier creoles and other vernaculars.

Studies and reports on evaluations of all three types of programs describe various positive results from using P/Cs in education: greater student participation rates, higher student scores on achievement tests that measure reading and writing skills in the standard language, and increases in overall academic achievement (see Siegel 1999b). There seem to be several obvious reasons for these results. First, for the instrumental programs, students find it easier to acquire literacy skills in a familiar variety of language and then to transfer these skills to the standard. Second, in all types of programs, students can express themselves better in a familiar language (without fear of correction), leading to better cognitive development. Third, teachers have more positive attitudes because of the nature of the programs, which make them aware of the legitimacy and complex rule-governed nature of their students' languages; therefore, they have higher expectations. Fourth, students have more positive attitudes toward their language and themselves, leading to greater interest and increased motivation.

Another reason, however, may be related to aspects of psycholinguistics and second language acquisition. As Craig (e.g., 1966, 1976, 1983) has pointed out, in educational situations involving a creole and the standard form of its lexifier, students often have trouble separating the two varieties because of the many similarities between them. Craig notes that in such cases "the learner fails to perceive the new target element in the teaching situation" (1966: 58). But, when students look at features of their own varieties in the classroom, they have a greater chance of noticing features of the standard that are different. This helps them to build the separate mental representation of the standard that is necessary for language acquisition (Siegel 1999b).

While problems of autonomy and negative attitudes continue to exist, it is unlikely that many communities would allow their pidgin or creole to be used as the primary language of education in an instrumental program. However, most of the educational benefits of such programs can still be obtained from accommodation or awareness programs, which would be much more acceptable to P/C-speaking communities. The establishment and evaluation of such programs will most likely be a future trend in the applied linguistics of pidgin and creole languages.

Language and the Law

Speakers of P/Cs also face inequities in the legal systems of most countries where a standard European language is the language of the law. Like others who do not know the official language, speakers of P/Cs suffer from not understanding police cautions, police interviews, and courtroom interactions (e.g., see Eades 1997). But these problems are exacerbated by the fact that P/Cs are not considered separate languages, and therefore that no interpreters are considered necessary. For example, Devonish (1986: 29–31) points out that English is the unquestioned language of the law in all Caribbean countries where English-lexifier creoles are spoken. Yet, monolingual creole-speaking witnesses often do not understand questions addressed to them in English, and lawyers, prosecutors, and magistrates have to translate them into the creole. Devonish contrasts this ad hoc court interpreting with that provided to speakers of other languages. He points out that a monolingual creole-speaking defendant is disadvantaged because "there is no official court-appointed interpreter, or anyone else for that matter, who ensures that he is able to follow the proceedings" (1986: 30). The erroneous assumption is that speakers of an English-lexifier creole should be able to follow the English used in court proceedings. Speakers of P/Cs are also disadvantaged by nonspeakers' mistaken impressions that they can understand evidence or testimony given in these languages (e.g., Koch 1991).

Linguists have attempted to serve as expert witnesses in order to deal with these inequities, but with varying success. Shuy (1993), for example, describes the case of a speaker of Hawai'i Creole on trial for perjury, and demonstrates the accused's misunderstanding, lack of comprehension, and confusion about the prosecutor's questions. Shuy notes: "The judge would not permit the expert witness testimony that could have clarified these issues" (1993: 148). The defendant was convicted on six counts of perjury.

In contrast, in the Supreme Court in Cairns, Australia, in 1995, Helen Harper was allowed to give evidence in the defense of a Torres Strait Creole speaker charged with attempted murder. Her evidence, based on an analysis of the recorded police interview, was that the accused did not have sufficient knowledge of standard English to deal with the complexities of the questions in the interview. Furthermore, she pointed out that, in Torres Strait Creole, the word *kill* may mean 'hurt or maim' rather than 'kill', so that the accused's statement *I wanted to kill him with that thing* did not necessarily indicate an intention to murder. As a result of this testimony, the charge was reduced to unlawful wounding (Trezise 1996).

Linguists in Australia have also been involved in the training of Kriol speakers as interpreters, in courses held since 1994 in Western Australia and the Northern Territory. The emphasis of the courses has been Kriol-English interpreting in legal and medical contexts. Teaching materials in Kriol have been developed, and several students have received paraprofessional accreditation from the National Association for Accreditation of Translators and Interpreters (NAATI).

Linguists in the United States, Canada, and Britain have also served as expert consultants and witnesses in cases involving creole speakers—in some for the defense and in some for the prosecution. In the most well-known case, a bilingual speaker of Hawai'i Creole and standard English unsuccessfully sued his employer for accent discrimination (Lippi-Green 1997: 44–45, Sato 1991). Matsuda notes: "The judge discounted the testimony of the linguist who stated that Hawaiian Creole pronunciation is not incorrect, rather it is one of the many varieties of pronunciation of standard English. The linguist, the judge stated, was not an expert in speech" (1991: 1345–1346). Other, more successful work has included the following: accent identification, determination of the reliability of a confession supposedly given in standard English by a creole speaker, translation and interpretation documents and recordings in creoles, and rating of intelligibility between a creole and standard English.

An interesting case described by Patrick (1999b) involved both wiretapped and consensual recordings of defendants speaking in Jamaican Creole. The crucial recordings were transcribed for the trial by a speaker of Jamaican Creole. The defense hired an unnamed linguist to contest the transcripts, and the prosecution hired Patrick (a near-native speaker of Jamaican Creole and an expert on the language) to review the defense version. He identified many examples of omissions, misunderstandings, mistranslation, misrepresentations, and other errors made by the defense linguist and appeared as a witness during the proceedings.

Patrick makes some interesting observations about involvement in criminal cases by linguists in general and by creolists in particular. First, he points out that prosecutors rarely hire experts, including linguists, and he adds: "Judges are also often sceptical about the need for expert testimony on the use of language, a subject which they themselves rule on every working day without the benefit of linguistic training" (1999b: 2). He also notes that, when linguists are consulted, lawyers have difficulty understanding exactly what they do. With regard to this particular case, Patrick observes that it was only because of the unwritten, non-standard status of Jamaican Creole that linguists, rather than translators, were consulted. Finally, he stresses the importance for creolists involved in criminal cases of being objective and absolutely certain of their conclusions (as opposed to the speculative argument that often takes place in creolistics). These observations will be important to keep in mind in this relatively new area of applied creolistics.

CONCLUSION

The nature of pidgin and creole languages, their role in society, and the continuing misconceptions about them provide a unique context for work in applied linguistics, especially in the areas of educational and forensic linguistics. But it remains to be seen whether more creolists will shift their attention from theoretical to applied issues in the years to come.

NOTES

I would like to thank the following people for providing information about various creoles in response to my inquiry over the CreoList in February 2000: Jacques Arends (Sranan), Ken Decker (Belize Creole), Michel DeGraff and Hugues St. Fort (Haitian Creole), Emmanuel Faure (Guadeloupean Creole), Ron Morren (San Andres Creole), and Peter Patrick (Jamaican Creole).

1. More information on any of the pidgins or creoles referred to here can be found in Holm (1989) or Arends, Muysken, and Smith (1994).

2. Nearly all expanded pidgins are English lexified, and the largest, Nigerian Pidgin, has more than 30 million speakers. The largest creole is Haitian Creole, spoken by more than 7.3 million. Creoles lexified by English have the most speakers (11.9 million), followed by French (9.4 million), Ngbandi (4.9 million), Malay (2.7 million), Arabic (1.8 million), and Portuguese (1.4 million).

3. For a good, although somewhat dated, overview, see Samarin (1980).

4. Baker (1991) calls the two types "nonautonomous" and "autonomous."

5. These results correspond with those of general research (such as Thomas and Collier 1997), which clearly shows that use of a familiar language in early eduction is advantageous both for overall academic performance and for acquisition of the mainstream educational language.

6. P/Cs have also been used instrumentally at the tertiary level. A degree-level course on the grammar of Bislama has been offered at the University of the South Pacific in the medium of Bislama (Crowley 1987). Furthermore, a successful master of arts thesis on the grammar of Tok Pisin was written in Tok Pisin by Dicks Raeparanga Thomas in 1996. (The two external examiners, Terry Crowley and Jeff Siegel, also wrote their evaluations and comments in Tok Pisin.)

7. This type of program is similar to some in the "language awareness" movement in Britain (see Hawkins 1987), but the emphasis is on pidgins and creoles or on nonstandard minority dialects.

8. It is ironic that the Caribbean Academic Program at Evanston Township High School, outside Chicago, may be the only place where students are taught to read and use the orthography developed by Cassidy for Caribbean English creoles.

CHAPTER 27

LANGUAGE SPREAD AND ITS STUDY: NARROWING ITS SPREAD AS A SCHOLARLY FIELD

OFELIA GARCÍA

LANGUAGE spread is, according to Cooper, "an increase, over time, in the proportion of a communication network that adopts a given language or language variety for a given communicative function" (1982a: 6). It is generally taken for granted that language, as a concomitant of culture, can spread. Even children begin to understand the spread of language as they become conscious that many of the sayings, stories, tales, legends, and songs that they're told have been repeated by others in different places, different times, and different languages.

Schoolchildren learn of the spread of Greek culture and language throughout the Mediterranean world, of the spread of Roman influence and Latin throughout the Roman Empire, and of the spread of Islam as a new world religion that accompanied the spread of the language of the *Koran*, Arabic. As children's world expands in historical and geographical dimensions, they begin to perceive how most sociocultural historical change has been accompanied by the spread of the culture, and consequently of the language, of the more powerful or high-status group. In some cases, the language of the more powerful has been forcefully imposed. In others, participation in the new sociocultural context has simply demanded the adoption of the new language or of new language features. Sometimes there is a social need for the new language or language variety in order to enjoy socioeconomic benefits or to achieve political integration. At other times the need is communicative because the new messages that the new cultural context creates cannot simply be transmitted in the old way, and a new way of communicating is needed (García and Otheguy 1989; Otheguy 1993, 1995).

Children in the Americas start becoming conscious that English, Spanish, Portuguese, and French may be their language but that these languages were not those of the indigenous people of the Americas—those languages being spoken even today by some. As children develop, they begin to understand that English, Spanish, Portuguese, and French were powerful languages that spread quickly and forcibly as the indigenous groups of the Americas were silenced and even killed. They learn from history books that other languages were brought to the New World, but yet there was no spread of either the many languages of African slaves or of the languages of less powerful immigrant groups. When students later compare the fate of Spanish in Latin America, brought by powerful conquerors, with that of Spanish in the United States, spoken originally by the less powerful conquerors in remote areas such as Florida or eventually by darker-skinned Mexicans in the Southwest who had by then adopted the Spanish language of their conquerors, they start to realize that language spread has much to do with dominance, power, prestige, and privilege.

Laypersons and even schoolchildren understand language spread as a normal historical process. In English, the term *language spread* combines two realities that they have known since childhood: spreading, such as butter on bread, and having language. It may be that it is the English language term, reflecting only a wide expansion on the surface, that has resulted in a scholarly field that has to date yielded little depth and that has worked at the theoretical level or merely described language spread without seriously studying the complex sociocultural processes that affect it in diverse ways. Descriptive studies of language spread, sometimes also referred to as language expansion, language diffusion, or language change, have little to do with the scholarly enterprise that modern language spread studies require (McConnell 1990).

The study of language spread or language diffusion (a prevalent term especially in non-Anglo American scholarship) is a fairly new scholarly enterprise. Fishman (1977b) formally introduced the complex conceptualization of the field of study in relationship to English-as-an-additional-language and as another perspective for the study of language maintenance and shift. Language spread studies were the object of attention at the Aberystwyth Conference, in Wales, in 1978. The first significant publication of studies devoted to language spread was compiled by Cooper (1982b).

Since Cooper's volume (1982b), there have been only a few serious comprehensive general studies of language spread (Ammon 1994; Ammon and Kleinedam 1992; Laforgue and McConnell 1990; Lowenberg 1988). The term is absent from encyclopedic works on language such as those by Baker and Jones (1998) and Crystal (1987). Yet, "language spread" has been increasingly used to describe the growth of English as a language of wider communication (LWC) in domains such as science, technology, finance, and higher education (Fishman 1977b; Fishman, Conrad, and Rubal-Lopez 1996; García and Otheguy 1989; Kachru 1986, 1992; Phillipson 1992). This emphasis on English responds to the more current definition of language spread as a consequence of modern globalization, and not simply of military conquest or imposition.

There are four main reasons for the dearth of studies on language spread:

1. The tendency of researchers to focus on questions that respond to a problem, rather than study phenomena of growth and development, even when those could also pose problems.
2. The lack of clarity in the term language spread because of its occasional overlap with other terms such as *language shift, language maintenance, reversing language shift,* and *language planning/policy.*
3. The complex interdisciplinary nature of language spread as a field of study, that involves economic, linguistic, political, psychological, and sociological behaviors toward language.
4. The difficulty of conducting empirical sociolinguistic research within the broad socio/geopolitical context required by the study of language spread.

This chapter synthesizes the theoretical literature on language spread, focusing on the defining characteristics of this field of study. The study of language spread has sometimes mimicked the phenomenon itself, thinly stretching to encompass many situations of different kinds of language change. This chapter also draws theoretical boundaries around the construct of language spread, making it easier to study it in the future.

The Study of Language Spread: What It Is and What It Is Not

The modern study of language spread, made possible by advances in the sociology of language and in psycholinguistics, as well as in ways of gathering and analyzing macro- and microsociolinguistic data, was preeminently shaped by Cooper, who has offered the classic definition: "the increase over time in the proportion of a communicative network that adopts a given language or language variety for a given communicative function" (1982a: 6).

Both Fishman (1977b) and Cooper (1982a) insist that the study of language spread is really not about language itself but is rather about *changes in the language behavior of speakers*. Sometimes these changes in behavior result in new speakers, but often they result simply in the adoption of the language, language variety, or features for new societal or communicative functions by existing speakers (Fishman 1977b).

According to Cooper (1982a) the study of language spread is really about human variability in four aspects of behavior toward language: awareness, evaluation, proficiency, and use. These four aspects of behavior toward language have different defining characteristics and are connected to different disciplines. The first two behaviors, Awareness and evaluation, involve being aware of being positively inclined toward a language or language variety and are of psychological import. Proficiency may be subdivided into the underlying knowledge or competence and the execution or speech performance in that language. Underlying competence is of psycholinguistic import, while performance is of sociolinguistic import and involves external behavior that may be directly observed and measured. Finally, the frequency of actual use, or adoption of the language or language variety, implicates both the narrower definition of sociolinguistics and the broader definition, sometimes explicitly referred to as sociology of language.

While studying the variance in human behavior toward language, language spread studies also focus on the contextual specificity and their dynamics in the change in language behavior. Three aspects of contextual specificity and their dynamics are taken into account:

Variance in overtness: whether the behavioral change toward language is in speaking, hearing, reading, or writing and whether it includes receptive or productive language behavior;

Variance in domain specificity: whether the behavioral change toward language occurs in relation to an institutional domain—that is, home and family, school, work, religion, or government—and in a specific communicative situation;

Variance in role-relationship specificity: whether the behavioral change toward language occurs depending on the social relationship of the interlocutors.

Language spread studies look at not only the degree and location of language behavior change but also the dynamics and interrelationship of the aspects of contextual specificity identified earlier (Fishman 1977b). But language spread studies go beyond the degree and location of language behavior to include the *sociocultural processes* that accompany the change. Brosnahan (1963) identified four sociocultural processes that explain the spread of Arabic, Greek, and Latin as mother tongues: military conquest or imposition, the length and duration of authority, the multilingualism and linguistic heterogeneity of the area in which the spread occurred, and the material incentives for learning the language.

However, in modern times, language spread has been increasingly associated with the acquisition of an additional language, and not simply with the acquisition of a second language that is characteristic of language shift. Fishman, Cooper, and Rosenbaum (1977) and Lewis (1982) identify the following additional sociocultural processes as important in this regard:

1. Factors related to modernization, especially:
   - Economic development, especially external exploitation of indigenous resources
   - Educational development
   - Political affiliation and global position vis-à-vis superpowers
   - Urbanization, with more linguistic heterogeneity, presence of governmental agencies and increased educational opportunity
   - Demographics and population mobility.
2. Factors related to between-group interactions, besides conquest, such as:
   - Colonization
   - Nature of the colonial center and the periphery
   - Geographical contiguity
   - Ease of communication.
3. Factors related to the religious and cultural characteristics of a group.

The study of language spread focuses, then, on the pervasiveness and variance of change in human behavior toward language (even when those are affective or cognitive, instead of interactional behavior per se), while identifying the contextual specificity and institutional domain of the behavior, as well as the sociocultural processes that shape the language behavior (Fishman 1977b).

Language spread studies, as a subfield of sociology of language studies, attempt to answer the summarizing question posed by Cooper: "Who adopts what, when, why, and how?" (1982a: 31). The framework proposed by Cooper asks that language spread studies determine:

Who: The sociolinguistic characteristics of individual and communicative network adopters
adopts: The interaction of the different levels of language behavior identified earlier
what: The structural/functional characteristics of the linguistic innovation
when: The time of adoption
where: The kinds of social interaction within the type of societal domain that lead to the adoption
why: The incentives for adoption
how: The language planning activities that accompany adoption.

Studies of language spread beginning after Cooper (1982b) mark a change in scholarship brought about not only by advances in the sociology of language (Fishman 1968) but also by the globalization of a new world order. We can speak of:

- The spread of Latin as a lingua franca in the western half of the Roman Empire until the Middle Ages
- The spread of Arabic during the Islamic expansion
- The spread of Spanish throughout Latin America during the conquest and colonization
- The spread of French, Portuguese, and English as colonial languages throughout Asia and Africa.

But all these cases of language spread, which resulted from direct military conquest and often resulting in a language shift in the population, have little to do with the study of language spread as we now know it. The study of language spread today looks at how global forces, less explicitly present than military conquest and interacting simultaneously at many social levels, impact language behaviors.

Language spread differs from language change, language shift, language maintenance, reversing language shift, and language planning and policy. When we speak of language change, we describe the change in the linguistic forms themselves, without considering human behavior as mediators or sources of change (Cooper 1982a) or the communicative reason for the occurrence of language change within a given sociocultural context.

Language shift, the process by which a speech community abandons a language or language variety and takes up another one, most often starts with the displacement of a language or a variety for low (L) functions—that is, with the erosion of diglossia. Language spread, however, most often responds to newly created communicative functions, usually high (H) functions that have not been previously occupied by the other language, and does not disturb the diglossic relationship of the first language with the other language. Thus, language spread most often refers to a communicative change within a stable speech community.

Language shift situations constitute the other side of the coin of language spread. When diglossia is eroded, language shift occurs as the other language spreads. But these situations are rarely studied from a language spread perspective. The study of language shift and language maintenance focuses on the more external human behavior toward language (that of proficiency and use), often using the more implicit behavior (that of awareness and evaluation) only as predictors of the change in external adoption, unlike language spread studies. Whereas studies of language shift and language maintenance concern themselves with measurement of habitual language use, language spread concerns itself with processes of sociocultural change and their impact on language behavior, including aware-ness, evaluation, proficiency, and use (Fishman 1977b).

Efforts to reverse language shift (RLS) often mimic the process of language spread, attempting to spread the use of one language in low (L) communicative functions for which another language is being used. But, whereas RLS efforts are often spurred by the speech community itself, language spread efforts are orches-trated generally by the state and its agencies and co-occur with more global forces such as trade or religion. And, as we said before, language spread concerns itself with high (H) functions.

Language planning is a "body of ideas, laws and regulations . . . , change rules, beliefs, and practices intended to achieve a planned change . . . in . . . language use," while *language policies* are the laws and regulations that constitute a part of language planning (Kaplan and Baldauf 1997a: 3). Language spread can be spurred on by language planning, which may be accompanied by language policy. But, as we will see, language spread can also be unplanned and can take place without the support of any policy (Baldauf 1994).

The Characteristics of Language Spread: Who, What, Where, and When?

Language spread has been characterized as taking an upbeat perspective (Fishman 1988), as the language adds speakers and functions. We use the acronym ADDS- B to contextualize language spread within its additive context while defining its characteristics: Additive, Dominant, Dynamic, Sustained over time, and Broad. We will look at each of these defining characteristics of language spread individ-ually.

Modern language spread most often results in additive bilingualism and even in multilingualism. According to Fishman, language spread often starts with the acquisition of a language or of a variety for H functions, such as technological, economic, governmental, high cultural, religious, and literacy-related functions in education. It is the increased globalization of the past two decades of the twentieth century that has spurred the spread of languages of wider communication (LWC), in particular of English, with bilingualism and multilingualism being desired out-comes. As globalization takes hold, new communicative functions are created that respond to the movement of capital and people around the globe and a prolifer-ation of new products and services. Speakers who wish to participate in this new world order are then increasingly aware and favorably inclined to learn and adopt the language or language variety that will enable them to partake of this new economic order. The increased use of English on the Internet is the most obvious example.

Kachru (1986) refers to the "alchemy of English," suggesting that the spread of English has resulted in nonnative varieties of English, used extensively in non-English society for H functions, for example, even in literature (Thumboo 1987). English, Phillipson (1994a, 1994b) tells us, has been globally marketed as the language of economic and technological progress, national unity, and international understanding. Thus, it has spread through ideological persuasion of access to socioeconomic incentives and favors.

Modern language spread doesn't usually result in subtractive bilingualism. Those subtractive situations are more aptly described as being situations of language shift, whereas groups of unequal power (whether immigrant populations or indigenous castelike populations like Native Americans) shift to the more dominant language. It is interesting that these subtractive situations occur today most commonly in the United States and England—contexts in which English continues to be forcibly imposed through a highly efficient school system. In the United States, the recent movement toward educational standards, especially in English, is an explicit manifestation of this effort.

It is precisely because of the additive nature of language spread that adoption of such language behavior usually starts, and is embraced by, indigenous populations, populations that are the victims of extensive power inequalities and for whom use of a second language, whether an international language like English or a colonial language like French, is an advantage. In countries of the Global South, where the divide between the poor and rich is great, it is only the elite that becomes bilingual. For example, Phillipson (1994a) points out that, in such "English speaking countries" as Kenya, Nigeria, and Pakistan, only a very few indigenous people are actually English speakers.

Combined with economic power, language spread also occurs only among groups that have a secure group language identity and for whom an additional language does not appear to be threatening. This is the difference, for example, between language spread in the Netherlands and language spread among the indigenous people of the Americas. In the former case, English has spread throughout the Netherlands, both in the Dutch-speaking and in the Frisian-speaking areas, without posing any threat to the language identity of the Dutch and the Frisians, because English does not compete with their languages. Yet, the spread of Dutch threatens the existence of Frisian, whose speakers have adopted protective policy against the spread of Dutch. Although Spanish has spread extensively throughout Latin America and has been vigorously imposed through conquest and colonization, there continues to be resistance against Spanish by members of impoverished and isolated indigenous groups who fear that the pull of economic advantages will lead to sure language death (Cobarrubias 1990; García 1999; Heath 1972).

Language spread responds to dominance of some kind, whether economic, political, ideological, or demographic, or dominance arising from communicative factors. It is the language that is contextually more powerful that spreads as a second or additional language because of the benefits that accrue to the adopters (Fishman 1977b, 1988). Scotton (1982: 85) reminds us that, in order for individuals to want to adopt another language or language variety, they must be dissatisfied with their socioeconomic status and confident that their lives will improve as a result of the new language behavior. Language spreads because there is dominance and because there are prospects for increased dominance. Language shift, however, concerns itself only with threatened languages.

To a lesser extent than economic, political, or demographic factors, religion can also account for the dominance that causes language spread. Religion, by insisting that prayer and ritual must be conducted in a certain language, may indeed be a very important factor in language spread (Ferguson 1982).

Because language spreads through dominance, it usually works from the top down; that is, it is the government or the cultural elite that first adopts and promotes the change. Dominance is also advanced through schools—especially through higher education—as well as through other special mechanisms controlled by the elite, such as the mass media, business, and employment (Fishman 1977b).

Language spread may be most effective in cities, where interaction is intensive and prevalent, where there is greater linguistic heterogeneity, which creates a communicative need for a lingua franca, and where there are governmental agencies and schools that can promote the spread of a different language.

Language spread is dynamic because the increase in pervasiveness of behavior toward language is a result of sociocultural change. Although language spread is always upbeat, its dynamism can hide the painful social dislocation of the adopters, sometimes resulting in conflict, pain, and loss (Fishman 1988).

Language spread takes place over an extended time. It is persistent, consistent, and repetitive, impacting duratively on language behavior. Mackey (1990) reminds us that the study of language spread is usually diachronic, and he uses demographic, geographic, and, especially, historic factors to explain the spread.

Finally, language spreads not only within groups, as does language shift and language maintenance, but also between groups. Thus, language spreads in a broad and extensive context, responsive to geopolitical interests. Language spreads among individuals and groups, as well as within a sociopolitical context. Scotton reminds us that "[i]t is misleading to study the spread of any language out of the context of change in the entire social system" (1982: 89).

Traditional diglossia allows for bilingual speakers who clearly differentiate between the L functions and the H functions for which the two languages are used. Language spread makes possible multiple language acquisition for H functions, a consequence of living in a modern globalized world. These H functions most often have to do with the globalization of trade and of the economy generally, therefore encouraging the acquisition of English; sometimes the H functions are influenced by the globalization of religion, as is the case in the acquisition of Arabic.

How and Why Language Spreads

The macro level of geopolitical interest may manifest itself consciously (as in language policy and language planning efforts), or it may be unplanned, with the pull toward the spreading language being a result of what Fishman refers to as the zeitgeist, in which "social mobility aspirations, hungers for material and leisure time gratifications and stylishness of the pursuit of modernity itself" (1988: 2) enter the picture. Yet Fishman himself believes that, if left unattended, the spreading language will eventually erode the other language(s) in the environment. Thus, for language spread to result in an additional language, it must be controlled through conscious language planning efforts.

Language spread also occurs because of the communicative needs in language contact situations. The spread of a trade pidgin along contact borders, its subsequent acquisition as a creole, and its eventual decreolization constitute examples of language spread (Holm 1988; Kaplan and Baldauf 1997; Stewart 1989).

Language spread is not subconscious, as is language maintenance because of its static characteristics. But language spreads only when people have some sense of power and control with which the language will interact (Scotton 1982). For example, the educated and the middle-class are more likely to adopt new language behaviors than are those for whom the acquisition of a new language will offer little change in the socioeconomic and political structure. Scotton herself provides evidence from Africa that the spread of a *lingua franca* depends upon the degree of socioeconomic integration. Fishman tells us that the spread of languages is facilitated by "the promise they hold to change the lives of their new speakers" (1988: 2).

Phillipson (1994a, 1994b), however, believes that, because language spread is tied to linguistic hierarchies in the new world order, it is never really left to chance and is most often accompanied by language planning, and often by language spread policy. Language spread policy is defined by Ammon as "attempts to entrench a language more deeply in its speakers, to increase their skills and improve their attitudes, or to enhance its status or extend its functions in any domain" (1997: 51). Ammon (1997) identifies the following five goals of language spread policy:

1. To increase communication
2. To spread one's ideology
3. To develop economic ties
4. To gain revenue from language study and products
5. To preserve national identity and pride.

Language spread policy, according to Ammon (1992: 47), can be explicit and declared, but it can also be undeclared (as in the case of Japan), covert (as in the case of Nazi Germany), or implicit (as in the case of Brazil). Language spread policy is not always directed by government or by independent organizations; it also involves the media, business, the scientific community, and institutions of higher education (Phillipson 1994a: 20). There are many agencies that promote or limit the spread of language by acting as motivators, propagandists, and pressure groups (Lewis 1982: 248). Among the most important agencies of language spread are the national language academies. Language planning deals with both corpus planning (especially standardization) and status planning. Ammon (1992, 1994) has described at length the Federal Republic of Germany's overt policy of spreading German. Although language spread policy is commonly top-down, there have been various attempts to contain it through bottom-up efforts, such as those described in Hornberger (1997) and Rivera (1999).

CONCLUSION

The questions raised in Cooper's (1982a) language spread framework ("Who adopts what, when, where, why and how?") can be summatively answered. Missing from such answers, however, are the complex interaction of all those factors that defines language spread:

1. Who adopts?
   - Those individuals who are high up in the social system, who stand to gain, who need to achieve, and who are secure in their language identity, thus being open to change
   - Those communicative networks that stand to gain from the spread of one language because it provides them with a lingua franca enabling both intergroup and intragroup communication, thus increasing trade,

improving economic and educational opportunity, or promoting religious/ideological fervor.

2. How does adoption work?
   • Generally adopters first become aware of the language innovation and become favorably disposed to it. Behaviors of psychological import (awareness and evaluation) precede behaviors of psycholinguistic and sociolinguistic import (knowledge and use).

3. What structural and functional characteristics of language are associated with adoption?
   • Functional characteristics dealing with domain-specific use and especially high-literacy/econotechnology spur the adoption. Whether the adoption includes receptive or productive language behaviors depends on the communicative need.

4. When does adoption take place? Why does it take place at different speeds?
   • The higher the benefit of adoption, and the higher the density and repeatedness of the language behavior, the faster the adoption.

5. Where does adoption take place?
   • First in H societal domains that are functionally restricted.

6. Why does adoption take place?
   • Because there are enough personal and societal incentives.

7. How does adoption take place?
   • It is most often spurred by language planning activities, but many times without them, as long as the incentive is high enough. To be adopted as an additional language, the spreading language must be curbed by language planning efforts, and even through language policy.

Language spread is not a new phenomenon, but it is a highly complex one. As the study of language spread has expanded and demanded a multidisciplinary and multidimensional level of analysis, the cases of language spread have contracted. Early in the twenty-first century, English is not the sole language that is spreading. Spanish and French as colonial languages continue to spread. Arabic and Hausa are also spreading. But, increasingly, the focus is on English, as it spreads not only around the Global South (which had been gaining English speakers since the days of colonization) but also significantly throughout the Global North. English has not only spread through cultures, but cultures have spread across English (García and Otheguy 1989).

In 1988, Kachru observed that one reason for the spread of English was its "propensity for acquiring new identities, its power of assimilation, its adaptability to decolonization as a language, its manifestation in a range of lects, and its provision of a flexible medium for literary and other types of creativity across languages and cultures" (1988: 222). Today we find that English spreads because it has increasingly become synonymous with globalization and with the economic and technological progress that accompanies it. English has also spread, however, because as English has spread across cultures, as cultures have spread across English, it has become a medium capable of expressing messages of global order.

In postimperialist times (Fishman, Conrad, and Rubal-Lopez 1996), English has succeeded in shedding its Anglo-American identity. As it has spread, it has gained new speakers and has spawned new nativized English varieties (Kachru 1982, 1992). Because of its global identity, English has spread even in Cuba, isolated by the United States through a forty-year-old economic embargo (Corona and García 1996).

The spread of English, increasingly focused on itself as it permeates the global economy, provides us with intensity and focus, coupled with the extensiveness and the multidisciplinary/multilevel perspective, that continue to make the study of language spread a difficult sociolinguistic enterprise.

CHAPTER 28

....

LANGUAGE SHIFT AND LANGUAGE REVITALIZATION

....

NANCY H. HORNBERGER

LANGUAGE shift refers to "the gradual displacement of one language by another in the lives of the community members" (Dorian 1982: 44), manifested as loss in number of speakers, level of proficiency, or range of functional use of the language. The contrasting term has traditionally been language maintenance, which "denotes the continuing use of a language in the face of competition from a regionally and socially more powerful or numerically stronger language" (Mesthrie 1999: 42). Implicitly, these terms connote a contact situation and power differential between two or more speech communities (Hyltenstam and Stroud 1996: 568; also Brenzinger 1997: 274); it is usually speakers of the minority language (in numerical or power terms) who shift away from or maintain use of their own language vis-à-vis the majority language.

Language shift and language maintenance as a field of inquiry dates back to the earliest days of sociolinguistics, in particular to the work of Joshua Fishman (1964, 1965) and above all his monumental and groundbreaking *Language Loyalty in the United States* (1966). Other early and influential studies in this field include Heinz Kloss's *American Bilingual Tradition* (1977), on immigrant language maintenance and shift in the United States; Susan Gal's *Language Shift* (1979), on the social determinants of the shift from Hungarian to German in the Austrian village of Oberwart; and Nancy Dorian's *Language Death* (1981), on morphological manifestations of language loss in older and younger speakers of East Sutherland Gaelic in northern Scotland. More recent studies, outside the United States and Europe, include Jane Hill and Kenneth Hill's *Speaking Mexicano* (1986), on central Mexican Nahuatl speakers' resistance to and incorporation of Spanish into their way of speaking, and Don Kulick's *Language Shift and Cultural Reproduction* (1992), on the "cosmological" reasons behind one Papua New Guinea village's shift away from its local language, Taiap, and toward Tok Pisin.

The factors that contribute to language maintenance and shift are diverse and complex, making the science of prediction elusive if not impossible, though scholars have proposed models and typologies of relevant factors. Conklin and Lourie (1983: 174–175) provide a comprehensive list of political, social, and economic factors, cultural factors, and linguistic factors that influence language maintenance and shift. Giles, Bourhis, and Taylor (1977) construct a model of the vitality of an ethnolinguistic group (and their language) in terms of status, demographic, and institutional support factors, specifically economic, social, sociohistorical, and language status; geographic distribution and numbers; and institutional support through mass media, religion, education, and government. (For recent studies using this model, see Evans 1996 on Spanish language maintenance among Mexican Americans in the U.S. Southwest and Yagmur et al. 1999 on Turkish in Australia.) Edwards (1992) proposes a typology of minority-language-situation variables that affect language maintenance and loss, organized as a grid attending to demographic, sociological, linguistic, psychological, historical, political, geographic, educational, religious, economic, and media perspectives on the speakers, their language, and the setting, respectively. (This work follows Haugen 1972 in taking an ecology of language approach; see Mühlhäusler, this volume.)

Language revitalization has arisen as a scholarly and activist focus of concern[1] primarily in the 1990s, in conjunction with the increasing recognition that an alarming portion of the world's languages are endangered (Krauss 1992). Defined as "the attempt to add new forms or new functions to a language which is threatened with language lost or death with the aim of increasing its uses and users" (King 2001: 4), language revitalization is closely related to earlier sociolinguistic concerns with vitality (Stewart 1968) and revival (Edwards 1993; Fellman 1974) and with more recent notions of renewal (Brandt and Ayoungman 1989: 43) and reversing language shift (Fishman 1991).

Language revitalization, renewal, or reversing language shift goes one step further than language maintenance, in that it implies recuperating and reconstructing something that is at least partially lost, rather than maintaining and strengthening what already exists. The change in emphasis is at least in part a reflection of the changing and increasingly threatened circumstances of the world's languages, in particular indigenous languages, in the last years of the twentieth century. Consider the case of Quechua, the largest indigenous language of South America, with some eight to twelve million speakers, but nevertheless a threatened language (Hornberger and King 2000). While Hornberger's dissertation research on Quechua in Peru in the early 1980s was formulated around the question of language maintenance (Hornberger 1988, 1989), a decade later her student King formulated her research on Quichua in Ecuador around the question of revitalization and reversing language shift (King 2001, Hornberger and King 1996), a change in research focus at least partially attributable to the growing threat to even such a large indigenous language as Quechua.

Whereas work on language maintenance (and shift) has focused as much on immigrant as on indigenous languages (or perhaps more so), language revitalization work carries a particular emphasis on indigenous languages; for example, Fishman's *Reversing Language Shift* (1991) includes among its thirteen cases Irish, Frisian, Basque, Catalan, Navajo, Maori, and Australian aboriginal languages, and his *Can Threatened Languages be Saved?* (2001) includes these, plus Ainu, Andamanese, Quechua, and indigenous languages of Mexico and Nigeria, as well. Likewise, while research on language maintenance and shift has been biased toward documenting cases of shift rather than maintenance (Hyltenstam and Stroud 1996: 568), documentation on language revitalization emphasizes the positive side of the equation, despite the seemingly insurmountable odds against survival of the languages in question. Another difference between maintenance and revitalization work is the relative emphasis placed on conscious and deliberate efforts by speakers of the language to affect language behavior, that is, on language planning. While language maintenance has long been recognized as a language planning goal (e.g., Nahir 1977, 1984), and language revitalization only more recently so, nevertheless it is also true that maintenance can describe a "natural" language phenomenon that does not require any deliberate planning on the part of its speakers, while revitalization cannot. Finally, whereas language maintenance efforts have often tended to emanate from the top down (in which someone takes benevolent initiative in "maintaining" someone else's language), language revitalization efforts tend to originate within the speech community itself. For that reason, and because there is another section in this volume devoted to the topic of language policy and planning, the present chapter emphasizes community-based rather than government-led language planning efforts (see Chapters in Part VIII this volume).

The following discussion focuses on work in the second half of the 1990s, and, given the recent trend toward greater attention to language revitalization and to endangered languages in particular, those are also emphasized here. I provide, first, an overview of selected work on endangered language shift and revitalization by geographic region of the world; this is followed by a highlighting of themes and trends in the field; the chapter concludes with some unresolved conceptual and methodological issues. Much of the work cited here is published in two journals that readers may want to consult for further detail and additional cases: the *International Journal of the Sociology of Language* (*IJSL*), edited, since its founding in 1974, by Joshua Fishman, and the *Journal of Multilingual and Multicultural Development* (*JMMD*), edited, since its founding in 1980, by John Edwards.[2]

ENDANGERED LANGUAGE SHIFT AND REVITALIZATION AROUND THE WORLD

Krauss announced (1992) and reaffirmed (1998b: 103) that only an estimated 5–10 percent of the world's six thousand extant languages are safe, and 20–50 percent are moribund, thus leaving 40–75 percent endangered. His and others' calls to both scholarship and action on behalf of endangered languages have been resoundingly taken up, especially in the past half-decade. (See Craig 1997: 268–269 for a brief history of the Linguistic Society of America's response to the situation of endangered languages.) International nonprofit organizations such as Terralingua and the Endangered Language Fund promote and advocate language revitalization efforts through their websites, newsletters, and project funding. Long-standing scholarly organizations such as the Society for the Study of the Indigenous Languages of the Americas, now more than twenty years old, also regularly report on colloquia, news items, and strategies of support for endangered languages.

Research attention to the maintenance and revitalization of endangered languages burgeoned in the 1990s, as well. By way of sketching the recent richness of cases and coverage, I cite here only selected works that have appeared since 1996. Edited collections on endangered indigenous languages in the Americas include volumes on North, South, and Meso-America (Hornberger 1996; McCarty and Zepeda 1998); on Latin America (Freeland 1999); on North American Indian and Alaska Native languages (Cantoni 1996; McCarty, Watahomigie, and Yamamoto 1999; Reyhner 1997; Reyhner et al. 1999); and on Alaska, California, Hawaii, and the Solomon Islands (Henze and Davis 1999).

In addition to the American cases cited, other cases of endangered language shift and revitalization discussed in the very recent literature include, by region of the world:

- Australia—immigrant languages (Clyne and Kipp 1997) and aboriginal languages (Lowell and Devlin 1999; Wurm 1999)
- New Zealand—community languages (Holmes 1997) and Maori language (Chrisp 1997; Durie 1999; May 1999a; Spolsky 1996)
- Africa—language revitalization among Western Bantu speakers in Uganda (Bernsten 1998); the rise of Lingala in eastern Zaire (Goyvaerts 1997); the

death of Berber in Tunisia (Battenburg 1999); and the status of K'emant, one of the most threatened languages of Ethiopia (Leyew 1998)

- Asia—Chinese speakers in Singapore (Wei et al. 1997); Sindhis in Malaysia (Khemlani-David 1998); indigenous languages in Japan and the Solomon Islands (Wurm 1999); and minority languages in Dehong, China (Xiao 1998)
- Siberia and Russia—Estonians shifting to Russian (Viikberg 1999); Evenki and Yukagir speakers shifting to Yakut or Russian (Wurm 1999); and Karelians shifting to Russian (Pyöli 1998)
- Europe—the Sami of Norway (Todal 1999); Iranian immigrants in Sweden (Sohrabi 1997); and Dutch language loss in French Flanders (Willemyns 1997)
- Middle East—minority languages in Israel (Spolsky and Shohamy 1999a, 1999b) and Judeo-Spanish speakers in Istanbul, Turkey (Altabev 1998).

This is by no means a comprehensive listing of cases reported on, but serves as a sample and basis for the following highlighting of trends and unresolved questions in the field.

THEMES AND TRENDS IN THE STUDY OF LANGUAGE SHIFT AND REVITALIZATION

I highlight here only four themes that permeate recent work in language shift and revitalization: linguistic human rights, literacy and education as vehicles for shift and revitalization, community-based revitalization efforts, and the controversial link between language and identity in revitalization initiatives.

There is a natural affinity between language revitalization efforts and the advocacy of linguistic human rights (Skutnabb-Kangas and Phillipson 1995); after all, the impetus behind language revitalization is speakers' desire—and their right—to speak their own language. Two articles in Hamel's special *IJSL* issue on *Linguistic Human Rights from a Sociolinguistic Perspective* (1997b) deal directly with language maintenance and shift (and others do so implicitly): Hamel (1997a), based on his research in Hñähñú (Otomí) and other indigenous areas of Mexico, proposes a sociolinguistic framework for defining and implementing linguistic human rights in contexts of language conflict and shift; and Hornberger (1997) draws on ethnographic research with Quechua speakers in Peru and with Puerto Ricans and Cambodian refugees in Philadelphia to explore the degree to which the development of literacy in a minority language does, or does not, contribute to minority linguistic human rights and minority language maintenance.

The ambiguous role of literacy and education in language maintenance and shift is a concern presaged by Gaarder (1977) and taken up in subsequent book-length ethnographic studies by Hornberger (1988), on Quechua in southern Peru, and McLaughlin (1992), on Navajo in the U.S. Southwest. Grenoble and Whaley (1998: 32) consider the role of literacy so important (though controversial) in language endangerment that they argue for its inclusion as a variable in their modified version of Edwards's (1992) typology. Despite the demonstrably complex and ambivalent relationships among literacy, education, and language shift/main-tenance/revitalization, literacy and education continue to be a productive focus of language revitalization efforts everywhere. McCarty and Zepeda (1995) bring to-gether papers concerned with the aims and effects of American Indian/Alaska Native bilingual and bicultural programs in relation to the survival of indigenous languages. Hornberger (1998) provides evidence from Shawandawa, in the Brazilan Amazon; Quechua, in the Andes; East Indian communities of South Africa; Khmer in Philadelphia; Welsh in the United Kingdom; Maori in New Zealand; Turkish in the United Kingdom, and Native Californian languages that language education (and language policy) can serve as vehicle(s) for promoting the vitality, versatility, and stability of indigenous and immigrant languages.

Very often the confluence of linguistic human rights with literacy or educa-tional initiatives directed toward language revitalization is in community-based education efforts, such as those reported in May's (1999b) edited volume. Indeed, May argues that indigenous community-based education is predicated on the prin-ciple of self-determination, which in turn encompasses the retention and pro-motion of indigenous languages and cultures (May 1999a: 1). Community-based education initiatives are also reported in the *IJSL* issue edited by McCarty and Zepeda (1998) and include efforts by Native California Indians to revive and main-tain community languages via such measures as the Master-Apprentice Language Learning Program which pairs older native speakers with younger members of the tribe who want to learn the ancestral language, as well as immersion preschool initiatives, the development of writing systems, and the formation of a committee of Advocates for Indigenous California Language Survival (Hinton 1998); and approaches being attempted in the Tohono O'odham community of Arizona to maintain their language via oral tradition and computer technology, not to men-tion the potential role of the lucrative gaming industry in turning the tide of their language loss (Zepeda 1998). In addition to accounts such as these by academic linguists, anthropologists, and educators, McCarty and Zepeda (1998) have inter-woven narratives by speakers of indigenous languages—"language autobiogra-phies" that attest powerfully to the compelling reasons why indigenous community members invest so much time, energy, and effort in revitalization efforts.

These narratives also point to the importance of identity in language revitalization efforts, a topic explored by contributors to Henze and Davis (1999). Warner, for example, argues forcefully against "an ideology whereby language is viewed as an autonomous entity distinct from the people from whom it evolved" (1999: 78); such an ideology, he suggests, is promoted by non-Hawaiians for political reasons of their own but is ultimately damaging to the cause of Hawaiian revitalization. Similarly, *A Place to Be Navajo*, a monograph by Teresa McCarty (2002), in honor of the thirtieth anniversary of the Rough Rock Community School, documents in rich detail how the community-based bilingual and bicultural program at the Rough Rock School provides a space not only for Navajo language to be maintained and revitalized but also for Navajo identity to flourish. Wurm asserts, with respect to Australian aboriginal languages, that "it was the very strong reawakened feeling of ethnic identity and a strong resurgence of Aboriginal pride . . . that led to efforts at maintaining and revitalizing languages" (1999: 169). Bernsten regards the language revitalization effort by Western Bantu speakers as an example of "an ethnic group working to maintain its identity by maintaining its language and expanding its domain" (1998: 104). Others, such as Jones (1998), on Breton; Wong (1999), on Hawaiian; and King (2001), on Ecuadorian Quichua, document the tensions around authenticity and identity that can arise between traditional speakers of a threatened language and younger speakers who learn the revitalized language through schooling and become advocates for a newly articulated authenticity and identity which may be somewhat at odds with the traditional ones. (See also Dorian 1994 on purism versus compromise in these matters.) Still others—such as Bankston and Henry (1998), on Cajun French in Louisiana, Khemlani-David (1998), on Sindhis in Malaysia, and Wei et al. (1997), on the Teochew community in Singapore—raise questions about the indissolubility of the language-identity bond, suggesting that speakers may place "the instrumental value of a language above [its] sentimental or symbolic value (Wei et al. 1997: 380). Further, it has been suggested that the language-and-identity ideology is in direct conflict with another powerful ideology that supports minority language survival, namely the ideology of language-and-territory (Myhill 1999).

Unresolved Conceptual and Methodological Issues

Myhill believes it is important to address the conflict in ideologies mentioned earlier, since the language-and-identity ideology "undermine[s] the efforts of those working to preserve indigenous minority languages threatened by demographic swamping, as speakers of mainstream languages move into areas historically dominated by indigenous languages but do not learn or use these indigenous languages"(1999: 34), while the language-and-territory ideology "undermines the immigrant language supporter who is trying to fight for public acceptance of the immigrant language" (1999: 36); furthermore, he suggests not the choice of one ideology over the other but rather a synthesis that provides "general principles regarding when one ideology should take priority over the other" (1999: 47).

Grenoble and Whaley (1998) argue for modifications to Edwards's (1992) typology, including the addition of literacy as a variable (mentioned earlier), the ranking of variables in terms of their predictive ability (e.g., the potential of economics to outweigh the other variables [Grenoble and Whaley 1998: 31]), and the expansion of the "setting" category into local, regional, national, and extranational settings. While providing three case studies to justify these proposals (the general pattern of language endangerment in sub-Saharan Africa, the decline of Evenki in Siberia, and the revitalization of Maori in New Zealand), they also acknowledge that many details remain to be filled in before the typology can be applied consistently (Grenoble and Whaley 1998: 52). Similarly, Fishman's eight-stage Graded Intergenerational Disruption Scale (GIDS) for reversing language shift is undergoing continuing criticism and refinement based on both theoretical concerns and the experience of applying it in different language revitalization contexts (e.g., Edwards 1993; Fishman 2001, Myhill 1999).

Scholars have recently begun to call for approaches to language shift and language revitalization that go beyond attention to surface linguistic structure on the one hand and macrolevel societal domains on the other. Wei and colleagues suggest that the "only coherent model which has been widely used in the study of language maintenance and language shift has been Fishman's domain analysis which focuses on the habitual language use of individual speakers" and that what is needed (and what they hope their work contributes to) is a model for analyzing underlying sociocultural processes, including both macrolevel social, political, and economic changes and linguistic and psychological processes of individual speakers in interaction, as they relate to changes in habitual language use (Wei et al. 1997: 365). Similarly, Holmes (1997: 33) warns that survey methods in and of themselves may unwittingly hasten the demise of community languages, since they focus on general trends and conceal detail, and she recommends the use of census/survey methods to document change in sociolinguistic norms over time, complemented by more detailed ethnographic research to provide information on how those changes came about (Holmes 1997: 26). Hamel, too, recommends finding ways to get at an understanding of underlying processes of language shift as "constituted and reproduced in verbal interaction" (Hamel 1997a: 109); he argues for a sociolinguistic framework that takes into account not only linguistic structure (i.e., phonology, morphology, syntax, semantics) but also discourse structure (i.e., discourse strategies, organization of interaction) and cultural models (i.e., discourse styles, habitus).

Grappling with these unresolved conceptual and methodological issues can only strengthen work in language shift and language revitalization. The overriding unresolved issue is, of course, the defining question of the field: How to predict which languages will shift, which will be maintained, and which successfully revitalized? Though this question is perhaps ultimately unanswerable, given the complexity and unpredictability of human existence, the rewards of pursuing an answer are immeasurable.

NOTES

1. Language revitalization thus becomes the third in the trinity of logical alternatives for minority language use and change in situations of language contact—language shift and maintenance being the other two.

2. In preparation for this chapter, the 1996–1999 issues of the following journals were searched and consulted, in addition to the *IJSL* and *JMMD*, already mentioned: *Anthropological Linguistics, Anthropology and Education Quarterly, Applied Linguistics, Bilingual Research Journal, Discourse and Society, International Journal of Bilingual Education and Bilingualism, Language and Education, Language in Society, Language Problems and Language Planning.* I am especially grateful to Doris S. Warriner for her timely and strategic assistance in identifying and summarizing relevant literature and for her invaluable feedback on the first draft of this chapter.

CHAPTER 29

ECOLOGY OF LANGUAGES

PETER MÜHLHÄUSLER

ERNST Haeckel, who coined the term *ecology* in 1866, characterized it in this way:

> By ecology we mean the body of knowledge concerning the economy of nature—
> the investigation of the total relations of the animal both to its inorganic and
> its organic environment; including, above all, its friendly and inimical relations
> with those animals and plants with which it comes directly or indirectly into
> contact—in a word, ecology is the study of all those complex interrelations re-
> ferred to by Darwin as the conditions of the struggle for existence. (Translation
> by R. Brewer 1988: 1)

Since this passage was written, a number of things have changed. One such
change is the extension of the ecology metaphor to new domains, such as the
ecology of mind or the ecology of language. A second change is the re-evaluation
of the notion of "the conditions of the struggle for existence." Functioning ecologies are characterized by predominantly mutually beneficial links and only to a
small degree by competitive relationships.

Ecological thinking has a number of distinguishing characteristics, including:

- Considerations not just of system internal factors but of wider environ-
  mental considerations
- Awareness of the dangers of monoculturalism
- Awareness of the limitations of both natural and human resources
- Long-term vision
- Awareness of those factors that sustain the health of ecologies.

The first use of the ecology metaphor in linguistics is found in a paper by
Voegelin, Voegelin and Schutz (1967) on the language varieties in Arizona, where

a distinction between intralanguage and interlanguage ecology is drawn. The meta-phor was introduced independently in Haugen's seminal paper, titled "The Ecol-ogy of Language" (1972, based on a lecture given in 1970), where he defines it as "the study of interactions between any given language and its environment" (1972: 325). The notion of environment includes the question "What concurrent lan-guages are employed by speakers of a given language?" (1972: 336). Since then, there has been a great deal of descriptive work on a number of multilingual ecologies (e.g., Denison 1982 for the European languages), as well as considerable conceptual refinement (e.g., Enninger and Haynes 1984). By the early 1980s, the importance of this notion to applied linguistics had become established, partic-ularly for the problem of language shift and loss (Mackey 1980).

ECOLOGY AS A STRUGGLE FOR EXISTENCE

Characteristics of most earlier work on language ecology is the dominance of the "struggle for existence" metaphor. Mackey highlights this competition:

> Languages too must exist in environments and these can be friendly, hostile or indifferent to the life of each of the languages. A language may expand, as more and more people use it, or it may die for lack of speakers. Just as com-petition for limited bio-resources creates conflict in nature, so also with lan-guages. (1980: 34)

The same emphasis is encountered in Denison:

> There is a sense in which all the languages and varieties in an area such as Europe constantly act in supplementation of each other and in competition with each other for geographical, social and functional *Lebensraum*; hence the metaphorical appropriateness of the term "ecology." (1982: 6)

Again, Nelde argues:

> I would like to put forward the argument here that an ecological viewpoint is not of paramount importance for the description of stable diglossic or multilin-gual linguistics areas or for open bilingual conflict ones, but rather for linguis-tics/ethnic contact areas in which one or more languages or variants are in danger of dying without any apparent political decisions, whether linguistic, ad-ministrative or repressive, being made. (1987: 40)

It seems extraordinary that Nelde reserves the ecological perspective for "patho-logical" situations and denies its use for gaining understanding of the many situations in the world where language contact did not result in conflict and where a large number of languages could co-exist in a single communal community.

Denison's and Nelde's views can, of course, be explained by their concentration on the effects of nation-states and national languages, two constructs that indeed have led to a great deal of linguistic conflict and to the endangerment of many smaller forms of speaking. To regard European conditions as the measure of all things has been unhelpful and remains problematic when it is applied to the strengthening of endangered languages around the globe. Empowering languages and making them more competitive by giving them grammars, lexicons, writing systems, and school syllabuses is a recipe that ignores a basic ecological fact: What supports one language may not support another language. Each language requires its own ecological system.

On the Inhabitants of Language Ecologies

Denison (1982: 8) drew attention to a weakness of Haugen's ecological metaphor, the notion of language itself, which Haugen equates with a code: "However, the picture is greatly complicated by the fact that each language (variety), far from being a separate, independent organism or species is rather to be seen as a symbiotic conglomerate" (1972: 325). The characterization of languages as fixed grammatical codes is at best unnecessarily reductionist and at worst a contributing factor in the loss of linguistic diversity. Before the advent of European nation-states, there were a number of dialect continua such as the Germanic, stretching from the north of Scandinavia to the north of Italy and consisting of an indefinite number of varieties, of which the proximate ones were mutually intelligible and the more distant ones were not. This continuum today has been overlaid by a number of superimposed official (standard) languages such as Swedish, Norwegian, German, Dutch, or Letze, each of them associated with a nation-state. Such national languages as Haugen points out are cultural artifacts. The ecological support system needed to sustain them consists of political and educational institutions, information technology, and such like. It would be unwise to regard the species "European national language" as the canonical case of an inhabitant of an ecology.

The label *language* is not applicable to the ways of speaking in pre–nation-state Europe and, indeed, to the ways humans communicate in more traditional settings. For the Pacific area, Grace (1993a, 1993b) has re-examined the notion of "languages" as employed by mainstream linguistics and demonstrated its insufficiency in cases other than a few mainstream standard national languages.

As in the case of Europe, in many parts of the Pacific we find long chains of interrelated dialects and languages with no clear internal boundaries. In Micronesia, a group of very closely related languages is spoken all the way from Truk, in the east, to Tobi, in the west. As observed by Bender (1971), "there are some indications that it is possible to establish a chain of dialectal connections from one end to the other with all contiguous dialects being mutually intelligible." The question as to how many distinct languages can be counted in the group remains difficult to answer, for those who regard it as a sensible question. Bender concludes that, "altogether there are between 10 and 20 languages indigenous to the cultural-geographic area of Micronesia, the indeterminacy in numbers reflects the indeterminacy as to language limit among certain of the nuclear languages" (1982: 46).

Professional linguists, nevertheless, have identified such languages as Sonsoralese, Ulithian, Satawalese, Puluwat, Namonuiti, and Trukese, the latter having become the language par excellence in this chain, as it is the best-described variety and is spoken at the center of economic and communicational activities. In many other areas, the place where missionaries, administrators, or linguists settle has become the focus of development of linguistic systems of "language" status. Arbitrary points on a linguistic continuum are made into discrete abstract entities called "languages," whereas all other reference points on the same continuum, unless of course some important outsider settles there, become marginalized, dialectal deviations from the standard.

A particular problem arises when it comes to labeling the "languages" brought into being by acts of power and other historical contingencies. The act of name giving by European linguists and missionaries can be compared to Europeans inscribing colonial landscapes with their place-names. An unintended but nevertheless real outcome is that only those ways of speaking that have been named are regarded as languages and can potentially feature in catalogues such as the UNESCO Redbook of Endangered Languages. Being a named language brings with it other rights and privileges, such as, financial support for recognized minority languages within the European Union, and has led to considerable competition for status and recognition. The emergence of named regional languages in post-Franco Spain is a case in point: Galician, Asturian, and Valencian are examples of ways of speaking that are becoming bounded and recognized, in the case of the latter in an atmosphere of considerable political conflict. Numerous other ways of speaking are left behind in this process, including some that have had tenuous labels attached to them. So-called controversial languages of Europe include Aromanian, Lallans, Piedmontese, Sater, Tsakonian, Zayrian, and about fifty others. One concludes (see Mühlhäusler 1996a) that the notion of a language is not a description of the actual nature of most inhabitants of language ecologies but a metaphor, based on linguists' experience of European national languages whose applicability to other societies stands in need of explanation and justification.

Contact without Conflict

Competition and conflict are the consequence of certain cultural practices that privilege particular ways of speaking, such as that of the Île de France, located in the center of Paris, or, in the case of Kôte of Papua New Guinea, the variety spoken around the main mission station. This is not to deny that a certain amount of linguistic conflict undoubtedly also occurred in pre–nation-state language ecologies, but it seems unwarranted to characterize language ecologies as a battlefield. Recent understanding of natural ecologies suggests that, of the interrelationship between the inhabitants of any given ecology, the vast majority are mutually beneficial.

Ecological linguistics in recent years has begun to examine the question of how, in many parts of the world, a large diversity of ways of speaking manages to co-exist side by side, often being used by the same communication community (e.g., Fill 1993). When applied to the language ecologies of Melanesia and Australia, the usefulness of Nelde's conflict hypothesis as a working hypothesis for sociolinguistic and applied sociolinguistic research seems much reduced. In a brilliant article about the functions of linguistic diversity in Melanesia, for instance, Laycock (1981) drew attention to the seemingly paradoxical situation in Papua New Guinea, where, in the most isolated areas, with the most difficult terrain, such as the New Guinea Highlands, we find not only the largest languages and the least linguistic diversity (languages with up to 150,000 speakers) but also the largest amount of violent intergroup conflict, whereas in the coastal areas, with a much easier terrain, we encounter the greatest linguistic variety, few languages with more than five hundred speakers, extensive trade and cultural contacts, and, apparently, a much lesser degree of inter-group conflict.

How is it, we might ask with Laycock (1979), that languages with as few as fifty speakers appear to have survived in an environment that comprises many larger surrounding languages? Or one may ask, with Sutton (1991: 63), about the language diversity of the Wik languages, in Northern Australia, where a dozen or more language groups manage to co-exist in a very small geographical area over thousands of years in conditions of constant contact. A tentative conclusion seems to be that social conflict and language contact are independent parameters, not part of the same package, and that unity and cooperation are compatible with both a high degree of linguistic diversity and contact as well as quasi-monolingualism and isolation. In many Australian languages, one encounters a special sublanguage, called "mother-in-law" language, that can differ lexically and structurally from the everyday languages spoken in a community. This additional language serves the principal function of conflict reduction.

When one studies the complex language situation in Papua New Guinea, one notes that, in addition to the very large number of languages spoken in the area, there are numerous structurally reduced intervillage pidgins used in trade relations between different language groups. The function of these intervillage pidgins appears to be conflict reduction, as they are restricted to use in a small domain of discourse of the type that makes it unlikely that controversial topics will arise. Dutton (1983), in his study of the ancient Hiri trade language of Papua, points out that the language is not used by women or for talking about women, a domain that might cause violent conflict from time to time. One is reminded of Hymes's final sentence in his forword to Pütz's "Language Contact and Language Conflict" (1994): "A viable future will require complex articulations between practices that bring us together and others that allow us to be apart, *access and privacy, what is shared and what is unique in our identities,* verbal repertoires that include both lingue franche and personal choice" [emphasis added].

The cases outlined here are suggestive of a class of languages whose principal function is that of conflict reduction. The mechanisms involved are of several types:

1. *Impoverishment.* "Mother-in-law" language and a number of trade languages are referentially impoverished to such a degree as to reduce dramatically their ability to refer to conflict-generating topics. Modern sublanguages of English such as maritime English or aviation English are of a similar nature. They enable North and South Korean captains and pilots to communicate in one of the few domains in which neither party wishes to be confrontational. Pidgin languages, of course, are the reduced languages par excellence, and again and again we find them used as neutral forms of speech between politically hostile communities, one of the earliest pidgin Englishes, Chinese Pidgin English (CPE), being an example. It was used initially as a medium of communicating about a small range of trade commodities (see Baker and Mühlhäusler 1990). Impoverishment of the type found in pidginization affords a balance between the desiderata of access (for trade) and privacy (for keeping interpersonal and cultural distance).

2. *Esotericity.* This represents the flip side of the coin in creating social distance and conflict reduction and consists of making the language formally and lexically so complex as to make it virtually unlearnable to outsiders. Examples again abound in the traditional language ecology of

areas such as Melanesia. Very small societies with only one hundred or
so speakers appear to have spent a great deal of energy on complicating
the language. The Anêm language, whose esotericity has been characterized by Thurston in a number of publications (e.g., 1987), is one example. The members of such communities spend an enormous amount of
energy on linguistic socialization. Such are the complexities of these languages that no one under about twenty-five years of age is regarded as a
proficient speaker. Contact with outsiders is made through easier neighboring languages. In Western societies, legal English, Church languages,
and professional jargons such as medical talk are the equivalent of such
esoteric languages. Their very complexity makes it difficult for outsiders
to come into conflict with their users.

3. *Intercommunication.* A third solution to conflict reduction is that found
in Kupwar village in India (Gumperz and Wilson 1971), where a combination of grammatical convergence and lexical divergence enables
members of a highly multilingual community to function as a single
communication network. More complex versions of this type of intercommunication and contact with little conflict used to be found in New
Caledonia. Each small community actively used its own endolexicon but
passively understood several synonyms (the exolexicon). This enabled
them to communicate while overtly signaling their own identities.

The examples on which I have just elaborated afford some interesting generalizations:

- All three conflict-reducing strategies involve people using two or more
  languages. This bi- or multilingualism is of a stable type and is not transitional to monolingualism in a dominant language. There is no agenda—
  as found, for instance, among many Esperantists and other Western designers of world languages—to have a single language shared by all.
- The solutions are very clearly intercultural, not monocultural. They exhibit a linguistic repertoire that combines private language for intergroup
  identity with access languages for intergroup communication. In the cases
  surveyed, these access languages were relatively powerless.
- The typical locus of the linguistic ecologies studied is not a nation-state.
- None of the solutions is predicated on the idea that a shared code reduces
  conflict.

It is further noted that the reduction of linguistic conflict appears to require two
functional types of languages: identity preserving, and linking languages (*lingue
franche*).

Conflict appears to arise most readily when these two functions are "fudged,"
that is, when a language that is the language of identity of a community is em-

ployed as a linking language. English and French as international languages, or indeed as languages of a nation such as Great Britain and France, are cases in point. Their dual function almost automatically enhances their power and thereby reduces the power of the other languages that come into contact with them. Additional conflict can arise if the speakers of a powerless language switch to English, or French, or whatever, as their language of identity.

THE INDEPENDENCY HYPOTHESIS OF LANGUAGES

Mackey (1980) identifies another problem with Haugen's equation of language with a code—the impossibility of separating linguistic from other communicative behavior: "One may question the very existence of non-linguistic social behaviour, since both language (*langue*) and language (*langage*) are inseparably connected with all social activity." This contrasts with the view of modern linguists that (1) languages are given, and (2) language is independent of other considerations. Smith and Wilson, for instance, argue: "It seems to us that there is no way of describing or defining a given language without invoking the notion of a linguistics rule" (1979: 1); and later: "A human language . . . is a rule governed system, defin-able in terms of a grammar which separates grammatical from ungrammatical sentences, assigning a pronunciation and meaning to each grammatical sentence" (1979: 31). The independency view of language is largely foreign to members of non-Westernized societies; in discussing the Javanese concept of *Basa* Anderson argues:

> Basa, just like bahasa in Classical Malay, meant "language"; but it always in-cluded in its broad semantic field the notions of civility, rationality, and truth. This conception of "true" language meant that in the profoundest sense Java-nese (or in their local habitats, Sundanese, Balinese and Buginese) was isomor-phic with the world, as it were glued to it. It was this isomorphism, this inher-ence, that made for the efficacy of mantra. Because words, or particular combinations of them, contained Power, like *kings, grasses, banyan-trees* and *sa-cred images,* their utterance could unleash that Power directly on, and in, the word. (1990: 28)

Thus, *Basa,* is an entirely different concept of language from modern *Bahasa,* which emerged as a translation equivalent of Dutch *taal* in the sense of modern nation-state language defined by its grammar and lexicon. The absence of a clear boundary between linguistics and other cultural practices is documented for numerous other groups, as well. Australian indigenous ways of speaking, for instance, recognize the holistic package of speaking, knowledge, land, dreaming, people, and cultural practices, and this view has prevailed among many speakers of pre–nation-state languages of Europe, despite a pretense among linguists and politicians to reduce them to closed systems of rules.

The metaphor of ecology does not lend itself readily to accommodating a holistic view of language and culture. Its etymology is *oikos* house/home—a cultural artifact that has boundaries and recognizes distinct inhabitants, furniture, fittings, and so on. Whilst *oikos* denotes a static object, a holistic perspective sees speaking as an activity or mode of being.

Ecologies as Adaptive Systems

Language change in mainstream linguistics has been variably characterized as being governed by natural laws or by fashions. By contrast, an ecological perspective highlights adaptation to external circumstances as a major force. In support of this view, one can point to the coincidence of tribal and language boundaries and local natural ecologies in Australia, and a recent study by Glausinsz (1997) suggests a close correlation between language size and rainfall: Geographically spread-out languages are encountered typically in dry areas, while small languages predominantly occur in high-rainfall areas. The unstoppable spread of English (a high-rainfall language) over the entire globe under this view suggests problems for discourses about the management of resources in desert areas.

Mühlhäusler (1998) argues that the hypothesis of adaptation can be tested most conveniently with evidence from recently occupied "desert" islands: A particularly revealing case is that of the Pitkern/Norfolk language, which developed on Pitcairn after 1792 and which was transported to Norfolk Island in 1856. While the constant scarcity of food and water on the overpopulated Pitcairn Island led to the development of a rich vocabulary for natural life forms, the subsistence affluence on the much larger Norfolk Island did not require the naming of every plant or animal, and the lexicon for life forms in the Norfolk variety is far less developed as a consequence. The predominance of grammar for effective causality (e.g., in European languages) in environments where human actions can control nature against the predominance of inherent causality (things are what they are because they are what they are) or commutative constructions (being with) in environments difficult to control may be another example, but this hypothesis requires considerably more research.

As languages get transported around the globe, the fit between them and the environment in which they are spoken of necessity weakens. As linguistic adaptation to a new environment takes several hundred years (e.g., the development of complex plant classification in Maori after the arrival of Eastern Polynesian, with a much less complex system in New Zealand), this misfit is likely to be a prolonged one and may turn out to be an important task for language planners.

Types of Linguistic Ecologies

Ecolinguistics emphasizes the uniqueness of forms of human speaking, rather than abstract universal principals, and the abstractions presented here have to be regarded as exploratory pre-theoretical categories. This section draws on insights from a number of sources, most of them not written from a specifically ecolinguistic perspective.

An overview of writings on the psychology and sociology of language ecologies is given by Fill (1993: 14–17). The parameters that determine ecological processes in language and society, as listed by Fill, include:

1. Status and intimacy
2. Similarity and difference of language in contact
3. Number of competing languages
4. Cultural, religious, and economic factors
5. Frequency of intermarriage
6. Functional distribution
7. Degree of codification
8. External intervention (1993: 15ff.).

Haarmann (1980: 199) has argued that these variables have to be ecologically interconnected but does not provide a theoretical framework for achieving this. In my view, there are a number of additional parameters that need to be considered:

i. Whether languages are endemic or exotic to an ecology
ii. Degree of esotericity (closed in-group language) or exotericity (for intercommunication)
iii. Degree of vitality of the languages in an ecology
iv. Whether languages are "packaged" with or disconnected from the ecology

   v. Whether the language exhibits continuity (e.g., dialect or chains) or dis-
      continuity (abrupt boundaries)
  vi. Whether the language is named or unnamed (i.e., degree of recognition
      by speakers and outsiders)
 vii. Types of solutions for intergroup communication with outside groups
      (bilingualism, *lingua francas*, pidgins).

I cannot offer a theoretical framework for connecting all these parameters,
but I believe there are a number of typical ecologies that combine at least some
of them. The following are suggested:

   Type 1: balanced equitable ecologies
   Type 2: mixed endemic/exotic ecologies
   Type 3: competitive ecologies
   Type 4: language continuance and networks
   Type 5: artificial ecologies
   Type 6: isolated monolingual communities.

Type 1 is represented by highly multilingual regions such as Papua New
Guinea (Laycock 1979), the Cape York Peninsula of Queensland (Sutton 1991), and
Brazil (Aikhenvald 1999). Communication between the speakers of multiple small
languages is achieved either by multilingualism, silent barter, or a layered language
ecology where local languages are employed mainly to express local identity and
discuss local knowledge, intergroup pidgins (often with a 50/50 mixed lexicon and
a common core grammar) are employed mainly for transactions between villagers,
and regional lingua francas are employed mainly for signaling regional identity
and exchanging regionally important information. Examples of such layered ecologies have been documented for Native (Indian) Americans in the southern United
States by Drechsel (1997).
   Type 2 typifies mixed endemic, exotic communities that are the consequence
of large-scale population movement such as have taken place many times in human history. The coexistence, after initial disruptions, of earlier Papuan and later
Melanesian languages in New Guinea or Timor prior to European colonization
are examples, as are *sprachbunds* such as that of the Balkans or Arnhemland.
Prolonged contacts tend to result in the leveling of grammatical differences (familiarity leads to similarity), with lexical differences sufficient to signal separate
identities. The social structures in such communities discourage social mobility,
and both original endemic and later introduced languages co-exist side by side
for prolonged periods of time. The co-existence of Spanish and Guarani in postcolonial Paraguay is another instance.
   Type 3 includes competitive language ecologies. The stability of types 1 and 2
is a result of the relative lack of power of the communities that inhabit these
ecologies, while type 3 ecologies are characterized both by power differential and

by constant restructuring of the ecology. The link between political and linguistic power is not a necessary one. Before the advent of European nation-states, for instance, centralized political power and tolerance of linguistic diversity were both present: Austria-Hungary before 1918 and Yugoslavia before its disintegration after Tito's demise are examples. There is a continuing trend toward streamlining the linguistic ecologies of nation-states, with the consequent marginalization and extinction of numerous smaller ways of speaking. The spread of Bahasa Indonesia or Mandarin today parallel the spread of French in France in the nineteenth century. With new transnational units becoming more important, smaller national languages are pushed out by a small number of super languages such as English.

Type 4 consists of language continua and networks (see type 3) that presuppose a lack of competition and an absence of national boundaries. Modern communication technology tends to require language standards and is ill suited to continua or structured diversity.

Type 5 includes artificial ecologies. One can argue that diversity is natural and streamlining is artificial and, further, that most contemporary language ecologies are located at the artificial end of a continuum, with examples of instances where exotic world languages were elevated to national languages being particularly artificial. Thus, the processes that have made English the national language of the Philippines and of Namibia are for the main part deliberate (artificial) interference in a language ecology. Attempts to create artificial languages as additions to or replacements of existing ones have been made from time to time. The promotion of Esperanto as the preferred language of the European Union is a recent example.

Last, Type 6 comprises isolated monolingual countries. While isolated desert islands with a single language are an important discursive category, there are very few examples of prolonged isolation of monolingual communities. Easter Island Rapanui (Fischer 1992) has been mentioned, though even in that instance there are doubts. Linguistic isolates (languages with no structural or historical affinity to surrounding languages, such as Basque) tend to be accounted for in complex ecologies, and it can be argued that structured contacts, rather than isolation, promotes unique ways of speaking.

APPLICATIONS OF
ECOLOGICAL LINGUISTICS

Applied linguistics involves the address of linguistic theories to a range of practical tasks, such as teaching language, increasing document readability, decreasing obsolete racist and sexist aspects of language, and many others. As a general principle, the applicability of a linguistic theory is determined by the number and type of parameters it contains; the fewer parameters, the smaller the range of its applications. Time-free theory has little to contribute to problems of language development; monostylistic (monolectal) theory has little to contribute to problems of variable language use. A clear advantage of ecological linguistics over other theories is that it accounts for a large number of parameters and hence is particularly applicable to a range of practical tasks, including at least the following:

1. Language planning
2. Language revival
3. Second language learning
4. Literacy teaching
5. Ecotourism language
6. Environmentally appropriate language.

It has become widely accepted that second language teaching involves more than structure and lexicon and that, for teaching/learning to be lasting, the learners, the classrooms, the attitudes of both teachers and students, and many other factors need to be considered. Similarly, literacy is much more than skill in writing and reading. When the ecological conditions for a literate community are not given (e.g., Desert Schools, DEETYA 1996), literacy programs cannot take off.

Applied ecological linguistics begins with the question "What are the minimum ecological requirements to sustain a given linguistic practice over long periods of time?" The ultimate aim of all ecological planning is to promote structured diversity—and such structural diversity implicates the different subdomains listed earlier:

1. The preservation of a number of smaller languages in a single communication ecology rather than preservation of the most widely spoken or best-documented language
2. The offering of a range of sociologically and structurally different languages for second language learners, rather than the focusing on a single world language
3. The inclusion of native speakers and nonspeakers, as well as semispeakers, in language revival programs.

Applied ecological linguistics also aims at greater harmony between languages and their physical environment, rather than at mere "greenspeaking" (Harré, Brockmeier, and Mühlhäusler 1999), which conceals and distorts this relationship. A recent study on the language of ecotourism (Mühlhäusler and Peace 1999) suggests that nonecological focusing on a few charismatic species and heavy emphasis on "survival of the fittest" were common in this domain. Some observers have argued for environmentally more suitable language, paralleling arguments for gender, race, and age sensitivity.

Generally speaking, ecological linguists are weary of control and prescriptivism, and, particularly, of single solutions. Because ecologies are complex and generated by many parameters, understanding this complexity, rather than focusing on single and simple formulas or universalist explanations, is favored. As yet, streamlining and simple formulas remain the norm in applied linguistics, and genuinely ecological approaches are rare.

OUTLOOK

The linguistics ecology of the earth, like its natural ecology, has become highly disturbed in the past two hundred years, mainly as a result of European expansion, with the consequent restriction and destruction of the habitats of the majority of the world's linguistic ecologies. The metaphor of ecology makes available both explanations for this process and solutions for reversing the current trends, which, if left unchecked, may result in the disappearance of up to 90 percent of the world's languages within two generations.

Since Haugen first created the term language ecology as an aid to description, there has been a gradual shift toward seeing it as a focus for action. Language ecologies provide the home in which different communities can co-exist, and their diversity is seen as a valuable resource for restoring the disturbed relationship between human beings and their natural environment.

The notion of language ecology and ecological linguistics can't be reconciled with the system-focused and universalist trend in modern linguistics. Ecologically aware linguists (e.g., the contributors to Fill's 1996 volume) regard modern linguistics as empirically unsustainable, as irrelevant, and as an obstacle to applied linguistics.

PART IX

LANGUAGE POLICY AND PLANNING

CHAPTER 30

METHODOLOGIES FOR POLICY AND PLANNING

RICHARD B. BALDAUF, JR.

ALTHOUGH a number of books have been written about research methodology appropriate for applied linguistics (e.g., Hatch and Lazaraton 1991) and for the subfields of (second) language learning (e.g., Brown 1988; Johnson 1992; Nunan 1992; Seliger and Shohamy 1989) and language testing (e.g., Henning 1987; Mc-Namara 1996), little attention has been paid to the methodology appropriate for one of the other major areas within applied linguistics—language policy and planning (cf. Eastman 1983b, Ch. 6; Kaplan and Baldauf 1997, Ch. 4). While journals like the TESOL Quarterly frequently discuss issues related to research methodology for language teaching (e.g., Brown 1991, 1992; *TESOL Quarterly* [28. 4.] 1994), there is very little in the way of substantive discussion of language policy and planning (hereafter LPP) methodology in the journals or in related literature.

Given the lack of easily recognizable material explicitly relating to LPP methodology, this chapter has been developed as a survey based on a corpus review of published LPP literature as found in *Linguistic and Language Behavior Abstracts* (*LLBA*) from 1973 to 1998 and as available on WebSPIRS. Using such a corpus of studies has advantages (e.g., there are abstracts, the material is published and usually readily available, the abstract is computer searchable, and it is widely used as an authoritative source) and disadvantages (e.g., it doesn't include government reports and other ephemeral material that may be the initial products of language planning; it probably has the limitations of other databases—selectivity, long lead time for item entry, different selection criteria at different times, bias in favor of articles in English or other "modernized languages"—for a discussion of these issues see Baldauf and Jernudd 1983). Nevertheless, the large number of studies in the corpus provides an initial starting point for doing a broadly based review of LPP methodology.

AN OVERVIEW OF LANGUAGE POLICY AND PLANNING PUBLICATION

It has been asserted that LLP is a relatively new but growing field, dating back to the late 1960s as language planning and to the late 1940s as language engineering. Its initial focus on polity-level solutions for language problems in emerging states has been replaced with a broader emphasis both in geography and scope (micro-, meso, and macrostudies). The LPP literature has always been scattered and diverse, with only a few specialist journals, reflecting at least partly the variety of disciplines that contribute to the field. To understand the nature and scope of the field better, the LPP literature, as defined by the *LLBA* database, was examined to construct a LPP corpus. The *LLBA* used for this study was an on-line version that covers a twenty-six-year period for data entered from 1973 to 1998; it also contains some earlier year of publication (PY) articles. The corpus for this study (see Table 30.1) are the 5,898 articles related either to "language policy" or "language planning" out of a total of 150,186 items related to "language" in the *LLBA* database. The references per 1,000 articles column shows how, in the 1970s, the LPP literature grew as a field relative to the language literature from only six articles per 1000 in 1973 to 41.1 articles per 1,000 in 1979. The ten-year period from 1979 to 1988 saw 1,840 or forty-nine articles per 1,000 published, while the period from 1989 to 1998 saw 3,546 or forty-three articles per 1,000 published, indicating the emerging strength of the field in the 1980s. However, from the total of 5,898 LPP articles, 565 book reviews must be deducted, leaving a corpus of 5,333 potentially research-related items. The decline in the number of articles published in 1998 (and 1997) is an artifact of the corpus data, as it takes several years for most articles from a particular year to be added to a database.

The diversity of sources in the total LPP corpus can be seen in part by the amount of non-English language material it contains; 3,364, or 57 percent, were in English; 783, or 13.3 percent, were in German; 731, or 12.4 percent, were in French; 173, or 2.9 percent, were in Spanish; 154, or 2.6 percent, were in Russian; 117, or 2.0 percent, were in Italian, while 576, or 9.8 percent, were in other languages (or the language was uncoded).

Table 30.1. Language policy and planning corpus items in the *Linguistics and Language Behavior Abstracts* database for 1973–1998

Year of publication	Language	Language planning	Language policy	Planning or policy	References per 1,000
1998	2307	71	31	82	35.5
1997	8490	309	240	417	49.1
1996	9943	396	232	491	49.4
1995	10526	323	181	395	37.5
1994	9994	293	172	369	36.9
1993	9440	351	196	434	46.0
1992	8855	283	169	358	40.4
1991	8261	315	201	394	47.7
1990	7918	258	207	362	45.7
1989	6776	170	152	244	36.1
1989–1998	82,500	2,769	1,781	3,546	43.0
1988	5,472	157	139	221	40.4
1987	5,077	224	172	310	61.1
1986	4,720	176	128	229	48.5
1985	3,349	108	93	154	46.0
1984	3,005	153	130	201	66.9
1983	2,981	126	98	163	54.7
1982	2,864	102	91	149	52.0
1981	3,250	94	92	146	44.9
1980[a]	3,349	64	81	124	37.0
1979	3,475	90	93	143	41.1
1979–1988	37,542	1,294	1117	1840	49.0
1978	4,451	113	83	166	37.3
1977[b]	4,550	69	48	104	22.8
1976	4,560	75	37	93	20.4
1975[c]	4,568	53	19	62	13.6
1974[d]	4,606	36	15	44	9.6
1973	4,337	16	15	26	6.0
1969–1972	3,003	9	9	16	5.3
1969–1978	30,075	371	226	511	17.0
Database[e]	150,186	4,435	3,125	5898	

[a]*Journal of Multilingual and Multicultural Development* begins publishing.
[b]*Language Problems and Language Planning* begins publishing.
[c]*Language Planning Newsletter* begins publishing.
[d]*International Journal of the Sociology of Language* begins publishing.
[e]There are sixty-nine pre-1969 language articles and one language planning or policy article.

This compares to the remaining "language"-related items[1] in LLBA, where 101,920 items, or 70.6 percent, were in English; 12,854, or 8.9 percent, were in German; 11,944, or 8.3 percent, were in French; 4,279, or 3.0 percent, were in Russian; 2,527, or 1.8 percent, were in Spanish; 2,367, or 1.6 percent, were in Italian, while 8,388, or 5.8 percent, were in other languages (or the language was uncoded). (See Ammon 1998 for a discussion of the decline of languages other than English—especially German—in databases in general.) Although not statistically significant, the LPP corpus had proportionally fewer items in English (57 percent vs. 70.6 percent) and more items in German, French, and other languages than the non-LPP language items in the database. This suggests that LPP items come from a more diverse set of language backgrounds than language items in general.

METHODOLOGY AS REPRESENTED IN THE LPP CORPUS

A variety of methodologies have been identified as ones appropriate to LPP research (e.g., Eastman 1983b; Kaplan and Baldauf 1997). Methodologies are related to the kinds of questions that the researcher wants to answer and are often discipline based. The variety of techniques used in LPP research reflects in part the multidisciplinary nature of the field. The LPP corpus was searched for instances of various methodological terms or their equivalents, and the number of studies found was noted. Such searching is imprecise, as it depends on what terms were used in the abstracting process, their spelling (e.g., color, colour) or form (e.g., methodology, methodologies), and so on. The subsets of studies were then weeded for "false friends" (e.g., "methodology" was frequently found to be related to "language teaching," rather than "research," "anthropology" was a term used in conjunction with the author's department, rather than in "anthropological linguistics") and then examined for examples that clearly demonstrated the methodology's use in LPP situations. Given a large number of potential examples, exemplary articles for this study were selected not only for their illustrative value but to show the variety of work being done in LPP around the world, the wide range of publications for LPP material, and the range of authors working in the field.

The studies were also selected to illustrate different types of LPP studies in the literature. They were classified under four categories: (1) as a comment on methodology, on the basis of what LPP methodology actually had been used in

(2) prelanguage policy and planning studies, or (3) what is reported in "evaluative studies" of LPP and (4) in "ex post facto" or descriptive studies. Originally it was intended also to classify studies under "unplanned sociolinguistic change" (see Baldauf 1994), but this proved too difficult to do working primarily with the abstracts in this corpus. This analysis is summarized in Table 30.2, where articles are listed by methodology and by type of study. In the following sections, for each methodology, a number of illustrative studies are briefly summarized. With the exception of methodology, the topics are ordered from the most frequently to the least frequently occurring[2] in the LPP corpus.

1. *Methodology(ical)*. Although methodology is not the focus of articles being written for the field, this does not mean that methodology is not discussed. For example, Haarmann (1990) reviews the functional ranges of language planning and methodology and presents an ideal typology that argues for the need to consider prestige planning and the roles of individuals and groups in that planning. Hamel (1986) attempts for language policy purposes to formulate theoretical-methodological criteria for research into the relationships between national and indigenous languages in Mexico. Schiffman (1994) provides an alternative approach to language policy that puts greater emphasis on the role of linguistic culture in LPP development. Labrie, Nelde, and Weber (1994) summarize the methodology to be used to study the situation of minority languages in the European Community. Blommaert (1996) evaluates the past performance of the tradition of language planning from the perspectives of theory, concepts, and methodology to improve future LPP studies. Holmes (1997) examines methods used by New Zealand researchers to collect community language data and the relationship between methodology and theory and concludes that the expressive functions may provide a basis for reversing language shift. Baldauf (1994) argues that "unplanned" LPP occurs regularly and is an important aspect of much LPP implementation. Poth (1996) provides a methodological outline of LPP for the introduction of national languages into schools in Africa. While these articles deal with methodological issues, they do not deal with methodology as a topic in its own right, as was the case in the references in the first section of this chapter.

2. *History(ical)*. A large number of items in the LPP corpus have a major historical focus. A few examples of items with this focus include Daud's (1996) historical overview of the five stages of the development of the Indonesian language; a description of the functions and activities of the Academy of the Hebrew Language (Bar Acher and Kaufmann 1998); an overview of the effect of the Soviet dictatorship on the Lithuanian language (Palionis 1997); a review of the developments in Quebec French during the past twenty years (Poirier 1998); a discussion of the implications of the historical context of African multilingualism for Ugandian language policy (Pawlikova-Vilhanova 1996), and the historical context for language policy in Australia (Clyne 1997). The historical context is nearly always important in understanding LPP in a particular polity and has been in-

Table 30.2 A summary of study methodologies used in language policy and planning

Methodology: language planning and policy	Pre-LPP studies	Evaluation of LPP studies	Descriptive LPP studies
Methodology(ical) issues: Eastman (1983a, Ch. 6); Kaplan and Baldauf (1997: Ch. 4); Baldauf (1994); Haarmann (1990); Hamel (1986); Schiffman (1994)	Labrie, Nelde, and Weber (1994)	Blommaert (1996); Holmes (1997)	Poth (1996)
Historical analysis: Kaplan and Baldauf (1997: 88)		Clyne (1997); Pawlikova-Vilhanova (1996); Henry (1997)	Bar-Acher and Kaufmann (1998); Daud (1996); Palionis (1997); Poirier (1998); Awoniyi (1995)
Measurements of language attitudes: Eastman (1983b: 190); Gorter (1987); Winter (1992)	Verhoef (1998)	Kennedy (1996); Guilford (1997)	Bourhis (1997); Varro (1997)
Implementation and evaluation surveys: Eastman (1983b: 196); Kaplan and Baldauf (1997:90); Rubin (1971)	Colomer (1996)	Daoust (1992); Dogançay-Aktuna (1995); Strubell (1996); Varga (1995)	Grin (1996)
Comparative method: Eastman (1983b:185)		Michelman (1995); Pakir (1993)	Hornberger (1996); Robinson (1994); Sonntag (1996); Sommer (1991)
Proficiency measures: Contextualized proficiency test Eastman (1983b: 199)	Van Weeren (1995)	Strubell (1996); Extra (1995)	Verhoeven (1997); Tucker (1997); Liddicoat (1996)

Corpus analysis: Kaplan and Baldauf (1997: 99); Bailey and Dyer (1992)	Gouadec (1994)	Piehl (1996); Planelles-Ivanez (1996); Kennedy (1996)	Glinert (1998); Kenrick (1996); Otto (1991)
Anthropological linguistics: Kaplan and Baldauf (1997: 100); Fishman (1993); Grillo (1989)		Hendry (1997); Henry (1997); Morphet (1996)	Jernudd (1971); Thornell (1997)
Sociolinguistic survey(s): Eastman (1983b: 192, 198); Kaplan and Baldauf (1997: 102); Tse (1982); Gorter (1987)	Apronti (1974); Dieu (1991)	O'Riagain (1988); LePage (1986)	Kayambazinthu (1999); Mehrotra (1985); Shevy-akov (1987); Crowley (1994)
Interlanguage: Eastman (1983b: 189)	Cavalli (1997)		Calvet (1997); Glenn (1997); Smalley (1988)
Ethnography of communication: Kaplan and Baldauf (1997: 101); *Sociolinguistic interview:* Eastman (1983b: 198); Fishman (1994)			Chick (1992); Cooper and Danet (1980)
Cost-benefit analysis: Eastman (1983b: 178); Kaplan and Baldauf (1997: 94)	Colomer (1996); Markee (1991); Mühlhaüsler (1996b)		

397

corporated into a number of recent politywide LPP studies (e.g., those in Baldauf and Kaplan 2000, Kaplan and Baldauf 1999, and Spolsky and Shohamy 1999b).

3. *Language attitudes.* Attitudes (and values) are an important aspect of language planning (see Haarmann 1990) as the attitudes of individuals can have a major impact on the success or failure of LPP or in the adoption of language change (e.g., Guilford [1997] on the acceptance of English loanwords in French). There are a number of studies in the corpus that discuss the general issue of attitudes and language planning (e.g., Bourhis [1997] in France and Canada or Verhoef [1998] about the new process to promote new language attitudes in South Africa). Winter (1992) discusses how discourse analysis can be used to collect information about language attitudes. Attitudes may also be an important indicator of the success (or failure) of certain language planning features (e.g., Kennedy [1996] on the use of nonsexist language in job advertisements). Attitudes are also important in our understanding of particular language problems (e.g., Varro [1997] on the source of pejorative social attitudes toward immigrants in France).

4. *Evaluation.* As Rubin (1971) indicated nearly thirty years ago, there is a dearth of data on the processes that actually characterize LPP. Little has changed. Although the corpus contains a substantial number of items relating LPP and evaluation, most are not specifically about the evaluation of LPP but relate more narrowly to testing and proficiency issues. There are also a number of studies in the corpus that use other methodologies and that make evaluative statements about LPP (see the category "Evaluation of LPP Studies" in Table 30.2). Some examples of evaluation studies include Daoust (1992), who examines the effectiveness of Quebec's language planning program in bringing French use to private business by examining the language choice of workplace terminology; Grin (1996), who reviews the language economics literature, commenting on a range of matters, including their use in the evaluation of language policies; Colomer (1996), who examines the economic efficiency of translation versus language learning in Europe; Dogançay-Aktuna (1995), who evaluates Turkish language reform after sixty years; Varga (1995), who evaluates the recent literary version of Rhaeto-Romance for the five groups who speak and write the language in the Grisons canton of Switzerland, or Strubell's (1996) evaluation of the Catalan government's language policy for normalizing Catalan. Most of these items represent quasi-evaluations, rather than detailed examinations of policy and practice. Perhaps such documents exist in the more ephemeral government literature, but they aren't abstracted in *LLBA*.

5. *Comparative studies.* It is often possible to get a better understanding of language planning and policy situations by using comparative data. For example, Hornberger (1996) uses a comparative approach to indigenous languages and literacies to highlight the common challenges that such languages face, especially because individual language work is often undertaken in isolation; Michelman (1995) highlights the differing impact that British and French colonial language

policies have had on the production of African literatures; Pakir (1993) provides a descriptive and evaluative look at bilingual education in Singapore, Malaysia, and Brunei Darussalam; Robinson (1994) compares policies to support minority languages in Canada and Cameroon; Sonntag (1996) compares the relationship between language and politics in India in Bihar State (relatively politically stable) and in Uttar Pradesh State (marked by high political conflict), while Sommer (1991) compares factors that affect language maintenance and shift for the Nubian in Egypt and the Yai in Botswana. Comparisons such as these allow for the development of LPP commonalties or allow hypotheses about differences in LPP approaches to be examined.

6. *Proficiency.* Much of the LPP-related literature on proficiency talks about proficiency needs in the LPP context (see, for example, Liddicoat [1996] for Australia, Tucker [1997] for the United States, or Verhoeven [1997] for bilingual proficiency), rather than actually evaluating proficiency. The literature also contains work about developing proficiency standards (e.g., Van Weeren 1995), but, as noted under evaluation, there is relatively little evaluation of proficiency (cf. Strubell [1996] who briefly evaluates policy outcomes for Catalan using language proficiency information from the census, while Extra [1995] presents data on the language proficiency of ethnic minority children in Holland). Language proficiency is clearly an important LPP goal, but its assessment is difficult, and not much of this sort of work is available in the literature.

7. *Corpus studies.* The literature also contains a substantial number of corpus-related studies, although quite a number of these relate to corpus planning, rather than corpus as a methodology. A number of other studies relate to lexicography (e.g., Glinert [1998] for an overview of the revernacularization of Hebrew) or to terminological development (e.g., Gouadec [1994] looks at official French computer terminological development). While such work is an important component of corpus planning, its connection with some specific LPP may be more difficult to discern. Another use of corpus analysis is to examine particular bodies of LPP literature (e.g., Piehl [1996] for Finnish language standardization, Kenrick [1996] for the written corpus of Romani, or this chapter) for LPP-related directions or trends. In other uses, Bailey and Dyer (1992) show how random samples from a corpus of speech data can be used to provide inferences about the language use of populations, while Planelles-Ivanez (1996), Kennedy (1996), and Otto (1991) use samples of written news media to look at linguistic policy related to the changing use of feminized job titles in French, sex discrimination in recruitment advertisements, or the promotion of German in France as assessed by language related job advertisements.

8. *Anthropology(ical).* Anthropological approaches normally involve the field study of a language in its social context. The corpus provided a substantial number of items that linked LPP and anthropology, but many were not clearly linked with fieldwork. Examples of this method include Hendry (1997), who, on the basis

of interviews in 1987 and 1995, examined the effects of the Spanish government's policy of official bilingualism in Rioja Alavesa (on the periphery of the Basque region) and found that the policy marginalized the identity of the population as neither Basque nor Spanish. Henry (1997) reviewed the impact of efforts since 1968 by the state government to develop French in Louisiana and noted modest success on the educational side. Thornell (1997) examined the social interaction and general characteristics of the lexicon of Songo, a newly developing lingua franca of the Central African Republic. Morphet (1996) provides an overview of an ethnographic study of the literacy practices of unschooled people in South Africa, showing that it was not illiteracy itself but issues of power and control that were problematic. Fishman (1993) argues for the necessity of ethnolinguistic consciousness, that is, he maintains that the involvement of the community in language maintenance and preservation is necessary for language revival. Jernudd (1971) used an anthropological linguistic approach to examine social change and aboriginal speech variation in Australia. As an introduction to a volume on the topic of social anthropology and the politics of language, Grillo (1989) provides a review that explores how anthropologists are concerned with issues of language and power. These studies indicate the usefulness of an anthropological approach to LPP problems.

9. *Sociolinguistic survey(s).* The corpus contains a fairly small number of examples of this method. Two (Tse [1982] for Taiwan and Gorter [1987] for Frisian in the Netherlands) have as their primary focus, discussion of the method, while Mehrotra (1985) for South Asia and Apronti (1974) and Shevyakov (1987) for Ghana provide brief reviews of these respective situations using survey data. O'Riagain (1988) compared the results of the 1973 and 1983 national language surveys to describe and explain the evolving pattern of bilingualism in Ireland. This could be classified as an evaluation of the state's language policy aimed at the maintenance and revival of Irish. Dieu (1991) reports on the use of a sociolinguistic survey to determine the most practical language for use for literacy development in the northern Cameroon, while LePage (1986) uses a sociolinguistic survey to collect data on Creole language development in Belize. Census data can also be used to provide sociolinguistic and LPP-related data (see Clyne 1997; Crowley 1994). Although sociolinguistic surveys can arguably be a foundation methodology for polity LPP (see Kaplan and Baldauf 1997), as well as for more micro situations, their reported used is not great, and it is noteworthy that sixteen of the eighteen studies in the corpus were published in the 1970s or 1980s. Although not part of the LLBA corpus, Kayambazinthu (1999) provides a more recent example of how survey data (for Malawi) can contribute to LPP.

10. *Interlanguage.* The traditional micro use of this term for learners at a stage of second language acquisition between L1 and L2 has been broadened to reflect the social extent to which languages, or certain deviations from mainstream language, are suggestive of a stable ethnic usage or dialect (Eastman 1983b: 190).

While Cavalli (1997) uses interlanguage in the individual sense, Calvet (1997, for the use of linguas francas of African cities), Glenn (1997, for the preservation of minority languages in Europe and North America), and Smalley (1988, for the hierarchy of languages in Thailand) use interlanguage in a macro context in examining the sociolinguistic and LPP relationship between languages. When searching the LPP corpus for the terms *interlanguage* (or *ethnography of communication*) and LPP, there was often a false relationship between co-occurance of the two, as they were found in volumes of collected papers but in separate chapters.

11. *Ethnography of communication.* Marxist and poststructuralist critiques of language planning have suggested that ethnographic LPP research would help to avoid the elitism, inequality, modernist approaches, and lack of support for multiculturalism found in classical LPP. Fishman (1994), while acknowledging the validity of such critiques, takes a minority language perspective, arguing that such critiques focus more on theory than on actual practice and that one needs to be careful not to replace one set of exploitations with another. Despite the call for the use of the technique, very few items were found in the corpus in which LPP was examined from the viewpoint of the ethnography of speaking/communication. Cooper and Danet (1980) discuss it in relation to language planning in Israel, while Chick (1992) uses it in a comparative micro LPP study of compliment and response in a South African university as an indicator of changes in postapartheid power relations.

12. *Cost-benefit analysis.* Cost-benefit analysis was an early method suggested in the LPP literature for evaluating language decision making. However, the difficulties of assigning monetary values to benefits in the language area, and the fact that many language decisions are often made for political and not for economic reasons, has limited the use of this technique. Colomer (1996) examines the economic efficiency of translation versus language learning in Europe using cost-benefit analysis; Mühlhäusler (1996b) discusses the benefits of learning lesser taught/learned languages in terms of their costs and benefits; and Markee (1991) uses cost-benefit analysis to look at language planning of communicative innovations. Reagan (1983) examines cost-benefit analysis as part of the potential of economics for LPP. As Fasold (1984) and Edwards (1985) indicate, very few cost-benefit analyses have been done or are available for scrutiny.

Other Methods

A number of methods originally suggested by Eastman (1983b) as possible tools for LPP that seem not to have been taken up in the corpus of LPP literature include *mutual intelligibility studies* (1983b: 195; cf. Rahman 1995; Gonzalez 1989), *language distance* (1983b: 186; cf. Khubchandani 1989), *transaction theory* (1983b: 200; cf. Laitin and Eastman 1989), *degrees of bilingualism* (1983b: 184; cf. Garmendia 1994), *glotoeconomics* (1983b: 180), *ethnic decision making* (1983b: 182), or *dominance configuration* (1983b: 185). Her analysis of emerging methodology was based on work in the 1970s (when LPP was in its formative stages as a field) and indicates that a wide range of methodologies have been considered for LPP work.

Misuses of Method

This is a difficult area to document, especially on the basis of a corpus study such as the one employed here. However, from LPP theses/dissertations I have been asked to read in which the methodological component was weak, and from verbal reports of problematic survey questions in large national studies I have heard about, methodology seems to be a problem. While these do not constitute a large or random sample, they further strengthen the suggestion that issues of methodology may be undervalued in the LPP field.

SUMMARY AND CONCLUSIONS

This corpus study demonstrates that LPP has grown into a substantial field of study since it first formally appeared in the database literature (as represented by LLBA). Between 4 percent and 5 percent of studies abstracted in LLBA related to language are related to language policy and planning. This literature is scattered across a wide range of publications related to many different disciplines and is published more frequently in a language other than English than is the LLBA literature in general. Unlike some other areas of applied linguistics, methodology and theory are, by and large, not issues for metadiscussion in the literature. It appears scholars bring to their LPP studies the more general traditions of the humanities and social sciences, with a lot of the work having a historical or comparative component or being merely descriptive. Statistical, survey-, or quantitative-data-based studies and evaluations seem to be relatively infrequent.

On the basis of this initial analysis of the LPP literature, the question needs to be asked whether this is a satisfactory state of affairs or whether, studies of LPP make unique methodological demands on scholars that should be better represented in the literature. What this brief survey of the literature points up, however, is the widely dispersed theoretical base of LPP—the nature of the underlying views of language, of language change, and of the politics of language change.

NOTES

1. There were 150,186 "language" items, less the 5,898 "language planning or policy" items, leaving 144,288 non-LPP language items.

2. As previously indicated, the imprecision of the search techniques makes the actual number of studies found relatively meaningless without detailed analysis of each of the studies located. Such an exercise was beyond the scope of this corpus review, which sought primarily to illustrate the methodologies in use.

CHAPTER 31

....

UNPLANNED LANGUAGE PLANNING

....

WILLIAM G. EGGINGTON

THE concept of "unplanned language planning" might appear to be an oxymoron, but, as this chapter indicates, unplanned language planning plays an important role in any language planning process. Since the term includes the semantic notion of an "unplanned" planned activity, precise definitions of something that is un-planned are difficult to construct. Kaplan and Baldauf (1997: 297–299), with reference to Baldauf (1994) and Luke and Baldauf (1990), suggest that unplanned language planning may involve language modification affected by accident, by a shared set of laissez-faire attitudes toward a language situation, and/or by an ad hoc solution to an immediate problem.

Recognizing the potential impact of unplanned language planning with respect to formal language planning, Kaplan and Baldauf (1997: 298–299) and Baldauf (1994) offer four reasons that a formal language planning activity needs to consider unplanned language planning activities in its planning stages. These are summarized as follows:

1. Planned and unplanned language planning attempts can co-exist in a symbiotic relationship, and thus a formal language plan is incomplete unless it considers existing unplanned language plans within the social ecosystem.
2. The existence or nonexistence of unplanned language planning can offer vital information, allowing the language planner to consider the social

and language related factors as to why an unplanned language planning exists or does not exist.

3. The relationship between planned and unplanned language planning and social power and control are such that any formal language plan needs to consider the power relationships revealed in all the unplanned language planning activities in the society.

4. The almost universal language competency that human beings share seems to give most people all the authority they need to become involved in language planning activities, especially at the local and microplanning level. This situation can create a myriad of mostly unplanned language planning activities and attitudes. Language planners need to address these attitudes and activities in any formal plan.

Obviously, when language planners attempt to develop and implement a formal language plan, unplanned language planning activities in the society need to be thoroughly considered. Ironically, neglecting the importance of unplanned language planning could easily lead to the formal language plan being sucked into an unplanned morass.

As this brief review indicates, to date, the discussion of unplanned language planning tends to cast rather benign descriptive attributes on this phenomenon. However, it could be argued that, when something happens in the social ecosystem by accident, or because of laissez-faire attitudes, or because of an ad hoc solution, underlying ideologies are being revealed. In a sense, unplanned language planning does not just "happen." There are reasons that "unplanning" occurs. Consequently, rather than blandly review instances of unplanned language planning, the following discussion attempts to get to the heart of unplanned language planning in terms of the ideologies and motivations that cause the accident, create the laissez-faire attitudes, and develop the ad hoc solutions. In so doing, the definition of unplanned language planning may be extended to include an ideological component that suggests that matters involving language issues in society do not unaccountably spring forth from the language ecosystem.

An Overview of Ideologies in Unplanned Language Planning

A review of some of the types of contemporary unplanned language planning activities suggests that there are at least two somewhat overlapping categories that reveal the ideological nature of unplanning in language planning: (1) unplanned language planning in social engineering planning and (2) unplanned language planning conducted by nonspecialists. Space does not permit an extensive elaboration of these two types of unplanned language planning in all settings and contexts, but it is evident that they occur at the national level, the state and regional level, the local level and the site-specific level. What follows is an elaboration of a number of unplanned language planning activities across a selection of these levels.

Unplanned Language Planning in Social Engineering Planning

The closest that formal language planning gets to "social engineering" is probably through "social purpose language planning" as described by Kaplan and Baldauf (1997: 122–152). However, it does appear that unplanned language planning is frequently utilized by those who wish to undertake various forms of social engineering. With respect to national social engineering, Sir Karl Popper, renowned philosopher of science, offers a typical "Popperian" critique. Popper divides social engineers into two groups—those who engage in "piecemeal" engineering and those with a more utopian, ideologically driven outlook who engage in "holistic" engineering. At the risk of quoting him excessively, he states:

> The piecemeal engineer [as opposed to the "holistic" or "Utopian engineer"] knows, like Socrates, how little he knows. He knows that we can learn only from our mistakes. Accordingly, he will make his way, step by step, carefully comparing the results expected with the results achieved, and always on the look-out for the unavoidable unwanted consequences of any reform; and he will avoid undertaking reforms of a complexity and scope which make it impossible for him to disentangle causes and effects, and to know what he is really doing. . . .
>
> The holists reject the piecemeal approach as being too modest. Their rejection of it, however, does not quite square with their practice; for in practice they always fall back on a somewhat haphazard and clumsy although ambitious and ruthless application of what is essentially a piecemeal method without its cautious and self-critical character. The reason is that, in practice, the holistic method turns out to be impossible; the greater the holistic changes attempted, the greater are their unintended and largely unexpected repercussions, forcing upon the holistic engineer the expedient of piecemeal improvization. In fact, this expedient is more characteristic of centralized or collectivistic planning than of the more modest and careful piecemeal intervention; and *it continually leads the Utopian engineer to do things which he did not intend to do; that is to say, it leads to the notorious phenomenon of unplanned planning.* (Popper 1961: 68–69; emphasis added)

The relevance to language planning of Popper's lengthy definition of unplanned planning is obvious. Language planning is an extremely complex undertaking, with a host of controllable and uncontrollable variables. As Kaplan and Baldauf (1997) explicate in detail, language planners working within a human-resource management mindset follow theories and practices that Popper would have no difficulty labeling as "piecemeal." This mindset has no doubt arisen because experienced language planners recognize the complexities involved in any language planning activity—and the potential for unintended consequences to derive from any overlooked variable. Consequently, piecemeal, language-as-human-resource language planners tend to construct elaborate empirical procedures for information gathering, usually through surveys. They then use the information analyzed in a survey report to inform their policy development and to develop their implementation plan. This plan is then implemented. At all stages in the language planning procedure, there is a series of "feedback" loops to ensure that there are no unintended consequences of any action. Most of these feedback loops involve seriously valuing the wishes and desires of the people immediately affected by the implementation of the policy within a bottom-up, top-down meeting of minds. As much as possible, the inculcation of scientific objectivity throughout this process reduces the potential for language planners to imprint their personal ideologies onto language planning outcomes. In this way, language planners hope to avoid being enmeshed in the repercussions that follow when resistance to a plan develops from segments in society that had been overlooked in the planning process.

On the other hand, language plans motivated by a desire to engineer a holistic solution to a perceived problem often fall into Popper's unplanned planning trap. These "social engineers" are usually motivated by an ideological framework that either longs for some form of Utopian society or attributes failure to achieve a Utopian ideal to a single causality. As such, any behavior exhibited by people in the society that does not fit "desired" behavior is seen as a "problem" that needs to be fixed—and, because it is a problem, it needs to be fixed as quickly, efficiently, and directly as possible.

Instances of this mentality to language-related issues in social contexts are plentiful. This is so probably because of the binding relationship between language and identity—and identity and ideology. In short, just about everyone in a speech community has an opinion of what should happen when that community is confronted with a perceived language problem, even though the problem may not really exist. Indeed, because there is some form of language behavior that does not meet the preferred or ideologically driven set of desired behaviors, the "problem" may be a figment of an ideologically driven imagination. Ironically, the solution to this virtual problem is also found in the ideologies that established the presence of the problem. To people outside the ideological loop, this process can be described as "a solution in search of a problem" (for example, Utah State

House minority leader Dave Jones as quoted in *the Deseret News*, 22 January 1999).

Nevertheless, for many people, a solution for the "problem" must be found—and it is found in some form of language planning process that usually leads to the enactment of a language policy. Not surprisingly, those most affected by the policy (those possessed of the "problem") are seldom consulted, or, if they are consulted, they are presented with a set of simplistic solutions to the virtual problem. These solutions often are supported by some form of "straw-man" argumentation. Eventually, the ideologically driven language plan is implemented through a top-down, bottom-up compliance process, and it is here that the plan meets its unplanned consequences. The people who were supposed to change their language behavior do not change. In fact, sometimes they behave in ways that suggest that the top-down language plan has contributed to the "problem," rather than provided a solution to the problem. Popper gives us one more insight into this phase of an unplanned language planning project. He states:

> It seems to escape the well-meaning Utopianist that this programme implies an admission of failure, even before he launches it. For it substitutes for his demand that we build a new society, fit for men and women to live in, the demand that we "mould" these men and women to fit into his new society. This, clearly, removes any possibility of testing the success or failure of the new society. For those who do not like living in it only admit thereby that they are not yet fit to live in it; that their "human impulses" need further "organizing."
> (Popper 1961: 70)

Considering the ideological foundations of this type of unplanned planning, it is not surprising that specific examples of unplanned language planning in social engineering can be provided from across the political spectrum: Two are reviewed in this chapter. They are the "Official English" movement in the United States, and the "language rights movement" also found in the United States, as well as in many international contexts.

Official English

As implied earlier, it appears that most people have a full and varied set of opinions about language behavior (grammar, pronunciation, usage, use) and behavior toward language (attitudes, motivations, opinions regarding existing formal or informal language policies and practices). Often these opinions are driven by a body of ideologies that, if implemented correctly, would contribute to the creation of Utopia. Eggington (1997) describes these ideologies in terms of socially shared metaphors. For example, dominant metaphors in English-as-first-language nations include "English as national language" where "English" is defined as a level of proficiency, closely approximating educated standard and "English as *our* language"—the language of "us." These dominant metaphors create a set of corollary socially shared ideologies that can be scripted as "If you don't speak (standard) English, you are not *us* or part of *our* nation."

Throughout the history of the United States, resistance to large, non-English speaking immigration movements is usually revealed through concerns that the preeminence of English (and "us") is under threat and that the essential national character will disappear. Even Benjamin Franklin weighed in on this subject by asking:

> Why should the Palatine Boors be suffered to swarm into our Settlements, and by herding together establish their Language and Manners to the exclusion of ours? Why should Pennsylvania, founded by the English, become a Colony of Aliens, who will shortly be so numerous as to Germanize us instead of our Anglifying them, and will never adopt our Language or Customs, any more than they can acquire our Complexion? (as quoted in Labaree 1959: 234)

In recent times, responses to the current wave of non-English speaking immigration have included various attempts to legislate English as the official language of the United States or of a particular state. Perhaps motivated by Utopian ideologies that might include the "English as 'us' "[1] set discussed earlier, and by a nostalgic longing for the mythological melting pot of the past (Dicker 1996: 34–71), most native English speakers, and a large number of non-native English speakers, seem to agree with sundry forms of legislation that would provide government services only in the English language, except for a narrow range of circumstances involving health and legal issues. Obviously, the legislators who are proposing official English laws are engaging in a form of language planning. However, a careful analysis of the underlying assumptions motivating these pieces of legislation reveals that the reality of the problem is questionable. Non-English speaking immigrants living in the United States are highly motivated to acquire English, and they are doing so at a remarkable rate (Dicker 2000: 54–55; Portes and Schauffler 1994). The English language has become the most powerful language in the macrohistory of humankind and thus is not under any form of threat (Graddol 1997). Indeed, far from being a language under threat, the English language is threatening numerous world languages through linguistic imperialism to a degree that some label it as a "killer language" (Skutnabb-Kangas 2000b: 22).

The proposed language planning solutions to these virtual problems are equally problematic and have the potential for ushering in a host of unintended consequences. There is no evidence that offering government services only in English will motivate people to acquire English any more efficiently or effectively than they are currently doing. Indeed, by withdrawing government services in languages other than English, class conditions are established that encourage immigrants to maintain closer ties to their ethnic and linguistic groupings (Picone

1997), which, in turn, retards "assimilation"—the primary objective of U.S. English. In addition, there is valid evidence that, in those states with official English laws, limited English speakers are paid less by nongovernment employers than those states without official English laws, primarily because of the second-class status the state endows on non-English speakers by declaring English the "official" language (Zavodny 1998). To reiterate, the Official English "language plan" promotes conditions that increase the likelihood of creating the problem the plan is designed to solve.

Space and the objectives of this chapter do not allow for a full rebuttal of the Official English position. Suffice it to say that the proponents of official English are engaged in an ideologically motivated enterprise, trying to solve a virtual problem with solutions that will create a host of unintended consequences—consequences that could easily devolve into further tribalization of the nation and that could ultimately create repercussions that will require solutions almost opposite of the intent of Official English. The Official English movement in the United States is a clear example of Popper's unplanned planning.

Linguistic Human Rights

A second instance of ideologically driven unplanned language planning comes from those who appear to have a knowledge of piecemeal objective (and scientific) language planning procedures designed to reduce the subjectivity and ideology of the planners. However, they have accepted the postmodern notion that ideologies of power inform and control every action, regardless of any attempts to create objective, or scientific, procedures in the language planning process. (See, e. g., Moore 1996.) Having bought into the sentiment that "all is power," these language planners have a tendency to disregard and even denigrate "Popperian" piecemeal language planning procedures, substituting for them holistic "ideologies-of-power" singular-causality, singular-outcome templates. For example, Moore (1996: 474), in her description and discussion of Australian language policy, introduces the topic by stating that "in this article, I use insights from Dorothy Smith and Anna Yeatman, both feminist scholars, to explore the nature of policy formation. They start with the premise that all description is partial and interested" (1996: 474). Casting aside the disturbing notions that Moore is either admitting that her subsequent discussion of Australian language policy is partial and interested, or that she alone holds the key that enables her to rise above partiality and self-interest, one must also ask what one will find when one examines anything from the point of view of a predetermined ideology other than what one's ideology has predetermined to find. A cookie cutter, when applied to pastry, always produces the desired outcome. Similarly, an ideologically driven template, regardless of whether it is from the political left or the political right, always creates the desired outcome, especially if that ideology rejects scientific objectivity. Thus, any language plan derived from an ideological template is predetermined to create unplanned consequences requiring improvised, unplanned "fixes."

One such ideological cookie cutter is the notion of "linguistic human rights"—defined by Skutnabb-Kangas as the right of all children to "have the opportunity to learn their parents' idiom fully and properly so that they become (at least) as proficient as the parents" (Skutnabb-Kangas 2000b: 25). In theory, such a right is a worthy goal supported by the majority of applied linguists, including the author of this chapter. However, in most social contexts (except for Utopia), huge problems lie in the development and implementation of any plan that is built exclusively on total, or at least widespread, acceptance and outcomes of a language-rights template. Regardless of the worthiness of the end objective, a language plan established solely upon this ideologically driven foundation is likely to overlook key variables that could impact the success of the plan.

For example, in both Australia and the United States, numerous maintenance and transition bilingual education plans for linguistic minorities (including immigrants and indigenous peoples) were implemented during the 1970s (the decade during which the language rights ideology initially flowered). These programs are now either nonexistent, floundering, and/or facing severe opposition partially because the generations of holistic language-in-education planners who informed these programs were so eager to implement an ideological Utopia that they overlooked a host of significant piecemeal processes and variables. These factors included the fervent desires of language-minority parents (and second language teachers and administrators) to ensure:

- That children received a quality education in the dominant language (English)
- That it is the parents' responsibility to ensure children's proficiency in the family language, while it is the education system's responsibility to teach in English (as revealed in Eggington 1985)
- That realistic cost-benefit analyses are necessary
- That there are difficulties faced in preparing high-quality bilingual teachers and in meeting the complexities and expenses of creating quality materials and evaluative measures
- That the development of realistic bilingual education outcomes is at best difficult
- That the development of quality testing and feedback mechanisms is also difficult
- Most important, that the creation of an ongoing procedure must ensure that the bilingual education plan reflects a meeting of the minds of those who wish to implement and continue the plan and of the parents and

students directly affected by the plan (Hansen 1999; Eggington and Baldauf 1990).

It is impossible to say that, had these more piecemeal approaches been followed, bilingual education programs would be flourishing. However, it is likely that if piecemeal approaches had been established, especially early in the development of bilingual education implementation models, procedures might have been put in place that would have identified growing resistance to bilingual education, not only from the dominant English-speaking society but also from parents eager for their children to acquire English as quickly as possible. Through community education programs and the involvement of parents in local language-in-education plans, many legitimate parental concerns could have been addressed. It should be noted that in both Australian aboriginal contexts and in the California bilingual education program, early and meaningful resistance to bilingual education came from parents of bilingual children (Hansen 1999). Now, in both aboriginal Australia and California, bilingual education is seen by many as a huge and costly mistake—yet another example of the wrongheadedness and ideologically driven "political correctness" of professional educators. As a consequence, language-minority children are daily facing the personal consequences of an exercise in unplanned language planning.

As the Official English and bilingual education movements demonstrate, ideologically driven unplanned language planning is not confined to a particular shade of the political spectrum. Rather, the commonality lies in the attempt to impose top-down, holistic, ideological "fixes" to a perceived language problem, without considering the probability of a host of unintended consequences.

Unplanned Language Planning Conducted by Nonspecialists

Although the term *global village* appears trite, it reflects accurately what is happening globally with regards to communication, immigration patterns, trade and business interactions, tourism, global information-storage-and-retrieval systems, and international media. Only sixty years ago, most speech and discourse communities (using Swales's [1990] definitions of these terms) had very limited intra- and/or intermultilingual contact. However, in contemporary society, we are regularly engaged in some activity that requires interaction with people who do not speak our language(s). In addition, the unanticipated arrival and rapid growth of the Internet has vastly increased cross-linguistic interactions. These events often require nonspecialists to engage in a form of language planning.

Recently, I personally witnessed the creation, design, construction, and implementation of a complex computer animation project in which the clients, initial design team, and production center were in Japan, the coordination group was in Los Angeles, the programmers were in Iceland, and the animators were in Utah. All communication between the various teams was conducted via the Internet in a specialized English. Aside from the requirement for all project teams to be available during Tokyo business hours, one could easily come to the conclusion that the project was being undertaken by teams housed in a single building in an English-speaking city. It is doubtful that there was a conscious decision to implement an English-as-language-of-project language plan. The decision probably just happened, and in that respect the project constitutes an example of unplanned language planning conducted by nonspecialists.[2]

This rather one-dimensional example does not imply that unplanned language planning by nonspecialists will always result in desired outcomes. When complexities increase, so-called common-sense language related solutions can easily lead to a host of unintended consequences, making any plan vulnerable to Popper's unplanned planning trap. Burningham (1998), in her study of language policy and planning in an urban U.S. school district, found an absence of any formal plan designed to address the needs of language-minority students. One administrator stated that the district language policy was "fairly clear," but, when asked to produce the policy, the administrator explained that he couldn't because the district "plan" consisted of "just kind of memos." When asked about how they deal with language planning issues, other administrators stated that they:

"Kind of operate from my own beliefs."
"Basically it's whatever you feel like as a humanitarian."
". . . professional and personal tendency."
"Anything in effect is kind of what [administrator #4] and I have decided
    to do." (Burningham 1998: 42–43)

After conducting extensive interviews with administrators and faculty, and after surveying language-minority parents, students, and teachers, Burningham concluded that the absence of a formal language plan in the district and the presence of a series of uncoordinated unplanned language plans are linked to what Wiley and Lukes (1996) label "individualism"—an attitude or ideology where the responsibility for any student failure is placed on the individual, thus freeing the institution and the society from any liability and, in turn, creating the foundation for significant, widespread student failure in the near future, with all the unintended consequences that accompany minority-group low academic achievement.

CONCLUSION

As is perhaps painfully obvious, this chapter has only skimmed the surface of the available instances of ideologically driven unplanned language planning. There are, however, a number of lessons to be gleaned from the discussion. Applied linguists and, more specifically, applied linguists engaged in language planning activities need to examine carefully the ideologies that inform and construct unplanned language planning efforts. At the same time, these applied linguists need to ensure that their own Utopian-driven ideological proclivities do not contribute to the formation of unplanned consequences that may derive from any language planning recommendations they may make. This can be done only by relying on established objective procedures and "piecemeal" approaches to language planning enterprises, rather than on attempts at holistic, sweeping social reconstruction.

A final lesson comes from Forrest Cuch, head of Utah's Office of Indian Affairs. When asked for his suggestions of what needs to be done to overcome a host of unplanned and uncoordinated language plans in Utah (see Sayers 1996), he suggested that:

> What you have to do is sit down and take a look at the needs and develop a policy systematically. . . . There's one thing that our state has going for it. Although we appear to be very narrow in our perceptions, at least I've found that the people at the top, once they hear the truth about the history of the state, once they obtain the information, they do change. They're not static; they don't resist the information. . . . It's just that they lack some information—some of the people at the top. But they do have a willingness to try to improve things. (Forrest Cuch, head of the Utah's Office of Indian Affairs, interview, March 1998)

By and large, public officials are amenable to the application of language planning procedures and will enact those recommendations that are supported by strong evidence. Consequently, it is the responsibility of language planners to be proactive in sharing their expertise with those outside academia.

NOTES

1. It is no coincidence that the national organization that is sponsoring official English legislation has named itself "U.S. English," playing on the ideologies of English as "U.S." and English as "us."

2. Those scholars invested in power ideologies might assume that the language plan was a result of the continuing hegemony of the English language. However, it is equally valid to assume that the decision was motivated by a practicality often overlooked by "power-is-everywhere" ideologues. That ideological factor might be labeled "communicative need" and fits along the social solidarity axis—an axis not encompassed by the plus/minus power construct.

CHAPTER 32

....

LIMITATIONS OF LANGUAGE POLICY AND PLANNING

....

JAMES W. TOLLEFSON

WHEN language policy and planning (LPP) first became widely practiced in the 1960s and 1970s, LPP specialists believed that their newly emerging understanding of language in society could be implemented in practical programs of "modern-ization" and "development" that would have important benefits for "developing" societies. Noting that "there is still no institution in the United States in which students can be adequately trained for either theoretical or applied involvement in the language problems of developing nations . . . ," Fishman, Ferguson, and Das Gupta, in their groundbreaking collection, argued that "few areas are more fruitful or urgent with respect to interdisciplinary attention" (1968: x–xi). The early period of LPP was characterized by an explosive growth in research (e.g., Fishman 1968, 1971, 1972, 1974; Rubin and Jernudd 1971; Rubin and Shuy 1973), as the new field of LPP was widely seen as having practical significance for the many newly in-dependent states of the postcolonial period, as well as theoretical value in provid-ing "new opportunities to tackle a host of . . . novel theoretical concerns" (1968: x) in sociology and political science.

Despite this early optimism, in less than twenty years, by the mid-1980s, dis-illusionment with LPP was widespread (Blommaert 1996; Williams 1992). The rapid disillusionment with LPP was due to several factors, which I outline here. More recently, a modest revival in academic interest in LPP has begun, though research is characterized by important differences from the early period. Following analysis of the limitations of early LPP, I summarize these recent trends in research and suggest future directions for the field.

Early Development in LPP

Major Concerns of Research

The linkage of LPP with development and modernization was crucial for the early history of the field. Influenced by modernization theory (e.g., Rostow 1960), early research focused primarily on the role of LPP in developing societies. For instance, of the nineteen case studies in Fishman, Ferguson, and Das Gupta (1968), eleven focused on Africa, while the others examined developing countries such as India, Haiti, Papua New Guinea, and Paraguay. (One article focused on Scandinavia.) Indeed, much of this early research seemed to restrict LPP to developing nations, as indicated by the subtitle of Rubin and Jernudd's (1971) influential book *Can Language Be Planned? Sociolinguistic Theory and Practice for Developing Nations.* It was widely believed that LPP could play a major role in achieving the goals of political/administrative integration and sociocultural unity (Das Gupta 1970). Thus, a major focus of this early research was analysis of the language planning needs specific to newly independent states, particularly language choice and literacy in processes of "nationism," and language maintenance, codification, and elaboration in processes of "nationalism" (Fishman 1968).

Although LPP was born out of a concern with development, researchers soon extended their work to include developed societies. By the end of its early "formative half decade" (Fishman 1971: 7), LPP research was being applied to language problems in the Soviet Union (Lewis 1972); Israel (Rabin 1971); Belgium, Luxembourg, and France (Verdoodt 1971); the United States (Entwisle 1971); and Ireland (Macnamara 1971), as well as to an expanding number of developing countries, including China, Indonesia, Malaysia, Pakistan, and the Philippines.

The major achievement of this early period of LPP was a deeper understanding of the relationship between language structure and language functions on the one hand and various forms of social organization (communities, ethnic groups, nations) on the other. On the theoretical level, this early work linked LPP with important research in microsociolinguistics on such issues as sequencing in interactions, code-switching, and systematicity in style and register variation.

Three Assumptions in Early LPP

In early LPP research, practitioners were seen as having the expertise to specify ways in which changes in the linguistic situation would lead to desired social and political transformations (eg., enhancing sociocultural unity, reducing economic inequalities, opening access to education). The historical link between LPP and modernization/development ensured that the implicit assumptions in LPP reflected widely held assumptions in the social sciences that have been subject to a great deal of critical reflection. Especially striking in hindsight is the optimism of early LPP, which conveyed an underlying ideological faith in development and modernization. This belief in economic and social progress was perhaps best expressed in Eastman's introduction to language planning (1983), in which language planners are depicted at the forefront of fundamental shifts in the organization of global society: "Modernization and preservation efforts are seemingly happening everywhere, to provide all people with access to the modern world through technologically sophisticated languages and also to lend a sense of identity through encouraged use of their first languages" (Eastman 1983a: 31). The belief that LPP would benefit ethnic and linguistic minorities was widespread in early LPP research, and cases could be found to confirm this optimism. For instance, the remarkable spread of Malay-Indonesian from the 1960s until the early 1980s indicated that LPP could have important consequences for newly independent multilingual and multiethnic states (Alisjahbana 1971). Subsequently, however, the failure of LPP to achieve its goals in many contexts and the intimate connection between early LPP and modernization theory meant that LPP was subject to the same criticisms as modernization theory generally, including the following:

- Economic models appropriate for one place may be ineffective elsewhere.
- National economic development will not necessarily benefit all sectors of society, especially the poor.
- Development fails to consider local contexts and the conflicting needs and desires of diverse communities.
- Development has a homogenizing effect on social and cultural diversity (Foster-Carter 1985; Worsley 1987).

A second key assumption of the early period of LPP was the emphasis on "efficiency," "rationality," and "cost-benefit analysis" as criteria for evaluating plans and policies in all contexts. For instance, Tauli (1968) proposed "clarity" and "economy," while Haugen (1966b) proposed "efficiency" as key criteria for evaluating the effectiveness of LPP decisions. The emphasis on the technical aspect of LPP led Jernudd and Das Gupta (1971) to argue that planners may be more able than political authorities to apply rational decision making in the solution to language problems. Such attempts to separate LPP from politics reflected not only a belief in the skills of technical specialists but also a broader failure to link LPP with a political analysis. The wide failure of early LPP to acknowledge that LPP is fundamentally political, involving a powerful mechanism for disciplining societies, is central to subsequent critiques of LPP.

A third assumption central to early LPP was that the nation-state is the appropriate focus for LPP research and practice. Indeed, this assumption is implicit in the perspective of LPP as a tool for political/administrative and sociocultural integration of the nation-state. Focusing on the nation-state had two important consequences. First, the main actors in LPP were assumed to be government agencies, and thus most research examined the work of such agencies. Second, many researchers adopted a top-down perspective, in which they were interested in national plans and policies, rather than local language practices. This emphasis on the nation-state continued in later LPP research as well, including research critical of other early assumptions in the field, such as research on linguistic imperialism (Phillipson 1992).

DISILLUSIONMENT AND CRITIQUE

The critique of early LPP was, in part, a manifestation of the general collapse of social planning that took place during the 1980s, as centrally planned economies gave way to market economies in which planning plays a relatively limited role. Yet criticisms specifically directed at the field of LPP can also be identified. I examine three of these criticisms here.

Perhaps the most important criticism of early LPP was the failure to analyze adequately the impact of local context on national policies and plans. In part, this failure was a result of the emphasis on technical, rather than political, evaluation of plans and policies, as well as the general separation of LPP from political analysis. As Blommaert (1996) argues, LPP "can no longer stand exclusively for practical issues of standardization, graphization, terminological elaboration, and so on. The link between language planning and sociopolitical developments is obviously of paramount importance" (p. 217). One consequence of the failure to link LPP to politics was that planners could not predict the impact of their plans and policies. Although early LPP specialists believed that unexpected outcomes could be avoided as long as adequate information was available, recent work in LPP assumes that unexpected outcomes are a normal feature of highly complex

social systems, where linear cause-effect relationships between language and society do not apply and where social groups may have covert goals for LPP (Ammon 1997).

With the failure of many plans and policies to achieve the goals of political/
administrative and sociocultural integration, the optimism of early LPP was soon
replaced by skepticism about the work of language planners (e.g., Cluver 1992).
Yet the failure of LPP to achieve its lofty goals is not surprising, given the complex
forces affecting various forms of national integration. As a result, researchers have
proposed what has been called a "systems approach" or an "ecological" perspective
for LPP (Clayton 1999; Cluver 1991; Ohly 1989; Skutnabb-Kangas 2000a). While
such work varies in the factors considered central to LPP, proponents agree that
specialists must understand the wide range of social, economic, and political forces
that affect, and are affected by, LPP processes. Within this framework, a widespread belief is that not enough is known about the complex relationships between
language and society for LPP to be used for "social engineering" (Cluver 1991: 44;
also see Kashoki 1982). Thus, recent work examines the capacity of LPP to achieve
limited aims, such as reducing social distance and stereotyping or increasing language learning and communicative interaction among groups that speak different
primary languages (e.g., Musau 1999).

A second criticism of early LPP was that it paid too little attention to the
language practices and attitudes of communities affected by LPP, particularly the
ways in which linguistic minorities accommodate, subvert, or transform national
plans within their local communities. In addition, early LPP research did not
adequately examine the involvement of business enterprises, nongovernmental organizations, professional associations (e.g., teachers' groups), and other institutions and organizations involved in LPP practice. In contrast, more recent work
emphasizes the capacity of local communities (even those that have relatively little
political power) to adopt multiple identities only partly determined by LPP and
to alter significantly the outcomes of plans and policies (Pennycook 1995).

A third criticism of early LPP is that, despite the hope that LPP would bring
a broad array of benefits to minority populations in developing nations, in practice
LPP was often used by dominant groups to maintain their political and economic
advantage. The clearest example is apartheid South Africa, where LPP isolated
black populations, increased conflict, and aided the white minority in its efforts
to hold on to power (Cluver 1992; de Klerk and Barkhuizen 1998; Kamwangamalu
1997; Ohly 1989). Indeed, the Afrikaner nationalist government promoted mother
tongue instruction and used codification and standardization as tools for segre-
gating different ethnic groups among the black population, while other policies
promoted Afrikaans rather than English (de Klerk 2000). As Cluver (1992) shows,
LPP was used in apartheid South Africa to confirm the ideology of racial separation that was at the heart of apartheid, and thus resistance to language policies
was an important factor behind the important Soweto uprising in June 1976 and

the eventual end of apartheid. In other states in Africa, LPP was used to overcome the immediate postindependence crisis of national integration, but often this goal was achieved only within the educated elite, leaving masses of the population largely cut off from economic and political power (Mazrui and Tidy 1984).

The use of LPP by dominant groups is not limited to developing nations. In the Soviet Union, for instance, the spread of Russian was selectively encouraged in regions where central planners sought to extend their authority (Kirkwood 1990). In the United Kingdom, the renewed prominence of standard English in the schools in the 1990s is linked to a wider effort to limit the role of immigrants' languages in education; and in the United States, federal policies suppressed indigenous languages (Shonerd 1990) and, more recently, official English legislation in some states has become a tool for restricting the political power of Latinos (Donahue 2001).

RECENT REVIVAL OF LPP

One of the most important changes in LPP since the 1980s is the recognition that LPP is not necessarily an aspect of development. Indeed, the recent revival in academic interest in LPP is in part a result of the growing recognition that LPP is involved in a broad range of social processes. Among the most important of these processes are migration and the rise of nationalism in Europe and Central Asia.

Migration is one of the major reasons for the increase in the number of people worldwide who are learning languages and for the resulting revival in LPP. With more than twenty million refugees worldwide, an equal number of people displaced within their own countries, and countless millions of economic migrants such as Bosnians and Turks in Germany, Filipinos in Hong Kong, South Asians in the United Kingdom, and Latinos in the United States, language teaching programs have been dramatically affected throughout the world. In many countries, LPP in education has been central to efforts to deal with this massive movement of people (Tollefson 1989). As a result of the global process of migration, new questions have gained importance in LPP:

- What should be the role of migrants' languages in education and other official domains of use?
- How are local languages affected by migrants?
- What should be the status of new varieties of English and other lingua francas?

- How can acquisition planning be most effectively carried out?
- What factors constrain acquisition planning?

A second area for LPP has emerged from the collapse of the Soviet Union and realignments in political boundaries in Eastern Europe and Central Asia. In these new states, language issues are intimately linked with ideological and political conflicts. Minority issues, including LPP, are at the center of conflicts between Russia and Ukraine, Georgia and South Ossetia, Armenia and Azerbaijan, Russia and Chechnya, Hungary and Slovakia, Slovenia and Austria, Turkey and its Kurdish minority, and elsewhere in the region, and they are central also to the efforts of new states to establish effective local institutions (e.g., Estonia, Latvia, and Lithuania). In the states of former Yugoslavia, for example, language policy has been a key issue for government leaders (Tollefson 1997). Indeed, the violent destruction of Yugoslavia has focused attention on the fundamental political problem of Europe and Central Asia: the relationship between minorities and nation states. The LPP choices made by state planners, legislative bodies, and citizens will play a key role in the management of political conflict in these new states for decades to come.

Finally, special mention should be made of the importance of South Africa in the recent interest in LPP. Blommaert (1996) argues that efforts by the post-apartheid government of South Africa to develop an ideology of multilingualism as a symbol of national revival and to use eleven official languages to enhance the process of democratization have forced LPP specialists to re-examine traditional assumptions about the costs of multilingualism and the benefits of monolingualism. The movement to deconstruct the ideology of monolingualism that pervades much LPP research (Williams 1992) has received new impetus from the innovative multilingual policies of postapartheid South Africa. Moreover, the linkage of multilingual policies and democratization is also an important part of political debates elsewhere, such as in Guatemala, where official recognition of the country's indigenous languages was an important part of the peace accords ending the country's civil war.

FUTURE DIRECTIONS IN LPP

Research in LPP is likely to continue to diverge from the limited focus on development that characterized the early period in the field. Indeed, it is now widely assumed that LPP is important for all states, not only developing ones. Moreover, in response to the critique of LPP, researchers have proposed new models, such as the systems approach or ecological model, incorporating new metaphors, such as networks (Cluver 1991; Kaplan and Baldauf 1997). This attention to the complex array of social forces involved in LPP presents a major challenge for LPP theory: Which social processes and factors are most relevant to LPP? Although LPP theory is not yet sufficiently developed to answer this question, it is likely that attention to both the local and global context and an interdisciplinary approach that considers issues of power will be essential. With these general guidelines in mind, I believe the following issues will receive attention by LPP researchers in the years ahead:

1. Although early LPP specialists assumed that LPP would lead to a general improvement in the conditions of less developed countries and minority groups, recent research has begun to examine how LPP exacerbates rather than reduces economic, social, and political inequalities (Phillipson 1992; Skuttnab-Kangas 2000; Tollefson 1995, 2001). In many instances, state policymakers have used LPP to further marginalize already domi- nated populations (e.g., Albanians in Kosovo). Rather than being a result of failed plans and policies, such exploitation is typical of LPP in many contexts, and thus should be a major focus for research.

2. Early LPP research seldom considered the local legal framework of plans and policies. For example, in the United States, the body of law sur- rounding the concept of "free speech" directly affects LPP debates about the English-only movement, state efforts to restrict languages other than English, and the use of nonstandard varieties in schools (Stephan 1999). LPP processes in the United States are constrained by this body of law, and policies have been overturned by the courts as violations of free speech (Donahue 2001). Similarly, language policies in the Philippines can be understood only within the framework of a long history of con- stitutional debates about the appropriate official role for English, Filipino, and other languages. Such "local" legal concerns must be incorporated into LPP research if LPP processes are to be understood across the full range of sociopolitical contexts in which LPP takes place.

3. The importance of linking LPP to political theory is at the heart of Wil- liams's (1992) claim that LPP specialists lack an understanding of the funda- mentally political nature of LPP processes. Though the academic discipline of LPP generally remains separate from political science, some recent theo- retical work in LPP has sought to connect LPP with political theory (e.g., Dua 1996). Understanding the central role of political processes in LPP will help specialists better understand how LPP is fundamentally involved in the pursuit and maintenance of power (see Cooper 1989).

4. Although they differ widely in their research orientations, Williams (1992) and Fishman (1992) concur in their concern for the failure of sociology

to confront issues in LPP and for the general lack of sociological expertise among LPP specialists in applied linguistics. Both Williams and Fishman call for LPP researchers to broaden their expertise beyond the traditional theoretical concerns and methodologies of applied linguistics and
to establish direct links with sociology. Although the influence of sociology on LPP continues to be minimal, efforts to understand the role of
LPP in migration, state formation, and political conflict may force LPP
specialists to develop new methodologies and to establish more direct
links with sociologists.

5. Recent work on discourse analysis demonstrates that ideology is an important factor in constraining plans and policies (e.g., Grove 1999; Pennycook 1998; Stephan 1999). Future research should continue to examine
the role of public political discourse and the mass media in LPP processes, particularly the role of political leaders in shaping public discussion of language issues.

6. Research on how the recipients of LPP control the process of social
change has led to a more complex understanding of social identity, the
various community affiliations that characterize individuals and groups,
and the importance of institutions other than the state for language use
and acquisition (Norton 1997a). Innovative work on language and social
identity should explore how communities undergo social change, quite
apart from actions of the state. Analysis of "real-life language planning"
(Dasgupta 1990: 87) should particularly examine the role of contact languages in promoting grass-roots dialogue. In this way, LPP research can
move away from a restricted focus on lingua francas as mechanisms for
state control and toward a deeper understanding of how they are involved in the multiple ways that power may be exercised in social life.

7. The diminishing role of the state and the growing importance of multinational corporations as institutions of global decision making require
new approaches to LPP research (Schubert 1990). How will global corporations manage the communication needs of business? What will be the
different functions within a united Europe for official languages and for
regional languages such as Catalan and Welsh? How will educational systems respond to the language needs of foreign workers? How will languages serve local community identity and communication needs, while
also meeting the demands of globalization? How will the global economy
change language acquisition and the structure of international languages?
These and many other important questions of language and globalization
will require new forms of LPP research, no longer focused exclusively on
the actions of state agencies, but instead linking LPP to related work in
the ethnography of communication, in mass media, and in microsociolinguistics, as well as in sociology and political theory.

8. Recent debates over language rights have affected LPP practitioners (e.g., South Africa, Guatemala). Moreover, as international organizations continue to adopt influential statements on language rights for linguistic minorities, the ground is being laid for language rights debates in additional settings (e.g., the United States). Thus, we can expect future research and practice in LPP to pay increasing attention to this important topic (Skutnabb-Kangas 2000).

PART X

TRANSLATION AND INTERPRETATION

CHAPTER 33

···

TRANSLATION

···

RODA P. ROBERTS

TRANSLATION is a polysemous word, which is often used in different senses, even in the same text. First, it stands for the act or operation of transferring a message from one language to another. Second, it refers to the product of the act of translating. Third, it designates the profession practiced by those performing the act or operation just mentioned. Finally, it has also been used for the academic discipline that studies or examines the operation or products of translation. These various senses of the word *translation* are illustrated by the following examples, all taken from Peter Newmark's *About Translation* (1991):

- Nida's (1975) classical definition of translation as "the reproduction of the closest natural equivalent of the source language message" could not be bettered (Newmark 1991: 34) [translation = act or operation].
- It is not possible to obtain any figures about the quantity and the areas of the total mass of translations (Newmark 1991: 16) [translation = product].
- Translation must now be recognized as a distinct and autonomous profession (Newmark 1991: 41) [translation = profession].
- Teaching such a necessary but tricky subject such as translation which is at once a skill, a science, an art and an area of taste has to be discussed (Newmark 1991: 137) [translation = discipline].

In each of these senses, translation can be considered as a generic, referring to both the written and oral transfer of a message from one language to another, or as a specific designating most often written transfer, although occasionally oral transfer (as in the expression "simultaneous translation").

In order to differentiate among these various senses, translation terminology has gradually evolved. The distinction between oral transfer and written transfer is now clearly made with "interpretation" being used for the former and "translation" being limited to the latter. "Translating" is increasingly used, instead of "translation," for the process. The academic discipline of translation is now called "translation studies."

Here, translation is treated in the narrower sense of written transfer, and particular emphasis is placed on the act of translating and on research in translation, although reference are also made to the translation product, as well as to the profession of translation.

Typologies of Translation

Even in the narrower sense of written transfer, both the process and the corresponding products of translation can be categorized in different ways, on the basis of different criteria, as demonstrated by Roberts (1995) in a comprehensive article on translation typologies.

Depending on who performs the act of translation (a person or the computer), the act itself and its result are classified as "human translation" or "machine translation" (MT) or "computer-assisted translation" (CAT). These names are fairly self-defining, with human translation being produced by a human being, machine translation by the computer using a specialized computer program (MT system), and computer-assisted translation by a human being using specialized computer programs that support the translator. However, it should be pointed out that, while, in theory, there is no human intervention in machine translation, since the computer program analyzes the text to be translated ("source text," or ST) and produces a translation ("target text," or TT), human intervention prior to or following the use of an MT system is nevertheless required in light of the current state of machine translation.

Both human translation and machine translation cover a variety of subtypes. For example, machine translation can be subdivided according to the type of system used by the computer. Two of the better known types are the following: the direct system, in which the processing of the ST leads directly to the TT without any intermediate stages, and the transfer system, which uses an indirect approach, interposing a bilingual transfer module between two intermediate representations, the source language representation and the target language representation, which are the result of analysis of the source text and the generation of the target text respectively (Hutchins and Somers 1992: 71–77). Another dimension that has been used to classify machine translation types is the nature of the human intervention required. This includes pre-editing (correcting or simplifying natural language before translation), creating source texts in controlled language using a limited range of syntax and vocabulary specifically for machine translation, and postediting (revising the raw machine translation output) (Lawson 1989: 212). Given that machine translation is in constant evolution, that much of the work done in this area is still experimental, and that it has become an area of specialization quite distinct from human translation, it is not treated further in this article.

Human translation, which is generally termed simply "translation" and which is the primary focus here, has also been classified in very different ways, both by translation scholars and by translation professionals. Typologies proposed by translation scholars focus more on the nature of the source text, while those suggested by translation professionals concentrate on the target text.

Source text-based typologies first group translation according to the function of the source text into two or three subcategories. Using this criterion, Delisle (1980: 29–34) distinguishes between pragmatic translation, which involves the translation of a predominantly informative text, and literary translation, which is the translation of a text in which the expressive and aesthetic functions predominate. Delisle's literary translation is more or less equivalent to what Newmark terms translation of an expressive text (1988), although in the latter's typology Delisle's "pragmatic translation" is further subdivided into translation of an informative text, which emphasizes the content, and translation of a vocative text, where the focus is on the reader. Another common characteristic used to classify translation on the basis of the source text is the degree of specialization in the source text. Thus, Delisle (1980: 25) differentiates between general translation, that is, translation of texts that require little or no specialized knowledge, and specialized translation, or translation of texts that require specialized knowledge. The content or subject matter of the source text also serves as a criterion of classification of translation. On this basis, Newmark (1991: 36–37) makes a distinction between scientific-technological translation, institutional-cultural translation, and literary translation.

Several authors, including translation scholars and translation professionals, take the general purpose of translating into consideration in their typologies of translation. Thus, Delisle (1980: 40–43) and Newmark (1991: 61–64) separate academic translation, whose goal is language acquisition for the person translating, from professional translation, whose objective is the transmission of a message to a translation user. On the same basis, Snell and Crampton (1983: 109) differentiate between noncommercial translation, which is done either for pleasure or as a language acquisition exercise, and professional translation, which is undertaken for a customer against remuneration.

Finally, some typologies of translation focus primarily on various aspects of the translation itself. Using the criterion of function of the translation, Snell and Crampton (1983: 111, 114) and Sager (1983: 124) distinguish between translation for publication and translation for information. The latter also takes into account the communicative function of the target text in relation to that of the source text, opposing translation with the same function as the original to translation with a new function in relation to the original. Based on the "integrality" of the translation, the same authors make a distinction between translation proper or full translation and extraction of information or selective translation. Sager (1983: 125) adds a further distinction on the basis of the degree of modification introduced in the target text, contrasting translation without modification of the original against translation with modification of the original. In fact, most typologies distinguish translation according to the translation approach used in producing the target text, approaches that are further considered in the following section.

THE TRANSLATION PROCESS

Whatever the nature of the source text and the differences in approach that can be adopted in its translation, the basic translation process remains much the same—the same factors and major stages are involved in each case.

The process of translation involves a number of different pairs of elements, a reality that may account for statements such as those claiming that translation is "probably the most complex type of event yet produced in the evolution of the cosmos" (Richards 1953: 250). The major elements are:

- Two authors (the author of the source text, called the "source," and the translator, who becomes the source of the target text)
- Two texts (a source text and the eventual target text), each containing a message
- Two (sets of) intended receptors (those of the source text and those of the target text)
- Two languages (the source language and the target language)
- Two cultures (that of the source, the source text's intended receptors and the source language, and that of the translator, the target text's intended receptors and the target language).

These elements, which are all inextricably linked, are briefly examined.

The author of the source text, like any individual involved in an act of communication, generally has a message that she wishes to convey to others.[1] "Message" is taken here in the sense given to it by Pergnier (1980: 22–23) as something particular that someone particular wishes to communicate to someone specific in specific circumstances. This message is conditioned by a number of factors, including the author's culture and language, her education, her socioprofessional background, and his linguistic skills. For instance, an author from a culture where divorce is taboo is unlikely to write on this topic; an author without much education, either formal or informal, would probably present a message on divorce from a personal point of view, rather than from a sociocultural or legal stance. In order to convey her message effectively, a good author will also take into consideration the background of her intended receptors. Thus, if she is writing a self-help guide on divorce, she will not, or should not, present divorce procedures in the same way as if she were writing on this topic in a legal textbook. The author's intended message is conveyed through a text, which involves not only content but also form. The linguistic and textual form in which the message is transmitted depends, on the one hand, on the linguistic and textual norms of the author's society and culture and, on the other hand, on the author's mastery of these norms. Thus, the alexandrine, a verse form that was popular in France (and therefore in French) in the seventeenth century, was not so in the English language and culture. Hence, poetry written in alexandrines in French would normally require transposition into another form in English translation. And, no matter how good a command the author has of her/her language,[2] the text she produces is often marked, to some degree at least, by her idiolect—that is, her personal speech habits. Given the number of factors involved in the production of the source text, the author's intended message may not be textually realized as clearly or as exactly as she may wish. However, it is on the message as realized in the source text and not on what the author may have intended to say that the translator works. The translator, who inevitably has a different background from that of the original author, has to grasp fully the source text message in order to translate it. Apart from a very good knowledge of the source language and culture, she also needs knowledge related to the topic with which she has to deal. And, of course, she needs to have an excellent command of the linguistic, textual, and cultural norms of the target language.[3]

Armed with her linguistic and extralinguistic knowledge, the translator undertakes the challenge of translating, a complicated process involving numerous steps and procedures. However, for practical purposes, the process is generally presented as consisting of three stages.[4] The first stage consists of analysis of the source text, the goal of which is a thorough comprehension of the message it intends to convey. This stage involves not only recognition of the words and their meaning and of the relationship between them (Nida and Taber 1974: 34–98) but also grasping the meaning that underlies the words and understanding exactly what is being referred to (Delisle 1980: 70–77). In principle, this leads to a nonlanguage-specific semantic representation in the translator's mind (Bell 1991:

45–58). The next stage involves transferring the source text message into the target language. This stage—called *transfer* by Nida and Taber (1974: 99–119), *reformulation* by Delisle (1980: 77–82), and *synthesis* by Bell (1991: 58–60)—is, to all intents and purposes, the reverse of the preceding one, in that the translator now transforms the nonlanguage-specific representation in her mind into words and a text in the target language. However, according to most translation scholars, this second stage results not in a final product, as Bell (1991) seems to imply, but in a draft translation, which is generally far from perfect from the point of view both of accuracy of content and of appropriateness of style. Hence, the need for the third stage of the translation process, termed *verification* by Delisle (1988: 66–68) and *restructuring* by Nida and Taber (1974: 120–162) but generally called *revision* (i.e., self-revision) by translators. At this point, the translator checks the target text against the source text to ensure that there are no omissions, additions or meaning distortions in her translation. She also reviews the translation to ensure that it is appropriate for the function that it is expected to fulfill.

While the three stages outlined here are part of every translation operation, there are differences in the way different translators work through them. Some analyze the source text in its entirety, then undertake sentence-by-sentence transfer, and finally revise the text as a whole. Others jump into the transfer stage with only minimal analysis and do further analysis as and when they feel the need. Some translation scholars propose specific (and often different) procedures to be used at each stage of the translation process. During analysis of structures, for instance, Nida and Taber (1974: 47–55) recommend the use of back-transformation of a surface structure to its underlying kernels, while Bell (1991: 44–56) proposes a combination of parsing, propositional analysis, and theme-rheme analysis. However, most translators do not seem to use any one procedure consistently and systematically. They also appear to work with differently sized units of translation, that is, the source text unit being translated. While there is general agreement among both translation scholars and translation professionals that the unit of translation must be larger than the word if one is to avoid a meaningless and ungrammatical translation, there is no consensus on the ideal unit of translation, although sentence-by-sentence translation is most often practiced. Indeed, Newmark (1988: 64–67) seems to suggest that the translation unit varies in size depending on the difficulty of (any portion of) the source text and on the translation approach adopted.

Translation approaches have long been a subject of debate and even dissension in the translation world, starting with the oft-cited but somewhat exaggerated quarrel on the topic between Augustine and Jerome. These approaches have traditionally been categorized around two poles, generally termed *literal* and *free*. Although the definitions given to literal translation and free translation have varied through the ages and according to the authors (Roberts 1988), the former approach consists essentially in maintaining the form of the source text, while the latter approach consists in conveying the content of the source text without consideration of its form. Over time, each of these overall approaches has developed subcategories. Literal translation, for instance, covers a range from word-for-word translation (which is often meaningless, since the source language word order is preserved and words are translated by their most common meanings without consideration of the context in which they occur) to Newmark's (1988: 45–46) semantic translation (which attempts to reproduce the precise contextual meaning of the original by using target language structures, while allowing for the translator's intuitive empathy with the original). Similarly, free translation covers a wide range of methods, from the extreme of adaptation, in which the source text serves merely as a starting point for a target text that is "rewritten," to idiomatic translation, which reproduces in the target language a text that communicates the same message as the source text but uses the natural grammatical and lexical choices of the target language. In fact, although much has been made of the literal and free translation dichotomy, there exists a continuum from one pole to the other, as Larson (1984: 17) has clearly shown. Moreover, it is currently acknowledged that no one approach is valid for all texts or all parts of a text. A legal text such as a statute, because of its status before the law, is likely to be translated more literally than an informative text, whose primary purpose is to convey content. If a part of a text is dense and difficult, the translator may either stick to a more literal translation or, after a thorough analysis of its meaning, present the meaning more freely without consideration of the source text form. A literary text may be translated very literally if the translator's intent is to show the specific characteristics of the source language text or quite freely if the translator translates it for the pleasure of the general reading public. Thus, many factors come into play in the choice of approach, including the nature of the source text, the function of the translation, and even the similarities between the source language and the target language.[5] These, in turn, influence the translation product. In fact, one of the key reasons for retranslation of a source text (and hence for the existence of more than one translation of a source text in any given language) is the need felt by a society to approach the original text and its translation from a different point of view. This has resulted in some of the world's more "popular" texts, such as the Bible, being translated into the major world languages not once but many times over the centuries.

RECENT TRANSLATION RESEARCH

While translation has been practiced since the beginnings of civilization and translators themselves have expressed their opinions on the translation process or the products of this process from early times, the more systematic study of translation began only in the 1950s and 1960s. This development was the result of a combination of factors, the most significant being a growing interest in machine translation and the emergence of university programs in translation both in Europe and in North America. Since that time, translation research has been wide ranging, covering the translation process, translation products, translation quality assessment, methods of training translators, bilingual terminology and lexicography, the use of technology in translation, and machine translation.[6] First, generalizations regarding translation and its problems and critical appraisals of specific translations gave way to the development of a number of theoretical models of the translation process,[7] often grouped according to their epistemological foundations into literary models, linguistic models, sociolinguistic or communicative models, interpretive models, and semiotic models (Delisle 1980; Nida 1976). But all these models, including the three-stage model presented earlier, have been criticized as being "speculative rather than empirical and concentrated on idealizations rather than on actually occurring data" (Lörscher 1991: 2). Such criticisms have led translation researchers to turn, in the past fifteen years, to more observational studies, which use as their starting point either translations themselves or translation performance.

The first innovative trend was the development of Descriptive Translation Studies (DTS) by Toury (1980), which focus on the observation of existing translations, that is, on actual products, rather than on the process of translation (1980: 7). Their goal is to account for translational phenomena—entire texts or parts of texts and groups of texts—in a systematic way within one unified framework. Toury's analyses begin, not with the source text as has generally been the case with product studies in the past, but with the target text or translation. According to him (1995: 29), "translations are facts of target cultures" and thus need proper contextualization in the polysystem of the target culture. Translation is, in effect, initiated by the target culture, as a way of filling in gaps in relation to other cultures. Translations are governed, first and foremost, by "preliminary norms," which establish the cultural context in which translation takes place; these include factors such as the translation policy of the target culture, the concept of translation during a given period, and the types of authors and works favored by the target culture. The translations are also governed by "initial norms," which categorize the decision of individual translators either to adhere closely to the source text and the norms of the source culture or to adapt the translation to the norms of the target culture or to adopt a compromise position. Finally, "operational norms" direct specific decisions made during the act of translation itself and affect the matrix of the target text. These translational norms can be reconstructed using both extratextual sources (such as statements made by translators, editors, and publishers) and textual sources, that is, translated texts, which are compared as necessary with their source texts.[8] But the focus of attention remains the translation itself, which is accepted without any judgments made regarding the correctness of the solutions adopted.[9] And since regular tendencies in translation can be identified only by studying a number of translations, DTSs examine multiple translations of the same source text produced at different times in one receiving culture or translations into one language and culture of the same type of work from predetermined source languages and literatures. Toury's entire approach is based on the belief that the translation process can be understood only by analyzing translated texts from within their cultural-linguistic context.

While DTSs were already using groups of translated texts as the basis for analysis, and while Toury had already used the word corpus to designate these groups of texts (e.g., Toury 1980: 81), until very recently corpora in translation studies were very modest in size and were searched manually. In 1993, Baker, inspired by the effective use of computerized corpora in linguistics, argued that "translation studies has reached a stage in its development as a discipline when it is both ready for and needs the techniques and methodology of corpus linguistics in order to make a major leap from prescriptive to descriptive statements" (Baker 1993: 248). Since then, a certain number of corpora appropriate for translation research have been developed, and a growing number of translation scholars have begun to consider the corpus-based approach as a viable and systematic way to study translation and translations. In fact, enough work has been done on, or using, the corpus-based approach for the translation journal *Meta* to publish a special issue on this topic, edited by Laviosa (1998a). The studies in this issue, which cover not only translation but also interpretation, are grouped into two main categories: first, discussions on theoretical issues relating to the scope, object of study, and methodology of corpus-based studies, and, second, empirical and pedagogical studies of translation.

One of the problems that the corpus-based approach is still grappling with is that of corpus establishment. While a number of unilingual corpora exist, especially in English (but also in other major languages), these corpora do not include translated texts. Moreover, translation studies require not only corpora of translations but corpora that allow for comparison of translations with source texts ("parallel corpora," according to Baker's 1995 terminology) or of original texts in two or more languages ("multilingual corpora," to use Baker's term) or of original texts and translations in a given language ("comparable corpora," according to Baker). Some such corpora do exist: TransBase, which consists of the French and English versions of the debates in the Canadian House of Commons from 1988 to 1995, is an example of a parallel corpus; the corpus compiled by the Council of Europe Multilingual Lexicography is given by Baker as an example of a multilingual corpus; the English Comparable Corpus is described by Laviosa (1998b: 557, 566) as a "monolingual, multi-source-language" corpus, consisting of two computerized collections of texts in English: the Translational English corpus, comprising English translations from a variety of source languages, and the Non-

Translational English Corpus, comprising original English texts of a similar type produced during a similar time span. But there is still a need for more and larger corpora suitable for translation research. Yet another problem is that of developing special tools for efficient and effective exploitation of data found in parallel, multilingual, and comparable corpora. Some programs such as TransSearch work on parallel corpora but not on multilingual corpora or comparable corpora; for others, such as PAT, the reverse is true. The development of suitable tools must be accompanied by the development of specific methods for interrogating corpora for translation-related research, methods that have been slow to emerge.

Despite these limitations, preliminary corpus-based studies have substantiated certain widespread generalizations about translation. For example, Baker's examination of a comparable English corpus for what she terms universal features of translation, such as explicitation, simplification, and grammatical conventionality (1993: 243–248), has yielded some proof that there is a tendency to use standard language in translation, which accounts for a striking homogeneity among texts translated into English as opposed to texts composed originally in English (1998: 482). Laviosa's study of lexical items in translated and original newspaper articles and narrative prose found in the English Comparable Corpus seems to confirm the fact that translators use simpler language, since she was able to identify the following "core patterns of lexical use":

- Translated texts, when compared with nontranslated texts, have a relatively lower percentage of content words versus grammatical words.
- Translated texts contain a higher proportion of frequent words than do nontranslated texts.
- The most frequent words are repeated more often in the former than in the latter, and, correspondingly, translated texts contain fewer lemmas (1998b: 565).

However, the majority of corpus-based translation studies have so far focused on the linguistic aspects of translation, rather than on the discourse aspects. While Munday (1998: 542–556) has analyzed a limited parallel corpus (a short story in Spanish and its English translation), using basic word statistics (type-token ratio and frequency lists on the one hand and KWIC concordances and intercalated text on the other hand) to identify and examine translation shifts (i.e., changes introduced in the process of going from SL to TL) related not only to vocabulary and structure but also to cohesion, he, like many other translation scholars working on corpora, is limited in the analysis of discourse by the corpus tools and methods presently available, many of which were developed with linguistic studies in mind. The challenge, then, for corpus-based translation studies is to develop tools and methods appropriate for the study not just of individual textual elements but of entire texts.

While corpus translation studies have opened up many possibilities for research (see Tymoczko 1998), they have not been able to account for the psychological reality of translating—what goes on in the translator's brain when she renders a source text into a target language. This is the goal of other observational studies, which borrow research tools and methods from psychology and psycholinguistics to study actual translation performance, that is, the translator working on a translation task, in an effort better to understand the complexity of the translation process. Krings's 1986 study is considered a pioneering work in this respect (Wilss 1996: 35). Krings introduced into translation studies the think-aloud protocol, which has since become one of the more popular of the experimental methods used in translation. This method involves asking translators to translate a text and, at the same time, to verbalize what they are thinking while they are performing the task; their performance is recorded on tape or video, and the recording is then transcribed, with the written transcript referred to as "think-aloud protocol," or TAP.

Krings's TAP study, whose subjects were university students of French who were asked to translate a text from French to German, analyzed translation problems, which the researcher identified by means of specific indicators in the protocols and which he classified into comprehension problems, combined comprehension and production problems, and pure production problems. The method he used has since been adopted by others to examine various aspects of the activity of translating, such as global translation strategies (Séguinot 1989), problem-solving strategies (Lörscher 1991), and criteria for decision making (Tirkkonen-Condit 1989).

TAP studies have given rise to some interesting conclusions; however, some of them appear to be contradictory. For example, while Séguinot's case study of a Canadian government translator supported the hypothesis that, for professional translators, the translation process is highly automatized, with few problems and little conscious decision making, Jääskeläinen's (1989) research has shown that professional translators identify more problems and spend more time and energy solving them than do language learners.

Some of the problems concerning TAP studies are related to "the danger of lack of representativeness in the sample of informants or in the tasks they are asked to do" (Bell 1998: 189). Thus, Séguinot's 1989 article was based on the analysis of a single subject's performance, whereas Lörscher's 1991 study was based on data collected from forty-eight subjects. Moreover, while Séguinot's subject was a professional translator, Lörscher's subjects were, for the most part, first- or second-year university foreign language students. And while, in most TAP studies on translation, subjects have been asked to produce a written translation of a written source text, often with the aid of dictionaries and other translation tools, Lörscher required his subjects to produce an oral translation of a written text without the use of aids of any kind.

Despite such methodological problems, as well as the general difficulty of observing what is basically a mental activity, the evidence of empirical studies not only has given rise to some interesting hypotheses that merit further attention but has also further revealed the complexity of the translation process which is not a straightforward three-stage process, but which involves much backtracking and recursiveness.

In summary, what characterizes recent translation research is diversity and openness. Diversity is evident in the methods used, in the topics examined and in the subjects and/or texts studied. The new openness with regard to borrowing approaches and methods from other disciplines, such as literary studies, corpus linguistics, and psychology, contrasts sharply with the dismissal, for example, of linguistically oriented traditions within translation studies in the 1970s and early 1980s (see, e.g., Seleskovitch 1984) when translation was still trying to establish itself as a separate discipline.

The Translation Profession

Just as translation research underwent major changes in the last two decades of the twentieth century, so did the translation profession. Wilss (1999: 181) identifies three basic trends that have affected the profession since the beginning of the 1990s: globalization, specialization, and technologization.

The abolition of trade barriers around the world, the merger of major companies, and the removal of border controls have led to economic globalization, which allows capital and products, information, and technology, as well as labor, to cross frontiers easily and speedily. This has led to an ever-increasing need for translation, especially into English, which is the acknowledged global language. Globalization has also led to greater competition in the translation market, since translators, like products and capital, can more easily work in countries other than their own.

If this is the era of globalization, it is also the age of specialization. Knowledge today is highly specialized, with the increasing sophistication of all disciplines—especially the scientific and technological disciplines. Specialized knowledge is communicated, at least among experts, through languages for special purposes or special languages. In order to be able to transmit such specialized knowledge accurately and appropriately in a target language, translators themselves need to be specialists, to some degree at least. They need both knowledge of the subject and knowledge of the special language used in the field (both the source special language and the target special language). They can no longer afford to be simply generalists who possess wide general knowledge and are willing to translate in any domain.

Finally, technologization not only has added more areas of specialization for translators to master (e.g., the whole Internet subfield), but has profoundly changed the way translators work. First, it has provided them with new tools that help them work more efficiently and, ideally at least, more rapidly. These include term banks and translation memory systems:

> *Term banks,* which are databases of term records intended to help translators to understand specialized vocabulary in the source language and to select an appropriate target language term, can now be accessed directly by translators from their personal computers.
>
> *Translation memories,* which are databases that contain source language text segments along with equivalent target language text segments, drawn from translations produced by human translators and segmented using simple linguistic algorithms, are also readily available.

Translators translating a new source text use a translation editor that automatically performs a segmentation of this text and looks up the segments in the translation memory database. If a segment is found, the translation stored with this segment is offered as a possible equivalent to the translator, who may choose to accept it as is, modify it, or reject it. Translation memory systems are particularly useful for source language texts that are updated versions of a former text and for texts that contain standardized components. Finally, there are a few operating machine translation systems such as SYSTRAN, although such systems are far from perfect and their output requires considerable postediting to make it easily readable. The few tools presented here show that translation technology has come a long way and is undoubtedly of great use to translators. But, despite fears in the 1960s and 1970s that translators would be replaced by machines, it is now clear that, at least in the foreseeable future, technological tools will remain merely aids in translation, with translators controlling the decision-making process.

Conclusion

The development of translation technology has created new challenges for translators by expanding their role to include aspects such as terminology management and postediting. Moreover, translators are now called upon to do not only full translations but also summary translations to keep up with the ever-growing need for interlingual communication. They are also asked to do parallel composition (i.e., to write a text in a second language at the same time as the unilingual author composes the "original" text in his language). Because of such additions to and permutations of the tasks of the translator, translator training has evolved to include editing, terminology production and management, and the use of translation technology. And some translation scholars have extended their areas of research to include aspects such as the comparison of original writing and translation and the dictionary needs of translators. In this rapidly evolving context, the very terms *translator* and *translation* seem too restrictive today and are often replaced by such usages as *language mediator* and *language mediation* and even by the generic terms *language professional* and *language industry*.[10]

NOTES

1. The major exception to this rule is poets, whose primary aim is often not to communicate a message but to express themselves in an original manner.

2. It is assumed here that the author of the source text is writing in his dominant language, that is, the language he knows best. However, this is not always the case.

3. This is why most professional translators choose to translate into their dominant language.

4. These stages have been designated and described somewhat differently by different translation scholars.

5. If the source language and target language are structurally similar, literal translation may result in a meaningful and even idiomatic target text, which is not the case when the two languages are very dissimilar.

6. While a number of books on translation are now being published, often in special series, by well-known publishers such as John Benjamins, much of the research is presented through the ever-growing number of specialized journals such as *Meta*.

7. We use "model" here in the sense presented by Roger Bell (1991: 23). He makes the link between theory and model as follows: "The explanation of the system is the theory of the scientist which, when passed on to others, is realized as a model."

8. According to Toury himself (1995: 80), "every comparison is partial only; it is not really performed on the objects as such, only certain aspects thereof."

9. As Gentzler (1993: 129) points out, "Toury now views 'original' texts as containing clusters of properties, meanings, possibilities. All translations privilege certain properties/meanings at the expense of others, and the concept of a 'correct' translation ceases to be a real possibility."

10. This term is generally used in the plural to cover a number of language-related activities such as translation, interpretation, editing, and even language planning.

CHAPTER 34

....

INTERPRETATION

....

NANCY L. SCHWEDA NICHOLSON

In 1995, in an article that presented an overview of the fields of translation and interpretation, I wrote that "research trends (especially in interpretation) clearly reveal a heightened awareness among many scholars of the value of interdisciplinary studies which provide enlightening psychological and physiological data on ... simultaneous interpretation" (Schweda Nicholson 1995: 44). This statement remains true today, as the body of literature in interpretation continues to focus on the "cognitive" approach. Whereas in the past publications tended to include personal accounts of interpreting experiences and lists of linguistic challenges presented by various language combinations as well as pedagogical frameworks that offered training advice, the current emphasis is on interdisciplinary studies that incorporate various components of processing activities (such as perception, comprehension, memory, monitoring, communication strategies, and so on). New journals such as *Interpreting* highlight research studies that look at interpretation from a wide range of perspectives. We currently see a growing trend in articles and books that focus on quantitative, as well as qualitative data.

Moreover, while many writings in the period from 1952 to 1988 are by French authors (often associated with the Ecole Supérieure d'Interprètes et de Traducteurs [ESIT]), recent work provides evidence of an increasing internationalization in the field. Authors from other European countries (i.e., Austria, Italy, and Switzerland), the United States, Canada, and Japan figure prominently (Pöchhacker 1995). Australia also makes a significant contribution. Perhaps one of the reasons for this is that the Internet and e-mail now provide an almost effortless medium of communication, making access to colleagues across the world as easy (and inexpensive) as getting in touch with someone across town. We have also seen a growing tendency toward collaboration among interpretation researchers and scholars working in related fields. Such cooperation is typified by the interdisciplinary efforts of Kurz (interpretation) and Petsche (neurophysiology) (Kurz 1995). In this connection, simultaneous interpretation (SI) is a more frequent subject of study than is consecutive interpretation (CI), probably because its real-time overlap of two codes permits the examination of interference, input-output, monitoring, ear-voice span (EVS), and other language interface issues as the interpretation takes place.

Another trend identified by Pöchhacker (1995) is that, during the six-year period he investigates (1989–1994), the majority of the publications were written in English. Finally, pedagogy still plays an important role in research and writing, as fully 25 percent of the material published during this interval concentrates on the teaching of interpretation, stressing the value of specific techniques and strategies. Additionally, many quantitative studies are conducted using interpretation students as subjects. (See, e.g., Russo 1995; Tonelli and Riccardi 1995.)

Conference interpreting is still the focus of numerous articles, but the growing fields of court and medical interpretation are now frequently treated by book-length manuscripts and more widely discussed in the literature (Carr et al. 1997; de Jongh 1992; Edwards 1995; González et al. 1991; Moore 1999).

CONFERENCE INTERPRETATION

As in the past, conference interpreting continues to be a popular research subject. Riccardi, Marinuzzi, and Zecchin (1998) describe interpreter stress, specifically in the context of remote interpreting (typified by videoconferencing). Gubertini (1998) discusses the validity of interpreter additions, making a case for the importance of producing a comprehensible rendition rather than a mere *transcodage*. Sergio (1998) examines the interpreter's role(s) in terms of mediating cultural differences. Ondelli (1998) deals with the interpreter's oral text production and also focuses on the text type of the source language (SL) material. Kohn and Kalina (1996) stress that interpretation differs sharply from monolingual communication. They provide a detailed description of the strategies employed by interpreters in order to understand initially and subsequently produce coherent output.

Simultaneous Interpretation (SI)

Kurz (1995) reports on her continuing research into SI processing activities using EEGs. Although the experiments were performed in a rather artificial situation (subjects were asked to interpret silently so as to avoid any motor activity interference in the EEG readings), Kurz states that a control experiment (in which interpreters did utter their renditions aloud) provided essentially the same outcome. She stresses that the aim of her study was to investigate cognitive processing activity, not articulatory or motor elements in SI. Kurz's results confirm right hemisphere involvement during language tasks in bilinguals (Green et al. 1994, 1990). She also suggests that interpretation into a nonnative language creates "greater coherence increases in the temporal region of the non-dominant hemisphere" (Kurz 1995: 13).

Messina (1998) revisits the ongoing problem of speakers who read prepared texts at conferences (Déjean le Féal 1978; Schweda Nicholson 1989). He offers some good suggestions regarding the preparation of speeches to be read aloud (which, unfortunately, are largely ignored by conference participants). Setton (1998) also touches on text type and delivery format in his discussion of how meaning develops incrementally as a speech unfolds during SI.

Van Besien (1999) analyzes German-to-French data taken from Lederer (1980, 1981) regarding simultaneous interpreters' use of anticipation techniques. He concludes that anticipation does play a role in SI, proposing that the strategies employed may also be language-specific. His data show that verbs were anticipated most frequently. He attributes this to the different syntactic patterns of the two languages (German = SOV and French = SVO). Van Besien also highlights the role of extralinguistic information, such as context, in the application of anticipation strategies.

Darò (1997) provides an overview of memory studies in conference interpretation. She stresses that memory is a multipartite and multifaceted phenomenon, not a single entity. In this connection, Darò indicates that different types of memory may be more or less involved in CI and SI. For example, she suggests that episodic memory may play a greater role in CI than in SI. Gran and Bellini (1996) report on a study of short-term memory in SI, focusing on verbatim recall. As demonstrated in other studies, the recency effect also played a role in this one. Chincotta and Underwood (1998), as well as Gernsbacher and Shlesinger (1997), discuss the consequences of concurrent articulation and suppression during SI. More specifically, the latter study examines a wide variety of material that may be suppressed during processing. This includes literal expressions as well as syntactic, anaphoric, and lexical interference.

Error analysis in interpretation has frequently been the subject of research (Barik 1994, 1969; Falbo 1998). Braun and Clarici (1997) describe the challenges posed to interpreters to represent numerals correctly in SI. Their study examined data collected from students working in a German-Italian combination and included shadowing, translation, and SI tasks.

Carlet (1998) tested Chernov's (1994) concept of probability prediction by including semantically unrelated, meaningless information in a SI passage. Subjects were jarred by these sentences, which did not fit into the logical progression of information input to that point in the speech. This material caused them to re-evaluate what they had already heard in terms of the new and implausible information. The resulting effect was frequent omissions. Carlet concludes that Chernov's approach is a valid tool for examining psycholinguistic processes in SI.

Over the years, a frequent topic of discussion has been the deleterious effects of simultaneous interpreters working longer than the average thirty-minute stint. Moser-Mercer, Künzli, and Korac (1998) conducted a small study and found that not only was there an increase in meaning errors during extended interpretation but also that interpreters became less effective at (a) monitoring their output and (b) recognizing the resulting reduction in the quality of their renditions. Zeier (1997) presents a broad overview of research on psychophysiological stress. He suggests that, in cases of mental overload in SI, interpreters may exhibit a careless attitude and take their work less seriously. Zeier stresses that this change in attitude occurs quite automatically, and interpreters are generally not conscious of decremental performance. Results such as these on extended turns and stress are currently being used to further the argument that court interpreters should also work in teams in order to combat the negative consequences of physiological and psychological fatigue (Festinger 1999). Frauenfelder and Schriefers (1997) propose a psycholinguistic approach to SI. From an historical perspective, Kaufmann (1998) discusses the history of SI in Israel. Mizuno (1995) reviews recent theoretical research in Japan.

Consecutive Interpretation (CI)

Falbo (1995) presents a general discussion of CI and focuses on the relevance of two pre-interpretation exercises, namely sight translation and memorization. Nguyen and Tochon (1998) discuss the role of concept maps and summaries during consecutive training of Vietnamese interpreters and conclude that the concept map is a useful learning tool. Kellet (1995) focuses on the importance of public speaking skills in CI and videotapes trainees in order to gather extralinguistic data regarding demeanor and presentation techniques. Giambagli (1998) questions whether attentional resource allocation to consecutive note-taking detracts from efficient listening activity.

In a study that looks at Portuguese-to-German interpretation of a political speech, Meyer (1998) applies the functional pragmatic framework with the goal of demonstrating that a reconstruction of mental processing activity during interpretation can be accomplished by examining transcriptions of output.

Dam (1998) reports on a Spanish-to-Danish study that examines lexical similarity and dissimilarity between source language (SL) and target language (TL) consecutive texts in an attempt to identify meaning-based versus form-based interpretation. Her results suggest that more interpretations are form based than are meaning based. This outcome is antithetic to the widespread belief that the identification of SL meaning and its transfer to the TL are at the heart of all interpretation.

TRAINING

Viaggio (1995) believes that exercises in sight translation are perhaps the most effective presimultaneous tool available to the interpreter trainer. Fusco (1995) presents a long list of problems and strategies in the context of training students to work between cognate languages.

On the basis of the results of research that examines speech proportion and accuracy during English-to-Korean SI, Lee (1999) suggests that training programs emphasize techniques that develop automatic (as opposed to controlled) processing capabilities and strengthen both prediction and anticipation skills.

In a study that focused on speech errors during shadowing tasks, Tonelli and Riccardi (1995) found that phonological errors are identified less frequently than are lexical and morphological ones. They conclude that subjects tend to be more conscious of mistakes at "deeper linguistic levels" than of those at the surface phonological level (1995: 72). Inasmuch as shadowing has always generated considerable controversy regarding its usefulness as a presimultaneous training technique, the authors propose some possible applications on the basis of their findings. Tonelli and Riccardi suggest that, in order to strengthen phonological focus, students shadow number lists in no apparent order. They also propose shadowing of prose passages that are characterized by frequent insertions of numbers and nonsense words that fit the phonotactic constraints of the specific language. The authors believe that the requirement of attention to surface form is most particularly evidenced in scientific and technical meetings.

Russo (1995) surveyed 135 conference interpretation students at the University of Trieste regarding their impressions after simultaneously paraphrasing a five-minute political talk in Italian. In this activity, no interpretation was involved, but the difficulty of the dual-task exercise of speaking and listening at the same time was compounded by the requirement to paraphrase (an assignment that is quite challenging even when the subject has a written text and simply paraphrases as she proceeds, reading the source text silently before uttering the paraphrased material aloud). After the exercise, an overwhelming majority (111 of the 135, or 82 percent) indicated that it was hard for them to continue listening and focus on the source content while at the same time trying to generate a paraphrase and utter it without reiterating the lexical items in the original. Trainees responded that, even though the task was an intralingual one, they still encountered difficulties with comprehension.

Déjean le Féal (1997) makes her case for preceding simultaneous training with consecutive skills acquisition. This approach is not new, for it has been the accepted norm for many years, especially in the European schools. She suggests a number of exercises to facilitate the transition from consecutive to simultaneous and offers critical comments on their usefulness.

Looking at SI from Arabic into English, Shakir and Farghal (1997) take a text-linguistic perspective on student error analysis when trainees fail to recognize the pragmatic effects of specific conjunctives and lexical items in Arabic. These components were frequently misinterpreted by the trainees, which resulted in a distortion of the source text's message when rendered in the TL. Taylor Torsello (1996) also employs a text-linguistic approach, stressing the important role of theme as a speech develops. She offers suggestions for training, including stopping a video- or audiotape just after important thematic components are introduced and having students predict what will follow on the basis of context and information up to that point.

Kurz et al. (1996) gathered data using a questionnaire developed by Casse (1981) and created a personality profile of translation and interpretation students at the University of Vienna. On the basis of their results, translation students are primarily *process and people oriented*, while interpretation trainees are *people and action oriented* (1996: 17). They also include comments about differences between beginning and advanced students.

Merlini (1996) suggests that students utilize computer software to assist them with the development of CI note-taking skills. She proposes her "Interprit" computer module, which presents a combination of aural and written tasks.

Viaggio (1996a) offers a very practical and novel look at training strategies related to building context and inferences. He selected a speech text in which the speaker neither (a) identifies himself, (b) states his country of origin, nor (c) names his employer. Viaggio played the speech for students and stopped at various intervals to gather input regarding their comprehension level and how they were going about constructing a mental framework of the unfolding text.

RESEARCH QUESTIONS, FRAMEWORKS, AND TECHNIQUES

Gambier et al. (1997) provide an overview of research trends in SI. In the same vein, Danks et al. (1997) offer an interdisciplinary perspective on a wide variety of cognitive processing aspects of SI.

Déjean le Féal (1998b) selects three of the most widely debated issues in the interpretation field:

1. Does deverbalization exist?
2. How does one choose interpreter trainees?
3. Should SI into a B language be encouraged or frowned upon?

She then proceeds to discuss ("in as dispassionate and impartial a fashion as possible" [1998b: 41]) various sides of each issue. Déjean le Féal concludes her analysis with suggestions for research that might provide some definitive answers to these contentious debates. She calls for cooperation among practitioners and researchers in the field, focusing on solidarity from within as a unifying force against those outside the interpretation world (whose effects are increasingly felt).

Garcia-Landa (1998) proposes a theoretical structure for research in both oral and written translation. Marzocchi (1998) examines the variety of settings in which interpretation takes place at the European Parliament. He suggests future research studies to investigate the goals of any given organization with respect to interpretation services, examining such factors as the treatment of culture within a particular context and the constraints imposed on interpretation by institution-specific parameters.

Focusing on SI, Massaro and Shlesinger (1997) discuss language processing and describe a computational approach to its study. They include an examination of the fuzzy logical model of perception, top-down and bottom-up processing, the role of introspection and some methodological challenges for SI researchers. Lonsdale (1997) presents a variety of methodological questions and concerns regarding the development of a cognitive model of SI. Among many other issues, he examines the potential relevance of research techniques available through technological advances, suggests which properties could be modeled, and questions how such a model would work.

Yagi (1999) applies a new technique, digital discourse analysis, to the study of SI. It is interesting to note that Yagi compared the time management data gathered via digital discourse analysis with traditional subjective measures and found a strong correlation between the two evaluation types. Shlesinger (1998) discusses the relevance of corpus-based studies (as used in translation) to interpretation.

Armstrong (1997) also writes about corpus-based methodology in natural language processing.

Alexieva (1997) proposes a typology to be applied to all events which involve interpreters (i.e., those that are "interpreter mediated"). She discusses the topic in terms of general human communication theory as well as intercultural communication. Alexieva focuses on two basic categories: (1) the delivery mode, and (2) the components of the communicative situation.

Grosjean (1997b) suggests some new parameters for the study of bilingualism that stress a holistic approach. He encourages "researchers to move away from the monolingual yardstick and develop a true linguistics and cognition of bilingualism" (1997b: 184).

Hoffman (1997) presents an overview of psychological research on expertise and proposes several "knowledge elicitation" techniques that may provide some insight into reasoning and memory activities during SI.

Moser-Mercer (1996) revisits the age-old issue of the identification of quality in interpreting. In this connection, she proposes a number of methodological questions and a variety of perspectives regarding quality assessment and measurement. Viaggio (1996b) offers an "outsider's" viewpoint on current research in interpretation.

COURT INTERPRETATION

The past ten years have witnessed a proliferation of court interpretation conferences, training courses, and research. Although no new certification tests have been developed for additional languages at the federal level, the National Center for State Courts (NCSC) has contributed much at the state level in terms of testing and certification of court interpreters. In 1995, it established the Consortium for State Court Interpreter Certification, which states may join for a fee (Gill and Hewitt 1996). Membership in the Consortium entitles the current twenty-five member states to use certification tests developed by the NCSC. Currently, there are nine languages represented, and multiple versions of tests for the most popular language (i.e., Spanish) exist. This program has obviated the need for each state to invest significant funds and human resources in test development, pilot testing, administration and grading.

The literature continues to examine weighty issues, especially ethics. Mikkelson (1998) questions whether the role of the interpreter should be expanded to allow for elucidation on often very disparate source and target cultural practices.

Fenton (1997), writing about New Zealand, examines the interpreter's role in the adversarial courtroom setting. Schweda Nicholson (1994b) presents an overview of critical ethical concerns, offering information taken from a variety of professional codes of ethics. Grabau (1996) writes about the role of the court interpreter from a judge's perspective.

Articles also deal with linguistic challenges. Hale (1997) writes about the importance of maintaining the same register when interpreting from the SL to the TL. Hewitt and Lee (1996) examine a number of linguistic issues in terms of accuracy and completeness, commenting especially on false cognates, slang, and idioms. They furnish test data that illustrate a wide variety of TL answers provided by examinees for specific scoring units. Richardson (1996) discusses the linguistic and cultural difficulties inherent in court interpreting for the deaf.

Comparative work continues to inform an international body of researchers and practitioners. A variety of articles has appeared on court interpretation in Australia (Spring 1999), Spain (Miguélez 1999), Spain and Colombia (Sherr 1999a), South Africa (Moeketsi 1999), Denmark (Schweda Nicholson 1997), Israel (Morris 1998), Japan (Tsuda 1997), England (Fowler 1997), and England and Wales (Banton 1998).

Community interpreting[1] as a whole is a growing field, especially in formerly English-dominant countries that are now faced with a burgeoning ethnic and linguistic minority population. (See, e.g., Benmaman 1997; Carr et al. 1997; Mikkelson 1996; Penning 1996; Schweda Nicholson 1994a, 1994c).

Currently, two of the most hotly debated issues in the court interpretation field are telephone interpreting and team interpreting. Regarding telephone interpreting, Mintz (1998) offers firsthand observations of the procedure. Heh and Hu (1997) (representing the AT&T Language Line Services) discuss the history of the program and present data from surveys that measured both (1) customer satisfaction and (2) job satisfaction among the Language Line interpreters. They call for standards development and the professionalization of over-the-phone Interpretation (OPI). Vidal (1998) is skeptical about OPI, stating that "[t]he question is one of the inherent unreliability of the telephone for meaningful communication of important legal matters" (1998: 1). One of the major concerns of opponents of telephone interpreting is the fact that all of the extralinguistic and nonverbal cues present in face-to-face interaction are missing in an OPI situation. Vidal asks whether OPI is a "technological advance or due process impediment" (1998: 1). Samborn (1996) offers an overview of the changing world of court interpretation, highlighting the development of testing for additional languages and the role of technology in evolving services, such as OPI.

In 1997, the NCSC launched an OPI initiative for the courts in the hopes of "assess[ing] the feasibility of providing high quality interpreting services to courts on short notice and at an affordable cost" (Hewitt 1997). This pilot project continued for six months and encompassed about 1,100 OPI calls. The conclusion of the study is that interpreters' preferences are not strongly against OPI. Furthermore, interpreter participants do not view OPI as a severe threat to quality interpreting. The most common response in favor of in-person interpreting is that the quality of the sound transmission is sometimes compromised, resulting in hearing difficulties (Hewitt 2000).

A more important concern is that court interpreters be competent to work in the judicial system. "[T]he use of unqualified individuals as interpreters in court *in person* is a far more commonplace and serious problem than those that arise when *qualified* interpreters work over the phone" (Hewitt 2000: 12; italics in original). The key lies in reducing the number of incompetent interpreters, regardless of whether services are provided via OPI or in person.

At the federal court level, a pilot project was launched in 1989 using special equipment developed by Chandler Thompson, a federally certified Spanish/English interpreter from Las Cruces, New Mexico. The apparatus permits *simultaneous* OPI (as opposed to consecutive only, which is the normal practice when one phone line is involved). In the late 1990s, the Administrative Office of the United States Courts (AO) devoted additional financial resources to the production of advanced prototypes. The new equipment was installed in the Houston, Los Angeles, Miami, New Mexico, Puerto Rico, and Washington, D.C., courts. It has proven to be dependable, efficient, and user-friendly. Recently, Rauch Companies, LLC, became involved in the commercial manufacture of this type of OPI equipment (Hewitt 2000).

Team interpreting (Festinger 1999; Resolution 1997) has been the norm in simultaneous conference interpretation. Inasmuch as working in court is extremely physically taxing, there has been a move in recent years to establish teams in the legal arena. Progress has been made, although some courts are resistant to it on financial grounds. Practitioners have reported on the success of effective teamwork at national and international conferences, and it appears that this approach will gain further acceptance as the new millennium unfolds.

A final comment on court interpreting is warranted. Judicial interpreters have been working for many years toward greater professionalization within the field. A constant bone of contention has been the generally low rates paid to contract, freelance interpreters, as well as the lack of benefits and job security in the workplace. Choate (1999) examines these issues in the California context. Aranguren and Moore (1999) respond to the issues raised by Choate. Roder (2000) writes about the two hundred-member Bay Area Court Interpreters' (BACI) decision to join the Newspaper Guild–Communications Workers of America, Northern California Media Workers Guild Local 39521, in October 1999. This unionization agreement was approved by more than 90 percent of BACI's voting members. M. Paz Perry, chair of BACI, stated: "Interpreters have realized that if we are to have any control over our profession, we must ally ourselves with the labor movement" (Roder 2000:

18). It will be interesting to see if this affiliation results in additional collective bargaining agreements for court interpreters in other parts of the United States.

A LOOK TO THE FUTURE

Déjean le Féal (1998a) describes the changing world of the conference interpreter from the perspective of differing employer requirements in the private and the institutional (primarily government) markets. As recently as only ten years ago, it was possible for a free-lance interpreter to move easily between the two markets. Now, however, a shift in focus regarding working languages has made this virtually impossible. To be more specific, in the private market, companies look for a bilingual combination: the national language and English. The institutional framework (most notably, the European Union [EU] and other international organizations), in contrast, looks for an "A" language (one of the eleven official languages of the EU) and as many "C" languages as possible.[2] Technological advances are also reshaping the interpreter's world. Videoconferences and telephone interpreting are becoming more and more prevalent in both the private and the public sectors (Mouzourakis 1996).

Déjean le Féal (1998a) boldly predicts that the profession of conference interpreter will not exist fifty years from now. She believes that because of the growing dominance of English throughout the world, the great majority of conferences will be conducted in that language alone.

Launer, Launer, and Pedro (1998) ask the question: "Do U.S.-based interpreters have a future?" The authors conducted a survey as well as personal interviews primarily of male, Russian native speakers who work in English and Russian. The sample consists of interpreters with extensive experience. Overall, they found that, with increasing frequency, interpreters for various U.S.–based companies and some federal agencies are now being hired abroad. Past policy involved taking U.S. interpreters along with a visiting delegation. The primary reason offered for this shift to foreign nationals is cost. Although this study looked at a small segment of the U.S. interpreting population, one can hypothesize that the same thing may be happening with other language groups as well. On the other hand, some private American companies continue their policy of taking Americans with them. They indicate that they feel more comfortable working with people they know, get along with, and trust—those who most definitely have their interests at heart in all types of business negotiations. The trust factor is critically important. Related to this consideration is the need for confidentiality to be strictly maintained when sensitive materials or trade secrets are involved. The authors conclude by mentioning that many of the overseas interpreters are actually contracted out by U.S.-based agencies and that this practice appears to violate the popular "Buy American" approach to securing goods and services.

In spite of these recent developments and potentially disturbing trends in conference interpretation, it appears clear that court interpreting will not disappear. This is especially true in the United States, where due process rights outlined in the Constitution provide the basis for the appointment of an interpreter when a non-English speaker is charged with a crime and comes into contact with the judicial system.

Taking into account Déjean le Féal's outlook, will more and more conference interpreters become involved in court interpreting? It is not always an easy task for a conference interpreter to make the transition to court interpreting. There are a number of important skill-related, linguistic, and subject matter considerations. First, many conference interpreters work primarily in SI. Some have never done CI and do not possess the requisite note-taking skills. Strong consecutive skills are required for witness testimony.[3] From the linguistic perspective, one trend, outlined earlier, is for conference interpreters to have an "A" language and a number of "C"s. The rule in SI has traditionally been that interpreters never work into a "C" language. A solid "B" language is required for court interpretation. If the interpreter is a nonnative English-speaker (and this is often the case), active English skills must be very strong because the language of the record is English.[4] In addition to substantial CI skills and a sound "B" language, court interpreters must be knowledgeable about the law in general (in both the United States and the country from which the defendant and the witnesses come), as well as legal procedure and terminology. The court interpreter must be comfortable being "in the thick of things," for isolation in the interpretation booth is not an option.

Moreover, conference interpreters who work in SI are permitted to paraphrase and to omit redundancies. The courts, however, require a verbatim translation of SL input and TL output (no additions, deletions, register changes, or editing of any kind). Conference interpreters may have difficulty adjusting their "mental set" to the stringent standards of the courts regarding completeness and pinpoint accuracy (Perez-Chambers 2000).

From a financial perspective, many conference interpreters are disinterested in courtroom work because the pay is generally much less than they are accustomed to earning. For example, as of January 3, 2000, federally certified interpreters (Spanish, Haitian Creole and Navajo) received a pay raise to $305 per day (Anon. 1999; Mecham 1999; Sherr 1999b). Many conference interpreters (depending on language combination and geographic location) earn significantly more.

Some conference interpreters object to court interpretation on purely aesthetic grounds. Those who are used to jetting all over the world and interacting with individuals who are at the top of their professions may not be interested in the prospect of sitting next to a defendant who is accused of serial murders or multiple rapes.

CONCLUSION

Moser-Mercer (1997) writes about the Ascona workshops, where researchers from a wide variety of disciplines got together to share their areas of expertise. These individuals brought different methodological perspectives to the study of processing components, all of which are relevant to interpretation. The goal of the workshops was to foster and advance an interdisciplinary approach to interpretation research.

It is clear that the growing emphasis on empirical, quantitative inquiry will continue. As technological advances become more accessible to interpretation researchers, the field will expand to include even more precise studies of neurolinguistic and cognitive processing activity. The search for more effective teaching tools will endure. Interpreter trainers will be able to take advantage of the information gleaned from detailed investigations and to develop instructional strategies that are empirically based. Additional quantitative and linguistic studies of court interpretation are definitely on the horizon, as well. The twenty-first century holds much promise for those who strive to better understand SI and CI. Slowly but surely, researchers and practitioners alike are chipping away at the shell that protects the secrets of the brain's processing activities during these complex cognitive tasks.

NOTES

1. There is some disagreement within the profession regarding the use of the term *community interpreting*. For some, it is an umbrella term that includes interpreting in the courts, in medical settings, and in social service and other government venues. Others prefer to distinguish between court interpreting and community interpreting, recognizing the former as a separate category. (See Benmaman 1997 for a discussion of this issue.)

2. An "A" language is considered to be one's dominant language. It is usually one's mother tongue. Simultaneous interpreters work *into* an "A" (output); it is characterized as an "active" language. On the other hand, a "C" language is considered a "passive." In

other words, an interpreter could work *from* a "C" language (input) into an "A," but not *into* a "C." A "B" language has traditionally been considered one that one can also work *into*, but only in CI.

3. Many courts (especially at the federal level) own SI equipment, which has traditionally been used to provide a running interpretation of the English proceedings to non-English-speaking defendants. In recent years, some courts have begun to use SI for witness testimony as well, thereby speeding up the proceedings.

4. The language of the court record in the United States is English. In the great majority of federal and state courts, court reporters are employed to keep a written verbatim account of what transpires. The presiding judicial officer can, at her discretion, require audio recording of the proceedings (Court Interpreter Amendments Act 1988). However, in the courts of the Executive Office for Immigration Review (which hear political asylum and deportation cases, for example), an audio recording is made of all proceedings (Schweda Nicholson 1999).

PART XI

LANGUAGE ASSESSMENT AND PROGRAM EVALUATION

CHAPTER 35

ISSUES IN LANGUAGE ASSESSMENT

GEOFF BRINDLEY

THE aim of this chapter is to identify some key current issues and approaches in the field of language assessment, to explore their theoretical and practical implications for testing and teaching practice, and briefly to indicate possible future directions for research and development. Since it would be impossible to do justice to the amount of research and test development activity that has occurred in the field over the past two decades (see Bachman 2000, Clapham and Corson 1997 for recent overviews), this review focuses on issues arising from four central themes that have been the subject of discussion and debate in the assessment literature in recent years. These are:

1. The nature of language ability
2. The assessment of language performance
3. The role of assessment in the language curriculum
4. The social, political, and ideological context of assessment.

Interfaces between language assessment and other branches of applied linguistics are also briefly canvassed.

For the purposes of this discussion, the term *assessment* is used as an umbrella term that encompasses formal measurement instruments such as tests, as well as other, more qualitative forms of assessment, such as observation, journals, or portfolio assessment (Brindley 2001; Clapham 2000; Lynch 2000).

DEFINING LANGUAGE PROFICIENCY:
APPROACHES TO CONSTRUCT DEFINITION

Although the notion of language proficiency may seem unproblematic to the lay observer, there is by no means unanimous agreement among researchers on what this term means, and construct definition remains a central issue in language assessment (Chapelle 1999a). In this regard, Spolsky (1985: 186) comments that "in practice it has turned out to be simpler to think up new tests and testing techniques than to explain precisely what it is that they are measuring."

"Real-Life" Approaches

Two broad approaches toward defining "what it means to know how to use a language" (Spolsky 1985) have been identified (McNamara 1996; Shohamy 1995, 1996; Skehan 1998a). The first, classified by McNamara (1996: 95) as "resolutely pragmatic and atheoretical," involves specifying as precisely as possible the features of the language performances that the language learner will have to carry out in the future situation of language use and using this information as the basis for defining the criteria against which the performance will be assessed. These criteria then become the functional definition of language proficiency in the context in question. Proficiency rating scales such as the U.S. Foreign Service Institute scale are one of the best-known manifestations of this approach to language performance assessment, classified by Bachman (1990) as the "real-life" approach. Such scales have been widely used for many years in language assessment for a variety of purposes, ranging from placement to certification (North 1993) and, as Shohamy (1996: 145) notes, have become de facto definitions of language proficiency. Specific purpose scales have also been developed for a range of vocational contexts (Douglas 2000).

   Although direct tests based on real-life language use have a certain face appeal for test users, a number of language testing researchers have argued that they should not be accepted as automatically valid measures of ability. Bachman (1990: 309) invokes Messick's (1989) argument that such tests confuse the observation of a performance with the ability itself and are limited in their generalizability beyond the specific context in which testing takes place. He proposes a somewhat different approach to authenticity by suggesting that authenticity lies not only in the resemblance between assessment tasks and real-world behavior but also in the extent to which different areas of language skills and knowledge are sampled in the task. This is what he refers to as "*interactional authenticity*": Bachman (1990: 322) argues that, in order to construct valid "authentic" assessments of communicative language ability, a theoretical framework is needed that includes both the language abilities of the test taker and the characteristics of the testing context.

Models of Language Ability

Partially because of the perceived shortcomings of the "real-life" approach, and the need to identify systematically the components of language ability that are the object of assessment, language test developers and researchers have increasingly turned to theoretical models as a guide for test construction and validation. Probably the best known and most influential of these are the models developed by Canale and Swain (1980) and by Bachman (1990), the latter subsequently updated by Bachman and Palmer (1996).

The Bachman (1990) model builds on and elaborates the Canale and Swain model. It contains three components: (1) language competence, (2) strategic competence and (3) psychophysiological mechanisms. Under the heading *language competence,* there are two components of *organizational competence* (creating and understanding grammatically correct utterances) and *pragmatic competence* (knowledge of rules of use and ability to produce and understand socially appropriate utterances). *Strategic competence* is not part of language ability and includes ability to identify the information needed to achieve particular communicative goals, planning, and execution. In addition, recognizing the crucial influence of test methods on test performance, Bachman sets out an extensive framework for describing specific features or "facets" of test method. These include facets of the testing environment, facets of the test rubric, facets of the input, facets of the expected response, and the relationship between input and response. In this way, the model is able to describe both underlying abilities and performance, thus allowing the possible effects of test method on task performance to be taken into account in test design.

Subsequently, the Bachman (1990) model has been amended by Bachman and Palmer (1996) in a number of ways. One of the most significant changes is the addition of personal characteristics of the individual language user. Under this category, the authors include *topical knowledge* and *affective schemata,* the latter being defined as "the affective or emotional correlates of topical knowledge" (Bachman and Palmer 1996: 72). Test method facets are renamed *task characteristics* and presented in the form of a checklist that can be used as a guide for describing and comparing target language use tasks and test tasks (1996: 57). Strategic competence is presented in the revised model as "a set of metacognitive components or strategies, which can be thought of as higher order executive processes that provide a cognitive management function in language use, as well as in other cognitive activities" (Bachman and Palmer 1996: 70).

Researchers have identified a number of useful features of the Bachman (1990) model and the subsequent Bachman/Palmer framework (McNamara 1996; Skehan

1998a). Foremost amongst these is explicitness. In this regard McNamara (1996: 71) notes that the Bachman model facilitates the investigation of claims concerning a candidate's ability that are made on the basis of test performance. In addition, according to McNamara (1996: 74), the inclusion of affective schemata in the Bachman and Palmer model represents an important attempt to incorporate Hymes' notion of "ability for use," which relates to affective and volitional attributes and thus marks an important step toward the development of a much-needed expanded model of language performance that can encompass nonlinguistic elements such as personality and emotional states.

Both the Bachman (1990) model and the Bachman and Palmer (1996) framework have been drawn on in the construction and validation of a range of assessments for a variety of purposes and populations (see, for example, Chalhoub-Deville et al. 1997). A number of these projects have used the components of language ability as a basis for identifying and describing aspects of language ability to be included in tests and assessment procedures. The Bachman (1990) test method "facets" have also been used by researchers in validation studies that seek to describe and compare the content of different tests (e.g., Bachman et al. 1995; Clapham 1996). More recently, there are signs that the framework of task characteristics proposed by Bachman and Palmer (1996) is being increasingly used as a practical model for test construction (see, e.g., Alderson 2000; Douglas 2000).

The Bachman and the Bachman/Palmer models are not without problems, however. From a theoretical point of view, McNamara (1996: 75) contends that the account of communication in the Bachman and Palmer model is "strangely one-sided" and fails to take into account the fact that communication is jointly constructed through social interaction. Problems have also been identified with the ability-based rating scales used in association with both models, including the vagueness of the descriptors, the subjectivity of their interpretation, and the difficulty of aligning scale descriptors to specific tasks (Brindley 1991; Davies 1995). Similarly, the test method facets/task characteristics have on occasions proved difficult for raters to interpret and use in test content analyses, leading to low levels of rater agreement on some facets (Clapham 1996). Other areas of concern with the Bachman/Palmer model, according to Skehan (1998a, 1998c) are a lack of detail regarding the role of strategic competence, the incapacity of the components of the model to predict real-world performance, and a lack of attention to underlying processing factors.

To address these perceived gaps, Skehan (1998a, 1998c), drawing on work by Kenyon (1992) and McNamara (1996), proposes a processing model that attempts to specify the complex range of influences on language performance. These include task characteristics and task conditions, as well as individual rater, interlocutor, and candidate variables. Skehan (1998c: 46) argues that the model provides a basis for investigating the generalizability of test performance across assessment contexts.

ISSUES IN
LANGUAGE PERFORMANCE ASSESSMENT

Task Variability and Generalizability

In recent years, researchers in second language acquisition and language assessment have begun to pursue the line of enquiry described by Skehan (1998a, 1998c) and have investigated the influence of a range of task conditions and task characteristics on language test performance. These include task type (Fulcher 1996), planning time (Wigglesworth 1997), interlocutor behavior (Morton et al. 1997; Wigglesworth 2000), and processing demands (Skehan and Foster 1997). A number of these studies have revealed considerable variability in learners' spoken or written production according to the type of elicitation tasks that are used and the conditions under which they are implemented. These findings are consistent with the results of a range of second language acquisition studies that have identified systematic variability in learner performance according to, inter alia, task, setting, and interlocutor (Ellis 1994; Tarone 1998). However, the existence of this variability in language performance poses a potentially serious problem for test developers. If the nature of the assessment tasks affects the type and amount of language that is produced (and hence the rating that is awarded), then it becomes very difficult to generalize from one elicitation context to another and thus to arrive at a meaningful interpretation of a test score or rating.

In view of these difficulties, some researchers in educational assessment have argued that, instead of trying to generalize across different kinds of tasks or to compare learners with each other, we should try to describe the context of the performance in sufficient detail to allow judgements on transferability across similar contexts of performance (Gipps 1994: 173). A similar approach is proposed by Tarone (1998: 86) in the context of language assessment. Since, in her view, task-related variation makes norm-referenced testing virtually impossible, she suggests that test scores could be reported as a kind of performance profile. In order to ensure a close correspondence between assessment tasks and the features of the real-world situation, Tarone (1998: 84) emphasizes the importance of carefully controlling task variables.

According to some language testers, however, adopting such an approach would greatly diminish the value of assessment information (Fulcher 1995). In a generalizability study of scores given in a group oral interview, Fulcher found that, "while task does have a significant effect upon scores, this effect is so small that it does not seriously reduce the ability to generalize from one task to another" (1996: 36). He hypothesizes that the large task effects that have been found in some studies may be artifacts of the task-specific rating scales that are used. This suggests the need for further research using generic rather than context-specific scales.

Rater Variability

Another major issue of concern in relation to language performance assessment is rater variability. Although high levels of rater agreement have been reported in some studies of speaking and writing proficiency (e.g., Dandonoli and Henning 1990), other investigations have revealed major differences in severity between raters (see, e.g., Brindley 2000; Upshur and Turner 1999). Findings from a range of studies of rater behavior suggest that these differences may be related to raters' previous experience, unconscious expectations, and subjective preferences regarding the relative importance of different communicative criteria (see, e.g., Brown, A., 1995; Chalhoub-Deville 1995). There is also evidence to suggest that individual rater behavior is not particularly susceptible to training and may change significantly over time (Lumley and McNamara 1995: 57).

The issue of rater variability has been addressed by researchers in a variety of ways. Some, like McNamara (1996, 1998), believe that the problems of rater differences should be addressed by modeling differences in severity using measurement technology, such as many-faceted Rasch analysis, and statistically compensating for them. Moss (1994), on the other hand, advocates a hermeneutic approach whereby judgments of performance are mediated through a social process involving those who are most familiar with the context of the assessment. Regardless of the approach taken, consistent emerging evidence suggests that, since different judges will have different perspectives on the same performance, there appears to be a strong case for using multiple ratings, particularly where high-stakes decisions are involved (McNamara and Lynch 1997).

ASSESSMENT IN THE
LANGUAGE CURRICULUM

Over the past decade, standardized tests of language knowledge have given way to more communicative forms of individualized assessment that reflect the context in which learning is taking place. However, these changes have occurred against a background of growing demands for accountability in language programs. In line with the introduction of corporate management principles into educational systems, educational authorities worldwide are now being increasingly required to demonstrate efficiency and cost-effectiveness by more rigorous reporting of program outcomes. The past decade has consequently seen the introduction of so-called outcomes-based approaches to assessment and reporting that use prespecified descriptions of attainment or ability, known variously as standards, curriculum profiles, attainment targets, benchmarks, bandscales, or competencies, to report learning outcomes in both school and vocational contexts (Brindley 1998b). In many outcomes-based schemes, student achievement is determined on the basis of teacher-conducted classroom performance assessments, sometimes in combination with standardized tests or assessment tasks (see, e.g., McKay 2000; Rea-Dickins and Gardner 2000). Such procedures include so-called alternative assessments, such as observations, portfolios, conferences, teacher-constructed performance tasks, projects, self-assessment, and journals (Brown and Hudson 1998; Genesee and Upshur 1996).

Outcomes-based approaches appear to offer a number of significant advantages over standardized tests, including closer alignment between assessment and learning, greater transparency of reporting, and improved communication between stakeholders. However, the introduction of such systems has, in some cases, proved problematic for a variety of political, technical, and practical reasons (see Brindley 1998b for an overview). Foremost among the former is the difficulty of using outcomes statements simultaneously to satisfy external demands for accountability and to provide diagnostic information for purposes of diagnosis and motivation (McKay 2000).

On the technical front, empirical studies of the teacher-conducted assessments used to gather information on progress and attainment have revealed a range of problems, some of which were noted in the discussion of performance assessment. These include low generalizability across tasks within the same domain (Brindley 2000), low levels of agreement between assessors on the quality of a given sample of work (Hamp-Lyons and Condon 1993), inconsistencies in teachers' observational records (Rea-Dickins and Gardner 2000), and lack of comparability across tasks (McKay 2000). Finally, from a practical perspective, evidence suggests that outcomes-based systems are difficult to implement successfully unless provision is made for adequate resourcing both at the planning and at the implementation stage (Breen et al. 1997; Brindley 1998b).

The Social, Political, and Ideological Context of Assessment

Challenges to the Psychometric Paradigm

The failure of some forms of performance assessment to satisfy the statistical requirements that are normally demanded of standardized tests has provoked considerable debate concerning the measurement properties of performance assessments. This debate reflects a fundamental clash between two opposing views of the nature of assessment: On the one hand a traditional psychological measurement view that treats ability as a quantifiable latent trait located in the individual and on the other hand one that holds that complex human performance is not readily amenable to quantitative measurement of the kind used in the physical sciences (Morrison and Wylie 1999; Teasdale and Leung 2000).

Although some language testing researchers maintain that the quality of alternative assessments should be judged according to the standard psychometric criteria for validity and reliability (Brown and Hudson 1998: 656), others have suggested that the application of these standards to assessments of curriculum-related language use is inappropriate (Rea-Dickins and Gardner 2000; Teasdale and Leung 2000). Lynch (2000: 19) claims that alternative assessment represents a different paradigm (an "assessment culture") and therefore cannot be evaluated from within the traditional positivist framework of educational measurement (a "testing culture"). McNamara (2000a, 2000b) suggests that proficiency is jointly constructed and questions the capacity of current measurement theories to capture the interactional nature of language performance.

Critical Language Testing

The social and political role of language assessment has also been the subject of searching critique. Shohamy (1997), drawing on insights from critical pedagogy, invokes the notion of *critical language testing*: "Critical language testing claims that the act of language testing is not neutral. Rather it is a product and agent of cultural, social, political, educational and ideological agenda that shape the lives of individual participants, teachers and learners" (1997: 2). In a far-reaching examination of the power of tests in society, Shohamy argues that tests are frequently used as controlling devices to serve the often unstated political agendas of educational authorities. She makes out a case for a radical reconceptualization of language assessment that would see a move away from centralized external testing toward more democratic models involving shared power between central and local stakeholder groups.

Social Consequences of Language Assessment: Test Impact and Fairness

Concerns relating to the misuse of tests such as those outlined earlier have been influenced to a significant degree by a reconceptualization of the notion of test validity over the past decade. In particular, Messick's (1989) expanded framework for validity, which incorporates the notion of "*consequential validity*" (the examination of intended and unintended consequences of test use), has been particularly influential in focusing attention on the social consequences of test use.

In line with this concern with social impact, assessment researchers have begun to examine the phenomenon of "washback"—the effect of assessment on teaching and learning (Alderson and Wall 1993; Wall 1997). Such studies have focused on such issues as the effects of test preparation (Alderson and Hamp-Lyons 1996), the interfaces between language policy and test use (Shohamy 1993), and the impact of changes in examination format on teaching practices (Cheng 1997). The findings of these studies suggest that the impact of a test or assessment system is by no means a simple phenomenon and that the type of washback that occurs may vary according to a range of contextual and individual variables.

These concerns with the consequences of assessment have been echoed in recent calls for those who work in the field of language assessment to consider their social and ethical responsibilities (Spolsky 1997). Davies (1997b) pleads a case for an "ethical milieu" that would be realized through a professional code of practice. Kunnan (1997), drawing on Messick's (1989) validity framework, proposes an agenda for conducting fairness research—which would involve investigation of the fairness implications at each stage of the test design and implementation process—as an integral part of test validation. Bachman (2000) sees the close link between ethical conduct and validity concerns as the basis for professionalization of the field.

INTERDISCIPLINARY INTERFACES

The search for expanded models of language ability that can include a complex range of performance factors has brought about a rapprochement between the fields of language assessment and second language acquisition (SLA) research, areas that until recently have tended to be somewhat compartmentalized (Bachman and Cohen 1998). Closer attention to the processing conditions that operate in language assessment (Skehan 1998c) has resulted in a range of studies that have explored factors such as the cognitive complexity and attentional demands of teaching and assessment tasks (Skehan and Foster 1997), test-taker strategies (Purpura 1998), and the relationship between test performance and characteristics such as background knowledge (Clapham 1996), gender (O'Loughlin 2000), and personality (Berry 1997). In addition, researchers have used a range of research techniques from language assessment and SLA to investigate the notion of "task difficulty" from both a cognitive and a psychometric perspective (Norris et al. 1998), with the aim not only of understanding better the effects of context on performance but also of informing teachers' task design practice.

This growing interest in the varying effects of contextual factors on assessment tasks has greatly expanded the range of analytical tools conventionally used in language testing. As well as drawing on traditional measurement approaches, recent studies of test performance and classroom assessment have employed a wide range of qualitative techniques from other disciplines such as cognitive psychology, sociolinguistics, anthropology and sociology (see Banerjee and Luoma 1997 for an overview). These admit including conversational and discourse analysis (Lazaraton 1996), verbal protocol analysis (Green, A., 1998), and various forms of ethnographic enquiry (Leung and Teasdale 1997).

Language assessment researchers have also benefited from recent advances in the field of educational measurement and have drawn a variety of quantitative techniques that can model the complex range of variables involved in language performance (Bachman 1997; Bachman and Eignor 1997; Kunnan 1998; McNamara 1996; Pollitt 1997).

FUTURE DIRECTIONS

It is clear from this survey that many challenges and unanswered questions remain in the field of language assessment. In relation to the crucial question of construct validation, a good deal more work needs to be done in order to build an expanded model of ability that can capture the complexity and multidimensionality of human communication and to develop assessment criteria that reflect current theories of language learning and language use. In pursuit of this aim, it is likely that we will see more attempts to specify features of various target language use domains in order to develop assessment tools that reflect the full range of parameters involved, including "nonlanguage" factors (Douglas 2000; Shohamy 1996). In addition, further research conducted within the framework of Skehan's (1998a, 1998c) processing approach should improve our understanding of the complex set of influences on assessment task performance, thus enabling better prediction from one language use situation to another and providing a better basis for making inferences about ability.

A second theme that emerges from this review is the ongoing tension between "assessment" and "testing" perspectives (Clapham 2000; Gipps 1994), reflected in the debate about the criteria for evaluating alternative assessment and in the challenges to the epistemological basis of traditional measurement approaches. In this context, a number of researchers have argued that the cause of classroom assessment has not been well served by language testing research, which, until recently, has tended to focus on large-scale summative tests that are unconnected to the learning process (Brindley 1997; Rea-Dickins and Gardner 2000). This concern has led to calls for a research agenda that would focus on ways in which teachers' assessment practices are realized in everyday contexts of monitoring and assessing classroom learning and achievement (Brindley 1989; McNamara 2000b; Rea-Dickins and Gardner 2000; Teasdale and Leung 2000). This question has been explored in some depth in general education (see, e.g., Mavrommatis 1997; Torrance and Pryor 1998) but is just beginning to be addressed in the context of language learning (Breen et al. 1997; Rea-Dickins and Gardner 2000). Given the increasing importance that is now being accorded to formative assessment as an indicator of student outcomes in many educational systems, in future we may expect to see a growth in this line of research.

CONCLUSION

The face of language assessment has changed considerably over the past decade. On the theoretical front, considerable progress has been made in building models of language ability that can guide test construction and validation. At the same time, processing approaches derived from cognitive psychology and second language acquisition research have provided a framework for examining the interactions between assessment tasks and contextual elements in real-life performance, the results of which can be applied to practical assessment situations. With respect to test impact and test use, the adoption of Messick's (1989) expanded validity framework and the increased focus on ethical behavior suggests that language tests and assessments of the future will be designed with greater attention to potential negative consequences to test-takers than has hitherto been the case.

Notwithstanding these positive developments, the critiques of the dominant psychometric paradigm and the repositioning of language assessment within a broader social and political context have raised fundamental questions concerning both the intellectual foundations and the social role of language assessment. They have also highlighted the great variety of subdisciplines that now contribute to the field, including second language acquisition, discourse analysis, measurement theory, critical theory, educational sociology, evaluation, and policy analysis. One of the major challenges to face assessment researchers in the new millennium will be to develop new methods of enquiry that can integrate these diverse fields.

CHAPTER 36

TECHNOLOGY IN STANDARDIZED LANGUAGE ASSESSMENTS

MICHELINE CHALHOUB-DEVILLE

WITHIN the past generation, computer technological advances have transformed our work environment, leisure activities, and educational practices. People have even argued that the emergence of computers represents a major turning point in our civilization, not unlike that experienced with the invention of the printing press in the late fifteenth century (Provenzo, Brett, and McCloskey 1999). It is to be expected, therefore, that computers have had, and will have, a large and even defining impact on second language (L2) assessment as well. Indeed, computer-based tests (CBTs) are not at all uncommon in the L2 field today. The computerized delivery of tests has become an appealing and a viable medium for the administration of standardized L2 tests in academic and nonacademic institutions. Given the growing use of CBTs, an important issue to reflect on is the nature of the change that CBTs have brought, and may in the future bring, to L2 assessment.

Researchers in various fields have characterized changes introduced by technology, including computers, in terms of two differentiated outcomes. Maddux (1986), in education, and Christensen (1997), in business, differentiate between two categories of computer technology applications. Maddux refers to these as "Type I" versus "Type II," and Christensen identifies them as "sustaining" versus "disruptive" applications. Type I or sustaining technology refers to innovations intended to simplify and facilitate current practices and products. Examples of this category in education include the use of the computer to administer learning drills. Type II or disruptive technologies, on the other hand, lead to the accomplishment of something that previously had not been considered plausible, such as utilizing the computer as part of new models of instruction, such as providing distance learning.

An examination of the changes introduced by L2 CBT shows that technology has been intended primarily to enhance current assessment practices, that is, as Type I or sustaining innovations. CBT allows, among other things, more flexible and individualized test administration, tracking of student performance, immediate test feedback, new item/task types, and enhanced test security. Perhaps one of the most exciting capabilities of L2 CBT, which can be viewed as a disruptive technology, is the adaptive approach. Computer adaptive testing (CAT) enables tailoring item difficulty to test-takers' performance, allowing a more accurate assessment of test-takers' L2 ability. In short, apart from the adaptive innovation, CBT has been utilized mainly to facilitate test delivery and administration. What is needed, however, is an exploration of how computer technology can lead to innovations in fundamental aspects of L2 testing.

The present chapter discusses issues in various areas of the CBT operation that will help promote this assessment more as the disruptive type of technology. Areas covered in this discussion include the representation of the L2 construct, overall test design and measurement issues, item/task construction, and test purpose. While the discussion highlights mainly the advantages—not the shortcomings—of certain models, measures, and procedures, this is intended not to promote any of these specifically but to explicate the type of changes needed. As background information to the central discussion, the chapter first provides an overview of several L2 CBTs that have been described in the literature. The review outlines the main features of these instruments, including test purpose, content, and scoring.

SECOND LANGUAGE CBT INSTRUMENTS

Because of limited space, I present, in Appendix A, a tabular description of several CBT and CAT projects that are either currently operational or under development. The following presents a brief description of a representative sample of these operational projects that have been developed in academic and nonacademic institutions. For more complete information on these projects see Chalhoub-Deville and Deville (1999) and Chalhoub-Deville (1999).

The Brigham Young University (BYU) assessments are among the first CBTs developed in the L2 field (Larson 1987; Larson 1989; Madsen 1991). The instruments include placement tests in French, German, Spanish, Russian, and English as second language (ESL). They assess test-takers' language ability in grammar, reading, and vocabulary. The ESL instrument includes a listening comprehension component. Items are restricted response, with an emphasis on multiple-choice. The BYU instruments use an adaptive algorithm based on the Rasch item response theory (IRT) model.

Another French placement test is the Computer Adaptive Proficiency Test (CAPT), developed by Laurier (1991, 1999) at the University of Montreal. CAPT uses multiple-choice items to assess test-takers' reading and listening comprehension, sociolinguistic judgment, lexical and grammatical knowledge, and self-assessment of oral skills. A three-parameter IRT and graded-response models are used for the adaptive algorithm.

Dunkel (1997, 1998, 1999) at Georgia State University, has developed an ESL and a Hausa CAT. These instruments are used to assess test-takers' listening comprehension for placement into and exit from language programs. Both instruments use Rasch estimation procedures for the adaptive algorithm. A variety of selected-response item types are included, such as, multiple-choice, matching, and identifying appropriate elements in a graphic.

Southern Illinois University also has an ESL placement CAT (Shermis 1996; Young et al. 1996). The instrument assesses test-takers' reading comprehension as they move from one course level to another within the ESL program. The instrument uses multiple-choice items and employs the Rasch model for the adaptive algorithm.

Since 1988, the Test of English as a Foreign Language (TOEFL) has been administered as CBT in the United States of America and in other countries around the world (ETS 1998). The purpose of CBT TOEFL, just like the paper-and-pencil (P&P) version, is to measure the English language proficiency of non-native speakers of English who seek admission into postsecondary institutions in North America. Also like the P&P version, CBT TOEFL includes a listening, structure, and reading component. CBT TOEFL includes traditional multiple-choice items, as well as other selected-response items, including, selection of a visual or part of a visual, matching, and ordering objects or text. Unique to CBT TOEFL is a writing component. Nonetheless, this writing component is a replication of the P&P Test of Written English. The listening and structure segments of the CBT TOEFL are adaptive and use a three-parameter IRT model.

The description of the various L2 CBTs illustrates that, except for the adaptive feature of item delivery, the tests employ largely P&P thinking in their approach to assessment. These instruments focus on the same aspects of the L2 construct as P&P tests, use unidimensional IRT models, employ predominantly selected-response items types (mainly multiple-choice), and generate an overall score(s) used for selection and placement purposes. In short, the various advantages of L2 CBTs function mainly to help make assessment more efficient and serviceable. As such, they can be characterized as Type I, or as representing sustaining technologies. Advances that can help make this assessment become Type II (or 'disruptive') are still needed. The following sections discuss some of the changes needed in several key areas in the CBT operation.

REPRESENTATION OF THE CONSTRUCT

Researchers (e.g., Bernhardt 1991, 1999; Buck 1994; Grabe 1999) present strong arguments that standardized tests, including CBTs, are not based on well-articulated theories of the L2 construct. These researchers question a representation of the L2 construct that depicts separate language skills or components and utilizes an additive unidimensional measurement framework. A number of researchers (e.g., Bernhardt 1991, 1999; Buck 1994; Grabe 1999; Schoonen et al. 2000) have argued persuasively that the L2 construct is multidimensional and involves a variety of interacting components and processes. The construct comprises a complex constellation of components that include knowledge of the language system, knowledge of the world, knowledge of the particular situation of language use, and a variety of strategies and processing skills needed to access, plan, and execute the communicative intents.

These researchers also contend that the make-up of the construct changes with different ability levels. The language ability of more proficient test-takers is different from that of less proficient ones—not simply in quantity but also in the nature of the construct. Test-takers at different ability levels differ in their command of linguistic and nonlinguistic concepts and knowledge, the richness of the connections among knowledge structures, the kinds of processes they employ, and the degree of automaticity governing these processes. While some abilities and processes are critical for beginning language learners, these become less salient and others emerge with more proficient learners. For example, Bernhardt (1991) shows that phonographemic features and word recognition are more critical in early stages of reading language development. As the processing of these word-based features becomes more automatic, learners can attend to more complex syntactic attributes of the text. Syntactic processing of text features becomes more critical as learners advance in their language/reading proficiency.

Test developers can use computer technology to measure such critical aspects of the construct and to trace learners' development better. For instance in reading, "a variety of measures of reading rate, word recognition and vocabulary and reading fluency could be developed for computer delivery" (Grabe 1999: 36). Additionally, the computer can collect reading protocols (Bernhardt 1991) or summary tests (Taylor, L., 1993) that allow test developers to investigate how test-takers organize and reconstruct texts. Although they are not readily available, computerized scoring templates can be feasibly incorporated (see Bernhardt 1991; Heinz 1993) for such assessments. Similarly, in assessing writing, the computer can be used to capture test-takers' outlines, drafts, uses of spell checkers, lookups in dictionaries, references to grammatical help, time spent on each of these aspects, and so on. Such a process would permit a more detailed examination of the linguistic and nonlinguistic components and the metacognitive processes that test-takers use while writing. The real challenge with such assessments is to organize, analyze, and interpret these rich data. This challenge is pertinent not only to language testing researchers but also to applied linguists in general. As Alderson (1999) argues, applied linguists need to make explicit the nature of the interactive components and processes involved in L2 performances in order to utilize the information to help explicate test performances.

Another issue to reconsider is the operationalization of the L2 construct in terms of separate skills. Current CBTs continue to emphasize the separation of the language skills, something incompatible with typical language use. As Widdowson (1978) and Grabe (1999) point out, language use typically involves more than one skill. For example, Widdowson states that "conversations" involve listening and speaking, and "correspondence" involves reading and writing. In short, the integration of skills provides for a more meaningful and appropriate depiction of language use. It is worth noting that the new TOEFL project is considering such an integration of skills.

In conclusion, CBT should allow test developers to move beyond P&P tests. Computer technology can be employed to advance assessment practices in terms of the representation of the L2 construct. Language testers need to utilize technology to design measures that increasingly explore and measure components and processes identified as salient to various language abilities.

OVERALL TEST DESIGN

The other area in which technological innovation can be explored to improve assessment is overall test design, with a related issue being the measurement model. Standardized P&P and CBT test developers have invested in procedures that seek to provide overall scores intended more to rank students than to provide rich documentation of the salient linguistic and nonlinguistic structures that underlie test-takers' performances. One important factor that has influenced current test design is related to the unidimensional measurement models used for ability estimation and item/test analysis. Unidimensional measurement models are at odds with the multidimensional representation of the L2 construct. The multidimensional conceptualization of the L2 construct discussed earlier necessitates an extension of current measurement models and perhaps even the use of a different measurement model. Extensions of and alternatives to current models (e.g., multidimensional IRT models, Bayesian inference networks, and latent class models) have been put forth in the measurement literature. These models differ in how they represent the construct; for example, while multidimensional IRT assumes a continuous latent trait, the latent class model assumes an underlying categorical variable. (See publications by researchers such as Haertel 1984, Embretson 1985, Tatsuoka 1993, Mislevy 1995, and Samejima 1995 for a thorough discussion of these measurement models.)

In addition to an alternative measurement model, an overall test design that yields meaningful representation of test-takers' abilities requires a coherent approach that closely links performance on test items to intended inferences about the underlying components and processes. One example of such an integrated overall test design is based on the work by Tatsuoka (1993), using rule-space methodology. This approach has been employed in the L2 field with reading and listening assessments (Buck and Tatsuoka 1998; Buck, Tatsuoka, and Kostin 1997). The approach entails a close examination of stimulus attributes such as text features, item/task characteristics, and the types of knowledge and processes these are likely to tap in test-takers. The researchers "begin with item characteristics, examine how these affect person performance, and then make assumptions about how these item characteristics map on to important aspects of linguistic knowledge or cognitive processes" (Buck and Tatsuoka 1998: 125). Rule-space methodology generates attributes related to text length, density of information, type of information, location of relevant information, processing speed, type of inferences, response requirements, and so on. The research conducted so far with rule-space methodology has focused on exploring the feasibility of the methodology to uncover attributes of existing, operational standardized L2 tests. The ultimate contribution of the approach occurs when performed at the test-design stage with items under development. In summary, research using rule-space methodology, although exploratory at this time, points to the future of test design, which emphasizes an explicit link among the intended knowledge and processes, targeted performances, and score interpretation.

Portal is an example of an approach that utilizes computer technology and alternative measurement models to advance a principled and construct-based approach to CBT design from the early stages of test construction. Portal is a test design system under development by Mislevy and his colleagues (see Mislevy 1996,

Mislevy et al. 1999) and is intended to design assessments that systematically link task characteristics to test-takers' abilities on the basis of test performance. The system combines three models: the student model, the task model, and the evidence model. The student model includes variables that describe the knowledge and processes to which the test developer makes inferences. The task model includes items/tasks that are, on the basis of task analysis, supposed to elicit performances that target identified aspects of the learner's knowledge and processes. The evidence model makes use of probabilistic modeling to relate salient features of test-takers' performance to the student model variables. Such a test design-approach works to create interrelations among task characteristics, test-takers' performances, and inferences about intended underlying abilities.

In conclusion, technological innovations and measurement advances can help CBT move beyond conventional test design practices. Information generated by the use of alternative measurement models and an integrated test design can greatly enhance the information and quality of inferences made about test-takers' L2 abilities.

ITEM/TASK CONSTRUCTION

The third area in which technological innovation can facilitate change needed is item/task (hereafter task) construction. Whereas the previous section focuses on overall test design, the present one addresses issues related specifically to test tasks. This section emphasizes a rational approach to task construction that can help facilitate the systematic links discussed earlier.

Typically, task development in standardized tests is more of an intuitive process than a principled procedure that deliberately represents the complex L2 construct and provides explicit links between task characteristics and the abilities needed to perform these tasks (see Peirce 1994 for an example). A meaningful approach to task development is one that provides a clear understanding of the ability features that are likely to be engaged in the test task. Bachman and Palmer provide a framework of "distinctive task characteristics" (1996: 107) intended as a tool to guide a principled approach for L2 task development. The framework requires considering characteristics related to:

- The setting (e.g., participants, time of task)
- The characteristics of the input and the expected response (e.g., organizational, pragmatic features, topical properties, and format—channel, form, language, length, speededness, type) and

- The relationship between input and expected response (e.g., scope of relationship, directness of relationship, and reactivity—reciprocal, nonreciprocal, adaptive).

Such a principled mechanism to constructing tasks helps test developers better understand and manipulate task features to target intended ability aspects. Hence, it affords more meaningful and appropriate test score inferences.

The measurement literature has been discussing use of computer technology to promote a principled approach to task construction. One example is response generative modeling (RGM) (Bejar 1993; Bennett 1999). RGM is intended to develop task prototypes, which entails task analysis, similar to that described using Bachman and Palmer's (1996) framework. These prototypes and their characteristics are then fed into a database used to generate new tasks with the desired linguistic, situational, cognitive, and measurement characteristics. Such prototypes enable test developers to draw more defensible inferences by establishing a close link between task creation and underlying abilities.

RGM can be used to generate a variety of task types, such as selected response multiple-choice or more elaborate types, such as simulations. Simulations have long been used in instructional settings (e.g., BaFá BaFá [Shirts 1977])—and to some extent in assessments (e.g., role plays, interviews, and other authentic tasks [see projects in Bachman and Palmer 1996]). Computer advances now permit the use of such complex tasks in standardized tests, as well. As Mislevy et al. (1999) state, "[t]asks in standardized tests are encapsulated and observations are spare mainly because, historically, we could not handle more. Computers and simulation capabilities shatter this barrier" (1999: 372). Simulation tasks would allow language test developers to elicit contextualized, integrated language performances that closely resemble those in real-life interactions. Remembering that real-world task features, such as face validity, are not the end-goal when designing simulations, test developers must ensure that simulations tap intended ability features. Controlled simulations allow relevant features to be manipulated in a structured manner in order to target intended knowledge and processes. Finally, CBT simulations are increasingly being used in professional licensure and certification, and it is only a matter of time before L2 CBT simulations will be developed as well. (For an example of a CBT simulation, see Mislevy et al. 1999.)

TEST PURPOSE

The main purpose of most standardized assessments, including CBT, is to help test users make accept/reject or classification decisions. Today's L2 CBT purposes reflect the "gatekeeping" (Spolsky 1997) practices that emerged as a response to the educational situation in the early part of the twentieth century. The demands and constraints educators faced at the beginning of the twentieth century—the introduction of education on a broader scale, coupled with limited instructional resources—led to the creation of large-scale standardized assessments for selection purposes (Messick 1999). A similar situation developed in the L2 field, where, because of limited learning opportunities, "efforts were made in the USA and elsewhere to develop prognostic tests that would justify decisions to exclude un-qualified students from high school foreign language classes. In the USA, after the second world war, USA government language programs supported research to improve selection techniques" (Spolsky 1995a: 321). The Modern Language Ap-titude (Carroll and Sapon 1959), Pimsleur's Language Aptitude Battery (Pimsleur 1966), the Defense Language Aptitude Battery (DLAB) (see MacWhinney 1995a), and TOEFL (see Spolsky 1995b) are examples of such prognosis/selection tests.

While historical circumstances have led to the creation of these selection tests, today's technological advances are changing learning environments (Bennett 1999; Layne and Lepeintre 1996; Messick 1999). In the L2 field,

> Increased demands for language instruction, together with advances in communication technology, have resulted in a proliferation of distance instruc-tion programs. . . . With each advance in communication technology, the poten-tial for meeting pedagogical requirements through distance instruction has in-creased, and it is now technically possible to provide effective distance instruction to widely diverse language learners scattered around the world.
> (Layne and Lepeintre 1996: 235)

Such changes in language learning opportunities will likely alter the traditionally dominant purpose of standardized assessment. Selection tests to limit students' access to universities will be needed less, as more students will be involved in distance instruction. Computer-delivered tests to assess students' progress in this environment will be more in demand.

Some of the circumstances that have led institutions to demand assessments for selection are changing and making way for an increased emphasis on achieve-ment and diagnostic tests. Bunderson, Inouye, and Olson (1989) point out that this shift will result in a new generation of CBT assessment, which they refer to as "continuous measurement" (CM) CBT. The CM CBT generation has distinct features:

- It emphasizes a close relationship between assessment and the curriculum in terms of learning objectives, tasks, and procedures.
- It is integrated into instructional plans in the form of exercises and activi-ties related to instructional units.
- It is intended to produce a rich profile of learners' strengths and weak-nesses to inform teaching and learning.

CM CBTs are learner centered, with an emphasis on meeting individual needs. While the CM generation of CBT corresponds in principle to current classroom assessments, its significance lies in its ability to transform large-scale standardized L2 assessment purposes and practices to accommodate changing learning and instructional environments.

The CM model of CBT may sound futuristic to some. Visualizing such changes is difficult because of our entrenched educational thinking. Nevertheless, continuing technological advances that produce new learning contexts and opportunities mean new CBTs in the future that will address changing purposes and needs.

CONCLUSION

CBT has made many of our L2 testing practices more efficient and introduced notable innovations such as CAT. But L2 CBTs, as currently conceived, fall short in providing any radical transformation of assessment practices. Rapidly changing computer technology should expand test developers' thinking beyond the realm of P&P testing. For CBT to be described as Type II or disruptive, it needs to be reconcepualized in terms of the opportunities computer technology can engender to make fundamental changes in the representation of the L2 construct, overall test design, task development, and even the context and purpose of tests. Changes along these lines can truly transform not only L2 CBTs but also the way language testers think about their field.

Appendix A: Computer Web-based projects

Instrument/institution	Purpose	Components and item types	Scores/algorithm
Test of English as a Foreign Language-CBT—ETS. References: ETS 1998; TOEFL CAT Scorer guide (on-line).	Proficiency test to measure the English proficiency of non-native speakers who intend to study in institutions of higher learning in the U.S. and Canada.	Listening; MC, selection of visual, selection of 2–4 choices, match ng/or-dering. Structure: Complete sentence, ID 1 of 4 acceptable words/phrase/sentences. Reading; MC, word/phrase selection, insert appropriate sentence. Writing: an essay.	Each section scored 0–30; Structure and Writing are combined and converted to scaled score of roughly 50% each. Listening and Structure parts are adaptive. 3-parameter IRT is used.
ESL Listening Comprehension—Georgia State University. References: Dunkel 1997, 1998	Listening comprehension test for placement into/exit from adult ESL programs.	Topics and authentic excerpts varying in extensiveness and cultural references; items require comprehension from discrete words and phrases to variable-length mono/dialogs, radio segments, scripted texts. Item types include MC, matching, and identifying appropriate elements in a graphic.	Rasch IRT is used; scores reported according to a nine-level scale representing the ACTFL scale continuum.
Hausa Listening CAT [HAST]—Georgia State University. References: Dunkel 1997, 1998	Listening comprehension test for placement into/exit from adult Hausa programs in the U.S.	Comparable to ESL Listening Comprehension CAT.	Rasch IRT is used; scoring is comparable to ESL Listening Comprehension CAT.

(continued)

Appendix A (continued)

Instrument/institution	Purpose	Components and item types	Scores/algorithm
French Computer Adaptive Proficiency Test (CAPT)—University of Montreal. References: Laurier 1991, 1999.	Placement test for English speakers enrolled in French courses at the postsecondary level.	MC for reading comprehension; sociolinguistic knowledge; lexical and grammatical knowledge; listening comprehension; and self-assessment of oral skills.	3-parameter IRT is used; score from each subtest provides entry point to subsequent subtest; final score determined by obtaining average of the five subtest scores.
Dutch Reading Proficiency CAT—Brigham Young University, CIA Language Training Division. References: Larson 1999	Reading proficiency; the test simulates four phases of the OPI: warm-up, level check, probe, and wind-down.	Texts are balanced in terms of content, context, abstract concrete passages, and cultural understanding. MC items are used; they focus on best meaning, best misfit, best restatement, best summary, and best logical completion.	Rasch IRT is used; scores span ILR reading proficiency scale, levels 1–5.
Spanish-CAPE, French-CAPE, German-CAPE, ESL-CAPE—Brigham Young University. References: Larson and Madsen 1985; Larson 1987, 1989; Madsen 1991; CAPE informational website (on-line).	Placement tests for incoming students in language curricula at the postsecondary level.	Each CAPE includes a grammar, reading, and vocabulary section; ESL also includes a listening section. Content sampling is random within each segment. MC items are used.	Rasch IRT is used; placement according to overall score obtained from the various sections.

ESL Reading Comprehension—Southern Illinois University. References: Shermis 1996; Young, Shermis, Brutten, and Perkins 1996.	Assess reading comprehension when progressing levels in a four-course ESL program.	Includes variable-length reading passages on diverse topics. Items used are MC.	Rasch IRT is used. Scores classify test takers into one of the four courses.
Multimedia Placement CAT (MultiCAT) in French, German, Spanish—Ohio State University. References: MultiCAT website.	Placement tests; also suggested as entrance/exit types of proficiency tests.	MultiCAT includes 3 subtests: Reading: Authentic texts, MC questions in English or target language, one question per text; Language in Context: cloze passages with MC options; Listening: (still under development) MC based on audio or video clip.	Rasch IRT is used; Scores rank students from beginning to superior.
Contextualized Reading Assessment (CoRA)—University of Minnesota. References: Chalhoub-Deville, Alcaya and Lozier 1997; Chalhouh-Deville 1997; CARLA website.	Entrance/Exit Reading Proficiency Tests for French, German, and Spanish language programs.	Authentic reading texts from a variety of sources are used. Multiple-choice items are used.	Algorithm information is not provided. Scores are based on total number of correct items within given time.
COMPASS—ACT. References: ACT COMPASS Planform (on-line).	English Placement Test into ESL or mainstream classes.	The test includes 3 segments: math, reading, and writing. MC items are used. The reading segment measures vocabulary and comprehension of a variety of text types. The writing segment focuses on mechanics, grammar, organization, and style.	3-parameter IRT is used. The 3 segments produce 7 possible scores (1 each in writing and reading skills and up to 5 in math).

(continued)

Appendix A (continued)

Instrument/institution	Purpose	Components and item types	Scores/algorithm
International English Language Testing System [IELTS]—UCLES. References: Charge and Taylor 1997.	English placement test with 2 foci: Academic and General Training.	Listening: MC, short answer/sentence completion, chart completion, label diagrams, classification, and matching. Reading: Same as listening plus identifying page/section, identification of writer's views.	Algorithm information is not provided. IELTS P&P bandscores are used.
CommuniCAT—University of Cambridge. References: UCLES CommuniCAT (on-line).	Assess proficiency in English, French, German, and Spanish for placement purposes and for monitoring learner progress and to determine appropriate certificate exam to take.	The tests include several question types, including MC listening and reading exercises, cloze tests, and sentence transformations.	Algorithm information is not provided. Levels of Ability categorized as with P&P KET, PET, FCE, CAE, and CPE exams.
DIALANG—European Commission. References: DIALANG website (on-line).	Diagnostic assessment in 14 languages.	The tests combine self-assessment information with other measures related to reading, writing, listening, speaking, vocabulary, and structure. Item type information is not provided.	Algorithm information is not provided. Scores are based on the European Commission Proficiency Scale.

PART XII

TECHNOLOGICAL APPLICATIONS IN APPLIED LINGUISTICS

CHAPTER 37

DIRECTIONS IN AUTOMATED ESSAY ANALYSIS

JILL BURSTEIN

MARTIN CHODOROW

COMPUTERS have been used to analyze essays since the early 1960s (Burstein et al. 1998b; Foltz, Kintsch, and Landauer 1998; Larkey 1998; Page 1966; Page and Petersen 1995). Recent advances have made it possible for computer systems to score essays in high-stakes testing, such as college entrance exams, and in lower-stakes Web-based writing practice. This chapter describes some of the linguistic and computational bases for automated essay analysis. Computer systems have been developed for *holistic scoring*, in which a reader (human or computer) assigns a single numerical score to the quality of writing in an essay. Others are being developed that produce *diagnostic analysis* based on features of writing, such as organization, grammar, and vocabulary.

An important issue for all forms of evaluation is test validity. Messick (1988) defines validity as the degree to which the empirical evidence and the theoretical rationales support the appropriateness of interpretations and actions based on test scores. In the context of automated essay analysis, the validity question might be phrased as "How adequately does computer-based scoring represent the underlying aspects of assessment?" When people rate essays, they are instructed to follow a set of scoring criteria based on the writer's organization of ideas, variety of syntactic constructions, and use of appropriate vocabulary. The challenge for computational linguistics is to develop methods to identify these features of writing and, for holistic scoring, to combine the features into a single score.

In the next three sections, we describe work on computational analyses of the lexical, syntactic, and discourse structure of essays within the context of three systems—an important early project known as the *Writer's Workbench* (WWB) and two contemporary systems, the *Intelligent Essay Assessor* (IEA) and the *Electronic Essay Rater* (E-rater). In the final section, we discuss future research directions and the importance of evaluating the impact of automated scoring on different gender and ethnic groups.

THREE SYSTEMS

The Writer's Workbench (MacDonald, Frase, Gingrich, and Keenan 1982) is a computer-based tool that was designed to be a general aid for text analysis. It looks for violations of rules believed to characterize good writing (e.g., avoid the passive voice) and analyzes text under three main categories: (1) proofreading (primarily spelling and punctuation), (2) stylistic analysis (e.g., readability measures, percentage of passives, nominalizations), and (3) English usage (on-line reference information about confusable words like "affect/effect"). The WWB was constructed by implementing rules in style guides such as Strunk and White (1959), a method that contrasts sharply with the more data-driven, statistical approaches of the IEA and E-rater.

IEA (Landauer, Foltz, and Laham 1998) and E-rater (Burstein et al. 1998b) base their assessment of an essay on a comparison between the essay and other essays that have been judged by human readers. For example, in holistic scoring, E-rater is trained on a few hundred essays that represent the full range of scores assigned by readers. (On many standardized tests, a 6-point scale is used, with 1 indicating the poorest quality of writing and 6 the best.) From this training set, it measures about fifty writing features reflecting lexical content, syntax, and discourse and then uses a regression model to select and weight the features that are most predictive of essay score. This avoids the need to code a model of writing competence manually. Additionally, the system can easily adapt to new essay topics (called "prompts") simply by processing a new set of training essays, and constructing a new regression model. IEA bases its scoring only on lexical content analysis, but it also uses human-judged training data, either as a set of scored essays or in the form of one or more "gold standard" versions of a good answer.

Both IEA and E-rater are used in operational applications. IEA is integrated with the Prentice-Hall book *Keys to Success* (Carter, Bishop, and Kravitz 1999). In this application, users read portions of the book and write answers to essay questions. They receive feedback on the quality of the content coverage of their essays. Since February 1999, Educational Testing Service (ETS) has successfully used E-rater as one of the two readers for the Graduate Management Admissions Test (GMAT) Analytical Writing Assessment (AWA). In its first year, E-rater scored approximately 400,000 essays, with performance comparable to that of a human reader. E-rater agreed with a human reader approximately 92 percent of the time, about as often as two humans agreed with each other.[1]

CONTENT ANALYSIS

Traditional readability measures (e.g., Coleman and Liau 1975) reflect at least one aspect of lexical content—overall word frequency (or grade-level). The WWB calculates standard readability indices and also provides information about the relative abstractness of writing by computing the percentage of words in the text that appear in a list of words rated as abstract in psychological research. Good documents were found to consist of fewer than 2.3 percent abstract terms, so, when this value is exceeded, the user is given an indication that the text should contain more concrete examples to increase its clarity.

E-rater evaluates the topical content of an essay by comparing its vocabulary to the vocabulary found in manually graded training essays. Good essays are relevant to the assigned topic. They also tend to use a more specialized and precise topical vocabulary than do poorer essays. Therefore, we expect a good essay to resemble other good essays in its choice of words and, conversely, a poor essay to resemble other poor ones. Resemblance is computed by means of content vector analysis (CVA), adapting a technique originally developed for information retrieval (Salton 1989).

The first step in CVA is to convert each training essay into a word frequency vector—a one-dimensional array in which each element represents the number of times a particular word type occurs in the essay. (Because this procedure discards positional information, it is referred to as the "bag of words" approach.) Usually, high frequency function words (e.g., "the," "of") are excluded, and each remaining word is converted to its base form using a morphological analyzer. The vectors can be viewed as representing points in a multidimensional space, and similarity between two essays can be measured as the cosine of the angle between their vectors. To illustrate this with highly simplified examples, suppose that each of these three sentences is an entire essay. Their word frequency vectors are shown in Table 37.1.

Essay 1   Training essays are converted into word frequency vectors, and new essays are compared to the training.
Essay 2   The words in a new essay are counted and transformed into a vector of frequencies.
Essay 3   Essays are represented by word counts.

The cosine is a measure of correlation; the more similar two vectors are, the closer their cosine will be to 1.0, and the less similar they are, the closer their cosine will be to 0. Cosines calculated for the frequency data in Table 37.1 would show essays 2 and 3 to be most similar.

In a variant of the procedure just described, word weights are used instead of frequencies (Salton 1989). The weights are computed so as to give greater importance to a word that is highly frequent in an essay. In Essay 1, the base form *train* is more frequent than *convert*, for example, and therefore has a higher weight. Additionally, the weighting scheme gives less importance to a word that is commonly found in many essays. If we consider our small collection to be the entire essay corpus, then the weights for *essay* and *word* are set to 0 because they appear in every essay and therefore do not discriminate among them. Cosines between the weight vectors show essays 1 and 2 to be most similar, a result that better captures our intuitions about the three essays than the frequency vector analysis did.

One of E-rater's measures of the lexical content of a new essay is the mean score assigned to the small set of training essays that are nearest (most similar) to it in the weight vector space (Burstein et al. 1998b; Burstein and Chodorow 1999; Landauer, Foltz, and Laham 1998). In this way, the vocabulary of a new essay can be assessed as, say, a 5 on the 6-point scale because 5 is the average score of the essays whose vocabulary most closely resembles it.

The actual *word X essay* matrices constructed from training sets tend to be extremely sparse (have numerous 0-frequency cells). These gaps can occur because of a failure to recognize synonymy. For example, *convert* and *transform* appear in essays 1 and 2, respectively, but the vectors miss the similarity of meaning of these two words, as each is represented on an independent row of the matrix. The Intelligent Essay Assessor uses a technique known as latent semantic analysis (LSA) to address this problem.

Table 37.1. Frequency word (weight) vectors for three example essays

Word	Essay 1	Essay 2	Essay 3
train	2 (1.1)	0 (0.0)	0 (0.0)
essay	2 (0.0)	1 (0.0)	1 (0.0)
convert	1 (0.5)	0 (0.0)	0 (0.0)
word	1 (0.0)	1 (0.0)	1 (0.0)
frequency	1 (0.2)	1 (0.4)	0 (0.0)
vector	1 (0.2)	1 (0.4)	0 (0.0)
new	1 (0.2)	1 (0.4)	0 (0.0)
compare	1 (0.5)	0 (0.0)	0 (0.0)
count	0 (0.0)	1 (0.4)	1 (0.4)
transform	0 (0.0)	1 (1.1)	0 (0.0)
represent	0 (0.0)	0 (0.0)	1 (1.1)

LSA begins with the same rectangular *word X document* matrix used in content vector analysis but applies to it a mathematical procedure known as singular value decomposition (SVD), a generalized form of factor analysis. SVD decomposes the overall matrix into a set of independent dimensions—a word matrix locating each word in the space of these dimensions and a document matrix locating each document in the same space. Together, the set of dimensions, the word matrix, and the document matrix can be used to reconstruct the original *word X document* matrix. However, the real value of the decomposition is that it allows "noise" to be eliminated by leaving out dimensions that account for only small amounts of variability in the original data. When only the most important dimensions are retained, the vectors for words with similar meaning (similar distributions across documents) are close together, and vectors for documents that are composed of similar word meanings are also near to one another. If LSA is used to process large corpora of general text (e.g., encyclopedia articles), it can create a kind of statistical thesaurus of the language. Thus, LSA can generalize across synonyms in ways that standard content vector analysis cannot.

Content measures are important not only in holistic scoring of writing quality but also in scoring content for a subject-based exam like the College Board's Advanced Placement (AP) writing assessment (Boodoo and Burstein, in press) or for answers that students write to questions from an instructional text (Landauer, Foltz, and Laham 1998). For example, the AP writing assessment requires the reader to consider not only the general quality of the writing in the response, but also the examinee's knowledge about the topic of the question.

SYNTACTIC ANALYSIS

Computational linguistics has developed many tools for syntactic analysis, ranging from tagging words for part-of-speech, to chunking words into phrases, to full-scale parsing of a sentence. The selection of syntactic analysis tools for use in essay scoring depends in part on the application. Holistic scoring criteria for college admissions tests generally emphasize syntactic variety as an indicator of good writing. Tests of nonnative speakers, such as the Test of English as a Foreign Language (TOEFL), use syntactic errors in their criteria as indicators of failure to master the grammar of English.

The WWB uses a part-of-speech tagger and heuristics to locate and count passive constructions. It then compares the proportion of passives to that found in a corpus of good documents of the same type, such as technical papers. E-rater tags each word for part-of-speech (Brill 1995), uses a syntactic "chunker" (Abney 1996) to find phrases, and assembles the phrases into trees on the basis of sub-categorization information for verbs (Grishman, Macleod, and Meyers 1994). Figure 37.1 shows part of the result for an example sentence. The tag *prp* stands for personal pronoun, *rb* for adverb, *vb* for verb, and *wdt* for *wh*-determiner. The nonterminal SCComp indicates the beginning of a subordinate clause of the complement type.

Detecting grammatical errors in the writing of nonnative speakers poses additional challenges. Some researchers (Park, Palmer, and Washburn 1997; Schneider and McCoy 1998) have approached this task by modifying parsers to look for specific errors that nonnative speakers might make. This requires considerable manual effort to modify the grammar that controls a broad-coverage parser. Recently, Chodorow and Leacock (2000) have explored a different strategy based on statistical methods and that requires little or no human supervision. Some of the errors that nonnative writers produce violate basic principles of English syntax, while others reflect a lack of word-specific knowledge. The statistical method looks at function words and part-of-speech tags that do not co-occur (or that co-occur much less often than expected) in large corpora of edited English text. For example, singular determiners and plural nouns almost never appear in adjacent positions, as in 'a books'. Singular determiners commonly precede singular nouns, but 'a knowledge' appears rarely even in a large corpus, a fact that reflects its

I also assume that shrinking high school enrollments . . .

S	NP |	prp	I
	VP |	rb	also
		vb	assume
	SCComp |	wdt	that

Fig. 37.1. Partial parse tree used by *e-rater*

status as a mass noun. In a test of this corpus-based approach, both general and word-specific errors were detected at a higher rate in TOEFL essays that received lower scores from human readers. In a blind evaluation of the statistical system's error judgments, a linguist found that 80 percent of them were indeed grammatical errors. Further refinement of this method could prove to be useful in applications for automated essay scoring and diagnostic analysis.

DISCOURSE ANALYSIS

Although the WWB does not analyze rhetorical structure per se, it does give the user an abstract of the essay by extracting the first and the last sentence of each paragraph. For writers who use the standard methods of beginning and ending paragraphs with topic and conclusion sentences, respectively, the claim is that viewing these sentences provides the writer with a sense of the organization of the essay and its flow of ideas.

E-rater identifies discourse cue words and terms and uses them to annotate each essay according to a discourse classification schema (Quirk et al. 1985). The annotation marks the beginnings of arguments (the main points of discussion) within a text, as well as the type of argument (e.g., a claim) and how it is developed. Discourse features based on the annotations ought to reflect the writer's organization of ideas, one of the scoring criteria. In fact, they have been shown to predict the holistic scores that human readers assign to essays. The discourse features are also used to refine the content analysis presented earlier. E-rater partitions essays into arguments and uses CVA to evaluate the content of each (Burstein et al. 1998a; Burstein and Chodorow 1999).

E-rater's discourse analysis produces a flat, linear sequence of units. For instance, in the essay text, E-rater's discourse annotation indicates that a contrastive relationship exists, based on discourse cue words, such as "however." The annotation does not show the sentences or clauses between which the relationship exists. Mann and Thompson (1988) have argued that a more realistic account of the structure of text must also encode hierarchical relationships. By contrast, Rhetorical Structure Theory (RST) provides logical connections between related sentences. For instance, RST relations can illustrate that two sentences are in *contrast* to one another, or that one sentence is an *elaboration* of another sentence. Rhetorical parsing tools (Marcu 2000) have made it possible for computer-based text analysis to use rhetorical relations. Preliminary experiments integrating RST features into E-rater indicate that they can increase the validity of E-rater scoring models (Burstein and Marcu 2000b).

Assessing Validity

From a purely data-driven, statistical point of view, validity of a holistic scoring model is measured by R^2, the proportion of variation in writing scores for which the model accounts. For example, E-rater builds a statistical model using a prompt-specific sample of training essays that have been scored by at least two human readers. More than fifty features related to lexical content, syntax, and discourse are identified for each essay in the training sample, and a linear regression selects the subset of features that best predict score—typically eight to twelve features. The regression weights for these features are used to assign scores to new essays. Discrepancies between predicted and reader-assigned scores form the basis for R^2.

There is, however, another sense of validity (more closely related to Messick's [1988] definition) that asks how adequately the model represents the underlying aspects of assessment. The distinction between these two senses can be seen when considering a feature such as essay length (number of words), which is reliably correlated with score but is not one of the criteria given to human readers. Including length in the model increases statistical validity, but at the expense of conceptual validity. In E-rater, an attempt has been made to base scores only on the kinds of features that human readers use.

We are continually exploring the inclusion of new features that relate to the scoring criteria, such as the relationship between RST features and the criterion "logical organization of ideas." In practice, it is desirable to have a balance between statistical and conceptual validity. The goal is to incorporate linguistically principled features into the model, while maintaining a good fit between actual and predicted scores. In an experiment where RST features were included in E-rater model building, we found consistent increases in R^2, indicating that linguistically motivated features can be used without sacrificing scoring accuracy (Burstein and Marcu 2000b). In this case, E-rater scoring performance remained stable, and the model validity was enhanced by the addition of the RST features.

How well do automatically generated essay scores correlate with other indicators of writing ability, such as grades in courses that require considerable writing, self-evaluations, and writing-related accomplishments (e.g., authoring a published paper)? A study by Powers et al. (2000) addressed this question by comparing E-rater scores on Graduate Record Examination (GRE) essays to these nontest indicators. The results showed that automated scores correlated significantly with the external criteria, though not quite as highly as the human reader scores. Landauer, Laham, Rehder, and Schreiner (1997) used IEA to evaluate student essays in content areas such as the structure and function of the human heart. IEA scores and human reader scores were significantly correlated with student performance on a forty-item short-answer test on the same topic, but IEA's correlation with this external measure was actually stronger than that of the human readers.

DIAGNOSTIC ANALYSIS

It has become apparent that the next step beyond generating a score for writing is to produce a text analysis that provides instructional feedback for facilitating the teaching and learning of writing. The WWB provides such information using a pedagogical approach and defining good features of writing on the basis of style guides. The approach is most similar to the kinds of corrections we can expect from grammar checkers in current word-processing software. The effectiveness of the WWB's feedback is documented in studies of those who have used it. MacDonald, Frase, Gingrich, and Keenan (1982) report that these writers' last drafts of documents have fewer passives, abstract words, and awkward phrases than their first drafts. Proofreading was also shown to be more accurate using the system.

Computational Modeling of Writing Components

E-rater was developed to predict a holistic score, rather than to assess individual aspects of writing. Diagnostic analysis, however, requires more specific information about particular components of writing. Breland, Bonner, and Kubota (1995) conducted a study using four hundred College Board English Composition Test

(ECT) essay responses. In addition to receiving holistic, over all scores, essays were scored by two independent readers who assigned separate scores to a number of writing components, of which the five most important were judged to be (1) thesis statement, (2) rhetorical structure, (3) noteworthy ideas, (4) organization and (5) how well the writer's ideas were supported in the essay. Burstein, Wolff, Breland, and Kubota (submitted) applied current E-rater techniques and a feature set augmented with RST features to the task of predicting the scores for each component. Using this approach, a future E-rater could rate individual characteristics of writing in essays, and the ratings could be used for diagnostic feedback and instruction. Results from this study indicated that E-rater was in agreement with the human readers as often as the humans agreed with each other, and for one component, rhetorical strategy, exact agreement between the human and E-rater scores was 8 to 10 percent higher than that between the two human readers.

Feedback in the Form of Summaries

As described earlier, the WWB can generate information about text organization in the form of a text abstract that includes the first (thesis) and the final (conclusion) sentences of each paragraph. In a similar spirit, automated text summarization techniques can be used to generate text abstracts. Since standardized essays are written under time constraints, there is little time for editing and smoothing out of the text. As a result, the essays tend to have a lot of "noise," such as repetitive statements and extraneous comments not central to the essay. Research indicates that salient summaries can be generated automatically from texts on the basis of their rhetorical structure (Marcu 1999) and that E-rater's lexical content analysis of these noise-reduced, cleaned-up summaries yields performance comparable to that of the full-text versions (Burstein and Marcu 2000b). We envision at least two uses for essay summaries. First, refinement of this technique could generate essay outlines. Second, salient information in summaries could be used to evaluate information in subject-based essays. If the main points in higher scoring essays could be identified, they could be used to illustrate the points that are missing in lower scoring ones.

FUTURE DIRECTIONS

Content scoring is likely to be an area of increasing interest. As noted earlier, IEA is already successfully used in this way. College Board–funded research on subject-based exams, such as the Advanced Placement essays in U.S. History and English Literature, suggests that E-rater can also score domain-specific prompts with reliability comparable to that achieved by readers (Boodoo and Burstein in press). Another increasingly important application will be in diagnostic analysis. E-rater's performance has motivated continued research in essay scoring across varied essay genres and populations, such as the GRE, TOEFL, the College Board's Advanced Placement (AP) tests, and ETS's English Proficiency Test (EPT).

As more and more writing assessments become automated, what impact will computer-generated scores have on racial, ethnic, and gender subgroups? GRE-funded research (Boodoo and Burstein in press) examined this question and found computer-generated scores to be as reliable as human reader scores for the general and subgroup populations. In TOEFL-funded research, Sheehan and Burstein (in preparation) are examining automated scoring performance on nonnative English speakers to reveal whether E-rater handles text differently depending on the writer's native language.

A goal of current research in automated essay analysis and scoring is to develop applications to ensure that systems maintain a relevant link to what writing experts and test developers believe are critical to the teaching and learning of writing. The WWB began with this approach by consulting classic style guides, and IEA and E-rater use data-driven techniques that relate scoring models to scoring criteria. Future research should continue to enhance the validity of automated scoring so that computer-based methods of essay analysis will be in line with the educational goals in writing instruction and so that systems can adequately represent the underlying aspects of writing assessments.

NOTES

We wish to thank Daniel Marcu, of the Information Sciences Institute of the University of Southern California, for generating rhetorical parses and summarizations of essays and for continued research collaborations. We are also indebted to Kathleen Sheehan and Bruce Kaplan, of Educational Testing Service, for statistical analyses and discussions and to Claudia Leacock, of ETS Technologies, for her contributions to the work on syntactic analysis. We gratefully acknowledge GMAT, GRE, TOEFL, the College Board, and Educational Testing Service for their continued support.

1. Agreement indicates that reader scores are within one point of each other on 6-point scale.

CHAPTER 38

COMPUTER-ASSISTED LANGUAGE LEARNING

CAROL A. CHAPELLE

COMPUTER-ASSISTED language learning (CALL), defined as "the search for and study of applications of the computer in language teaching and learning" (Levy 1997: 1), covers a broad spectrum of concerns, including the pedagogies implemented through technology and their evaluation. As a consequence, CALL draws from other areas within and beyond applied linguistics for conceptual and technical tools to develop and evaluate computer-based learning. However, because other areas fail to provide pedagogical or evaluative methods for the specific needs of L2 learners and learning, the perennial issue in CALL is how best to apply research and practice in L2 pedagogy to CALL.

Almost twenty years ago, John Underwood took up this challenge, outlining the then-current comprehensible input theory of Krashen (1982) and drawing from it pedagogical principles for designing CALL activities. He summarized his thinking this way: "Input theory tells us that classroom activities should be directed more toward the unconscious acquisition of language than the conscious learning of rules. Acquisition will take place if we provide our students with sufficient quantities of comprehensible input" (Underwood 1984: 18). Principles for 'communicative' CALL based on this theory included, for example, at least the following: "Communicative CALL will aim at acquisition practice rather than learning practice," and "grammar will always be implicit rather than explicit." On the basis of these principles, Underwood described CALL activities that, for example, allowed learners to "communicate" with CALL programs through interactive written language concerning topics such as family.

Most CALL practitioners would point out that the technology has changed dramatically since the publication of Underwood's book, but equally important are the changes in pedagogically oriented SLA theory. Whereas Krashen's theory asserts that the L2 must be acquired unconsciously, Schmidt claims the opposite: "subliminal language learning is impossible, and that [what might be learned] is what learners consciously notice. This requirement of noticing is meant to apply equally to all aspects of language (lexicon, phonology, grammatical form, pragmatics)" (1990: 149). Schmidt's claim is consistent with findings that suggest that acquisition requires interaction with the target language, rather than exposure to input alone (Gass 1997; Long 1996); interaction draws attention to language. Recognition of the importance of interaction, in addition to an expanded view of factors related to selection of pedagogical materials (Doughty and Williams 1998a; Skehan 1998a), has resulted in the need to reconsider the relationship between theory-based L2 pedagogy and CALL. One of the most important developments comes from research on pedagogical tasks in L2 classrooms, because this work underscores the importance of guiding principles for pedagogy and empirical research methods for their evaluation.

Principles for CALL Pedagogues

In designing CALL tasks, decisions must be made concerning, for example, task goals, learners' activity, specifics of software design, and the number and roles of learners. The many types of suggested CALL activities need to be judged for a particular learning situation on the basis of principles from the theory and research for instructed SLA (Pica 1997b). Whereas, twenty years ago, "communicative CALL" might have been judged relative to the qualities outlined by Underwood, today "appropriate CALL" can be defined by the following qualities: (1) Language learning potential, (2) learner fit, (3) meaning focus, (4) authenticity, (5) positive impact, and (6) practicality.

Language learning potential refers to the extent to which a CALL activity can be expected to be beneficial for language learning. Current theory and research suggest that language learning is most likely to result when learners engage in three types of processes. First, learners should focus on linguistic form periodically during otherwise meaning-based activities. One way that learners can be directed to notice some aspects of the linguistic input is through explicit "input enhancement" (Sharwood-Smith 1993), in other words, highlighting linguistic features in the input for learners. Second, learners should engage in interactional modifications; in other words, they should interrupt the "normal" interaction if they do not comprehend the language to obtain "modification" of input through simplification, elaboration, or added redundancy (Larsen-Freeman and Long 1991). One form of interactional modification can be seen in CALL materials when the learner stops aural input to request a simplification, repetition, or definition, for example. Another type is seen in interactive discourse (e.g., in a chat room) when the learner requests and receives clarification from interlocuters. Third, learners should notice and correct errors in their linguistic output (Swain 1985), either on their own or with help from the computer, other learners or the teacher. What the three ideal processes have in common is that they prompt learners to attend to language and therefore reflect current perspectives on the importance of attention in language learning (Robinson 1995).

Learner fit refers to the appropriate fit of CALL materials to learners' linguistic ability level and individual characteristics. If the language of a CALL task is already known to the learner, the task presents no opportunity for development, but language that is beyond the learners' grasp relative to their ability is equally ineffective. In addition, important learner characteristics such as willingness to communicate (MacIntyre, Clément, Dörnyei, and Noels 1998), age, and learning style also come into play in task choice (Skehan 1998a).

Meaning focus denotes the direction of learners' attention primarily toward the meaning of the language required to accomplish the task. The clearest example of L2 tasks with meaning focus are communication tasks that require the learners to solve a problem, such as deciding how to spend funds for a party (Pica, Kanagy, and Falodun 1993). Meaning focus can occur during tasks that involve reading and writing when learners use the written language for constructing and interpreting meaning for a purpose. Meaning-focused tasks require learners to use the target language to accomplish something, rather than manipulate language as they would be likely to do while filling in correct verb tenses in isolated sentences, for example.

Authenticity refers to the degree of correspondence between a CALL task and the language use the learner is likely to engage in outside the classroom. Current theory of communicative language ability (Bachman 1990; Bachman and Palmer 1996) as situation-specific implies that development of ability in language for particular purposes requires practice in using language for those purposes. Moreover, the choice of pedagogical tasks that learners see as relevant to their language use beyond the classroom should help to engage learners' interest and therefore participation.

The *positive impact* of a CALL task refers to its effects beyond its language learning potential. Ideally, classroom language learning tasks teach more than language; they should help learners develop their metacognitive strategies (Oxford 1990) in a way that allows them to develop accountability for their learning in the classroom and beyond. They should engage learners' interest in the target culture to help develop their willingness to communicate in the L2. They should learn pragmatic abilities that will serve them beyond the classroom, which, as Warschauer (1998) has argued, includes situations in which electronic communication is normal. Parallel to the concept of washback or impact in language testing (Bachman and Palmer 1996), positive impact in CALL can include effects on the learners and teachers as well as on the educational system as a whole.

Practicality refers to how easily learners and teachers can implement the CALL task within the particular constraints of a class or language program. Relevant constraints include the availability of adequate hardware and software for the activities, as well as knowledgeable personnel who can assist with unforeseen problems. Early experience with CALL showed how essential adequate access to well-maintained software and hardware was for CALL (Marty 1981). This observation is equally valid today, because, even though learners use computers regardless of the infrastructure provided by language programs, they cannot be expected to use computers for language learning without guidance, and solid guidance requires resources.

Empirical CALL Research

Judgments concerning qualities of CALL activities can help to guide selection of CALL for a particular context. In fact, twenty years ago, many observes relied solely on judgmental evaluation of the extent to which CALL activities were "communicative" in the light of Underwood's premises. However, another contribution from research on instructed SLA has been the development of methods for investigating L2 teaching and learning. Empirical research methods include process-oriented and product-oriented approaches, with particular focus on outcomes that can be attributed to features of instruction.

Process-Oriented Research

Process-oriented research investigates interactions, discourse, or other aspects of learner performance during CALL use. Empirical evidence for language learning potential can be seen in data that reveal that learners have noticed linguistic form, engaged in interactional modifications, and corrected errors in their linguistic output. Noticing linguistic form, of course, is not directly observable; however, some researchers infer that noticing is taking place when they observe learners engage in "reflective conversation" (i.e., conversation about language) during CALL tasks (Lamy and Goodfellow 1999).

Interactional modifications are evident any time the learner interrupts to request help. For example, when learners read or listen to a text that provides opportunities for them to request modified input, "normal" interaction for reading a text on a screen is considered to consist of the learner's receiving input and requesting more input (i.e., scrolling down the page); this normal sequence is interrupted or modified when the learner clicks on a word to receive a definition. For example, an L2 French activity, *Language now*, by Transparent Language, displays lines of a dialog on the screen (e.g, an interviewer asks a vineyard owner: *"Combien de types de vignes, de cépages cultivez-vous?"*). A learner who does not know the word *cépages* can click on it. The computer returns help: "Word meaning—*varieties.*" Modified interaction may also be apparent when a learner requests and receives a clarification during a chat room conversation or when learners interrupt themselves to request help during writing. The latter behavior was documented in research by Bland, Noblitt, Armington, and Gay (1990), who examined the process learners used to construct a text using *System-D*, which supports queries about the vocabulary and grammar of French while the learners are writing their French texts.

Error correction can best be observed in sequences of data consisting of the learners' unsuccessful attempts at expression followed by their linguistic modification. These data are like those used to infer "self-monitoring" strategies that have been documented in CALL (Jamieson and Chapelle 1987): The data include the learner's original form, the process of correction, and the learner's final form.

Evidence for learner fit should indicate that CALL is the appropriate level of difficulty and type of pedagogy, given the learners' characteristics. Process data that indicate good learner fit overlap those used to infer language learning potential because an activity can hold potential for language learning only if it is at the appropriate level for the learner. Observations of behaviors can be supplemented by introspective methods that require learners to think aloud as they work. For example, Park's study of the use of ESL multimedia through think-aloud data identified revealing thoughts such as "I think I have a lot of vocabulary that I don't know" (1994: 147). This statement, indicating a need for task-related vocabulary, was made while the learner was clicking on one of the words in the input.

Learner fit can also be investigated through process data containing the language that learners produced. For example, Kern (1995) examined the linguistic characteristics of his students' language in a computer-assisted classroom discussion, and found that learners were able to engage in language at an appropriate level of complexity for their development. Issues of learner fit are also explored through consideration of individual differences, such as field independence/dependence, motivation, and gender, as they relate to interaction in CALL activities, with the most important result being the apparent diminishing of individual differences that can hamper communication in oral face-to-face activities in the classroom (Meunier 1995/1996; Warschauer 1995/1996).

Discourse analysis of learners' language and learners' reports can help to provide empirical evidence about meaning focus and authenticity of CALL tasks. Meaning focus is evident in language from computer-mediated communication (CMC) tasks if it develops a topic or topics during a conversation about something such as family or the content of a story learners have read (e.g., Kelm 1992; Kern 1995). Examples of meaning-focused target language use contrast with observations of one- or two-word target language utterances used for guessing responses to a game, for example. Learners' reports of their attention while working on a CALL task can add another dimension to the analysis. In a study of ESL learners' strategies while working on interactive multimedia software, Park (1994) identified clear instances in learners' reports of attending to meaning in the input they were receiving.

Investigation of authenticity requires evidence that learners' performance in CALL tasks corresponds to what one would expect to see outside the CALL task (Esling 1991). Research that investigated learners' oral language as they worked on CALL programs has found that the computer program influences learners' language, but points of comparison with out-of-class language have not been articulated (Abraham and Liou 1991; Mohan 1992; Piper 1986). Similarly, the research that has examined the language of computer-mediated communication in CALL has drawn comparisons between oral classroom language and the written language of CMC (Kern 1995; Warschauer 1995/1996). Today, interpretation of such an analysis would undoubtedly need to be recast in view of the registers of language use outside the classroom that include language about computer programs and through electronic communication. In particular, analysis would compare the pedagogic CALL discourse and discourse outside the classroom in terms of the input provided to the learner, the learner's output, and the interaction between the learner and the interlocutor from the perspectives of pragmatic function, linguistic characteristics, quantity, nonlinguistic moves and forms, and medium (Chapelle 1999b). An additional consideration for investigation of authenticity is evidence obtained through introspective methods that indicate that learners see the connection between the CALL task and tasks outside the classroom.

Qualitative studies that might reveal evidence about the impact and practicality are yet to be undertaken. CALL researchers might look to work in language testing that is beginning to explore methodologies for the study of impact of language tests (Alderson and Hamp-Lyons 1996). Issues of practicality are closely tied to characteristics of institutional, social, and cultural practices that allow some members the power to make decisions about the amount and type of the resources to be made available to CALL. Practicality might therefore be examined through critical methods (Pennycook 1999b).

Product-Oriented Research

The most definitive evidence for language learning potential and learner fit comes from studies that have investigated outcomes from CALL tasks. Despite the difficulty of defining and assessing what is taught through CALL, progress requires evidence about the features of CALL tasks that succeed in particular circumstances.

The definition of language learning potential makes predictions about the value of particular conditions. Even though little research has been conducted on the effects of CALL activities that focus learners' attention on particular linguistic forms in the L2 input, one carefully conducted study yielded results that favored the condition in which linguistic form (relative clauses) was highlighted in a text that learners were reading for meaning (Doughty 1991). Several studies have found evidence for learning in conditions that allow interactional modifications, as well. Chun and Plass (1996) found vocabulary gains for German learners who read text that contained hyperlinked annotations for words, and Hegelheimer (1998) found similar vocabulary gains for ESL learners who took advantage of annotations for vocabulary during on-line reading. In an interactive listening task for learners of L2 French, Borrás and Lafayette (1994) found learners with access to L1 (English) subtitles outperformed learners who did not have this option for interactional modification. Hsu (1994) found increases in ESL listening comprehension related to use of interactional modification during a CALL listening activity. The results of these studies appear to suggest that opportunities for noticing and interactional modifications may be a feature of CALL that makes a positive difference.

Less evidence exists for the value of opportunities for error identification and correction; however, one study of outcomes indicated the value of pinpointing learners' errors as carefully as possible (Nagata 1993). Unfortunately, other studies of feedback that one would think might speak to error correction investigated structure tasks for which meaning clearly was not central, if relevant at all, and, therefore, learners' output on such tasks cannot be considered "comprehensible output," as Swain (1985) defined it. It is not clear how hypotheses about noticing errors in comprehensible output apply to error correction during explicit grammar instruction in which the learners' attention is directed to the forms of the language. Additional research is needed to help assess the language learning potential of various types of feedback in comprehensible output in both computer-learner interactions and learner-learner interactions in CALL.

Studies that examine learning outcomes are crucial for developing arguments about language learning potential. Therefore, future research needs to examine exactly what features of performance should be related to outcomes. The question is not whether the *provision for* particular interactions increases acquisition, but whether the *use of* these interactions is related to those forms for which, noticing, interactional modifications or error correction occurred. Swain (1998) makes this point in her discussion of the methodology used for examining the effectiveness of a classroom language learning task. She observed learners while they were participating in the task and then assessed outcomes with measures designed specifically for individual students to assess their knowledge of the linguistic elements *they chose to focus on* during task completion. In CALL research, Hsu's (1994) study used a similar methodology, investigating the relationships between interactional modifications used for specific segments of the input and subsequent comprehension of the same segments on the posttest.

Examination of past CALL research at the close of the twentieth century reveals more potential than results; however, an elaborate conceptual framework on the role of interaction in L2 development (Gass 1997; Pica 1994) makes possible links between SLA theory and CALL research and practice (Chapelle 1998; Renié and Chanier 1995). As the opportunities for software development and computer use by language learners expand, questions about the qualities outlined above need to be investigated systematically.

CALL in the Twenty-first Century

The topic of CALL makes an ideal closing chapter for the *Handbook of Applied Linguistics* because it is likely to be the vehicle by which many of the concepts and findings in other aspects of applied linguistics will be explored and developed in the twenty-first century. However, if CALL is to contribute substantively to teaching practice and theoretical developments concerning language teaching and learning, applied linguists' view of what constitutes appropriate CALL activities must constantly be updated on the basis of developments in theory and research in language teaching, in addition to those in technology.

PART XIII

CONCLUSION

CHAPTER 39

WHERE TO FROM HERE?

ROBERT B. KAPLAN

APPLIED linguistics looks to be alive and well, judging by the chapters in this collection. However, in some quarters, the very diversity represented here has led to the belief that not only is applied linguistics not "linguistics applied" but also that it has no particular relationship with linguistics at all and should instead be seen as the name given to any concern with language in the real world, whether or not such a concern is informed by any discipline. What it should be informed by, instead, it is argued, is a critical attitude to established authority and a political commitment to the cause of social justice. The discussions in this volume that are reflective of concerns with the goals and principles of applied linguistics have, in recent years, produced a good deal of debate. (See, e.g., Brumfit 1997; Davies 1999a; Kaplan and Grabe 2000; Rampton 1995a, 1997b, Spolsky 1999; Widdowson 1998c, 2000a, 2000b). This debate can be seen as an expression of uncertainty about the status of applied linguistics as an independent discipline. On the other hand, more positively, the scope and range of this volume can be seen as evidence of a continuing and critical evaluation of how the defining principle of relevance in applied linguistics can be most effectively satisfied.

While the various debates have by no means produced general agreement, there are some points on which, I believe, most practitioners of applied linguistics would agree. This despite the fact that the debates intermingle a number of issues that ought to be teased apart, namely the scope of the field, its status, its emergence, and its viability as a discipline (alternatively, the paradigms that inform the field, the political place of the field in the academic landscape, and the means for and content of training the next generation[s] of applied linguists).

The commonalities, while few and seemingly meager, nonetheless provide the anchor for discussing applied linguistics as an interdisciplinary field. Most applied linguists would agree on at least the following points:

- Applied linguistics is grounded in real-world, language-driven problems and issues (primarily by linkages to practical issues that involve language use, language evaluation, language contact and multilingualism, language policies, and language learning, teaching, and assessment). There is, however, a recognition that these practically driven problems have extraordinary range and that this range tends to diminish the sense of common purpose or professional identity among practitioners.
- Applied linguistics typically incorporates knowledge of disciplines beyond linguistics in its efforts to address language-based problems. Applied linguists commonly draw upon, and are often well trained in, such areas as anthropology, computer programming, economics, education, literature, measurement, political science, psychology, and/or sociology.
- Applied linguistics often defines itself in such a way as to include additional fields of language-related studies (e.g., first language composition studies, first language literacy research, language and literature, language history, language pathology, and natural language processing). The great majority of individuals in these fields do not necessarily see themselves as applied linguistics, but applied linguists have license to investigate these disciplines in the interests of the goals of applied linguistics.
- Applied linguistics, then (following from the preceding points), is by definition an interdisciplinary field, since few real-world language issues can be addressed through the resources of any single discipline.
- Applied linguistics commonly includes a core set of issues and practices that are readily identified as the kind of work regularly undertaken by many applied linguists (e.g., language teaching, language teacher preparation, and language curriculum development).
- Applied linguistics generally incorporates or includes several identifiable sub-fields of linguistics, such as corpus linguistics, forensic linguistics, language pathology, language testing, lexicography and dictionary making, literacy, pragmatics, second language acquisition, second language writing research, and translation and interpretation. Some members of these sub-fields also do not see themselves as applied linguists, though their work clearly addresses practical language issues.
- Applied linguistics already has many of the characteristics of an academic discipline, including academic license to practice and teach, a large population of individuals who see themselves as applied linguists, funding resources for research projects, international recognition of the field, professional associations, professional journals, students who want to become

applied linguists, together with the mechanism that permits training such students to become applied linguists, and trained professionals who are hired in academic institutions (and elsewhere) as applied linguists.

- There is a general recognition that linguistics needs to be included as the core in the work of applied linguistics, even though the purpose of most applied linguistics work is not merely to "apply linguistics" to the achievement of a solution to a problem.

These points bring to awareness a number of basic questions that have in the past beset the field and continue to do so:

- What is the locus of applied linguistics in the architecture of the "university"?
- Where does applied linguistics belong in the greater sociology of knowledge?
- What are the questions that applied linguistics ought to be addressing? That is, what are the research paradigms that should guide research in the field?
- What part(s) of linguistics can be applied to real-world, language-based problems that applied linguistics undertakes to mediate?
- To the extent that linguistics alone is clearly necessary but not sufficient, what other disciplines must be involved and to what extent?
- What kind(s) of real-world problems can be mediated by applied linguistics?
- What does an applied linguist need to know? That is, of what should the graduate curricula in applied linguistics consist?

It is apparent that the questions just enumerated span a number of different kinds of issues, some purely pragmatic, some more philosophical. On the one hand, the locus of applied linguistics in the architecture of the university is a more pragmatic question, but it is critical to the survival of the field; without a "home," the work of the field is significantly circumscribed. Scholars working in the field cannot exist in a vacuum; they need academic departments in which to work, academic titles in those departments—those titles awarded according to standardized processes within the institutional framework, the institutional authority to enroll students and to award them degrees, some definition of the work required to achieve a degree, classrooms in which to deliver that work, and the panoply of other practical issues involved in survival within the academic community, including recognized standing within the broader academic community.

On the other hand, the definition of the research paradigms to guide research in the field constitutes a more philosophical matter, since it implicates at least questions of epistemology. The very term applied linguistics raises fundamental difficulties, if for no other reason than that it is difficult to determine what counts as "linguistics." This issue really belongs to linguistics proper. Does linguistics incorporate the range of competing theoretical views of language description commonly identified as theories? Does linguistics include the work of descriptive grammarians and corpus linguists? Does linguistics include the work of prescriptive grammarians and stylists? Does linguistics include the hyphenated sub fields—computational linguistics, critical linguistics, forensic linguistics, historical linguistics, pragmatics, psycholinguistics, sociolinguistics, and so on? Does linguistics operate on "sentences" and other smaller clausal structural units, or does it operate on whole discourses, whether spoken or written? Is so, what are the limits of a "discourse"? More important, what assumptions underlie the competing views of what counts as linguistics? The answer to most of these questions has to be "it depends." Given these difficulties within linguistics proper, it is perhaps unreasonable to expect clean solutions and clear boundaries in defining the field of *applied* linguistics.

These questions, while not necessarily explicitly addressed in the chapters of the present volume, are implied in every discussion herein. Indeed, while the volume reflects the diversity of applied linguistics, that diversity does not necessarily represent a Balkanization of the field. There have, historically, been two quite different ways of looking at the nature of language, and these divergent views have supported the independent development of applied linguistics. On the one hand, in what has been called "autonomous" linguistics, the object of inquiry has traditionally been seen as an independent language system composed of unique and invariant structural and semantic rules. In contemporary thinking, this system has been seen as innate to human beings—a species-specific phenomenon encoded into the human genetic structure. Given this biological explanation of its ontogeny, it has been, in this paradigm, perfectly reasonable to investigate language as a separate entity, because it has an independent existence unrelated to human production or use. The relationship in that system between the investigator and language is quite straightforward and unproblematic—"subject > object." The objective of formal inquiry is systematic description in neutral scientific language quite isolated from the value-laden characteristics of everyday language in use. Such neutral description is seen to give rise to rational predictions about the internal operations of the system and about the directions of its future development. This perspective derives from the traditions of logical positivism and scientific realism and is thought to provide parsimonious and invariant description. This view identifies language with grammatical theory, leading to an exclusive preoccupation with form and a disregard of, or skepticism toward, language use and function. But a parallel between linguistics and natural science may be challenged.

> When one uses a physical theory T, containing claims about unobservables, to make a prediction P, one explains the truth of P by positing the truth of T, and showing that it entails P. Since T says there are unobservables, one is

thereby committed to their existence. This is not what happens when one uses a grammar to make predictions about grammaticality. Since a grammar is made up of rules, it does not state anything, let alone that its rules are internalized by specific people. As a result, the claim that S is a grammatical sentence of L is entailed not by a grammar G but by a principle which says that a sequence of words is a grammatical sentence of L if and only if it is generated by G. It is the truth of this principle to which the [autonomous] linguist is committed when adopting G. Thus the abstract concept does not violate any presumption of truth regarding explanatory principles that are used to make predictions. (Soames 1992: 192)

There is an alternative view more generally associated with applied linguistics. In this perspective, language is seen not as an independent system but rather as a human product and a social tool. The ontogenesis of this view is influenced by hermeneutic philosophy—a position essentially antagonistic to scientific realism and logical positivism. The perception is that, while the physical sciences deal with inanimate objects outside the human sphere, language is the product of the human mind and is therefore inseparable from it and from the attendant subjectivity, value orientation, and emotion. In scientific realism, the object of empirical research is to capture an invariant objective reality through repeated testing of hypothetical correspondences that occur between models and observed phenomena; that is, empirical research is a tool through which to test, repeatedly, the consistency, and thus to verify the validity, of any observed correspondences. In the alternative view, deriving at least in part from the ideas of Husserl, that sort of empiricism was conceived as an error traceable to Galilean systematization, because the notion "hypothesis > test > verification" is based on an assumption of the constancy of any given phenomenon. Such an assumption ignores even the practical problems inherent in setting up a consistent measurement system with respect to language. In the alternative view, the investigator is simultaneously both the subject and the object of inquiry; the study of language is the study of human beings. Such a perception challenges, on logical grounds, the notion of an independent existence and objectification of language, as well as the possibility of devising an invariant abstract model. Given the complexity of language, given the fact that language changes over time, and given the fact that language exists within various cultural systems, it would be impossible to discover invariant laws as in the physical sciences. Thus, the study of language, at certain levels at least, must be descriptive, rather than predictive and explanatory. In addition, it would be impossible, from this perspective, to describe language in a context-free, neutral scientific sense. Applied linguistics perceives language as constituting much more than grammar. This is not to suggest an extreme relativist position; applied linguists generally believe that data are worth gathering and that generalizations are possible and may indeed lead to useful responses to problems. It is important to distinguish between theoretical constructivism on the one hand and a healthy recognition of the difficulties of valid generalization from data as well as the limitations of data creation and interpretation on the other.

Given these differing underlying assumptions, certain predictions can be made about the future development of applied linguistics. Applied linguistics is likely to be marked by a more powerful version of descriptive linguistics as the central linguistic resource for research. The development of corpus linguistics, for example, is now revealing facts about language use and language variation across registers that are essential for addressing practical issues but that are largely incompatible with most current theoretical models in linguistics proper. Applied linguists, who must be anchored in a "realistic" linguistics that is discourse based and grounded in attested occurrences, are likely to move toward the analysis of new data, rather than continue to argue new theory, despite the reality that theory building is not only possible but desirable within a descriptive framework. Goals will center around understanding new facts about language, rather than around having language facts manipulated to fit preconceived theory. In the face of this disjuncture, descriptive linguistics, with its increasing power to enhance understanding of language uses, is likely to provide more fertile ground for applied linguistics. The recycling to descriptively powerful research will be enhanced by computer applications; by studies of language uses in the "professions"—law, medicine, science (more broadly), and business; by research at the discourse level (rather than the clause level), defining the basic analytic unit; and by the power of descriptive analysis to provide relatively theory-neutral data for future linguistic theorizing.

It is likely that applied linguistics will be characterized by the much greater uses of technology and computer applications, making these essential components of training for new applied linguists. These computer-based applications will be seen in computer-based testing and language learning, connectionist research on learning, corpus linguistics research and lexicography, new statistical approaches (particularly in assessment, better to reflect recent views on validity and performance assessment), and translation research. Assessment practices are likely to implicate new dimensions that result from the development of appropriate technology resources that are not yet ready for application or that have not yet been developed in practical ways. The rapid growth in computational power available to everyone will bring these changes about sooner rather than later.

These changes will result in new definitions of student learning—both for students learning languages and for students undertaking applied linguistics. Language students will become familiar with new technologies for learning, becoming more engaged in autonomous learning while also working collaboratively with groups. They will have greater access to resources to support their learning, receiving more rapid feedback on their learning progress. These features of language learning are likely to be even more prominent among programs that train applied linguists. Applied linguistics students will need to master a wide range of technological resources as central components of their training. They will need to learn to work collaboratively on research projects, as interdisciplinary cooperation and research teams become increasingly essential to deal with larger problems involving more variables, more disciplines, and more person power. Students are likely to become engaged in research practices that require expert knowledge of both quantitative and qualitative methods, as well as of their complementary contributions to knowledge making. Students may be required to carry out complex and extensive field-work projects as application takes on a role larger than a formal knowledge base in training programs. Additionally, student of applied linguistics will inevitably need current and deep understanding of developments in linguistics and, in all likelihood, of at least one related field. Finally, applied linguistics students will need to have a command of at least two natural languages, in addition to their first language. These latter requirement, however, are not new; they are characteristic of contemporary training in the field.

That, it seems to me, responds to the question "Where to from here?" I believe this view is substantiated by the various contributions to this volume. However, as noted in the Preface, the answer to the question ultimately must rest in the hands of those who are now working at the cutting edges of the field, as well as those who are just entering the field and who will work actively to define it through their research and teaching, rather than to those at or near the end of their active careers. No handbook like this has appeared before. Encyclopedias (or encyclopedic dictionaries) tend to appear at roughly decade-long intervals. Because applied linguistics is developing at such a rapid rate, it would probably be useful to revise and extend this handbook, not ten years from now but much sooner. Those who would wish to contribute to such an enterprise should make known their desires and thus should capture the definition of the field.

REFERENCES

Abbs, B., and I. Freebairn (1977) *Starting strategies.* London: Longman.

Abbs, B., and I. Freebairn (1975) *Strategies.* Harlow, Essex: Longman

Abbs, B., and M. Sexton (1978) *Challenges.* London: Longman.

Abney, S. (1996) Part-of-speech tagging and partial parsing. In S. Young and G. Blooth-ooft (eds.) *Corpus-based methods in language and speech.* Dordrecht, Netherlands: Kluwer Academic. 118–136.

Abraham, R., and H.-C. Liou (1991) Interaction generated by three computer programs: Analysis of functions of spoken language. In P. Dunkel (ed.) *Computer-assisted language learning and testing: Research issues and practice.* New York: Newbury House. 85–109.

ACT COMPASS Planform. [Online.] Available: ⟨http://www.act. org/compass⟩.

Adams, M. (1990) *Beginning to read: Thinking and learning about print.* Cambridge, MA: MIT Press.

Adamson, H. D. (1988) *Variation theory and second language acquisition.* Washington, D.C.: Georgetown University Press.

Aikhenvald, A. Y. (1999) Areal diffusion and language contact in the Içana-Vaupés basin, North West Amazonia. In R. M. W. Dixon and A. Y. Aikhenvald (eds.) *The Amazonian languages.* Cambridge: Cambridge University Press. 385–415.

Alderson, J. C. (2000) *Assessing reading.* Cambridge: Cambridge University Press.

Alderson, J. C. (1999) Reading constructs and reading assessment. In M. Chalhoub-Deville (ed.) *Issues in computer-adaptive testing of reading proficiency.* Cambridge: Cambridge University Press. 49–78.

Alderson, J. C., and L. Hamp-Lyons (1996) TOEFL preparation courses: A study of washback. *Language Testing* 13: 280–297.

Alderson, J. C., and D. Wall (1993) Does washback exist? *Applied Linguistics* 14: 115–129.

Alexander, L. G. (1967) *New concept English: First things first.* London: Longman.

Alexieva, B. (1997) A typology of interpreter-mediated events. *The Translator* 3: 153–174.

Alisjahbana, S. T. (1971) Language policy, language engineering, and literacy in Indonesia and Malaysia. In A. Sebeok (ed.) *Current trends in linguistics.* The Hague: Mouton. Vol. 8: 1087–1109.

Aljaafreh, A., and J. P. Lantolf (1994) Negative feedback as regulation and second language learning in the zone of proximal development. *The Modern Language Journal* 78: 465–483.

Allen, J. P. B., and S. P. Corder (1973/1974/1975) *Papers in applied linguistics: The Edinburgh course in applied linguistics.* 3 Vols. Oxford: Oxford University Press. [A 4th volume, Allen and Davies, appeared in 1977.]

Allen, P. (1989) *COLT observation scheme: Definition categories.* Toronto, Ontario.

Allen, P. (1983) A three-level curriculum model for second language education. *The Canadian Modern Language Review* 40: 23–43.

Allen, P., J. Howard, and R. Ullman (1984) Module making research. In P. Allen, and M. Swain (eds.) *Language issues and educational policies.* [ELT Documents 119.] Oxford: Pergamon. 83–98.

Allen, P., M. Swain, B. Harley, and J. Cummins (1990) Aspects of classroom treatment: Toward a more comprehensive view of second language education. In B. Harley, P. Allen, J. Cummins, and M. Swain (eds.) *The development of bilingual proficiency.* Cambridge: Cambridge University Press. 57–81.

Alleyne, M. (1994) Problems of standardization of creole languages. In M. Morgan (ed.) *The Social construction of identity in creole situations.* Los Angeles: Center for Afro-American Studies, UCLA. 7–18.

Alleyne, M. (1980) *Comparative Afro-American: An historical-comparative study of English-based Afro-American dialects of the New World.* Ann Arbor: Karoma.

Allwright, R. (1984) The importance of interaction in classroom language learning. *Applied Linguistics* 5: 156–171.

Altabev, R. (1998) The effect of dominant discourses on the vitality of Judeo-Spanish in the Turkish social context. *Journal of Multilingual and Multicultural Development* 19: 263–281.

Altarriba, J., and M. K. Mathis (1997) Conceptual and lexical development in second language acquisition. *Journal of Memory and Language* 36: 550–568.

Altmann, G. T. M., and M. Steedman (1988) Interaction with context during human sentence processing. *Cognition* 30: 191–238.

Alvarez-Torres, M., and S. Gass (forthcoming.) From input and interaction to learning.

Ammon, U. (1998) *Ist Deutsch noch internationale Wissenschaftssprache? Englishe auch für die Lehre an den deutschsprachigen Hochschulen* [*Is German still an international language of science? English teaching at German-language colleges.*] Berlin: Walter de Gruyter.

Ammon, U. (1997) Language spread policy. *Language Problems and Language Planning* 21: 51–57.

Ammon, U. (1994) *Language spread policy.* Vol. 2: *Languages of the former colonial powers and former colonies.* Special issue of the *International Journal of the Sociology of Language* 107.

Ammon, U. (1992) The Federal Republic of Germany's policy of spreading German. *International Journal of the Sociology of Language* 95: 33–50.

Ammon, U., and H. Kleinedam (eds.) (1992) *Language spread policy.* Vol. 1: *Languages of former colonial powers.* Special issue of the *International Journal of the Sociology of Language* 95.

Anderson, A., and T. Lynch (1988) *Listening.* Oxford: Oxford University Press.

Anderson, B. R. (1990) Language, fantasy, revolution in Java: 1900–1945. *Prisma* 50: 25–39.

Anderson, B. R. (1983) *Imagined communities: Reflections on the origins and spread of nationalism.* London: Verso.

Anderson, F. (1995) Classroom discourse and language socialization in a Japanese elementary-school setting: An ethnographic-linguistic study. Ph.D. diss., University of Hawai'i, Honolulu.

Anderson, J. R. (1985/1983) *Cognitive psychology and its implications.* New York: Freeman.

Anderson, J. R. (1982) Acquisition of cognitive skill. *Psychological Review* 89. 4: 369–406.

Anderson, K. O., W. Allen, and L. Narvaéz (1993) The applied foreign language component in the humanities and the sciences. In M. Krueger and F. Ryan (eds.) *Language and content: Discipline- and content-based approaches to language study.* Lexington, MA: D.C. Heath. 103–113.

Anderson, S., and E. Keenan (1985) Deixis. *Language typology and syntactic description, Vol. 3.* Cambridge: Cambridge University Press. 3–56.

Angelil-Carter, S. (1997) Second language acquisition of spoken and written English: Acquiring the skeptron. *TESOL Quarterly* 31: 263–287.

Angelis, P. (1987) Applied linguistics: Realities and projections. Paper presented at the 1987 Annual Conference of the American Association for Applied Linguistics, San Francisco, December.

Antón, M. (1999) A learner-centered classroom: Sociocultural perspectives on teacher-learner interaction in the second language classroom. *The Modern Language Journal* 83: 303–318.

Antón, M., and F. J. DiCamilla (1998) Socio-cognitive functions of L1 collaborative interaction in the L2 classroom. *Canadian Modern Language Review* 54: 314–342.

Appel, G., and J. P. Lantolf (1994) Speaking as mediation: A study of L1 and L2 text recall tasks. *The Modern Language Journal* 78: 437–452.

Appel, R., and L. Verhoeven (1994) Decolonization, language planning and education. In J. Arends, P. Muysken, and N. Smith (eds.) *Pidgins and creoles: An introduction.* Amsterdam: John Benjamins. 65–74.

Apronti, E. O. (1974) Sociolinguistics and the question of a national language: The case of Ghana. *Studies in African Linguistics* 5: 1–20. [Supplement.]

Aranguren, M. L., and S. Moore (1999) Reply to Choate. *Proteus* 8: 21.

Archibald, J. (1998) *Second language phonology.* Philadelphia: John Benjamins.

Archibald, J. (1993) *Language learnability and L2 phonology: The acquisition of metrical parameters.* Dordrecht, Netherlands: Kluwer Academic.

Archibald, J. (ed.) (2000) *Second language acquisition and linguistic theory.* Oxford: Basil Blackwell.

Arends, J., P. Muysken, and N. E. Smith (eds.) (1994) *Pidgins and creoles: An introduction.* Amsterdam: John Benjamins.

Armstrong, S. (1997) Corpus-based methods for NLP and translation studies. *Interpreting* 2: 141–162.

Arndt, V. (1987) Six writers in search of texts: A protocol based study of L1 and L2 writing. *ELT Journal* 41: 257–267.

Arsenian, S. (1945) Bilingualism in the post-war world. *Psychological Bulletin* 42: 65–86.

Artigal, J. (1997) The Catalan immersion program. In R. K. Johnson and M. Swain (eds.) *Immersion education: International perspectives.* Cambridge: Cambridge University Press. 133–150.

Asher, J. (1977) *Learning another language through actions: The complete teachers' guidebook.* Los Gatos, CA: Sky Oaks Publications.

Atkinson, D. (1999a) Language and science. In W. Grabe et al. (eds.) *Annual Review of Applied Linguistics 19: Survey of applied linguistics.* New York: Cambridge University Press. 193–214.

Atkinson, D. (1999b) Toward a sociocognitive approach to second language acquisition. Unpublished manuscript. [Contact author at Dwightatki@aol.com.]

Auer, P. (1992) Introduction: John Gumperz' approach to contextualization. In P. Auer and A. di Luzio (eds.) *The contextualization of language.* Amsterdam: John Benjamins. 1–37.

Auerbach, E. R. (1989) Toward a social-contextual approach to family literacy. *Harvard Educational Review* 59: 165–181.

August, D., and K. Hakuta (1997) *Improving schooling for language-minority children.* Washington, DC: National Academy Press.

Austin, J. L. (1962) *How to do things with words.* Oxford: Oxford University Press.

Awoniyi, T. A. (1995) Problems related to curriculum development and teaching mother tongues in Nigeria: A historical survey 1800–1974. *Audio Visual Language Journal* 13(1): 31–41.

Bachman, L. F. (2000) Modern language testing at the turn of the century: Assuring that what we count counts. *Language Testing* 17: 1–42.

Bachman, L. F. (1997) Generalizability theory. In C. Clapham and D. Corson (eds.) *Encyclopedia of language and education.* Vol. 7: *Language testing and assessment.* Dordrecht, Netherlands: Kluwer Academic. 255–262.

Bachman, L. F. (1990) *Fundamental considerations in language testing.* Oxford: Oxford University Press.

Bachman, L. F., and A. D. Cohen (1998) Language testing-SLA interfaces: An update. In L. F. Bachman and A. D. Cohen (eds.) *Interfaces between second language acquisition and language testing research.* Cambridge: Cambridge University Press. 1–31.

Bachman, L. F., F. Davidson, K. Ryan, and I.-C. Choi (1995) *An investigation into the comparability of two tests of English as a foreign language.* Cambridge: Cambridge University Press.

Bachman, L. F., and D. Eignor (1997) Recent advances in quantitative test analysis. In C. Clapham and D. Corson (eds.) *Encyclopedia of language and education.* Vol. 7: *Language testing and assessment.* Dordrecht, Netherlands: Kluwer Academic. 227–242.

Bachman, L., and A. Palmer (1996) *Language testing in practice.* Oxford: Oxford University Press.

Bachman, L., and A. Cohen (eds.) (1998) *Interfaces between second language acquisition and language testing research.* New York: Cambridge University Press.

Backus, A. (1992) *Patterns of language mixing: A study of Turkish-Dutch bilingualism.* Wiesbaden: Harrassowitz.

Bacon, S. M. (1992) The relationship between gender, comprehension, processing strategies, and cognitive and affective response in foreign language listening. *The Modern Language Journal* 76: 160–178.

Baetens-Beardsmore, H. (1993) European school model. In H. Baetens Beardsmore (ed.) *European models of bilingual education.* Clevedon, Avon, UK: Multilingual Matters.

Bailey, G., and M. Dyer (1992) An approach to sampling in dialectology. *American Speech* 67: 3–20.

Bailey, G., and N. Maynor (1998) Decreolization? In P. Trudgill and J. Cheshire (eds.) *The sociolinguistics reader.* London: Arnold. 240–262. Originally published in 1987 in *Language in Society, 16.*

Bailey, K., and D. Nunan (eds.) (1996) *Voices from the language classroom.* New York: Cambridge University Press.

Baker, C. (1997) Survey methods in researching language and education. In N. Hornberger and D. Corson (eds.) *Encyclopedia of Language and Education.* Vol. 8: *Research methods in language and education.* Dordrecht, Netherlands: Kluwer Academic. 35–46.

Baker, C. (1996) *Foundations of bilingual education and bilingualism.* 2nd ed. Clevedon, Avon, UK: Multilingual Matters.

Baker, C., and M. P. Jones (1999) *Continuity in Welsh language education.* Cardiff: Welsh Language Board.

Baker, C., and S. P. Jones (1998) *Encyclopedia of bilingualism and bilingual education.* Clevedon, Avon, UK: Multilingual Matters.

Baker, K. A., and A. A. de Kanter (1983) *Bilingual education.* Lexington, MA: Lexington Books.

Baker, M. (1998) Réexplorer la langue de la traduction: Une approche par corpus. [Reexploring the language of translation: A corpus-based approach.] *Meta* 43. 4: 480–485.

Baker, M. (1995) Corpora in translation studies: An overview and some suggestions for future research. *Target* 7: 223–243.

Baker, M. (1993) Corpus Linguistics and Translation Studies. In M. Baker, G. Francis, and E. Tognini-Bonelli (eds.) *Text and technology. In honour of John Sinclair.* Amsterdam: John Benjamins. 233–250.

Baker, P. (1991). Column: Writing the wronged. *Journal of Pidgin and Creole Languages* 6: 107–122.

Baker, P., and P. Mühlhäusler (1990) From business to pidgin. *Journal of Asian Pacific Communication* 1: 87–115.

Bakhtin, M. (1984) *Problems of Dostoevsky's poetics.* Tr. C. Emerson. Minneapolis: University of Minnesota Press.

Bakhtin, M. (1981) *The dialogic imagination: Four essays by M. M. Bakhtin.* Austin: University of Texas Press.

Baldauf, R. B., Jr. (1994) "Unplanned" language policy and planning. In W. Grabe et al. (eds.) *Annual Review of Applied Linguistics 14: Language policy and planning.* Cambridge: Cambridge University Press. 82–89.

Baldauf, R. B., Jr., and B. H. Jernudd (1983) Language of publications as a variable in scientific communication. *Australian Review of Applied Linguistics* 6(1): 97–108.

Baldauf, R. B., Jr., and R. B. Kaplan (2000) *Language planning in Nepal, Taiwan and Sweden.* Clevedon, Avon, UK: Multilingual Matters.

Bamberg, M. G. W. (ed.) (1998) Oral versions of personal experience: Three decades of narrative analysis. *Journal of Narrative and Life History* 7: 1–4.

Bandura, A. (1982) Self-efficacy mechanism in human agency. *American Psychologist* 37: 122–147.

Banerjee, J., and S. Luoma (1997) Qualitative approaches to test validation. In C. Clapham and D. Corson (eds.) *Encyclopedia of language and education.* Vol. 7: *Language testing and assessment.* Dordrecht, Netherlands: Kluwer Academic. 275–287.

Banks, J. A. (1991) Ethnicity, class, cognitive styles and motivational styles: Research and teaching implications. *Journal of Negro Education* 57: 452–466.

Bankston, C. L., and J. M. Henry (1998) The silence of the gators: Cajun ethnicity and intergenerational transmission of Louisiana French. *Journal of Multilingual and Multicultural Development* 19: 1–22.

Banton, M. (1998) Research note: Judicial training in ethnic minority issues in England and Wales. *Journal of Ethnic and Migration Studies* 24: 561–573.

Bar-Acher, M., and F. Kaufmann (1998) The functions and activities of the Academy of the Hebrew Language in the orientation and development of Hebrew. *Meta* 43: 10–18.

Barcelos, A. (2000) Relationships between Brazilian students' beliefs and their teachers' beliefs in an intensive ESL institute. Ph.D. diss. University of Alabama, Tuscaloosa.

Bardovi-Harlig, K. (1999a) The interlanguage of interlanguage pragmatics: A research agenda for acquisitional pragmatics. *Language Learning* 49: 677–713.

Bardovi-Harlig, K. (1999b) Researching method. In L. F. Bouton (ed.) *Pragmatics and Language Learning*. Urbana-Champaign: University of Illinois, Division of English as an International Language [DEIL]. 9: 237–264.

Bardovi-Harlig, K. (1996) Pragmatics and language teaching: Bringing pragmatics and pedagogy together. In L. F. Boulton (ed.) *Pragmatics and language learning*. Urbana-Champaign: University of Illinois, Division of English as an International Language [DIEL] 7: 21–39.

Bardovi-Harlig, K., and Z. Dörnyei (1998) Do language learners recognize pragmatic violations? Pragmatic vs. grammatical awareness in instructed L2 learning. *TESOL Quarterly* 32: 233–259.

Bardovi-Harlig, K., and B. S. Hartford (1993) Learning the rules of academic talk: A longitudinal study of pragmatic development. *Studies in Second Language Acquisition* 15: 279–304.

Bardovi-Harlig, K., and B. S. Hartford (1990) Congruence in native and nonnative conversations: Status balance in the academic advising session. *Language Learning* 40: 467–501.

Bargiela-Chiappini, F., and S. Harris (eds.) (1997) *The languages of business: An international perspective*. Edinburgh: Edinburgh University Press.

Barik, H. (1994) A description of various types of omissions, additions and error translation encountered in simultaneous interpretation. In S. Lambert and B. Moser-Mercer (eds.) *Bridging the gap: Empirical research in simultaneous interpretation*. Amsterdam: John Benjamins. 121–137.

Barik, H. (1969) A study of simultaneous interpretation. Ph.D. diss., University of North Carolina, Chapel Hill.

Barsalou, L. (1999) Language comprehension: Archival memory or preparation for situated action? *Discourse Processes* 28(1): 61–80.

Battenburg, J. (1999) The gradual death of the Berber language in Tunisia. *International Journal of the Sociology of Language* 137: 147–161.

Bayley, R. (1991) Variation theory and second language learning: Linguistic and social constraints on interlanguage tense marking. Ph.D. diss., Stanford University, Stanford, CA.

Bayley, R., and D. R. Preston (1996) *Second language acquisition and linguistic variation*. Amsterdam: John Benjamins.

Beattie, G. W. (1980) The role of language production processes in the organisation of behaviour in face-to-face interaction. In B. Butterworth (ed.) *Language production*. Vol. 1. London: Academic Press. 69–107.

Beaugrande, R. de (1997) Theory and practice in applied linguistics: Disconnection, conflict, or dialectic? *Applied Linguistics* 18: 279–313.

Bebel-Gisler, D. (1981) *La langue créole force jugulée*. [*Creole language: A suppressed force.*] Paris and Montréal: L'Harmattan and Nouvelle-Optique.

Beck, M.-L. (1998a) L2 acquisition and obligatory head-movement: English-speaking learners of German and the local impairment hypothesis. *Studies in Second Language Acquisition* 20: 311–348.

Beck, M.-L. (ed.) (1998b) *Morphology and its interfaces in second language acquisition.* Philadelphia: John Benjamins.

Beck, M.-L. (1997) Regular verbs, past tense and frequency: Tracking down a potential source of NS/NSS competence differences. *Second Language Research* 13: 93–115.

Becker, H., B. Geer, E. Hughes, and A. Strauss (1961) *Boys in white: Student culture in medical school.* Chicago: University of Chicago Press.

Beebe, L. (1985) Input: Choosing the right stuff. In S. Gass and C. Madden (eds.), *Input in second language acquisition.* Rowley, MA: Newbury House. 404–414.

Beebe, L., T. Takahashi, and R. Uliss-Weltz (1990) Pragmatic transfer in ESL refusals. In R. Scarcella, E. Andersen, and S. Krashen (eds.) *Developing communicative competence in a second language.* New York: Newbury House. 55–73.

Bejar, I. I. (1993) A generative approach to psychological and educational measurement. In N. Frederiksen, R. J. Mislevy, and I. I. Bejar (eds.) *Test theory for a new generation of tests.* Hillsdale, NJ: Lawrence Erlbaum. 323–357.

Belcher, D. (1997) An argument for nonadversarial argumentation: On the relevance of the feminist critique of academic discourse to L2 writing pedagogy. *Journal of Second Language Writing* 6: 1–21.

Bell, A. (1991) *The language of news media.* Oxford: Blackwell.

Bell, A. (1984) Language style as audience design. *Language in Society* 13: 145–204.

Bell, R. T. (1998) Psycholinguistic/cognitive approaches. In M. Baker (ed.) *Routledge encyclopedia of translation studies.* London: Routledge. 185–190.

Bell, R. T. (1991) *Translation and translating: Theory and practice.* London: Longman.

Bender, B. W. (1982) Proto-Micronesian wordlist. Ms. Honolulu: University of Hawai'i.

Bender, B. W. (1971) Micronesian Languages. In T. A. Sebeok (ed.) *Current Trends in Linguistics.* The Hague: Mouton. 8: 426–65.

Benesch, S. (1998) Anorexia: A feminist EAP curriculum. In T. Smoke (ed.) *Adult ESL: Politics, pedagogy, and participation in classroom and community programs.* Mahwah, NJ: Lawrence Erlbaum. 101–114.

Benesch, S. (1993) ESL, ideology, and the politics of pragmatism. *TESOL Quarterly* 27: 705–717.

Benhabib, S. (1999) Citizens, residents, and aliens in a changing world: Political membership in the global era. *Social Research* 66: 709–744.

Benhabib, S. (1997) Strange multiplicities: The politics of identity and difference in a global context. In A. Samatar (ed.) *The divided self: Identity and globalization.* St. Paul, MN: Macalester College International Studies and Programming. 27–56.

Benmaman, V. (1997) Legal interpreting by any other name is still legal interpreting. In S. E. Carr, R. Roberts, A. Dufour, and D. Steyn (eds.) *The critical link: Interpreters in the community.* Amsterdam: John Benjamins. 179–190.

Bennett, R. E. (1999) Using new technology to improve assessment. *Educational Measurement: Issues and Practice* 18: 5–12.

Benson, P., and P. Voller (eds.) (1997) *Autonomy and independence in language learning.* New York: Longman.

Bentahila, A. (1987) Haitian Creole: a challenge for education. *Diogenes* 137: 73–87.

Beretta, A. (ed.) (1993) *Theory construction in SLA*. [Special issue of *Applied Linguistics* 14(3).]

Beretta, A., G. Crookes, K. Gregg, and M. H. Long (1994) Comment on van Lier (1994). *Applied Linguistics* 15: 347.

Bernhardt, E. (1999) If reading is reader-based, can there be a computer-adaptive test of reading? In M. Chalhoub-Deville (ed.) *Issues in computer-adaptive testing of reading proficiency*. Cambridge: Cambridge University Press. 1–10.

Bernhardt, E. (1991) A psycholinguistic perspective on second language literacy. *AILA Review* 8: 45–60.

Bernsten, J. (1998) Runyakitara: Uganda's 'new' language. *Journal of Multilingual and Multicultural Development* 19: 93–107.

Berry, R., and J. Hudson (1997) *Making the jump: A resource book for teachers of aboriginal students*. Broome: Catholic Education Office, Kimberley Region.

Berry, V. (1997) Ethical considerations when assessing oral proficiency in pairs. In A. Huhta, V. Kohonen, L. Kurki-Suonio, and S. Luoma (eds.) *Current developments and alternatives in language assessment*. Jyväskylä: University of Jyväskylä. 107–123.

Besnier, N. (1988) The linguistic relationships of spoken and written Nukulaelae registers. *Language* 64: 707–736.

Bhabha, H. (1994) *The location of culture*. New York: Routledge.

Bialystok, E. (1994) Analysis and control in the development of second language proficiency. *Studies in Second Language Acquisition* 16: 157–168.

Bialystok, E. (1993) Symbolic representation and attentional control in pragmatic competence. In G. Kasper and S. Blum-Kulka (eds.) *Interlanguage pragmatics*. New York: Oxford University Press. 43–59.

Bialystok, E. (1990) *Communication strategies*. Oxford: Blackwell.

Biber, D. (1988) *Variation across speech and writing*. Cambridge: Cambridge University Press.

Biber, D. (1986) Spoken and written textual dimensions in English: Resolving the contradictory findings. *Language* 62: 384–414.

Biber, D., S. Conrad, and R. Reppen (1998) Corpus-based approaches in applied linguistics. *Applied Linguistics* 15: 169–189.

Biber, D., S. Johansson, G. Leech, S. Conrad, and E. Finegan (1999) *Longman grammar of spoken and written English*. London: Longman.

Bickerton, D. (1990) *Language and species*. Chicago: University of Chicago Press.

Bickerton, D. (1984) The Language Bioprogram Hypothesis. *Behavioral and Brain Sciences* 7: 173–221.

Bickerton, D. (1981) *Roots of language*. Ann Arbor: Karoma.

Bickerton, D. (1975) *Dynamics of a creole system*. Cambridge: Cambridge University Press.

Bickerton, D. (1971) Inherent variability and variable rules. *Foundations of Language* 7: 457–92.

Bickerton, D., and C. Odo (1976) *Change and variation in Hawaiian English*. Vol. 1: *General phonology and Pidgin syntax*. Honolulu: Social Sciences and Linguistics Institute, University of Hawai'i.

Billmyer, K. (1990) "I really like your lifestyle": ESL learners learning how to compliment. *Pennsylvania working papers in educational linguistics* 62: 31–48.

Birdsong, D. (1989) *Metalinguistic performance and interlinguistic competence.* New York: Spinger Verlag.

Blackledge, A. (2000) *Literacy, power and social justice.* Stoke-on-Trent: Trentham Books.

Bland, S. K., J. S. Noblitt, S. Armington, and G. Gay (1990) The naive lexical hypothesis: Evidence from computer-assisted language learning. *The Modern Language Journal* 74: 440–450.

Blau, E. K., and E. Dayton (1992) Puerto Rico as an English-using society: Implications for teaching. Paper presented at the Conference on World Englishes Today, University of Illinois, Champaign-Urbana.

Bley-Vroman, R. (1989) What is the logical problem of foreign language learning? In S. M. Gass and J. Schachter (eds.) *Linguistic perspectives on second language acquisition.* Cambridge: Cambridge University Press. 41–68.

Bley-Vroman, R., and L. Loschky (1993) Grammar and task-based methodology. In S. M. Gass and G. Crookes (eds.) *Tasks and language learning: Integrating theory and practice.* Clevedon, Avon, UK: Multilingual Matters. 123–167.

Bliss, P. A. (1993) Emphasis on English. *San Juan Star,* March 9, pp. F8–F9.

Block, D. (1996) Not so fast: Some thoughts on theory culling, relativism, accepted findings, and the heart and soul of SLA. *Applied Linguistics* 17: 63–83.

Blommaert, J. (1996) Language planning as a discourse on language and society: The linguistic ideology of a scholarly tradition. *Language Problems & Language Planning* 20: 199–222.

Bloom, A. (1981) *The linguistic shaping of thought.* Hillsdale, NJ: Lawrence Erlbaum.

Blum-Kulka, S. (1982) Learning to say what you mean in a second language: A study of speech act performance of learners of Hebrew as a second language. *Applied Linguistics* 3: 29–59.

Blum-Kulka, S., J. House, and G. Kasper (eds.) (1989) *Cross-cultural pragmatics.* Norwood, NJ: Ablex.

Blum-Kulka, S., and E. Olshtain (1986) Too many words: Length of utterance and pragmatic failure. *Studies in Second Language Acquisition* 8: 165–180.

Blum-Kulka, S., and E. Olhstain (1984) Requests and apologies: A cross-cultural study of speech act realization patterns [CCSARP]. *Applied Linguistics* 5: 196–213.

Blundell, L. (1983) *Task listening.* London: Longman.

Bock, K., and W. J. M. Levelt (1994) Language production: Grammatical encoding. In M. Gernsbacher (ed.) *Handbook of psycholinguistics.* San Diego: Academic Press. 945–984.

Boekaerts, M. (1986) The measurement of state and trait motivational orientation: Refining our measures. In J. H. L. van denBercken, E. E. J. De Bruyn and Th. C. M. Bergen (eds.) *Achievement and task motivation.* Lisse: Swets and Zeitlinger. 229–245.

Bogdan, R. C., and S. K. Biklen (1992) *Qualitative research for education.* 2nd ed. Boston: Allyn and Bacon.

Boggs, S. T. (1985) *Speaking, relating, and learning: A study of Hawaiian children at home and at school.* Norwood, NJ: Ablex.

Boland, J. E. (1997) The relationship between syntactic and semantic processes in sentence comprehension. *Language and Cognitive Processes* 12(4): 423–484.

Bolinger, D. (1975) Meaning and memory. *Forum Linguisticum* 1: 2–14.

Bollée, A. (1993) Language policy in the Seychelles and its consequences. *International Journal of the Sociology of Language* 102: 85–99.

Bongaerts, T., E. Kellerman, and A. Bentlage (1987) Perspective and proficiency in L2 referential communication. *Studies in Second Language Acquisition* 9: 171–200.

Boodoo, G., and J. Burstein (submitted.) Automated scoring for advanced placement essay responses for U.S. History and English Literature. New York: College Entrance Examination Board.

Boodoo, G., and J. Burstein (in press.) Evaluation of e-rater scoring performance for GREAE essay responses. [GRE 97-14.] Princeton, NJ: Educational Testing Service.

Bordo, S. (1990) Feminism, post-modernism and gender skepticism. In L. Nicholson (ed.) *Feminism/postmodernism.* New York: Routledge.

Borrás I., and R. C. Lafayette (1994) Effects of multimedia courseware subtitling on the speaking performance of college students of French. *The Modern Language Journal* 78: 61–75.

Borsley, R. (1998) *Syntactic theory.* Oxford: Arnold.

Bourdieu, P. (1984) *Distinction: A social critique of the judgement of taste.* Tr. R. Nice. London: Routledge and Kegan Paul.

Bourdieu, P. (1977) The economics of linguistic exchanges. *Social Science Information* 16: 645–668.

Bourdieu, P., and J. Passeron (1977) *Reproduction in education, society, and culture.* Beverly Hills, CA: Sage Publications.

Bourhis, R. Y. (1997) Language policies and language attitudes: Le Monde de la Francophone. [. . . The world of the Francophone.] In N. Coupland and A. Jaworski (eds.) *Sociolinguistics: A reader.* New York: St. Martin's Press. 306–322.

Bouton, L. F. (1994) Can NNS skill in interpreting implicatures in American English be improved through explicit instruction? In L. F. Bouton and Y. Kachru (eds.) *Pragmatics and language learning.* Urbana-Champaign: University of Illinois, Division of English as an International Language [DEIL]. 5: 88–109.

Brandt, E. A., and V. Ayoungman (1989) Language renewal and language maintenance: A practical guide. *Canadian Journal of Native Education* 16: 42–77.

Braun, S., and A. Clarici (1997) Inaccuracy for numerals in simultaneous interpretation: Eurolinguistic and neuropsychological perspectives. *The Interpreters' Newsletter* 7: 85–102.

Breen, M. P. (1987) Learner contributions to task design. In C. Candlin and D. F. Murphy (eds.) *Language learning tasks.* Englewood Cliffs, NJ: Prentice-Hall. 23–46.

Breen, M. P., C. Barratt-Pugh, B. Derewianka, H. House, C. Hudson, T. Lumley, and M. Rohl (1997) *Profiling ESL children.* Vol. 1: *Key issues and findings.* Canberra: Department of Employment, Education, Training and Youth Affairs.

Breen, M. P., and C. N. Candlin (1980) The essentials of a communicative curriculum in language teaching. *Applied Linguistics* 1: 89–112.

Breinberg, P. (1986) Language attitudes: The case of Caribbean language. In D. Sutcliffe and A. Wong (eds.) *The language of Black experience.* Oxford: Blackwell. 136–142

Breland, H., M. Bonner, and M. Kubota (1995) *Factors in performance on brief, impromptu essay examinations.* College Board Report No. 95-4. New York: College Entrance Examination Board.

Bremer, K., C. Roberts, M. Vasseur, M. Simonot, and P. Broeder (1996) *Achieving understanding: Discourse in international encounters.* London: Longman.

Brenzinger, M. (1997) Language contact and language displacement. In F. Coulmas (ed.) *Handbook of sociolinguistics.* Oxford: Blackwell. 273–284.

Bresnan, J. (2000) *Lexical-functional grammar.* Oxford: Blackwell.

Brewer, R. (1988) *The science of ecology.* Philadelphia: Saunders College Publications.

Brill, E. (1995) *Unsupervised learning of disambiguation rules for part of speech tagging: Proceedings of the third Association for Computational Linguistics workshop on very large corpora.* Cambridge, MA: Association for Computational Linguistics. 1–13.

Brindley, G. (2001) Assessment. In R. Carter and D. Nunan (eds.) *The Cambridge TESOL guide.* Cambridge: Cambridge University Press. 137–143.

Brindley, G. (2000) Task difficulty and task generalisability in competency-based writing assessment. In G. Brindley (ed.) *Issues in immigrant English language assessment.* Sydney: National Centre for English Language Teaching and Research, Macquarie University.45–80.

Brindley, G. (1998a) Assessing listening abilities. In W. Grabe et al. (eds.) *Annual Review of Applied Linguistics 18: Foundations of second language teaching.* New York: Cambridge University Press. 171–191.

Brindley. G. (1998b) Outcomes-based assessment and reporting in language programs: A review of the issues. *Language Testing* 15: 45–85.

Brindley, G. (1997) Assessment and the language teacher: Trends and transitions. *Language Teacher* 21: 37, 39.

Brindley, G. (1991) Defining language ability: The criteria for criteria. In S. Anivan (ed.) *Current developments in language testing.* Singapore: Regional Language Centre. 139–164.

Brindley. G. (1989) *Assessing achievement in the learner-centred curriculum.* Sydney: National Centre for English Language Teaching and Research, Macquarie University.

Brinton, D., and P. Master (eds.) (1997) *New ways in content based instruction.* Alexandria. VA: Teachers of English to Speakers of Other Languages.

Brinton, D., M. Snow, and M. Wesche (1989) *Content-based second language teaching.* Rowley, MA: Newbury House.

Broeder, P., and K. Plunkett (1994) Connectionism and second language acquisition. In N. Ellis (ed.) *Implicit and explicit learning of languages.* San Diego, CA: Academic Press. 421–454.

Broner, M., and E. Tarone (2000) Language play in immersion classroom discourse: Some suggestions for language teaching. *Australian Review of Applied Linguistics* 16: 121–133.

Brooks, F. B., and R. Donato (1994) Vygotskyan approaches to understanding foreign language learner discourse during communicative tasks. *Hispania* 77: 262–274.

Brooks, F. B., R. Donato, and J. V. McGlone (1997) When are they going to say 'it' right? Understanding learner talk during pair-work activity. *Foreign Language Annals* 30: 523–541.

Broselow, E., and H.-B. Park (1995) Morae conservation in second language prosody. In J. Archibald (ed.) *Phonological acquisition and phonological theory.* Hillsdale, NJ: Lawrence Erlbaum. 151–68.

Brosnahan, L. F. (1963) Some historical cases of language imposition. In J. Spencer (ed.) *Language in Africa.* Cambridge: Cambridge University Press. 7–24.

Broughton, G. (1968–70). *Success with English.* 3 Vols. Harmondsworth: Penguin.

Brown, A. (1995) The effect of rater variables in the development of an occupation-specific language performance test. *Language Testing* 12: 1–15.

Brown, C. (2000) The interrelation between speech perception and phonological acquisition. In J. Archibald (ed.) *Second language acquisition and linguistic theory*. Oxford: Blackwell. 4–63.

Brown, C. (1998) The role of the L1 grammar in the acquisition of L2 segmental structure. *Second Language Research* 14: 136–193.

Brown, G. (1995) *Speakers, listeners and communication*. Cambridge: Cambridge University Press.

Brown, G. (1986) Investigating listening comprehension in context. *Applied Linguistics* 7: 284–302.

Brown, G. (1977) *Listening to spoken English*. Harlow, Essex: Longman.

Brown, G., and G. Yule (1983a) *Discourse analysis*. Cambridge: Cambridge University Press.

Brown, G., and G. Yule (1983b) *Teaching the spoken language*. Cambridge: Cambridge University Press.

Brown, J. D. (1992) Statistics as a foreign language. Part 2: More things to consider in reading statistical language studies. *TESOL Quarterly* 26: 629–664.

Brown, J. D. (1991) Statistics as a foreign language. Part 1: What to look for in reading statistical language studies. *TESOL Quarterly* 25: 569–586.

Brown, J. D. (1988) *Understanding research in second language learning*. Cambridge: Cambridge University Press.

Brown, J. D., and T. Hudson (1998) The alternatives in language assessment. *TESOL Quarterly* 32: 653–675.

Brown, P., and S. Levinson (1988) *Politeness: Some universals of language usage*. Cambridge: Cambridge University Press.

Brumfit, C. J. (1997) Theoretical practice: Applied linguistics as pure and practical science. *AILA Review*. 12: 18–30.

Brumfit, C. J. (1984) *Communicative methodology in language teaching*. Cambridge: Cambridge University Press.

Brumfit, C. J., and K. Johnson (eds.) (1979) *The communicative approach to language teaching*. Oxford: Oxford University Press.

Brysbaert, M. (1998) Word recognition in bilinguals: Evidence against the existence of two separate lexicons. *Psychologica Belgica* 38: 163–175.

Buck, G. (1994) The appropriacy of psychometric measurement models for testing second language listening comprehension. *Language Testing* 11: 145–170.

Buck, G. (1990) Testing second language comprehension. Ph.D. diss., University of Lancaster, U.K.

Buck, G., and K. Tatsuoka (1998) Application of the rule-space procedure to language testing: Examining attributes of a free-response listening test. *Language Testing* 15: 119–157.

Buck, G., K. Tatsuoka, and I. Kostin (1997) The subskills of reading: Rule-space analysis of a multiple-choice test of second language reading comprehension. *Language Learning* 47: 423–466.

Bunderson, C. V., D. K. Inouye, and J. B. Olson (1989) The four generations of computerized educational measurement. In R. L. Linn (ed.) *Educational measurement*. Washington, DC: American Council on Education. 367–407.

Burger, S., M. Wesche, and M. Migneron (1997) Late, late immersion, or discipline-based second language teaching at the University of Ottawa. In R. K. Johnson and

M. Swain (eds.) *Immersion education: International perspectives.* Cambridge: Cambridge University Press. 65–84.

Burningham, L. (1998) Factors influencing language policy and planning in a Utah school district. MA thesis, Brigham Young University, Provo, UT.

Burstein, B., L. Bank, and L. E. Jarvik (1980) Sex differences in cognitive functioning: Evidence, determinants, implications. *Human Development* 23:289–313.

Burstein, J., and M. Chodorow (1999) Automated essay scoring for nonnative English speakers. In *Proceedings of a workshop on computer-mediated language assessment and evaluation of natural language processing.* Joint Symposium of the Association of Computational Linguistics and the International Association of Language Learning Technologies. College Park, MD: Association of Computational Linguistics and the International Association of Language Learning Technologies. 68–75.

Burstein, J., K. Kukich, S. Wolff, C. Lu, and M. Chodorow (1998a) Enriching automated scoring using discourse marking. In *Proceedings of the workshop on discourse relations and discourse marking*: Annual meeting of the Association of Computational Linguistics. Montreal. 15–21.

Burstein, J., K. Kukich, S. Wolff, C. Lu, M. Chodorow, L. Braden-Harder, and M. Dee Harris (1998b) Automated scoring using a hybrid feature identification technique. In *Proceedings of the annual meeting of the Association of Computational Linguistics.* Montreal. 206–210.

Burstein, J., and D. Marcu (2000a) Benefits of modularity in an automated scoring system. In *Proceedings of the workshop on using toolsets and architectures to build NLP systems, at the 18th international conference on Computational Linguistics,* Luxembourg, August. 49–55.

Burstein, J., and D. Marcu (2000b) Towards using text summarization for essay-feedback. In *Le 7ᵉ Conference Annuella sur le traitment automatique des languages naturelles* [TALN 2000.] [*The 7th annual conference on the automatic treatment of natural languages*]. Lausanne. October. 51–59.

Burstein, J., S. Wolff, H. Breland, and M. Kubota (submitted) *Computational modeling of writing feature scores.* New York: College Entrance Examination Board.

Burtoff, M. (1985) *Haitian Creole literacy evaluation study: Final report.* Washington, DC: Center for Applied Linguistics.

Butler, J. (1990) *Gender trouble: Feminism and the subversion of identity.* New York: Routledge.

Bygate M. (2001) Effects of task repetition on the structure and control of oral language. In M. Bygate, P. Skehan, and M. Swain (eds.) *Researching pedagogic tasks: Second language learning, teaching and testing.* London: Longman. 23–48.

Bygate, M. (1999) Task as context for the framing, reframing and unframing of language. *System* 27: 33–48.

Bygate, M. (1996) Effects of task repetition: Appraising the developing language of learners. In D. Willis and J. Willis (eds.) *Challenge and change in language teaching.* London: Heinemann. 136–146.

Calderón, M., and E. Díaz (1993) Retooling teacher preparation programs to embrace Latino realities in schools. In Tomás Rivera Center (ed.) *Reshaping teacher education in the Southwest: A response to the needs of Latino students and teachers.* Los Angeles: Tomás Rivera Center. 51–70.

Call, E. (1985) Auditory short-term memory, listening comprehension and the input hypothesis. *TESOL Quarterly* 19: 765–781.

Calvé, P. (1991) Vingt-cinq ans d'immersion au Canada: 1965–1990 [Twenty-five years of immersion in Canada]. *Études de linguistique appliquée: L'immersion au Canada [Studies in applied linguistics: Immersion in Canada].* [P. Calvé, Coordinator.] 82: 7–23.

Calvet, L. J. (1997) Cities and languages. *Diagonales* 42: 32–33.

Cameron, D. (1992) *Feminism and linguistic theory.* 2nd ed. New York: St. Martin's Press.

Cameron, D., E. Frazer, P. Harvey, M. B. H. Rampton, and K. Richardson (eds.) (1992) *Researching language: Issues of power and method.* London: Routledge.

Cameron, L., J. Moon, and M. Bygate (1996) Language development of bilingual pupils in the mainstream. *Language and Education* 10: 221–236.

Canagarajah, A. S. (1997) Safe houses in the contact zone: Coping strategies of African-American students in the academy. *College Composition and Communication* 48: 173–196.

Canagarajah, A. S. (1993a) Comment on Ann Raimes's "Out of the Woods: Emerging traditions in The teaching of writing": Up the garden path: Second language writing approaches, local knowledge, and pluralism. *TESOL Quarterly* 27: 301–306.

Canagarajah, A. S. (1993b) Critical ethnography of a Sri Lankan classroom: Ambiguities in student opposition to reproduction through ESOL. *TESOL Quarterly* 27: 601–626.

Canale, M., and M. Swain (1980) Theoretical bases of communicative approaches to second language teaching and testing. *Applied Linguistics* 1: 1–17.

Candlin, C. N. (1987) Towards task-based language learning. In C. Candlin and D. Murphy (eds.) *Language learning tasks.* Englewood Cliffs, NJ: Prentice Hall. 5–22

Cantoni, G. (ed.) (1996) *Stabilizing indigenous languages.* Flagstaff: Center for Excellence in Education, Northern Arizona University.

CAPE website. Brigham Young University Humanities Research Center. [Online.] Available: ⟨http://creativeworks.byu.edu/hrc⟩.

CARLA website. University of Minnesota Computer Adaptive Tests. [Online.] Available: ⟨http://carla.ucad.umn.edu/CAT.html⟩.

Carlet, L. (1998) G.V. Chernov's psycholinguistic model in simultaneous interpretation: An experimental contribution. *The Interpreters' Newsletter* 8: 75–92.

Carpenter, P. A., A. Miyake, and M. A. Just (1995) Language comprehension: Sentence and discourse processing. *Annual Review of Psychology* 46: 91–120.

Carpenter, P. A., A. Miyake, and M. A. Just (1994) Working memory constraints in comprehension: Evidence from individual differences, aphasia, and aging. In M. A. Gernsbacher (ed.) *Handbook of psycholinguistics.* San Diego: Academic Press. 1075–1122.

Carr, S. E., R. Roberts, A. Dufour, and D. Steyn (eds.) (1997) *The critical link: Interpreters in the community.* Amsterdam: John Benjamins.

Carroll, B. J. (1980) *Testing communicative performance: An interim study.* Oxford: Pergamon.

Carroll, J. B., and S. M. Sapon (1959) *Modern language aptitude test.* New York: Psychological Corporation.

Carroll, S. E. (1995) The hidden dangers of computer modeling: Remarks on Sokolik and Smith's connectionist learning model of French gender. *Second Language Research* 11: 193–205.

Carter, C., J. Bishop, and S. L. Kravitz (1999) *Keys to success.* 2nd ed. New York: Prentice-Hall.

Carter, R., and M. McCarthy (1997) *Exploring spoken English.* Cambridge: Cambridge University Press

Casanave, C. (1998) Transitions: The balancing act of bilingual academics. *Journal of Second Language Writing* 7: 175–203.

Casse, P. (1981) *Training for the cross-cultural mind: A handbook for cross-cultural trainers and consultants.* Washington, DC: Sietar.

Cassidy, F. G. (1993) Short note: On creole orthography. *Journal of Pidgin and Creole Languages* 8: 135–137.

Cassidy, F. G. (1961) *Jamaica talk: Three hundred years of the English language in Jamaica.* London: Macmillan.

Catholic Education Office, Kimberley Region (1994) *FELIKS: Fostering English language in Kimberley schools.* Broome: Catholic Education Commission of Western Australia.

Cavalli, M. (1997) Social representations and linguistic planning: The case of Val d'Aoste. *Travaux neuchatelois de linguistique.* [Neuchatel Studies in Linguistics.] 27: 83–97.

Cazden, C. (1992) *Language minority education in the United States: Implications of the Ramirez report.* Santa Cruz, CA: National Center for Research on Cultural Diversity and Second Language Learning.

Cazden, C. (1987) *Classroom discourse: The language of teaching and learning.* Portsmouth, NH: Heinemann.

Celce-Murcia, M. (1997) Direct approaches in L2 instruction: A turning point in communicative language teaching? *TESOL Quarterly* 31: 141–152.

Cenoz, J. (1998) Multilingual education in the Basque country. In J. Cenoz and F. Genesee (eds.) *Beyond bilingualism: Multilingualism and multilingual education.* Clevedon, Avon, UK: Multilingual Matters. 175–191.

Cenoz, J., and F. Genesee (eds.) (1998) *Beyond bilingualism: Multilingualism and multilingual education.* Clevedon, Avon, UK: Multilingual Matters.

Chafe, W. L. (1985) Linguistic differences produced by differences between speaking and writing. In D. R. Olson, N. Torrance, and A. Hildyard (eds.) *Literacy, language and learning.* Cambridge: Cambridge University Press. 105–124.

Chalhoub-Deville, M. (1997) Theoretical models, operational frameworks, and test construction. *Language Testing* 14: 3–22.

Chalhoub-Deville, M. (1995) Deriving oral assessment scales across different tasks and rater groups. *Language Testing* 12: 16–33.

Chalhoub-Deville, M., C. Alcaya, and V. Lozier (1997) Language and measurement issues in developing computer-adaptive tests of reading ability: The University of Minnesota model. In A. Huhta, V. Kohonen, L. Kurki-Suonio, and S. Luoma (eds.) *Current developments and alternatives in language assessment.* Jyväskylä, Finland: University of Jyväskylä. 545–585.

Chalhoub-Deville, M., and C. Deville (1999) Computer adaptive testing in second language contexts. In W. Grabe et al. (eds.) *Annual Review of Applied Linguistics 19: A survey of applied linguistics.* New York: Cambridge University Press. 273–299.

Chalhoub-DeVille, M. (ed.) (1999) *Issues in computer-adaptive testing of reading proficiency.* Studies in Language Testing. Cambridge: Cambridge University Press.

Chambers, J. K., and P. Trudgill (1998) *Dialectology.* 2nd ed. Cambridge: Cambridge University Press.

Chamot, A. U., S. Barnhardt, P. El-Dinary, and J. Robbins (1996) Methods for teaching learning strategies in the foreign language classroom. In R. Oxford (ed.) *Language learning strategies around the world: Crosscultural perspectives.* Honolulu: University Press of Hawai'i. 175–188.

Chapell, E., and M. DeCourcy (1993) Using immersion to train primary school teachers of French in Australia. *Canadian Modern Language Review* 49: 316–337.

Chapelle, C. A. (1999a) Validity in language assessment. In W. Grabe et al. (eds.) *Annual Review of Applied Linguistics 19: Survey of applied linguistics.* New York: Cambridge University Press. 154–272.

Chapelle, C. A. (1999b) Investigation of "Authentic L2 tasks." In J. Egbert and E. Hanson-Smith (eds.) *Computer-enhanced language learning.* Alexandria, VA: TESOL Publications. 101–115.

Chapelle, C. A. (1998) Multimedia CALL: Lessons to be learned from research on instructed SLA. *Language Learning and Technology* 2: 22–34. [Available at http://polyglot. cal.msu. edu/llt/].

Chapelle, C. A. (1995) Field-dependence/field-independence in the L2 classroom. In J. M. Reid (ed.) *Learning styles in the ESL/ESL classroom.* Boston: Heinle and Heinle. 158–168.

Charge, N., and L. Taylor (1997) Recent developments in IELTS. *ELT Journal* 51: 374–80.

Charniak, E. (1993) *Statistical language learning.* Cambridge, MA: MIT Press.

Charpentier, J.-M. (1997) Literacy in a pidgin vernacular. In A. Tabouret-Keller, R. B. LePage, P. Gardner-Chloros, and G. Varro (eds.) *Vernacular literacy: A re-evaluation.* Oxford: Clarendon Press. 222–245.

Chaudenson, R. (1992) *Des îles, des hommes, des langues.* [Islands, men and languages.] Paris: L'Harmattan.

Chaudron, C. (1988) *Second language classrooms.* Cambridge: Cambridge University Press.

Chaudron, C. (1985) Intake: On models and methods for discovering learners' processing of input. *Studies in Second Language Acquisition* 7: 1–14.

Chen, H.-C. (1992) Lexical processing in bilingual or multilingual speakers. In R. J. Harris (ed.) *Cognitive processing in bilinguals.* Amsterdam: Elsevier. 253–264.

Chen, H.-C., and Y.-S. Leung (1989) Patterns of lexical processing in a nonnative language. *Journal of Experimental Psychology: Learning, Memory, and Cognition* 15: 316–325.

Chen, L.-C. (1999) The organization of teacher-student interaction in Chinese EFL classroom lessons. MA thesis, San Diego State University, CA.

Cheng, Y. (1997) How does washback influence teaching? Implications for Hong Kong. *Language and Education* 11: 38–54.

Chernov, G. V. (1994) Message redundancy and message anticipation in simultaneous interpretation. In S. Lambert and B. Moser-Mercer (eds.) *Bridging the gap: Empirical research in simultaneous interpretation.* Amsterdam: John Benjamins. 139–154.

Chick, J. K. (1996) Safe-talk: Collusion in apartheid education. In H. Coleman (ed.) *Society and the language classroom.* Cambridge: Cambridge University Press. 21–39.

Chick, J. K. (1992) Addressing contextual issues relevant to language teaching in South

Africa: Implications for policy and practice. *Working Papers in Educational Linguistics* 8(2): 1–16.

Chick, J. K. (1988) Contribution of ethnography to applied linguistics and to the in-service education of English language teachers. Unpublished paper presented at the 22nd Annual Convention of Teachers of English to Speakers of Other Languages, Chicago, March 8–13.

Chincotta, D., and G. Underwood (1998) Simultaneous interpreters and the effect of concurrent articulation on immediate memory. *Interpreting* 3: 1–20.

Choate, D. L. (1999) Labor issues and interpreters in the California courts: An exchange. (Letter to the Editors). *Proteus* 8.3 and 4: 20–21.

Chodorow, M., and C. Leacock (2000) An unsupervised method for detecting grammatical errors. In *Proceedings of the first conference of the North American Chapter of the Association of Computational Linguistics,* Seattle. 140–147.

Chomsky, N. (1995). *The minimalist program.* Cambridge, MA: MIT Press.

Chomsky, N. (1991). Some notes on economy of derivation and representation. In R. Freidin (ed.) *Principles and parameters in generative grammar.* Cambridge, MA: MIT Press. 417–454.

Chomsky, N. (1988) *Language and problems of knowledge: the Managua lectures.* Cambridge, MA: MIT Press.

Chomsky, N. (1986) *Knowledge of language.* New York: Praeger.

Chomsky, N. (1981) *Lectures on government and binding.* Dordrecht, Netherlands: Foris.

Chomsky, N. (1959) Review of "Verbal Behavior" by B. F. Skinner. *Language* 35: 26–58.

Chomsky, N., and M. Halle (1968) *The sound pattern of English.* New York: Harper Row.

Chrisp, S. (1997) He Taonga Te Reo: The use of a theme year to promote a minority language. *Journal of Multilingual and Multicultural Development* 18: 100–106.

Christian, D. (1999) Applied linguistics in 2000 and beyond. *AAALetter* 21: 6–9.

Christian, D., C. Montone, K. Lindholm, and I. Carranza (eds.) (1997) *Profiles of two-way immersion education.* McHenry, IL: Delta Systems.

Christiansen, C. (1997) *The innovator's dilemma: When new technologies cause great firms to fail.* Boston, MA: Harvard Business School Press.

Christiansen, M. H., and N. Chater (1999) Connectionist natural language processing: The state of the art. *Cognitive Science* 23: 417–430.

Christiansen, M. H., and N. Chater (1994) Generalization and connectionist language learning. *Mind and Language* 9: 273–287.

Chun, D. M., and J. L. Plass (1996) Effects of multimedia annotations on vocabulary acquisition. *Modern Language Journal* 80: 183–198.

Churchill, E. F. (1999) Pragmatic development in L2 request strategies by lower level learners. Paper presented at the Second Language Research Forum, Minneapolis, MN.

Churchland, P. (1995) *The engine of reason, the seat of the soul.* Cambridge, MA: MIT Press.

Cicourel, A. (1992) The interpenetration of communicative contexts: Examples from medical encounters. In A. Duranti and C. Goodwin (eds.) *Rethinking context.* Cambridge: Cambridge University Press. 291–322.

Clahsen, H. (ed.) (1996) *Generative perspectives on language acquisition.* Philadelphia: John Benjamins.

Clahsen, H., M. Rothweiler, A. Woest, and G. Marcus (1993) Regular and irregular inflection in the acquisition of German noun plurals. *Cognition* 45: 225–255.

Clapham, C. (2000) Assessment and testing. In W. Grabe et al. (eds.) *Annual Review of Applied Linguistics 20: Applied linguistics as an emerging discipline.* New York: Cambridge University Press. 147–161.

Clapham, C. (1996) *An investigation into the comparability of two tests of English as a foreign language.* Cambridge: Cambridge University Press.

Clapham, C., and D. Corson (eds.) (1997) *Encyclopedia of language and education.* Vol. 7: *Language testing and assessment.* Boston: Kluwer.

Clark, A. (1993) *Associative engines.* Cambridge, MA: MIT Press.

Clark, R., and R. Ivanic (1997) *The politics of writing.* New York: Routledge.

Clarke, D. F. (1991) The negotiated syllabus: What is it and how is it likely to work? *Applied Linguistics* 12: 13–28.

Clayton, T. (1999) Decentering language in world-system inquiry. *Language Problems & Language Planning* 23: 133–156.

Clément, R. (1980) Ethnicity, contact and communicative competence in a second language. In H. Giles, W. P. Robinson, and P. M. Smith (eds.) *Language: Social psychological perspectives.* Oxford: Pergamon Press. 147–159.

Clément, R., Z. Dörnyei, and K. A. Noels (1994) Motivation, self-confidence, and group cohesion in the foreign language classroom. *Language Learning* 44: 417–448.

Clément, R., and R. C. Gardner (2000) Second language mastery. In H. Giles and W. P. Robinson (eds). *The new handbook of language and social psychology.* Chichester, UK: Wiley. 489–504.

Clément, R., and B. G. Kruidenier (1983) Orientations in second language acquisition: The effects of ethnicity, milieu and target language on their emergence. *Language Learning* 33: 273–291.

Clements, G. (1985) The geometry of phonological features. *Phonology Yearbook* 2: 225–252.

Clennell, C. (1999) Promoting pragmatic awareness and spoken discourse skills with EAP classes. *ELT Journal* 53: 83–91.

Clifford, J. (1988) *The predicament of culture.* Cambridge, MA: Harvard University Press.

Clifton, C. J., L. Frazier, and K. Rayner (eds.) (1994) *Perspectives on sentence processing.* Hillsdale, NJ: Lawrence Erlbaum.

Cluver, A. D. de V. (1992) Language planning models for a post-apartheid South Africa. *Language Problems & Language Planning* 16: 105–136.

Cluver, A. D. de V. (1991) A systems approach to language planning: The case of Namibia. *Language Problems & Language Planning* 15: 43–64.

Clyne, M. (1997) Managing language diversity and second language programmes in Australia. *Current Issues in Language & Society* 4: 94–119.

Clyne, M. (1994) *Intercultural communication at work: Cultural values in discourse.* Cambridge: Cambridge University Press.

Clyne, M. (1987) Constraints on code-switching: How universal are they. *Linguistics* 25: 739–764.

Clyne, M., and S. Kipp (1997) Trends and changes in home language use and shift in Australia, 1986–1996. *Journal of Multilingual and Multicultural Development* 18: 451–473.

Cobarrubias, J. (1990) The spread of the Spanish language in the Americas. In L. Laforgue and G. D. McCommell (eds.) *Language spread and social change: Dynamics and measurement.* Ste.-Foy, Québec: Les Presses de l'Université Laval. 49–92.

Cobarrubias, J. (1983) Ethical issues in status planning. In J. Cobarrubias and J. A. Fishman (eds.) *Progress in language planning.* Berlin: Mouton. 41–85.

Coelho, E. (1991) *Caribbean students in Canadian schools.* Book 2. Toronto: Pippin Publishing.

Coelho, E. (1988) *Caribbean students in Canadian schools.* Book 1. Toronto: Carib-Can Publishers.

Cohen, A. D. (1998) *Strategies in learning and using a second language.* London: Longman.

Cohen, A. D. (1997) Developing pragmatic ability: Insights from accelerated study of Japanese. In H. M. Cook, K. Hijirida, and M. Tahara (eds.) *New trends and issues in teaching Japanese language and culture.* Honolulu: University of Hawai'i, Second Language Teaching and Curriculum Center. Technical Report 15: 133–159.

Cohen, A. D. (1996) Developing the ability to perform speech acts. *Studies in Second Language Acquisition* 18: 253–267.

Cohen, A. D. (1991) Feedback on writing: The use of verbal report. *Studies in Second Language Acquisition* 13: 133–159.

Cohen, J. (1988) *Statistical power analysis for the behavioral sciences.* 2nd ed. Hillsdale, NJ: Lawrence Erlbaum.

Cohen, L., and L. Manion (1994) *Research methods in education.* 4th ed. London: Routledge.

Cole, P., G. Hermon and L.-M. Sung (1990) Principles and parameters of long-distance reflexives. *Linguistic Inquiry* 21: 1–22.

Cole, P., and L.-M. Sung (1994) Head movement and long-distance reflexives. *Linguistic Inquiry* 25: 355–406.

Coleman, M., and T. Liau (1975) A computer readability formula designed for machine scoring. *Journal of Applied Psychology* 60: 283–284.

Colomer, J. M. (1996) To translate or learn languages? An evaluation of social efficiency. *International Journal of the Sociology of Language* 121: 181–197.

CommuniCAT. University of Cambridge Language Examination Syndicate. [Online.] Available: ⟨http://www.ucles.org.uk⟩.

Computerized Adaptive Placement Test (CAPT) informational website. [Online.] Available: ⟨http://www.uqtr.uquebec.ca/eif/u-montr.html⟩.

Comrie, B. (1985) *Tense.* Cambridge: Cambridge University Press.

Comrie, B. (1976) *Aspect.* Cambridge: Cambridge University Press.

Conklin, N., and M. Lourie (1983) *A host of tongues: Language communities in the U.S.* New York: Free Press.

Conley, J. M., and W. M. O'Barr (1998) *Just words: Law, language, and power.* Chicago: University of Chicago Press.

Conley, J. M., and W. M. O'Barr (1990) *Rules versus relationships: The ethnography of legal discourse.* Chicago: University of Chicago Press.

Connor, U. (1996) *Contrastive rhetoric: Cross-cultural aspects of second language writing.* Cambridge: Cambridge University Press.

Conrad, S., and L. Goldstein (1999) ESL student revision after teacher-written comments: Text, contexts, and individuals. *Journal of Second Language Writing* 8: 147–179.

Cook, G. (1989) *Discourse*. Oxford: Oxford University Press.

Cook, H. M. (1999) Language socialization in Japanese elementary schools: Attentive listening and reaction turns. *Journal of Pragmatics* 31: 1443–1465.

Cook, V. J. (1993) *Linguistics and second language acquisition*. London: Longman.

Cook, V. J. (1988) *Chomsky's Universal Grammar*. Oxford: Basil Blackwell.

Cook-Gumperz, J., and K. Hanna (1997) Nurses' work, women's work: Some recent issues of professional literacy and practice. In G. Hull (ed.) *Changing work, changing workers: Critical perspectives on language, literacy, and skills*. Albany: State University of New York Press. 316–334.

Cooper, R. L. (1989). *Language planning and social change*. Cambridge: Cambridge University Press.

Cooper, R. L. (1982a) A framework for the study of language spread. In R. Cooper (ed.) *Language spread: Studies in diffusion and social change*. Bloomington: Indiana University Press. 5–36.

Cooper, R. L., and B. Danet (1980) Language in the melting pot: The sociolinguistic context for language planning in Israel. *Language Problems & Language Planning* 4: 1–28.

Cooper, R. L. (ed.) (1982b) *Language spread: Studies in diffusion and social change*. Bloomington: Indiana University Press.

Cope, B., and M. Kalantzis (eds.) (1993) *The powers of literacy: A genre approach to teaching writing*. London: Falmer.

Coppieters, R. (1987) Competence differences between native and fluent non-native speakers. *Language* 63: 544–573.

Corder, S. P. (1973) *Introducing applied linguistics*. Harmondsworth: Penguin Books.

Corona, D., and O. García (1996) English in Cuba: From imperialist design to imperative need. In J. A. Fishman, A. Conrad, and A. Rubal-Lopez (eds.) *Post-Imperialist English*. Berlin: Mouton de Gruyter. 85–112.

Corson, D. (1998) *Changing education for diversity*. London: Open University Press.

Cortés, C. (1986) Sociocultural resources in instruction: A context-specific approach. In D. Holt (ed.) *Beyond language: Social and cultural factors in schooling language minority students*. Los Angeles: Evaluation, Dissemination and Assessment Center, California State University, Los Angeles. 3–34.

Costa, A., and A. Caramazza (1999) Is lexical selection in bilingual speech production language-specific? Further evidence from Spanish-English and English-Spanish bilinguals. *Bilingualism: Language and Cognition* 2: 231–244.

Costa, A., M. Miozzo and A. Caramazza (1999) Lexical selection in bilinguals: Do words in the bilingual's two lexicons compete for selection? *Journal of Memory and Language* 41: 365–397.

Coughlan, P., and P. A. Duff (1994) Same task, different activities: Analysis of a SLA task from an activity theory perspective. In J. P. Lantolf and G. Appel (eds.) *Vygotskian approaches to second language learning*. Norwood, NJ: Ablex. 173–194.

Coulthard, R. M. (1977) *An introduction to discourse analysis*. London: Longman.

Coulthard, R. M. (ed.) (1991) *Advances in spoken discourse*. London: Routledge.

Council of Europe (1998) *Modern languages: Learning, teaching, assessment: A common European framework of reference*. Strasbourg: Council of Europe.

Court Interpreter Amendments Act of 1988. (1988) Title VII: Sections 701–712.

Craig, C. G. (1997) Language contact and language degeneration. In F. Coulmas (ed.) *Handbook of sociolinguistics*. Oxford: Blackwell. 257–270.

Craig, D. R. (1999) *Teaching language and literacy: Policies and procedures for vernacular situations.* Georgetown, Guyana: Education and Development Services.

Craig, D. R. (1983) Teaching standard English to nonstandard speakers: Some methodological issues. *Journal of Negro Education* 52: 65–74.

Craig, D. R. (1976) Bidialectal education: Creole and standard in the West Indies. *International Journal of the Sociology of Language* 8: 93–134.

Craig, D. R. (1966) Teaching English to Jamaican Creole speakers: A model of a multidialect situation. *Language Learning* 16: 49–61.

Crain, S., and M. Steedman (1985) On not being led up the garden path: The use of context by the psychological parser. In D. R. Dowry, L. Kartunnen and A. Zwicky (eds.) *Natural language parsing: Psychological, computational and theoretical perspectives.* Cambridge: Cambridge University Press. 320–358.

Crandall, J. (2000) Language teacher education. In W. Grabe et al. (eds.) *Annual Review of Applied Linguistics 20: Applied linguistics as an emerging discipline.* New York: Cambridge University Press. 34–55.

Crawford, J. (1999) *Bilingual education: History, politics, theory and practice.* Los Angeles: Bilingual Educational Services.

Creswell, J. (1994) *Research design: Qualitative and quantitative approaches.* Thousand Oaks, CA: Sage.

Crocker, M. W. (1994) On the nature of the principle-based parser. In C. J. Clifton, L. Frazier and K. Rayner (eds.) *Perspectives on sentence processing.* Hillsdale, NJ: Lawrence Erlbaum. 245–266.

Crookes, G. (1997) SLA and language pedagogy: A socioeducational perspective. *Studies in Second Language Acquisition* 19: 93–116.

Crookes, G. (1989) Planning and interlanguage variability. *Studies in Second Language Acquisition* 11: 367–83.

Crookes, G., and R. W. Schmidt (1991) Motivation: Reopening the research agenda. *Language Learning* 41: 469–512.

Crookes, G., and S. M. Gass (eds.) (1993) *Tasks in a pedagogical context: Integrating theory and practice.* Clevedon, Avon, UK: Multilingual Matters.

Crowley, S. (1998) *Composition in the university.* Pittsburgh, PA: University of Pittsburgh Press.

Crowley, T. (1996) Bislama: Orthographic and attitudinal evolution. *Language and Linguistics in Melanesia* 26: 119–146.

Crowley, T. (1994) Linguistic demography: Interpreting the 1989 census results in Vanuatu. *Journal of Multilingual and Multicultural Development* 15: 1–16.

Crowley, T. (1987) *Introdaksen long stadi blong Bislama (Kos buk wan, Kos buk tu, Buk blong ridim).* [Introduction to the study of Bislama (Course book one, Course book two, Book of readings)]. Suva: Extension Services, University of the South Pacific.

Crystal, D. (1987) *The Cambridge encyclopedia of language.* Cambridge: Cambridge University Press.

Csapó, B. (ed.) (1998) *Az iskolai tudás [School knowledge].* Budapest: Osiris.

Csikszentmihalyi, M. (1990) *Flow.* New York: Basic Books.

Culicover, P. W., and R. S. Jackendoff (1995) Something else for the binding theory. *Linguistic Inquiry* 26: 249–276.

Cumming, A. (1998) Theoretical perspectives on writing. In W. Grabe et al. (eds.) *An-*

nual Review of Applied Linguistics 18: Foundations of second language teaching. New York: Cambridge University Press. 61–78.

Cumming, A. (1989) Writing expertise and second language proficiency. *Language Learning* 39: 81–141.

Cumming, A., and A. Riazi (2000) Building models of adult second-language writing instruction. *Learning and Instruction* 10: 55–71.

Cumming, A. (ed.) (1994) Alternatives in TESOL research: Descriptive, interpretive, and ideological orientations. *TESOL Quarterly* 28: 673–703.

Cummins, J. (2000a) Biliteracy, empowerment, and transformative pedagogy. In J. Tinajero and R.A. DeVillar (eds.) *The power of two languages 2000.* New York: McGraw Hill. 9–19.

Cummins, J. (2000b) *Language, power and pedagogy: Bilingual children in the crossfire.* Clevedon, Avon, UK: Multilingual Matters.

Cummins, J. (1999) Alternative paradigms in bilingual education research: Does theory have a place? *Educational Researcher* 28: 26–32, 41.

Cummins, J. (1996) *Negotiating identities: Education for empowerment in a diverse society.* Ontario, CA: California Association for Bilingual Education.

Cummins, J. (1986). The role of primary language development in promoting success for language minority students. In D. Holt (ed.) *Schooling and language minority students: A theoretical framework.* Los Angeles: Evaluation, Dissemination and Assessment Center, California State University, Los Angeles. 3–49.

Cummins, J. (1984) *Bilingualism and special education: Issues in assessment and pedagogy.* Clevedon, Avon, UK: Multilingual Matters.

Cummins, J., and D. Corson, D. (eds.) (1997) Bilingual education. *Encyclopedia of language and education.* Vol. 5: *Bilingual education.* Dordrecht, Netherlands: Kluwer Academic.

Cunningham, S., and P. Moor (1998) *Cutting edge: A practical approach to task-based learning: Students' book.* London: Longman.

Cutting, J. C., and V. S. Ferreira (1999) Semantic and phonological information flow in the production lexicon. *Journal of Experimental Psychology: Learning, Memory, and Cognition* 25: 318–344.

Da Pidgin Coup (1999) Pidgin and education. Unpublished position paper. Honolulu: University of Hawai'i.

Dagenais, D., and E. Day (1999) Home language practices of children in French immersion. *Canadian Modern Language Review* 56: 99–123.

Dalphinis, M. (1991) The Afro-English creole speech community. In S. Alladina and V. Edwards (eds.) *Multilingualism in the British Isles.* Vol. 2:. *Africa, the Middle East and Asia.* London: Longman. 42–56.

Dalphinis, M. (1985) *Caribbean and African languages: Social history, language, literature and education.* London: Karia Press.

Dam, H. V. (1998) Lexical similarity vs. lexical dissimilarity in consecutive interpreting. *The Translator* 4: 49–68.

Damian, M. F., and R. C. Martin (1999) Semantic and phonological codes interact in single word production. *Journal of Experimental Psychology: Learning, Memory, and Cognition* 25: 345–361.

Dandonoli, P., and G. Henning (1990) An investigation of the construct validity of the ACTFL proficiency guidelines and oral interview procedure. *Foreign Language Annals* 23: 11–22.

Danks, J., G. M. Shreve, S. B. Fountain, and M. K. McBeath (eds.) (1997) *Cognitive processes in translation and interpreting.* Thousand Oaks, CA: Sage Publications.

Daoust, D. (1992) The role of occupation as a factor of change in the terminological habits of a Montreal private business. *Revue de l'ACLA* [Canadian Association of Applied Linguistics (ACLA) Review] 14(2): 71–93.

Darò, V. (1997) Experimental studies on memory in conference interpretation. *Meta* 42: 622–628.

Darrah, C. (1997) Complicating the concept of skill requirements: Scenes from a workplace. In G. Hull (ed.) *Changing work, changing workers: Critical perspectives on language, literacy, and skills.* Albany, NY: State University of New York Press. 249–272.

Darrah, C. (1990) Skills in context: An exploration in industrial ethnography. Ph.D. diss., Stanford University.

Darwin, C. (1872/1979) *The expression of emotion in man and animals.* London: Julian Friedmann.

Das Gupta, J. (1970) *Language conflict and national development.* Berkeley: University of California Press.

Dasgupta, P. (1990) Editorial perspectives: A new decade and a new direction. *Language Problems & Language Planning* 14: 85–88.

Daud, B. (1996) Bahasa Indonesia: The struggle for a national language. *Working Papers in Linguistics—University of Melbourne* 16: 17–28.

Davies, A. (1999a) *An introduction to applied linguistics: From practice to theory.* Edinburgh: The Edinburgh University Press.

Davies, A. (1999b) Ethics in educational linguistics. In B. Spolsky (ed.) *Concise encyclopedia of educational linguistics.* Amsterdam: Elsevier. 21–25

Davies, A. (1997b) Introduction: The limits of ethics in language testing. *Language Testing* 14: 235–241.

Davies, A. (1995) Testing communicative language or testing language communicatively: What? How? *Melbourne Papers in Language Testing* 4: 1–20.

Davies, A. (ed.) (1997a) *Ethics in language testing.* Special issue of *Language and Testing* 14(3).

Davis, K. (1995) Qualitative theory and methods in applied linguistics research. *TESOL Quarterly* 29: 427–453.

Davison, C. (2001) Identity and ideology: The problem of defining and defending ESLness. In B. Mohan, C. Leung, and C. Davison (eds.) *English as a second language in the mainstream: Issues of teaching, learning and identity.* London: Pearson Longman.

Day, E. (1999) Identity formation in a kindergarten English language learner: An ethnographic case study. Ph.D. diss., Simon Fraser University, Vancouver, BC.

Day, R., and J. Bamford (1998) *Extensive reading in the second language classroom.* New York: Cambridge University Press.

de Bot, K. (1997) Nelde's law revisited. In W. Wölck and A. De Houwer (eds.) *Recent studies in contact linguistics.* Bonn: Duemmler. 51–59.

de Bot, K. (1992) A bilingual production model: Levelt's Speaking model adapted. *Applied Linguistics* 13: 1–24.

de Bot, K., and M. Clyne (1994) A 16-year longitudinal study of language attrition in Dutch immigrants in Australia. *Journal of Multilingual and Multicultural Development* 15: 17–28.

de Bot, K., T. S. Paribaklit, and M. B. Wesche (1997) Toward a lexical processing model for the study of second language vocabulary acquisition. *Studies in Second Language Acquisition* 19: 309–329.

de Bot, K., and R. Schreuder (1993) Word production and the bilingual lexicon. In R. Schreuder and B. Weltens (eds.) *The bilingual lexicon.* Amsterdam: John Benjamins. 191–214.

Decker, K. (1995) Orthography development for Belize Creole. Paper presented at the Society for Caribbean Linguistics Conference, Georgetown, Guyana.

Deetz, S. (1995) *Transforming communication, transforming business.* Cresskill, NJ: Hampton Press.

DeGraff, M. (ed.) (1999) *Language creation and language change: Creolization, diachrony and development.* Cambridge, MA: MIT Press.

De Groot, A. M. B. (1995) Determinants of bilingual lexicosemantic organization. *Computer Assisted Language Learning* 8: 151–180.

De Groot, A. M. B. (1993) Word-type effects in bilingual processing tasks: Support for a mixed representational system. In R. Schreuder and B. Weltens (eds.) *The bilingual lexicon.* Amsterdam: John Benjamins. 27–51.

De Groot, A. M. B., L. Dannenburg, and J. G. Van Hell (1994) Forward and backward word translation by bilinguals. *Journal of Memory and Language* 33: 600–629.

De Groot, A. M. B., P. Delmaar, and S. J. Lupker (2000) The processing of interlexical homographs in a bilingual and a monolingual task: Support for nonselective access to bilingual memory. *Quarterly Journal of Experimental Psychology* 53A: 397–428.

De Groot, A. M. B., and R. Poot (1997) Word translation at three levels of proficiency in a second language: The ubiquitous involvement of conceptual memory. *Language Learning* 47: 215–264.

de Guerrero, M. C. M. (1999) Inner speech as mental rehearsal: The case of advanced L2 learners. *Issues in Applied Linguistics* 10: 27–55.

de Guerrero, M. C. M., and O. Villamil (2000) Activating the ZPD: Mutual scaffolding in L2 peer revision. *Modern Language Journal* 84: 51–68.

Dejean, Y. (1993) An overview of the language situation in Haiti. *International Journal of the Sociology of Language* 102: 73–84.

Déjean le Féal, K. (1998a) Acquisition d'une langue de travail supplémentaire. Expérience récente d'une interpréte de conférence. [Acquiring an additional working language: A conference interpreter's recent experience.] *Traduire* [Translation] 178–179: 71–84.

Déjean le Féal, K. (1998b) Non nova, sed nove. *The Interpreters' Newsletter* 8: 41–49.

Déjean le Féal, K. (1997) Simultaneous interpretation with "training wheels." *Meta* 42: 616–621.

Déjean le Féal, K. (1978) Lectures et improvisations: Incidences de la forme de l'énonciation sur la traduction simultaneé [Lectures and improvisations: Incidents of the form of enunciation in simultaneous translation] Ph.D. diss., Université de la Sorbonne Nouvelle. Paris.

de Jongh, E. M. (1992) *An introduction to court interpreting.* Lanham, MD: University Press of America.

DeKeyser, R. (1995) Learning second language grammar rules: An experiment with a miniature linguistic system. *Studies in Second Language Acquisition* 17: 379–410.

de Klerk, G. (2000). Mother tongue instruction and military dictatorships: How fascist ideology can set the stage for human rights. Paper presented at the Colloquium on Revisiting the Mother Tongue Question in Language Policy. American Association for Applied Linguistics, Annual Conference, Vancouver.

de Klerk, V., and G. P. Barkhuizen (1998) Language policy in the SANDF: A case for biting the bullet? *Language Problems & Language Planning* 22: 215–236.

Dekydspotter, L., R. A. Sprouse and K. A. B. Swanson (2000) The primacy of syntax and second language acquisition: The interpretation of *combien* extractions in English-French interlanguage. In A. Juffs, T. W. Talpas, G. Mizera and B. Burtt (eds.) *Proceedings of GASLA IV*. Pittsburgh, PA: University of Pittsburgh Working Papers in Linguistics. 73–84.

Delisle, J. (1988) *Translation: An interpretive approach.* (Tr. P. Logan and M. Creery.) Ottawa, Canada: University of Ottawa Press.

Delisle, J. (1980) *L'Analyse du discours comme méthode de traduction: Initiation à la traduction française de textes pragmatiques anglais: Théorie et pratique.* [*Discourse analysis as a translation method: Introduction to the translation into French of English pragmatic texts: Theory and practice.*] Ottawa, Canada: University of Ottawa Press.

Dell, G. S. (1988) The retrieval of phonological forms in production: Tests of predictions from a connectionist model. *Journal of Memory and Language* 27: 124–142.

Dell, G. S., and P. G. O'Seaghdha (1991) Mediated and convergent lexical priming in language production: A comment on Levelt et al. (1991). *Psychological Review* 98: 604–614.

Denison, N. (1982) A linguistics ecology for Europe? *Folia Linguistica* 16: 1–16.

Denzin, N., and Y. Lincoln (eds.) (1994) *Handbook of qualitative research.* Thousand Oaks, CA: Sage.

Department of Employment, Education, Training and Youth Affairs [DEETYA]. (1996) *Desert schools.* Vol. 1. Canberra: Department of Employment, Education, Training and Youth Affairs.

Devlin, K., and D. Rosenberg (1996) *Language at work: Analyzing communication breakdown in the workplace to inform system design.* Stanford, CA: Center for the Study of Language and Information.

Devonish, H. (1986) *Language and liberation: Creole language and politics in the Caribbean.* London: Karia Press.

DIALANG Computer Adaptive Test informational website. [Online.] Available: ⟨www.jyu.fi/~dialang/general.html⟩.

Diaz, R. M., and L. E. Berk. (eds.) (1992) *Private speech: From social interaction to self-regulation.* Hillsdale, NJ: Lawrence Erlbaum.

Díaz, S., L. Moll, and H. Mehan (1986) Sociocultural resources in instruction: A context-specific approach. In D. Holt (ed.) *Beyond language: Social and cultural factors in schooling language minority students.* Los Angeles: Evaluation, Dissemination and Assessment Center, California State University, Los Angeles. 187–230.

DiCamilla, F. J., and M. Antón (1997) The function of repetition in the collaborative discourse of L2 learners. *Canadian Modern Language Review* 53: 609–633.

Dicker, S. J. (2000) Official English and bilingual education: The controversy over language pluralism in the U.S. society. In J. K. Hall and W. Eggington (eds.) *The sociopolitics of English language teaching.* Clevedon, Avon, UK: Multilingual Matters. 45–66.

Dicker, S. J. (1996) *Languages in America: A pluralist view.* Clevedon, Avon, UK: Multilingual Matters.

Dieu, M. (1991) National languages and rice cultivation in Northern Cameroon. *Terminologies Nouvelles* [New Terminologies] 6 (Dec): 7–12.

Dijkhoff, M. (1993) [Report on the Netherlands Antilles]. *Pidgins and Creoles in Education (PACE) Newsletter* 4: 1–2.

Dijkstra, A., E. De Bruijn, H. Schriefers and S. Ten Brinke (2000) More on interlingual homograph recognition: Language intermixing versus explicitness of instruction. *Bilingualism: Language and Cognition* 3: 69–78.

Dijkstra, A., J. Grainger and W. J. B. Van Heuven (1999) Recognizing cognates and interlingual homographs: The neglected role of phonology. *Journal of Memory and Language* 41: 496–518.

Dijkstra, A., M. Timmermans and H. Schriefers (2000) On being blinded by your other language: Effects of task demands on interlingual homograph recognition. *Journal of Memory and Language* 42: 445–464.

Dijkstra, A., and W. J. B. Van Heuven (1998) The BIA model and bilingual word recognition. In J. Grainger and A. Jacobs (eds.) *Localist connectionist approaches to human cognition.* Mahwah, NJ: Lawrence Erlbaum. 189–225.

Dijkstra, A., W. J. B. Van Heuven and J. Grainger (1998) Simulating cross-language competition with the Bilingual Interactive Activation model. *Psychologica Belgica* 38: 177–197.

Dijkstra, A., H. Van Jaarsveld and S. Ten Brinke (1998) Interlingual homograph recognition: Effects of task demands and language intermixing. *Bilingualism: Language and Cognition* 1: 51–66.

Dirven, R., and M. Pütz (1996–1997) *Sprachkonflikt.* [Language conflict.] In P. H. Nelde et al. (eds.) *Contact linguistics: An international handbook of contemporary research.* Berlin: de Gruyter. 684–691.

Dodson, C., and S. Thomas (1988) The effect of total L2 immersion education on concept development. *Journal of Multilingual and Multicultural Development* 9: 467–485.

Doğançay-Aktuna, S. (1995) An evaluation of the Turkish language reform after 60 years. *Language Problems & Language Planning* 19: 221–249.

Donahue, T. S. (2001) Language planning and the perils of ideological solipsism. In J. W. Tollefson (ed.) *Language policies in education: Critical issues.* Mahwah, NJ: Lawrence Erlbaum.

Donato, R. (1994) Collective scaffolding in second language learning. In J. P. Lantolf and G. Appel (eds.) *Vygotskian approaches to second language research.* Norwood, NJ: Ablex. 33–56.

Donato, R., and B. Adair-Hauck (1992) Discourse perspectives on formal instruction. *Language Awareness* 1: 73–90.

Dorian, N. (1994) Purism vs. compromise in language revitalization and language revival. *Language in Society* 23: 479–494.

Dorian, N. (1982) Language loss and maintenance in language contact situations. In R. D. Lambert and B. F. Freed (eds.) *The loss of language skills.* Rowley, MA: Newbury House. 44–59.

Dorian, N. (1981) *Language death: The life cycle of a Scottish Gaelic dialect.* Philadelphia: University of Pennsylvania Press.

Dörnyei, Z. (1994) Motivation and motivating in the language foreign language classroom. *The Modern Language Journal* 78: 273–284.

Dörnyei, Z. (1990) Conceptualizing motivation in foreign-language learning. *Language Learning* 40: 45–78.

Dörnyei, Z., and J. Kormos (1998) Problem-solving mechanisms in L2 communication. *Studies in Second Language Acquisition* 20: 349–385.

Dörnyei, Z., E. Nyilasi and R. Clément (1996) Hungarian school children's motivation to learn languages: A comparison of target languages. *Novelty* 3: 6–16.

Dörnyei, Z., and S. Thurrell (1992) *Conversation and dialogues in action.* New York: Prentice-Hall International.

Doughty, C. (in press) Cognitive underpinnings of focus on form. In P. Robinson (ed.) *Cognition and second language instruction.* Cambridge: Cambridge University Press.

Doughty, C. (1991) Second language instruction does make a difference: Evidence from an empirical study of SL relativization. *Studies in Second Language Acquisition* 13: 431–469.

Doughty, C., and T. Pica (1986) "Information gap" tasks: Do they facilitate second language acquisition? *TESOL Quarterly* 20: 305–325.

Doughty, C., and J. Williams (1998a) Pedagogical choices in focus on form. In C. Doughty and J. Williams (eds.) *Focus on form in classroom second language acquisition.* Cambridge: Cambridge University Press. 197–261.

Doughty, C., and J. Williams (eds.) (1998b) *Focus on form in classroom second language acquisition.* Cambridge: Cambridge University Press.

Douglas, D. (2000) *Assessing languages for specific purposes.* Cambridge: Cambridge University Press.

Drechsel, E. (1997) *Mobilian jargon.* London: Oxford University Press.

Dreyer, C. (1998) Teacher-student styles wars in South Africa: The silent battle. *System* 26: 115–126.

Dreyer, C., and R. Oxford (1996) Learning strategies and other predictors of ESL proficiency among Afrikaans-speakers in South Africa. In R. Oxford (ed.) *Language learning strategies around the world: Crosscultural perspectives.* Honolulu: University Press of Hawai'i. 61–74.

Dua, H. (1996) The politics of language conflict: Implications for language planning and political theory. *Language Problems & Language Planning* 20: 1–17.

Dubin, F., and E. Olshtain (1986) *Course design: Developing programs and materials for language learning.* Cambridge: Cambridge University Press.

Dudley-Evans, T., and M. J. St John (1998) *Developments in English for specific purposes.* New York: Cambridge University Press.

Duff, P. A. (forthcoming.) *Case study research in second language acquisition.* Mahwah, NJ: Lawrence Erlbaum.

Duff, P. A. (1995) An ethnography of communication in immersion classrooms in Hungary. *TESOL Quarterly* 29: 505–537.

Duff, P. A. (1993a) Syntax, semantics, and SLA: The convergence of possessive and existential constructions. *Studies in Second Language Acquisition* 15: 1–34.

Duff, P. A. (1993b) Tasks and interlanguage performance: An SLA perspective. In G. Crookes and S. M. Gass (eds.) *Tasks and language learning: Integrating theory and practice.* Clevedon, Avon, UK: Multilingual Matters. 57–95.

Duff, P. A., and Y. Uchida (1997) The negotiation of teachers' sociocultural identities and practices in post-secondary EFL classrooms. *TESOL Quarterly* 31: 451–486.

Dulay, H., M. Burt, and S. Krashen (1982) *Language two.* New York: Oxford University Press.

Dunkel, P. (1999) Research and development of a computer-adaptive test of listening comprehension in the less-commonly taught language Hausa. In M. Chalhoub-Deville (ed.) *Issues in computer-adaptive testing of reading proficiency.* Cambridge: Cambridge University Press. 119–121.

Dunkel, P. (1998) Considerations in developing or using second/foreign language proficiency computer-adaptive tests. *Language Learning and Technology* 2: 77–93.

Dunkel, P. (1997) Computer-adaptive testing of listening comprehension: A blueprint for CAT development. *Language Teacher Online.* 21: 10 [Online]. Available: ⟨http://langue.hyper.chubu.ac.jp/jalt/pub/tlt/97/oct/dunkel.html⟩.

Durgunoglu, A., and L. Verhoven (eds.) (1998) *Literacy development in a multilingual context: Cross-cultural perspectives.* Mahwah, NJ: Lawrence Erlbaum.

Durie, A. (1999) Emancipatory Maori education: Speaking from the heart. In S. May (ed.) *Indigenous community-based education.* Clevedon, Avon, UK: Multilingual Matters. 67–78.

Dutcher, N. (1995) *The use of first and second languages in education: A review of international experience.* Washington, DC: World Bank.

Dutton, T. E. (1983) *Hiri Motu—Iena Sivarai. [Hiri Motu—its story.]* Port Moresby: University of Papua New Guinea Press.

Eades, D. (1997) Language in court: The acceptance of linguistic evidence about Indigenous Australians in the criminal justice system. *Australian Aboriginal Studies* 1:15–27.

Eades, D. (1994) A case of communicative clash: Aboriginal English and the legal system. In J. Gibbons (ed.) *Language and the law.* London: Longman. 234–264.

Eagleson, R. (1994) Forensic analysis of personal written texts: A case study. In J. Gibbons (ed.) *Language and the law.* London: Longman. 362–373.

Early, M., B. Mohan and H. Hooper (1989) The Vancouver School Board Language and Content Project. In J. Esling (ed.) *Multicultural education and policy: ESL in the 1990s.* Toronto: Ontario Institute for Studies in Education Press.

Eastman, C. M. (1983a) *Language planning: An introduction.* San Francisco: Chandler and Sharp.

Eastman, C. M. (1983b) Language-planning method. In C. M. Eastman (ed.) *Language planning: An introduction.* San Francisco: Chandler and Sharp. 177–203.

Eckman, F. R. (1996) A functional-typological approach to second language acquisition theory. In W. C. Ritchie and T. K. Bhatia (eds.) *Handbook of second language acquisition.* New York: Academic. 195–211.

Eckman, F. R., and G. K. Iverson (2000) Principles of L2 phonology: The question of learnability. In A. Juffs, T. W. Talpas, G. Mizera, and B. Burtt (eds.) *Proceedings of GASLA IV.* Pittsburgh, PA: University of Pittsburgh Working Papers in Linguistics. 85–105.

Edelsky, C. (1993) Democracy and the teaching of English. Keynote address to the NCTE national conference, Indianapolis, IN, November.

Edelsky, C. (1991) *With literacy and justice for all: Rethinking the social in language and education.* New York: Falmer Press.

Edelsky, C. (1986) *Writing in a bilingual program: Había una vez.* Norwood, NJ: Ablex.

Edge, J., and K. Richards (1998) May I see your warrant, please?: Justifying outcomes in qualitative research. *Applied Linguistics* 19: 334–356.

Edmondson, W., and J. House (1981) *Let's talk and talk about it.* Munich: Urban and Schwarzenberg.

Edwards, A. B. (1995) *The practice of court interpreting.* Amsterdam: John Benjamins.

Edwards, J. (1993) Language revival: Specifics and generalities. *Studies in Second Language Acquisition* 15: 107–113.

Edwards, J. (1992) Sociopolitical aspects of language maintenance and loss: Towards a typology of minority language situations. In W. Fase, K. Jaspaert and S. Kroon (eds.) *Maintenance and loss of minority languages.* Philadelphia: John Benjamins. 37–54.

Edwards, J. (1985) *Language, society and identity.* Oxford: Basil Blackwell.

Edwards, V. (1979) *The West Indian language issue in British schools: Challenges and responses.* London: Routledge and Kegan Paul.

Edwards, W. (1983) Code selection and code shifting in Guyana. *Language in Society* 12: 295–311.

Eggington, W. G. (1997) The English language metaphors we live by. In W. Eggington and H. Wren (eds.) *Language policy: Dominant English, pluralist challenges.* Amsterdam: John Benjamins. 29–46.

Eggington. W. G. (1985) Toward a language plan for the Southern California area: The Hacienda-La Puente sociolinguistic survey. Ph.D. diss., University of Southern California, Los Angeles.

Eggington, W. G., and R. B. Baldauf, Jr. (1990) Towards evaluating the Aboriginal bilingual education program in the Northern Territory. In R. B. Baldauf, Jr., and A. Luke (eds.) *Language planning and education in Australasia and the South Pacific.* Clevedon, Avon, UK: Multilingual Matters. 89–105

Eggins, S., and D. Slade (1997) *Analyzing casual conversation.* London: Cassell.

Ehrlich, S. (1997) Gender as social practice. *Studies in Second Language Acquisition* 19: 421–446.

Ehrman, M. (1996) *Understanding second language learning difficulties.* Thousand Oaks, CA: Sage.

Ehrman, M., and R. L. Oxford (1995) Cognition plus: Correlates of adult language proficiency. *The Modern Language Journal* 79: 67–89.

Ehrman, M., and R. L. Oxford (1990) Adult language learning styles and strategies in an intensive training setting. *The Modern Language Journal* 74: 311–327.

Ehrman, M., and R. L. Oxford (1989) Effects of sex differences, career choice, and psychological type on adult language learning strategies. *The Modern Language Journal* 73: 1–13.

Eisenhart, M. (1995) The fax, the jazz player and the self-story teller: How do people organize culture? *Anthropology and Education Quarterly* 26: 3–26.

Ellis, N. C. (1999) Cognitive approaches to SLA. In W. Grabe et al. (eds.) *Annual Review of Applied Linguistics 19: A survey of applied linguistics.* New York: Cambridge University Press. 22–42.

Ellis, N. C. (1998) Emergentism, connectionism and language learning. *Language Learning* 48: 631–644.

Ellis, N. C., and R. Schmidt (1998) Rules or associations in the acquisition of morphol-

546   REFERENCES

ogy? The frequency by regularity interaction in human and PDP learning of morphosyntax. *Language and Cognitive Processes* 13: 307–336.

Ellis, N. C., and R. Schmidt (1997) Morphology and long-distance dependencies: Laboratory research illuminating the A in SLA. *Studies in Second Language Acquisition* 19: 145–171.

Ellis, R. (1999) Task-based research and language pedagogy. Unpublished manuscript.

Ellis, R. (1997) *SLA research and language teaching.* Oxford: Oxford University Press.

Ellis, R. (1994) *The study of second language acquisition.* Oxford: Oxford University Press.

Ellis, R. (1992) Learning to communicate in the classroom: A study of two language learners' requests. *Studies in Second Language Acquisition* 14: 1–23.

Ellis, R. (1990) *Instructed second language acquisition.* Cambridge: Basil Blackwell.

Ellis, R., Y. Tanaka, and A. Yamazaki (1994) Classroom interaction, comprehension, and the acquisition of L2 word meanings. *Language Learning* 44: 449–491.

Elman, J. L. (1993) Learning and development in neural networks: The importance of starting small. *Cognition* 48: 71–99.

Elman, J. L., E. A. Bates, M. H. Johnson, A. Karmiloff-Smith, D. Parisi, and K. Plunkett (1996) *Rethinking innateness: A connectionist perspective on development.* Cambridge, MA: MIT Press.

Elsasser, N., and P. Irvine (1987) English and Creole: The dialectics of choice in a college writing program. In I. Shor (ed.) *Freire for the classroom: A sourcebook for literacy teaching.* Portsmouth, MA: Boynton/Cook. 129–149.

Elugbe, B. O. (1994) Minority language development in Nigeria: A situation report on Rivers and Bendel states. In R. Fardon and G. Furniss (eds.) *African languages, development and the state.* London: Routledge. 62–75.

Embretson, S. E. (1985) Multicomponent content trait models for test design. In S. E. Embretson (ed.) *Test design: Developments in psychology and psychometrics.* Orlando, FL: Academic Press. 195–218.

Emig, J. (1971) *The composing process of twelfth graders.* Urbana, IL: National Council of Teachers of English.

Engeström, Y. (1999) Activity theory and individual and social transformation. In Y. Engeström, R. Miettenen, and R-L Punamake (eds.) *Perspectives on activity theory.* Cambridge: Cambridge University Press. 19–38.

Engeström, Y. (1993) Developmental studies of work as a testbench of activity theory: The case of primary care medical practice. In S. Chaiklin and J. Lave (eds.) *Understanding practice.* Cambridge: Cambridge University Press. 64–103.

English Language Services (1964) *English 900.* New York: Collier Macmillan.

Enninger, W., and L. M. Haynes (eds.) (1984) *Studies in language ecology.* Wiesbaden: Steiner.

Entwisle, D. R. (1971) Developmental sociolinguistics: Inner-city children. *American Journal of Sociology* 74: 37–49.

Enyedi, Á., and P. Medgyes (1998) ELT in Central and Eastern Europe. *Language Teaching* 31: 1–12.

Epstein, S. D., S. Flynn, and G. Martohardjono (1996) Second language research: Theoretical and experimental issues in contemporary research. *Behavioral and Brain Sciences* 19: 677–749.

Ericsson, K. A., R. T. Krampe, and C. Tesch-Römer (1993) The role of deliberate practice in the acquisition of expert performance. *Psychological Review* 100: 363–406.

Escamilla, K. (1994) The sociolinguistic environment in a bilingual school: A case study introduction. *Bilingual Research Journal* 18: 21–47.

Escamilla, K. (1992) Theory into practice: A look at maintenance bilingual classrooms. *Journal of Educational Issues of Language Minority Students* 11: 1–25.

Esling, J. (1991) Researching the effects of networking: Evaluating the spoken and written discourse generated by working with CALL. In P. Dunkel (ed.) *Computer-assisted language learning and testing: Research issues and practice.* New York: Newbury House. 111–131.

ETS [Educational Testing Service]. (1998) *Computer-based TOEFL: Score user guide.* Princeton, NJ: Educational Testing Service.

Etzioni, A. (1969) *The semi-professions and their organization: Teachers, nurses, and social workers.* New York: Free Press.

Eubank, L. (1993/1994) On the transfer of parametric values in L2 development. *Language Acquisition* 3: 183–208.

Eubank, L. (1993) Optionality and the initial state in L2 development. In B. D. Schwartz and T. Hoekstra (eds.) *Language Acquisition Studies in Generative Grammar.* Philadelphia: John Benjamins. 369–388.

Eubank, L., J. Bischof, A. Huffstutler, P. Leek, and C. West (1997) "Tom eats slowly cooked eggs": Thematic verb raising in L2 knowledge. *Language Acquisition* 6: 171–199.

Evans, C. (1996) Ethnolinguistic vitality, prejudice, and family language transmission. *Bilingual Research Journal* 20: 177–207.

Extra, G. (1995) Ethnic minorities, language diversity, and home language instruction: Crosscultural perspectives on the Netherlands. In T. F. Shannon and J. P. Snapper (eds.) *Berkeley conference on Dutch linguistics 1993: Dutch linguistics in a changing Europe.* Lanham, MD: University Press of America. 17–39.

Færch, C., and G. Kasper (1986) The role of comprehension in second language learning. *Applied Linguistics* 7: 257–274.

Færch, C., and G. Kasper (1983a) Plans and strategies in foreign language communication. In C. Færch and G. Kasper (eds.) *Strategies of interlanguage communication.* London: Longman. 20–60.

Færch, C., and G. Kasper. (eds.) (1983b) *Strategies of interlanguage communication.* London: Longman.

Fairclough, N. (1997) Discourse across disciplines: Discourse analysis in researching social change. *AILA Review* 12: 3–17.

Fairclough, N. (1995) *Critical discourse analysis.* London: Longman.

Fairclough, N. (1995) *Media discourse.* London: Edward Arnold.

Fairclough, N. (1989) *Language and power.* Longman: New York.

Falbo, C. (1998) Analyse des erreurs en interprétation simultaneé. [Error analysis in simultaneous interpretation.] *The Interpreters' Newsletter* 8: 107–120.

Falbo, C. (1995) Interprétation consécutive et exercices préparatoires. [Consecutive interpretion and preparatory exercises.] *The Interpreters' Newsletter* 6: 87–91.

Faltis, C. (1997) Case study methods in researching language and education. In N. Hornberger and D. Corson (eds.) *Encyclopedia of language and education* Vol. 8: *Research methods in language education.* Dordrecht, Netherlands: Kluwer Academic. 145–152

Faltis, C., and S. Hudelson (1998) *Bilingual education in elementary and secondary school communities: Toward understanding and caring.* Needham Heights, MA: Allyn & Bacon.

Fasold, R. (1984) *The sociolinguistics of society.* Oxford: Basil Blackwell.

Federal rates to rise (1999) *Proteus* 8(2): 1.

Feldman, C. F., A. Stone, and B. Renderer (1990) Stage, transfer, and academic achievement in dialect-speaking Hawaiian adolescents. *Child Development* 61: 472–484.

Fellman, J. (1974) The role of Eliezer Ben Yehuda in the revival of the Hebrew language: An assessment. In J. A. Fishman (ed.) *Advances in language planning.* The Hague: Mouton. 427–455.

Fenton, S. (1997) The role of the interpreter in the adversarial courtroom. In S. E. Carr, R. Roberts, A. Dufour, and D. Steyn (eds.) *The critical link: Interpreters in the community.* Amsterdam: John Benjamins. 29–34.

Ferguson, C. A. (1982) Religious factors in language spread. In R. L. Cooper (ed.) *Language spread: Studies in diffusion and social change.* Bloomington: Indiana University Press. 95–106.

Ferguson, C. A. (1975) Towards a characterization of English foreigner talk. *Anthropological Linguistics* 17: 1–14.

Ferguson, C. A. (1971) Absence of copula and the notion of simplicity: A study of normal speech, baby talk, foreigner talk and pidgins. In D. Hymes (ed.) *Pidginization and creolization of languages.* Cambridge: Cambridge University Press. 141–150.

Ferrara, K. W. (1994) *Therapeutic ways with words.* New York: Oxford University Press.

Ferreira, F., and C. Clifton (1986) The independence of syntactic processing. *Journal of Memory and Language* 25: 348–368.

Ferris, D. (1999) The case for grammar correction in L2 writing classes: A response to Truscott (1996). *Journal of Second Language Writing* 8: 1–11.

Ferris, D. (1997) Influence of teacher commentary on student revision. *TESOL Quarterly* 31: 315–339.

Festinger, N. (1999) When is a team not a team? *Proteus* 8: 6–7.

Fettes, M. (1998) Life on the edge: Canada's aboriginal languages under official bilingualism. In T. Ricento and B. Burnaby (eds.) *Language and politics in the United States and Canada: Myths and realities.* Mahwah, NJ: Lawrence Erlbaum. 117–149.

Fettes, M. (1997) Language planning and education. In R. Wodak and D. Corson (eds.) *Encyclopedia of language and education.* Vol. 1: *Language policy and political issues in education.* Dordrecht, Netherlands: Kluwer Academic. 13–22.

Field, J. (2000) 'Not waving but drowning': Do we measure the depth of the water or throw a lifebelt? *ELT Journal* 54: 186–195.

Field, J. (1998) Skills and strategies: towards a new methodology for listening. *ELT Journal* 52: 110–118.

Fill, A. (1993) *Ökolinguistik: Eine Einführung. [Ecolinguistics: An introduction.]* Tubingen: Narr.

Fill, A. (ed.) (1996) *Sprachökologie und Ökolinguistik. [Ecology of language and ecolinguistics.]* Tübingen: Stauffenburg.

Firth, A. (1996) The discursive accomplishment of normality: On 'lingua franca' English and conversation analysis. *Journal of Pragmatics* 26: 237–259.

Fischer, K. (1992) Educating speakers of Caribbean English in the United States. In J. Siegel (ed.) *Pidgins, creoles and nonstandard dialects in education.* Melbourne: Applied Linguistics Association of Australia. 99–123.

Fischer, S. A. (1992) Homogeneity in Old Rapanui. *Oceanic Linguistics* 31: 181–190.

Fisher, S. (1995) *Nursing wounds: Nurse practitioners, doctors, women patients and the negotiation of meaning.* New Brunswick, NJ: Rutgers University Press.

Fisher, S., and A. D. Todd (eds.) (1983) *The social organization of doctor-patient communication.* Washington, D.C.: Center for Applied Linguistics.

Fishman, J. A. (1994) Critiques of language planning: A minority language perspective. *Journal of Multilingual and Multicultural Development* 15: 91–99.

Fishman, J. A. (1993) The content of positive ethnolinguistic consciousness. *Geolinguistics* 19: 16–26.

Fishman, J. A. (1992) Forward: What can sociology contribute to the sociolinguistic enterprise? In G. Williams (ed.) *Sociolinguistics: A sociological critique.* London: Routledge. vii-ix.

Fishman, J. A. (1991) *Reversing language shift: Theoretical and empirical foundations of assistance to threatened languages.* Clevedon, Avon, UK: Multilingual Matters.

Fishman, J. (1989) *Language and ethnicity in minority sociolinguistic perspective.* Clevedon, Avon, UK: Multilingual Matters.

Fishman, J. A. (1988) Language spread and language policy for endangered languages. In P. Lowenberg (ed.) *Language spread and language policy issues: Implications and case studies.* Washington, D.C.: Georgetown University Press. 1–15.

Fishman, J. A. (1980) Prefatory notes. In P. H. Nelde (ed.) *Languages in contact and in conflict.* Wiesbaden: Steiner. xi.

Fishman, J. A. (1977a) The sociology of language yesterday, today, and tomorrow. In R. W. Cole (ed.) *Current issues in linguistic theory.* Bloomington: Indiana University Press. 51–75.

Fishman, J. A. (1977b) The spread of English as a new perspective for the study of language maintenance and language shift. In J. A. Fishman, R. L. Cooper, and A. W. Conrad (eds.) *The spread of English: The sociology of English as an additional language.* Rowley, MA: Newbury House. 108–136.

Fishman, J. A. (1972) *The sociology of language.* Rowley, MA: Newbury House.

Fishman, J. A. (1968) The sociology of language. In J. A. Fishman (ed.) *Readings in the sociology of language.* Vol. 1. The Hague: Mouton. 5–13.

Fishman, J. A. (1966) *Language loyalty in the United States: The maintenance and perpetuation of non-English mother-tongues by American ethnic and religious groups.* The Hague: Mouton.

Fishman, J. A. (1965) Language maintenance and language shift: The American immigrant case within a general theoretical perspective. *Sociologus* 16: 19–38.

Fishman, J. A. (1964) Language maintenance and language shift as a field of inquiry: A definition of the field and suggestions for its further development. *Linguistics* 9: 32–70.

Fishman, J. A., R. L. Cooper, and Y. Rosenbaum (1977) English around the world. In J. A. Fishman, R. L. Cooper, and A. Conrad (eds.) *The spread of English. The sociology of English as an additional language.* Rowley, MA: Newbury House. 77–107.

Fishman, J. A. (ed.) (2001) *Can threatened languages be saved? "Reversing language shift" revisited.* Clevedon, Avon, UK: Multilingual Matters.

Fishman, J. A. (ed.) (1974) *Advances in language planning.* The Hague: Mouton.

Fishman, J. A. (ed.) (1971) *Advances in the sociology of language.* 2 vols. The Hague: Mouton.

Fishman, J. A., A. Conrad, and A. Rubal-Lopez (eds.) (1996) *Post Imperialist English.* Berlin: Mouton de Gruyter.

Fishman, J. A., C. A. Ferguson, and J. Das Gupta (eds.) (1968) *Language problems of developing nations.* New York: Wiley.

Flege, J. E. (1990) English vowel production by Dutch talkers: More evidence for the 'similar' vs. 'new' distinction. In J. Leather and A. James (eds.) *New sounds '90. Proceedings of the 1990 Amsterdam symposium on the acquisition of second language speech.* Amsterdam: University of Amsterdam. 255–293.

Flowerdew, J. (1999) Problems in writing for scholarly publication in English: The case of Hong Kong. *Journal of Second Language Writing* 8: 253–264.

Flynn, S. (1996). A parameter-setting approach to second language acquisition. In W. C. Ritchie and T. K. Bhatia (eds.) *Handbook of second language acquisition.* New York: Academic Press. 121–158.

Flynn, S. (1988) Second language acquisition and grammatical theory. In F. Newmeyer (ed.) *Linguistics: The Cambridge Survey.* Vol. 2: *Linguistic theory extensions and implications.* Cambridge: Cambridge University Press. 53–73.

Flynn, S., G. Martohardjono, and W. O'Neill (eds.) (1998) The generative study of second language acquisition. Hillsdale, NJ: Lawrence Erlbaum.

Fodor, J. A. (1975) *The Language of Thought.* New York: Thomas Crowell.

Fodor, J. A., and B. P. McLaughlin (1990) Connectionism and the problem of systematicity: Why Smolensky's solution doesn't work. *Cognition* 35: 183–204.

Fodor, J. A., and Z. Pylyshyn (1988) Connectionism and cognitive architecture: A critical analysis. *Cognition* 28: 3–71.

Foley, J. (1991) A psycholinguistic framework for task-based approaches to language teaching. *Applied Linguistics* 12: 62–75.

Foley, J. (1990) Task-based approaches to language learning from the learner's point of view. *Language and Education* 4: 81–101.

Foltz, P. W., W. Kintsch, and T. Landauer (1998) The measurement of textual coherence with latent semantic analysis. *Discourse Processes* 25: 285–307.

Fontaine, N., and J. Leather (1992) *Kwéyòl usage and attitudes of Dominican second-formers.* Canefield, Dominica: Folk Research Institute.

Foster, P., and P. Skehan (1996) The influence of planning on performance in task-based learning. *Studies in Second Language Acquisition* 18: 299–324

Foster-Carter, A. (1985) The sociology of development. In M. Haralambos (ed.) *Sociology: New directions.* Ormskirk, UK: Causeway Press. 1–21.

Foucault, M. (1980) *Power/knowledge: Selected interviews and other writings 1972–1977.* Tr. C. Gordon. New York: Pantheon Books.

Foucault, M. (1972) *The archaeology of knowledge.* London: Tavistock.

Fowler, Y. (1997) The courtroom interpreter: Paragon *and* intruder? In S. E. Carr, R. Roberts, A. Dufour, and D. Steyn (eds.) *The critical link: Interpreters in the community.* Amsterdam: John Benjamins. 191–201.

Fox, E. (1996) Cross-language priming from ignored words: Evidence for a common representational system in bilinguals. *Journal of Memory and Language* 35: 353–370.

Francis, W. (1999) Cognitive integration of language and memory in bilinguals: Semantic representation. *Psychological Bulletin* 125: 193–222.

Frank, D. B. (1993) Political, religious, and economic factors affecting language choice in St Lucia. *International Journal of the Sociology of Language* 102: 39–56.

Frauenfelder, U., and H. Schriefers (1997) A psycholinguistic perspective on simultaneous interpretation. *Interpreting* 2: 55–89.

Frawley, W. J. (1997) *Vygotsky and cognitive science: Language and the unification of the social and computational mind.* Cambridge, MA: Harvard University Press.

Frawley, W. J., and L. P. Lantolf (1985) Second language discourse: A Vygotskyan perspective. *Applied Linguistics* 6: 19–44.

Frazier, L. (1989) Against lexical generation of syntax. In W. Marslen-Wilson (ed.) *Lexical representation and process.* Cambridge, MA: MIT Press. 505–528.

Frazier, L. (1987) Sentence processing: A tutorial review. In M. Coltheart (ed.) *Attention and performance XII: The psychology of reading.* Hillsdale, NJ: Erlbaum. 601–681.

Frazier, L., and J. Fodor (1978) The sausage machine: A new two-stage parsing model. *Cognition* 6: 1–34.

Frederiksen, N., R. J. Mislevy, and I. I. Bejar (eds.) (1993) *Test theory for a new generation of tests.* Hillsdale, NJ: Erlbaum.

Freed, B. (1995) Language learning and study abroad. In B. Freed (ed.) *Second language acquisition in a study abroad context.* Philadelphia: John Benjamins. 3–33.

Freeland, J. (ed.) (1999) *Indigenous language maintenance in Latin America.* Special Issue of *International Journal of Bilingual Education and Bilingualism* 2(3).

Freeman, D. (1998) *Doing teacher research: From inquiry to understanding.* Pacific Grove, CA: Heinle and Heinle.

Freeman, R. D. (1997) Researching gender in language use. In N. Hornberger and D. Corson (eds.) *Encyclopedia of Language and Education.* Vol. 8: *Research methods in language and education.* Dordrecht, Netherlands: Kluwer Academic. 47–56.

Freidson, E. (ed.) (1973) *The professions and their prospects.* Beverly Hills, CA: Sage.

Frenck-Mestre, C., and P. Prince (1997) Second language autonomy. *Journal of Memory and Language* 37: 481–501.

Friedlander, A. (1990) Composing in English: Effects of a first language on writing in English as a second language. In B. Kroll (ed.) *Second language writing: Research insights for the classroom.* New York: Cambridge University Press. 109–125.

Fries, C. C. (1945) *Teaching and learning English as a foreign language.* Ann Arbor, MI: University of Michigan Press.

Frost, R. (1998) Toward a strong phonological theory of visual word recognition: True issues and false trails. *Psychological Review* 123: 71–99.

Fulcher, G. (1995) Variable competence in second language acquisition: A problem for research methodology? *System* 23: 25–33.

Fullan, M. (1982) *The meaning of educational change.* New York: Columbia University, Teachers College Press.

Fusco, M. A. (1995) On teaching conference interpretation between cognate languages: Towards a workable methodology. *The Interpreters' Newsletter* 6: 93–109.

Fyle, C. M. (1994) Official and unofficial attitudes and policy towards Krio as the main language of Sierra Leone. In R. Fardon and G. Furniss (eds.) *African languages, development and the state.* London: Routledge. 44–54.

Gaarder, A. B. (1977) Language maintenance or language shift. In W. F. Mackey and T. Andersson (eds.) *Bilingualism in early childhood.* Rowley, MA: Newbury House. 409–434.

Gal, S. (1979) *Language shift: Social determinants of linguistic change in bilingual Austria.* New York: Academic Press.

Gall, M. D., W. R. Borg, and J. P. Gall. (1996) *Educational Research*. 6th ed. London: Longman.

Gambier, Y., D. Gile, and C. Taylor. (eds.) (1997) *Conference interpreting: Current trends in research*. Amsterdam: John Benjamins.

García, O. (1999) Latin America. In J. A. Fishman (ed.) *Latin America: Handbook of language and ethnic identity*. Oxford: Oxford University Press. 226–243.

García, O., and R. Otheguy (1989) *English across cultures: Cultures across English. A reader in cross-cultural communication*. Berlin: Mouton de Gruyter.

Garcia-Landa, M. (1998) A theoretical framework for oral and written translation research. *The Interpreters' Newsletter* 8: 5–40.

Gardner, R. (1998) Between speaking and listening: The vocalisation of understandings. *Applied Linguistics* 19: 204–224.

Gardner, R. C. (2000) Correlation, causation, motivation and second language acquisition. *Canadian Psychology* 41:10–24.

Gardner, R. C. (1985) *Social psychology and second language learning: The role of attitudes and motivation*. London: Edward Arnold.

Gardner, R. C., and W. E. Lambert. (1972) *Attitudes and motivation in second-language learning*. Rowley, MA: Newbury House.

Gardner, R. C., and W. E. Lambert (1959) Motivational variables in second language acquisition. *Canadian Journal of Psychology* 13: 266–272.

Gardner, R. C., and P. D. MacIntyre (1991) An instrumental motivation in language study: Who says it isn't effective? *Studies in Second Language Acquisition* 13: 57–72.

Gardner, R. C., and P. C. Smythe (1975) *Second language acquisition: A social psychological approach*. Research Bulletin No. 332, London, Canada: Department of Psychology, University of Western Ontario.

Garmendia, M.C. (1994) The linguistic normalisation process in Basque country: Data of a decade. *International Journal of the Sociology of Language* 109: 97–107.

Gass, S. M. (1997) *Input, interaction and the second language learner*. Mahwah, NJ: Lawrence Erlbaum.

Gass, S. M. (1988) Integrating research areas: A framework for second language studies. *Applied Linguistics* 9: 198–217.

Gass, S. M. (1987) The resolution of conflicts among competing systems: A bi-directional perspective. *Applied Psycholinguistics* 8: 329–350.

Gass, S. M., and J. Ard (1984) Second language acquisition and the ontology of language universals. In W. Rutherford (ed.) *Universals in second language acquisition*. Amsterdam: John Benjamins. 33–68.

Gass, S. M., and A. Mackey (2000) *Stimulated recall in second language research*. Mahwah, NJ: Lawrence Erlbaum.

Gass, S. M., and L. Selinker (1994) *Second language acquisition*. Hillsdale, NJ: Lawrence Erlbaum.

Gass, S. M., I. Svetics, and S. Lemelin (forthcoming) The differential role of attention in SLA.

Gass, S. M., and E. Varonis (1994) Input, interaction and second language production. *Studies in Second Language Acquisition Research* 16: 283–302.

Gass, S. M., and E. Varonis (1989) Incorporated repairs in NNS discourse. In M. Eisenstein (ed.) *The dynamic interlanguage*. New York: Plenum Press. 71–86.

Gass, S. M., and E. Varonis (1985) Variation in native speaker speech modification to non-native speakers. *Studies in Second Language Acquisition* 7: 37–57.

Gasser, M. (1990) Connectionism and universals of second language acquisition. *Studies in Second Language Acquisition* 12: 179–199.

Gebhard, M. (1999) Debates in SLA studies: Redefining classroom SLA as an institutional phenomenon. *TESOL Quarterly* 33: 544–557.

Geddes, M. (1986) *Fast Forward 3.* Oxford: Oxford University Press.

Geddes, M., and G. Sturtridge (1981) *Reading links.* London: Heineman.

Geddes, M., and G. Sturtridge (1979) *Listening links.* London: Heinemann.

Geddes, M., and G. Sturtridge (1978) Jigsaw listening. *Modern English Teacher* 6: 1.

Gee, J. (1996/1990) *Social linguistics and literacies: Ideology in discourses.* 2nd ed. London: Falmer.

Genesee, F. (1987) *Learning through two languages: Studies of immersion and bilingual education.* Rowley, MA: Newbury House.

Genesee, F., and J. Upshur (1996) *Classroom-based evaluation in second language education.* Cambridge: Cambridge University Press.

Genesee, F. (ed.) (1994) *Educating second language children.* Cambridge: Cambridge University Press.

Gentil, G. (2000) Language, power and identity: Insights from moral philosophy. Unpublished paper delivered at the Annual Conference of the American Association of Applied Linguistics, Vancouver, BC.

Gentzler, E. (1993) *Contemporary translation theories.* London: Routledge.

Gernsbacher, M. A., and M. Shlesinger (1997) The proposed role of suppression insimultaneous interpretation. *Interpreting* 2: 119–140.

Gersten, B. F., and C. Faltis (2000) Linking sociocultural contexts to classroom practices: Language identity in bilingual Hungarian-Slovak school in Slovakia. In H. T. Trueba and L. Bartolomé (eds.) *Immigrant Voices.* Lanham, MD: Rowen & Littlefield. 132–150.

Giambagli, A. (1998) La prise de notes peut-elle détourner d'une bonne qualité de l'écoute en interprétation consécutive [Can note-taking detract from good quality listening in consecutive interpretation]? *The Interpreters' Newsletter* 8: 121–134.

Gibbons, J. (1999) Language and the law. In W. Grabe et al. (eds.) *Annual Review of Applied Linguistics 19: Survey of applied linguistics.* New York: Cambridge University Press. 156–173.

Giles, H., R. Y. Bourhis, and D. M. Taylor (1977) Towards a theory of language in ethnic group relations. In H. Giles (ed.) *Language, ethnicity, and intergroup relations.* New York: Academic Press. 307–348.

Gill, C., and W. E. Hewitt (1996) Improving court interpreting services: What the states are doing. *State Court Journal* 20: 34–41.

Gillette, B. (1994) The role of learner goals in L2 success. In J. P. Lantolf and G. Appel (eds.) *Vygotskian approaches to second language research.* Norwood, NJ: Ablex. 195–214.

Gipps, C. (1994) *Beyond testing.* London: Falmer Press.

Givon, T. (1979) *On understanding grammar.* New York: Academic Press.

Glausinsz, J. (1997) The ecology of language (link between rainfall and language diversity). *Discover* 18: 30.

Gleitman, L. (1990) The structural sources of verb meaning. *Language Acquisition* 1: 3–55.

Glenn, C. L. (1997) The languages of immigrants. *READ Perspectives* 4: 17–58.

Glinert, L. (1998) Lexicographic function and the relation between supply and demand. *International Journal of Lexicography* 11: 111–124.

Goffman, E. (1961) *Asylums*. Garden City, NY: Doubleday.

Goffman, E. (1959) *The presentation of self in everyday life*. Garden City, NY: Doubleday.

Goh, C. (1997) Metacognitive awareness and second language listeners. *ELT Journal* 51: 361–369.

Goldsmith, J. (1976) An overview of autosegmental phonology. *Linguistic Analysis* 2: 23–68.

Goldstein, L., and S. Conrad. (1990) Student input and negotiation of meaning in ESL writing conferences. *TESOL Quarterly* 24: 443–460.

Goldstein, T. (1997) *Two languages at work: Bilingual life on the production floor*. Berlin: Mouton de Gruyter.

Gollan, T., K. I. Forster, and R. Frost. (1997) Translation priming with different scripts: Masked priming with cognates and noncognates in Hebrew-English bilinguals. *Journal of Experimental Psychology: Learning, Memory, and Cognition* 23: 1122–1139.

Gonsalves, G. E. (1999) [Report.] *Pidgins and Creoles in Education (PACE) Newsletter* 10: 1.

Gonsalves, G. E. (1996) Language policy and education reform: The case of Cape Verdean. In C. E. Walsh (ed.) *Education reform and social change: Multicultural voices, struggles and visions*. Mahwah, NJ: Lawrence Erlbaum. 31–36.

Gonzalez, A. (1989) Sociolinguistics in the Philippines. *Philippine Journal of Linguistics* 20: 57–58.

González, R. D., V. F. Vásquez, and H. Mikkelson. (1991) *Fundamentals of court interpretation*. Durham, NC: Carolina Academic Press.

Goodwin, C., and A. Duranti. (1992) Rethinking context: An introduction. In C. Goodwin and A. Duranti (eds.) *Rethinking context: Language as an interactive phenomenon*. New York: Cambridge University Press. 1–42.

Gorter, D. (1987) Surveys of the Frisian language situation: Some considerations of research methods on language maintenance and shift. *International Journal of the Sociology of Language* 68: 41–56.

Gottlob, L.R., S. D. Goldinger, G. O. Stone, and G. C. Van Orden (1999) Reading homographs: Orthographic, phonologic, and semantic dynamics. *Journal of Experimental Psychology: Human Perception and Performance* 25: 561–574.

Gouadec, D. (1994) The introduction of official computer terminology: Attestations, gallicization, normalization, assimilation. *Terminologies Nouvelles* [New Terminologies] 12 (Dec): 141–147.

Goyvaerts, D. L. (1997) Power, ethnicity, and the remarkable rise of Lingala in Bukavu, eastern Zaire. *International Journal of the Sociology of Language* 128: 25–44.

Grabau, C. M. (1996) Court interpreting: View from the bench. *State Court Journal* 20: 6–11.

Grabe, W. (2001) Reading-writing relations: Theoretical perspectives and instructional practices. In D. Belcher and A. Hirvela (eds.) *Proceedings of the Ohio State Conference on Second Language Reading/Writing Connections*. Ann Arbor: University of Michigan Press. 15–47.

Grabe, W. (2000) Reading research and its implications for reading assessment. In A. Kunnan (ed.) *Fairness and validation in language assessment.* Cambridge: Cambridge University Press. 226–262.

Grabe, W. (1999) Developments in reading research and their implications for computer-adaptive reading assessment. In M. Chaloub-DeVille (ed.) *Issues in computer-adaptive testing of reading proficiency.* Cambridge: Cambridge University Press. 11–47.

Grabe, W. (1996) Reading in an ESP Context: Dilemmas and possible solutions. *ESP Malaysia* 4: 1–28.

Grabe, W., and R. B. Kaplan (eds.) (1992) *Introduction to applied linguistics.* Reading, MA: Addison-Wesley.

Grabe, W., and F. Stoller (1997) Content-based instruction: Research foundations. In M. A. Snow and D. M. Brinton (eds.) *The content-based classroom: Perspectives on integrating language and content.* New York: Longman. 158–174.

Grabe, W. et al. (eds.) (1998) *Annual Review of Applied Linguistics 18: Foundations of second language teaching.* New York: Cambridge University Press.

Grabe, W. et al. (eds.) (1997) *Annual Review of Applied Linguistics 17: Multilingualism.* New York: Cambridge University Press.

Grabe, W. et al. (eds.) (1996) *Annual Review of Applied Linguistics 16. Technology and language.* New York: Cambridge University Press.

Graddol, D. (1997) *The future of English? A guide to forecasting the popularity of the English language in the 21st century.* London: British Council.

Gran, L., and B. Bellini (1996) Short-term memory and simultaneous interpretation: An experimental study on verbatim recall. *The Interpreters' Newsletter* 7: 103–112.

Green, A. (1998) *Verbal protocol analysis in language testing research.* Cambridge: Cambridge University Press.

Green, A., N. Schweda-Nicholson, J. Vaid, N. White, and R. Steiner (1990) Hemispheric involvement in shadowing vs. interpretation: A time-sharing study of simultaneous interpreters with matched bilingual and monolingual controls. *Brain and Language* 39: 107–133.

Green, A., J. Vaid, N. Schweda-Nicholson, N. White, N. Steiner, and R. Steiner (1994) Lateralization for shadowing vs. interpretation: A comparison of interpreters with bilingual and monolingual controls. In S. Lambert and B. Moser-Mercer (eds.) *Bridging the gap: Empirical research in simultaneous interpretation.* Amsterdam: John Benjamins. 331–355.

Green, D. W. (1998) Mental control of the bilingual lexico-semantic system. *Bilingualism: Language and Cognition* 1: 67–81.

Green, D. W. (1993) Towards a model of L2 comprehension and production. In R. Schreuder and B.Weltens (eds.) *The bilingual lexicon.* Amsterdam: John Benjamins. 249–278.

Green, D. W. (1986) Control, activation, and resource: A framework and a model for the control, of speech in bilinguals. *Brain and Language* 27: 210–223.

Green, J. M., and R. L. Oxford (1995) A closer look at learning strategies, L2 proficiency, and gender. *TESOL Quarterly* 29: 263–297.

Green, S. (1994) *Principles of biopsychology.* Hove, UK: Erlbaum.

Greenberg, J. (1991) Typology/universals and second language acquisition. In T. Huebner and C. A. Ferguson (eds.) *Crosscurrents in second language acquisition and linguistic theories.* Amsterdam: John Benjamins. 37–43.

Greene, J. P. (1998) *A meta-analysis of the effectiveness of bilingual education.* Claremont, CA: Tomas Rivera Policy Institute.

Gregg, K. R. (1996) The logical and developmental problems of second language acquisition. In W. C. Ritchie and T. Bhatia (eds.) *Handbook of second language acquisition.* San Diego: Academic Press. 49–81.

Gregg, K. R. (1991) The Variable Competence Model of second language acquisition and why it isn't. *Applied Linguistics* 11: 364–83.

Gregg, K. R. (1989) Second language acquisition theory: The case for a generative perspective. In S. Gass and J. Schachter (eds.) *Linguistic perspectives on second language acquisition.* Cambridge: Cambridge University Press. 15–40.

Gregg, K., M. H. Long, G. Jordan, and A. Beretta. (1997) Rationality and its discontents in SLA. *Applied Linguistics* 18: 538–558.

Gregorc, A. F. (1979) Learning/teaching styles: Potent forces behind them. *Educational Leadership* 16: 234–236.

Grenoble, L. A., and L. J. Whaley. (1998) *Endangered languages: Current issues and future prospects.* Cambridge: Cambridge University Press.

Grice, H. P. (1975) Logic and conversation. In P. Cole and J. L. Morgan (eds.) *Syntax and semantics: Speech acts.* New York: Academic Press. 41–58.

Grillo, R. (1989) Anthropology, language, politics. *Sociological Review Monograph* 36: 1–24. [*Social Anthropology and the Politics of Language.*]

Grimes, B. (ed.) (1999) *Ethnologue: Languages of the world.* 13th ed. Dallas: Summer Institute of Linguistics.

Grin, F. (1996) The economics of language: Survey assessment, prospects. *International Journal of the Sociology of Language* 121: 17–44.

Grishman, R. C., C. Macleod, and A. Meyers (1994) Complex syntax: Building a computational lexicon. In Proceedings of the 15th International Conference on Computational Linguistics [COLING '94]. Kyoto, Japan. 268–272.

Grosjean, F. (2001) The bilingual's language modes. In J. L. Nicol (ed.) *One mind, two languages: Bilingual language processing.* Cambridge, MA: Blackwell. 1–22.

Grosjean, F. (1998) Studying bilinguals: Methodological and conceptual issues. *Bilingualism: Language and Cognition* 1: 131–149.

Grosjean, F. (1997a) Processing mixed language: Issues, findings, and models. In A. M. B. De Groot and J. F. Kroll (eds.) *Tutorials in bilingualism: Psycholinguistic perspectives.* Mahwah, NJ: Lawrence Erlbaum. 225–254.

Grosjean, F. (1997b) The bilingual individual. *Interpreting* 2: 163–187.

Grosjean, F. (1988) Exploring the recognition of guest words in bilingual speech. *Language and Cognitive Processes* 3: 233–274.

Grove, C. D. (1999). The Official English debate in the United States Congress: A critical analysis. Ph.D. diss., University of Washington, Seattle.

Guba, E. G., and Y. S. Lincoln (1994) Competing paradigms in qualitative research. In N. K. Denzin and Y. S. Lincoln (eds.) *Handbook of qualitative research.* Thousand Oaks, CA: Sage. 105–117.

Gubertini, M. C. P. (1998) Des ajouts en interprétation. Pourquoi pas? [Additions in interpretation. Why not?] *The Interpreters' Newsletter* 8: 135–149.

Guerrero, M. (1997) Spanish language academic language proficiency: The case of bilingual education teachers in the U.S. *Bilingual Research Journal* 21: 65–84.

Guilford, J. (1997) The attitudes of French youth toward English loan words. *Linguistique* [*Linguistics*] 33: 117–135.

Gumperz, J. (1983) *Discourse strategies.* Cambridge: Cambridge University Press.

Gumperz, J. J., and R. Wilson. (1971) Convergence and creolization: A case from the IndoAryan/Dravidian border. In D. Hymes (ed.) *Pidginization and creolization of languages.* Cambridge: Cambridge University Press. 151–168.

Gunnarsson, B.-L. (1997) Applied discourse analysis. In T. A. Van Dijk (ed.) *Discourse as social interaction.* Thousand Oaks, CA: Sage. 285–312.

Gunnarsson, B.-L., P. Linell, and B. Nordberg (eds.) (1997) *The construction of professional discourse.* London: Longman.

Gutiérrez, K. (1993) How talk context and script shape contexts for learning: A cross case comparison of journal sharing. *Linguistics and Education* 5: 335–365.

Gutiérrez, K., P. Baquedano-Lopes, and C. Tejada (1999) Rethinking diversity: Hybridity and hybrid language practices in the third space. *Mind, Culture and Activity* 6: 286–303.

Gutiérrez, K., and J. Larson. (1994) Language borders: Recitation as hegemonic discourse. *International Journal of Education Reform* 3: 22–36.

Haarmann, H. (1990) Language planning in the light of a general theory of language: A methodological framework. *International Journal of the Sociology of Language* 86: 103–126.

Haarmann, H. (1980) *Multilingualismus 2: Elemente einer Sprachökologie* [Elements of an ecology of language]. 2 vols. Tübingen: Narr.

Hadfield, J. (1987) *Advanced communicative games.* Walton-upon-Thames, UK: Nelson.

Haertel, E. H. (1984) An application of latent class models for assessment data. *Applied Psychological Measurement* 8: 333–346.

Hale, K., and S. J. Keyser (1993) On argument structure and the lexical expression of syntactic relations. In K. Hale and S. J. Keyser (eds.) *The view from Building 20: Essays in linguistics in honor of Sylvain Bromberger.* Cambridge, MA: MIT Press. 53–110.

Hale, S. (1997) The treatment of register variation in court interpreting. *Translator* 3: 39–54.

Hall, C. (1995) Formal linguistics and mental representation: Psycholinguistic contributions to the identification and explanation of morphological and syntactic competence. *Language and Cognitive Processes* 10: 169–187.

Hall, J. K. (1998) Differential teacher attention to student utterances: The construction of different opportunities for learning in the IRF. *Linguistics and Education* 9: 287–311.

Hall, J. K. (1995) "Aw, man, where you goin'?" Classroom interaction and the development of L2 interactional competence. *Issues in Applied Linguistics* 6: 37–62.

Hall, S. (1996) Introduction: Who needs 'identity'? In S. Hall and P. Du Gay (eds.) *Questions of cultural identity.* London: Sage. 1–17.

Halliday, M. A. K. (1978) *Language as social semiotic: The social interpretation of language and meaning.* London: Edward Arnold.

Halliday, M. A. K., A. McIntosh, and P. Strevens. (1964) *The linguistics sciences and language teaching.* London: Longman.

Hamel, R. E. (1997a) Language conflict and language shift: A sociolinguistic framework for linguistic human rights. *International Journal of the Sociology of Language* 127: 105–134.

Hamel, R. E. (ed.) (1997b) *Linguistic human rights from a sociolinguistic perspective.* Special Issue of *International Journal of the Sociology of Language* 127.

Hamel, R. E. (1986) Language policy and interethnic conflict. Sociolinguistic research issues. *Escritos [Writing]* 1(2): 7–36.

Hamp-Lyons, L. (2001) Fourth generation writing assessment. In T. Silva and P. Matsuda (eds.) *On second language writing.* Mahwah, NJ: Erlbaum. 117–127.

Hamp-Lyons, L. (1991a) Pre-text: Task-related influences on the writer. In L. Hamp-Lyons (ed.) *Assessing second language writing in academic contexts.* Norwood, NJ: Ablex. 97–107.

Hamp-Lyons, L. (1991b) Reconstructing "academic writing proficiency." In L. Hamp-Lyons (ed.) *Assessing second language writing in academic contexts.* Norwood, NJ: Ablex. 127–153.

Hamp-Lyons, L., and W. Condon (1993) Questioning assumptions about portfolio-based assessment. *College Composition and Communication* 44: 176–190.

Haneda, M. (1997) Second language learning in a 'community of practice': A case study of adult Japanese learners. *Canadian Modern Language Review* 54: 11–27.

Hannahs, S. J., and M. Young-Scholten (eds.) (1997) *Focus on phonological acquisition.* Philadelphia: John Benjamins.

Hansen, M. (1999) *Historical summary of the Unz Initiative.* MA thesis, Brigham Young University, Provo, UT.

Harklau, L. (2000) From the "good kids" to the "worst": Representations of English language learners across educational settings. *TESOL Quarterly* 34: 35–67.

Harklau, L. (1999) Representing culture in the ESL writing classroom. In E. Hinkel (ed.) *Culture in second language teaching and learning.* Cambridge: Cambridge University Press. 109–130.

Harklau, L. (1994) ESL versus mainstream classes: Contrasting L2 learning environments. *TESOL Quarterly* 28: 241–272.

Harley, B. (1993) Instructional strategies and second language acquisition in French immersion. *Studies in Second Language Acquisition* 15: 245–259.

Harley, B. (1989) Transfer in the written compositions of French immersion students. In H. Dechert and M. Raupach (eds.) *Transfer in language production.* Norwood, NJ: Ablex. 3–19.

Harley, B. (1984) The interlanguage of immersion students and its implications for second language teaching. In A. Davies, C. Criper, and A. Howatt (eds.) *Interlanguage.* Edinburgh: Edinburgh University Press. 291–311.

Harré, R., J. Brockmeier, and P. Mühlhäusler (1999) *Greenspeak.* Beverley Hills, CA: Sage.

Harrington, M. (forthcoming) Sentence processing. In P. J. Robinson (ed.) *Cognition and second language instruction.* Cambridge: Cambridge University Press.

Harrington, M. (1987) Processing strategies as a source of interlanguage variation. *Applied Psycholinguistics* 8: 351–378.

Harris, S. (1994) Ideological exchanges in British magistrates courts. In J. Gibbons (ed.) *Language and the law.* London: Longman. 156–170.

Harris, S., and F. Bargiela-Chiappini (1997) The languages of business: Introduction and overview. In F. Bargiela-Chiappini and S. Harris (eds.) *The languages of business: An international perspective.* Edinburgh: Edinburgh University Press. 1–18.

Hart-Landsberg, S., and S. Reder (1997) Teamwork and literacy: Teaching and learning at Hardy Industries. In G. Hull (ed.) *Changing work, changing workers: Critical perspectives on language, literacy, and skills.* Albany: State University of New York Press. 350–382.

Hassall, T. J. (1997) Requests by Australian learners of Indonesian. Ph.D. diss. Australian National University, Canberra.

Hatch, E. M. (1992) *Discourse and language education.* Cambridge: Cambridge University Press.

Hatch, E. M. (1983) *Psycholinguistics: A second language approach.* Rowley, MA: Newbury House.

Hatch, E. M. (ed.) (1978) *Second language acquisition.* Rowley, MA: Newbury House.

Hatch, E. M., and A. Lazaraton (1991) *The research manual: Design and statistics for applied linguistics.* Boston: Newbury House.

Hatch, E. M., and M. Long (1980) Discourse analysis: What's that? In D. Larsen-Freeman (ed.) *Discourse analysis in second language research.* Rowley, MA: Newbury House. 1–40.

Haugen, E. (1983) The implementation of corpus planning: Theory and practice. In J. Cobarrubias and J. A. Fishman (eds.) *Progress in language planning.* Berlin: Mouton. 269–289

Haugen, E. (1972) *The ecology of language.* Stanford, CA: Stanford University Press.

Haugen, E. (1966a) *Language planning and language conflict: The case of modern Norwegian.* Cambridge, MA: Harvard University Press.

Haugen, E. (1966b) Linguistics and language planning. In W. Bright (ed.) *Sociolinguistics: Proceedings of the UCLA Sociolinguistics Conference, 1964.* Janua Linguarum, Series Maior, 20. The Hague: Mouton. 50–71.

Hawkins, E. (1987) *Awareness of language: An introduction.* Rev. ed. Cambridge: Cambridge University Press.

Hazäel-Massieux, M.-C. (1993) *Ecrire en créole* [Writing in Creole]. Paris: l'Harmattan.

Heath, S. B. (2000) Linguistics in the study of language in education. *Harvard Educational Review* 70: 49–59.

Heath, S. B. (1982) What no bedtime story means: Narrative skills at home and school. *Language in Society* 11: 49–77.

Heath, S. B. (1972) *Telling tongues: Language policy in Mexico. Colony to nation.* New York: Teachers College Press.

Hegelheimer, V. (1998) Effects of textual glosses and sentence-level audio glosses on reading comprehension and vocabulary recall. Ph.D. diss., University of Illinois, Urbana.

Heh, Y.-C. (W), and Q. Hu (1997) Over-the-phone interpretation: A new way of communication between speech communities. In M. Jérôme-O'Keeffe (ed.) *Proceedings of the 1997 American Translators Association Annual Conference.* Medford, NJ: Information Today, 51–62.

Heinz, P. (1993) Towards enhanced, authentic second language reading comprehension assessment, research, and theory building: The development and analysis of an automated recall protocol scoring system. Ph.D. diss., Ohio State University, Columbus.

Heller, M. (1999) *Linguistic minorities and modernity: A sociolinguistic ethnography.* London: Longman.

Hendry, B. (1997) Constructing linguistic and ethnic boundaries in a Basque borderland: Negotiating identity in Rioja Alavesa, Spain. *Language Problems & Language Planning* 21: 216–233.

Henning, G. (1987) *A guide to language testing: Development, evaluation, research.* New York: Newbury House.

Henriques, J., W. Hollway, C. Urwin, C. Venn, and V. Walkerdine (1984) *Changing the subject.* New York: Methuen.

Henry, J. (1997) The Louisiana French movement: Actors and actions in social change. In A. Valdman (ed.) *French and Creole in Louisiana.* New York: Plenum. 183–213.

Henze, R., and K. A. Davis (eds.) (1999) *Authenticity and identity: Lessons from indigenous language education.* Special Issue of *Anthropology and Education Quarterly* 30(1).

Hermans, D. (2000) Language production in bilinguals. Ph.D. diss., University of Nijmegen Netherlands.

Hermans, D., T. Bongaerts, K. de Bot, and R. Schreuder (1998) Producing words in a foreign language: Can speakers prevent interference from their first language? *Bilingualism: Language and Cognition* 1: 213–229.

Hewitt, W. E. (2000) *Language interpreting over the telephone: A primer for court policy makers and managers.* Williamsburg, VA: National Center for State Courts.

Hewitt, W. E. (1997) Letter announcing the National Center for State Courts' Court Telephone Interpretation Service, May 15. Williamsburg, VA: National Center for State Courts.

Hewitt, W. E., and R. J. Lee (1996) Beyond the language barrier, or "You say you were eating an orange?" *State Court Journal* 20: 23–31.

Hill, J., and K. Hill (1986) *Speaking Mexicano: Dynamics of syncretic language in central Mexico.* Tucson: University of Arizona Press.

Hill, T. (1997) The development of pragmatic competence in an EFL context. Ph.D. diss., Temple University Japan, Tokyo.

Hinkel, E. (ed.) (1999) *Culture in second language teaching and learning.* Cambridge: Cambridge University Press.

Hinton, L. (1998) Language loss and revitalization in California: Overview. *International Journal of the Sociology of Language* 132: 83–93.

Hintzman, D. L. (1993) Twenty-five years of learning and memory: Was the cognitive revolution a mistake? In D. E. Meyer and S. Kornblum (eds.) *Attention and performance XIV.* Cambridge, MA: MIT Press. 359–391.

Ho M.-L., and J. Platt (1993) *Dynamics of a contact continuum: Singaporean English.* Oxford: Oxford University Press.

Hockett, C. (1961/1966) The problem of universals in language. In J. Greenberg (ed.) *Universals of language.* Cambridge, MA: MIT Press. 1–29.

Hoey, M. (1991) Some properties of spoken discourses. In R. Bowers and C. J. Brumfit (eds.) *Applied linguistics and English language teaching.* London: Modern English Publications in association with the British Council. 65–84.

Hoffman, R. R. (1997) The cognitive psychology of expertise and the domain of interpreting. *Interpreting* 2: 189–230.

Hofstede, G. (1986) Cultural differences in teaching and learning. *International Journal of International Relations* 10: 301–320.

Hofstede, G. (1980) *Culture's consequences: International differences in work-related values.* Beverly Hills, CA: Sage.

Holland, D., W. Lachiotte, D. Skinner, and C. Cain (1998) *Identity and agency in cultural worlds.* Cambridge, MA: Harvard University Press.

Holliday, A. (1999) Small cultures. *Applied Linguistics* 20: 237–264.

Holliday, A. (1994) *Appropriate methodology and social context.* Cambridge: Cambridge University Press.

Holm, J. (1989) *Pidgins and creoles.* Vol. 2: *Reference survey.* Cambridge: Cambridge University Press.

Holm, J. (1988) *Pidgins and creoles.* Cambridge: Cambridge University Press.

Holmes, J. (1997) Keeping tabs on language shift in New Zealand: Some methodological considerations. *Journal of Multilingual and Multicultural Development* 18: 17–39.

Hornberger, N. H. (1998) Language policy, language education, language rights: Indigenous, immigrant, and international perspectives. *Language in Society* 27: 439–458.

Hornberger, N. H. (1997) Literacy, language maintenance, and linguistic human rights: Three telling cases. *International Journal of the Sociology of Language* 127: 87–103.

Hornberger, N. H. (1989) Can Peru's rural schools be agents for Quechua language maintenance? *Journal of Multilingual and Multicultural Development* 10: 145–159.

Hornberger, N. H. (1988) *Bilingual education and language maintenance: A Southern Peruvian Quechua case.* Berlin: Mouton.

Hornberger, N. H., and K. A. King (2000) Reversing Quechua language shift in South America. In J. A. Fishman (ed.) *Can threatened languages be saved?: "Reversing language shift" revisited: A 21st century perspective.* Clevedon, Avon, UK: Multilingual Matters. 166–194.

Hornberger, N. H., and K. A. King (1996) Language revitalisation in the Andes: Can the schools reverse language shift? *Journal of Multilingual and Multicultural Development* 17: 427–441.

Hornberger, N. H. (ed.) (1996) *Indigenous literacies in the Americas: Language planning from the bottom up.* Berlin: Mouton de Gruyter.

Hornberger, N. H., and D. Corson (eds.) (1997) *Encyclopedia of Language and Education.* Vol. 8: *Research methods in language and education.* Dordrecht, Netherlands: Kluwer Academic.

Hornstein, N., and D. Lightfoot (eds.) (1981) *Explanation in linguistics: The logical problem of language acquisition.* London: Longman.

Horwitz, E. K., and D. J. Young (1991) *Language anxiety: From theory and research to classroom practice.* Englewood Cliffs, NJ: Prentice Hall.

Houck, N., and S. M. Gass (1996) Non-native refusals: A methodological study. In S. M. Gass and J. Neu (eds.) *Speech acts across cultures: Challenge to communication in a second language.* Berlin: Mouton de Gruyter. 45–64.

House, J. (1996) Developing pragmatic fluency in English as a foreign language: Routines and metapragmatic awareness. *Studies in Second Language Acquisition* 17: 225–252.

Howatt, A. P. R. (1984) *A history of English language teaching.* Oxford: Oxford University Press.

Howson, C., and P. Urbach (1989) *Scientific reasoning: The Bayesian approach.* La Salle, IL: Open Court.

Hsu, J. (1994) Computer assisted language learning (CALL): The effect of ESL students' use of interactional modifications on listening comprehension. Ph.D. diss., Iowa State University, Ames.

Hudelson, S. (2000) Developing a framework for writing in dual language settings. In J. Tinajero and R. A. DeVillar (eds.) *The power of two languages 2000.* New York: McGraw-Hill. 9–19.

Hudelson, S., and I. Serna (1994) Beginning literacy in English in a whole language bilingual program. In A. Flurkey and R. Meyer (eds.) *Under the whole language umbrella: Many cultures, many voices.* Urbana, IL: National Council of Teachers of English. 278–294.

Hull, G. (ed.) (1997) *Changing work, changing workers: Critical perspectives on language, literacy, and skills.* Albany: State University of New York Press.

Hulsen, M. (2000) Between two worlds: Social networks, language shift and language processing in three generations of Dutch migrants in New Zealand. Ph.D. diss., University of Nijmegen, Netherlands.

Hulstijn, J. H. (1990) A comparison between information processing and the analysis/control approach to language learning. *Applied Linguistics* 11: 30–45.

Hulstijn, J. H., and R. DeKeyser. (eds.) (1997) *Testing SLA theory in the research laboratory.* Special issue of *Studies in Second Language Acquisition* 19(2).

Hulstijn, J. H., and W. Hulstijn (1984) Grammatical errors as a function of processing constraints and explicit knowledge. *Language Learning* 34: 23–43.

Humboldt, W. von (1836/1988) *On language.* Cambridge: Cambridge University Press.

[Hungarian Ministry of Education.] (1995.) *Nemzeti alaptanterv* [National core curriculum]. Budapest: Hungarian Ministry of Education.

[Hungarian Ministry of Education.] (1992.) *Nemzeti alaptanterv* [National core curriculum]. Budapest: Hungarian Ministry of Culture and Education.

[Hungarian Ministry of Education.] (1990). Nemzeti alaptanterv [National core curriculum]. First Draft. Elsō fogalmazvány. Székesfehérvár. [Manuscript.]

Hunter, J. (1997) Multiple perceptions: Social identity in a multilingual elementary classroom. *TESOL Quarterly* 31: 603–611.

Hutchins, W. J., and H. L. Somers (1992) *An introduction to machine translation.* London: Academic Press.

Hyden, L.-C., and E. Mishler (1999) Language and medicine. In W. Grabe et al. (eds.) *Annual review of applied linguistics, 19: Survey of applied linguistics.* New York: Cambridge University Press. 174–192.

Hyland, F. (1998) The impact of teacher-written feedback on individual writers. *Journal of Second Language Writing* 7: 255–286.

Hyland, K. (1999) Disciplinary discourses: Writer stance in research articles. In C. Candlin and K. Hyland (eds.) *Writing: Text, processes and practices.* New York: Longman. 99–121.

Hyltenstam, K., and C. Stroud (1996) Language maintenance. In H. Göble, P. H. Nelde, A. Starý, and W. Wölck *Contact linguistics: An international handbook of contemporary research.* Berlin: Walter de Gruyter. 567–578.

Hymes, D. (1994) The concept of communicative competence revisited. In M. Pütz (ed.) *Thirty years of linguistic evolution.* Amsterdam: John Benjamins. 31–58.

Hymes, D. (1972) On communicative competence. In J. Pride and J. Holmes (eds.) *Sociolinguistics.* Harmondsworth, UK: Penguin. 269–293.

Hymes, D. (1971a) Competence and performance in linguistic theory. In R. Huxley and E. Ingram (eds.) *Language acquisition: Models and methods.* London: Academic Press. 3–28.

Hymes, D. (1971b) *On communicative competence.* Philadelphia: University of Pennsylvania Press.

Hymes, D. (1967) Models of the interaction of language and social setting. *Journal of Social Issues* 23: 8–38.

Iaccino, J. F. (1993) *Left brain-right brain differences: Inquiries, evidence, and new approaches.* Hillsdale, NJ: Lawrence Erlbaum.

Ibrahim, A. (1999) Becoming Black: Rap and hip-hop, race, gender, identity and the politics of ESL learning. *TESOL Quarterly* 33: 349–370.

Ijaz, I. H. (1986) Linguistic and cognitive determinants of lexical acquisition in a second language. *Language Learning* 36: 401–451.

ILEA Afro-Caribbean Language and Literacy Project in Further and Adult Education (1990) *Language and power.* London: Harcourt Brace Jovanovich.

Inglehart, R. F., and M. Woodward (1972) Language conflicts and political community. In P. P. Giglioli (ed.) *Language and social context.* Baltimore: Penguin. 358–377.

Irvine, J. (1982) Language and affect. In H. Byrnes (ed.) *Contemporary perceptions of language.* Washington, DC: Georgetown University Press. 31–47.

Itô, J. (1986) Syllable theory in prosodic phonology. Ph.D. diss., University of Massachusetts, Amherst.

Ivanič, R. (1998) *Writing and identity: The discoursal construction of identity in academic writing.* Amsterdam: John Benjamins.

Jääskeläinen, R. (1989) Translation assignment in professional vs. non-professional translation: A think-aloud protocol study. In C. Séguinot (ed.) *The translation process.* Toronto, Canada: H. G. Publications, School of Translation, York University. 87–98.

Jackendoff, R. S. (1992) Mme Tussaud meets the Binding theory. *Natural Language and Linguistic Inquiry* 10: 1–31.

Jackendoff, R. S. (1990) *Semantic structures.* Cambridge, MA: MIT Press.

Jackson, Q. (1995) *Doing social research methods.* Scarboro, Ontario, Canada: Prentice Hall.

Jackson, P. W. (ed.) (1992) *Handbook of research on curriculum: A project of the American Educational Research Association.* New York: Macmillan.

Jacobson, R. and C. Faltis. (eds.) (1990) *Language distribution issues in bilingual school.* Clevedon, Avon, UK: Multilingual Matters.

James, C. T. (1975) The role of semantic information in lexical decisions. *Journal of Experimental Psychology: Human Perception and Performance* 1: 130–136.

Jamieson, J., and C. Chapelle (1987) Working styles on computers as evidence of second language learning strategies. *Language Learning* 37: 523–544.

Janks, H. (1997) Teaching language and power. In R. Wodak and D. Corson (eds.) *Encyclopedia of Language and Education.* Vol. 1: *Language policy and political issues in education.* Dordrecht, Netherland: Kluwer Academic. 241–252.

Janney, R., and H. Arndt (1993) Universality and relativity in cross-cultural politeness research: A historical perspective. *Multilingua* 12: 13–50.

January, A. (1996) An interactional analysis of an L2 jigsaw reading activity. MA thesis, San Diego State University, CA.

Jarvis, S. (1998) *Conceptual transfer in the interlanguage lexicon*. Bloomington: Indiana University Linguistics Club.

Jarvis, S., and T. Odlin (2000) Morphological type, spatial reference, and language transfer. *Studies in Second Language Acquisition* 22: 535–556.

Jensen, C., and C. Hansen (1995) The effect of prior knowledge on EAP listening test performance. *Language Testing* 12: 99–119.

Jernudd, B. H. (1971) Social change and Aboriginal speech variation in Australia. *Anthropological Linguistics* 13: 16–32.

Jernudd, B. H., and J. Das Gupta (1971) Towards a theory of language planning. In J. Rubin and B. H. Jernudd (eds.) *Can language be planned? Sociolinguistic theory and practice for developing nations*. Honolulu: University Press of Hawai'i. 195–216.

Jescheniak, J. D., and K. I. Schriefers (1998) Discrete serial versus cascading processing in lexical access in speech production: Further evidence from the coactivation of near-synonyms. *Journal of Experimental Psychology: Learning, Memory, and Cognition* 24: 1256–1274.

Jiang, N. (1999) Testing processing explanations for the asymmetry in masked cross-language priming. *Bilingualism: Language and Cognition* 2: 59–75.

Jin, H. G. (1994) Topic prominence and subject prominence in L2 acquisition. *Language Learning* 44: 101–122.

Johns, A. M. (1997) *Text, role and context: Developing academic literacies*. Cambridge: Cambridge University Press.

Johns, A. M. (1991a) English for specific purposes (ESP): Its history and contributions. In M. Celce-Murcia (ed.) *Teaching English as a second or foreign language*. Boston: Heinle and Heinle. 67–78.

Johns, A. M. (1991b) Interpreting an English competency examination: The frustrations of an ESL science student. *Written Communication* 8: 379–401.

Johns, A. M. (ed.) (2001) *Genre and pedagogy: Research and practice*. Mahwah, NJ: Lawrence Erlbaum.

Johns, A. M., and T. Dudley-Evans (1991) English for special purposes: International in scope, specific in purpose. *TESOL Quarterly* 25: 297–315.

Johnson, D. M. (1992) *Approaches to research in second language learning*. New York: Longman.

Johnson, J., and E. Newport (1989) Critical period effects in second language learning: The influence of maturational state on the acquisition of English as a second language. *Cognitive Psychology* 21: 60–90.

Johnson, K. (1996) *Language teaching and skill learning*. Oxford: Blackwell.

Johnson, K. (1979) Communicative approaches and communicative processes. In C. J. Brumfit and K. Johnson (eds.) *The communicative approach to language teaching*. Oxford: Oxford University Press. 195–205.

Johnson, R. K. (ed.) (1989) *The second language curriculum*. Cambridge: Cambridge University Press.

Johnson, R. K., and M. Swain. (eds.) (1997) *Immersion education: International perspectives*. Cambridge: Cambridge University Press.

Johnstone, B. (2000) *Qualitative methods in sociolinguistics*. New York: Oxford University Press.

Jones, A. (1994) The limits of voice identification. In J. Gibbons (ed.) *Language and the law*. London: Longman. 346–361.

Jones, M. C. (1998) Death of a language, birth of an identity: Brittany and the Bretons. *Language Problems & Language Planning* 22: 129–142.

Joseph, C. M. B. (1997) Haitian Creole in New York. In O. García and J. A. Fishman (eds.) *The multilingual apple: Language in New York City.* Berlin: Mouton de Gruyter. 281–299.

Judd, E. (1992) Language-in-education policy and planning. In W. Grabe and R. B. Kaplan (eds.) *Introduction to applied linguistics.* Reading, MA: Addison-Wesley. 169–188.

Juffs, A. (2000) An overview of the second language acquisition of the links between verb semantics and morpho-syntax. In J. Archibald (ed.) *Second language acquisition and linguistic theory.* Oxford: Blackwells. 187–227.

Juffs, A. (1998a) Some effects of first language argument structure and morphosyntax on second language sentence processing. *Second Language Research* 14: 406–424.

Juffs, A. (1998b) Main verb versus reduced relative clause ambiguity resolution in L2 sentence processing. *Language Learning* 48: 107–147.

Juffs, A. (1996) *Learnability and the lexicon: Theories and second language acquisition research.* Amsterdam: John Benjamins.

Juffs, A., and M. Harrington (1996) Garden path sentences and error data in second language sentence processing. *Language Learning* 46: 283–326.

Juffs, A., and M. Harrington (1995) Parsing effects in L2 sentence processing: Subject and object asymmetries in WH-extraction. *Studies in Second Language Acquisition* 17: 483–512.

Juffs, A., T. W. Talpas, G. Mizera, and B. Burtt (eds.) (2000) *Proceedings of GASLA IV.* Working Papers in Linguistics. Pittsburgh: University of Pittsburgh.

Jupp, T., C. Roberts, and J. Cook-Gumperz (1982) Language and disadvantage: The hidden process. In J. J. Gumperz (ed.) *Language and social identity.* Cambridge: Cambridge University Press. 232–256.

Kachru, B. B. (1988) The spread of English and sacred linguistic cows. In P. Lowenberg (ed.) *Language spread and language policy issues: Implications and case studies.* Georgetown University Round Table on Languages and Linguistics. Washington, D.C.: Georgetown University Press. 207–228.

Kachru, B. B. (1986) *The alchemy of English: The spread, functions and models of non-native Englishes.* Oxford: Pergamon.

Kachru, B. B. (1982) *The Indianization of English.* New Delhi: Oxford University Press.

Kachru, B. B. (ed.) (1992) *The other tongue: English across cultures.* 2nd ed. Urbana: University of Illinois Press.

Kahle, J. B., and M. K. Lakes (1983) The myth of equality in science classrooms. *Journal of Research in Science Teaching* 20: 131–140.

Kalat, J. W. (1995) *Biological psychology.* Pacific Grove, CA: Brooks/Cole.

Kamide, Y., and D. C. Mitchell (1999) Incremental pre-head attachment in Japanese parsing. *Language and Cognitive Processes* 14: 631–662.

Kamwangamalu, N. M. (1997) Multilingualism and education policy in post-apartheid South Africa. *Language Problems & Language Planning* 21: 234–253.

Kanagy, R., and K. Igarashi (1997) Acquisition of pragmatic competence in a Japanese immersion kindergarten. In L. F. Bouton and Y. Kachru (eds.) *Pragmatics and language learning.* Urbana-Champaign: University of Illinois, Division of English as an International Language [DEIL]. 8: 243–265.

Kanno, Y. (1996) There's no place like home: Japanese returnees' identities in transition. Ph.D. diss., University of Toronto, Canada.

Kaplan, R. B. (2000) Applied Linguistics: (Yesterday,) Today and Tomorrow. *Selected papers from AILA '99 Tokyo*. Tokyo: Waseda University Press.

Kaplan, R. B. (1992) Applied linguistics and language policy and planning. In W. Grabe and R. B. Kaplan (eds.) *Introduction to applied linguistics*. Reading, MA: Addison-Wesley. 143–165.

Kaplan, R. B. (1990) Concluding essay: On applied linguistics and discourse analysis. In R. B. Kaplan et al. (eds.) *Annual Review of Applied Linguistics 11: Discourse analysis*. New York: Cambridge University Press. 199–204.

Kaplan, R. B. (1966) Cultural thought patterns in intercultural education. *Language Learning* 16: 1–20.

Kaplan, R. B., and R. B. Baldauf, Jr. (1997a) *Language planning from practice to theory*. Clevedon, Avon, UK: Multilingual Matters.

Kaplan, R. B., and R. B. Baldauf, Jr. (1997b) Language planning processes. In *Language planning from practice to theory*. Clevedon, Avon, UK: Multilingual Matters. 87–121.

Kaplan, R. B., and W. Grabe. (2000) Applied linguistics and the *Annual review of applied linguistics*. In William Grabe et al. (eds.) *Annual Review of Applied Linguistics 20: Applied linguistics as an emerging discipline*. New York: Cambridge University Press. 3–17.

Kaplan, R. B., and H. G. Widdowson (in preparation) Applied linguistics. In William Frawley et al. (eds.) *International Encyclopedia of Linguistics*. 2nd ed. New York: Oxford University Press.

Kaplan, R. B., and H. G. Widdowson (1992) Applied linguistics: An overview. In W. Bright, (ed.) *International encyclopedia of linguistics*. 4 Vols. Oxford: Oxford University Press. 1: 76–80

Kaplan, R. B. (ed.) (1980) *On the scope of applied linguistics*. Rowley, MA: Newbury House.

Kaplan, R. B., and R. B. Baldauf Jr. (eds.) (1999) *Language planning in Malawi, Mozambique and the Philippines*. Clevedon, Avon, UK: Multilingual Matters.

Kaplan, R. B., et al. (eds.) (1981) *Annual Review of Applied Linguistics 1. 1980*. Rowley, MA: Newbury House.

Karavas-Doukas, E. (1996) Using attitude scales to investigate teachers' attitudes to the communicative approach. *ELT Journal* 50: 187–198.

Karmiloff-Smith, A. (1994) Innate constraints and developmental change. In P. Bloom (ed.) *Language Acquisition*. Cambridge, MA: MIT Press. 563–590.

Kashoki, M. E. (1982) Achieving nationhood through language: The challenge of Namibia. *Third World Quarterly* 4: 182–190.

Kasper, G. (1998) Analyzing verbal protocols. *TESOL Quarterly* 32: 358–362.

Kasper, G. (1997) Beyond reference. In G. Kasper and E. Kellerman (eds.) *Communication strategies: Psycholinguistic and sociolinguistic perspectives*. London: Longman. 345–360.

Kasper, G. (1992) Pragmatic transfer. *Second Language Research* 8: 203–231.

Kasper, G., and M. Dahl. (1991) Research methods in interlanguage pragmatics. *Studies in Second Language Acquisition* 13: 215–247.

Kasper, G., and K. R. Rose (1999) Pragmatics and SLA. In W. Grabe et al. (eds.) *Annual*

Review of Applied Linguistics 19: A Survey of applied linguistics. New York: Cambridge University Press. 81–104.

Kasper, G., and R. Schmidt (1996) Developmental issues in interlanguage pragmatics. *Studies in Second Language Acquisition* 18: 149–169.

Kasper, G., and S. Blum-Kulka (eds.) (1993) *Interlanguage pragmatics.* New York: Oxford University Press.

Kasper, G., and R. Grotjahn (eds.) (1991) *Methods in second language research.* Special issue of *Studies in Second Language Acquisition* 13(2).

Kasper, G., and E. Kellerman. (eds.) (1997) *Communication strategies: Psycholinguistic and sociolinguistic perspectives.* London: Longman.

Kaufmann, F. (1998) Eléments pour une histoire de l'interprétation simultaneé en Israël. [Elements for a history of simultaneous interpretation in Israel]. *Meta* 43: 98–109.

Kawamoto, A. H. (1993) Nonlinear dynamics in the resolution of lexical ambiguity: A parallel distributed processing account. *Journal of Memory and Language* 32: 474–516.

Kawamoto, A. H., and J. H. Zemblidge (1992) Pronunciation of homographs. *Journal of Memory and Language* 31: 349–374.

Kayambazinthu, E. (1999) The language planning situation in Malawi. In R. B. Kaplan and R. B. Baldauf Jr. (eds.) *Language planning in Malawi, Mozambique and the Philippines.* Clevedon, Avon, UK: Multilingual Matters. 15–85.

Keatley, C., J. Spinks, and B. De Gelder (1994) Asymmetrical semantic facilitation between languages. *Memory & Cognition* 22: 70–84.

Kellerman, E. (1995) Crosslinguistic influence: Transfer to nowhere? In W. Grabe et al. (eds.) *Annual Review of Applied Linguistics 15: A broad survey of the entire field of applied linguistics.* Cambridge: Cambridge University Press. 125–150.

Kellerman, E. (1977) Towards a characterization of the strategy of transfer in second language learning. *Interlanguage Studies Bulletin* 2: 58–145.

Kellet, C. J. M. (1995) Video-aided testing of student delivery and presentation in consecutive interpretation. *The Interpreters' Newsletter* 6: 43–66.

Kelley, E. (2000) Task design, pair work and L2 classroom interaction. MA thesis, San Diego State University, CA.

Kelm, O. R. (1992) The use of synchronous computer networks in second language instruction: A preliminary report. *Foreign Language Annals* 25: 441–454.

Kempe, V., and B. MacWhinney (1998) Acquisition of case marking by adult learners of German and Russian. *Studies in Second Language Acquisition* 20: 543–587.

Kempen, G., and E. Hoenkamp (1987) An incremental procedural grammar for sentence formulation. *Cognitive Science* 11: 201–258.

Kendall, S., and D. Tannen (1997) Gender and language in the workplace. In R. Wodak (ed.) *Gender and discourse.* London: Sage. 81–105.

Kennedy, C. (1996) 'La crème de la crème': Coercion and corpus change—an example from recruitment advertisements. In H. Coleman and L. Cameron (eds.) *Change and language.* Clevedon, Avon, UK: British Association for Applied Linguistics. 28–38.

Kennedy, C. (1988) Evaluation of the management of change in ELT projects. *Applied Linguistics* 9: 329–342.

Kenrick, D. (1996) Romani literacy at the crossroads. *International Journal of the Sociology of Language* 119: 109–123.

Kenyon, D. (1992) Introductory remarks: Introduction to a symposium on the development and use of rating scales in language testing. *Language Testing Research Colloquium.* Vancouver, British Columbia. March.

Kephart, R. F. (1992) Reading creole English does not destroy your brain cells! In J. Siegel (ed.) *Pidgins, creoles and nonstandard dialects in education.* Melbourne: Applied Linguistics Association of Australia. 67–86.

Kerekes, J. (1992) Development in nonnative speakers' use and perceptions of assertiveness and supportiveness in a mixed-sex conversation. Occasional Paper, No. 21. Honolulu: University of Hawai'i at Manoa, Department of English as a Second Language.

Kern, R. G. (1995) Restructuring classroom interaction with networked computers: Effects on quantity and characteristics of language production. *The Modern Language Journal* 79: 457–476.

Khemlani-David, M. (1998) Language shift, cultural maintenance and ethnic identity; a study of a minority community: The Sindhis of Malaysia. *International Journal of the Sociology of Language* 129: 67–76.

Khubchandani, L. M. (1989) Language demography in the Indian context. *Sociolinguistics* 18: 75–84.

Kilborn, K. (1989) Sentence processing in a second language: The timing of transfer. *Language and Speech* 32: 1–23.

Kimura, D. (1992) Sex differences in the brain. *Scientific American* 160: 119–125.

King, K. A. (2000) *Language revitalization processes and prospects: Quichua in the Ecuadorian Andes.* Clevedon, Avon, UK: Multilingual Matters.

Kinginger, C., and S. J. Savignon (1991) Four conversations: Task variation and classroom learner discourse. In M. McGroarty and C. J. Faltis (eds.) *Languages in school and society: Policy and pedagogy.* Berlin: Mouton de Gruyter. 85–106.

Kinsella, K., and K. Sherak. (1998) Designing ESL classroom collaboration to accommodate diverse work styles. In J. M. Reid (ed.) *Understanding learning styles in the second language classroom.* Upper Saddle River, NJ: Prentice Hall Regents. 85–99.

Kintsch. W. (1998) *Comprehension: A framework for cognition.* Cambridge: Cambridge University Press.

Kirkwood, M. (ed.) (1990) *Language Planning in the Soviet Union.* New York: St. Martin's.

Kjisik, F., and J. Nordlund (2000) From here to autonomy: The role of language learning strategies. Invited presentation. New York: Teachers College, Columbia University.

Kjolseth, R. (1970) Bilingual education programs in the United States: For assimilation or pluralism? In P. Turner (ed.) *Bilingualism in the southwest.* Tucson: University of Arizona Press. 3–28.

Klee, C., and A. Ocampo (1995) The expression of past reference in Spanish narratives of Spanish-English bilingual speakers. In C. Silva-Corvalán (ed.) *Spanish in four continents.* Washington, DC: Georgetown University Press. 52–70.

Klee, C., and D. Tedick (1997) The undergraduate foreign language immersion program in Spanish at the University of Minnesota. In S. Stryker and B. Leaver (eds.) *Content-based instruction in foreign language education: Models and methods.* Washington, DC: Georgetown University Press. 140–173.

Klein, E., and G. Martohardjono (eds.) (1999) *The development of second language grammars: A generative approach.* Philadelphia: John Benjamins.

Klippel, F. (1984) *Keep talking: Communicative fluency activities for language learning.* Cambridge: Cambridge University Press.

Kloss, H. (1998/1977) *The American bilingual tradition.* Washington, DC, and McHenry, IL: Center for Applied Linguistics and Delta Systems. [Intro. R. Macias and T. G. Wiley.]

Koch, H. (1991) Language and communication in Aboriginal Land Claim hearings. In S. Romaine (ed.) *Language in Australia.* Cambridge: Cambridge University Press. 94–103.

Koda, K. (1997) Orthographic knowledge in L2 lexical processing. In J. Coady and T. Huckin (eds.) *Second language vocabulary acquisition.* Cambridge: Cambridge University Press. 35–52.

Koda, K. (1996) L2 word recognition research: A critical review. *Modern Language Journal* 80: 450–460.

Kohn, K., and S. Kalina (1996) The strategic dimension of interpreting. *Meta* 41: 118–138.

Koike, D. A. (1996) Transfer of pragmatic competence and suggestions in Spanish. In S. M. Gass and J. Neu (eds.) *Speech acts across cultures: Challenge to communication in a second language.* Berlin: Mouton de Gruyter. 257–281.

Koshik, I. (1999) Practices of pedagogy in ESL writing conferences: A conversation analytic study of turns and sequences that assist student revision. Ph.D. diss., University of California, Los Angeles.

Koschmann, T. (1999) *Meaning making.* Special issue of *Discourse Processes* 27(2).

Kouritzen, S. (1999) *Face[t]s of first language loss.* Mahwah, NJ: Lawrence Erlbaum.

Kouwenberg, S., and P. Muysken (1994) Papiamento. In J. Arends, P. Muysken, and N. Smith (eds.) *Pidgins and creoles: An introduction.* Amsterdam: John Benjamins. 205–218.

Kowal, M., and M. Swain (1997) From semantic to syntactic processing: How can we promote it in the immersion classroom? In R. K. Johnson and M. Swain (eds.) *Immersion education: International perspectives.* Cambridge: Cambridge University Press. 284–309.

Kramsch, C. (2000a) Expansion of the field. *AAAL Newsletter* 20: 1–2.

Kramsch, C. (2000b) Social discourse constructions of self in L2 learning. In J. P. Lantolf (ed.) *Sociocultural theory and second language learning.* Oxford: Oxford University Press. 135–156.

Kramsch, C. (1998) *Language and culture.* Oxford: Oxford University Press.

Kramsch, C. (1993) Redrawing the boundaries of foreign language study. In M. Krueger and F. Ryan (eds.) *Language and content: Discipline- and content-based approaches to language study.* Lexington, MA: Heath. 203–217.

Krapels, A. (1990) An overview of second language writing process research. In B. Kroll (ed.) *Second language writing: Research insights for the classroom.* Cambridge: Cambridge University Press. 37–56.

Krashen, S. D. (1999) *Condemned without a trial: Bogus arguments against bilingual education.* Portsmouth, NH: Heinemann.

Krashen, S. D. (1996) *Under attack: The case against bilingual education.* Culver City, CA: Language Education Associates.

Krashen, S. D. (1993) *The power of reading*. Englewood, CO: Libraries Unlimited.

Krashen, S. D. (1985) *The input hypothesis: Issues and implications*. London: Longman.

Krashen, S. D. (1984) *Writing: Research, theory, and applications*. Oxford: Pergamon.

Krashen, S. D. (1982) *Principles and practice in second language acquisition*. Oxford: Pergamon.

Krashen, S. D., and T. D. Terrell (1983) *The Natural Approach: Language acquisition in the classroom*. Oxford: Pergamon.

Krauss, M. (1998) The scope of the language endangerment crisis and recent response to it. In K. Matsumara (ed.) *Studies in Endangered Languages*. Tokyo, Japan: Hituzi Syobo. 101–114.

Krauss, M. (1992) The world's languages in crisis. *Language* 68: 4–10.

Kress, G. (2000) Design and transformation: New theories of meaning. In B. Cope and M. Kalantzis (eds.) *Multiliteracies: Literacy learning and the design of social futures*. London: Routledge. 153–161.

Kress, G. (1993) Genre as social process. In B. Cope and M. Kalantzis (eds.) *The powers of literacy: A genre approach to teaching writing*. London: Falmer Press. 22–37.

Kress, G. (1989) *Linguistic processes in sociocultural practice*. Oxford: Oxford University Press.

Krings, H. (1986) *Was in den Köpfen von Übersetzern vorgeht. Eine empirische Untersuchung zur Struktur des Übersetzungsprozesses an fortgeschrittenen Französischlernern.* [What is happening in the mind of the translator: An empirical investigation of the structure of translation processes in advanced learners of French.] Tübingen: Narr.

Kroll, J. F. (1993) Accessing conceptual representation for words in a second language. In R. Schreuder and B. Weltens (eds.) *The bilingual lexicon*. Amsterdam: John Benjamins. 53–81.

Kroll, J. F., and J. Curley (1988) Lexical memory in novice bilinguals: The role of concepts in retrieving second language words. In M. Gruneberg, P. Morris, and R. Sykes (eds.) *Practical aspects of memory*. London: Wiley. 389–395.

Kroll, J. F., and A. M. B. De Groot (1997) Lexical and conceptual memory in the bilingual: Mapping form to meaning in two languages. In A. M. B. De Groot and J. F. Kroll (eds.) *Tutorials in bilingualism: Psycholinguistic perspectives*. Mahwah, NJ: Lawrence Erlbaum. 169–199.

Kroll, J. F., F. Dietz, and D. W. Green (in preparation) Language switch costs in bilingual picture naming and translation. University Park: Pennsylvania State University. Unpublished ms.

Kroll, J. F., A. Dijkstra, N. Janssen, and H. Schriefers (1999) Cross-language lexical activity during production: Evidence from cued picture naming. Invited paper presented as part of a symposium, Bilingualism. Ghent, Belgium: European Society for Cognitive Psychology.

Kroll, J. F., E. Michael, and A. Sankaranarayanan (1998) A model of bilingual representation and its implications for second language acquisition. In A. F. Healy and L. E. Bourne (eds.) *Foreign Language Learning: Psycholinguistic Experiments on Training and Retention*. Mahwah, NJ: Lawrence Erlbaum. 365–395.

Kroll, J. F., and A. Peck (1998) Competing activation across a bilingual's two languages: Evidence from picture naming. Paper presented at the 43rd Annual Meeting of the International Linguistic Association, New York University.

Kroll, J. F., and E. Stewart (1994) Category interference in translation and picture naming: Evidence for asymmetric connections between bilingual memory representations. *Journal of Memory and Language* 33: 149–174.

Kroll, J. F., and N. Tokowicz (2001) The development of conceptual representation for words in a second language. In J. L. Nicol (ed.) *One mind, two languages: Bilingual Language Processing*. Cambridge, MA: Blackwell. 49–71.

Krueger, M., and F. Ryan (eds.) (1993) *Language and content: Discipline- and content-based approaches to language study*. Lexington, MA: Heath.

Kubota, R. (1999) Japanese culture constructed by discourses: Implications for applied linguistics research and ELT. *TESOL Quarterly* 33: 9–35.

Kucan, L., and I. Beck (1997) Thinking aloud and reading comprehension research: Inquiry, instruction and social interaction. *Review of Education Research* 67: 271–299.

Kuczaj, S. A., II (1983) *Crib speech and language play*. New York: Springer-Verlag.

Kulick, D. (1992) *Language shift and cultural reproduction: Socialization, self, and syncretism in a Papua New Guinea village*. Cambridge: Cambridge University Press.

Kumaravadivelu, B. (1994) The postmethod condition: (E)merging strategies for second/foreign language teaching. *TESOL Quarterly* 28: 27–48.

Kunda, G. (1992) *Engineering culture: Control and commitment in a high-tech corporation*. Philadelphia: Temple University Press.

Kunnan, A. J. (1999) Recent developments in language testing. In W. Grabe, et al. (eds.) *Annual Review of Applied Linguistics 19: A survey of applied linguistics*. New York: Cambridge University Press. 235–253.

Kunnan, A. J. (1998) An introduction to structural equation modeling for language assessment research. *Language Testing* 15: 295–332.

Kunnan, A. J. (1997) Connecting fairness with validation in language assessment. In A. Huhta, V. Kohonen, L. Kurki-Suonio, and S. Luoma (eds.) *Current developments and alternatives in language assessment*. Jyväskylä: University of Jyväskylä. 85–105.

Kurz, I. (1995) Watching the brain at work: An exploratory study of EEG changes during simultaneous interpreting (SI). *The Interpreters' Newsletter* 6: 3–16.

Kurz, I., E. Basel, D. Chiba, W. Patels, and J. Wolfframm (1996) Scribe or actor? A survey paper on personality profiles of translators and interpreters. *The Interpreters' Newsletter* 7: 3–18.

Labaree, L. W. (1959) *The papers of Benjamin Franklin*. Vol. 4. New Haven: Yale University Press.

Labov, W. (1972) *Sociolinguistic patterns*. Philadelphia: University of Pennsylvania Press.

Labov, W., and D. Fanshel (1977) *Therapeutic discourse: Psychotherapy as conversation*. New York: Academic Press.

Labrie, N., P. Nelde, and P. J. Weber (1994) Project for the study of less widely used languages of the European community. *Europa Ethnica*. [Ethnic Europe.] 51: 67–70.

Lado, R. (1964) *Language teaching*. New York: McGraw Hill.

Lado, R., and C. C. Fries (1957) *English sentence patterns. Understanding and producing English grammatical structures: An oral approach*. Ann Arbor: University of Michigan Press.

Laforgue, L., and G. D. McConnell (eds.) (1990) *Language spread and social change: Dynamics and measurement*. Ste.-Foy, Québec: Les Presses de l'Université Laval.

La Heij, W. (1988) Components of Stroop-like interference in picture naming. *Memory and Cognition* 16: 400–410.

La Heij, W., E. De Bruyn, E. Elens, R. Hartsuiker, D. Helaha, and L. Van Schelven.

(1990) Orthographic facilitation and categorical interference in a word-translation variant of the Stroop task. *Canadian Journal of Psychology* 44: 76–83.

La Heij, W., R. Kerling, and E. Van der Velden (1996) Nonverbal context effects in forward and backward translation: Evidence for concept mediation. *Journal of Memory and Language* 35: 648–665.

Laitin, D., and C. M. Eastman (1989) Language conflict: Transactions and games in Kenya. *Cultural Anthropology* 4: 51–72.

Lakoff, R. (1975) *Language and woman's place*. New York: Harper Colophon.

Lambert, W. E. (1974) Culture and language as factors in learning and education. In F. E. Aboud and R. D. Meade (eds.) *Cultural factors in learning and education*. Bellingham, WA: Fifth Western Symposium on Learning. 91–122.

Lambert, W. E. (1967) A social psychology of bilingualism. *Journal of Social Issues* 23: 91–109.

Lambert, W. E. (1956a) Developmental aspects of second-language acquisition. I: Associational fluency, stimulus provocativeness, and word-order influence. *Journal of Social Psychology* 43: 83–89.

Lambert, W. E. (1956b) Developmental aspects of second-language acquisition. II: Associational stereotypy, associational form, vocabulary commonness, and pronunciation. *Journal of Social Psychology* 43: 91–98.

Lambert, W. E. (1956c) Developmental aspects of second-language acquisition. III: A description of developmental changes. *Journal of Social Psychology* 43: 99–104.

Lambert, W. E. (1955) Measurement of the linguistic dominance of bilinguals. *Journal of Abnormal and Social Psychology* 50: 197–200.

Lamy, M.-N., and R. Goodfellow (1999) Reflective conversation in the virtual language classroom. *Language Learning and Technology* 2: 43–61.

Landauer, T., P. Foltz, and D. Laham (1998) An introduction to latent semantic analysis. *Discourse Processes* 25: 259–284.

Landauer, T. K., D. Laham, B. Rehder, and M. E. Schreiner (1997) How well can passage meaning be derived without using word order? A comparison of latent semantic analysis and humans. In M. G. Shafto and P. Langleyy (eds.) *Proceedings of the 19th annual meeting of the Cognitive Science Society*. Mahwah, NJ: Lawrence Erlbaum. 412–417.

Lantolf, J. P. (1997) The function of language play in the acquisition of Spanish as a second language. In W. R. Glass and A. T. Perez-Leroux (eds.) *Contemporary perspectives on the acquisition of Spanish*. 2 Vols. Somerville, MA: Cascadilla Press. 2: 3–25.

Lantolf, J. (1996) SLA theory building: 'Letting all the flowers bloom.' *Language Learning* 46: 713–749.

Lantolf, J. P., and W. Frawley (1984) Second language performance and Vygotskyan psycholinguistics: Implications for L2 instruction. In A. Manning, P. Martin, and K. McCalla (eds.) *The tenth LACUS forum 1983*. Columbia, SC: Hornbeam Press. 425–440.

Lantolf, J. P. (ed.) (2000) *Sociocultural theory and second language learning*. Oxford: Oxford University Press.

Lantolf, J. P. (ed.) (1994) *Sociocultural theory and second language learning*. [Special issue of *Modern Language Journal* 78(4).

Lardiere, D. (2000) Mapping features to forms in second language acquisition. In J. Archibald (ed.) *Second language acquisition and linguistic theory*. Oxford: Basil Blackwell. 102–129.

Larkey, L. (1998) Automatic essay grading using text categorization techniques. In *Proceedings of the 21st ACM-SIGIR conference on research and development in information retrieval*. Melbourne, Australia. 90–95.

Larsen-Freeman, D., and M. H. Long (1991) *An introduction to second language acquisition research*. New York: Longman.

Larson, J. W. (1999) Considerations for testing reading proficiency via computer-adaptive testing. In M. Chalhoub-Deville (ed.) *Issues in computer-adaptive testing of reading proficiency*. Cambridge: Cambridge University Press. 71–90.

Larson, J. W. (1989) S-SCAPE: A Spanish computerized adaptive placement exam. In W. F. Smith (ed.) *Modern technology in foreign language education: Applications and projects*. New York: ACTFL Foreign Language Series.

Larson, J. W. (1987) Computerized adaptive language testing: A Spanish placement exam. In K. M. Bailey, T. L. Dale, and R. T. Clifford (eds.) *Language testing research: Papers from the 1986 Colloquium*. Monterey, CA: Defense Language Institute.

Larson, J. W., and H. S. Madsen (1985) Computerized adaptive language testing: Moving beyond computer-assisted testing. *CALICO Journal* 2: 32–36.

Larson, M. (1984) *Meaning-based translation: A guide to cross-language equivalence*. Lanham, MD: University Press of America.

Lasnik, H. (1999) *Minimalist analysis*. Oxford: Blackwell.

Launer, M. K., T. L. Launer, and M. L. Pedro. (1998) Do US-based interpreters have a future? *ATA Chronicle* April: 18–20, 23.

Laurier, M. (1999) The development of an adaptive test for placement in French. In M. Chalhoub-Deville (ed.) *Issues in computer-adaptive testing of reading proficiency*. New York: Cambridge University Press. 119–132.

Laurier, M. (1991) What we can do with computerized adaptive testing—and what we cannot do. In S. Anivan (ed.) *Current developments in language testing*. Singapore: SEAMEO Regional Language Centre. 244–255.

Lave, J., and E. Wenger. (1991) *Situated learning: Legitimate peripheral participation*. Cambridge: Cambridge University Press.

Laviosa, S. (1998a) Core patterns of lexical use in a comparable corpus of English narrative prose *Meta* 43: 557–577.

Laviosa, S. (ed.) (1998b) *L'Approche basée sur le corpus* [The corpus-based approach] *Meta* 43(4) [Special issue.]

Lawrence, G. (1984) A synthesis of learning style research involving the MBTI. *Journal of Psychological Type* 8: 2–15.

Lawson, V. (1989) Machine translation. In C. Picken (ed.) *The translator's handbook*. 2nd ed. London: Aslib. 203–213.

Lawton, D. (1980) Language attitude, discreteness and code shifting in Jamaican Creole. *English World-Wide* 1: 221–226.

Laycock, D. C. (1981) Melanesian linguistic diversity: A Melanesian choice? In R. J. May and N. Hughes (eds.) *Melanesian beyond diversity*. Canberra: Research School of Pacific Studies. 33–38.

Laycock, D. C. (1979) Multilingualism: Linguistics boundaries and unsolved problems in Papua New Guinea. In S. A. Wurm (ed.) *New Guinea and neighbouring areas: A sociolinguistic laboratory*. The Hague: Mouton. 81–100.

Layne, P., and S. Lepeintre (1996) Distance instruction. In W. Grabe et al. (eds.) *Annual Review of Applied Linguistics 16: Technology and language.* Cambridge: Cambridge University Press. 226–239.

Lazaraton, A. (2000) Current trends in research methodology and statistics in applied linguistics. *TESOL Quarterly* 34: 175–181.

Lazaraton, A. (1996) Interlocutor support in oral proficiency interviews: The case of CASE. *Language Testing* 13: 151–172.

Lazaraton, A. (1995) Qualitative research in applied linguistics: A progress report. *TESOL Quarterly* 29: 455–472.

Lazarus, R. (1991) Progress on a cognitive-motivational-relational theory of emotion. *American Psychologist* 46: 819–834.

Leather, J., and A. James (1996) Second language speech and the influence of the first language. In W. Ritchie and T. K. Bhatia (eds.) *Handbook of second language acquisition.* New York: Academic. 269–316.

LeCompte, M. D., W. L. Millroy, and J. Preissle (eds.) (1992) *The handbook of qualitative research in education.* New York: Academic Press.

Lederer, M. (1981) *La traduction simultanée. Expérience et théorie.* [Simultaneous translation: Experience and theory.] Paris: Minard.

Lederer, M. (1980) *La traduction simultanée. Fondements théoriques.* [Simultaneous translation: Theoretical foundations.] Lille: Université de Lille III.

Lee, J. F., and B. VanPatten (1995) *Making communicative language teaching happen: Directions for language learning and teaching.* Vol. 1. Blacklick, OH: McGraw-Hill.

Lee, T.-H. (1999) Speech proportion and accuracy in simultaneous interpretation from English to Korean *Meta* 44: 260–267.

Lefebvre, C. (1999) *Creole genesis and the acquisition of grammar: The case of Haitian Creole.* Cambridge: Cambridge University Press.

Legutke, M., and H. Thomas. (1991) *Process and experience in the language classroom.* London: Longman.

Leidner, R. (1993) *Fast food, fast talk: Service work and the routinization of everyday life.* Berkeley: University of California Press.

Leki, I. (submitted) A critical examination of the limits of L2 writing: Is writing overrated? In B. Kroll (ed.) *Exploring second language writing.* Cambridge: Cambridge University Press.

Leki, I. (1999) "Pretty much I screwed up": Ill-served needs of a permanent resident. In L. Harklau, K. Losey, and M. Siegal (eds.) *Generation 1.5 meets college composition.* Mahwah, NJ: Erlbaum. 17–43.

Leki, I. (1991) Twenty-five years of contrastive rhetoric: Text analysis and writing pedagogies. *TESOL Quarterly* 25: 123–144.

Leki, I. (1990) Coaching from the margins: Issues in written response. In B. Kroll (ed.) *Second language writing: Research insights for the classroom.* Cambridge: Cambridge University Press. 57–68.

Leki, I., and J. Carson (1997) "Completely different worlds": EAP and the writing experiences of ESL students in university courses. *TESOL Quarterly* 31: 39–69.

Lemke, J. (1992) Intertextuality and educational research. *Linguistics and Education* 4: 257–267.

Lennon, P. (1998) Approaches to the teaching of idiomatic language. *International Review of Applied Linguistics* 36: 11–30.

Lennon, P. (1996) Getting 'easy' verbs wrong at the advanced level. *International Review of Applied Linguistics* 34: 23–36.

Lennon, P. (1990) Investigating fluency in EFL: A quantitative approach. *Language Learning* 40: 387–417.

LePage, R. B. (1986) Acts of identity. *English Today* 8 (Oct.–Dec.): 21–24.

LePage, R. B. (1977) Processes of pidginization and creolization. In A. Valdman (ed.) *Pidgin and creole linguistics.* Bloomington: University of Indiana Press. 222–255.

LePage, R. B. (1968) Problems to be faced in the use of English as a medium of education in four West Indian territories. In J. A. Fishman et al. (eds.) *Language problems of developing nations.* New York: Wiley. 431–443.

LePage, R. B., and A. Tabouret-Keller (1985) *Acts of identity: Creole-based approaches to ethnicity and language.* Cambridge: Cambridge University Press.

Leung, C., R. Harris, and B. Rampton (1997) The idealized native speaker, reified ethnicities and classroom realities. *TESOL Quarterly* 31: 543–560.

Leung, C., and A. Teasdale (1997) What do teachers mean by speaking and listening? A contextualized study of assessment in multilingual classrooms in the English national curriculum. In A. Huhta, V. Kohonen, L. Kurki-Suonio, and S. Luoma (eds.) *Current developments and alternatives in language assessment.* Jyväskylä: University of Jyväskylä. 291–324.

Levelt, W. J. M. (1993) Language use in normal speakers and its disorders. In G. Blanken et al. (eds.) *Linguistic disorders and pathologies: An international handbook.* Berlin: Walter de Gruyter. 1–15.

Levelt, W. J. M. (1989) *Speaking: From intention to articulation.* Cambridge, MA: MIT Press.

Levelt, W. J. M., A. Roelofs, and A. S. Meyer (1999) A theory of lexical access in speech production. *Behavioural and Brain Sciences* 22: 1–75.

Levelt, W. J. M., H. Schriefers, D. Vorberg, A. S. Meyer, T. Pechman, and J. Havinga (1991) The time course of lexical access in speech production: A study of picture naming. *Psychological Review* 98: 122–142.

Levinson, S. C. (1983) *Pragmatics.* Cambridge: Cambridge University Press.

Levy, M. (1997) *Computer-assisted language learning: Context and conceptualization.* Oxford: Clarendon Press.

Lewis, E. G. (1982) Movements and agencies of language spread: Wales and the Soviet Union compared. In R. L. Cooper (ed.) *Language spread: Studies in diffusion and social change.* Bloomington: Indiana University Press. 214–259.

Lewis, E. G. (1981) *Bilingualism and bilingual education.* Oxford: Pergamon.

Lewis, E. G. (1972) *Multilingualism in the Soviet Union.* The Hague: Mouton.

Leyew, Z. (1998) An Ethiopian language on the verge of extinction: K'emant, a preliminary sociolinguistic survey. *International Journal of the Sociology of Language* 134: 69–84.

Li, D.-F. (1998) "It's always more difficult than you plan and imagine": Teachers' perceived difficulties in introducing the communicative approach in South Korea. *TESOL Quarterly* 32: 679–703.

Li, P. (1996) Spoken word recognition of code-switched words by Chinese-English bilinguals. *Journal of Memory and Language* 35: 757–774.

Liddicoat, A. (1996) The narrowing focus: Australia's changing language policy. *Babel* 31(1): 4–7, 33.

Lightbown, P. M. (1998) The importance of timing in focus on form. In C. Doughty and J. Williams (eds.) *Focus on Form in Classroom Second Language Acquisition.* Cambridge: Cambridge University Press. 177–196.

Lightbown, P. M., and L. White (1987) The influence of linguistic theories on language acquisition research: Description and explanation. *Language Learning* 37: 483–510.

Lin, A. (1999) Doing-English-lessons in the reproduction or transformation of social worlds? *TESOL Quarterly* 33: 393–412.

Lindholm, K. (1994) Promoting positive cross-cultural attitudes and perceived competence in culturally and linguistically diverse classrooms. In R. A. DeVillar, C. Faltis, and J. Cummins (eds.) *Cultural diversity in schools: From rhetoric to practice.* Albany: State University of New York Press. 189–206.

Lindholm, K., and R. Molina (2000) Two-way bilingual education: The power of two languages in promoting success. In J. Tinajero and R. A. DeVillar (eds.) *The power of two languages 2000.* New York: McGraw Hill. 163–174.

Lippi-Green, R. (1997) *English with an accent.* London: Routledge.

Littlewood, W. T. (1981) *Communicative language teaching. An introduction.* Cambridge: Cambridge University Press.

Liu, J. (1999) Nonnative-English-speaking professionals in TESOL. *TESOL Quarterly* 33: 85–102.

Loasby, H. A. (1998) A study of the effects of language switching and priming in a picture naming task. Unpublished manuscript, Oxford University.

Long, D. (1990) What you don't know can't help you: An exploratory study of background knowledge and second language listening comprehension. *Studies in Second Language Acquisition* 12: 65–80.

Long, M. (1998) SLA: Breaking the siege. *University of Hawai'i Working Papers in Linguistics* 17: 79–129.

Long, M. (1996) The role of the linguistic environment in second language acquisition. In W. Ritchie and T. Bhatia (eds.) *Handbook of second language acquisition.* San Diego: Academic Press. 413–468.

Long, M. (1990) The least a second language acquisition theory needs to explain. *TESOL Quarterly* 24: 649–666.

Long, M. (1989) Task, group, and task-group interactions. *University of Hawai'i Working Papers in ESL* 8: 1–26.

Long, M. (1983) Linguistic and conversational adjustments to non-native speakers. *Studies in Second Language Acquisition* 5: 177–193.

Long, M. (1981) Input, interaction, and second language acquisition. In H. Winitz (ed.) *Native Language and Foreign Language Acquisition.* New York: New York Academy of Sciences. 259–278.

Long, M. (1980) Input, interaction, and second language acquisition. Ph.D. diss., University of California at Los Angeles.

Long, M., and G. Crookes (1992) Three approaches to task-based syllabus design. *TESOL Quarterly* 26: 27–56.

Long, M., S. Inagaki, and L. Ortega (1998) The role of implicit negative feedback in SLA: Models and recasts in Japanese and Spanish. *The Modern Language Journal* 82: 357–371.

Long, M., and C. J. Sato (1983) Classroom foreigner talk discourse: Forms and functions of teachers' questions. In H. W. Seliger and M. H. Long (eds.) *Classroom oriented research in second language acquisition.* Rowley: Newbury House. 268–286.

Lonsdale, D. (1997) Modeling cognition in SI: Methodological issues. *Interpreting* 2: 91–117.

Lörscher, W. (1991) *Translation performance, translation process, and translation strategies: A psycholinguistic investigation.* Tübingen: Narr.

Loschky, L. (1994). Comprehensible input and second language acquisition. What is the relationship? *Studies in Second Language Acquisition* 16: 303–324.

Lowell, A., and B. Devlin (1999) Miscommunication between Aboriginal students and their non-Aboriginal teachers in a bilingual school. In S. May (ed.) *Indigenous community-based education.* Clevedon, Avon, UK: Multilingual Matters. 137–159.

Lowenberg, P. (ed.) (1988) *Language spread and language policy: Issues, implications, and case studies.* Georgetown University Round Table on Languages and Linguistics. Washington, D.C.: Georgetown University Press.

Lucy, J. (1992) *Grammatical categories and cognition.* Cambridge: Cambridge University Press.

Luke, A. (1988) *Literacy, textbooks and ideology.* Basingstoke: Falmer Press.

Luke, A., and R. B. Baldauf, Jr. (1990) Language planning and education: A critical re-reading. In R. B. Baldauf, Jr., and A. Luke (eds.) *Language planning and education in Australasia and the South Pacific.* Clevedon, Avon, UK: Multilingual Matters. 349–56.

Lumley, T., and T. F. McNamara (1995) Rater characteristics and rater bias: Implications for training. *Language Testing* 12: 54–71.

Lutz, C., and G. White (1986) The anthropology of emotions. *Annual Review of Anthropology* 15: 405–436.

Lynch, B. K. (2000) Re-thinking assessment from a critical perspective. Paper presented at the American Association for Applied Linguistics annual conference, Vancouver, British Columbia. March.

Lynch, B. K., and T. F. McNamara. (1998) Using G-theory and many-facet Rasch measurement in the development of performance assessments of the ESL speaking skills of immigrants. *Language Testing* 15: 158–180.

Lynch, T. (1998) Theoretical perspectives on listening. In W. Grabe, et al. (eds.) *Annual Review of Applied Linguistics 18: Foundations of second language teaching.* New York: Cambridge University Press. 3–19.

Lynch, T. (1997) Life in the slow lane: Observations of a limited L2 listener. *System* 25: 385–398.

Lynch, T. (1991) Questioning roles in the classroom. *ELT Journal* 45: 201–210.

Lynch, T., and J. MacLean (2001) 'A case of exercising': Effects of immediate task repetition on learners' performance. In M. Bygate, P. Skehan, and M. Swain (eds.) *Researching pedagogic tasks: Second language learning, teaching and testing.* London: Longman. 141–162.

Lynch, T., and J. Maclean (2000) Exploring the benefits of task repetition and recycling for classroom language learning. *Language Teaching Research* 4(3): 221–250.

Lyons, J. (1977) *Semantics.* 2 vols. Cambridge: Cambridge University Press.

Lyotard, J.-F. (1984/1979) *La condition postmoderne.* Paris: Minuit. Tr. G. Bennington and B. Massumi, as *The postmodern condition: A report on knowledge.* Manchester: Manchester University Press.

Lyster, R. (1998) Recasts, repetition, and ambiguity in L2 classroom discourse. *Studies in Second Language Acquisition* 20: 51–81.

Lyster, R., and L. Ranta. (1997) Corrective feedback and learner uptake: Negotiation of form in communicative classrooms. *Studies in Second Language Acquisition* 19: 37–66.

Macaulay, R. K. S. (1978) Variation and consistency in Glaswegian English. In P. Trudgill (ed.) *Sociolinguistic patterns in British English.* London: Arnold. 105–124.

MacDonald, C., and G. MacDonald. (eds.) (1995) *Connectionism: Debates on psychological explanation.* Oxford: Basil Blackwell.

MacDonald, M. C. (1994) Probablistic constraints and syntactic ambiguity resolution. *Language and Cognitive Processes* 9(2): 157–120.

MacDonald, M. C., N. J. Perlmutter, and M. S. Seidenberg (1994) The lexical nature of syntactic ambiguity resolution. *Psychological Review* 101: 676–703.

MacDonald, N. H., L. T. Frase, P. S. Gingrich, and S. A. Keenan (1982) The writer's workbench: Computer aids for text analysis. *IEEE Transactions on Communications* 30: 105–110.

MacFarlane, A. (1997) The linguistic and attitudinal aspects of school year group exchanges: Their immediate and long-term outcomes for participants. Ph.D. diss., University of Ottawa.

MacFarlane, A., and M. Wesche (1995) Immersion outcomes: Beyond language proficiency. *Canadian Modern Language Review* 51: 250–273.

MacIntyre, P. D., R. Clément, Z. Dörnyei, and K. A. Noels (1998) Conceptualizing willingness to communicate in a L2: A situational model of L2 confidence and affiliation. *The Modern Language Journal* 82: 545–562.

Mack, M. (1986) A study of semantic and syntactic processing in monolinguals and fluent early bilinguals. *Journal of Psycholinguistic Research* 15: 463–488.

Mackey, A. (1999) Input, interaction and second language development. *Studies in Second Language Acquisition* 21: 557–587.

Mackey, A., S. M. Gass, and K. McDonough (2000) How do learners perceive implicit negative feedback? *Studies in Second Language Acquisition* 22: 471–497.

Mackey, A., and J. Philp (1998) Conversational interaction and second language development: Recasts, responses, and red herrings. *The Modern Language Journal* 82: 338–356.

Mackey, W. F. (1990) Données et mesure de la dynamique de diffusion des languages: Quelques hypotheses. [Principles and measurements of the dynamics of language diffusion: Some hypotheses.] In L. Laforgue and G. D. McConnell (eds.) *Language spread and social change: Dynamics and measurement.* Ste.-Foy, Québec: Les Presses de l'Université Laval. 23–40.

Mackey, W. F. (1980) The ecology of language shift. In P. H. Nelde (ed.) *Sprachkontakt und sprachkonflikt* [Language contact and language conflict]. Weisbasden. 35–41.

Mackey, W. F. (1965) *Language teaching analysis.* London: Longmans, Green.

Macnamara, J. (1973) Nurseries, streets and classrooms: Some comparisons and deductions. *The Modern Language Journal* 57: 250–255.

Macnamara, J. (1971) Successes and failures in the movement for the restoration of Irish. In J. Rubin and B. Jernudd (eds.) *Can language be planned? Sociolinguistic theory and practice for developing nations.* Honolulu: University Press of Hawai'i. 65–94.

MacWhinney, B. (1997) Second language acquisition and the Competition Model. In A.

De Groot and J. Kroll (eds.) *Tutorials in bilingualism: Psycholinguistic perspectives*. Mahwah, NJ: Lawrence Erlbaum. 113–142.

MacWhinney, B. (1995a) Language-specific prediction in foreign language learning. *Language Testing* 12: 292–320.

MacWhinney, B. (1995b) *The CHILDES project: Tools for analyzing talk*. 2nd ed. Mahwah, NJ: Lawrence Erlbaum.

MacWhinney, B. (1987) Applying the competition model to bilingualism. *Applied Psycholinguistics* 8: 315–327.

MacWhinney, B. (ed.) (1999) *The emergence of language*. Mahwah, NJ: Lawrence Erlbaum.

Madden, C., and S. Reinhart (1987) *Pyramids: Structural based tasks for ESL Learners*. Ann Arbor: University of Michigan Press.

Maddux, C. D. (1986) Issues and concerns in special education microcomputing. *Computers in the Schools* 3: 3–4.

Madsen, H. S. (1991) Computer-adaptive testing of listening and reading comprehension: The Brigham Young University approach. In P. Dunkel (ed.) *Computer-assisted language learning and testing: Research issues and practice*. New York: Newbury House. 237–257.

Maeshiba, N., N. Yoshinaga, G. Kasper, and S. Ross (1996) Transfer and proficiency in interlanguage apologizing. In S. M. Gass and J. Neu (eds.) *Speech acts across cultures: Challenge to communication in a second language*. Berlin: Mouton de Gruyter. 155–187.

Maguire, M. H. (1998) A bilingual child's discourses, choices and voices: Lesson in listening, noticing and understanding. In E. Franklin (ed.) *Reading and writing in more than one language*. Washington DC: TESOL. 115–149.

Maley, A., A. Duff, and F. Grellet (1980) *The mind's eye*. Cambridge: Cambridge University Press.

Mann, W. C., and S. A. Thompson (1988) Rhetorical structure theory: Toward a functional theory of text organization *Text* 8: 243–281.

Manyak, P. (2000) Borderlands literacy in a primary-grade immersion class. In T. Shanahan and F. Rodriguez-Brown (eds.) *1999 Yearbook of the National Reading Conference*. Chicago: National Reading Conference.

Marantz, A. (1995) The Minimalist Program. In G. Webelhuth (ed.) *Government and Binding theory and the Minimalist program*. Oxford: Blackwell. 351–382.

Marckwardt, A. M. (1948/1988) Motives for the study of modern languages. *Language Learning* 1: 1–11. [Reprinted in *Language Learning* 38: 159–169.]

Marcu, D. (1999) Discourse trees are good indicators of importance of text. In I. Mani and M. Maybury (eds.) *Advances in automatic text summarization*. Cambridge, MA: MIT Press. 123–136.

Marcu, D. (1997) The rhetorical parsing of natural language texts. In *Proceedings of the 35th annual meeting of the Association for Computational Linguistics*. Madrid. 96–103.

Marcus, G. F. (1998) Can connectionism save constructivism? *Cognition* 66: 153–182.

Markee, N. P. (2000) *Conversation analysis*. Mahwah, NJ: Lawrence Erlbaum.

Markee, N. P. (1997) *Managing curricular innovation*. Cambridge: Cambridge University Press.

Markee, N. P. (1991) Toward an integrated approach to language planning. *Studies in the Linguistic Sciences* 21: 107–123.

Martin-Jones, M., and M. Heller. (1996) Introduction to the special issue on Education in multilingual settings: Discourse, identities, and power. *Linguistics and Education* 8: 3–16.

Marty, F. (1981) Reflections on the use of computers in second language acquisition. *System* 9: 85–98.

Marzocchi, C. (1998) The case for an institution-specific component in interpreting research. *The Interpreters' Newsletter* 8: 51–74.

Masgoret, A-M., and R. C. Gardner (1999) A causal model of Spanish immigrant adaptation in Canada. *Journal of Multilingual and Multicultural Development* 20: 216–236.

Massaro, D. W., and M. Shlesinger (1997) Information processing and a computational approach to the study of simultaneous interpretation. *Interpreting* 2: 13–53.

Master, P. (1987) A cross-linguistic interlanguage analysis of the acquisition of the English article system. Ph.D. diss. University of California at Los Angeles.

Matoesian, G. (1999) The grammaticalization of participant roles in the constitution of expert identity. *Language in Society* 28: 491–521.

Matsuda, M. J. (1991) Voices of America: Accent, antidiscrimination law, and a jurisprudence for the last reconstruction. *Yale Law Journal* 100: 1329–1407.

Matsuda, P. K. (1999) Composition studies and ESL writing: A disciplinary division of labor. *College Composition and Communication* 50: 699–721.

Matsuda, P. K. (1998) Situating ESL writing in a cross-disciplinary context. *Written Communication* 15: 99–121.

Mattheier, K. A. (1984) Sprachkonflikte in einsprachigen Ortsgemeinschaften. [Language conflicts in monolingual settings.] In E. Oksaar (ed.) *Spracherwerb—Sprachkontakt—Sprachkonflikt* [Language acquisition—language contact—language conflict]. Berlin: de Gruyter. 197–204.

Matthews, A., and C. Read (1981) *Tandem*. London: Evans.

Mavrommatis, Y. (1997) Understanding assessment in the classroom: Phases of the assessment process—the assessment episode. *Assessment in Education* 4: 381–399.

May, S. (1999a) Language and education rights for indigenous peoples. In S. May (ed.) *Indigenous community-based education*. Clevedon, Avon, UK: Multilingual Matters. 42–66.

May, S. (ed.) (1999b) *Indigenous community-based education*. Clevedon, Avon, UK: Multilingual Matters.

Maynard, D. W. (1992) On clinicians co-implicating recipients' perspective in delivery of diagnostic news. In P. Drew and J. Heritage (eds.) *Talk at work: Interaction in institutional settings*. Cambridge: Cambridge University Press. 331–359.

Mazrui, A. A., and M. Tidy. (1984) *Nationalism and new states in Africa*. Nairobi: Heinemann.

McCafferty, S. (1994) The use of private speech by adult ESL learners at different levels of proficiency. In J. P. Lantolf and G. Appel (eds.) *Vygotskian approaches to second language research*. Norwood, NJ: Ablex. 117–134.

McCafferty, S., and A. Ahmed (2000) The appropriation of gestures of the abstract by L2 learners. In J. P. Lantolf (ed.) *Sociocultural theory and second language learning*. Oxford: Oxford University Press. 199–218.

McCarthy, M. (1998) *Spoken language and applied linguistics*. Cambridge: Cambridge University Press.

McCarthy, M., and R. Carter (1994) *Language as discourse: Perspectives for language teaching*. London: Longman.

McCarty, T. L. (2001) *A place to be Navajo: Rough Rock and the struggle for self-determination in indigenous schooling*. Mahwah, NJ: Lawrence Erlbaum.

McCarty, T. L., L. J. Watahomigie, and A. Y. Yamamoto (eds.) (1999) *Reversing language shift in indigenous America: Collaborations and views from the field*. Special Issue of *Practicing Anthropology* 20.

McCarty, T. L., and O. Zepeda (eds.) (1998) *Indigenous language use and change in the Americas*. Special Issue of *International Journal of the Sociology of Language* 132.

McCarty, T. L., and O. Zepeda (eds.) (1995) *Indigenous language education and literacy*. Special Issue of *Bilingual Research Journal* 19.

McClelland, J. L., and D. E. Rumelhart (1981) An interactive activation model of context effects in letter perception, Part 1: An account of basic findings. *Psychological Review* 88: 375–405.

McClelland, J. L., D. E. Rumelhart, and G. Hinot (1986) The appeal of parallel distributed processing. In D. E. Rumelhart and J. L. McClelland (eds.) *Parallel distributed processing*. Cambridge, MA: MIT Press. 3–44.

McCollum, P. (1994) Language use in two-way bilingual programs. *Intercultural Development Research Association Newsletter* 21: 1, 9–11.

McConnell, G. D. (1990) Language spread as a phenomenon and concept. In L. Laforgue and G. D. McConnell (eds.) *Language spread and social change: Dynamics and measurement*. Ste.-Foy, Québec: Les Presses de l'Université Laval. 9–16.

McDermott, R. (1993) The acquisition of a child by a learning disability. In J. Lave and S. Chaiklin (eds.) *Understanding practice: Perspectives on activity and context*. Cambridge: Cambridge University Press. 269–305.

McGroarty, M. (1998) Constructive and constructivist challenges for applied linguistics. *Language Learning* 48: 591–622.

McGroarty, M. (1996) Language contact in social service institutions. In H. Goebl, P. Nelde, Z. Starý, and W. Wolck (eds.) *Contact linguistics: An international handbook of contemporary research*. Berlin: Walter de Gruyter. 1: 865–871.

McKay, P. (2000) On ESL standards for school-age learners. *Language Testing* 17: 185–214.

McKay, S., and N. Hornberger (eds.) (1996) *Sociolinguistics and language teaching*. Cambridge: Cambridge University Press.

McKay, S., and S.-L. Wong (1996) Multiple discourses, multiple identities: Investment and agency in second-language learning among Chinese adolescent immigrant students. *Harvard Educational Review* 66: 577–608.

McLane, J. B. (1987) Interaction, context and the zone of proximal development. In M. Hickmann (ed.) *Social and functional approaches to language and thinking*. Orlando, FL: Academic Press. 267–286.

McLaughlin, B. (1990) Restructuring. *Applied Linguistics* 11: 113–128.

McLaughlin, B., and R. Heredia (1996) Information-processing approaches to research on second language acquisition and use. In W. C. Ritchie and T. K. Bhatia (eds.) *Handbook of second language acquisition*. San Diego, CA: Academic Press. 213–228.

McLaughlin, D. (1992) *When literacy empowers: Navajo language in print*. Albuquerque: University of New Mexico Press.

McNamara, T. F. (2000a) *Language testing*. Oxford: Oxford University Press.

McNamara, T. F. (2000b) Shaking the foundations: Confronting the alternatives. Paper presented at AAAL meeting, Vancouver, British Columbia. March.

McNamara, T. F. (1998) Policy and social considerations in language assessment. In W. Grabe et al. (eds.) *Annual Review of Applied Linguistics 18: Foundations of second language teaching*. New York: Cambridge University Press. 304–319.

McNamara, T. F. (1997) What do we mean by social identity? Competing frameworks, competing discourses. *TESOL Quarterly* 31: 561–566.

McNamara, T. F. (1996) *Measuring second language performance*. London: Longman.

McNamara, T. F. (1995) Modelling performance: Opening Pandora's Box. *Applied Linguistics* 16: 159–179.

McNamara, T. F., and B. K. Lynch. (1997) A generalisability theory study of ratings and test design in the oral interaction and writing modules. In G. Brindley and G. Wigglesworth (eds.) *access: Issues in language test design and delivery*. Sydney: National Centre for English Language Teaching and Research, Macquarie University. 197–214.

McNeill, D. (1992) *Hand in mind*. Chicago: University of Chicago Press.

McWhorter, J. H. (1998) Identifying the creole prototype: Vindicating a typological class. *Language* 74: 788–818.

Mecham, L. R. (1999) Memorandum to all clerks, United States District Courts: Fees for contract court interpreters. June 10. Washington, DC: Administrative Office of the United States Courts.

Medgyes, P. (1986) Queries from a communicative teacher. *ELT Journal* 40: 107–112.

Medgyes, P., and K. Miklósy. (2000) The language situation in Hungary. *Current Issues in Language Planning* 1(2): 148–242.

Mehan, H. (1986) The role of language and the language of role in institutional decision making. In S. Fisher and A. D. Todd (eds.) *Discourse and institutional authority: Medicine, education, and law*. Norwood, NJ: Ablex. 140–163.

Mehan, H. (1979) *Learning lessons: Social organization in the classroom*. Cambridge: Cambridge University Press.

Mehnert, U. (1998) The effects of different lengths of time for planning on second language performance. *Studies in Second Language Acquisition* 20: 83–108

Mehrotra, R. R. (1985) Sociolinguistic surveys in South Asia: An overview. *International Journal of the Sociology of Language* 55: 115–124.

Melinkoff, D. (1963) *The language of the law*. Boston, MA: Little, Brown.

Mellow, J. D., K. Reeder, and E. Forster (1996) Using time-series research designs to investigate the effects of instruction on SLA. *Studies in Second Language Acquisition* 18: 325–350.

Mendelsohn, D. (1998) Teaching listening. In W. Grabe et al. (eds.) *Annual Review of Applied Linguistics 18: Foundations of second language teaching*. New York: Cambridge University Press. 81–101.

Mendelsohn, D. (1994) *Learning to listen*. San Diego, CA: Dominie Press.

Merlini, R. (1996) Interprit: Consecutive interpretation module. *The Interpreters' Newsletter* 7: 31–41.

Messick, S. (1999) Technology and the future of higher education assessment. In S. Messick (ed.) *Assessment in higher education: Issues of access, student development, and public policy*. Hillsdale, NJ: Lawrence Erlbaum. 245–254.

Messick, S. (1988) Validity. In R. L. Linn (ed.) *Educational measurement.* New York: Macmillan. 13–103.

Messina, A. (1998) The reading aloud of English language texts in simultaneously interpreted conferences. *Interpreting* 3: 147–161.

Mesthrie, R. (1999) Language loyalty. In B. Spolsky (ed.) *Concise encyclopedia of educational linguistics.* Amsterdam: Elsevier. 42–47.

Met, M., and E. Lorenz (1997) Lessons from U.S. immersion programs: Two decades of experience. In R. K. Johnson and M. Swain (eds.) *Immersion education: International perspectives.* Cambridge: Cambridge University Press. 243–264.

Métellus, J. (1998) The process of creolization in Haiti and the pitfalls of the graphic form. In K. M. Balutansky and M.-A. Sourieau (eds.) *Caribbean creolization: Reflections on the cultural dynamics of language, literature, and identity.* Gainesville: University Press of Florida and Barbados: University Press of the West Indies. 118–128.

Meunier, L. E. (1995/1996) Human factors in a computer-assisted foreign language environment: The effects of gender, personality and keyboard control. *CALICO Journal* 13: 47–72.

Meuter, R. F. I., and A. Allport (1999) Bilingual language switching in naming: Asymmetrical costs of language selection. *Journal of Memory and Language* 40: 25–40.

Meyer, A., and K. Bock (1992) The tip-of-the-tongue phenomenon: Blocking or partial activation? *Memory and Cognition* 20(6): 715–726.

Meyer, B. (1998) What transcriptions of authentic discourse can reveal about interpreting. *Interpreting* 3: 65–83.

Michelman, F. (1995) French and British colonial policies: A comparative view of their impact on African Literature. *Research in African Literatures* 26: 216–225.

Miguélez, C. (1999) Current issues in court interpreting: Spain, a case study. *Proteus* 8(2): 5–8.

Mikkelson, H. (1998) Towards a redefinition of the role of the court interpreter. *Interpreting* 3: 21–45.

Mikkelson, H. (1996) Community interpreting: An emerging profession. *Interpreting* 1: 125–129.

Miles, M. B., and A. M. Huberman (1994) *Qualitative data analysis.* 2nd ed. Newbury Park, CA: Sage.

Miller, J. (1998) Speaking English and social identity: Migrant students in Queensland high schools. Ph.D. diss., University of Queensland, Brisbane. Australia.

Miller, N. (1997) The influence of word form and meaning in bilingual language production. M.A. thesis, Pennsylvania State University, University Park.

Mills, S. (ed.) (1995) *Language and gender.* London: Longman.

Mintz, D. (1998) Hold the phone: Telephone interpreting scrutinized. *Proteus* 7(1): 1, 3–5.

Mishler, E. (1984) *The discourse of medicine: Dialectics of medical interviews.* Norwood, NJ: Ablex.

Mislevy, R. J. (1996) Test theory reconceived. *Journal of Educational Measurement* 33: 379–416.

Mislevy, R. J. (1995) Probability-based inference in cognitive diagnosis. In P. Nichols, S. Chipman, and R. Brennan (eds.) *Cognitively diagnostic assessment.* Hillsdale, NJ: Lawrence Erlbaum. 43–71.

Mislevy, R. J., L. S. Steinberg, F. J. Breyer, R. G. Almond, and L. Johnson (1999) A cognitive analysis, with implications for designing simulation-based performance assessment. *Computers in Human Behavior* 15: 335–374.

Mitchell, D. C. (1994) Sentence parsing. In M. Gernsbacher (ed.) *Handbook of psycholinguistics*. San Diego, CA: Academic Press. 375–409.

Mitchell, R., and F. Myles (1998) *Second language learning theories*. London: Edward Arnold.

Mizuno, A. (1995) A brief review of interpretation research in Japan. *Hermes* 14: 131–144.

Moeketsi, R. H. (1999) Redefining the role of the South African court interpreter. *Proteus* 8(3 and 4): 12–15.

Mohan, B. (1992) Models of the role of the computer in second language development. In M. Pennington and V. Stevens (eds.) *Computers in applied linguistics: An international perspective*. Clevedon, Avon, UK: Multilingual Matters. 110–126.

Mohan, B. (1986) *Language and content*. Reading, MA: Addison-Wesley.

Mohan, B., C. Leung, and C. Davison (eds.) (2001) *English as a second language in the mainstream: Teaching, learning, identity*. London: Pearson Education.

Montrul, S. A. (1999) Causative errors with unaccusative verbs in L2 Spanish. *Second Language Research* 15: 191–219.

Montrul, S. A. (1998) The L2 acquisition of dative experiencer subjects. *Second Language Research* 14: 27–61.

Moore, H. (1996) Language policies as virtual realities: Two Australian examples. *TESOL Quarterly* 30: 473–497.

Moore, J. I. (ed.) (1999) *Immigrants in courts*. Seattle: University of Washington Press.

Morgan, B. (1998) *The ESL classroom: Teaching, critical practice, and community development*. Toronto: University of Toronto Press.

Morimoto, Y. (1999) Making words in two languages: A prosodic account of Japanese-English language mixing. *International Journal of Bilingualism* 3(1): 23–44.

Morphet, T. (1996) Afterword. In M. Prinsloo and M. Breier (eds.) *The social uses of literacy: Theory and practice in contemporary South Africa*. Bertsham, South Africa: Sached Books. 257–264.

Morris, R. (1998) Justice in Jerusalem: Interpreting in Israeli legal proceedings. *Meta* 43: 110–118.

Morrison, H., and C. Wylie (1999) Why national curriculum testing is based on a methodological thought disorder. *Evaluation and Research in Education* 13: 92–105.

Morrow, K. (1979) Communicative language testing. In C. J. Brumfit and K. Johnson (eds.) *The communicative approach to language teaching*. Oxford: Oxford University Press. 143–157.

Morrow, K., and K. Johnson (1979) *Communicate 1*. Cambridge: Cambridge University Press.

Morton, J., G. Wigglesworth, and D. Williams (1997) Approaches to the evaluation of interviewer behaviour in oral tests. In G. Brindley and G. Wigglesworth (eds.) *access: Issues in language test design and delivery*. Sydney: National Centre for English Language Teaching and Research, Macquarie University. 175–196.

Moser-Mercer, B. (1997) Editorial: Methodological issues in interpreting research: An introduction to the Ascona workshops. *Interpreting* 2: 1–11.

Moser-Mercer, B. (1996) Quality in interpreting: Some methodological issues. *The Interpreters' Newsletter* 7: 43–55.

Moser-Mercer, B., A. Künzli, and M. Korac (1998) Prolonged turns in interpreting: Effects on quality, physiological and psychological stress (pilot study). *Interpreting* 3: 47–64.

Moskowitz, G. (1978) *Caring and sharing in the foreign language class.* Rowley, MA: Newbury House.

Moss, P. (1994) Can there be validity without reliability? *Educational Researcher* 23: 5–12.

Mouzourakis, P. (1996) Videoconferencing: Techniques and challenges. *Interpreting* 1: 21–38.

Mufwene, S. S. (1997) Jargons, pidgins, creoles, and koines: What are they? In A. Spears and D. Winford (eds.) *The structure and status of pidgins and creoles.* Amsterdam: John Benjamins. 35–70

Mufwene, S. S. (1986) The universalist and substrate hypotheses complement one another. In P. Muysken and N. Smith (eds.) *Substrate versus universals in creole genesis.* Amsterdam: John Benjamins. 129–162.

Mühlhäusler, P. (1998) Some Pacific island utopias and their languages. *Plurilinguismes* 15: 27–47.

Mühlhäusler, P. (1996a) *Linguistic ecology: Language change and linguistic imperialism in the Pacific region.* London: Routledge.

Mühlhäusler, P. (1996b) The value of low candidature languages at university level. *Australian Language Matters* 4(1): 8–9, 15.

Mühlhäusler, P. (1995) Attitudes to literacy in the pidgins and creoles of the Pacific area. *English World-Wide* 16: 251–271.

Mühlhäusler, P., and A. Peace. (1999) Mind your language: Ecolinguistics as a resource for peace, ecotourism. Unpublished conference paper presented at the Ecotourism Association of Australia, Fraser Island. MultiCAT informational website. [Online.] Available: ⟨http://www.cohums.ohio-state.edu/flc/cic/multicat.htm⟩.

MultiCAT informational web site [online]. Avaialble: ⟨http://www.cohums.ohio-state.edu/flc/cic/multicat.htm⟩

Munby, J. (1978) *Communicative syllabus design.* Cambridge: Cambridge University Press.

Munday, J. (1998) A computer-assisted approach to the analysis of translation shifts. *Meta* 43: 542–556.

Murray, D. (1995) *Knowledge machines: Language and information in a technological society.* London: Longman.

Murtagh, E. J. (1982) Creole and English as languages of instruction in bilingual education with Aboriginal Australians: Some research findings. *International Journal of the Sociology of Language* 36: 15–33.

Musau, P. M. (1999) Constraints on the acquisition planning of indigenous African languages: The case of Kiswahili in Kenya. *Language, Culture, and Curriculum* 12: 117–127.

Myers, G. (1999) *Ad worlds: Brands, media, audiences.* London: Arnold.

Myers, I. B., and M. McCaulley (1985) *Manual: A guide to the developmental and use of the Myers-Briggs Type Indicator.* Palo Alto, CA: Counseling Psychologists Press.

Myers-Scotton, C. (1995) A lexically based model of code switching. In L. Milroy and P. Muysken (eds.) *One speaker, two languages: Cross-disciplinary perspectives on code-switching.* Cambridge: Cambridge University Press. 233–256.

Myhill, J. (1999) Identity, territoriality, and minority language survival. *Journal of Multilingual and Multicultural Development* 20: 35–50.

Myles, F. (1995) Interaction between linguistic theory and language processing in SLA. *Second Language Research* 11: 235–265.

Nagata, N. (1993) Intelligent computer feedback for second language instruction. *The Modern Language Journal* 77: 330–339.

Nagy, W., E. McClure, and M. Mir (1997) Linguistic transfer and the use of context by Spanish-English bilinguals. *Applied Psycholinguistics* 18: 431–452.

Nahir, M. (1984) Language planning goals: A classification. *Language Problems & Language Planning* 8: 294–327.

Nahir, M. (1977) The five aspects of language planning: A classification. *Language Problems & Language Planning* 1: 107–122.

Naiman, N., M. Fröhlich, H. H. Stern, and A. Todesco (1978) *The good language learner.* Toronto: Ontario Institute for Studies in Education.

Nassaji, H., and M. Swain (2000) A Vygotskyan perspective towards corrective feedback in L2: The effect of random vs. negotiated help on the acquisition of English articles. *Language Awareness* 9: 34–51.

[National Core Curriculum: First draft (1990)] *Nemzeti alaptanterv: Első fogalmazvány* Székesfehérvár. [Manuscript.]

Nattinger, J. R., and J. S. DeCarrico (1992) *Lexical phrases and language teaching.* Oxford: Oxford University Press.

Nelde, P. H. (1995) *Euromosaic: The production and reproduction of the minority language groups in the European Union.* Luxemburg: Office for Official publications of the European Community.

Nelde, P. H. (1987) Language contact means language conflict. In G. Mac Eoin, A. Ahlqvist, and C. Óh Aodha (eds.) *Third international conference on minority languages.* Clevedon, Avon, UK: Multilingual Matters. 33–42.

Nelde, P. H., H. Göebl, Z. Starý, and W. Wolck (eds.) (1996) *Contact linguistics: An international handbook of contemporary research.* Berlin: de Gruyter.

Nelson, C. (1999) Sexual identities in ESL: Queer theory and classroom enquiry. *TESOL Quarterly* 33: 371–392.

Nelson, G., and J. Carson (1998) ESL students' perceptions of effectiveness in peer response groups. *Journal of Second Language Writing* 7: 113–131.

Nelson, G., and J. Murphy (1992) An L2 writing group: Task and social dimensions. *Journal of Second Language Writing* 1: 171–194.

Neuman, W. L. (1994) *Social research methods: Qualitative and quantitative approaches.* 2nd ed. Boston: Allyn and Bacon.

Newell, A., P. S. Rosenbloom, and J. E. Laird (1989) Symbolic architecture for cognition. In M. I. Posner (ed.) *Foundations of cognitive science.* Cambridge, MA: MIT Press. 93–131.

New London Group (1996) A pedagogy of multiliteracies: Designing social futures. *Harvard Educational Review* 66: 60–92.

Newmark, L., and D. Reibel (1968) Necessity and sufficiency in language learning. *International Review of Applied Linguistics in Language Teaching* 6: 145–164.

Newmark, P. (1991) *About translation.* Clevedon, Avon, UK: Multilingual Matters.

Newmark, P. (1988) *A textbook of translation.* Hemel Hempstead, UK: Prentice Hall International.

Newmeyer, F. J. (1987) The current convergence in linguistic theory: Some implications for second language research. *Second Language Research* 3: 1–19.

Nguyen, T. C. P., and F. V. Tochon (1998) Influence comparée de la carte de concepts et du résumé sur la compréhension et la production orales durant l'interprétation consécutive. [English translation of article titles: Comparative influence of concept mapping and summary on oral comprehension and production during consecutive interpretation.] *Meta* 43: 220–235.

Nichols, P. C. (1996) Pidgins and creoles. In S. L. McKay and N. H. Hornberger (eds.) *Sociolinguistics and language teaching.* Cambridge: Cambridge University Press. 195–217.

Nida, E. A. (1976) A framework for the analysis and evaluation of theories of translation. In R. W. Brislin (ed.) *Translation: Applications and research.* New York: Gardner Press. 47–91.

Nida, E. A. (1975) *Language, structure and translation* [Essays selected and introduced by A.S. Dill]. Stanford: Stanford University Press.

Nida, E. A. (1956) Motivation in second language learning. *Language Learning* 7: 11–16.

Nida, E. A., and C. Taber (1974) *The theory and practice of translation.* Leiden, Netherlands: E. J. Brill.

Nidue, J. (1988) A survey of teachers' attitudes towards the use of Tok Pisin as a medium of instruction in community schools in Papua New Guinea. *Papua New Guinea Journal of Education* 24: 214–231.

Nikolov, M. (1999a) The socio-educational and sociolinguistic context of the examination reform. In H. Fekete, É. Major, and M. Nikolov (eds.) *English language education in Hungary: A baseline study.* Budapest: British Council. 7–20.

Nikolov, M. (1999b) Classroom observation project. In H. Fekete, É. Major, and M. Nikolov (eds.) *English language education in Hungary: A baseline study.* Budapest: British Council. 221–245.

Noels, K. A., G. Pon, and R. Clément (1996) Language, identity and adjustment: The role of linguistic self-confidence in the adjustment process. *Journal of Language and Social Psychology* 15: 246–264.

Nolan, F. (1994) Auditory and acoustic analysis in speaker recognition. In J. Gibbons (ed.) *Language and the law.* London: Longman. 326–345.

Norgate, S. (1997) Research methods for studying the language of blind children. In N. Hornberger and D. Corson (eds.) *Encyclopedia of Language and Education.* Vol. 8: *Research methods in language and education.* Dordrecht, Netherlands: Kluwer Academic. 165–173.

Norris, J., J. D. Brown, T. Hudson, and J. Yoshioka (1998) *Designing second language performance assessments.* Honolulu: University of Hawai'i at Manoa, Second Language Teaching and Curriculum Center.

North, B. (1993) *The development of descriptors on scales of language proficiency.* Washington, DC: National Foreign Language Center.

Northern Territory Department of Education (1995) *1994 annual reports from specialist staff in bilingual programs in Northern Territory Schools.* Darwin: Northern Territory Department of Education.

Nortier, J. (1989) Dutch and Moroccan Arabic in contact: Code-switching among Moroccans in the Netherlands. Ph.D. diss., University of Utrecht, Netherlands.

Norton, B. (2001) Non-participation, imagined communities, and the language classroom. In M. Breen (ed.) *Learner contributions to language learning: New directions in research.* London: Longman/Pearson Education. 159–171.

Norton, B. (2000) *Identity and language learning: Gender, ethnicity and educational change.* London: Longman/Pearson Education.

Norton, B. (1997a) Language, identity, and the ownership of English. *TESOL Quarterly* 31: 409–430.

Norton, B. (ed.) (1997b) *Language and identity.* [Special issue of *TESOL Quarterly* 31(3).]

Norton Peirce, B. (1995) Social identity, investment, and language learning. *TESOL Quarterly* 29: 9–31.

Norton Peirce, B. (1994) The test of English as a foreign language: Developing items for reading comprehension. In C. Hill and K. Parry (eds.) *From testing to assessment.* New York: Longman. 39–60.

Nunan, D. (1995a) *Atlas 1.* New York: Heinle and Heinle.

Nunan, D. (1995b) *Atlas 2.* Boston: Heinle and Heinle.

Nunan, D. (1992) *Research methods in language learning.* Cambridge: Cambridge University Press.

Nunan, D. (1991) Communicative tasks and the language curriculum. *TESOL Quarterly* 25: 279–295.

Nunan, D. (1989) *Designing tasks for the communicative classroom.* Cambridge: Cambridge University Press.

Nwenmely, H. (1996) *Language reclamation: French Creole language teaching in the UK and the Caribbean.* Clevedon, Avon, UK: Multilingual Matters.

Nyikos, M. (1996) The conceptual shift to learner-centered classrooms: Increasing teacher and student strategic awareness. In R. Oxford (ed.) *Language learning strategies around the world: Crosscultural perspectives.* Manoa: University Press of Hawai'i. 109–118.

O'Barr, W. M., and J. M. Conley. (1996) Ideological dissonance in the American legal system. In C. Briggs (ed.) *Disorderly discourse: Narrative, conflict, and inequality.* New York: Oxford University Press. 114–134.

Ochs, E. (1997) From the past president. *AAALetter* 19: 2.

Ochs, E. (1992) Indexing gender. In A. Duranti and C. Goodwin (eds.) *Rethinking context.* Cambridge: Cambridge University Press. 335–358.

Ochs, E. (1988) *Culture and language development: Language acquisition and language socialization in a Samoan village.* Cambridge: Cambridge University Press.

Ochs, E., and C. Taylor. (1992) Family narrative as political activity. *Discourse and Society* 3: 301–340.

Ockenden. M. (1972) *Situational dialogues.* London: Longman.

Odlin, T. (1998) On the affective and cognitive bases for language transfer. In R. Cooper (ed.) *Compare or contrast?* Tampere, Finland: University of Tampere Studies in English. 81–106.

Odlin, T. (1991) Irish English idioms and language transfer. *English World-Wide* 12: 175–193.

Odlin, T. (1989) *Language transfer.* Cambridge: Cambridge University Press.

Ogbu, J. (1983) Minority status and schooling in plural societies. *Comparative Education Review* 27: 168–190.

Ogbu, J., and M. E. Matute-Bianchi (1986) Understanding sociocultural factors: Knowledge, identity, and school adjustment. In D. Holt (ed.) *Beyond language: Social and cultural factors in schooling language minority students.* Los Angeles: Evaluation, Dissemination and Assessment Center, California State University, Los Angeles. 73–142.

Ogbu, J., and H. Simons (1998) Voluntary and involuntary minorities: A cultural-ecological theory of school performance with some implications for education. *Anthropology and Education Quarterly* 29: 155–188.

O'Grady, W. (1996) *Syntactic development.* Chicago: University of Chicago Press.

Ohly, R. (1989) Linguistic ecology: The African language case. *Logos* 9: 79–90.

Ohta, A. (2001) *Second language acquisition processes in the classroom: Learning Japanese.* Mahwah, NJ: Lawrence Erlbaum.

Oksaar, E. (1980) *Mehrsprachigkeit, Sprachkontakt, Sprachkonflikt* [Multilingualism, language contact, language conflict]. In P. H. Nelde (ed.) *Sprachkontakt und Sprachkonflikt* [Language contact and language conflict]. Wiesbaden: Steiner. 43–52.

Oliver, R. (1995) Negative feedback in child NS-NNS conversation. *Studies in Second Language Acquisition* 17: 459–481.

Oller, J. W., Jr. (1979) *Language tests at school.* London: Longman.

O'Loughlin, K. (2000) Gender bias in oral proficiency testing. Paper presented at Language Testing Research Colloquium, Vancouver, British Columbia. March.

Olsher, D. (2000) Text, task and talk: A multi-modal perspective on ESL pair work interaction. Paper presented at the annual meeting of the American Association for Applied Linguistics [AAAL]. Vancouver, BC. March.

Olshtain, E., and S. Blum-Kulka (1985) Degree of approximation: Nonnative reactions to native speech act behavior. In S. M. Gass and C. Madden (eds.) *Input in second language acquisition.* Rowley, MA: Newbury House. 303–325.

O'Malley, J., and A. Chamot (1990) *Learning strategies in second language acquisition.* Cambridge: Cambridge University Press.

Omar, A. S. (1992) Conversational openings in Kiswahili: The pragmatic performance of native and nonnative speakers. In L. F. Bouton and Y. Kachru (eds.) *Pragmatics and language learning.* Urbana-Champaign: University of Illinois, Division of English as an International Language [DEIL]. 3: 20–32.

Ondelli, S. (1998) Medium shift in interpretation: Do interpreters produce oral texts? *The Interpreters' Newsletter* 8: 181–193.

O'Neill, R. (1981) *American kernel lessons: Beginning.* New York: Longman.

O'Neill, R. (1970) *English in situations.* Oxford: Oxford University Press.

O'Riagain, P. (1988) Bilingualism in Ireland 1973–1983: An overview of national sociolinguistic surveys. *International Journal of the Sociology of Language* 70: 29–51.

Ortega, L. (1999) Planning and focus on form in L2 oral performance. *Studies in Second Language Acquisition* 21: 109–148.

Otheguy, R. (1995) When contact speakers talk, linguistic theory listens. In E. Contini-Morova and B. Goldberg (eds.) *Meaning as explanations: Advances in linguistic sign theory.* Berlin: Mouton de Gruyter. 213–242.

Otheguy, R. (1993) A reconsideration of the notion of loan translation in the analysis of U.S. Spanish. In A. Roca and J. Lipski (eds.) *Spanish in the United States: Linguistic contact and diversity.* Berlin: Mouton de Gruyter. 21–41.

Otto, S. (1991) German as a second language in France—a view from the outside. *Germanistische Mitteilungen* [Germanic Studies Communications] 34: 81–88.

Oxford, R. L. (2001). "The bleached bones of a story": Learners' constructions of language teachers. In M. Breen (ed.) *Learners contributions to language learning: New directions in research.* Cambridge: Cambridge University Press.

Oxford, R. L. (1996a) *Language learning strategies: Crosscultural perspectives.* Honolulu: University Press of Hawai'i.

Oxford, R. L. (1996b) *Language learning motivation: Pathways to the new century.* Honolulu: University Press of Hawai'i.

Oxford, R. L. (1996c) Personality type in the foreign or second language classroom: Theoretical and empirical perspectives. In A. Horning and R. Sudol (eds.) *Understanding literacy: Personality preferences in rhetorical and psycholinguistic contexts.* Cresskill, NJ: Hampton Press. 1–35.

Oxford, R. L. (1996d) New pathways of language learning motivation. In R. L. Oxford (ed.) *Language Learning Motivation: Pathways to the New Century.* Honolulu: University Press of Hawai'i. 1–8.

Oxford, R. L. (1990) *Language learning strategies: What every teacher should know.* New York: Newbury House.

Oxford, R. L., and N. Anderson (1995) A crosscultural view of learning styles. *Language Teaching* 28: 201–215.

Oxford, R. L., and M. Ehrman. (1993) Second language research on individual differences. In W. Grabe et al. *Annual Review of Applied Linguistics 13: Issues in second language teaching and learning.* Cambridge: Cambridge University Press. 188–205.

Oxford, R. L., M. Ehrman, and M. Lavine (1991) Style wars: Teacher-student style conflicts in the language classroom. In S. S. Magnan (ed.) *Challenges in the 1990s for college foreign language programs.* Boston: Heinle and Heinle. 1–25.

Oxford, R. L., and M. Nyikos (1989) Variables affecting choice of language learning strategies by university students. *The Modern Language Journal* 73: 219–300.

Page, E. B. (1966) The imminence of grading essays by computer. *Phi Delta Kappan* March: 238–243.

Page, E. B., and N. Petersen (1995) The computer moves into essay grading: Updating the ancient test. *Phi Delta Kappan* March: 561–565.

Pakir, A. (1993) Making bilingualism work: Developments in bilingual education in ASEAN. *Language, Culture and Curriculum* 6: 209–223.

Palionis, J. (1997) On the Lithuanian language during the Soviet dictatorship. *Gimtoji Kalba* [Native Language] 6(362): 1–3.

Palmer, S. E., and R. Kimchi (1986) The information processing approach to cognition. In T. J. Knapp and L. C. Robertson (eds.) *Approaches to cognition: Contrasts and controversies.* Hillsdale, NJ: Lawrence Erlbaum. 37–77.

Palys, T. (1997) *Research decisions: Quantitative and qualitative perspectives.* 2nd ed. Toronto: Harcourt, Brace, Jovanovich.

Paradis, M. (1998) Aphasia in bilinguals: How atypical is it? In P. Coppens, Y. Lebrun, and A. Basso (eds.) *Aphasia in atypical populations.* Mahwah, NJ: Lawrence Erlbaum. 35–66.

Paradis, M. (1981) Neurolinguistic organization of a bilingual's two languages. In J. E. Copeland and P. W. Davis (eds.) *The Seventh LACUS Forum.* Columbia, SC: Hornbeam Press. 486–494.

Park, G. (1994) Language learning strategies: Why do adults need them? Austin: University of Texas. [Unpublished manuscript.]

Park, J. C., M. Palmer, and G. Washburn (1997) Checking grammatical mistakes for

English-as-a-second-language (ESL) students. *Proceedings of KSEA-NERC*. New Brunswick, NJ.

Park, Y. (1994) Incorporating interactive multimedia in an ESL classroom environment: Learners' interactions and learning strategies. Ph.D. diss., Iowa State University, Ames.

Parks, S. (2000) Professional writing and the role of incidental collaboration: Evidence from a medical setting. *Journal of Second Language Writing* 9: 101–122.

Patrick, P. L. (1999a) *Urban Jamaican Creole: Variation in the mesolect* [Varieties of English around the world. G 17.] Amsterdam: John Benjamins.

Patrick, P. L. (1999b) Applied creolistics in court: Linguistic, methodological and ethical dimensions of expert testimony. Paper presented at the Conference of the Society for Pidgin and Creole Linguistics, Los Angeles.

Patthey-Chavez. G. G. (1993) High school as an arena for cultural conflict and acculturation for Latino Angelinos. *Anthropology and Education Quarterly* 24: 33–60.

Patthey-Chavez, G. G., and L. Clare (1996) Task, talk and text: The influence of instructional conversation on transitional bilingual writers. *Written Communication* 13: 515–563.

Patthey-Chavez, G. G., and D. R. Ferris (1997) Writing conferences and the weaving of multi-voiced texts in college composition. *Research in the Teaching of English* 31: 51–90.

Pavlenko, A. (1999) New approaches to concepts in bilingual memory. *Bilingualism: Language and Cognition* 2: 209–230.

Pavlenko, A., and J. P. Lantolf (2000) In J. P. Lantolf (ed.) *Sociocultural theory and second language learning*. Oxford: Oxford University Press. 155–178.

Pawley, A., and F. H. Syder (1983) Two puzzles for linguistic theory: Nativelike selection and nativelike fluency. In J. C. Richards and R. W. Schmidt (eds.) *Language and Communication*. London: Longman. 191–226.

Pawlikova-Vihanova, V. (1996) Swahili and the dilemma of Ugandan language policy. *Asian and African Studies* 5: 158–170.

Pearson, B. A., and R. W. Berch (1994) Video depositions: Linguistic endorsement and caveats. In J. Gibbons (ed.) *Language and the law*. London: Longman. 171–187.

Pearson, P. D., and L. Fielding (1991) Comprehension instruction. In R. Barr et al. (eds.) *Handbook of reading research*. 2 vols. New York: Longman. 2: 815–860.

Pease-Alvarez, L. (1993) *Moving in and out of bilingualism: Investigating native language maintenance and shift in Mexican-descent children*. Santa Cruz, CA: National Center for Research on Cultural Diversity and Second Language Learning.

Peck, S. (1980). Language play in child second language acquisition. In D. Larsen-Freeman (ed.) *Discourse analysis in second language research*. Rowley, MA: Newbury House. 154–164.

Pederson, E., E. Danziger, D. Wilkins, S. Levinson, S. Kita, and G. Senft (1998) Semantic typology and spatial conceptualization. *Language* 74: 557–589.

Peirce, B. N. (1995) Social identity, investment, and language learning. *TESOL Quarterly* 29: 9–31.

Peirce, B. N. (1994) The test of English as a foreign language: Developing items for reading comprehension. In C. Hill and K. Parry (eds.) *From testing to assessment*. New York: Longman. 39–60.

Penning, R. (1996) History of the community interpreting industry: Gaining respect for the profession. In M. Jérôme-O'Keeffe (ed.) *Proceedings of the 1997 American Translators Association Annual Conference.* Medford, NJ: Information Today, 91–97.

Pennycook, A. (1999a) Introduction: Critical approaches to TESOL. *TESOL Quarterly* 33: 329–348.

Pennycook, A. (1998) *English and the discourses of colonialism.* New York: Routledge.

Pennycook, A. (1997a) Borrowing others' words: Text, ownership, memory, and plagiarism. *TESOL Quarterly* 30: 201–230.

Pennycook, A. (1997b) Critical applied linguistics and education. In R. Wodak and D. Corson (eds.) *Encyclopedia of language and education.* Vol. 1: *Language policy and political issues in education.* Dordrecht, Netherlands: Kluwer Academic. 23–31.

Pennycook, A. (1995) English in the world/The world in English. In J. W. Tollefson (ed.) *Power and inequality in language education.* Cambridge: Cambridge University Press. 34–58.

Pennycook, A. (1994a) Incommensurable discourses? *Applied Linguistics* 15: 115–138.

Pennycook, A. (1994b) *The cultural politics of English as an international language.* New York: Longman.

Pennycook, A. (ed.) (1999b) *Critical approaches to TESOL.* [Special issue of *TESOL Quarterly* 33(3).]

Perez-Chambers, M. (2000) Personal communication. March 20.

Pergnier, M. (1980) *Les fondements sociolinguistiques de la traduction* [The sociolinguistic foundations of translation]. Paris: Honoré Champion.

Peters, A. (1983) *Units of language acquisition.* Cambridge: Cambridge University Press.

Peterson, R. R., and P. Savoy (1998) Lexical selection and phonological encoding during language production: Evidence for cascaded processing. *Journal of Experimental Psychology: Learning, Memory, and Cognition* 24: 539–557.

Philips, S. U. (1998) *Ideology in the language of judges: How judges practice law, politics, and courtroom control.* Oxford: Oxford University Press.

Phillipson, R. (1994a) English language spread policy. *International Journal of the Sociology of Language* 107: 7–24.

Phillipson, R. (1994b) The spread of dominant languages (English, French, German) in multilingual Europe. ROLIG Paper No. 51. Roskilde, Denmark: Roskilde Universitets. 18–22.

Phillipson, R. (1992) *Linguistic imperialism.* Oxford: Oxford University Press.

Philp, J. (1999) Interaction, noticing and second language acquisition: An examination of learners' noticing of recasts in task-based interaction. Ph.D. diss., University of Tasmania, Hobart, Australia.

Pica, T. (1997a) Second language research methods. In N. Hornberger and D. Corson (eds.) *Encyclopedia of Language and Education.* Vol. 8: *Research methods in language and education.* Dordrecht, Netherlands: Kluwer Academic. 89–99.

Pica, T. (1997b) Second language teaching and research relationships: A North American view. *Language Teaching Research* 1: 48–72.

Pica, T. (1994) Research on negotiation: What does it reveal about second-language learning conditions, processes, and outcomes? *Language Learning* 44: 493–527.

Pica, T. (1988) Interlanguage adjustments as an outcome of NS-NNS negotiated interaction. *Language Learning* 38: 45–73.

Pica, T. (1987) Second language acquisition, social interaction, and the classroom. *Applied Linguistics* 8: 3–21.

Pica, T., and C. Doughty (1985) Input and interaction in the communicative language classroom: A comparison of teacher-fronted and group activities. In S. M. Gass and C. Madden (eds.) *Input in second language acquisition.* Rowley, MA: Newbury House. 115–132.

Pica, T., C. Doughty, and R. Young (1986) Making input comprehensible: Do interactional modifications help? *ITL Review of Applied Linguistics* 72: 1–25.

Pica, T., R. Kanagy, and J. Falodun (1993) Choosing and using communication tasks for second language instruction. In G. Crookes and S. M. Gass (eds.) *Tasks and language learning.* Clevedon, Avon, UK: Multilingual Matters. 9–34.

Pica, T., R. Young, and C. Doughty (1987) The impact of interaction on comprehension. *TESOL Quarterly* 21: 737–758.

Picone, M. (1997) Enclave dialect contraction: An external overview of Louisiana French. *American Speech* 72: 117–144.

Piehl, A. (1996) Language standardization and guidance on correct usage in *Virttaja. Virittaja.* [The Inquirer]. 100: 490–503.

Piggott, G. (1992) Variability in feature dependency: The case of nasality. *Natural Language and Linguistic Theory* 10: 33–77.

Piller, I. (1999) 'Something tattooed on my forehead': Gendered performances and perceptions of linguistic and national identity. In U. Pasero and B. Friederike (eds.) *Wahrnehmung und Herstellung von Geschlecht—Perceiving and Performing Gender.* Wiesbaden: Westdeutscher Verlag. 117–126.

Pimsleur, P. (1966) *Language aptitude battery.* New York: Harcourt, Brace, and Jovanovich.

Pinker, S. (1994) *The Language Instinct.* New York: Morrow.

Pinker, S. (1991) Rules of language. *Science* 253: 530–536.

Pinker, S. (1989) *Learnability and cognition: The acquisition of argument structure.* Cambridge, MA: MIT Press.

Pinker, S., and A. Prince (1994) Regular and irregular morphology and the psychological status of rules. In S. D. Lima, R. L. Corrigan, and G. K. Iverson (eds.) *The reality of linguistic rules.* Philadelphia: John Benjamins. 321–351.

Pinker, S., and A. Prince (1988) On language and connectionism: Analysis of a parallel distributing model of language acquisition. *Cognition* 28: 73–193.

Pintrich, P., and D. Schunk (1996) *Motivation in education: Theory, research, and application.* Englewood Cliffs, NJ: Prentice Hall.

Piper, A. (1986) Conversation and the computer: A study of the conversational spin-off generated among learners of English as a second language working in groups. *System* 14: 187–198.

Planelles-Ivanez, M. (1996) The influence of linguistic planning on the feminization of job titles in France and Quebec: Two different results concerning usage. *Revue quebecoise de linguistique* [Quebec review of linguistics] 24: 71–106.

Platt, E., and S. Troudi (1997) Mary and her teachers: A Grego-speaking child's place in the mainstream classroom. *The Modern Language Journal* 81: 28–59.

Plough, I. (1995) Indirect negative evidence, inductive inferencing and second language acquisition. In L. Eubank, L. Selinker, and M. Sharwood Smith (eds.) *The current state of interlanguage: Studies in honor of William E. Rutherford*. Amsterdam: John Benjamins. 89–105.

Plough, I. (1994) A role for indirect negative evidence in second language acquisition. Ph.D. diss., Michigan State University, East Lansing.

Plunkett, K., and V. Marchman (1993) From rote learning to system building: Acquiring verb morphology in children and connectionist nets. *Cognition* 48: 21–69.

Pöchhacker, F. (1995) Writings and research on interpreting: A bibliographic analysis. *The Interpreters' Newsletter* 6: 17–31.

Poirier, C. (1998) Toward a new image of Québec French: Twenty years of Tresor. *French Review* 71: 912–929.

Polio, C., C. Fleck, and N. Leder. (1998) "If only I had more time": ESL learners' changes in linguistic accuracy on essay revisions. *Journal of Second Language Writing* 7: 43–68.

Politzer, R. L. (1983) Research notes: An explanatory study of self reported language learning behaviors and their relation to achievement. *Studies in Second Language Acquisition* 6: 54–68.

Pollard, C. J., and I. Sag (1994) *Head-driven phrase structure grammar*. Chicago: University of Chicago Press.

Pollard, V. (1993) *From Jamaican Creole to standard English: A handbook for teachers*. Brooklyn, NY: Caribbean Research Center, Medgar Evers College.

Pollitt, A. (1997) Rasch measurement in latent trait models. In C. Clapham and D. Corson (eds.) *Encyclopedia of language and education. Vol. 7: Language testing and assessment*. Dordrecht, Netherlands: Kluwer Academic. 243–253.

Pollock, J.-Y. (1989) Verb Movement, Universal Grammar, and the structure of IP. *Linguistic Inquiry* 20: 365–424.

Poole, D. (1994a) Routine testing practices and the linguistic construction of knowledge. *Cognition and Instruction* 12: 125–150.

Poole, D. (1994b) Differentiation as an interactional consequence of routine classroom testing. *Qualitative Studies in Education* 7: 1–17.

Poole, D. (1992) Language socialization in the second language classroom. *Language Learning* 42: 593–616.

Poplack, S. (1985) Contrasting Patterns of code-switching in two communities. In H. J. Warkentyne (ed.) *Methods V: papers from the Fifth International Conference on Methods in Dialectology*. Sydney, Australia: University of Victoria Press. 363–386.

Popper, K. (1961) *The poverty of historicism*. London: Routledge.

Porter-Ladousse, G. (1987) *Role play*. Cambridge: Cambridge University Press.

Portes, A., and R. Schauffler (1994) Language and the second generation: Bilingualism yesterday and today. *International Migration Review* 28: 640–661.

Poth, J. (1996) A methodological outline of language planning in Africa. *Etudes de Linguistiqe Appliquée* [Studies in applied linguistics] 103: 351–356.

Potter, M. C., K.-F. So, B. Von Eckardt, and L. B. Feldman (1984) Lexical and conceptual representation in beginning and more proficient bilinguals. *Journal of Verbal Learning and Verbal Behavior* 23: 23–38.

Poulisse, N. (1999) *Slips of the tongue: Speech errors in first and second language production*. Amsterdam: John Benjamins.

Poulisse, N. (1997) Language production in bilinguals. In A. M. B. de Groot and J. F.

Kroll (eds.) *Tutorials in bilingualism: Psycholinguistic perspectives.* Mahwah, NJ: Lawrence Erlbaum. 201–224.

Poulisse, N., and T. Bongaerts (1994) First language use in second language production. *Applied Linguistics* 15: 36–57.

Powers, D. E., J. Burstein, M. Chodorow, M. E. Fowles, and K. Kukich (2000) Comparing the validity of automated and human essay scoring. GRE No. 98–08a. Princeton, NJ: Educational Testing Service.

Prabhu, N. S. (1987) *Second language pedagogy.* Oxford: Oxford University Press.

Prasada, S., and S. Pinker (1993) Similarity-based and rule-based generalizations in inflectional morphology. *Language and Cognitive Processes* 8: 1–56.

Pratt, D., and E. C. Short (1994) Curriculum management. In T. Husén and T. N. Postlethwaite (eds.) *The international encyclopedia of education.* 2nd ed. Oxford: Pergamon. 1320–1325.

Pratt-Johnson, Y. (1993) Curriculum for Jamaican Creole-speaking students in New York City. *World Englishes* 12: 257–264.

Pressley, M. (1998) *Reading instruction that works: The case for balanced teaching.* New York: Guilford.

Pressley, M., and V. Woloshyn (1995) *Cognitive strategy instruction that really improves children's academic performance.* Cambridge, MA: Brookline Books.

Preston, D. R. (2000) Three kinds of sociolinguistics and SLA: A psycholinguistic perspective. In. B. Swierzbin, F. Morris, M. E. Anderson, C. A. Klee, and E. Tarone (eds.) *Social and cognitive factors in second language acquisition: Selected proceedings of the 1999 Second Language Research Forum.* Somerville, MA: Cascadilla Press. 3–30.

Preston, D. R. (1996a) Variationist perspectives on second language acquisition. In R. Bayley and D. R. Preston (eds.) *Second language acquisition and linguistic variation.* Amsterdam: John Benjamins. 1–45.

Preston, D. R. (1996b) Variationist linguistics and second language acquisition. In W. C. Ritchie and T. K. Bhatia (eds.) *Handbook of second language acquisition.* New York: Academic. 229–265.

Preston, D. R. (1991a) Style, status, and change: Three sociolinguistic axioms. In F. Byrne and T. Huebner (eds.) *Development and structures of creole languages. Essays in honor of Derek Bickerton.* Creole Language Library, Vol. 9. Amsterdam: John Benjamins. 43–59.

Preston, D. R. (1991b) Sorting out the variables in sociolinguistic theory. *American Speech* 66: 33–56.

Preston, D. R. (1991c) Variable rules and second language acquisition: An integrationist attempt. *PALM* [Papers in Applied Linguistics Michigan] 6: 1–12.

Preston, D. R. (1989) *Sociolinguistics and second language acquisition.* Oxford: Blackwell.

Prévost, P., and L. White (2000) Missing surface inflection or impairment in second language acquisition. *Second Language Research* 16: 103–134.

Prior, P. (1998) *Writing/Disciplinarity.* Mahwah, NJ: Lawrence Erlbaum.

Pritchett, B. (1992) *Grammatical competence and parsing performance.* Chicago: University of Chicago Press.

Provenzo, E. F., Jr., A. Brett, and G. N. McCloskey (1999) *Computers, curriculum, and cultural change: An introduction for teachers.* Mahwah, NJ: Lawrence Erlbaum.

Pucci, S. (1994) Supporting Spanish language literacy: Latino children and free reading resources in schools. *Bilingual Research Journal* 18: 67–82.

Purpura, J. (1998) Investigating the effects of strategy use and second language test performance with high- and low-ability groups. *Language Testing* 15: 333–379.

Pyöli, R. (1998) Karelian under pressure from Russian—internal and external Russification. *Journal of Multilingual and Multicultural Development* 19: 128–142.

Quine, W. V. O. (1960) *Word and object.* Cambridge, MA: MIT Press.

Quirk, R., S. Greenbaum, S. Leech, and J. Svartik (1985) *A comprehensive grammar of the English language.* New York: Longman.

Rabin, C. (1971) Spelling reform—Israel 1968. In J. Rubin and B. H. Jernudd (eds.) *Can language be planned? Sociolinguistic theory and practice for developing nations.* Honolulu: University Press of Hawai'i. 95–122.

Radecki, P., and J. Swales (1988) ESL student reaction to written comments on their written work. *System* 16: 355–365.

Rahman, T. (1995) The Siraiki movement in Pakistan. *Language Problems & Language Planning* 19: 1–25.

Raimes, A. (1985) What unskilled writers do as they write: A classroom study of composing. *TESOL Quarterly* 19: 229–258.

Ramanathan, V., and D. Atkinson (1999) Ethnographic approaches and methods in L2 writing research: A critical guide and review. *Applied Linguistics* 20: 44–70.

Ramírez, J. D., and B. Merino (1990) Classroom talk in English immersion, early-exit and late-exit transitional bilingual education programs. In R. Jacobson and C. Faltis (eds.) *Language distribution issues in bilingual schooling.* Clevedon, Avon, UK: Multilingual Matters. 61–103.

Rampton, B. (1997a) A socio-linguistic perspective on L2 communication strategies. In G. Kasper and E. Kellerman (eds.) *Communication strategies: Psycholinguistic and sociolinguistic perspectives.* London: Longman. 279–303.

Rampton, B. (1997b) Retuning in applied linguistics. *International Journal of Applied Linguistics* 7: 3–25.

Rampton, B. (1995a) Politics and change in research in applied linguistics. *Applied Linguistics* 12: 229–248.

Rampton, B. (1995b) *Crossings: Language and ethnicity among adolescents.* London: Longman.

Ravel, J.-L., and P. Thomas (1985) *État de la réforme de l'enseignement aux Seychelles (1981–1985)* [The state of education reform in the Seychelles]. Paris: Ministère des Relations Extérieures, Coopération et Développement.

Rea-Dickins, P., and S. Gardner (2000) Snares and silver bullets: Disentangling the construct of formative assessment. *Language Testing* 17: 215–243.

Ready, D., and M. Wesche (1992) An evaluation of the University of Ottawa's sheltered program: Language teaching strategies that work. In R. Courchàne, J. Glidden, J. St. John, and C. Thérien (eds.) *Comprehension-based second language instruction.* Ottawa: University of Ottawa. 389–405.

Reagan, T. (1983) The economics of language: Implications for language planning. *Language Problems & Language Planning* 7: 148–161.

Reid, J. M. (1994) Responding to ESL students' texts: The myths of appropriation. *TESOL Quarterly* 28: 273–292.

Reid, J. M. (1987) The learning style preferences of ESL students. *TESOL Quarterly* 21: 87–111.

Reid, J. M. (ed.) (1998) *Understanding learning styles in the second language classroom.* Upper Saddle River, NJ: Prentice Hall.

Reid, J. M. (ed.) (1995) *Learning styles in the ESL/EFL classroom.* Boston: Heinle and Heinle.

Renié, D., and T. Chanier (1995) Collaboration and computer-assisted acquisition of a second language. *Computer Assisted Language Learning* 8: 3–29.

Resolution (1997) Presented to the Judicial Council Court Interpreter Advisory Panel on June 7 by the Bay Area Court Interpreters (BACI). Berkeley, CA.

Reyhner, J. (ed.) (1997) *Teaching indigenous languages.* Flagstaff: Center for Excellence in Education, Northern Arizona University.

Reyhner, J., G. Cantoni, R. N. St. Clair, and E. P. Yazzie (eds.) (1999) *Revitalizing indigenous languages.* Flagstaff: Center for Excellence in Education, Northern Arizona University.

Rhodes, N., D. Christian, and S. Barfield (1997) Innovations in immersion: The Key School two-way model. In R. K. Johnson and M. Swain (eds.) *Immersion education: International perspectives.* Cambridge: Cambridge University Press. 265–283.

Riazi, A. (1997) Acquiring disciplinary literacy: A social-cognitive analysis of text production and learning among Iranian graduate students of education. *Journal of Second Language Writing* 6: 105–137.

Riccardi, A., G. Marinuzzi, and S. Zecchin (1998) Interpretation and stress. *The Interpreters' Newsletter* 8: 93–106.

Richards, I. A. (1953). Toward a theory of translation. In A. F. Wright (ed.) *Studies in Chinese thought.* Vol. 55. Chicago: University of Chicago Press.

Richards, J. B. (1987) Spanish language and classroom dynamics: School failure in a Guatemalan Mayan community. In H. T. Trueba (ed.) *Success or failure: Learning and the language minority student.* Rowley, MA: Newbury House. 109–130.

Richards, J. C. (1990) *The language teaching matrix.* Cambridge: Cambridge University Press.

Richards, J. C., J. Hull, and S. Proctor (1991) *Interchange 2.* Cambridge: Cambridge University Press.

Richards, J. C., and T. Rodgers (1986) *Approaches and methods in language teaching: A description and analysis.* Cambridge: Cambridge University Press.

Richardson, J. G. (1996) Court interpreting for deaf persons: Culture, communication, and the courts. *State Court Journal* 20: 16–22.

Rickford, J. R. (1999) *African American Vernacular English: Features, evolution, educational implications.* Oxford: Blackwell.

Rickford, J. R. (1997) Unequal partnership: Sociolinguistics and the African American speech community. *Language and Society* 26: 161–197.

Rickford, J. R., and J. McWhorter (1997) Language contact and language generation: Pidgins and creoles. In F. Coulmas (ed.) *The handbook of sociolinguistics.* Oxford: Blackwell. 238–256.

Rickford, J. R., and E. C. Traugott (1985) Symbol of powerlessness and degeneracy, or symbol of solidarity and truth? Paradoxical attitudes toward pidgins and creoles. In S. Greenbaum (ed.) *The English language today.* Oxford: Pergamon Institute of English. 252–261.

Ricoeur, P. (1992) *Oneself as another*. Chicago: University of Chicago Press.

Riggenbach, H. (1999) *Discourse analysis in the language classroom*. Vol. 1: *The spoken language*. Ann Arbor: University of Michigan Press.

Riggenbach, H., and V. Samuda (2000) *Grammar dimensions: Form, meaning and use 2*. Boston: Heinle and Heinle.

Riggins, S. H. (ed.) (1997) *The language and politics of exclusion: Others in discourse*. Thousand Oaks, CA: Sage.

Riley, R. W. (1998) *Helping all children learn English*. Washington, DC: U.S. Department of Education.

Ringbom, H. (1992) On L1 transfer in L2 comprehension and production. *Language Learning* 42: 85–112.

Ringbom, H. (1987) *The role of the first language in foreign language learning*. Clevedon, Avon, UK: Multilingual Matters.

Rintell, E. (1989) That reminds me of a story: The use of language to express emotion by second language learners and native speakers. In M. Eisenstein (ed.) *The dynamic interlanguage*. New York: Plenum. 237–257.

Ritchie, W., and T. Bhatia (eds.) (1996) *Handbook of second language acquisition*. New York: Academic Press.

Rivera, K. (1999) From developing one's voice to making oneself heard: Affecting language policy from the bottom up. In T. Huebner and K. Davis (eds.) *Sociopolitical perspectives on language policy and planning in the USA*. Amsterdam: John Benjamins. 333–346.

Rivers, W. (1968) *The psychologist and the foreign language teacher*. Chicago: University of Chicago Press.

Rivers, W., and M. S. Temperley (1978) *A practical guide to the teaching of English as a second language*. New York: Oxford University Press.

Roberts, C., E. Davies, and T. Jupp (1992) *Language and discrimination*. New York: Longman.

Roberts, R. (1995) Towards a typology of translations. *Hieronymus Complutensis. El Mundo de la Traducción* [The world in translation] 1: 69–78.

Roberts, R. (1988) Literal translation: Different concepts underlying the term. *Terminology Update* 21: 11–13.

Robinson, C. D. W. (1994) Is sauce for the goose sauce for the gander? Some comparative reflections on minority language planning in North and South. *Journal of Multilingual and Multicultural Development* 15: 129–145.

Robinson, J. D. (1998) Getting down to business: Talk, gaze, and body orientation during openings of doctor-patient consultations. *Human Communication Research* 25: 97–123.

Robinson, M. A. (1992) Introspective methodology in interlanguage pragmatics research. In G. Kasper (ed.) *Pragmatics of Japanese as a native and target language*. Honolulu: University Press of Hawai'i. 27–82.

Robinson, P. (1997) Generalizability and automaticity of second language learning under implicit, incidental, enhanced and instructed conditions. *Studies in Second Language Acquisition* 19: 223–247.

Robinson, P. (1996) *Consciousness, rules, and instructed second language instruction*. New York: Peter Lang.

Robinson, P. (1995) Review article: Attention, memory and the "noticing" hypothesis. *Language Learning* 45: 285–331.

Robinson, P. (ed.) (2001) *Cognition and second language instruction.* New York: Cambridge University Press.

Roca de Larios, J., L. Murphy, and R. Manchon (1999) The use of restructuring strategies in EFL writing: A study of Spanish learners of English as a Foreign Language. *Journal of Second Language Writing* 8: 13–44.

Roder, T. (2000) Court interpreters join Communications Workers of America. *ATA Chronicle* (January) 18.

Roebuck, R. (1998) *Reading and recall in L1 and L2: A sociocultural approach.* Stamford, CT: Ablex.

Roelofs, A. (1992) A spreading-activation theory of lemma retrieval in speaking. *Cognition* 41(1, 2): 107–142.

Rogers, C. R. (1969) *Freedom to learn for the 80s.* Columbus, Ohio: Charles Merrill.

Romaine, S. (1994a) Language standarization and linguistic fragmentation in Tok Pisin. In M. Morgan (ed.) *The social construction of identity in creole situations.* Los Angeles: Center for Afro-American Studies, UCLA. 19–42.

Romaine, S. (1994b) Hawai'i Creole as a literary language. *Language in Society* 23: 527–554.

Romaine, S. (1992) *Language, education and development: Urban and rural Tok Pisin in Papua New Guinea.* Oxford: Oxford University Press.

Rommetveit, R. (1985) Language acquisition as increasing linguistic structuring of experience and symbolic behavior control. In J. V. Wertsch (ed.) *Culture, communication, and cognition: Vygotskian perspectives.* Cambridge: Cambridge University Press. 183–204.

Rosaldo, R. (1993) *Culture and truth: The remaking of social analysis.* Boston: Beacon Press.

Rosch, E. (1974) Linguistic relativity. In A. Silverstein (ed.) *Human communication.* Hillsdale, NJ: Lawrence Erlbaum. 95–121.

Rose, K. R. (2000) An exploratory cross-sectional study of interlanguage pragmatic development. *Studies in Second Language Acquisition* 22: 27–67.

Rose, K. R., and G. Kasper (eds.) (in press) *Pragmatics in language teaching.* Oxford: Oxford University Press.

Rosenthal, J. (ed.) (2000) *Handbook of undergraduate second language education.* Mahwah, NJ: Lawrence Erlbaum.

Ross, S. (1997) An introspective analysis of listener inferencing on a second language listening test. In G. Kasper and E. Kellerman (eds.) *Communication strategies: Psycholinguistic and sociolinguistic perspectives.* London: Longman. 216–237.

Rossell, C., and K. Baker (1996) The educational effectiveness of bilingual education. *Research in the Teaching of English* 30: 7–74.

Rost, M. (1994) On-line summaries as representations of lecture understanding. In J. Flowerdew (ed.) *Academic listening: Research perspectives.* Cambridge: Cambridge University Press. 93–127.

Rost, M. (1990) *Listening in language learning.* London: Longman.

Rost, M., and S. Ross (1991) Learner use of strategies in interaction: Typology and teachability. *Language Learning* 41: 235–271.

Rostow, W. W. (1960) *The stages of economic growth.* Cambridge: Cambridge University Press.

Rotter, J. B. (1966) Generalized expectancies for internal versus external locus of control. *Psychological Monographs* 80(1). [Whole No. 609.]

Rounds, P. L., and R. Kanagy (1998) Acquiring linguistic cues to identifying AGENT: Evidence from children using Japanese as a second language. *Studies in Second Language Acquisition* 20: 509–541.

Rubin, J. (1994) A review of second language listening comprehension research. *The Modern Language Journal* 78: 199–221.

Rubin, J. (1987) Learner strategies: Theoretical assumptions, research history and typology. In A. L. Wenden and J. Rubin (eds.) *Learner strategies in language learning.* Englewood Cliffs, NJ: Prentice Hall. 15–30.

Rubin, J. (1975) What the "good language learner" can teach us. *TESOL Quarterly* 9: 41–51.

Rubin, J. (1971) Evaluation and language planning. In J. Rubin and B. H. Jernudd (eds.) *Can language be planned? Sociolinguistic theory and practice for developing nations.* Honolulu: University Press of Hawai'i. 217–252.

Rubin, J., and B. H. Jernudd (eds.) (1971) *Can language be planned? Sociolinguistic theory and practice for developing nations.* Honolulu: University Press of Hawai'i.

Rubin, J., and R. Shuy (eds.) (1973) *Language planning: Current issues and research.* Washington, DC: Georgetown University School of Languages and Linguistics.

Rumelhart, D. E., and J. L. McClelland (eds.) (1986) *Parallel distributed processing.* Cambridge, MA: MIT Press.

Russell, D. (1991) *Writing in the academic disciplines, 1870–1990.* Carbondale: Southern Illinois University Press.

Russo, M. (1995) Self-evaluation: The awareness of one's own difficulties as a training tool for simultaneous interpretation. *The Interpreters' Newsletter* 6: 75–85.

Rutherford, W. E. (1983) Language typology and language transfer. In S. Gass and L. Selinker (eds.) *Language transfer in language learning.* Rowley, MA: Newbury House. 358–370.

Rymes, B. (1998) Dropping out and dropping in: Discourse genres in an urban charter school. Ph.D. diss., University of Southern California, Los Angeles.

Rynkofs, J. T. (1993) Culturally responsive talk between a second grade teacher and Hawaiian children during writing workshop. Ph.D. diss., University of New Hampshire, Plymouth.

Sabban, A. (1982) *Gälisch-Englischer Sprachkontakt* [Gaelic-English language contact]. Heidelberg, Germany: Julius Groos.

Sacks, H., E. A. Schegloff, and G. Jefferson (1974) A simplest systematics for the organization of turn-taking for conversation. *Language* 50: 696–735.

Sager, J. C. (1983) Quality and standards: The evaluation of translations. In C. Picken (ed.) *The translator's handbook.* London: Aslib. 121–128.

Saleh, A. (1997) The nexus of brain hemisphericity, personality types, temperaments, learning styles, learning strategies, gender, majors, and cultures. Ph.D. diss., University of Alabama, Tuscaloosa.

Salomon, G. (1991) On the cognitive effects of technology. In L. T. Landsman (ed.) *Culture, schooling and psychological development.* Norwood, NJ: Ablex. 185–204.

Salsbury, T., and K. Bardovi-Harlig (2000) Oppositional talk and the acquisition of modality in L2 English. In B. Swierzbin, F. Morris, M. E. Anderson, C. A. Kleem, and E. Tarone (eds.) *Social and cognitive factors in second language acquisition: Selected proceedings of the 1999 second language research forum.* Sommerville, MA: Cascadilla Press. 57–76.

Salton G. (1989) *Automatic text processing: The transformation, analysis, and retrieval of information by computer.* Reading, MA: Addison-Wesley.

Samarin, W. J. (1980) Standardization and instrumentalization of creole languages. In A. Valdman and A. Highfield (eds.) *Theoretical orientations in creole studies.* New York: Academic Press. 213–236.

Samborn, H. V. (1996) Tongue-tied. *ABA Journal* February: 22–23.

Samejima, F. (1995) A cognitive diagnosis method using latent trait models: Competency space approach and its relationship with Dibello and Stout's unified cognitive psychometric diagnosis model. In P. Nichols, S. Chipman, and R. Brennan (eds.) *Cognitively diagnostic assessment.* Hillsdale, NJ: Lawrence Erlbaum. 391–410.

Samuda, V. (2001) Guiding relationships between form and meaning during task performance: The role of the teacher. In M. Bygate, P. Skehan, and M. Swain (eds.) *Researching pedagogic tasks: Second language learning, teaching and testing.* London: Pearson Educational.

Samuels, S., and R. Flor (1997) The importance of automaticity for developing expertise in reading. *Reading and Writing Quarterly* 13: 107–121.

Santos, T., D. Atkinson, M. Erickson, P. Matsuda, and T. Silva (2000) On the future of second language writing: A colloquium. *Journal of Second Language Writing* 9: 1–20.

Sapiens, A. (1982) The use of Spanish and English in a high school bilingual civics class. In J. Amastae and L. Elías-Oliveras (eds.) *Spanish in the United States: Sociolinguistic aspects.* New York: Cambridge University Press. 386–412.

Sarangi, S., and M. Baynham (1996) Discursive construction of educational identities: Affirmative readings. *Language and Education* 10: 77–81.

Sasaki, M. (1993) Relationships among second language proficiency, foreign language aptitude and intelligence: A structural equation modeling approach. *Language Learning* 43: 313–344.

Sasaki, Y. (1994) Paths of processing strategy transfers in learning Japanese and English as foreign languages: A Competition Model approach. *Studies in Second Language Acquisition* 16: 43–72.

Sato, C. J. (1991) Sociolinguistic variation and attitudes in Hawaii. In J. Cheshire (ed.) *English around the world.* Cambridge: Cambridge University Press. 647–663

Sato, C. J. (1985) Linguistic inequality in Hawaii: The post-creole dilemma. In N. Wolfson and J. Manes (eds.) *Language of inequality.* Berlin: Mouton. 255–272

Saussure, F. de (1966) *Course in general linguistics.* Tr. W. Baskin [1916]. New York: McGraw-Hill.

Savignon, S. J. (1991) Communicative language teaching: State of the art. *TESOL Quarterly* 25: 261–278.

Saville-Troike, M. (1988) Private speech: Evidence for second language learning strategies during the "silent" period. *Journal of Child Language* 15: 567–590.

Sawyer, M. (1992) The development of pragmatics in Japanese as a second language: The sentence-final particle *ne.* In G. Kasper (ed.) *Pragmatics of Japanese as a native and foreign language.* Technical Report 3. Honolulu: University of Hawai'i at Manoa, Second Language Teaching and Curriculum Center. 83–125.

Saxton, M. (1997) The contrast theory of negative input. *Journal of Child Language* 24: 139–161.

Sayers, J. (1996) Accidental language policy: Creating an ESL/Bilingual teacher endorsement program in Utah. *TESOL Quarterly* 30: 611–615.

Scarcella, R. (1979) On speaking politely in a second language. In C. A. Yorio, K. Perkins, and J. Schachter (eds.) *On TESOL '79*. Washington, DC: TESOL. 275–287.

Scarcella, R., and R. Oxford (1992) *The tapestry of language learning*. Boston: Heinle and Heinle.

Schachter, J. (1996) Maturation and Universal Grammar. In W. Ritchie and T. K. Bhatia (eds.) *Handbook of second language acquisition*. New York: Academic Press. 159–193.

Schachter, J. (1989) Testing a proposed universal. In S. M. Gass and J. Schachter (eds.) *Linguistic perspectives on second language acquisition*. Cambridge: Cambridge University Press. 73–88.

Schachter, J., and V. Yip (1990) Why does anyone object to subject extraction? *Studies in Second Language Acquisition* 12: 379–392.

Schecter, S., and R. Bayley (1997) Language socialization practices and cultural identity: Case studies of Mexican descent families in California and Texas. *TESOL Quarterly* 31: 513–542.

Schegloff, E. A. (1991) Reflections on talk and social structure. In D. Boden and D. H. Zimmerman (eds.) *Talk and social structure: Studies in ethnomethodology and conversation analysis*. Berkeley: University of California Press. 44–70.

Schegloff, E. A., and H. Sacks (1973) Opening up closings. *Semiotica* 8: 289–327.

Schenke, A. (1996) Not just a 'social issue': Teaching feminist in ESL. *TESOL Quarterly* 30: 155–159.

Schieffelin, B. B., and R. C. Doucet (1994) The "real" Haitian Creole: Ideology, metalinguistics, and orthographic choice. *American Ethnologist* 21: 176–200.

Schieffelin, B. B., and E. Ochs (1986) Language socialization. *Annual Review of Anthropology* 15: 163–191.

Schiffman, H. F. (1994) Diglossia, linguistic culture and language policy in Southeast Asia. In K. L. Adams and T. J. Huduk (eds.) *Papers from the second annual meeting of the Southeast Asian Linguistics Society 1992*. Tempe: Arizona State University. 279–307.

Schiffrin, D. (1994) *Approaches to discourse*. Oxford: Blackwell

Schmeck, R. R. (1988) *Learning strategies and learning styles*. New York: Plenum.

Schmidt, R. (1993) Consciousness, learning and interlanguage pragmatics. In G. Kasper and S. Blum-Kulka (eds.) *Interlanguage pragmatics*. Oxford: Oxford University Press. 21–42.

Schmidt, R. (1992) Psychological mechanisms underlying second language fluency. *Studies in Second Language Acquisition* 14: 357–385.

Schmidt, R. (1990) The role of consciousness in second language learning. *Applied Linguistics* 11: 129–158.

Schmidt, R. (1983) Interaction, acculturation, and the acquisition of communicative competence: A case study of an adult. In E. Judd and N. Wolfson (eds.) *Sociolinguistics and language acquisition*. Rowley, MA: Newbury House. 137–174.

Schmidt, R., and S. N. Frota (1986) Developing basic conversational ability in a second language: A case study of a learner of Portuguese. In R. Day (ed.) *Talking to learn*. Rowley, MA: Newbury House. 237–326.

Schmidt, R., O. Kassabgy, D. Boraie, S. Jacques, and R. Moody (1996) Motivation, reported strategy use, and preferences for activities in the foreign language class. Colloquium presented at the annual meeting of Teachers of English to Speakers of Other Languages. Chicago, IL.

Schmidt, R. (ed.) (1995) *Attention and awareness in foreign language teaching.* Honolulu: University Press of Hawai'i.

Schneider, D. A., and K. F. McCoy (1998) Recognizing syntactic errors in the writing of second language learners. In Proceedings of the 17th International Conference on Computational Linguistics and the 36th Annual Meeting of the Association of Computational Linguistics [Coling-ACL-98], Montreal. 1198–1204.

Schneider, W., and R. Shiffrin (1977) Controlled and automatic human processing. I: Detection, search and attention. *Psychological Review* 84: 1–66.

Schön, D. (1983) *The reflective practitioner: How professionals think in action.* Aldershot, UK: Ashgate Arena.

Schoonen, R., K. de Glopper, J. Hulstijn, A. Simis, M. Stevenson, A. van Gelderen, and P. Snellings (2000) Secondary school writing in EFL and L1 (Dutch): The role of higher-order and lower-order skills. Paper presented at the Annual Meeting of the American Association of Applied Linguistics, Vancouver, British Columbia. March.

Schriefers, H. A., A. Meyer, and W. J. M. Levelt (1990) Exploring the time-course of lexical access in speech production: Picture-word interference studies. *Journal of Memory and Language* 29: 86–102.

Schubert, K. (1990) Editorial perspectives: A new decade and a new direction. *Language Problems & Language Planning* 14: 88–90.

Schumann, J. (1997) *The neurobiology of affect in language.* Malden, MA: Blackwell.

Schumann, J. (1994) Where is cognition? Emotion and cognition in second language acquisition. *Studies in Second Language Acquisition* 16: 231–242.

Schwartz, B. D. (1999) Let's make up your mind: "Special Nativist" perspectives on language, modularity of mind, and nonnative language acquisition. *Studies in Second Language Acquisition* 21: 635–654.

Schwartz, B. D., and T. Hoekstra (eds.) (1994) *Language acquisition studies in generative grammar: Papers in honor of Kenneth Wexler from the 1991 GLOW workshops.* Amsterdam: John Benjamins.

Schwartz, B. D., and R. A. Sprouse (2000) When syntactic theories evolve: Consequences for L2 acquisition research. In J. Archibald (ed.) *Second language acquisition and linguistic theory.* Oxford: Blackwell. 156–186.

Schwartz, B. D., and R. A. Sprouse (1996) L2 cognitive states and the full transfer/full access model. *Second Language Research* 12: 40–72.

Schwartz, B. D., and R. A. Sprouse (1994) Word order and nominative case in nonnative language acquisition: A longitudinal study of (L1 Turkish) German interlanguage. In T. Hoekstra and B. D. Schwartz (eds.) *Language acquisition studies in generative grammar.* Amsterdam: John Benjamins. 317–368.

Schweda Nicholson, N. (1999) Language policy development for interpreter services at the Executive Office for Immigration Review. *Language Problems & Language Planning* 23: 37–63.

Schweda Nicholson, N. (1997) Court interpretation in Denmark. In S. E. Carr, R. Roberts, A. Dufour, and D. Steyn (eds.) *The critical link: Interpreters in the community.* Amsterdam: John Benjamins, 259–270.

Schweda Nicholson, N. (1995) Translation and interpretation. In W. Grabe, et al. (eds.) *Annual Review of Applied Linguistics 15: A broad survey of the entire field of applied linguistics.* New York: Cambridge University Press. 42–62.

Schweda Nicholson, N. (1994a) Community interpreter training in the United States and the United Kingdom: An overview of selected initiatives. *Hermes* 12: 127–139.

Schweda Nicholson, N. (1994b) Professional ethics for court and community interpreters. In D. Hammond (ed.) *Professional issues for translators and interpreters.* Amsterdam: John Benjamins. 79–97.

Schweda Nicholson, N. (1994c) Training for refugee mental health interpreters. In C. Dollerup and A. Lindegaard (eds.) *Teaching translation and interpreting 2: Insights, aims, visions.* Amsterdam: John Benjamins. 211–215.

Schweda Nicholson, N. (1989) Documentation and text preparation for simultaneous interpretation. In D. L. Hammond (ed.) *Proceedings of the 1989 American Translators Association Conference.* Medford, NJ: Learned Information. 163–182.

Schweers, C. W. (1993) Variation in cross-linguistic influence on interlanguage lexicon as a function of perceived first-language distance. Ph.D. diss., New York University.

Scollon, R., and S. B. K. Scollon (1983) Face in interethnic communication. In J. C. Richards and R. W. Schmidt (eds.) *Language and communication.* London: Longman. 156–188.

Scotton, C. M. (1982) Learning lingua francas and socioeconomic integration: Evidence from Africa. In R. L. Cooper (ed.) *Language spread: Studies in diffusion and social change.* Bloomington: Indiana University Press. 63–97.

Scotton, C. M., and W. Ury (1977) Bilingual strategies: The social functions of code-switching. *Linguistics* 193: 5–20.

Scovel, T. (1998) *Psycholinguistics.* Oxford: Oxford University Press.

Scribner, S., and M. Cole (1981) *The psychology of literacy.* Cambridge, MA: Harvard University Press.

Searle, J. R. (1976) A classification of illocutionary acts. *Language and Society* 5: 1–23.

Searle, J. R. (1969) *Speech acts.* Cambridge: Cambridge University Press.

Sebba, M. (1997) *Contact languages: Pidgins and creoles.* New York: St. Martin's.

Séguinot, C. (1989) The translation process. An experimental study. In C. Séguinot (ed.) *The translation process.* Toronto: H. G. Publications, School of Translation, York University. 21–53.

Seidenberg, M. S., and M. C. McDonald (1999) A probabilistic constraints approach to language acquisition and processing. *Cognitive Science* 23: 569–588.

Seleskovitch, D. (1984) La traductologie entre l'exégèse et la linguistique [Translation studies between exegesis and linguistics]. In D. Seleskovitch and M. Lederer (eds.) *Interpréter pour traduire* [Interpreting for the purpose of translating]. Paris: Didier Érudition. 264–272.

Seliger, H. W., and E. Shohamy (1989) *Second language research methods.* New York: Oxford University Press.

Selinker, L., and D. Douglas (1985) Wrestling with 'context' in interlanguage theory. *Applied Linguistics* 6: 190–204.

Selinker, L., and U. Lakshmanan (1992) Language transfer and fossilization: The "Multiple Effects Principle." In S. M. Gass and L. Selinker (eds.) *Language transfer in language learning.* Amsterdam: John Benjamins. 197–216.

Sergio, F. S. (1998) Notes on cultural mediation. *The Interpreters' Newsletter* 8: 151–168.

Setton, R. (1998) Meaning assembly in simultaneous interpretation. *Interpreting* 3: 163–199.

Shakir, A., and M. Farghal (1997) When the focus of the text is blurred: A textlinguistic approach for analyzing student interpreters' errors. *Meta* 42: 629–640.

Shannon, S. (1995) The hegemony of English: A case study of one bilingual classroom as a site of resistance. *Linguistics and Education* 7: 175–200.

Sharkey, J., and C. Layzer (2000) Whose definition of success? Identifying factors that affect English language learners' access to academic success and resources. *TESOL Quarterly* 34: 352–368.

Sharkey, N. E. (1996) Fundamental issues in connectionist processing. In G. Brown, K. Malmkjær, and J. Williams (eds.) *Performance and competence in second language acquisition.* Cambridge: Cambridge University Press. 155–184.

Sharwood Smith, M. (1993) Input enhancement in instructed SLA: Theoretical bases. *Studies in Second Language Acquisition* 15: 165–179.

Sharwood Smith, M. (1991) Speaking to many minds: On the relevance of different types of language information for the L2 learner. *Second Language Research* 7: 118–132.

Sharwood Smith, M. (1979) Strategies, language transfer and the simulation of second language learners' mental operations. *Language Learning* 29: 345–361.

Shaw, P. (1996) Voices for improved learning: The ethnographer as co-agent of pedagogic change. In K. M. Bailey and D. Nunan (eds.) *Voices from the language classroom.* Cambridge: Cambridge University Press. 318–337.

Sheehan, K., and J. Burstein (in preparation). An analysis of e-rater scoring for TOEFL-CBT essays. Princeton, NJ: Educational Testing Service.

Shermis, M. (1996) Computerized adaptive testing for reading placement and diagnostic assessment. *Journal of Developmental Education* 38: 45–52.

Sherr, D. (1999a) Interpreting in Spain and Colombia: Two perspectives. *Proteus* 8(3 and 4): 1, 3–4.

Sherr, D. (1999b) Freelance interpreters mobilize for rate increase. *Proteus* 8(1): 1, 3–6.

Shevyakov, M. B. (1987) On language policy in Ghana. *Vestnik Leningradskogo Universiteta, Istoriya yazyk literatura* [Bulletin of the University of Leningrad; History, Language, Literature] 42(4): 88–91.

Shimron, J., and T. Savon (1994) Reading proficiency and orthography: Evidence from Hebrew. *Language Learning* 44: 5–27.

Shirts, R. G. (1977) *BaFa' BaFa': A cross-culture simulation.* Del Mar, CA: Simulation Training Systems.

Shlesinger, M. (1998) Corpus-based interpreting studies as an offshoot of corpus-based translation studies. *Meta* 43: 486–493.

Shnukal, A. (1992) The case against a transfer bilingual program of Torres Strait Creole to English in Torres Strait schools. In J. Siegel (ed.) *Pidgins, creoles and nonstandard dialects in education.* Melbourne: Applied Linguistics Association of Australia. 1–12.

Shohamy, E. (1997) Critical language testing and beyond. Plenary talk presented at Annual American Association for Applied Linguistics [AAAL] meeting, Orlando, FL. March.

Shohamy, E. (1996) Competence and performance in language testing. In G. Brown, K. Malmkjaer, and J. Williams (eds.) *Performance and competence in second language acquisition.* Cambridge: Cambridge University Press. 136–151.

Shohamy, E. (1995) Performance assessment in language testing. In W. Grabe et al.

(eds.) *Annual Review of Applied Linguistics 15: A broad survey of the entire field of applied linguistics.* Cambridge: Cambridge University Press. 188–211.

Shohamy, E. (1993) *The power of tests: The impact of language tests on teaching and learning.* Washington, DC: National Foreign Language Center.

Shohamy, E. (1985) *A practical handbook in language testing for the second language teacher.* Tel Aviv: Tel Aviv University Press.

Shohamy, E., and O. Inbar (1991) Validation of listening comprehension tests: The effect of text and question type. *Language Testing* 8: 23–40.

Sholl, A., A. Sankaranarayanan, and J. F. Kroll (1995) Transfer between picture naming and translation: A test of asymmetries in bilingual memory. *Psychological Science* 6: 45–49.

Shonerd, H. G. (1990) Domesticating the barbarous tongue: Language policy for the Navajo in historical perspective. *Language Problems & Language Planning* 14: 193–208.

Shrimpton, N. (1995) Standardizing the Krio language. In P. Baker (ed.) *From contact to creole and beyond.* London: University of Westminster Press. 217–228.

Shuy, R. W. (1998) *The language of confession, interrogation and deception.* Thousand Oaks, CA: Sage.

Shuy, R. W. (1993) *Language crimes: The use and abuse of language evidence in the courtroom.* Oxford: Blackwell.

Siegal, M. (1996) The role of learner subjectivity in second language sociolinguistic competency: Western women learning Japanese. *Applied Linguistics* 17: 356–382.

Siegel, J. (1999a) Transfer constraints and substrate influence in Melanesian Pidgin. *Journal of Pidgin and Creole Languages* 19: 1–44.

Siegel, J. (1999b) Stigmatized and standardized varieties in the classroom: Interference or separation? *TESOL Quarterly* 33: 701–728.

Siegel, J. (1999c) Creole and minority dialects in education: An overview. *Journal of Multilingual and Multicultural Development* 20: 508–531.

Siegel, J. (1998) Literacy in Melanesian and Australian pidgins and creoles. *English World-Wide* 16: 104–133

Siegel, J. (1997a) Pidgins and English in Melanesia: Is there a continuum? *World Englishes* 16: 185–204.

Siegel, J. (1997b) Using a pidgin language in formal education: Help or hindrance? *Applied Linguistics* 18: 86–100.

Siegel, J. (1996).*Vernacular education in the South Pacific.* International Development Issues No. 45. Canberra: Australian Agency for International Development.

Siegel, J. (1993) Pidgins and creoles in education in Australia and the Southwest Pacific. In F. Byrne and J. Holm (eds.) *Atlantic meets Pacific: A global view of pidginization and creolization.* Amsterdam: John Benjamins. 299–308.

Silva, T. (1993) Toward an understanding of the distinct nature of L2 writing: The ESL research and its implications. *TESOL Quarterly* 24: 657–671.

Simon, R. (1992) *Teaching against the grain: Texts for a pedagogy of possibility.* New York: Bergin and Garvey.

Simpson, G. B. (1984) Lexical ambiguity and its role in models of word recognition. *Psychological Bulletin* 96: 316–340.

Sinclair, J. McH. (1987) Classroom discourse: Progress and prospects. *RELC Journal* 18: 1–14.

Sinclair, J. McH., and M. Coulthard (1975) *Towards an analysis of discourse: The English used by teachers and pupils.* Oxford: Oxford University Press.

Singleton, D. (1989) *Language acquisition: The age factor.* Clevedon, Avon, UK: Multilingual Matters.

Singleton, D., and Z. Lengyel (1995) *The age factor in second language acquisition: A critical look at the critical period hypothesis.* Clevedon, Avon, UK: Multilingual Matters.

Sjöholm, K. (1983) Problems in "measuring" L2-learning strategies. In H. Ringbom (ed.) *Psycholinguistics and Foreign Language Learning.* Turku, Finland: Åbo Akademi Foundation. 174–200. [ERIC ED 276 309.]

Skehan, P. (2001) Tasks and language performance assessment. In M. Bygate, P. Skehan, and M. Swain (eds.) *Researching pedagogic tasks: Second language learning, teaching and testing.* London: Longman. 167–185.

Skehan, P. (1998a) *A cognitive approach to language learning.* Oxford: Oxford University Press.

Skehan, P. (1998b) *Cognition and second language acquisition.* Oxford: Oxford University Press.

Skehan, P. (1998c) Task-based approaches to language testing. In E. Li and G. James (eds.) *Testing and evaluation in second language education.* Hong Kong: Language Centre, Hong Kong University of Science and Technology. 34–49.

Skehan, P. (1998d) Task-based instruction. In W. Grabe, et al. (eds.) *Annual Review of Applied Linguistics 18: Foundations of second language teaching.* Cambridge: Cambridge University Press. 268–286.

Skehan, P. (1996) A framework for the implementation of task-based instruction. *Applied Linguistics* 17: 38–62.

Skehan, P. (1991) Individual differences in second language learning. *Studies in Second Language Acquisition.* 13: 272–298.

Skehan, P. (1989) *Individual differences in second-language learning.* London: Edward Arnold.

Skehan, P. (1984) Issues in the testing of English for Specific Purposes. *Language Testing.* 1: 202–220

Skehan, P., and P. Foster (in preparation) The effects of post-task dictation activities on the accuracy of task-based oral performance. London: King's College. Unpublished manuscript.

Skehan, P., and P. Foster (1997) Task type and task processing conditions as influences on foreign language performance. *Language Teaching Research* 13: 185–211.

Skilbeck, M. (1994) Curriculum renewal. In T. Husén and T. N. Postlethwaite (eds.) *The international encyclopedia of education.* 2nd ed. Oxford: Pergamon. 1338–1343.

Skilton-Sylvester, E. (1997) Inside, outside, and in-between: Identitites, literacies and educational policies in the lives of Cambodian women and girls in Philadelphia. Ph.D. diss., University of Pennsylvania, Philadelphia.

Skutnabb-Kangas, T. (2000a) *Linguistic genocide in education—or worldwide diversity and human rights?* Mahwah, NJ: Lawrence Erlbaum.

Skutnabb-Kangas, T. (2000b) Linguistic human rights and teachers of English. In J. K. Hall and W. Eggington (eds.) *The sociopolitics of English language teaching.* Clevedon, Avon, UK: Multilingual Matters. 22–44.

Skutnabb-Kangas, T., and R. Phillipson (eds.) (1995) *Linguistic human rights: Overcoming linguistic discrimination.* Berlin: Mouton.

Slaughter, H. (1997) Indigenous language immersion in Hawai'i: A case study of Kula Kaiapuni Hawai'i, an effort to save the indigenous language of Hawai'i. In R. K. Johnson and M. Swain (eds.) *Immersion education: International perspectives.* Cambridge: Cambridge University Press. 105–129

Slobin, D. (1993) Adult language acquisition: A view from child language study. In C. Perdue (ed.) *Adult language acquisition: Cross-linguistic perspectives.* Cambridge: Cambridge University Press. 239–252.

Small, S. L., G. W. Cottrell, and L. Shastri (1982) *Toward connectionist parsing.* Paper presented at the Proceedings of the National Conference on Artificial Intelligence, Pittsburgh, PA.

Smalley, W. A. (1988) Thailand's hierarchy of multilingualism. *Language Sciences* 10: 245–261.

Smith, H. L. (1999) Bilingualism and bilingual education: The child's perspective. *International Journal of Bilingual Education and Bilingualism* 2(4): 267–281.

Smith, M. C. (1997) How do bilinguals access lexical information? In A. M. B. De Groot and J. F. Kroll (eds.) *Tutorials in bilingualism: Psycholinguistic Perspectives.* Mahwah, NJ: Lawrence Erlbaum. 145–168.

Smith, N. (1994) An annotated list of creoles, pidgins, and mixed languages. In J. Arends, P. Muysken, and N. Smith (eds.) *Pidgins and creoles: An introduction.* Amsterdam: John Benjamins. 331–374

Smith, S., and A. Yamashiro (1998) Introduction. *Language Teacher* 22: 5.

Smith, W. (1994) Computers, statistics, and disputed authorship. In J. Gibbons (ed.) *Language and the law.* London: Longman. 374–413.

Snell, B., and P. Crampton (1983) Types of translations. In C. Picken (ed.) *The translator's handbook.* London: Aslib. 109–120.

Snow, C. (1990) Rationales for native language instruction: Evidence from research. In A. M. Padilla, H. H. Fairchild, and C. M. Valdez (eds.) *Bilingual education: Issues and strategies.* Newbury Park, CA: Sage. 60–74

Snow, C., W. Barnes, J. Chandler, I. Goodman, and L. Hemphill (1991) *Unfulfilled expectations: Home and school influences on literacy.* Cambridge, MA: Harvard University Press.

Snow, C., M. S. Burns, and P. Griffin (1998) *Preventing reading difficulties in young children.* Washington, DC: National Academy Press.

Snow, M. A. (1998) Trends and issues in content-based instruction. In W. Grabe, et al. (eds.) *Annual Review of Applied Linguistics 18: Foundations of second language teaching.* New York: Cambridge University Press. 243–267.

Snow, M. A. (1997) Teaching academic literacy skills: Discipline faculty take responsibility. In M. A. Snow and D. M. Brinton (eds.) *The content-based classroom: Perspectives on integrating language and content.* New York: Longman. 290–304.

Snow, M. A., and D. Brinton (eds.) (1997) The *content-based classroom: Perspectives on integrating language and content.* New York: Longman.

Snow, M. A., M. Met, and F. Genessee (1989) A conceptual framework for the integration of language and content in second/foreign language instruction. *TESOL Quarterly* 23: 201–217.

Soames, S. 1992. Philosophy of language. In W. Bright (ed.) *International encyclopedia of linguistics.* 4 vols. New York: Oxford University Press. 3: 188–193.

Sohrabi, B. (1997) Ethnolinguistic vitality and patterns of communication among the second generation of Iranian immigrants in Sweden. *International Journal of the Sociology of Language* 128: 45–72.

Sokolik, M. E. (1990) Learning without rules: PDP and a resolution of the adult language learning paradox. *TESOL Quarterly* 24: 685–696.

Sokolik, M. E., and M. E. Smith (1992) Assignment of gender to French nouns in primary and secondary language: A connectionist model. *Second Language Research* 8: 39–58.

Sommer, G. (1991) Gradual language shift in Egypt and Botswana: Two case examples. *Afrikanistische-Arbeitspapiere* [African studies—working papers] Special issue: 351–368.

Sonntag, S. K. (1996) The political saliency of language in Bihar and Uttar Pradesh. *Journal of Commonwealth and Comparative Politics* 34: 1–18.

Sorace, A. (2000) Introduction: Optionality in second language acquisition. *Second Language Research* 16: 93–102.

Sorjonen, M.-L. (1999) From textbook cues to dialogue: Interaction between students in an ESL classroom. Los Angeles: University of California, Los Angeles, Department of Applied Linguistics and TESL. Unpublished manuscript.

Spack, R. (1997) The acquisition of academic literacy in a second language: A longitudinal case study. *Written Communication* 14: 3–62.

Spada, N. M. (1997) Form-focused instruction and second-language acquisition: A review of classroom and laboratory research. *Language Teaching* 30: 73–87.

Spada, N. M., and M. Fröhlich (1995) *Communicative Orientation of Language Teaching Observation Scheme: Coding conventions and applications.* Sydney: Macquarie University, NCELTR.

Spilka, R. (ed.) (1993) *Writing in the workplace: New research perspectives.* Carbondale: Southern Illinois University Press.

Spivey, M. J., and V. Marian (1999) Cross talk between native and second languages: Partial activation of an irrelevant lexicon. *Psychological Science* 10: 281–284.

Spolsky, B. (1998) *Sociolinguistics.* Oxford: Oxford University Press.

Spolsky, B. (1997) The ethics of gatekeeping tests: What have we learned in a hundred years? *Language Testing* 14: 242–247.

Spolsky, B. (1996) Conditions for language revitalization: A comparison of the cases of Hebrew and Maori. In S. Wright (ed.) *Language and the state: Revitalization and revival in Israel and Eire.* Clevedon, Avon, UK: Multilingual Matters. 5–29.

Spolsky, B. (1995a) Prognostication and language aptitude testing, 1925–62. *Language Testing* 12: 321–340.

Spolsky, B. (1995b) *Measured words.* Oxford: Oxford University Press.

Spolsky, B. (1994) Comprehension testing, or can understanding be measured? In G. Brown, K. Malmkjaer, A. Pollitt, and J. Williams (eds.) *Language and understanding.* Oxford: Oxford University Press. 139–152.

Spolsky, B. (1989) Communicative competence, language proficiency, and beyond. *Applied Linguistics* 10: 138–156.

Spolsky, B. (1985) What does it mean to know how to use a language? An essay on the theoretical basis of language testing. *Language Testing* 2: 180–191.

Spolsky, B. (1973) What does it mean to know a language, or how do you get someone to perform his competence? In J. W. Oller and J. C. Richards (eds.) *Focus on the learner: Pragmatic perspectives for the language teacher.* Rowley, MA: Newbury House. 164–176.

Spolsky, B., and E. Shohamy (1999a) Language in Israeli society and education. *International Journal of the Sociology of Language* 137: 93–114.

Spolsky, B., and E. Shohamy (1999b) *The languages of Israel: Policy, ideology and practice.* Clevedon, Avon, UK: Multilingual Matters.

Spolsky, B. (ed.) (1999) *Concise encyclopedia of educational linguistics.* Amsterdam: Elsevier.

Spring, M. (1999) A view from down under. *Proteus* 8(2): 3–4.

Springer, S. P., and G. Deutsch (1989) *Left brain-right brain.* New York: W. H. Freeman.

Sprouse, R. (1998) Some notes on the relationship between inflectional morphology and parameter setting in first and second language acquisition. In M.-L. Beck (ed.) *Morphology and its interfaces in second language knowledge.* Philadelphia: John Benjamins. 41–68.

Stahl, S., K. Heuback, and B. Cramond (1997) *Fluency-oriented reading instruction.* Reading Research Report No. 79. Athens: National Reading Research Center, University of Georgia.

Stalnaker, R. C. (1972) Pragmatics. In D. Davidson and G. Harman (eds.) *Semantics of natural language.* Dordrecht: Reidel. 380–397.

Stanovich, K., and P. Stanovich (1995) How research might inform the debate about early reading acquisition. *Journal of Research in Reading* 18: 87–105.

Stansfield, C. W., and J. Hansen (1983) Field dependence-independence as a variable in second language cloze test performance. *TESOL Quarterly* 17: 29–38.

Starfield, S. (in press) "I'll go with the group": Rethinking "discourse community" in EAP. In J. Flowerdew and M. Peacock (eds.) *Research perspectives on English for Academic Purposes.* Cambridge: Cambridge University Press.

Starreveld, P. A. (2000) On the interpretation of onsets of auditory context effects in word production. *Journal of Memory and Language* 42: 497–525.

Starreveld, P. A., and W. La Heij (1995) Semantic interference, orthographic facilitation, and their interaction in naming tasks. *Journal of Experimental Psychology: Learning, Memory, and Cognition* 21: 686–698.

Steedman, M. (1999) Connectionist sentence processing in perspective. *Cognitive Science* 23: 615–634.

Stein, P. (2000) Rethinking resources: Multimodal pedagogies in the ESL classroom. *TESOL Quarterly* 34: 333–336.

Steinmetz, D. L., K. A. Bush, and N. Joseph-Goldfarb (1994) Integrating ESL and Lakota Indian culture. *TESOL Journal* 3: 12–14.

Stenhouse, L. (1975) *An introduction to curriculum research and development.* London: Heinemann.

Stephan, L. (1999) Political correctness versus freedom of speech: Social uses of language ideology. Ph.D. diss., University of Washington, Seattle.

Stern, H. H. (1989) Analysis and experience as variables in second language pedagogy. In B. Harley, P. Allen, J. Cummins, and M. Swain (eds.) *The development of bilingual proficiency.* Cambridge: Cambridge University Press. 93–109

Stern, H. H. (1983) *Fundamental concepts of language teaching.* Oxford: Oxford University Press.

Stern, H. H. (1981) The formal-functional distinction in language pedagogy: A conceptual clarification. In J. G. Savard and L. Laforge (eds.) *Proceedings of the 5th Congress of L'Association internationale de linguistique appliquée.* Quebec: Les Presses de l'Université Laval.

Stevick, E. W. (1990) *Humanism in language teaching.* Oxford: Oxford University Press.

Stevick, E. W. (1980) *Teaching languages: A way and ways.* Rowley, MA: Newbury House.

Stewart, W. A. (1989) Structural mimicry in decreolization and its effect on pseudo-comprehension. In O. García and R. Otheguy (eds.) *English across cultures: Cultures across English. A reader in cross-cultural communication.* Berlin: Mouton de Gruyter. 263–280.

Stewart, W. (1968) A sociolinguistic typology for describing national multilingualism. In J. A. Fishman (ed.) *Readings in the sociology of language.* The Hague: Mouton. 531–545.

St. Fort, H. (2000) What is Haitian Creole?/*Ki sa kreyòl ayisyen ye?* http://www.ahad-kreyol.org/Newsletter/Number20/haitiancreole.htm.

Stilling, N. A., S. E. Weisler, C. H. Chase, M. H. Feinstein, J. L. Garfield, and E. L. Rissland (1995) *Cognitive science: An introduction.* Cambridge, MA: MIT Press.

Stolcke, A. (1991) Syntactic category information with vector space grammars. Paper presented at the Thirteenth Annual Conference of the Cognitive Science Society, Hillsdale, NJ.

Stoller, F. (1999) Time for change: A hybrid curriculum for EAP programs. *TESOL Journal* 8: 9–13.

Strevens, P. (1992) Applied linguistics: An overview. In W. Grabe and R. B. Kaplan (eds.) *Introduction to applied linguistics.* Reading, MA: Addison-Wesley. 13–31

Strevens, P. (1980) Toward a redefinition of applied linguistics. In R. B. Kaplan (ed.) *On the scope of applied linguistics.* Rowley, MA: Newbury House. 17–20.

Stroop, J. R. (1935) Studies of interference in serial verbal reactions. *Journal of Experimental Psychology* 18: 643–662.

Strubell, M. (1996) Language planning and bilingual education in Catalonia. *Journal of Multilingual and Multicultural Development* 17: 262–275.

Strunk, W., and E. B. White (1955) *The elements of style.* New York: Macmillan.

Stryker, S. B., and B. L. Leaver (eds.) (1997) *Content-based instruction in foreign language education: Models and methods.* Washington DC: Georgetown University Press.

Stuart, S. (1993) Dominican Patwa—mother tongue or cultural relic? *International Journal of the Sociology of Language* 102: 57–72.

Sturt, P., and M. W. Crocker (1996) Monotonic syntactic processing: A cross-linguistic study of attachment and reanalysis. *Language and Cognitive Processes* 11: 449–494.

Sullivan, P. (2000) Playfulness as mediation in communicative language teaching in a Vietnamese classroom. In J. P. Lantolf (ed.) *Sociocultural theory and second language learning.* Oxford: Oxford University Press. 115–132.

Sutton, P. (1991) Language in Aboriginal Australia: Social dialects in a geographic idiom. In S. Romaine (ed.) *Language in Australia.* Cambridge: Cambridge University Press. 49–66.

Svanes, B. (1992) En undersoekelse av realisasjonsmoenstret for spraakhandlingen "aa be noen om aa gjoere noen" [A study of the realization pattern of the linguistic action "to ask someone to do something"]. *Maal og Minne* 1–2: 89–107.

Swain, M. (2000) The output hypothesis and beyond: Mediating acquisition through collaborative dialogue. In J. P. Lantolf (ed.) *Sociocultural theory and second language learning*. Oxford: Oxford University Press. 99–116.

Swain, M. (1998) Focus on form through conscious reflection. In C. Doughty and J. Williams (eds.) *Focus on form in classroom second language acquisition*. Cambridge: Cambridge University Press. 64–81.

Swain, M. (1995) Three functions of output in second language learning. In G. Cook and B. Seidlhofer (eds.) *Principle and practice in applied linguistics: Studies in honour of H. G. Widdowson*. Oxford: Oxford University Press. 125–144.

Swain, M. (1985) Communicative competence: Some roles of comprehensible input and comprehensible output in its development. In S. M. Gass and C. Madden (eds.) *Input in second language acquisition*. Rowley, MA: Newbury House. 235–253.

Swain, M., and S. Lapkin (2001) Focus on form through collaborative dialogue: Exploring tasks effects. In M. Bygate, P. Skehan, and M. Swain (eds.) *Task-based learning: Language teaching, learning and assessment*. London: Longman. 99–118.

Swain, M., and S. Lapkin (2000) Task-based language learning: The uses of first language use. *Special issue of Language Teaching Research: Tasks in language pedagogy* 4: 251–274.

Swain, M., and S. Lapkin (1998) Interaction and second language learning: Two adolescent French immersion students working together. *The Modern Language Journal* 82: 320–337.

Swain, M., and S. Lapkin (1995) Problems in output and the cognitive processes they generate: A step toward second language learning. *Applied Linguistics* 16: 371–391.

Swain, M., and S. Lapkin (1982) *Evaluating bilingual education: A Canadian case study*. Clevedon, Avon, UK: Multilingual Matters.

Swales, J. M. (2000) Language for specific purposes. In W. Grabe et al. (eds.) *Annual Review of Applied Linguistics 20: Applied linguistics as an emerging discipline*. Cambridge: Cambridge University Press. 59–76.

Swales, J. M. (1990) *Genre analysis: English in academic and research settings*. Cambridge: Cambridge University Press.

Swan, M. (1985) A critical look at the communicative approach. *ELT Journal* 39: 1–12, 76–87.

Swan, M., and C. Walter (1992) *The new Cambridge English course, 3*. Cambridge: Cambridge University Press.

Sweedler-Brown, C. (1993) ESL essay evaluation: The influence of sentence-level and rhetorical features. *Journal of Second Language Writing* 2: 3–17.

Swigart, L. (1992) Two codes or one? The insider's view and the description of codeswitching in Dakar. In C. Eastman (ed.) *Codeswitching*. Clevedon, Avon, UK: Multilingual Matters. 71–82.

Tabor, W., C. Juliano, and M. K. Tanenhaus (1997) Parsing in a dynamical system: An attractor-based account of the interaction of lexical and structural constraints in sentence processing. *Language and Cognitive Processes* 12: 211–271.

Takahashi, S. (1996) Pragmatic transferability. *Studies in Second Language Acquisition* 18: 189–223.

Takahashi, S., and M. A. DuFon (1989) *Cross-linguistic influence in indirectness: The case of English directives performed by native Japanese speakers*. Honolulu: University of Hawai'i at Manoa. [ERIC ED 370 439.]

Takahashi, T., and L. Beebe (1987.) The development of pragmatic competence by Japanese learners of English. *JALT Journal* 8: 131–155.

Takenoya, M. (1995) Address terms in Japanese: Patterns of use by native and nonnative speakers. Ph.D. diss., Indiana University, Bloomington.

Takeuchi, O. (1999) Language learning strategies used by Japanese college learners of English: A synthesis of four empirical studies. Paper presented at the World Congress of the International Association of Applied Linguistics, Tokyo, Japan. August.

Takeuchi, O. (1993) Language learning strategies and their relationship to achievement in EFL listening comprehension. *Language Laboratory* 30: 17–34.

Tanenhaus, M. K., and J. C. Trueswell (1995) Sentence comprehension. In J. L. Miller and P. D. Eimas (eds.) *Speech, language, and communication.* San Diego: Academic Press. 217–262.

Tang, G. (1992) The effects of graphic representation of knowledge structures on ESL reading comprehension. *Studies in Second Language Acquisition* 14: 177–195.

Tannen, D., and C. Wallat (1993) Doctor/mother/child communication: Linguistic analysis of a pediatric interaction. In A. D. Todd and S. Fisher (eds.) *The social interaction of doctor-patient communication.* 2nd ed. Norwood, NJ: Ablex. 31–47.

Tarone, E. (1998) Research on interlanguage variation: Implications for language testing. In L. F. Bachman and A. D. Cohen (eds.) *Interfaces between second language acquisition and language testing research.* Cambridge: Cambridge University Press. 71–89.

Tarone, E. (1988) *Variation in interlanguage.* London: Edward Arnold.

Tarone, E., and M. Broner (2001) Is it fun? Language play in a fifth grade Spanish immersion classroom. *The Modern Language Journal* 85(3).

Tarone, E., S. M. Gass, and A. Cohen (1994) *Research methodology in second-language acquisition.* Mahwah, NJ: Lawrence Erlbaum.

Tatsuoka, K. K. (1993). Item construction and psychometric models appropriate for constructed responses. In R. E. Bennet and W. C. Ward (eds.) *Construction versus choice in cognitive measurement: Issues in constructed response, performance testing, and portfolio assessment.* Hillsdale, NJ: Lawrence Erlbaum. 107–134.

Tauli, V. (1968) *Introduction to a theory of language planning.* Acta Universitatis Upsaliensis, Studia Philologiae Scandinavicae Upsaliensia, 6. Uppsala: University of Uppsala.

Tauroza, S. (1997) Using students' listening comprehension problems. *Perspectives* 9: 161–178.

Taylor, C. (1991) The dialogical self. In D. Hiley, J. Bohman, and R. Shusterman (eds.) *The interpretive turn: Philosophy, science and culture.* Ithaca, NY: Cornell University Press. 304–314.

Taylor, C. (1989) *Sources of the self: The making of the modern identity.* Cambridge, MA: Harvard University Press.

Taylor, C. (1985) *Human agency and language: Philosophical papers, 1.* Cambridge: Cambridge University Press.

Taylor, L. (1993) Text-removed summary completion as a means of assessing reading comprehension ability. Paper presented at the Language Testing Forum, Lancaster University, UK. November.

Taylor, L., and A. Pollitt (1996) The reading process and reading assessment. Paper presented at the 18th Annual Language Testing Research Colloquium. Tampere, Finland.

Taylor Torsello, C. (1996) Theme as the interpreter's path indicator through the unfolding text. *The Interpreters' Newsletter* 7: 113–149.

Teasdale, A., and C. Leung (2000) Teacher assessment and psychometric theory: A case of paradigm crossing? *Language Testing* 17: 165–186.

Temple, C. (1993) *The brain: An introduction to the psychology of the human brain and behaviour.* London: Penguin.

Terestyéni, T. (1996) Vizsgálat az idegennyelv-tudásról [A survey on foreign language knowledge]. *Modern Nyelvoktatás* 2: 3–16.

Thatcher, B. (2000) L2 professional writing in a U.S. and South American context. *Journal of Second Language Writing* 9: 41–70.

Thesen, L. (1997.) Voices, discourse and transition: In search of new categories in EAP. *TESOL Quarterly* 31: 487–512.

Thomas, J. (1983) Cross-cultural pragmatics. *Applied Linguistics* 4: 91–112.

Thomas, J., and M. Short (eds.) (1996) *Using corpora for language research.* London: Longman.

Thomas, M. (1998) Programmatic ahistoricity in second language acquisition theory. *Studies in Second Language Acquisition* 20: 387–405.

Thomas, M. (1995) Acquisition of the Japanese reflexive *zibun* and movement of anaphors in Logical Form. *Second Language Research* 11: 206–234.

Thomas, M. (1993) *Knowledge of reflexives in a second language.* Amsterdam: John Benjamins.

Thomas, M. (1991) Universal grammar and the interpretation of reflexives in second language. *Language* 67: 211–239.

Thomas, W. P., and V. Collier (1997) *School effectiveness for language minority students.* Washington, DC: National Clearinghouse for Bilingual Education.

Thompson, G. (1996) Some misconceptions about communicative language teaching. *ELT Journal* 50: 9–15.

Thompson, I. (1995) Assessment of second/foreign language listening comprehension. In D. Mendelsohn and J. Rubin (eds.) *A guide for the teaching of second language listening.* San Diego: Dominie Press. 31–58.

Thompson, I., and J. Rubin (1996) Can strategy instruction improve listening comprehension? *Foreign Language Annals* 29: 331–342.

Thorne, S. (1999) An activity theoretical analysis of foreign language electronic discourse. Ph.D. diss., University of California, Berkeley.

Thornell, C. (1997) The Songo language and its lexicon. *Travaux de l'Institut de Linguistique de Lund* [Papers of the Lund Institute of Linguistics] 32: 3–195.

Thumboo, E. (1987) The literary dimension of the spread of English: Creativity in a second tongue. In P. Lowenberg (ed.) *Language spread and language policy issues: Implications and case studies.* Washington, DC: Georgetown University Press. Georgetown University Round Table on Languages and Linguistics. 361–401.

Thurston, W. R. (1987) Process of changes in the language of North-Western New Britain. *Pacific Linguistics.* Canberra: Linguistic Circle of Canberra.

Tiersma, P. M. (1999) *Legal language.* Chicago: University of Chicago Press.

Tirkkonen-Condit, S. (1989) Professional vs. non-professional translation: A think-aloud protocol study. In C. Séguinot (ed.) *The translation process.* Toronto: H.G. Publications, School of Translation, York University. 73–85.

Todal, J. (1999) Minorities with a minority: Language and the school in the Sámi areas of Norway. In S. May (ed.) *Indigenous community-based education.* Clevedon, Avon, UK: Multilingual Matters. 124–136.

Todd, A. D. (1993) A diagnosis of doctor-patient communication in the prescription of contraception. In A. D. Todd and S. Fisher (eds.) *The social organization of doctor-patient communication.* 2nd ed. Norwood, NJ: Ablex. 183–209.

Todd, A. D., and S. Fisher (eds.) (1993) *The social organization of doctor-patient communication.* 2nd ed. Norwood, NJ: Ablex.

Todd, L. (1990) *Pidgins and creoles.* 2nd ed. London: Routledge.

Tollefson, J. W. (1997). Language policy in independent Slovenia. *International Journal of the Sociology of Language* 124: 29–50.

Tollefson, J. W. (1995) *Power and inequality in language education.* Cambridge: Cambridge University Press.

Tollefson, J. W. (1989) *Alien winds: The reeducation of America's Indochinese refugees.* New York: Praeger.

Tollefson, J. W. (ed.) (2001) *Language policies in education: Critical issues.* Mahwah, NJ: Lawrence Erlbaum.

Tonelli, L., and A. Riccardi (1995) Speech errors, shadowing and simultaneous interpretation. *The Interpreters' Newsletter* 6: 67–74.

Toohey, K. (2000) *Learning English at school: Identity, social relations and classroom practice.* Clevedon, Avon, UK: Multilingual Matters.

Toohey, K. (1998) 'Breaking them up, taking them away': ESL students in grade one. *TESOL Quarterly* 32: 61–84.

Toohey, K. (1996) Learning English as a second language in kindergarten: A community of practice perspective. *Canadian Modern Language Review* 52: 549–576.

Torrance, E. P. (1988) *Style of learning and thinking administrator's manual.* Bensenville, IL: Scholastic Testing Service.

Torrance, E. P., B. Taggart, and W. Taggart (1984). *Human information processing survey.* Bensenville, IL: Scholastic Testing Service.

Torrance, H., and J. Pryor (1998) *Investigating formative assessment.* Buckingham: Open University Press.

Toury, G. (1995) *Descriptive translation studies and beyond.* Amsterdam: John Benjamins.

Toury, G. (1980) *In search of a theory of translation.* Tel Aviv: Porter Institute for Poetics and Semiotics, Tel Aviv University.

Towell, R., and R. Hawkins (1994) *Approaches to second language acquisition.* Clevedon, Avon, UK: Multilingual Matters.

Towell, R., R. Hawkins, and N. Bazergui (1996) The development of fluency in advanced learners of French. *Applied Linguistics* 17: 84–119.

Trahey, M., and L. White (1993) Positive evidence and pre-emption in the second language classroom. *Studies in Second Language Acquisition* 15: 181–204.

Tremblay, P. F., and R. C. Gardner (1995) Expanding the motivation construct in language learning. *The Modern Language Journal* 79: 505–520.

Trezise, P. (1996) Use of language and the Anunga Rules: R v Jean Denise Izumi. *Aboriginal Law Bulletin* 79: 17–18.

Triandis, H. C. (1989) The self and social behavior in differing cultural indices as a means of confirming cultural differences. *International Journal of Psychology* 59: 1006–1020.

Trim, J. (1980/1978) *Developing a unit/credit scheme of adult language learning.* Oxford: Pergamon.

Trosborg, A. (1995) *Interlanguage pragmatics: Requests, complaints and apologies.* Berlin: Mouton de Gruyter.

Trosborg, A. (1987) Apology strategies in natives/non-natives. *Journal of Pragmatics* 11: 147–167.

Trudgill, P. (1972) Sex, covert prestige and linguistic change in the urban British English of Norwich. *Language in Society* 1: 179–95.

Trueswell, J. C. (1996) The role of lexical frequency in syntactic ambiguity resolution. *Journal of Memory and Language* 35: 566–585.

Trueswell, J. C., and M. K. Tanenhaus (1994) Toward a constraint-based lexicalist approach to syntactic ambiguity resolution. In C. Clifton, L. Frazier, and K. Rayner (eds.) *Perspectives on sentence processing.* Hillsdale, NJ: Lawrence Erlbaum. 155–179.

Trueswell, J. C., M. K. Tanenhaus, and S. M. Garnsey (1994) Semantic influences on parsing: Use of semantic role information in syntactic ambiguity resolution. *Journal of Memory and Language* 33: 285–318.

Truscott, J. (1998) Noticing in second language acquisition: A critical review. *Second Language Research* 14: 103–135.

Truscott, J. (1996) The case against grammar correction in L2 writing classes. *Language Learning* 46: 327–369.

Tse, J. K. P. (1982) Some advantages of sociolinguistic surveys for language planning purposes. *Ying Yu Yen Chiu Chi K'an* [Studies in English Literature and Linguistics] 8 (April): 157–167.

Tsuda, M. (1997) Human rights problems of foreigners in Japan's criminal justice system. *Migrationworld* 25: 22–28.

Tsui, A., and J. Fullilove (1998) Bottom-up or top-down processing as a discriminator of L2 listening performance. *Applied Linguistics* 19: 432–451.

Tucker, G. R. (2000) Concluding thoughts: Applied linguistics at the juncture of millennia. In W. Grabe et al. (eds.) *Annual Review of Applied Linguistics 20: Applied linguistics as an emerging discipline.* Cambridge: Cambridge University Press. 241–249.

Tucker, G. R. (1997) Developing a language competent American society: Implications of the English-only movement. In T. Bongaerts and K. de Bot (eds.) *Perspectives on foreign-language policy: Studies in honour of Theo Van Els.* Amsterdam: John Benjamins. 87–98.

Tucker, G. R. (1996) Applied linguistics [http://www.lsadc.org/web2/fldfr.htm].

Tudor, I. (1997) *Learner-centredness as language education.* Cambridge: Cambridge University Press.

Turner, C. (1997) The Injinoo Home Language Program: A positive community response to marginalisation and institutional racism. *Australian Journal of Indigenous Education* 25: 1–9.

Tymoczko, M. (1998) Computerized corpora and the future of translation studies. *Meta* 43: 652–659.

Uber Gross, C., and G. Voght (1991) The evolution of languages for specific purposes in the United States. *The Modern Language Journal* 2: 181–195.

UCLES [University of Cambridge Local Examinations Syndicate.] Computerized Adaptive Placement Examination (CAPE) informational website. [Online.] Available: http://aaunk.unk.edu/asmt/ forltest.html.

Underwood, J. (1984) *Linguistics, computers, and the language teacher.* Rowley, MA: Newbury House.

UNESCO (1968) The use of vernacular languages in education: The report of the UNESCO meeting of specialists, 1951. In J. A. Fishman (ed.) *Readings in the sociology of language*. The Hague: Mouton. 688–716.

Upshur, J., and C. Turner (1999) Systematic effects in the rating of second-language speaking ability: Test method and learner discourse. *Language Testing* 16: 82–111.

Ur, P. (1996) *A course in language teaching: Practice and theory.* Cambridge: Cambridge University Press.

Ur, P. (1981) *Discussions that work.* Cambridge: Cambridge University Press.

Urquhart, S., and C. Weir (1999) *Reading in a second language: Process, product and practice.* London: Longman.

Vaik, F. (1992) Radio talk-show therapy and the pragmatics of possible worlds. In A. Duranti and C. Goodwin (eds.) *Rethinking context.* Cambridge: Cambridge University Press. 271–289.

Vainikka, A., and M. Young-Scholten (1998) Morphosyntactic triggers in adult second language acquisition. In M.-L. Beck (ed.) *Morphology and interfaces in second language acquisition knowledge.* Philadelphia: John Benjamins. 89–113.

Vainikka, A., and M. Young-Scholten (1996) The gradual development of L2 phrase structure. *Second Language Research* 12: 7–39.

Vainikka, A., and M. Young-Scholten (1994) Direct access to X'-theory: Evidence from Turkish and Korean adults learning German. In B. D. Schwartz and T. Hoekstra (eds.) *Language acquisition studies in generative grammar.* Philadelphia: John Benjamins. 265–316.

Valdés, G. (1998) The world inside and outside schools: Language and immigrant children. *Educational Researcher* 27: 4–18.

Valdés, G. (1997) Dual language immersion programs: A cautionary note concerning the education of language-minority students. *Harvard Educational Review* 67: 391–429.

Valdman, A. (1991) Decreolization or dialect contact in Haiti? In F. Byrne and T. Huebner (eds.) *Development and structures of creole languages: Essays in honor of Derek Bickerton.* Amsterdam: John Benjamins. 75–88.

Valdman, A. (1989) The use of Creole as a school medium and decreolization in Haiti. In W. Z. Sonino (ed.) *Literacy in school and society: Multidisciplinary perspectives.* New York: Plennum Press. 55–79.

Van Besien, F. (1999) Anticipation in simultaneous translation. *Meta* 44: 250–259.

Vandergrift, L. (1999) Facilitating second language listening comprehension: Acquiring successful strategies. *ELT Journal* 53: 168–176.

Vandergrift, L. (1997a) The strategies of second language (French) listeners: A descriptive study. *Foreign Language Annals* 30: 387–409.

Vandergrift, L. (1997b) The Cinderella of communication strategies: Reception strategies in interactive listening. *Modern Language Journal* 81: 494–505.

Vandrick, S. (1998) Promoting gender equity in the postsecondary ESL class. In T. Smoke (ed.) *Adult ESL: Politics, pedagogy, and participation in classroom and community programs.* Mahwah, NJ: Lawrence Erlbaum. 73–88.

van Ek, J. A. (1977) *The Threshold Level for modern language learning in schools.* Strasbourg: Council of Europe.

van Ek, J. A. (1975) *The Threshold Level in a European unit/credit system for modern language learning by Adults: Systems Development in Adult Language Learning.* Strasbourg: Council of Europe.

Van Heuven, W. J. B., A. Dijkstra, and J. Grainger (1998) Orthographic neighborhood effects in bilingual word recognition. *Journal of Memory and Language* 39: 458–483.

van Lier, L. (1997) Apply within, apply without? *International Journal of Applied Linguistics* 7: 95–105.

van Lier, L. (1996) *Interaction in the language curriculum*. London: Longman.

van Lier, L. (1995) *Introducing language awareness*: Harmondsworth: Penguin Books.

van Lier, L. (1994) Forks and hopes: Pursuing understanding in different ways. *Applied Linguistics* 15: 328–346.

van Lier, L. (1988) *The classroom and the language learner*. New York: Longman.

van Lier, L., and D. Corson (eds.) (1997) *Encyclopedia of language and education*. Vol. 6: *Knowledge about language*. Boston: Kluwer.

Vann, R., and R. Abraham (1990) Strategies of unsuccessful language learners. *TESOL Quarterly* 24: 177–198.

VanPatten, B., and T. Cadierno (1993) Explicit instruction and input processing. *Studies in Second Language Acquisition* 15: 225–244.

Van Valin, R., and R. La Polla (1997) *Syntax: Structure, meaning and function*. Cambridge: Cambridge University Press.

Van Weeren, J. (1995) European language qualifications: Information on standards of proficiency. *System* 23: 481–490.

Varga, D. (1995) Creation of a language: Rumantsch Grischun. *Studia Romancia et Anglica Zabrabiensia* [Romance and English studies overseas] 40: 181–190.

Varonis, E., and S. M. Gass (1985a) Non-native/non-native conversations: A model for negotiation of meaning. *Applied Linguistics* 6: 71–90.

Varonis, E., and S. M. Gass (1985b) Miscommunication in native/non-native conversation. *Language in Society* 14: 327–343.

Varro, G. (1997) Bilinguals sacrificed, or what are native languages good for? *Cahiers de l'Institut de Linguistique de Louvain* [Working papers of the Linguistics Institute of Louvain] 23: 61–70.

Verdoodt, A. (1971) The differential impact of immigrant French speakers on indigenous German speakers: A case study in the light of two theories. *International Migration Review* 5: 138–146.

Verhoef, M. (1998) Toward a theory of language attitude planning in South Africa. *South African Journal of Linguistics* 16: 27–33.

Verhoeven, L. (1997) Acquisition of literacy by immigrant children. In L. Verhoven (ed.) *Writing development: An interdisciplinary view*. Amsterdam: John Benjamins. 219–240.

Viaggio, S. (1996a) Elementary, my dear colleague! Educating our students' guesses. *The Interpreters' Newsletter* 7: 57–71.

Viaggio, S. (1996b) Research in simultaneous interpretation: An outsider's overview. *The Interpreters' Newsletter* 7: 73–84.

Viaggio, S. (1995) The praise of sight translation (and squeezing the last drop thereout of). *The Interpreters' Newsletter* 6: 33–42.

Vidal, M. (1998) Telephone interpreting: Technological advance or due process impediment? *Proteus* 7(3): 1, 3–6.

Viikberg, J. (1999) Language shift among Siberian Estonians: Pro and contra. *International Journal of the Sociology of Language* 139: 105–124.

Villamil, O., and M. C. M. de Guerrero (1996) Peer revision in the L2 classroom: Social-cognitive activities, mediating strategies, and aspects of social behavior. *Journal of Second Language Writing* 5: 51–75.

Voegelin, C. F., F. M. Voegelin, and N. W. Schutz, Jr. (1967) The language situation in Arizona as part of South West cultural area. In D. Hymes and W. E. Bittle (eds.) *Studies in South Western ethnolinguistics.* The Hague: Mouton. 403–451.

Von Studnitz, R., and D. Green (submitted) Interlingual homograph interference in German-English bilinguals: Its modulation and locus of control. London: University College. Unpublished manuscript.

Vygotsky, L. S. (1987) Thinking and speech. In R. W. Rieber and A. S. Carton (eds.) *The collected works of L. S. Vygotsky;* Vol. 1: *Problems of general psychology.* New York: Plenum. 39–285.

Vygotsky, L. S. (1978) *Mind in society: The development of higher psychology processes.* Cambridge, MA: Harvard University Press.

Wagner-Gough, J., and E. Hatch (1975) The importance of input data in second language acquisition studies. *Language Learning* 25: 297–307.

Wall, D. (1997) Impact and washback in language testing. In C. Clapham and D. Corson (eds.) *Encyclopedia of language and education.* Vol 7: *Language testing and assessment.* Dordrecht, Netherlands: Kluwer Academic. 291–302.

Wallace, B., and R. L. Oxford (1992) Disparity in learning styles and teaching styles in the ESL classroom: Does this mean war? *AMTESOL Journal* 1: 45–68.

Walsh, M. (1994) Interactional styles in the courtroom: An example from northern Australia. In J. Gibbons (ed.) *Language and the law.* London: Longman. 217–233.

Warner, S. L. N. (1999) Kuleana: The right, responsibility, and authority of indigenous peoples to speak and make decisions for themselves in language and cultural revitalization. *Anthropology and Education Quarterly* 30: 68–93.

Warschauer, M. (1998) Researching technology in TESOL: Determinist, instrumental, and critical approaches. *TESOL Quarterly* 32: 757–761.

Warschauer, M. (1995/1996) Comparing face to face and electronic discussion in the foreign language classroom. *CALICO Journal* 13: 7–26.

Watson, J. L. (ed.) (1997) *Golden arches east: McDonald's in East Asia.* Stanford, CA: Stanford University Press.

Watson, T. J. (1997) Languages within languages: A social constructivist perspective on multiple managerial discourses. In F. Bargiela-Chiappini and S. Harris (eds.) *The languages of business: An international perspective.* Edinburgh: Edinburgh University Press. 211–227.

Watson-Gegeo, K. A. (1994) Language and education in Hawai'i: Sociopolitical and economic implications of Hawai'i Creole English. In M. Morgan (ed.) *The Social construction of identity in creole situations.* Los Angeles: Center for Afro-American Studies, UCLA. 101–120.

Watson-Gegeo, K. A. (1988) Ethnography in ESL: Defining the essentials. *TESOL Quarterly* 22: 575–592.

Weedon, C. (1997) *Feminist practice and poststructuralist theory.* 2nd ed. London: Blackwell.

Wei, L., V. Saravanan, and J. N. L. Hoon (1997) Language shift in the Teochew community in Singapore: A family domain analysis. *Journal of Multilingual and Multicultural Development* 18: 364–384.

Weiner, B. (1986) *An attributional theory of motivation and emotion.* New York: Springer-Verlag.

Weinreich, U. (1953) *Languages in contact.* New York: Mouton.

Weir, C. (1983) Identifying the language problems of overseas students in tertiary education in the United Kingdom. Ph.D. diss., University of London.

Weir, R. (1962) *Language in the crib.* The Hague: Mouton.

Weissberg, B. (2000) Developmental relationships in the acquisition of English syntax: Writing vs. speech. *Learning and Instruction* 10: 37–53.

Weitzman, E., and M. B. Miles (1995) *Computer programs for qualitative data analysis.* Thousand Oaks, CA: Sage.

Wells, G. (1999) *Dialogic inquiry.* New York: Cambridge University Press.

Welsh Language Board (1999) *The Welsh language: A vision and mission for 2000–2005.* Cardiff: Welsh Language Board.

Wenden, A. L. (ed.) (1995) *Autonomy, self-direction, and self access in language teaching and learning: The history of an idea.* [Special issue of *System* 23(2).]

Wenger, E. (1998) *Communities of practice: Learning, meaning and identity.* Cambridge: Cambridge University Press.

Wenzell, V. (1989) Transfer of aspect in the English oral narratives of native Russian speakers. In H. Dechert and M. Raupach (eds.) *Transfer in language production.* Norwood, NJ: Ablex. 71–97.

Wertsch, J. V. (1991) *Voices of the mind: A sociocultural approach to mediated action.* Cambridge, MA: Harvard University Press.

Wesche, M. (2000) A Canadian perspective: Second language teaching and learning in the university. In J. Rosenthal (ed.) *Handbook of undergraduate second language education.* Mahwah, NJ: Lawrence Erlbaum. 187–208.

Wesche, M. (1994) Input and interaction in second language acquisition. In C. Gallaway and B. Richards (eds.) *Input and interaction in language acquisition.* Cambridge: Cambridge University Press. 219–249.

Wesche, M. (1993a) Discipline-based approaches to foreign and second language study: Research issues and outcomes. In M. Krueger and F. Ryan (eds.) *Language and content: Discipline-based approaches to language study.* Lexington, MA: D.C. Heath. 57–58.

Wesche, M (1993b) French immersion graduates at university and beyond: What difference has it made? In J. Alatis (ed.) *Language, communication and social meaning. Georgetown University Round Table on Languages and Linguistics.* Washington, DC: Georgetown University Press. 208–240.

Wesche, M. (1987) Second language performance testing: The Ontario Test of ESL as an example. *Language Testing* 4: 28–47.

Wesche, M. (1985) What can the universities offer to the bilingual student? *Canadian Modern Language Review* 41: 956–961.

White, G. (1998) *Listening.* Oxford: Oxford University Press.

White, H. (1990) School library collections and services: Ranking the states. *School Library Media Quarterly* 19: 13–26.

White, L. (2000a) Second language acquisition: From initial to final state. In J. Archibald (ed.) *Second language acquisition and linguistic theory.* Oxford: Blackwell. 130–155.

White, L. (2000b) Universal grammer in second language acquisition: The nature of interlanguage representation. In A. Juffs, T. W. Talpas, G. Mizera, and B. Burtt (eds.)

Proceedings of GASLA IV. Working Papers in Linguistics. Pittsburgh, PA: University of Pittsburgh. 3–14.

White, L. (1998) Introduction to the Special Issue: Implications of divergent outcomes in second language acquisition. *Second Language Research* 14: 321–324.

White, L. (1996a) Clitics in L2 French. In H. Clahsen (ed.) *Generative perspectives on language acquisition.* Philadelphia: John Benjamins. 334–368.

White, L. (1996b) Universal grammar and second language acquisition: Current trends and new directions. In T. Bhatia and W. Ritchie (eds.) *Handbook of language acquisition.* New York: Academic Press. 85–120.

White, L. (1992) Long and short verb movement in second language acquisition. *Canadian Journal of Linguistics* 37: 273–286.

White, L. (1991a) Adverb placement in second language acquisition: Some effects of positive and negative evidence in the classroom. *Second Language Research* 7: 133–161.

White, L. (1991b) The verb-movement parameter in second language acquisition. *Language Acquisition* 1: 337–360.

White, L. (1989) *Universal Grammar and second language acquisition.* Amsterdam: John Benjamins.

White, L., J. Bruhn-Garavito, T. Kawasaki, J. Pater, and P. Prévost (1997) The researcher gave the subject a test about himself: Problems of ambiguity and preference in the investigation of reflexive binding. *Language Learning* 47: 145–172.

White, M. (1994) Language in job interviews: Differences relating to success and socio-economic variables. Ph.D. diss., Northern Arizona University, Flagstaff.

White, R. V. (1993) Innovation in curriculum planning and program development. In W. Grabe et al. (eds.) *Annual Review of Applied Linguistics 13: Issues in second-language teaching and learning.* Cambridge: Cambridge University Press. 244–259.

White, R. V. (1988) *The ELT curriculum: Design, innovation and management.* Oxford: Blackwell.

Widdowson, H. G. (2000a) Object language and the language subject: On the mediating role of applied linguistics. In W. Grabe et al. (eds.) *Annual Review of Applied Linguistics 20: Applied linguistics as an emerging discipline.* New York: Cambridge University Press. 21–33.

Widdowson, H. G. (2000b) On the limitations of linguistics applied. *Applied Linguistics* 21: 3–25.

Widdowson, H. G. (1998a) Skills, abilities, and contexts of reality. In W. Grabe et al. (eds.) *Annual Review of Applied Linguistics 18: Foundations of second language teaching.* New York: Cambridge University Press. 323–333.

Widdowson, H. G. (1998b) The theory and practice of critical discourse analysis. *Applied Linguistics* 19: 136–151.

Widdowson, H. G. (1998c) Retuning, calling the tune, and paying the piper: A reaction to Rampton. *International Journal of Applied Linguistics* 8: 131–140.

Widdowson, H. G. (1979/1984) *Explorations in applied linguistics.* 2 vols. Oxford: Oxford University Press.

Widdowson, H. G. (1983) *Learning purpose and language use.* Oxford: Oxford University Press.

Widdowson, H. G. (1980) Applied linguistics: The pursuit of relevance. In R. B. Kaplan (ed.) *On the scope of applied linguistics.* Rowley, MA: Newbury House. 74–87.

Widdowson, H. G. (1978) *Teaching language as communication.* London: Oxford University Press.

Wigglesworth, G. (2000) Issues in the development of oral tasks for competency-based assessments of second language performance. In G. Brindley (ed.) *Issues in immigrant English language assessment.* Sydney: National Centre for English Language Teaching and Research, Macquarie University. 81–124.

Wigglesworth, G. (1997) An investigation of planning time and proficiency level on oral test discourse. *Language Testing* 14: 85–106.

Wiley, T. G., and M. Lukes (1996) English-only and standard English ideologies in the U.S. *TESOL Quarterly* 30: 511–525.

Wilkins, D. A. (1999) Applied linguistics. In B. Spolsky (ed.) *Concise Encyclopedia of educational linguistics.* Amsterdam: Elsevier. 6–17.

Wilkins, D. A. (1976) *Notional syllabuses.* Oxford: Oxford University Press.

Willemyns, R. (1997) Language shift through erosion: The case of the French-Flemish 'Westhoek.' *Journal of Multilingual and Multicultural Development* 18: 54–66.

Willett, J., J. Solsken, and J. Wilson-Keenan (1998) The (im)possibilities of constructing multicultural language practices in research and pedagogy. *Linguistics and Education* 10: 165–218.

Williams, G. (1992) *Sociolinguistics: A sociological critique.* London: Routledge.

Williams, J. (1999) Learner-generated attention to form. *Language Learning* 49: 583–625.

Williams, J., R. Inscoe, and T. Tasker (1997) Communication strategies in an interactional context: The mutual achievement of comprehension. In G. Kasper and E. Kellerman (eds.) *Communication strategies: Psycholinguistic and sociolinguistic perspectives.* London: Longman. 304–322.

Williams, M., and R. L. Burden (1997) *Psychology for language teachers: A social constructivist approach.* Cambridge: Cambridge University Press.

Williams, R. M. (1947) The reduction of intergroup tensions. *Social Sciences Research Council Bulletin* 57: 40–43.

Willig, A. C. (1985) A meta-analysis of selected studies on the effectiveness of bilingual education. *Review of Educational Research* 55: 269–317.

Willing, K. (1992) *Talking it through: Clarification and problem-solving in professional work.* Sydney: Macquarie University, National Centre for English Language Teaching and Research.

Willis, J. (1996) *A framework for task-based learning.* London: Longman.

Willis, J., and D. Willis (1988) *Collins COBUILD English course.* London: Collins.

Willis, J., and D. Willis. (1987) *COBUILD BOOK 1.* London: Collins.

Wilss, W. (1999) *Translation and interpreting in the 20th century: Focus on German.* Amsterdam: John Benjamins.

Wilss, W. (1996) *Knowledge and skills in translator behavior.* Amsterdam: John Benjamins.

Winer, L. (1993) Teaching speakers of Caribbean English Creoles in North American classrooms. In A. W. Glowka and D. M. Lance (eds.) *Language variation in North American English: Research and teaching.* New York: Modern Language Association of America. 191–198.

Winer, L. (1990) Orthographic standardization for Trinidad and Tobago: Linguistic and sociopolitical considerations. *Language Problems & Language Planning* 14: 237–268.

Winer, L. (1989) Variation and transfer in English Creole—Standard English language learning. In M. R. Eisenstein (ed.) *The dynamic interlanguage: Empirical studies in second language variation.* New York: Plenum. 155–173.

Winer, L., and L. Jack (1997) Caribbean English Creole in New York. In O. García and J. A. Fishman (eds.) *The multilingual apple: Language in New York City.* Berlin: Mouton de Gruyter. 301–337.

Winford, D. (1998) On the origins of African American Vernacular English—A creolist perspective. Part II: Linguistic features. *Diachronica* 15: 99–154.

Winford, D. (1997) On the origins of African American Vernacular English—A creolist perspective. Part I: The sociohistorical background. *Diachronica* 14: 305–344.

Winford, D. (1994) Sociolinguistic approaches to language use in the Anglophone Caribbean. In M. Morgan (ed.) *The social construction of identity in creole situations.* Los Angeles: Center for Afro-American Studies, UCLA. 43–62.

Winter, J. (1992) Discourse as a resource: Methods of collecting language attitudes. *Australian Review of Applied Linguistics* 15: 1–22.

Witkin, H. A., C. A. Moore, D. R. Goodenough, and P. W. Cox (1977) Field-dependence and field-independence cognitive styles and their educational implications. *Review of Educational Research* 47: 1–64.

Wodak, R. (1997) Introduction: Some important issues in the research of gender and discourse. In R. Wodak (ed.) *Gender and discourse.* London: Sage. 1–20.

Wodak, R. (1995) The development and forms of racist discourse in Austria since 1989. In D. Graddol and S. Thomas (eds.) *Language in a changing Europe.* Clevedon, Avon, UK: Multilingual Matters. 1–15.

Wolfe, P. (1999) Situated learning in a transactional, secondary, English as a second language classroom. Ph.D. diss., Arizona State University, Tempe.

Wolfe, P., and C. Faltis (1999) Gender and ideology in secondary ESL and bilingual classrooms. In C. Faltis and P. Wolfe (eds.) *So much to say: Adolescents, bilingualism and ESL in the secondary school.* New York: Teachers College Press. 83–104.

Wolfe-Quintero, K. (1996) Nativism does not equal Universal Grammar. *Second Language Research* 12: 335–373.

Wong, L. (1999) Authenticity and the revitalization of Hawaiian. *Anthropology and Education Quarterly* 30: 94–115.

Wong Fillmore, L. (1991) When learning a second language means losing the first. *Early Childhood Research Quarterly* 6: 323–346.

Wong-Fillmore, L. (1979) Individual differences in second language acquisition. In C. J. Fillmore, D. Kempler, and W.-S. Y. Wang (eds.) *Individual differences in language ability and language behavior.* New York: Academic Press. 17–50.

Wong Fillmore, L., and C. Valadez (1986) Teaching bilingual learners. In M. C. Wittrock (ed.) *Handbook on research in teaching.* 3rd ed. New York: Macmillan. 648–685.

Woolard, K.A. (1999) Simultaneity and bivalency as strategies in bilingualism. *Journal of Linguistic Anthropology* 8: 3–29.

Worsley, P. (1987) Development. In P. Worsley (ed.) *Sociology.* Harmondsworth: Penguin Books. 48–83.

Wray, A. (2000) Formulaic sequences in second language teaching: Principle and practice. *Applied Linguistics* 21(4).

Wu, Y. (1998) What do tests of listening comprehension test? A retrospection study of EFL test-takers performing a multiple-choice task. *Language Testing* 15: 21–44.

Wurm, S. A. (1999) Language revivalism and revitalization in Pacific and Asian areas. *International Journal of the Sociology of Language* 137: 163–172.

Wurm, S. A. (1985) Writing systems and the orthography of Tok Pisin. In S. A. Wurm and P. Mühlhäusler (eds.) *Handbook of Tok Pisin (New Guinea Pidgin)*. Pacific Linguistics No. C-70. Canberra: Australian National University. 167–176.

Wurm, S. A. (1980) Standardisation and intrumentalisation in Tok Pisin. In A. Valdman and A. Highfield (eds.) *Theoretical orientations in creole studies*. New York: Academic Press. 237–244.

Xiao, H. (1998) Minority languages in Dehong, China: Policy and reality. *Journal of Multilingual and Multicultural Development* 19: 221–235.

Yagi, S. M. (1999) Computational discourse analysis for interpretation. *Meta* 44: 268–279.

Yagmur, K., K. de Bot, and H. Korzilius (1999) Language attrition, language shift and ethno-linguistic vitality of Turkish in Australia. *Journal of Multilingual and Multicultural Development* 20: 51–69.

Yalden, J. (1987) *Principles of course design for language teaching*. Cambridge: Cambridge University Press.

Yamagata, A., and D. R. Preston (1999) Variation in katakana representations. Paper presented at the NWAV conference. Toronto. October.

Yang, N. D. (1992) Second language learners' beliefs about language learning and their use of learning strategies: A study of college students of English in Taiwan. Ph.D. diss., University of Texas, Austin.

Yin, R. (1994) *Case study research: Design and methods*. Thousand Oaks, CA: Sage.

Ying, H. G. (1996) Multiple constraints on processing ambiguous sentences: Evidence from adult L2 learners. *Language Learning* 46: 681–711.

Yip, V., and G. Tang (1998) English reflexive binding by Cantonese learners. In M.-L. Beck (ed.) *Morphology and its interfaces in second language knowledge*. Philadelphia: John Benjamins. 167–193.

Young, D. J. (ed.) (1998) *Affect in L2 learning: A practical guide for dealing with learner anxieties*. Englewood Cliffs, NJ: Prentice Hall.

Young, R. (1989) Variation in interlanguage morphology: (s) plural-marking in the speech of Chinese learners of English. Ph.D. diss., University of Pennsylvania, Philadelphia.

Young, R., and R. Bayley (1996) VARBRUL analysis for second language acquisition research. In R. Bayley and D. Preston (eds.) *Second language acquisition and linguistic variation*. Amsterdam: John Benjamins. 253–306.

Young, R., and A. W. He (1998) *Talking and testing: Discourse approaches to the assessment of oral proficiency*. Amsterdam: John Benjamins.

Young, Y., M. D. Shermis, S. R. Brutten, and K. Perkins (1996) From conventional to computer-adaptive testing of ESL reading comprehension. *System* 24: 23–40.

Young-Scholten, M., and J. Archibald (2000) Second language syllable structure. In J. Archibald (ed.) *Second language acquisition and linguistic theory*. Oxford: Blackwell. 64–102.

Yule, G. (1997) *Referential comunication tasks*. Mahwah, NJ: Lawrence Erlbaum.

Yule, G. (1996) *Pragmatics*. Oxford: Oxford University Press.

Zamel, V. (1983) The composing processes of advanced ESL students: Six case studies. *TESOL Quarterly* 17: 165–187.

Zavodny, M. (1998) *The effects of Official English laws on limited-English-proficient work-ers.* Working Paper 98–4a. Atlanta GA: Federal Reserve Bank of Atlanta.

Zeier, H. (1997) Psychophysiological stress research. *Interpreting* 2: 231–249.

Zepeda, O. (1998) Voices in the desert: Contemporary approaches to language mainte-nance and survival of an ancient language, Tohono O'odham. *International Journal of the Sociology of Language* 132: 47–57.

Zéphir, F. (1997) Haitian Creole language and bilingual education in the United States: Problem, right, or resource? *Journal of Multilingual and Multicultural Development* 18: 223–237.

Zhang, S. (1995) Re-examining the affective advantage of peer feedback in the ESL writ-ing class. *Journal of Second Language Writing* 4: 209–222.

Zobl, H. (1998) Representational changes: From listed representations to independent representations of verbal affixes. In M.-L. Beck (ed.) *Morphology and its interfaces in second language acquisition.* Philadelphia: John Benjamins. 339–371.

Index

aboriginal languages, 367, 368, 371
academic settings, 8, 223
accommodation language programs, 347, 348
accuracy, speech, 33, 37, 38, 223–24
acquisition hypothesis, 215
acrolect, 337
ACT* theory, 291
action research, 7, 17
activity theory, 104, 110–13
Adair-Hauck, B., 105
additive bilingualism, 163, 358
Administrative Office of the United States
    Courts, 452
advertising, 272
Advocates for Indigenous California
    Language Survival, 370
affect, 12, 245, 249–51, 260, 261
affective schemata, 461, 462
African American Vernacular English, 337–38
Afrikaans, 332, 338, 420
age, 148, 231, 252
agency, 111–12, 114, 122
agreement, 89, 93, 94, 135
Ahmed, A., 109–10
Ainu, 367
Alderson, J. C., 58, 475
Aljaafreh, A., 105, 107
Alleyne, M., 340
allophones, 99
Allport, A., 318
ambiguity, tolerance of, 246
Ammon, U., 361–62
anaphors, 96
Andamanese, 367
Anderson, J. R., 40, 291
Anêm, 380
anthropological linguistics, 6, 399–400
anticipation, interpretive, 445, 447
Antón, M., 106, 107, 108
anxiety, 251
applied linguistics
    current status, 3–12
    discourse analysis and, 73–84

future considerations, 509–15
    research approaches, 13–23
appropriacy, speech, 28, 30, 32
Arabic, 352, 355–56, 357, 361, 363
Archibald, J., 88, 100–102
argument structures, 128, 131, 133
Armenia, 422
Arnhemland, 384
Aromanian, 377
article (part of speech), 256
articulation, 32, 36, 445
articulator, 289, 290
artifact mediation, 105, 110–13
artificial language conflict, 333–34
artificial languages, 385
Aruba, 343
aspect, 89, 257, 258
associative memory, 134
Asturian, 377
Atkinson, D., 8, 66
attention, 7, 32, 38, 51, 500
    interactionist theory, 178–81, 212
attitude, 12, 163, 164, 167, 398
Attitude/Motivation Test Battery, 164
audiolingual method, 35, 36, 200, 208–9
August, D., 239, 285
Austin, J. L., 75
Australia, 197, 223, 378–79, 382, 384
    aboriginal languages, 367, 368, 371
    bilingual education, 411, 412
    pidgins and creoles, 338, 339, 346, 347, 349
Australian Kriol, 338, 339, 346, 347, 349
Austria, 422
Austria-Hungary, 385
automated essay analysis, 487–97
    content analysis, 489–92
    discourse analysis, 493–94
    syntactic analysis, 492–93
autonomous linguistics, 512
aviation English, 379
awareness language education programs, 347,
    348
Azerbaijan, 422

DATE DUE

APR 2 3 2003

RECD APR 2 3 2003

RECD DEC 0 9 2003

RECD JUL 1 0 2005

RECD DEC 27 2008

OC 0 3 2008

MAR 0 9 2009

RECD AUG 1 1 2010

RESERVE

OCT 3 1 2010

NOV 1 0 2010

01-17-1

"DPF" reserve

Demco, Inc. 38-293